英语文学系列教材

美国文学选读新编·20世纪卷

罗良功　李汝成　主编

曹　曼　郭晶晶　张生珍　副主编

華中師範大學出版社

2015年·武汉

新出图证(鄂)10 号

图书在版编目(CIP)数据

美国文学选读新编·20 世纪卷/罗良功　李汝成主编.
—武汉:华中师范大学出版社,2010.8(2015.2 重印)
ISBN 978-7-5622-4274-1

Ⅰ.①美…　Ⅱ.①罗…②李…　Ⅲ.①英语-阅读教学-高等学校-教材②文学-作品-简介-美国-20 世纪　Ⅳ.H319.4:I

中国版本图书馆 CIP 数据核字(2010)第 060390 号

美国文学选读新编·20 世纪卷

作者:罗良功　李汝成©
责任编辑:李郭倩
责任校对:王　炜　　封面设计:甘　英
编 辑 室:高校教材编辑室　　电　话:027－67867364
出版发行:华中师范大学出版社
社址:湖北省武汉市珞瑜路 152 号
电话:027－67863426(发行部)　027－67861321(邮购)
传真:027－67863291
网址:http://www.ccnupress.com　　电子邮箱:hscbs@public.wh.hb.cn
印刷:武汉理工大印刷厂　　督印:章光琼
字数:817 千字
开本:787mm×960mm　1/16　　印张:43
版次:2010 年 8 月第 1 版　　印次:2015 年 2 月第 2 次印刷
印数:3001－5000　　定价:49.00 元

欢迎上网查询、购书

前　言

《美国文学选读新编·20世纪卷》是一部在新的社会文化历史语境下编写的英语专业高年级本科生或研究生的教材，也是一部文学研究者的参考书。当历史进入国家十二五规划时期，我国社会和高校对文学以及高校英语专业文学教育的观念发生了很大变化，对英语专业文学课程的教学时数、内容、手段和方法、教材编写与使用等都提出了新的要求。随着时代的发展和文学观念的更新，国内外对于20世纪美国文学的认识也发生了变化。

为了适应新时代高校文学教学的要求和文学史观的特点，也为了更充分地体现教材在文学教学和学术研究中的意义和价值，我们根据下列原则编写了本书：第一，力求体现新形势下研究型教学的要求和探究式学习的特点。本书以作品选读为主，兼顾文学史的梳理，强调基于作品研读的问题探究，注重学生的课外学习与课堂研讨相结合，适度引导学生进行深度的阅读和研究。第二，注重教材内容的时代性。本书在作家作品的选择上兼顾学界关于文学经典的传统的和当下的观点，在内容的分布上则强调现当代部分，兼及21世纪美国文学。第三，适度打破文学史的时间框架，按照文学流派和文学体裁建构章节，帮助学生更好地把握作家作品的共性与个性。第四，教材性与资料性并重。本书选材丰富、内容系统、体系完整，既是教材也是文集，适度超过教学时数的限制，供教师根据实际选择使用和供学生进行拓展学习，同时也可供文学研究者参考使用。

全书共分为九章：1945年以前的美国现实主义文学、"迷惘的一代"文学、南方文学、1945年之后的现实主义文学、后现代主义小说和先锋俗文艺、美国族裔文学、诗歌（二战前后各一章）、戏剧，较全面、系统地反映了20世纪美国文学的精髓。本书各章分为概述和作家作品选读两大部分。概述部分注重历史梳理和文学概念厘清；作家作品部分则主要是针对重要文学流派及其代表作家作品选材，分为预习问题、作品选读与问题、补充阅读材料等三个板块，补充阅读材料一般为作家本人或其他学者撰写的学术性文章，便于本书的使用者进行深度研究。

本书由来自国内近10所高校的专业教师共同编写而成。第一、二章由曹蔓、张俊、刘晖负责，第三章由邓小红、丁艳雯负责，第四章由刘芳负责，第五章由张海霞、赵晶负责，第六章由刘东霞负责，第七章由王卓负责，第八章由罗良功负责，第九章由张生珍负责。此外，李漫萍、丁玫、易立君、黄晓燕、彭家海、李汝成等老师也参加了编写。本书统稿工作由罗良功、李汝成共同完成，华中师范大学的李淑春老师和硕士生朱方芳、马媛、王琨、蔡萍、何乙罂、沈慧、丁春笋参与了部分稿件的编辑和统筹工作。本书的编辑出版得到了华中师范大学出版社范军社长、段维总编、曾巍副社长以及高校教材编辑室刘晓嘉主任、李郭倩编辑等的大力支持，我们在此一并致谢。

文学选读的编写的难度远比看上去的大。我们在学习国内外同类教材和相关著作的经验和优点的同时，也力图在视角、结构、体系、作家作品选择、问题设计等方面都能体现新时代的特点和我们自己的学术观点。但是由于时间仓促、资料难寻、编者学养有限，不足之处在所难免，敬请广大师生和学者批评指正。

编　者

2010年6月

CONTENTS

Chapter 1 Realistic Literature Before 1945

1. Introduction

The era between the Civil War (1861—1865) and World War I is variously labeled as the Gilded Age, the Age of Realism, the Age of Energy, the Age of Darwin, and the Age of Colonialism and Empire. It was a time of great change in America. The country began to move from a southern, farming, wealthy, Protestant group of colonies to an industrialized nation which pushed its boundary west, and it was struggling with the implications of Darwinism, and saw huge numbers of poor immigrants working in factories in the cities (even imperialist expansion in the Spanish-American War). By the 1870s New England Renaissance had waned. Hawthorne and Thoreau were dead, Emerson, Longfellow and other New England celebrities, though still writing, were old and feeble. The age of Romanticism and Transcendentalism was by and large over. Boston and New England ceased to be the cultural center of the country. Meanwhile, younger writers appeared on the scene. Mark Twain (1835—1910) and a good number of "local colorists" began to publish their works. The age of realism had arrived.

The Local Color movement which followed the war and frontier humor tales are often considered contributing factors to American realism. Regionalism and the desire to preserve expressions of modes of life before industrialization became an important impulse in American writing. Focusing on specific regions within the nation, writers such as Mark Twain, and Kate Chopin (1851—1904) captured the sensibilities of particular places. Women writers such as Harriet Beecher Stowe (1811—1896) offered the additional perspective of women's experiences. They drew upon the sometimes grim realities of everyday life, showing the breakdown of traditional values and the growing plight of the new urban poor. American realists built their plots and characters around people's ordinary, everyday lives. Additionally, their works contained regional dialects and extensive dialogue which connected well with the public. Conversely, the public had little patience for the slow paced narratives, allegory and symbolism of the romantic writers, but they had interest in life in contemporary cities and small towns, and the aspirations and struggles of people like themselves in an era of mobility and social dislocation. The realists thus had a moral and social role: to hold up a mirror to ordinary life, and help an emerging society understand itself and achieve its own voice. Local Color fiction reached its peak of popularity in the 1880s, but by the turn of the century it had begun to decline due to its limited resources.

Regionalism was followed by a deeper, wider and more insightful trend—realism. According to William Dean Howells (1837—1920), "Realism is nothing more and nothing less than the truthful treatment of material"①. It is to offer an objective rather than an idealized view of human nature and experience. William Dean Howells, Mark Twain and Henry James (1843—1916) are the three representatives of American Realism. Their realistic works helped the development of American realism which replaced the earlier romantic writing. William Dean Howells was a literary critic and writer. He was the advocator of realism. Howells' major works are *A Modern Instance* (1882), and *The Rise of Silas Lapham* (1885). Mark Twain was a social critic and the first great American satirist. He portrayed the lives of the common people and dealt with social problems at that time. In one of his most important works *The Adventures of Huckleberry Finn* (1883), Mark Twain used a distinctively American idiom which reflected the way Americans actually talked. He wrote in the vernacular of different classes and ethnic groups. His creative writing had great influence in the development of American literature. Ernest Hemingway once said that "All modern American literature comes from one book by Mark Twain called *Huckleberry Finn* ... it's the best book we've had ... There has been nothing so good since"②. Henry James' major writing concerned the international theme—the drama of Americans (young

---

① William Dean Howells. Editor's Study. *Harper's New Monthly Magazine*, 1889 (11). p. 966.

② George McMichael. *Concise Anthology of American Literature*. New York: Macmillan Publishing Co. Inc., 1974. p. 1063.

culture) encountering Europe (old culture). His major works are *Daisy Miller* (1878), *Portrait of a Lady* (1881), *The Wings of the Dove* (1902), *The Ambassadors* (1903), *The Golden Bowl* (1904). He was famous for his psychological realism.

The leading spokesman of 19th century literary realism was William Dean Howells who had argued for the treatment of the "smiling aspects of life" as being the more "American." But by the end of the 19th century, a generation of writers arose "whose ideas of the workings of the universe and whose perception of society's disorders led them to a new and harsher realism, a naturalism that attempted to achieve extreme objectivity and frankness. America's literary naturalists portrayed characters of low social and economic orders who were shaped by their environment and heredity and moved by animal passions"①. Their writings dealt with cities like Chicago and San Francisco as well as Boston, with working class characters as well as middle-class intellectuals. The mood was documentary and the language was deliberately blunt and unliterary. Realism and naturalism were products of the events and ideals of the 19th century which witnessed their final triumph at the early part of the 20th century.

With the opening of the 20th century, the exposure of injustice and abuses of national life became a popular literary subject. In politics the 1900s were the era of Theodore Roosevelt's progressivism and "trust-busting" which was reflected in literature as the era of "muckrakers," those who were accused of raking up the much of life for all to see. The American realistic writers depicted life around them and they tried to work out new techniques to fit their new ideas. Edith Wharton (1862—1937), in her stories and novels, was concerned about the upper-class, the world of aristocracy in which she had grown up. One of her finest books, *The Age of Innocence* (1920), probed the moral values and the conflict between the social conformity and personal fulfillment. The decent people were the major characters. At about the same time, some other authors such as Theodore Dreiser (1871—1945), Stephen Crane (1871—1900), Hamlin Garland (1860—1940) and Frank Norris (1870—1902) showed their sympathy toward ordinary people. They wrote

① George McMichael. *Concise Anthology of American Literature*. New York: Macmillan Publishing Co. Inc., 1974. p. 875.

about political corruption, economic inequality, business deception and the exploitation of labor. Stephen Crane, best known for his Civil War novel *The Red Badge of Courage* (1895), depicted the life of New York prostitutes in *Maggie: A Girl of the Streets* (1893). He was highly praised for his realistic treatment of the sordidness of city life in *Maggie*. Theodore Dreiser, who came from lower class of society, portrayed a country girl who moved to Chicago and became a kept woman in *Sister Carrie* (1900). Dreiser's other important novels are *The Financier* (1912), *The Titan* (1914), *The "Genius"* (1915), and *An American Tragedy* (1925). Greatly impressed by scientific thought, Dreiser aimed to give his fiction the precision of a scientific statement. Its view of society or of people would be true and completely objective. As one of the great realists and naturalists, Dreiser showed sympathy for the oppressed and he criticized the debased American values. Frank Norris and Hamlin Garland wrote about the problems of American farmers and other social issues from a naturalist perspective. Frank Norris' best work *McTeague* (1899) and *The Octopus* (1901) dealt with the lower classes, with coarse and usually inarticulate people. His narrative style is as simple and direct as his subject. Hamlin Garland was from the Midwest. His important books are *Main-Traveled Roads* (1891) and *Prairie Folks* (1893).

Between the two world wars, the United States became a modern nation, fraught with internal fractures. Literature of the period struggled to understand the new and diverse responses to the advent of modernity. Some writers celebrated the changes, others lamented the loss of old ways of being; some imagined future utopias, others searched for new forms to speak of the new realities. World War I was followed by two decades which were distinctly different from one another and clearly defined. The first, the "Twenties," lasted from the signing of the Treaty of Versailles in 1919 until the collapse of the Stock Market in New York at the end of 1929. The second decade, the "Thirties," lasted from 1929, through the Depression years, until the outbreak of the Second World War in 1939. The 1920s was a period marked by rampant social and economic change. It was the Roaring Twenties and the Jazz Age. During World War I, 4 million Americans were involved in the war. Many young men were killed and wounded. They were shocked by the way of the war. The innocence, naivety and optimism of the intellectuals were changed. To many writers, the war seemed to be a senseless slaughter. The American dream of a better world was shattered. The writers such as Ernest Hemingway (1899—1961), F. Scott Fitzgerald (1896—1940), Thomas Wolfe (1900—1938) and John Dos Passos (1896—1970) voluntarily moved to Paris. Gertrude Stein told the young Ernest Hemingway: "You are all a lost generation." They were "lost" because they were cut off from the life of their own country, and the continuity of their culture. At the same time they were searching for the meaning of life. They observed the American life objectively as outsiders. In the following ten years after the World War Ⅰ, the writers wrote about the typical extravagant life of the 1920s, about the disillusionment of the war and the American Dream. They criticized the American life as a whole, and they depicted the failure of American society, the failure of communication among the people.

Ernest Hemingway has been considered as the spokesman of the Lost Generation. His best novels are *The Sun Also Rises* (1926), *A Farewell to Arms* (1929), and *For Whom the Bell Tolls* (1940). His subjects and themes of war, hunting, bullfighting that deal with courage and endurance spoke for his generation. F. Scott Fitzgerald remained both as an insider and an outsider of the life of the 1920s. The novel *The Great Gatsby* (1925) is considered his best work. His other important works are: *This Side of Paradise* (1920) and *Tender is the Night* (1934). John Dos Passos wrote about the war and also *The USA* (1937)—a trilogy consisting of three parts: *The 42nd Parallel* (1930), *Nineteen Nineteen* (1932), *The Big Money* (1936) that which extended into the Depression. Thomas Wolfe was famous for his novel *Look Homeward, Angel* (1929). During the 1920s, writers such as Sinclair Lewis (1885—1951) and Sherwood Anderson (1876—1941) also wrote novels with critical depictions of American life. Sinclair Lewis is the author of *Main Street* (1920) and *Babbitt*(1922). He wrote about the life of small town people in Midwest. He exposed and ridiculed the pretentiousness of the middle-class businessmen as selfish and hypocritical. Sherwood Anderson was born in Camden, Ohio. He wrote *Windy Mcpherson's Son* (1916) and *Marching Men* (1917), novels about successful men who abandoned their own selfish aims to become Populist heroes, helping the "little people." In 1919 he published *Winesburg, Ohio*, his masterpiece, a collection of tales of the "grotesque" characters he had known during his youth in Ohio. Anderson's successful volumes of short stories, *The Triumph of the Egg* (1921), *Horses and*

Men (1923), and *Death in the Woods* (1933), contained work of great merit.

Anderson was preoccupied by a desire to describe the agonies, failures, and the complex groping of the unsuccessful, the deprived, and the inarticulate. His sensitive depictions of poverty and eccentricity, and his deceptively simple style, with its colloquial rhythms and matter-of-fact Midwestern sentences, opened new perspectives for 20th-century literature and influenced a wide range of American writers: Hart Crane, John Steinbeck, Thomas Wolfe, Ernest Hemingway, and William Faulkner who, in 1956, acknowledged Anderson as "the father of my generation of American writers and the tradition of American writing which our successors will carry on"①.

Literature during the 1930s was direct in its social criticism. Following the crash of the stock market in 1929, a depression set in, causing social unrest and economic upheaval on a global scale. During the period of depression, the writers were not outsiders but deeply involved in social affairs. They showed great concern for the common people, their suffering and struggle. The writers mirrored the emotions of the people—the despair of the homeless, the anxiety of the unemployed. One of the representative writers during the Great Depression, John Steinbeck (1902—1968), wrote about the migration workers and the mutual help of the ordinary people. He condemned the social system and asked for social reformation. His style was simple and evocative, winning him the favor of the readers but not of the critics. Steinbeck often wrote about poor, working-class people and their struggle to lead a decent and honest life. *The Grapes of Wrath* (1939), considered his masterpiece, is a strong, socially-oriented novel that tells the story of the Joads, a poor family from Oklahoma and their journey to California in search of a better life. In the novel, John Steinbeck protested the lack of economic opportunity that was blighting the lives of countless Americans. His other popular novels include *Tortilla Flat* (1935), *Of Mice and Men* (1937), *Cannery Row*, and *East of Eden* (1952). He was awarded the Nobel Prize in

---

① George McMichael. *Concise Anthology of American Literature*. New York: Macmillan Publishing Co. Inc., 1974. p. 1390.

Literature in 1962.

In the early part of the 20th century, the two world wars had greatly affected the American society as well as writing. The United States of America entered the new period of development in the field of modern science and technology. And it has ever since become a superpower of the world. The writers in this era especially during the 1920s and 1930s wrote truthfully and vividly about the country and the life of the people. They contributed to the treasure of world literature with their efforts and creativity. Six writers were awarded the Noble Prize in Literature.

Key words

Realism

Realism first appeared in France as a literary doctrine that called for "reality and truth" and the presentation of the minute details of ordinary life. In American literature, the Age of Realism began with the end of the Civil War and the Romantic Period. American authors turned from the romantic exoticism of an earlier age and sought to create an objective portrayal of American life, insisting that the ordinary and the local were as suitable for artistic portrayal as the magnificent and the remote. Realism turned from an emphasis on the strange toward a faithful rendering of the ordinary, a slice of life as it is really lived. It expresses the concern for the commonplace and the low, and offers an objective rather than an idealistic view of human nature and human experience.

Naturalism

Naturalism is a new and harsher realism, which prevailed in America in the late 19th century and early 20th century. Naturalism attempts to achieve extreme objectivity and frankness, presenting characters of low social and economic classes who are determined by their environment and heredity. In presenting the extremes of life, the naturalists sometimes display an affinity to the sensationalism of early romanticism, but emphasize that the world is amoral, that human beings have no free will, that lives are controlled by heredity and environment. Although naturalistic literature describes the world with sometimes brutal realism, it sometimes also aims at bettering the world through social reform.

2. Sherwood Anderson

2.1 Presentation Topics

(1) Sherwood Anderson as a story-teller, the "writer of writers," and the first "psychological" fiction writer.

(2) Anderson's efforts to see beneath the surface of lives: the loss of love and the failure of communication among the people.

(3) Artistic features of his works.

2.2 Selected Reading

Ⅰ. Central issue of concern

Anderson wrote about the mental state of the people in the modern society. The theme of his writings centers on the conflicts between the organized industrial society and the subconscious instincts of the individuals, whose spiritual and emotional sterility of a success-oriented material world is obviously depicted.

Ⅱ. Text

Sophistication

It was early evening of a day in the late fall and the Winesburg County Fair had brought crowds of country people into town. The day had been clear and the night came on warm and pleasant. On the Trunion Pike, where the road after it left town stretched away between berry fields now covered with dry brown leaves, the dust from passing wagons arose in clouds. Children, curled into little balls, slept on the straw scattered on wagon beds. Their hair was full of dust and their fingers black and sticky. The dust rolled away over the fields and the departing sun set it ablaze with colors.

In the main street of Winesburg crowds filled the stores and the sidewalks. Night came on, horses whinnied, the clerks in the stores ran madly about, children became lost and cried lustily, an American town worked terribly at the task of amusing itself.

Pushing his way through the crowds in Main Street, young George Willard concealed himself in the stairway leading to Doctor Reefy's office and looked at the people. With feverish eyes he watched the faces drifting past under the store lights. Thoughts kept coming into his head and he did not want to think. He stamped impatiently on the wooden steps and looked sharply about. "Well, is she going to stay with him all day? Have I done all this waiting for nothing?" he muttered.

George Willard, the Ohio village boy, was fast growing into manhood and new thoughts had been coming into his mind. All that day, amid the jam of people at the Fair, he had gone about feeling lonely. He was about to leave Winesburg to go away to some city where he hoped to get work on a city newspaper and he felt grown up. The mood that had taken possession of him was a thing known to men and unknown to boys. He felt old and a little tired. Memories awoke in him. To his mind his new sense of maturity set him apart, made him a half-tragic figure. He wanted someone to understand the feeling that had taken possession of him after his mother's death.

There is a time in the life of every boy when he for the first time takes the backward view of life. Perhaps that is the moment when he crosses the line into manhood. The boy is walking through the street of his town. He is thinking of the future and of the figure he will cut in the world. Ambitions and regrets awake within him. Suddenly something happens; he stops under a tree and waits as for a voice calling his name. Ghosts of old things creep into his consciousness; the voices outside of himself whisper a message concerning the limitations of life. From being quite sure of himself and his future he becomes not at all sure. If he be an imaginative boy a door is torn open and for the first time he looks out upon the world, seeing, as though they marched in procession before him, the countless figures of men who before his time have come out of nothingness into the world, lived their lives and again disappeared into nothingness. The sadness of sophistication has come to the boy. With a little gasp he sees himself as merely a leaf blown by the wind through the streets of his village. He knows that in spite of all the stout talk of his fellows he must live and die in uncertainty, a thing blown by the winds, a thing destined like corn to wilt in the sun. He shivers and looks eagerly about. The eighteen years he has lived seem but a moment, a breathing space in the long march of humanity. Already he hears death calling. With all his heart he wants to come close to some other human, touch someone with his hands, be touched by the hand of another. If he prefers that the other be a woman, that is because he believes that a woman will be gentle, that she will understand. He wants, most of all, understanding.

When the moment of sophistication came to George Willard his mind turned to Helen White, the Winesburg banker's daughter. Always he had been conscious of the girl growing into womanhood as he grew into manhood. Once on a summer night when he was eighteen, he had walked with her on a country road and in her presence had given way to an impulse to boast, to make himself appear big and significant in her eyes. Now he wanted to see her for another purpose. He wanted to tell her of the new impulses that had come to him. He had tried to make her think of him as a man when he knew nothing of manhood and now he wanted to be with her and to try to make her feel the change he believed had taken place in his nature.

As for Helen White, she also had come to a period of change. What George felt, she in her young woman's way felt also. She was no longer a girl and hungered to reach into the grace and beauty of womanhood. She had come home from Cleveland, where she was attending college, to spend a day at the Fair. She also had begun to have memories. During the day she sat in the grand-stand with a young man, one of the instructors from the college, who was a guest of her mother's. The young man was of a pedantic turn of mind and she felt at once he would not do for her purpose. At the Fair she was glad to be seen in his company as he was well dressed and a stranger. She knew that the fact of his presence would create an impression. During the day she was happy, but when night came on she began to grow restless. She wanted to drive the instructor away, to get out of his presence. While they sat together in the grand-stand and while the eyes of former schoolmates were upon them, she paid so much attention to her escort that he grew interested. "A scholar needs money. I should marry a woman with money," he mused.

Helen White was thinking of George Willard even as he wandered gloomily through the crowds thinking of her. She remembered the summer evening when they had walked together and wanted to walk with him again. She thought that the months she had spent in the city, the going to theaters and the seeing of great crowds wandering in lighted thoroughfares, had changed her profoundly. She wanted him to feel and be conscious of the change in her nature.

The summer evening together that had left its mark on the memory of both the young man and woman had, when looked at quite sensibly, been rather stupidly spent. They had walked out of town along a country road. Then they had stopped by a fence near a field of young corn and George had taken off his coat and let it hang on his arm. "Well, I've stayed here in Winesburg—yes—I've not yet gone away but I'm growing up," he had said. "I've been reading books and I've been thinking. I'm going to try to amount to something in life"①.

"Well," he explained, "that isn't the point. Perhaps I'd better quit talking."

The confused boy put his hand on the girl's arm. His voice trembled. The two started to walk back along the road toward town. In his desperation George boasted, "I'm going to be a big man, the biggest that ever lived here in Winesburg," he declared. "I want you to do something, I don't know what. Perhaps it is none of my business. I want you to try to be different from other women. You see the point. It's none of my business I tell you. I want you to be a beautiful woman. You see what I want."

The boy's voice failed and in silence the two came back into town and went along the street to Helen White's house. At the gate he tried to say something impressive. Speeches he had thought out came into his head, but they seemed utterly pointless. "I thought—I used to think—I had it in my mind you would marry Seth Richmond. Now I know you won't," was all he could find to say as she went through the gate and toward the door of her house.

On the warm fall evening as he stood in the stairway and looked at the crowd drifting through Main Street, George thought of the talk beside the field of young corn and was ashamed of the figure he had made of himself. In the street the people surged up and down like cattle confined in a pen. Buggies and wagons almost filled the narrow thoroughfare. A band played and small boys raced along the sidewalk, diving between the legs of men. Young men with shining red faces walked awkwardly about with girls on their arms. In a room above one of the stores, where a dance was to be held, the fiddlers tuned their instruments. The broken

---

① Try to achieve great success.

sounds floated down through an open window and out across the murmur of voices and the loud blare of the horns of the band. The medley of sounds got on young Willard's nerves. Everywhere, on all sides, the sense of crowding, moving life closed in about him. He wanted to run away by himself and think. "If she wants to stay with that fellow she may. Why should I care? What difference does it make to me?" he growled and went along Main Street and through Hern's Grocery into a side street.

George felt so utterly lonely and dejected that he wanted to weep but pride made him walk rapidly along, swinging his arms. He came to Wesley Moyer's livery barn and stopped in the shadows to listen to a group of men who talked of a race Wesley's stallion, Tony Tip, had won at the Fair during the afternoon. A crowd had gathered in front of the barn and before the crowd walked Wesley, prancing up and down and boasting. He held a whip in his hand and kept tapping the ground. Little puffs of dust arose in the lamplight. "Hell, quit your talking," Wesley exclaimed. "I wasn't afraid, I knew I had 'em beat all the time. I wasn't afraid."

Ordinarily George Willard would have been intensely interested in the boasting of Moyer, the horseman. Now it made him angry. He turned and hurried away along the street. "Old windbag,"① he sputtered②. "Why does he want to be bragging? Why don't he shut up?"

George went into a vacant lot and, as he hurried along, fell over a pile of rubbish. A nail protruding from an empty barrel tore his trousers. He sat down on the ground and swore. With a pin he mended the torn place and then arose and went on. "I'll go to Helen White's house, that's what I'll do. I'll walk right in. I'll say that I want to see her. I'll walk right in and sit down, that's what I'll do," he declared, climbing over a fence and beginning to run.

On the veranda of Banker White's house Helen was restless and distraught. The instructor sat between the mother and daughter. His talk wearied the girl. Although he had also been raised in an Ohio town, the instructor began to put on the airs of the city. He wanted to appear cosmopolitan. "I like the chance you have

① Informal derog, means a person who talks too much, especially about uninteresting things.

② To speak or say in confusion.

given me to study the background out of which most of our girls come," he declared. "It was good of you, Mrs. White, to have me down for the day." He turned to Helen and laughed. "Your life is still bound up with the life of this town?" he asked. "There are people here in whom you are interested?" To the girl his voice sounded pompous and heavy.

Helen arose and went into the house. At the door leading to a garden at the back she stopped and stood listening. Her mother began to talk. "There is no one here fit to associate with a girl of Helen's breeding"①, she said.

Helen ran down a flight of stairs at the back of the house and into the garden. In the darkness she stopped and stood trembling. It seemed to her that the world was full of meaningless people saying words. Afire with eagerness she ran through a garden gate and, turning a corner by the banker's barn, went into a little side street. "George! Where are you, George?" she cried, filled with nervous excitement. She stopped running, and leaned against a tree to laugh hysterically. Along the dark little street came George Willard, still saying words. "I'm going to walk right into her house. I'll go right in and sit down," he declared as he came up to her. He stopped and stared stupidly. "Come on," he said and took hold of her hand. With hanging heads they walked along the street under the trees. Dry leaves rustled under foot. Now that he had found her George wondered what he had better do and say.

At the upper end of the Fair Ground, in Winesburg, there is a half decayed old grand-stand. It has never been painted and the boards are all warped out of shape. The Fair Ground stands on top of a low hill rising out of the valley of Wine Creek and from the grand-stand one can see at night, over a cornfield, the lights of the town reflected against the sky.

George and Helen climbed the hill to the Fair Ground, coming by the path past Waterworks Pond. The feeling of loneliness and isolation that had come to the young man in the crowded streets of his town was both broken and intensified by the presence of Helen. What he felt was reflected in her.

In youth there are always two forces fighting in people. The warm unthinking little animal struggles against the thing that reflects and remembers, and the older,

① To join in a relationship based in friendship, business, or a shared purpose.

the more sophisticated thing had possession of George Willard. Sensing his mood, Helen walked beside him filled with respect. When they got to the grand-stand they climbed up under the roof and sat down on one of the long bench-like seats.

There is something memorable in the experience to be had by going into a fair ground that stands at the edge of a Middle Western town on a night after the annual fair has been held. The sensation is one never to be forgotten. On all sides are ghosts, not of the dead, but of living people. Here, during the day just passed, have come the people pouring in from the town and the country around. Farmers with their wives and children and all the people from the hundreds of little frame houses have gathered within these board walls. Young girls have laughed and men with beards have talked of the affairs of their lives. The place has been filled to overflowing with life. It has itched and squirmed with life and now it is night and the life has all gone away. The silence is almost terrifying. One conceals oneself standing silently beside the trunk of a tree and what there is of a reflective tendency in his nature is intensified. One shudders at the thought of the meaninglessness of life while at the same instant, and if the people of the town are his people, one loves life so intensely that tears come into the eyes.

In the darkness under the roof of the grand-stand, George Willard sat beside Helen White and felt very keenly his own insignificance in the scheme of existence. Now that he had come out of town where the presence of the people stirring about, busy with a multitude of affairs, had been so irritating, the irritation was all gone. The presence of Helen renewed and refreshed him. It was as though her woman's hand was assisting him to make some minute readjustment of the machinery of his life. He began to think of the people in the town where he had always lived with something like reverence. He had reverence for Helen. He wanted to love and to be loved by her, but he did not want at the moment to be confused by her womanhood. In the darkness he took hold of her hand and when she crept close put a hand on her shoulder. A wind began to blow and he shivered. With all his strength he tried to hold and to understand the mood that had come upon him. In that high place in the darkness the two oddly sensitive human atoms held each other tightly and waited. In the mind of each was the same thought. "I have come to this lonely place and here is this other," was the substance of the thing felt.

In Winesburg the crowded day had run itself out into the long night of the late fall. Farm horses jogged away along lonely country roads pulling their portion of weary people. Clerks began to bring samples of goods in off the sidewalks and lock the doors of stores. In the Opera House a crowd had gathered to see a show and further down Main Street the fiddlers, their instruments tuned, sweated and worked to keep the feet of youth flying over a dance floor.

In the darkness in the grand-stand Helen White and George Willard remained silent. Now and then the spell that held them was broken and they turned and tried in the dim light to see into each other's eyes. They kissed but that impulse did not last. At the upper end of the Fair Ground a half dozen men worked over horses that had raced during the afternoon. The men had built a fire and were heating kettles of water. Only their legs could be seen as they passed back and forth in the light. When the wind blew the little flames of the fire danced crazily about.

George and Helen arose and walked away into the darkness. They went along a path past a field of corn that had not yet been cut. The wind whispered among the dry corn blades. For a moment during the walk back into town the spell that held them was broken. When they had come to the crest of Waterworks Hill they stopped by a tree and George again put his hands on the girl's shoulders. She embraced him eagerly and then again they drew quickly back from that impulse. They stopped kissing and stood a little apart. Mutual respect grew big in them. They were both embarrassed and to relieve their embarrassment dropped into the animalism of youth. They laughed and began to pull and haul at each other. In some way chastened and purified by the mood they had been in, they became, not man and woman, not boy and girl, but excited little animals.

It was so they went down the hill. In the darkness they played like two splendid young things in a young world. Once, running swiftly forward, Helen tripped George and he fell. He squirmed and shouted. Shaking with laughter, he rolled down the hill. Helen ran after him. For just a moment she stopped in the darkness. There was no way of knowing what woman's thoughts went through her mind but, when the bottom of the hill was reached and she came up to the boy, she took his arm and walked beside him in dignified silence. For some reason they could not have explained they had both got from their silent evening together the thing needed. Man or boy, woman or girl, they had for a moment taken hold of the thing that makes the mature life of men and women in the modern world possible.

[Selected from Sherwood Anderson. *Winesburg, Ohio.* New York: Penguin Books Ltd., 1976.]

Ⅲ. Questions for discussion

(1) What leads to George Willard's and Helen's new sense of maturity?

(2) Throughout the story, what does the word "darkness" possibly symbolize?

(3) How does the author give us a realistic picture of the life of a small Midwestern town at the turn of the 20th century?

(4) Sherwood Anderson was one of the first writers who used Freud's theory to do psychoanalysis. Reread the 5th paragraph, which describes the moment a boy "crosses the line into manhood." How does this passage sharpen your insight into George's mental confusion?

(5) Anderson is noted for his efforts to create the effect of a moment of aliveness—epiphany. How does the author tell George's story?

(6) What's the author's attitude towards these two young people?

(7) Why does the author use George Willard, the young reporter to connect the separate stories and to whom the grotesques approach and place their hopes and wishes (after the readers finish the whole book)?

2.3 Assigned Reading

Introduction to *Winesburg, Ohio*

Irving Howe

I must have been no more than fifteen or sixteen years old when I first chanced upon *Winesburg, Ohio.* Gripped by these stories and sketches of Sherwood Anderson's small-town "grotesques," I felt that he was opening for me new depths of experience, touching upon half-buried truths which nothing in my young life had prepared me for. A New York City boy who never saw the crops grow or spent time in the small towns that lay sprinkled across America, I found myself overwhelmed by the scenes of wasted life, wasted love (was this the "real" America?) that Anderson sketched in Winesburg. In those days only one other book seemed to offer so powerful a revelation, and that was Thomas Hardy's *Jude the Obscure*.

Several years later, as I was about to go overseas as a soldier, I spent my last weekend pass on a somewhat quixotic journey to Clyde, Ohio, the town upon which

Winesburg was partly modeled. Clyde looked, I suppose, not very different from most other American towns, and few of its residents I tried to engage in talk about Anderson seemed quite interested. This indifference would not have surprised him; it certainly should not surprise anyone who reads his book.

Once freed from the army, I started to write literary criticism, and in 1951 I published a critical biography of Anderson. It came shortly after Lionel Trilling's influential essay attacking Anderson, an attack from which Anderson's reputation would never quite recover. Trilling charged Anderson with indulging a vaporous sentimentalism, a kind of vague emotional meandering in stories that lacked social or spiritual solidity. There was a certain cogency in Trilling's attack, at least with regard to Anderson's inferior work, most of which he wrote after *Winesburg, Ohio*. In my book I tried, somewhat awkwardly, to bring together the kinds of judgment Trilling had made with my still keen affection for the best of Anderson's writings. By then, I had read writers more complex, perhaps more distinguished than Anderson, but his muted stories kept a firm place in my memories, and the book I wrote might be seen as a gesture of thanks for the light—a glow of darkness, you might say—that he had brought to me.

Decades passed, I no longer read Anderson, perhaps fearing I might have to surrender an admiration of youth. (There are some writers one should never return to.) But now, in the fullness of age, when asked to say a few introductory words about Anderson and his work, I have again fallen under the spell of *Winesburg, Ohio*, again responded to the half-spoken desires, the flickers of longing that spot its pages. Naturally, I now have some changes of response: a few of the stories no longer haunt me as once they did, but the long story "Godliness," which years ago I considered a failure, I now see as a quaintly effective account of the way religious fanaticism and material acquisitiveness can become intertwined in American experience.

[...]

And then, in 1912, occurred the great turning point in Anderson's life. Plainly put, he suffered a nervous breakdown, though in his memoirs he would elevate this into a moment of liberation in which he abandoned the sterility of commerce and turned to the rewards of literature. Nor was this, I believe, merely a deception on Anderson's part, since the breakdown painful as it surely was, did help precipitate a basic change in his life. At the age of 36, he left behind his business and moved to Chicago, becoming one of the rebellious writers and cultural bohemians in the group that has since come to be called the "Chicago Renaissance." Anderson soon adopted the posture of a free, liberated spirit, and like many writers of the time, he presented himself as a sardonic critic of American provincialism and materialism. It was in the freedom of the city, in its readiness to put up with deviant styles of life, that Anderson found the strength to settle accounts with—but also to release his affection for—the world of small-town America. The dream of an unconditional personal freedom, that hazy American version of utopia, would remain central throughout Anderson's life and work. It was an inspiration; it was a delusion.

[...]

In 1915—1916 Anderson had begun to write and in 1919 he published the stories that comprise *Winesburg, Ohio*, stories that form, in sum, a sort of loosely-strung episodic novel. The book was an immediate critical success, and soon Anderson was being ranked as a significant literary figure. In 1921 the distinguished literary magazine The Dial awarded him its first annual literary prize of $2,000, the significance of which is perhaps best understood if one also knows that the second recipient was T. S. Eliot. But Anderson's moment of glory was brief, no more than a decade, and sadly, the remaining years until his death in 1940 were marked by a sharp decline in his literary standing. Somehow, except for an occasional story like the haunting "Death in the Woods," he was unable to repeat or surpass his early success. Still, about *Winesburg, Ohio* and a small number of stories like "The Egg" and "The Man Who Became a Woman" there has rarely been any critical doubt.

No sooner did *Winesburg, Ohio* make its appearance than a number of critical labels were fixed on it: the revolt against the village, the espousal of sexual freedom, the deepening of American realism. Such tags may once have had their point, but by now they seem dated and stale. The revolt against the village (about which Anderson was always ambivalent) has faded into history. The espousal of sexual freedom would soon be exceeded in boldness by other writers. And as for the effort to place *Winesburg, Ohio* in a tradition of American realism, that now seems dubious. Only rarely is the object of Anderson's stories social verisimilitude, or the "photographing" of familiar appearances, in the sense, say, that one might use to describe a novel by Theodore Dreiser or Sinclair Lewis. Only occasionally, and then with a very light touch, does Anderson try to fill out the social arrangements of his imaginary town—although the fact that his stories are set in a mid-American place like Winesburg does constitute an important formative condition. You might even say, with only slight overstatement, that what Anderson is doing in *Winesburg, Ohio* could be described as "antirealistic," fictions notable less for precise locale and social detail than for a highly personal, even strange vision of American life. Narrow, intense, almost claustrophobic, the result is a book about extreme states of being, the collapse of men and women who have lost their psychic bearings and now hover, at best tolerated, at the edge of the little community in which they live. It would be a gross mistake, though not one likely to occur by now, if we were to take *Winesburg, Ohio* as a social photograph of "the typical small town" (whatever that might be). Anderson evokes a depressed landscape in which lost souls wander about; they make their flitting appearances mostly in the darkness of night, these stumps and shades of humanity. This vision has its truth, and at its best it is a terrible if narrow truth—but it is itself also grotesque, with the tone of the authorial voice and the mode of composition forming muted signals of the book's content. Figures like Dr. Parcival, Kate Swift, and Wash Williams are not, nor are they meant to be "fully-rounded" characters such as we can expect in realistic fiction; they are the shards of life, glimpsed for a moment, the debris of suffering and defeat. In each story one of them emerges, shyly or with a false assertiveness, trying to reach out to companionship and love, driven almost mad by the search for human connection. In the economy of Winesburg these grotesques matter less in their own right than as agents or symptoms of that "indefinable hunger" for meaning which is Anderson's preoccupation.

Brushing against one another, passing one another in the streets or the fields, they see bodies and hear voices, but it does not really matter— they are disconnected, psychically lost. Is this due to the particular circumstances of small-town America as Anderson saw it at the turn of the century? Or does he feel that he is sketching an inescapable human condition which makes all of us bear the burden of loneliness? Alice Hindman in the story "Adventure" turns her face to the wall and tries "to force herself to face the fact that many people must live and die alone, even in Winesburg." Such impressions have been put in more general terms in Anderson's only successful novel, *Poor White*:

All men lead their lives behind a wall of misunderstanding they have themselves built, and most men die in silence and unnoticed behind the walls. Now and then a man, cut off from his fellows by the peculiarities of his nature, becomes absorbed in doing something that is personal, useful and beautiful. Word of his activities is carried over the walls.

These "walls" of misunderstanding are only selfdom due to physical deformities (Wing Biddlebaum in "Hands") or oppressive social arrangements (Kate Swift in "The Teacher"). Misunderstanding, loneliness, the inability to articulate, are all seen by Anderson as virtually a root condition, something deeply set in our natures. Nor are these people, the grotesques, simply to be pitied and dismissed; at some point in their lives they have known desire, have dreamt of ambition, have hoped for friendship. In all of them there was once something sweet, "like the twisted little apples that grow in the orchards in Winesburg." Now, broken and adrift, they clutch at some rigid notion or idea, a "truth" which turns out to bear the stamp of monomania, leaving them helplessly sputtering, desperate to speak out but unable to. *Winesburg, Ohio* registers the losses inescapable to life, and it does so with a deep fraternal sadness, a sympathy casting a mild glow over the entire book. "Words," as the American writer Paula Fox has said, "are nets through which all truth escapes." Yet what do we have but words?

They want, these Winesburg grotesques, to unpack their hearts, to release emotions buried and festering. Wash Williams tries to explain his eccentricity but hardly can; Louise Bentley "tried to talk but could say nothing"; Enoch Robinson retreats to a fantasy world, inventing "his own people to whom he could really talk and to whom he explained the things he had been unable to explain to living people."

In his own somber way, Anderson has here touched upon one of the great themes of American literature, especially Midwestern literature, in the late 19th and early 20th centuries: the struggle for speech as it entails a search for the self. Perhaps the central Winesburg story, tracing the basic movements of the book, is "Paper Pills," in which the old Doctor Reefy sits "in his empty office close by a window that was covered with cobwebs," writes down some thoughts on slips of paper ("pyramids of truth," he calls them) and then stuffs them into his pockets where they "become round hard balls" soon to be discarded. What Dr. Refry's "truths" may be we never know; Anderson simply persuades us that to this lonely old man they are utterly precious and thereby incommunicable, forming a kind of blurred moral signature.

After a time the attentive reader will notice in these stories a recurrent pattern of theme and incident: the grotesques, gathering up a little courage, venture out into the streets of Winesburg, often in the dark, there to establish some initiatory relationship with George Willard, the young reporter who hasn't yet lived long enough to become a grotesque. Hesitantly, fearfully, or with a sputtering incoherent rage, they approach him, pleading that he listen to their stories in the hope that perhaps they can find some sort of renewal in his youthful voice. Upon this sensitive and fragile boy they pour out their desires and frustrations. Dr. Parcival hopes that George Willard "will write the book I may never get written," and for Enoch Robinson, the boy represents "the youthful sadness, young man's sadness, the sadness of a growing boy in a village at the year's end (which may open) the lips of the old man."

What the grotesques really need is each other, but their estrangement is so extreme that they cannot establish direct ties—they can only hope for connection through George Willard. The burden placed on the boy is more than he can bear. He listens to them attentively, he is sympathetic to their complaints, but finally he is too absorbed in his own dreams. The grotesques turn to him because he seems "different"—younger, more open, not yet hardened—but it is precisely this "difference" that keeps him from responding as warmly as they want. It is hardly the boy's fault; it is simply in the nature of things. For George Willard, the grotesques form a moment in his education; for the grotesques, their encounters with George Willard come to seem like a stamp of hopelessness.

The prose Anderson employs in telling these stories may seem at first glance to be simple: short sentences, a sparse vocabulary, uncomplicated syntax. In actuality, Anderson developed an artful style in which, following Mark Twain and preceding Ernest Hemingway, he tried to use American speech as the base of a tensed rhythmic prose that has an economy and a shapeliness seldom found in ordinary speech or even oral narration. What Anderson employs here is a stylized version of the American language, sometimes rising to quite formal rhetorical patterns and sometimes sinking to a self-conscious mannerism. But at its best,

Anderson's prose style in *Winesburg, Ohio* is a supple instrument, yielding that "low fine music" which he admired so much in the stories of Turgenev.

One of the worst fates that can befall a writer is that of self-imitation: the effort later in life, often desperate, to recapture the tones and themes of youthful beginnings. Something of the sort happened with Anderson's later writings. Most critics and readers grew impatient with the work he did after, say, 1927 or 1928; they felt he was constantly repeating his gestures of emotional "groping"—what he had called in *Winesburg, Ohio* the "indefinable hunger" that prods and torments people. It became the critical fashion to see Anderson's "gropings" as a sign of delayed adolescence, a failure to develop as a writer. Once he wrote a chilling reply to those who dismissed him in this way: "I don't think it matters much, all this calling a man a muddler, a groper, etc.... The very man who throws such words as these knows in his heart that he is also facing a wall." This remark seems to me both dignified and strong, yet it must be admitted that there was some justice in the negative responses to his later work. For what characterized it was not so much "groping" as the imitation of "groping," the self-caricature of a writer who feels driven back upon an earlier self that is, alas, no longer available.

But *Winesburg, Ohio* remains a vital work, fresh and authentic. Most of its stories are composed in a minor key, a tone of subdued pathos—pathos marking both the nature and limit of Anderson's talent. (He spoke of himself as a "minor writer.") In a few stories, however, he was able to reach beyond pathos and to strike a tragic note. The single best story in *Winesburg, Ohio* is, I think, "The Untold Lie," in which the urgency of choice becomes an outer sign of a tragic element in the human condition. And in Anderson's single greatest story, "The Egg," which appeared a few years after *Winesburg, Ohio*, he succeeded in bringing together a surface of farce with an undertone of tragedy. "The Egg" is an American masterpiece.

Anderson's influence upon later American writers, especially those who wrote short stories, has been enormous. Ernest Hemingway and William Faulkner both praised him as a writer who brought a new tremor of feeling, a new sense of introspectiveness to the American short story. As Faulkner put it, Anderson "was the fumbling for exactitude, the exact word and phrase within the limited scope of a vocabulary controlled and even repressed by what was in him almost a fetish of simplicity...to seek always to penetrate to thought's uttermost end." And in many younger writers who may not even be aware of the Anderson influence, you can see touches of his approach, echoes of his voice.

Writing about the Elizabethan playwright John Ford, the poet Algernon Swinburne once said: "If he touches you once he takes you, and what he takes he keeps hold of; his work becomes part of your thought and parcel of your spiritual furniture forever." So it is, for me and many others, with Sherwood Anderson.

[Selected from Sherwood Anderson. *Winesberg, Ohio*. New York: Penguin Books Ltd., 1976.]

3. John Steinbeck

3.1 Presentation Topics

(1) John Steinbeck as a realistic and regionalist writer and Nobel laureate.

(2) Social protest characteristic of much of Steinbeck's writings.

(3) Artistic feature(s) of his works: a. Steinbeck's prose style for a poetic quality which heightens the realism of his naturalistic writings. b. His method of "interchapters" which helps to unify the themes, symbols and actions.

3.2 Selected Reading

Ⅰ. Central issue of concern

The central theme of his works is the unremitting struggle of people who depend on the soil for their livelihood and the quiet dignity he saw in them.

Ⅱ. Text

The Leader of the People

On Saturday afternoon Billy Buck, the ranch hand, raked together the last of the old year's haystack and pitched small forkfuls over the wire fence to a few mildly interested cattle. High in the air small clouds like puffs of cannon smoke were driven eastward by the March wind. The wind could be heard whishing in the brush on the ridge crests, but no breath of it penetrated down into the ranch-cup.

The little boy, Jody, emerged from the house eating a thick piece of buttered bread. He saw Billy working on the last of the haystack. Jody tramped down scuffing his shoes in a way he had been told was destructive to good shoe leather. A flock of white pigeons flew out of the black cypress tree as Jody passed, and circled the tree and landed again. A half-grown tortoise-shell cat leaped from the bunkhouse porch, galloped on stiff legs across the road, whirled, and galloped back again. Jody picked up a stone to help the game along, but he was too late, for the cat was under the porch before the stone could be discharged. He threw the stone into the cypress tree and started the white pigeons on another whirling flight.

Arriving at the used-up haystack, the boy leaned against the bared-wire fence. "Will that be all of it, do you think?" he asked.

The middle-aged ranch hand stopped his careful raking and stuck his fork into the ground. He took off his black hat and smoothed down his hair. "Nothing left of it that isn't soggy from ground moisture," he said. He replaced his hat and rubbed his dry leathery hands together.

"Ought to be plenty mice," Jody suggested.

"Lousy with them," said Billy. "Just crawling with mice."

"Well, maybe, when you get all through, I could call the dogs and hunt the mice."

"Sure, I guess you could," said Billy Buck. He lifted a forkful of the damp ground hay and threw it into the air. Instantly three mice leaped out and burrowed frantically under the hay again.

Jody sighed with satisfaction. Those plump, sleek, arrogant mice were doomed. For eight months they had lived and multiplied in the haystack. They had been immune from cats, from traps, from poison, and from Jody. They had grown smug in their security, overbearing and fat. Now the time of disaster had come; they would not survive another day.

Billy looked up at the top of the hills that surrounded the ranch. "Maybe you better ask your father before you do it," he suggested.

"Well, where is he? I'll ask him now."

"He rode up to the ridge ranch after dinner. He'll be back pretty soon."

Jody slumped against the fencepost. "I don't think he's care."

As Billy went back to his work he said ominously, "You'd better ask him anyway. You know how he is."

Jody did know. His father, Carl Tiflin insisted upon giving permission for anything that was done on the ranch, whether it was important or not. Jody sagged farther against the post until he was sitting on the ground. He looked up at the little puffs of wind-driven cloud. "Is it like to rain, Billy?"

"It might. The wind's good for it, but not strong enough."

"Well, I hope it don't rain until after I kill those damn mice." He looked over his shoulder to see whether Billy had noticed the mature profanity①. Billy worked on without comment.

Jody turned back and looked at sidehill where the road from the outside world came down. The hill was washed with lean March sunshine. Silver thistles, blue lupines, and a few poppies bloomed among the sage bushes②. Halfway up the hill Jody could see Double-tree Mutt, the black dog, digging in a squirrel hole. He paddled for a while and then paused to kick bursts of dirt out between his hind legs, and he dug with an earnestness which belied the knowledge he must have had that no dog had ever caught a squirrel by digging in a hole.

Suddenly, while Jody watched, the black dog stiffened, and backed out of the hole and looked up the hill toward the cleft in the ridge where the road came through. Jody looked up too. For a moment Carl Tiflin on houseback stood out against the pale sky, and then he moved down the road toward the house. He carried something white in his hand.

The boy started to his feet. "He's got a letter," Jody cried. He trotted away toward the ranch house, for the letter would probably be read aloud and he wanted to be there. He reached the house before his father did, and ran in. He heard Carl dismount form his creaking saddle and slap the horse on the side to send it to the barn where Billy would unsaddle it and turn it out.

Jody ran into the kitchen. "We got a letter!" he cried.

His mother looked up from a pan of beans. "Who has?"

"Father has. I saw it in his hand."

Carl strode into the kitchen then, and Jody's mother asked, "Who's the letter from, Carl?"

---

① Adult cursing words.

② Bushy evergreen shrubs in North America.

He frowned quickly. "How did you know there was a letter?"

She nodded her head in the boy's direction. "Big-Britches[①] Jody told me."

Jody was embarrassed.

His father looked down at him contemptuously. "He is getting to be a big-britches," Carl said. "He's minding everybody's business but his own. Got his big nose into everything."

Mrs. Tiflin relented a little. "Well, he hasn't enough to keep him busy. Who's the letter from?"

Carl still frowned on Jody. "I'll keep him busy if he isn't careful." He held out a sealed letter. "I guess it's from your father."

Mrs. Tiflin took a hairpin from her head and slit open the flap. Her lips pursed judiciously. Jody saw her eyes snap back and forth over the lines. "He says," she translated, "he says he's going to drive out Saturday to stay for a little while. Why, this is Saturday. The letter must have been delayed." She looked at the postmark. "This was mailed day before yesterday. It should have been here yesterday." She looked up questioningly at her husband, and then her face darkened angrily. "Now what have you got that look on you for? He doesn't come often."

Carl turned his eyes away from her anger. He could be stern with her most of the time, but when occasionally her temper rose, he could not combat it.

"What's the matter with you?" she demanded again.

In his explanation there was a tone of apology Jody himself might have used. "It's just that he talks," Carl said lamely. "Just talks."

"Well, what of it? You talk yourself."

"Sure I do. But your father only talks about one thing."

"Indians!" Jody broke in excitedly. "Indians and crossing the plains!"

Carl turned fiercely on him. "You get out, Mr. Big-Britches! Go on, now! Get out!"

Jody went miserably out the back door and closed the screen with elaborate quietness. Under the kitchen window his shamed, down-cast eyes fell upon a curiously shaped stone, a stone of such fascination that he squatted down and

① [oral] Bit breeches, shorts.

picked it up and turned it over in his hands.

The voices came clearly to him through the open kitchen window. "Just Indians and crossing the plains. I've heard that story about how the horses got driven off about a thousand times. He just goes on and on, and he never changes a word in the things he tells."

When Mrs. Tiflin answered, her tone was so changed that Jody, outside the window, looked up from his study of the stone. Her voice had become soft and explanatory. Jody knew how her face would have changed to match the tone. She said quietly, "Look at it this way, Carl. That was the big thing in my father's life. He led a wagon train clear across the plains to the west coast, and when it was finished, his life was done. It was a big thing to do, but it didn't last long enough. Look!"She continued, "It's as though he was born to do that, and after he finished it, there wasn't anything more for him to do but think about it and talk about it. If there'd been any farther west to go, he's have gone. He's told me so himself. But at last there was the ocean. He lives right by the ocean where he had to stop."

She had caught Carl, caught and entangled him in her soft tone.

"I've seen him," he agreed quietly. "He goes down and stares off west over the ocean." His voice sharpened a little. "And then he goes up to the Horseshoe Club in Pacific Grove, and he tells people how the Indians drove off the horses."

She tried to catch him again. "Well, it's everything to him. You might be patient with him and pretend to listen."

Carl turned impatiently away. "Well, if it gets too bad. I can always go down to the bunkhouse and sit with Billy," he said irritably. He walked through the house and slammed the front door after him.

Jody ran to his chores. He dumped the grain to the chickens without chasing any of them. He gathered the eggs from the nests. He trotted into the house with the wood and interlaced it so carefully in the woodbox that two armloads seemed to fill it to overflowing.

His mother had finished the beans by now. She stirred up the fire and brushed off the stove top with a turkey wing. Jody peered cautiously at her to see whether any rancor toward him remained. "Is he coming today?" Jody asked.

"That's what his letter said."

"Maybe I better walk up the road to meet him."

Mrs. Tiflin clanged the stove lid shut. "That would be nice," she said. "He'd probably like to be met."

"I guess I'll just do it then."

Outside, Jody whistled shrilly to the dogs. "Come on up the hill," he commanded. The two dogs waved their tails and ran ahead. Along the roadside the sage had tender new tips. Jody tore off some pieces and rubbed them on his hands until the air was filled with the sharp wild smell. With a rush the dogs leaped from the road and yapped into the brush after a rabbit. That was the last Jody saw of them, for when they failed to catch the rabbit, they went back home.

Jody plodded on up the hill toward the ridge top. When he reached the little cleft where the road came through, the afternoon wind struck him and blew up his hair and ruffled his shirt. He looked down on the little hills and ridges below and then out at the huge green Salinas Valley. He could see the white town of Salinas far out in the flat and the flash of its windows under the waning sun. Directly below him, in an oak tree, a crow congress had convened①. The tree was black with crows all cawing at once.

Then Jody's eyes followed the wagon road down from the ridge where he stood, and lost it behind a hill, and picked it up again on the other side. On that distant stretch he saw a cart slowly pulled by a bay horse. It disappeared behind the hill. Jody sat down on the ground and watched the place where the cart would reappear again. The wind sang on the hilltops and the puff-ball clouds hurried eastward.

Then the cart came into sight and stopped. A man dressed in black dismounted from the seat and walked to the horse's head. Although it was so far away, Jody knew he had unhooked the checkrein, for the horse's head dropped forward. The horse moved on, and the man walked slowly up the hill beside it. Jody gave a glad cry and ran down the road toward them. The squirrels bumped along off the road, and a road runner flirted its tail and raced over the edge of the hill and sailed out like a glider.

Jody tried to leap into the middle of his shadow at every step. A stone rolled under his foot and he went down. Around a little bend he raced, and there, a short

① There is a cloud of crows.

distance ahead, were his grandfather and the cart. The boy dropped from his unseemly running and approached at a dignified walk.

The horse plodded stumble-footedly up the hill and the old man walked beside it. In the lowering sun their giant shadows flickered darkly behind them. The grandfather was dressed in a black broadcloth suit and he wore kid congress gaiters① and a black tie on a short, hard collar. He carried his black slouch hat in his hand. His white beard was cropped close and his white eyebrows overhung his eyes like mustaches. The blue eyes were sternly merry. About the whole face and figure there was a granite dignity, so that every motion seemed an impossible thing. Once at rest, it seemed the old man would be stone, would never move again. His steps were slow and certain. Once make, no step would ever be retraced; once headed in a direction, the path would never bend nor the pace increase nor slow.

When Jody appeared around the bend, Grandfather waved his hat slowly in welcome, and he called, "Why, Jody! Come down to meet me, have you?"

Jody sidled near and turned and matched his step to the old man's step and stiffened his body and dragged his heels a little. "Yes, sir," he said. "We got your letter only today."

"Should have been here yesterday." Said grandfather. "It certainly should. How are all the folks?"

"They're fine, sir." He hesitated and then suggested shyly, "Would you like to come on a mouse hunt tomorrow, sir?"

"Mouse hunt, Jody?" Grandfather chuckled. "Have the people of this generation come down to hunting mice? They aren't very strong the new people, but I hardly thought mice would be game for them."

"No, sir. It's just play. The haystack's gone. I'm going to drive out the mice to the dogs. You can watch, or even beat the hay a little."

The stern, merry eyes turned down on him. "I see. You don't eat them, then. You haven't come to that yet."

Jody explained, "The dogs eat them, sir. It wouldn't be much like hunting Indians, I guess."

---

① Congress boots, high shoes with elastic sides, by the stretching of which they are drawn onto the feet.

"No, not much—but then later, when the troops were hunting Indians and shooting children and burning tepees, it wasn't much different from your mouse hunt."

They topped the rise and started down into the ranch-cup, and they lost the sun from their shoulders. "You've grown," Grandfather said. "Nearly an inch, I should say."

"More," Jody boasted. "Where they mark me on the door, I'm up more than an inch since Thanksgiving even."

Grandfather's rich throaty voice said, "Maybe you're getting too much water and turning to pith and stalk. Wait until you head out, and then we'll see."

Jody looked quickly into the old man's face to see whether his feelings should be hurt, but there was no will to injure, no punishing, nor putting-in-your-place light in the keen blue eyes. "We might kill a pig," Jody suggested.

"Oh, no! I couldn't let you do that. You're just humoring me. It isn't the time and you know it."

"You know Riley, the big boar, sir?"

"Yes, I remember Riley well."

"Well, Riley ate a hole into that same haystack, and it fell down on him and smothered him."

"Pigs do that when they can," said Grandfather.

"Riley was a nice pig, for a boar, sir. I rode him sometimes, and he didn't mind."

A door slammed at the house below them, and they saw Jody's mother standing on the porch waving her apron in welcome. And they saw Carl Tiflin walking up from the barn to be at the house for the arrival.

The sun had disappeared from the hills by now. The blue smoke from the house chimney hung in flat layers in the purpling ranch-cup. The puff-ball clouds, dropped by the falling wind, hung listlessly in the sky.

Billy Buck came out of the bunkhouse and flung a wash basin of soapy water on the ground. He had been shaving in midweek, for Billy held Grandfather in reverence, and Grandfather said that Billy was one of the few men of the new generation who had not gone soft. Although Billy was in middle age, Grandfather considered him a boy. Now Billy was hurrying toward the house too.

When Jody and Grandfather arrived, the three were waiting for them in front of the yard gate.

Carl said, "Hello, sir. We've been looking for you."

Mrs. Tiflin kissed Grandfather on the side of his beard, and stood still while his big hand patted her shoulder. Billy shook hands solemnly, grinning under his straw mustache. "I'll put up your horse," said Billy, and he led the rig away.

Grandfather watched him go, and then, turning back to the group, he said as he had said a hundred times before, "There is a good boy. I knew his father, old Mule-tail Buck. I never knew why they called him Mule-tail Buck except he packed mules①."

Mrs. Tiflin turned and led the way into the house. "How long are you going to stay, Father? Your letter didn't say."

"Well, I don't know. I thought I'd stay about two weeks. But I never stay as long as I think I'm going to."

In a short while they were sitting at the white oilcloth table eating their supper. The lamp with the reflector hung over the table. Outside the dining-room windows the big moths battered softly against the glass.

Grandfather cut his steak into tiny pieces and chewed slowly. "I'm hungry," he said. "Driving out here got my appetite up. It's like when we were crossing. We all got so hungry every night we could hardly wait to let the meat get done. I could eat about five pounds of buffalo meat every night."

"It's moving around, does it," said Billy. "My father was a government packer②. I helped him when I was a kid. Just the two of us could about clean up a deer's ham."

"I knew your father, Billy," said Grandfather. "A fine man he was. They called him Mile-tail Buck. I don't know why except he packed mules."

"That was it," Billy agreed. "He packed mules."

Grandfather put down his knife and fork and looked around the table, "I remember one time we ran out of meat—" His voice dropped to a curious low singsong, dropped into a tonal groove the story had worn for itself. "There was no

---

① Billy's father was in charge of a string of mules which carried goods or provisions.

② One who ran a string of mules owned by the government.

buffalo, no antelope, not even rabbits. The hunters couldn't even shoot a coyote. That was the time for the leader to be on the watch. I was the leader, and I kept my eyes open. Know why? Well, just the minute the people began to get hungry they'd start slaughtering the team oxen. Do you believe that? I've heard of parties that just ate up their draft cattle. Started from the middle and worked toward the ends. Finally they'd eat the lead pair, and then the wheelers①. The leader of a party had to keep them from doing that."

In some manner a big moth got into the room and circled the hanging kerosene lamp. Billy got up and tried to clap it between his hands. Carl struck with a cupped palm and caught the moth and broke it. He walked to the window and dropped it out.

"As I was saying," Grandfather began again, but Carl interrupted him. "You'd better eat some more meat. All the rest of us are ready for our pudding."

Jody saw a flash of anger in his mother's eyes. Grandfather picked up his knife and fork. "I'm pretty hungry, all right," he said. "I'll tell you about that later."

When supper was over, when the family and Billy Buck sat in front of the fireplace in the other room, Jody anxiously watched Grandfather. He saw the signs he knew. The bearded head leaned forward; the eyes lost their sternness and looked wonderingly into the fire; the big lean fingers laced themselves on the black knees. "I wonder," he began, "I just wonder whether I ever told you how those thieving Piutes② drove off thirty-five of our horses."

"I think you did," Carl interrupted. "Wasn't it just before you went up into the Tahoe country③?"

Grandfather turned quickly toward his son-in-law. "That's right. I guess I must have told you that story."

"Lots of times," Carl said cruelly, and he avoided his wife's eyes. But he felt the angry eyes on him, and he said, "'Course I'd like to hear it again."

---

① The lead pair were the animals harnessed first in a team; the wheelers were placed immediately in front of the wheels of a wagon.

② A term applied to various Shoshone Indian tribes who were scattered from Arizona and Utah to Nevada, California, and Oregon.

③ The high forested land near Lake Tahoe, a lake which lies at the base of the Sierra Nevada Mountains on the Nevada-California boundary.

Grandfather looked back at the fire. His fingers unlaced and laced again. Jody knew how he felt, how his insides were collapsed and empty. Hadn't Jody been called a big-britches that very afternoon? He arose to heroism and opened himself to the term big-britches again. "Tell about Indians," he said softly.

Grandfather's eyes grew stern again. "Boys always want to hear about Indians. It was a job for men, but boys want to hear about it. Well, let's see. Did I ever tell you how I wanted each wagon to carry a long iron plate?"

Everyone but Jody remained silent. Jody said, "No. You didn't."

"Well, when the Indians attacked, we always put the wagons in a circle and fought form between the wheels. I thought that if every wagon carried a long plate with rifle holes, the men could stand the plates on the outside of the wheels when the wagons were in the circle and they would be protected. It would save lives and that would make up for the extra weight of the iron. But of course the party wouldn't do it. No party had done it before, and they couldn't see why they should go to the expense. They lived to regret it, too."

Jody looked at his mother, and knew from her expression that she was not listening at all. Carl picked at a callus on his thumb and Billy Buck watched a spider crawling up the wall.

Grandfather's tone dropped into its narrative groove again. Jody knew in advance exactly what words would fall. The story droned on, speeded up for the attack, grew sad over the wounds, struck a dirge at the burials on the great plains. Jody sat quietly watching Grandfather. The stern blue eyes were detached. He looked as though he were not very interested. He looked as though he were not very interested in the story himself.

When it was finished, when the pause had been politely respected as the frontier of the story, Billy Buck stood up and stretched and hitched his trousers. "I guess I'll turn in," he said. Then he faced Grandfather. "I've got an old powder horn and a cap and ball pistol down to the bunkhouse. Did I ever show them to you?"

Grandfather nodded slowly. "Yes, I think you did, Billy. Reminds me of a pistol I had when I was leading the people across." Billy stood politely until the little story was done, and then he said, "Good night," and went out of the house.

Carl Tiflin tried to turn the conversation then. "How's the country between here and Monterey? I've heard it's pretty dry."

"It is dry," said Grandfather. "There's not a drop of water in the Laguna Seca. But it's a long pull from '87. The whole country was powder then, and in '61 I believe all the coyotes starved to death. We had fifteen inches of rain this year."

"Yes, but it all came too early. We could do with some now." Carl's eye fell on Jody. "Hadn't you better be getting to bed?"

Jody stood up obediently. "Can I kill the mice in the old haystack, sir?"

"Mice? Oh! Sure, kill them all off. Billy said there isn't any good hay left."

Jody exchanged a secret and satisfying look with Grandfather. "I'll kill every one tomorrow," he promised.

Jody lay in his bed and thought of the impossible world of Indians and buffaloes, a world that had ceased to be forever. He wished he could have been living in the heroic time, but he knew he was not of heroic timber. No one living now, save possibly Billy Buck, was worthy to do the things that had been done. A race of giants had lived then, fearless men, men of a stanchness unknown in this day. Jody thought of the wide plains and of the wagons moving across like centipedes. He thought of Grandfather on a huge white horse, marshaling the people. Across his mind marched the great phantoms, and they marched off the earth and they were gone.

He came back to the ranch for a moment, then. He heard the dull rushing sound that space and silence make. He heard one of the dogs, out in the doghouse, scratching a flea and bumping his elbow against the floor with every stroke. Then the wind arose again, and the black cypress groaned, and Jody went to sleep.

He was up half an hour before the triangle sounded for breakfast. His mother was rattling the stove to make the flames roar when Jody went through the kitchen. "You're up early," she said. "Where are you going?"

"Out to get a good stick. We're going to kill the mice today."

"Who is 'we'?"

"Why, Grandfather and I."

"So you've got him in it. You always like to have someone in with you in case there's blame to share."

"I'll be right back," said Jody. "I just want to have a good stick ready for after breakfast."

He closed the screen door after him and went out into the cool blue morning. The birds were noisy in the dawn and the ranch cats came down from the hill like blunt snakes. They had been hunting gophers in the dark, and although the four cats were full of gopher meat, they sat in a semicircle at the back door and mewed piteously for milk. Doubletree Mutt and Smasher moved sniffling along the edge of the brush, performing the duty with rigid ceremony, but when Jody whistled, their heads jerked up and their tails waved. They plunged down to him, wriggling their skins and yawning. Jody patted their heads seriously, and moved on to the weathered scrap pile. He selected an old broom handle and a short piece of inch-square scrap wood. From his pocket he took a shoelace and tied the ends of the sticks loosely together to make a flail. He whistled his new weapon through the air and struck the ground to look over the field of slaughter, but Billy Buck, sitting patiently on the back steps, called to him, "You better come back. It's only a couple of minutes till breakfast."

Jody changed his course and moved toward the house. He leaned his flail against the steps. "That's to drive the mice out," he said. "I'll bet they're fat. I'll bet they don't know what's going to happen to them today."

"No, nor you either," Billy remarked philosophically, "nor me, nor anyone."

Jody was staggered by this thought. He knew it was true. His imagination twitched away from the mouse hunt. Then his mother came out on the back porch and struck the triangle, and all thoughts fell in a heap.

Grandfather hadn't appeared at the table when they sat down. Billy nodded at his empty chair. "He's all right? He isn't sick?"

"He takes a long time to dress," said Mrs. Tiflin. "He combs his whiskers and rubs up his shoes and brushes his clothes."

Carl scattered sugar on his mush. "Don't do that, Carl! Please don't!" There was more of threat than of request in her tone. And the threat irritated Carl.

"Well, how many times do I have to listen to the story of the iron plates, and the thirty-five horses? That time's done. Why can't he forget it, now it's done?" He grew angrier while he talked, and his voice rose. "Why does he have to tell them over and over? He came across the plains. All right! Now it's finished. Nobody wants to hear about it over and over."

The door into the kitchen closed softly. The four at the table sat frozen. Carl laid his mush spoon on the tale and touched his chin with his fingers.

Then the kitchen door opened and Grandfather walked in. His mouth smiled tightly and his eyes were squinted. "Good morning," he said, and he sat down and looked at his mush dish.

Carl could not leave it there. "Did—did you hear what I said?"

Grandfather jerked a little nod.

"I don't know what got into me, sir. I didn't mean it. I was just being funny."

Jody glanced in shame at his mother, and he saw that she was looking at Carl, and that she wasn't breathing. It was an awful thing that he was doing. He was tearing himself to pieces to talk like that. It was a terrible thing to him to retract a word, but to retract it in shame was infinitely worse.

Grandfather looked sidewise. "I'm trying to get right side up," he said gently. "I'm not being mad. I don't mind what you said, but it might be true, and I would mind that."

"It isn't true," said Carl. "I'm not feeling well this morning. I'm sorry I said it."

"Don't be sorry, Carl. An old man doesn't see things sometimes. Maybe you're right. The crossing is finished. Maybe it should be forgotten, now it's done."

Carl got up from the table. "I've had enough to eat. I'm going to work. Take your time, Billy!" He walked quickly out of the dining room. Billy gulped the rest of his food and followed soon after. But Jody could not leave his chair.

"Won't you tell any more stories?" Jody asked.

"Why, sure I'll tell them, but only when—I'm sure people want to hear them."

"I like to hear them, sir."

"Oh! Of course you do, but you're a little boy. It was a job for men, but only little boys like to hear about it."

Jody got up from his place. "I'll wait outside for you, sir. I've got a good stick for those mice."

He waited by the gate until the old man came out on the porch. "Let's go down and kill the mice now," Jody called.

"I think I'll just sit in the sun, Jody. You go kill the mice."

"You can use my stick if you like."

"No, I'll just sit here a while."

Jody turned disconsolately away, and walked down toward the old haystack. He tried to whip up his enthusiasm with thoughts of the fat juicy mice. He beat the ground with his flail. The dogs coaxed and whined about him, but he could not go. Back at the house he could see Grandfather sitting on the porch, looking small and thin and black.

Jody gave up and went to sit on the steps at the old man's feet.

"Back already? Did you kill the mice?"

"No, sir. I'll kill them some other day."

The morning flies buzzed close to the ground and the ants dashed about in front of the steps. The heavy smell of sage slipped down the hill. The porch boards grew warm in the sunshine.

Jody hardly knew when Grandfather started to talk. "I shouldn't stay here, feeling the way I do."

He examined his strong old hands. "I feel as though the crossing wasn't worth doing." His eyes moved up the sidehill and stopped on a motionless hawk perched on a dead limb. "I tell those old stories, but they're not what I want to tell. I only know how I want people to feel when I tell them.

"It wasn't Indians that were important, nor adventures, nor even getting out here. It was a whole bunch of people made into one big crawling beast. And I was the head. It was westering and westering. Every man wanted something for himself, but the big beast that was all of them wanted only westering. I was the leader, but if I hadn't been there, someone else would have been the head. The thing had to have a head.

"Under the little bushes the shadows were black at white noonday. When we saw the mountains at last, we cried—all of us. But it wasn't getting here that mattered, it was movement and westering.

"We carried life out here and set it down the way those ants carry eggs. And I was the leader. The westering was as big as God, and the slow steps that made the movement piled up and piled up until the continent was crossed.

"Then we came down to the sea, and it was done." He stopped and wiped his eyes until the rims were red. "That's what I should be telling instead of stories."

When Jody spoke, Grandfather started and looked down at him. "Maybe I could lead the people someday," Jody said.

The old man smiled. " There's no place to go. There's the ocean to stop you. There's a line of old men along the shore hating the ocean because it stopped them. "

"In boats I might, sir. "

"No place to go, Jody. Every place is taken. But that's not the worst—no, not the worst. Westering has died out of the people. Westering isn't a hunger any more. It's all done. Your father is right. It is finished. " He laced his fingers on his knee and looked at them.

Jody felt very sad. "If you'd like a glass of lemonade, I could make it for you. "

Grandfather was about to refuse, and then he saw Jody's face. "That would be nice," he said. "Yes, it would be nice to drink a lemonade. "

Jody ran into the kitchen where his mother was wiping the last of the breakfast dishes. "Can I have a lemon to make a lemonade for Grandfather?"

His mother mimicked—"And another lemon to make a lemonade for you. "

"No, ma'am. I don't want one. "

"Jody! You're sick!" then she stopped suddenly. "Take a lemon out of the cooler," she said softly. "Here, I'll reach the squeezer down to you. "

[Selected From John Steinbeck. *The Long Valley*. London: Marderin, 1990.]

Ⅲ. Questions for discussion

(1) Both of Jody's parents call him "Big Britches. " Why is Jody's reaction to his father's use of the term different from his feeling when his mother uses it? Contrast Jody's relationship with his grandfather to his relationship with his father and explain why.

(2) What ideas about the Westward Movement does Grandfather express? What is the spirit of Westering? Grandfather tells Jody that he believes "Westering has died out of the people," why Grandfather has reached this conclusion?

(3) What is the narrative point of view of The Leader of the People? During the course of the story Jody overhears his father and mother discussing grandfather. How does this overheard conversation illustrate the difficulties inherent in handling this point of view? Later Jody is present when his father utters the criticism that Grandfather overhears. Explain why, using the point of view that

Steinbeck had adopted, Jody's presence is necessary.

(4) Because of Steinbeck's tone, the reader sympathizes with Grandfather and admires Jody's capacity for understanding. Why is this so? In what way can you tell the writer is a "primitivist"?

(5) John Steinbeck shows the artistry with which a writer uses figures of speech to convey exact and vivid meaning to the story. Comment on his strong poetic quality of the story and pick out sentences which contain figurative language.

(6) Can you find out the symbols in the story and what they are symbolic of?

3.3 Assigned Reading

The Nobel Prize in Literature 1962 Presentation Speech

Anders Osterling①

John Steinbeck, the author awarded this year's Nobel Prize in Literature, was born in the little town of Salinas, California, a few miles from the Pacific coast near the fertile Salinas Valley. This locality forms the background for many of his descriptions of the common man's everyday life. He was raised in moderate circumstances, yet he was on equal terms with the workers' families in this rather diversified area. While studying at Stanford University, he often had to earn his living by working on the ranches. He left Stanford without graduating and, in 1925, went to New York as a freelance writer. After bitter years of struggling to exist, he returned to California, where he found a home in a lonely cottage by the sea. There he continued his writing.

Although he had already written several books by 1935, he achieved his first popular success in that year with *Tortilla Flat*. He offered his readers spicy and comic tales about a gang of paisanos, a social individuals who, in their wild revels, are almost caricatures of *King Arthur's Knights of the Round Table*. It has been said that in the United States this book came as a welcome antidote to the gloom of the then prevailing depression. The laugh was now on Steinbeck's side.

But he had no mind to be an unoffending comforter and entertainer. The topics

① Permanent Secretary of the Swedish Academy.

he chose were serious and denunciatory, as for example the bitter strikes on California's fruit and cotton plantations which he depicted in his novel *In Dubious Battle* (1936). The power of his literary style increased steadily during these years. The little masterpiece *Of Mice and Men* (1937), which is the story of Lennie, the imbecile giant who, out of tenderness, alone squeezes the life out of every living creature that comes into his hands, was followed by those incomparable short stories which he collected in the volume *The Long Valley* (1938). The way had now been paved for the great work that is principally associated with Steinbeck's name, the epic chronicle *The Grapes of Wrath* (1939). This is the story of the emigration to California which was forced upon a group of people from Oklahoma through unemployment and abuse of power. This tragic episode in the social history of the United States inspired in Steinbeck a poignant description of the experiences of one particular farmer and his family during their endless, heartbreaking journey to a new home.

In this brief presentation it is not possible to dwell at any length on individual works which Steinbeck later produced. If at times the critics have seemed to note certain signs of flagging powers, of repetitions that might point to a decrease in vitality, Steinbeck belied their fears most emphatically with *The Winter of Our Discontent* (1961), a novel published last year. Here he attained the same standard which he set in *The Grapes of Wrath*. Again he holds his position as an independent expounder of the truth with an unbiased instinct for what is genuinely American, be it good or bad.

In this recent novel, the central figure is the head of a family who has come down in the world. After serving in the war, he fails at whatever he tries until at last he is employed in the simple work of a grocery store clerk in the New England town of his forefathers. He is an honest man and he does not complain without due cause, although he is constantly exposed to temptation when he sees the means by which material success must be purchased. However, such means require both hard scrupulousness and moral obduracy, qualities he cannot muster without risking his personal integrity. Tellingly displayed in his sensitive conscience, irradiated like a prism, is a whole body of questions which bear on the nation's welfare problems. This is done without any theorizing, using concrete, or even trivial, everyday situation, which are nonetheless convincing when described with all of Steinbeck's vigorous and realistic verve. Even with his insistence on the factual, there are harmonic tones of daydreaming, fumbling speculations around the eternal theme of life and death.

Steinbeck's latest book is an account of his experiences during a three-month tour of forty American states *Travels with Charley* (1962). He traveled in a small truck equipped with a cabin where he slept and kept his stores. He travelled incognito, his only companion being a black poodle. We see here what a very experienced observer and raisonneur he is. In a series of admirable explorations into local color, he rediscovers his country and its people. In its informal way this book is also a forceful criticism of society. The traveler in Rosinante—the name which he gave his truck—shows a slight tendency to praise the old at the expense of the new, even though it is quite obvious that he is on guard against the temptation. "I wonder why progress so often looks like destruction," he says in one place when he sees the bulldozers flattening out the verdant forest of Seattle to make room for the feverishly expanding residential areas and the skyscrapers. It is, in any case, a most topical reflection, valid also outside America.

Among the masters of modern American literature who have already been awarded this Prize—from Sinclair Lewis to Ernest Hemingway—Steinbeck more than holds his own, independent in position and achievement. There is in him a strain of grim humor which, to some extent, redeems his often cruel and crude motif. His sympathies always go out to the oppressed, to the misfits and the distressed; he likes to contrast the simple joy of life with the brutal and cynical craving for money. But in him we find the American temperament also in his great feeling for nature, for the tilled soil, the wasteland, the mountains, and the ocean coasts, all an inexhaustible source of inspiration to Steinbeck in the midst of, and beyond, the world of human beings.

The Swedish Academy's reason for awarding the prize to John Steinbeck reads, "for his realistic as well as imaginative writings, distinguished by a sympathetic humor and a keen social perception."

Dear Mr. Steinbeck, you are not a stranger to the Swedish public any more than to that of your own country and of the whole world. With your most distinctive works you have become a teacher of good will and charity, a defender of human values, which can well be said to correspond to the proper idea of the Nobel

Prize. In expressing the congratulations of the Swedish Academy, I now ask you to receive this year's Nobel Prize in Literature from the hands of His Majesty, the King.

[Selected from Horst Frenz, (ed.). *Nobel Lectures, Literature 1901—1967*. Amsterdam: Elsevier Publishing Company, 1969.]

Chapter 2 "Lost Generation" Literature

1. Introduction

The 20th century began with a strong sense of social breakdown. A series of wars fought on the international scene during the first part of the century were to affect the life of Americans and their literary writings. The United States' participation in World War Ⅰ marked a crucial stage in the nation's evolution to a world power. It had become the most powerful industrialized nation in the world. Despite its booming industry and material prosperity, there was a sense of unease and restlessness underneath. World War Ⅰ had made a great impact on the life of the American people. They became less certain about what might arise in this changing world and more cynical about accepted standards of honesty and morality. The idea of "seize the day" or "enjoy the present" was pervasive, as opposed to placing all hope in the future.

There was a spiritual crisis in this period, a full blossoming of literary writings. The most recognizable literary movement that gave rise to the 20th century American literature is the expatriate movement.

The years immediately after World War Ⅰ brought a highly vocal rebellion against established social, sexual, and aesthetic conventions and a vigorous attempt to establish new values. Disillusionment after the war led to many people drifting morally and spiritually. The soldiers went into the war with expectations of making the world a safer place, but after many lost lives and much suffering, the world did not feel safer to those who gave up so much. The soldiers were disappointed; those back home were feeling the effects of the war, and no one was particularly pleased with the outcome and their current conditions. The dissatisfaction made many people question where they were, where they were going, and what it all meant.

They were a "lost generation." Young artists flocked to Greenwich Village, Chicago, and San Francisco, determined to protest and intent on making a new art. Others went to Europe, living mostly in Paris as expatriates. In Paris in the 1920s, writers and artists soon found their way to 27 Rue de Fleurus, the home of Gertrude Stein, Ernest Hemingway and F. Scott Fitzgerald. Of them, Miss Stein remarked to Hemingway, "You are all a lost generation." Out of their disillusion and rejection, the expatriates used their pens to rebel against established social, sexual, and aesthetic conventions and to attempt to establish new values. They rediscovered the vitality of the American scenes, its people and its speech, and built a new literature, impressive in the glittering 1920s and the years that followed.

The "Lost Generation," a phrase coined by Gertrude Stein and made popular by Ernest Hemingway in the epigraph to his first published novel *The Sun Also Rises*. Often it is used to refer to a group of American literary notables who lived in Paris and other parts of Europe, for example, F. Scott Fitzgerald, Ernest Hemingway, John Dos Passos, E. E. Cummings, T. S. Eliot, Djuna Barnes, Margaret Anderson, Sherwood Anderson, Kay Boyle, Hart Crane, Ford Maddox Ford and Zelda Fitzgerald to name a few. It also refers to the period from the end of World War Ⅰ to the beginning of the Great Depression. More generally, the term is used for the generation of young people coming of age in the United States during and shortly after World War Ⅰ. Broadly, the term is often used to refer to the younger literary modernists.

The Lost Generation's writers held many common points. At first, all of them were weary of the imperialistic wars but couldn't find the way out. Expatriation was another common point. Many young writers had an experience living in the European countries, especially in Paris. Although the government pronounced "recovering the atmosphere before the war," the war had left deep hurt in people's heart. Therefore, the writers' self-exile became a way of escaping from the reality.

America's Lost Generation expatriates had discussions with European celebrated authors and articulated their desire to admonish unsophisticated American society. During that time they advanced literary form and style in support of their discontent. Many of the authors experimented differently, but they all seemed to agree on their dedication to a new literature absent of the idealism and narrative simplicity of the previous century. The writers during this period tended to be anti-Romantic and tried to rid the world of mysterious aspects to uncover the true nature of life without the confinement of American life. Romantic clichés were abandoned for extreme realism or for complex symbolism and created myth. Language grew so frank that there were bitter quarrels over censorship. The influences of new psychology and of Marxian social theory were also very strong. Out of this highly active boiling of new ideas and new forms came writers of recognizable stature in the world. The Lost Generation writers all gained prominence in the 20th century literature. Their innovations challenged assumptions about writing and expression and changed the course for future.

American writers expressed the disillusionment following upon the war. The stories and novels of F. Scott Fitzgerald (1896—1940) capture the restless, pleasure-hungry, defiant mood of the 1920s. His works, including the early novels *This Side of Paradise* (1920) and *The Beautiful and Damned* (1922), and the story collections *Tales of the Jazz Age* (1922) and *All the Sad Young Men* (1926), captured the Jazz Age's vulgarity and dazzling promise. His brilliant *The Great Gatsby* (1925), a story of American wealth and corruption, was eventually acclaimed one of the century's greatest novels. Fitzgerald's characteristic theme, expressed poignantly in *The Great Gatsby*, is the tendency of youth's golden dreams to dissolve in failure and disappointment. Fitzgerald also elucidated the collapse of some key American ideals, set out in the Declaration of Independence, such as liberty, social unity, good governance and peace, with features which were severely threatened by the pressures of the modern early 20th century society.

Sinclair Lewis and Sherwood Anderson also wrote novels with critical depictions of American life. John Dos Passos wrote about the war and also the U. S. A. trilogy which extended into the Depression. In his fiction, Dos Passos is said to have mingled the naturalism of Theodore Dreiser with the modernism of James Joyce. His first successful novel, *Three Soldiers* (1921), belonged to the group of socially conscious novels of disillusionment that appeared after the war. With *Manhattan Transfer* (1925) his major creative period began. Intertwining accounts of a succession of unrelated characters, the novel presents a composite picture of the meaninglessness and decadence of the life of the typical early 1920s New Yorker. In his finest achievement, the trilogy *U. S. A.* (1937), composed of *The 42nd Parallel* (1930), *1919* (1932), and *The Big Money* (1936), he developed the kaleidoscopic technique introduced in Manhattan Transfer. By skillfully weaving together narration, stream of consciousness, biographies of representative figures, and quotations from newspapers and magazines, Dos Passos portrayed the first three decades of the 20th century in America.

Ernest Hemingway (1899—1961) saw violence and death first-hand as an ambulance driver in World War Ⅰ. With the publication of *The Sun Also Rises* (1926), he was recognized as the spokesman of the "lost generation." His next important novel, *A Farewell to Arms* (1929), tells of a tragic wartime love affair between an ambulance driver and an English nurse. From his experience in the Spanish Civil War came Hemingway's great novel, *For Whom the Bell Tolls* (1940), which in detailing an incident in the war argues for human brotherhood. His novella *The Old Man and the Sea* (1952) celebrates the indomitable courage of an aged Cuban fisherman. In 1954, he won the Nobel Prize in Literature. Hemingway's fiction usually focuses on people living essential, dangerous lives—soldiers, fishermen, athletes, bullfighters—who meet the pain and difficulty of their existence with stoic courage. His celebrated literary style, influenced by Ezra Pound and Gertrude Stein, is direct, terse, muscular, and often monotonous, yet particularly suited to his elemental subject matter. He adhered to a moral code that emphasized grace under pressure, and his protagonists are strong, silent men who often deal awkwardly with women.

Key words

Jazz Age

Jazz Age describes the period after the end of World War Ⅰ, through the Roaring Twenties, ending with the onset of the Great Depression. Traditional values of the previous period declined while the American stock market soared. The age took its name from popular music, which saw a tremendous surge in popularity. Among the prominent concerns and trends of the period were the public embrace of technological developments typically seen as progress—cars, air travel and the telephone—as well as new modernist trends in social behavior, the arts, and culture.

Iceberg Theory

Iceberg Theory is a writing theory advanced by American writer Ernest

Hemingway. According to him, "If a writer of a prose knows enough about what he is writing about he may omit things that he knows and the reader, if the writer is writing truly enough, will have a feeling of those things as strongly as though the writer had stated them. The dignity of movement of the iceberg is due to only one-eighth of it being above water. The writer who omits things because he does not know them only makes hollow places in his writing."

2. F. Scott Fitzgerald

2.1 Presentation Topics

(1) F. Scott Fitzgerald as the spokesman of the Lost Generation.

(2) The Jazz Age and its features.

(3) Fitzgerald known as a stylist.

2.2 Selected Reading

Ⅰ. Central issue of concern

Fitzgerald's concern with moral issues.

Ⅱ. Text

Babylon Revisited

(1)

"And where's Mr. Campbell?" Charlie asked.

"Gone to Switzerland. Mr. Campbell's a pretty sick man, Mr. Wales."

"I'm sorry to hear that. And George Hardt?" Charlie inquired.

"Back in America, gone to work."

"And where is the Snow Bird?"

"He was in here last week. Anyway, his friend, Mr. Schaeffer, is in Paris."

Two familiar names from the long list of a year and a half ago. Charlie scribbled an address in his notebook and tore out the page.

"If you see Mr. Schaeffer, give him this," he said. "It's my brother-in-law's address. I haven't settled on a hotel yet."

He was not really disappointed to find Paris was so empty. But the stillness in the Ritz bar was strange and portentous. It was not an American bar any more—he felt polite in it, and not as if he owned it. It had gone back into France. He felt the stillness from the moment he got out of the taxi and saw the doorman, usually in a frenzy of activity at this hour, gossiping with a *chasseur* by the servants' entrance.

Passing through the corridor, he heard only a single, bored voice in the once-clamorous women's room. When he turned into the bar he travelled the twenty feet of green carpet with his eyes fixed straight ahead by old habit; and then, with his foot firmly on the rail, he turned and surveyed the room, encountering only a single pair of eyes that fluttered up from a newspaper in the corner. Charlie asked for the head barman, Paul, who in the latter days of the bull market had come to work in his own custom-built car—disembarking, however, with due nicety at the nearest corner. But Paul was at his country house today and Alix giving him information.

"No, no more," Charlie said, "I'm going slow these days."

Alix congratulated him: "You were going pretty strong a couple of years ago."

"I'll stick to it all right," Charlie assured him. "I've stuck to it for over a year and a half now."

"How do you find conditions in America?"

"I haven't been to America for months. I'm in business in Prague, representing a couple of concerns there. They don't know about me down there."

Alix smiled.

"Remember the night of George Hardt's bachelor dinner here?" said Charlie. "By the way, what's become of Claude Fessenden?"

Alix lowered his voice confidentially: "He's in Paris, but he doesn't come here any more. Paul doesn't allow it. He ran up a bill of thirty thousand francs, charging all his drinks and his lunches, and usually his dinner, for more than a year. And when Paul finally told him he had to pay, he gave him a bad check."

Alix shook his head sadly.

"I don't understand it, such a dandy fellow. Now he's all bloated up—" He made a plump apple of his hands.

Charlie watched a group of strident queens installing themselves in a corner.

"Nothing affects them," he thought. "Stocks rise and fall, people loaf or work, but they go on forever." The place oppressed him. He called for the dice and shook with Alix for the drink.

"Here for long, Mr. Wales?"

"I'm here for four or five days to see my little girl."

"Oh-h! You have a little girl?"

Outside, the fire-red, gas-blue, ghost-green signs shone smokily through the tranquil rain. It was late afternoon and the streets were in movement; the bistros gleamed. At the corner of the Boulevard des Capucines he took a taxi. The Place de la Concorde moved by in pink majesty; they crossed the logical Seine, and Charlie felt the sudden provincial quality of the Left Bank.

Charlie directed his taxi to the Avenue de l'Opéra, which was out of his way. But he wanted to see the blue hour spread over the magnificent fasçade, and imagine that the cab horns, playing endlessly the first few bars of La Plus que Lent, were the trumpets of the Second Empire. They were closing the iron grill in front of Brentano's Book-store, and people were already at dinner behind the trim little bourgeois hedge of Duval's. He had never eaten at a really cheap restaurant in Paris. Five-course dinner, four francs fifty, eighteen cents, wine included. For some odd reason he wished that he had.

As they rolled on to the Left Bank and he felt its sudden provincialism, he thought, "I spoiled this city for myself. I didn't realize it, but the days came along one after another, and then two years were gone, and everything was gone, and I was gone."

He was thirty-five, and good to look at. The Irish mobility of his face was sobered by a deep wrinkle between his eyes. As he rang his brother-in-law's bell in the Rue Palatine, the wrinkle deepened till it pulled down his brows; he felt a cramping sensation in his belly. From behind the maid who opened the door darted a lovely little girl of nine who shrieked "Daddy!" and flew up, struggling like a fish, into his arms. She pulled his head around by one ear and set her cheek against his.

"My old pie," he said.

"Oh, daddy, daddy, daddy, daddy, dads, dads, dads!"

She drew him into the salon, where the family waited, a boy and girl his daughter's age, his sister-in-law and her husband. He greeted Marion with his voice pitched carefully to avoid either feigned enthusiasm or dislike, but her response was more frankly tepid, though she minimized her expression of unalterable distrust by directing her regard toward his child. The two men clasped hands in a friendly way and Lincoln Peters rested his for a moment on Charlie's shoulder.

The room was warm and comfortably American. The three children moved intimately about, playing through the yellow oblongs that led to other rooms; the cheer of six o'clock spoke in the eager smacks of the fire and the sounds of French activity in the kitchen. But Charlie did not relax; his heart sat up rigidly in his body and he drew confidence from his daughter, who from time to time came close to him, holding in her arms the doll he had brought.

"Really extremely well," he declared in answer to Lincoln's question. "There's a lot of business there that isn't moving at all, but we're doing even better than ever. In fact, damn well. I'm bringing my sister over from America next month to keep house for me. My income last year was bigger than it was when I had money. You see, the Czechs—"

His boasting was for a specific purpose; but after a moment, seeing a faint restiveness in Lincoln's eye, he changed the subject:

"Those are fine children of yours, well brought up, good manners."

"We think Honoria's a great little girl too."

Marion Peters came back from the kitchen. She was a tall woman with worried eyes, who had once possessed a fresh American loveliness. Charlie had never been sensitive to it and was always surprised when people spoke of how pretty she had been. From the first there had been an instinctive antipathy between them.

"Well, how do you find Honoria?" she asked.

"Wonderful. I was astonished how much she's grown in ten months. All the children are looking well."

"We haven't had a doctor for a year. How do you like being back in Paris?"

"It seems very funny to see so few Americans around."

"I'm delighted," Marion said vehemently. "Now at least you can go into a store without their assuming you're a millionaire. We've suffered like everybody, but on the whole it's a good deal pleasanter."

"But it was nice while it lasted," Charlie said. "We were a sort of royalty, almost infallible, with a sort of magic around us. In the bar this afternoon"—he stumbled, seeing his mistake—"there wasn't a man I knew."

She looked at him keenly. "I should think you'd have had enough of bars."

"I only stayed a minute. I take one drink every afternoon, and no more."

"Don't you want a cocktail before dinner?" Lincoln asked.

"I take only one drink every afternoon, and I've had that."

"I hope you keep to it," said Marion.

Her dislike was evident in the coldness with which she spoke, but Charlie only smiled; he had larger plans. Her very aggressiveness gave him an advantage, and he knew enough to wait. He wanted them to initiate the discussion of what they knew had brought him to Paris.

At dinner he couldn't decide whether Honoria was most like him or her mother. Fortunate if she didn't combine the traits of both that had brought them to disaster. A great wave of protectiveness went over him. He thought he knew what to do for her. He believed in character; he wanted to jump back a whole generation and trust in character again as the eternally valuable element. Everything wore out.

He left soon after dinner, but not to go home. He was curious to see Paris by night with clearer and more judicious eyes than those of other days. He bought a strapontin for the Casino and watched Josephine Baker go through her chocolate arabesques.

After an hour he left and strolled toward Montmartre, up the Rue Pigalle into the Place Blanche. The rain had stopped and there were a few people in evening clothes disembarking from taxis in front of cabarets, and cocottes prowling singly or in pairs, and many Negroes. He passed a lighted door from which issued music, and stopped with the sense of familiarity; it was Bricktop's, where he had parted with so many hours and so much money. A few doors farther on he found another ancient rendezvous and incautiously put his head inside. Immediately an eager orchestra burst into sound, a pair of professional dancers leaped to their feet and a maître d'hôtel swooped toward him, crying, "Crowd just arriving, sir!" But he withdrew quickly.

"You have to be damn drunk," he thought.

Zelli's was closed, the bleak and sinister cheap hotels surrounding it were dark; up in the Rue Blanche there was more light and a local, colloquial French crowd. The Poet's Cave had disappeared, but the two great mouths of the Café of Heaven and the Café of Hell still yawned—even devoured, as he watched, the meager contents of a tourist bus—a German, a Japanese, and an American couple who glanced at him with frightened eyes.

So much for the effort and ingenuity of Montmartre. All the catering to vice and waste was on an utterly childish scale, and he suddenly realized the meaning of the word "dissipate"—to dissipate into thin air; to make nothing out of something. In the little hours of the night every move from place to place was an enormous human jump, an increase of paying for the privilege of slower and slower motion.

He remembered thousand-franc notes given to an orchestra for playing a single number, hundred-franc notes tossed to a doorman for calling a cab.

But it hadn't been given for nothing.

It had been given, even the most wildly squandered sum, as an offering to destiny that he might not remember the things most worth remembering, the things that now he would always remember—his child taken from his control, his wife escaped to a grave in Vermont.

In the glare of a brasserie a woman spoke to him. He bought her some eggs and coffee, and then, eluding her encouraging stare, gave her a twenty-franc note and took a taxi to his hotel.

(2)

He woke upon a fine fall day—football weather. The depression of yesterday was gone and he liked the people on the streets. At noon he sat opposite Honoria at Le Grand Vatel, the only restaurant he could think of not reminiscent of champagne dinners and long luncheons that began at two and ended in a blurred and vague twilight.

"Now, how about vegetables? Oughtn't you to have some vegetables?"

"Well, yes."

"Here's épinards and chou-fleur and carrots and haricots."

"I'd like chou-fleur."

"Wouldn't you like to have two vegetables?"

"I usually only have one at lunch."

The waiter was pretending to be inordinately fond of children. "Qu'elle est mignonne la petite? Elle parle exactement comme une Française."

"How about dessert? Shall we wait and see?"

The waiter disappeared. Honoria looked at her father expectantly.

"What are we going to do?"

"First, we're going to that toy store in the Rue Saint-Honoré and buy you anything you like. And then we're going to the vaudeville at the Empire."

She hesitated. "I like it about the vaudeville, but not the toy store."

"Why not?"

"Well, you brought me this doll." She had it with her. "And I've got lots of things. And we're not rich any more, are we?"

"We never were. But today you are to have anything you want."

"All right," she agreed resignedly.

When there had been her mother and a French nurse he had been inclined to be strict; now he extended himself, reached out for a new tolerance; he must be both parents to her and not shut any of her out of communication.

"I want to get to know you," he said gravely. "First let me introduce myself. My name is Charles J. Wales, of Prague."

"Oh, daddy!" her voice cracked with laughter.

"And who are you, please?" he persisted, and she accepted a role immediately: "Honoria Wales, Rue Palatine, Paris."

"Married or single?"

"No, not married. Single."

He indicated the doll. "But I see you have a child, madame."

Unwilling to disinherit it, she took it to her heart and thought quickly: "Yes, I've been married, but I'm not married now. My husband is dead."

He went on quickly, "And the child's name?"

"Simone. That's after my best friend at school."

"I'm very pleased that you're doing so well at school."

"I'm third this month," she boasted. "Elsie"—that was her cousin—"is only about eighteenth, and Richard is about at the bottom."

"You like Richard and Elsie, don't you?"

"Oh, yes. I like Richard quite well and I like her all right."

Cautiously and casually he asked: "And Aunt Marion and Uncle Lincoln—which do you like best?"

"Oh, Uncle Lincoln, I guess."

He was increasingly aware of her presence. As they came in, a murmur of "... adorable" followed them, and now the people at the next table bent all their silences upon her, staring as if she were something no more conscious than a flower.

"Why don't I live with you?" she asked suddenly. "Because mamma's dead?"

"You must stay here and learn more French. It would have been hard for daddy to take care of you so well."

"I don't really need much taking care of any more. I do everything for myself."

Going out of the restaurant, a man and a woman unexpectedly hailed him.

"Well, the old Wales!"

"Hello there, Lorraine... Dunc."

Sudden ghosts out of the past: Duncan Schaeffer, a friend from college. Lorraine Quarrles, a lovely, pale blonde of thirty; one of a crowd who had helped them make months into days in the lavish times of three years ago.

"My husband couldn't come this year," she said, in answer to his question. "We're poor as hell. So he gave me two hundred a month and told me I could do my worst on that.... This your little girl?"

"What about coming back and sitting down?" Duncan asked.

"Can't do it." He was glad for an excuse. As always, he felt Lorraine's passionate, provocative attraction, but his own rhythm was different now.

"Well, how about dinner?" she asked.

"I'm not free. Give me your address and let me call you."

"Charlie, I believe you're sober," she said judicially. "I honestly believe he's sober, Dunc. Pinch him and see if he's sober."

Charlie indicated Honoria with his head. They both laughed.

"What's your address?" said Duncan sceptically.

He hesitated, unwilling to give the name of his hotel.

"I'm not settled yet. I'd better call you. We're going to see the vaudeville at the Empire."

"There! That's what I want to do," Lorraine said. "I want to see some clowns and acrobats and jugglers. That's just what we'll do, Dunc."

"We've got to do an errand first," said Charlie. "Perhaps we'll see you there."

"All right, you snob .... Good-by, beautiful little girl."

"Good-by."

Honoria bobbed politely.

Somehow, an unwelcome encounter. They liked him because he was functioning, because he was serious; they wanted to see him, because he was stronger than they were now, because they wanted to draw a certain sustenance from his strength.

At the Empire, Honoria proudly refused to sit upon her father's folded coat. She was already an individual with a code of her own, and Charlie was more and more absorbed by the desire of putting a little of himself into her before she crystallized utterly. It was hopeless to try to know her in so short a time.

Between the acts they came upon Duncan and Lorraine in the lobby where the band was playing.

"Have a drink?"

"All right, but not up at the bar. We'll take a table."

"The perfect father."

Listening abstractedly to Lorraine, Charlie watched Honoria's eyes leave their table, and he followed them wistfully about the room, wondering what they saw. He met her glance and she smiled.

"I liked that lemonade," she said.

What had she said? What had he expected? Going home in a taxi afterward, he pulled her over until her head rested against his chest.

"Darling, do you ever think about your mother?"

"Yes, sometimes," she answered vaguely.

"I don't want you to forget her. Have you got a picture of her?"

"Yes, I think so. Anyhow, Aunt Marion has. Why don't you want me to forget her?"

"She loved you very much."

"I loved her too."

They were silent for a moment.

"Daddy, I want to come and live with you," she said suddenly.

His heart leaped; he had wanted it to come like this.

"Aren't you perfectly happy?"

"Yes, but I love you better than anybody. And you love me better than anybody, don't you, now that mummy's dead?"

"Of course I do. But you won't always like me best, honey. You'll grow up and meet somebody your own age and go marry him and forget you ever had a daddy."

"Yes, that's true," she agreed tranquilly.

He didn't go in. He was coming back at nine o'clock and he wanted to keep himself fresh and new for the thing he must say then.

"When you're safe inside, just show yourself in that window."

"All right. Good-by, dads, dads, dads, dads."

He waited in the dark street until she appeared, all warm and glowing, in the window above and kissed her fingers out into the night.

(3)

They were waiting. Marion sat behind the coffee service in a dignified black dinner dress that just faintly suggested mourning. Lincoln was walking up and down with the animation of one who had already been talking. They were as anxious as he was to get into the question. He opened it almost immediately:

"I suppose you know what I want to see you about—why I really came to Paris."

Marion played with the black stars on her necklace and frowned.

"I'm awfully anxious to have a home," he continued. "And I'm awfully anxious to have Honoria in it. I appreciate your taking in Honoria for her mother's sake, but things have changed now"—he hesitated and then continued more forcibly—"changed radically with me, and I want to ask you to reconsider the matter. It would be silly for me to deny that about three years ago I was acting badly—"

Marion looked up at him with hard eyes.

"—But all that's over. As I told you, I haven't had more than a drink a day for over a year, and I take that drink deliberately, so that the idea of alcohol won't get too big in my imagination. You see the idea?"

"No," said Marion succinctly.

"It's a sort of stunt I set myself. It keeps the matter in proportion."

"I get you," said Lincoln. "You don't want to admit it's got any attraction for you."

"Something like that. Sometimes I forget and don't take it. But I try to take it. Anyhow, I couldn't afford to drink in my position. The people I represent are more than satisfied with what I've done, and I'm bringing my sister over from Burlington to keep house for me, and I want awfully to have Honoria too. You know that even when her mother and I weren't getting along well we never let anything that happened touch Honoria. I know she's fond of me and I know I'm able to take care of her and—well, there you are. How do you feel about it?"

He knew that now he would have to take a beating. It would last an hour or two hours, and it would be difficult, but if he modulated his inevitable resentment to the chastened attitude of the reformed sinner, he might win his point in the end.

Keep your temper, he told himself. You don't want to be justified. You want Honoria.

Lincoln spoke first: "We've been talking it over ever since we got your letter last month. We're happy to have Honoria here. She's a dear little thing, and we're glad to be able to help her, but of course that isn't the question—"

Marion interrupted suddenly. "How long are you going to stay sober, Charlie?" she asked.

"Permanently, I hope."

"How can anybody count on that?"

"You know I never did drink heavily until I gave up business and came over here with nothing to do. Then Helen and I began to run around with—"

"Please leave Helen out of it. I can't bear to hear you talk about her like that."

He stared at her grimly; he had never been certain how fond of each other the sisters were in life.

"My drinking only lasted about a year and a half—from the time we came over until I—collapsed."

"It was time enough."

"It was time enough," he agreed.

"My duty is entirely to Helen," she said. "I try to think what she would have wanted me to do. Frankly, from the night you did that terrible thing you haven't really existed for me. I can't help that. She was my sister."

"Yes."

"When she was dying she asked me to look out for Honoria. If you hadn't been in a sanitarium then, it might have helped matters."

He had no answer.

"I'll never in my life be able to forget the morning when Helen knocked at my door, soaked to the skin and shivering, and said you'd locked her out."

Charlie gripped the sides of the chair. This was more difficult than he expected; he wanted to launch out into a long expostulation and explanation, but he only said: "The night I locked her out—" and she interrupted, "I don't feel up to going over that again."

After a moment's silence Lincoln said: "We're getting off the subject. You want Marion to set aside her legal guardianship and give you Honoria. I think the main point for her is whether she has confidence in you or not."

"I don't blame Marion," Charlie said slowly, "but I think she can have entire confidence in me. I had a good record up to three years ago. Of course, it's within human possibilities I might go wrong any time. But if we wait much longer I'll lose Honoria's childhood and my chance for a home." He shook his head, "I'll simply lose her, don't you see?"

"Yes, I see," said Lincoln.

"Why didn't you think of all this before?" Marion asked.

"I suppose I did, from time to time, but Helen and I were getting along badly. When I consented to the guardianship, I was flat on my back in a sanitarium and the market had cleaned me out. I knew I'd acted badly, and I thought if it would bring any peace to Helen, I'd agree to anything. But now it's different. I'm functioning, I'm behaving damn well, so far as—"

"Please don't swear at me," Marion said.

He looked at her, startled. With each remark the force of her dislike became more and more apparent. She had built up all her fear of life into one wall and faced it toward him. This trivial reproof was possibly the result of some trouble with the cook several hours before. Charlie became increasingly alarmed at leaving Honoria in this atmosphere of hostility against himself; sooner or later it would come out, in a word here, a shake of the head there, and some of that distrust would be irrevocably implanted in Honoria. But he pulled his temper down out of his face and shut it up inside him; he had won a point, for Lincoln realized the absurdity of

Marion's remark and asked her lightly since when she had objected to the word "damn."

"Another thing," Charlie said. "I'm able to give her certain advantages now. I'm going to take a French governess to Prague with me. I've got a lease on a new apartment—"

He stopped, realizing that he was blundering. They couldn't be expected to accept with equanimity the fact that his income was again twice as large as their own.

"I suppose you can give her more luxuries than we can," said Marion. "When you were throwing away money we were living along watching every ten francs.... I suppose you'll start doing it again."

"Oh, no," he said. "I've learned. I worked hard for ten years, you know—until I got lucky in the market, like so many people. Terribly lucky. It didn't seem any use working any more, so I quit. It won't happen again."

There was a long silence. All of them felt their nerves straining, and for the first time in a year Charlie wanted a drink. He was sure now that Lincoln Peters wanted him to have his child.

Marion shuddered suddenly; part of her saw that Charlie's feet were planted on the earth now, and her own maternal feeling recognized the naturalness of his desire; but she had lived for a long time with a prejudice—a prejudice founded on a curious disbelief in her sister's happiness, and which, in the shock of one terrible night, had turned to hatred for him. It had all happened at a point in her life where the discouragement of ill health and adverse circumstances made it necessary for her to believe in tangible villainy and a tangible villain.

"I can't help what I think!" she cried out suddenly. "How much you were responsible for Helen's death, I don't know. It's something you'll have to square with your own conscience."

An electric current of agony surged through him; for a moment he was almost on his feet, an unuttered sound echoing in his throat. He hung on to himself for a moment, another moment.

"Hold on there," said Lincoln uncomfortably. "I never thought you were responsible for that."

"Helen died of heart trouble," Charlie said dully.

"Yes, heart trouble." Marion spoke as if the phrase had another meaning for her.

Then, in the flatness that followed her outburst, she saw him plainly and she knew he had somehow arrived at control over the situation. Glancing at her husband, she found no help from him, and as abruptly as if it were a matter of no importance, she threw up the sponge.

"Do what you like!" she cried, springing up from her chair. "She's your child. I'm not the person to stand in your way. I think if it were my child I'd rather see her—" She managed to check herself. "You two decide it. I can't stand this. I'm sick. I'm going to bed."

She hurried from the room; after a moment Lincoln said:

"This has been a hard day for her. You know how strongly she feels—" His voice was almost apologetic: "When a woman gets an idea in her head."

"Of course."

"It's going to be all right. I think she sees now that you—can provide for the child, and so we can't very well stand in your way or Honoria's way."

"Thank you, Lincoln."

"I'd better go along and see how she is."

"I'm going."

He was still trembling when he reached the street, but a walk down the Rue Bonaparte to the quais set him up, and as he crossed the Seine, fresh and new by the quai lamps, he felt exultant. But back in his room he couldn't sleep. The image of Helen haunted him. Helen whom he had loved so until they had senselessly begun to abuse each other's love, tear it into shreds. On that terrible February night that Marion remembered so vividly, a slow quarrel had gone on for hours. There was a scene at the Florida, and then he attempted to take her home, and then she kissed young Webb at a table; after that there was what she had hysterically said. When he arrived home alone he turned the key in the lock in wild anger. How could he know she would arrive an hour later alone, that there would be a snowstorm in which she wandered about in slippers, too confused to find a taxi? Then the aftermath, her escaping pneumonia by a miracle, and all the attendant horror. They were "reconciled," but that was the beginning of the end, and Marion, who had seen with her own eyes and who imagined it to be one of many scenes from her sister's martyrdom, never forgot.

Going over it again brought Helen nearer, and in the white, soft light that steals upon half sleep near morning he found himself talking to her again. She said that he was perfectly right about Honoria and that she wanted Honoria to be with him. She said she was glad he was being good and doing better. She said a lot of other things—very friendly things—but she was in a swing in a white dress, and swinging faster and faster all the time, so that at the end he could not hear clearly all that she said.

(4)

He woke up feeling happy. The door of the world was open again. He made plans, vistas, futures for Honoria and himself, but suddenly he grew sad, remembering all the plans he and Helen had made. She had not planned to die. The present was the thing—work to do and someone to love. But not to love too much, for he knew the injury that a father can do to a daughter or a mother to a son by attaching them too closely: afterward, out in the world, the child would seek in the marriage partner the same blind tenderness and, failing probably to find it, turn against love and life.

It was another bright, crisp day. He called Lincoln Peters at the bank where he worked and asked if he could count on taking Honoria when he left for Prague. Lincoln agreed that there was no reason for delay. One thing—the legal guardianship. Marion wanted to retain that a while longer. She was upset by the whole matter, and it would oil things if she felt that the situation was still in her control for another year. Charlie agreed, wanting only the tangible, visible child.

Then the question of a governess. Charlie sat in a gloomy agency and talked to a cross Béarnaise and to a buxom Breton peasant, neither of whom he could have endured. There were others whom he would see tomorrow.

He lunched with Lincoln Peters at Griffons, trying to keep down his exultation.

"There's nothing quite like your own child," Lincoln said. "But you understand how Marion feels too."

"She's forgotten how hard I worked for seven years there," Charlie said. "She just remembers one night."

"There's another thing." Lincoln hesitated. "While you and Helen were tearing around Europe throwing money away, we were just getting along. I didn't touch any of the prosperity because I never got ahead enough to carry anything but my insurance. I think Marion felt there was some kind of injustice in it—you not even working toward the end, and getting richer and richer."

"It went just as quick as it came," said Charlie.

"Yes, a lot of it stayed in the hands of chasseurs and saxophone players and maîtres d'hôtel—well, the big party's over now. I just said that to explain Marion's feeling about those crazy years. If you drop in about six o'clock tonight before Marion's too tired, we'll settle the details on the spot."

Back at his hotel, Charlie found a pneumatique that had been redirected from the Ritz bar where Charlie had left his address for the purpose of finding a certain man.

DEAR CHARLIE: You were so strange when we saw you the other day that I wondered if I did something to offend you. If so, I'm not conscious of it. In fact, I have thought about you too much for the last year, and it's always been in the back of my mind that I might see you if I came over here. We did have such good times that crazy spring, like the night you and I stole the butcher's tricycle, and the time we tried to call on the president and you had the old derby rim and the wire cane. Everybody seems so old lately, but I don't feel old a bit. Couldn't we get together some time today for old time's sake? I've got a vile hang-over for the moment, but will be feeling better this afternoon and will look for you about five in the sweat-shop at the Ritz.

Always devotedly,
LORRAINE.

His first feeling was one of awe that he had actually, in his mature years, stolen a tricycle and pedalled Lorraine all over the Étoile between the small hours and dawn. In retrospect it was a nightmare. Locking out Helen didn't fit in with any other act of his life, but the tricycle incident did—it was one of many. How many weeks or months of dissipation to arrive at that condition of utter irresponsibility?

He tried to picture how Lorraine had appeared to him then—very attractive; Helen was unhappy about it, though she said nothing. Yesterday, in the restaurant, Lorraine had seemed trite, blurred, worn away. He emphatically did not want to see her, and he was glad Alix had not given away his hotel address. It was a relief to think, instead, of Honoria, to think of Sundays spent with her and of saying good morning to her and of knowing she was there in his house at night, drawing her breath in the darkness.

At five he took a taxi and bought presents for all the Peters—a piquant cloth doll, a box of Roman soldiers, flowers for Marion, big linen handkerchiefs for Lincoln.

He saw, when he arrived in the apartment, that Marion had accepted the inevitable. She greeted him now as though he were a recalcitrant member of the family, rather than a menacing outsider. Honoria had been told she was going; Charlie was glad to see that her tact made her conceal her excessive happiness. Only on his lap did she whisper her delight and the question "When?" before she slipped away with the other children.

He and Marion were alone for a minute in the room, and on an impulse he spoke out boldly:

Family quarrels are bitter things. They don't go according to any rules. They're not like aches or wounds; they're more like splits in the skin that won't heal because there's not enough material. I wish you and I could be on better terms.

"Some things are hard to forget," she answered. "It's a question of confidence." There was no answer to this and presently she asked, "When do you propose to take her?"

"As soon as I can get a governess. I hoped the day after tomorrow."

"That's impossible. I've got to get her things in shape. Not before Saturday."

He yielded. Coming back into the room, Lincoln offered him a drink.

"I'll take my daily whisky," he said.

It was warm here, it was a home, people together by a fire. The children felt very safe and important; the mother and father were serious, watchful. They had things to do for the children more important than his visit here. A spoonful of medicine was, after all, more important than the strained relations between Marion and himself. They were not dull people, but they were very much in the grip of life and circumstances. He wondered if he couldn't do something to get Lincoln out of his rut at the bank.

A long peal at the door-bell; the bonne *à* tout faire passed through and went down the corridor. The door opened upon another long ring, and then voices, and the three in the salon looked up expectantly; Lincoln moved to bring the corridor within his range of vision, and Marion rose. Then the maid came back along the corridor, closely followed by the voices, which developed under the light into Duncan Schaeffer and Lorraine Quarrles.

They were gay, they were hilarious, they were roaring with laughter. For a moment Charlie was astounded; unable to understand how they ferreted out the Peters' address.

"Ah-h-h!"Duncan wagged his finger roguishly at Charlie. "Ah-h-h!"

They both slid down another cascade of laughter. Anxious and at a loss, Charlie shook hands with them quickly and presented them to Lincoln and Marion. Marion nodded, scarcely speaking. She had drawn back a step toward the fire; her little girl stood beside her, and Marion put an arm about her shoulder.

With growing annoyance at the intrusion, Charlie waited for them to explain themselves. After some concentration Duncan said:

"We came to invite you out to dinner. Lorraine and I insist that all this shishi, cagy business 'bout your address got to stop."

Charlie came closer to them, as if to force them backward down the corridor.

"Sorry, but I can't. Tell me where you'll be and I'll phone you in half an hour."

This made no impression. Lorraine sat down suddenly on the side of a chair, and focussing her eyes on Richard, cried, "Oh, what a nice little boy! Come here, little boy." Richard glanced at his mother, but did not move. With a perceptible shrug of her shoulders, Lorraine turned back to Charlie:

"Come and dine. Sure your cousins won' mine. See you so sel'om. Or solemn."

"I can't," said Charlie sharply. "You two have dinner and I'll phone you."

Her voice became suddenly unpleasant. "All right, we'll go. But I remember once when you hammered on my door at four A. M. I was enough of a good sport to give you a drink. Come on, Dunc."

Still in slow motion, with blurred, angry faces, with uncertain feet, they retired along the corridor.

"Good night," Charlie said.

"Good night!" responded Lorraine emphatically.

When he went back into the salon Marion had not moved, only now her son was standing in the circle of her other arm. Lincoln was still swinging Honoria back and forth like a pendulum from side to side.

"What an outrage!" Charlie broke out. "What an absolute outrage!" Neither of them answered. Charlie dropped into an armchair, picked up his drink, set it down again and said:

"People I haven't seen for two years having the colossal nerve—"

He broke off. Marion had made the sound "Oh!" in one swift, furious breath, turned her body from him with a jerk and left the room.

Lincoln set down Honoria carefully.

"You children go in and start your soup," he said, and when they obeyed, he said to Charlie:

"Marion's not well and she can't stand shocks. That kind of people make her really physically sick."

"I didn't tell them to come here. They wormed your name out of somebody. They deliberately—"

"Well, it's too bad. It doesn't help matters. Excuse me a minute."

Left alone, Charlie sat tense in his chair. In the next room he could hear the children eating, talking in monosyllables, already oblivious to the scene between their elders. He heard a murmur of conversation from a farther room and then the ticking bell of a telephone receiver picked up, and in a panic he moved to the other side of the room and out of earshot.

In a minute Lincoln came back. "Look here, Charlie. I think we'd better call off dinner for tonight. Marion's in bad shape."

"Is she angry with me?"

"Sort of," he said, almost roughly. "She's not strong and—"

"You mean she's changed her mind about Honoria?"

"She's pretty bitter right now. I don't know. You phone me at the bank tomorrow."

"I wish you'd explain to her I never dreamed these people would come here. I'm just as sore as you are."

"I couldn't explain anything to her now."

Charlie got up. He took his coat and hat and started down the corridor. Then he opened the door of the dining room and said in a strange voice, "Good night, children."

Honoria rose and ran around the table to hug him.

"Good night, sweetheart," he said vaguely, and then trying to make his voice more tender, trying to conciliate something, "Good night, dear children."

(5)

Charlie went directly to the Ritz bar with the furious idea of finding Lorraine and Duncan, but they were not there, and he realized that in any case there was nothing he could do. He had not touched his drink at the Peters', and now he ordered a whisky-and-soda. Paul came over to say hello.

"It's a great change," he said sadly. "We do about half the business we did. So many fellows I hear about back in the States lost everything, maybe not in the first crash, but then in the second. Your friend George Hardt lost every cent, I hear. Are you back in the States?"

"No, I'm in business in Prague."

"I heard that you lost a lot in the crash."

"I did," and he added grimly, "but I lost everything I wanted in the boom."

"Selling short."

"Something like that."

Again the memory of those days swept over him like a nightmare—the people they had met travelling; then people who couldn't add a row of figures or speak a coherent sentence. The little man Helen had consented to dance with at the ship's party, who had insulted her ten feet from the table; the women and girls carried screaming with drink or drugs out of public places—

The men who locked their wives out in the snow, because the snow of twenty-nine wasn't real snow. If you didn't want it to be snow, you just paid some money.

He went to the phone and called the Peters' apartment; Lincoln answered.

"I called up because this thing is on my mind. Has Marion said anything definite?"

"Marion's sick," Lincoln answered shortly. "I know this thing isn't altogether your fault, but I can't have her go to pieces about it. I'm afraid we'll have to let it slide for six months; I can't take the chance of working her up to this state again."

"I see."

"I'm sorry, Charlie."

He went back to his table. His whisky glass was empty, but he shook his head when Alix looked at it questioningly. There wasn't much he could do now except send Honoria some things; he would send her a lot of things tomorrow. He thought rather angrily that this was just money—he had given so many people money....

"No, no more," he said to another waiter. "What do I owe you?"

He would come back some day; they couldn't make him pay forever. But he wanted his child, and nothing was much good now, beside that fact. He wasn't young any more, with a lot of nice thoughts and dreams to have by himself. He was absolutely sure Helen wouldn't have wanted him to be so alone.

[Selected from F. S. Fitzgerald. *Babylon Revisited and Other Stories*. New York: Scribner, 1996.]

Ⅲ. Questions for discussion

(1) What is the purpose of Charlie's return to Paris? What does it suggest in terms of values?

(2) How does Charlie think of the role of money in his life, particularly in his relationship with his daughter?

(3) How do you think a reformed Charlie is characterized in this story?

(4) What is the metaphorical meaning of the frequent appearance and disturbance of Lorraine and Duncan?

(5) Make an analysis of the themes of this story.

(6) The technique of impressionism is employed in the short story. Please take some examples and explain the use and effect of this technique.

2.3 Assigned Reading

Fitzgerald's "Babylon Revisited"

James M. Harrison

The usual interpretation of F. Scott Fitzgerald's "Babylon Revisited" has been summarized by Ray B. West (*The Short Story in America*, 1952). Charlie Wales, returning to Paris, "accidentally becomes involved with some of his old friends; and despite his present dislike of the old life—his knowledge that ... it was something he had to escape if possible, not recover—he appears to have succumbed and thus loses, once and for all, the hope of regaining his child. The pathos in 'Babylon

Revisited' is deepened and enriched by Charlie Wales' recognition that he is, in part at least, merely reaping the harvest of his earlier years.... [He is] doomed because he still carries the burden of his early irresponsibility, even in the years of maturity and knowledge."

According to this interpretation the effect is, as West suggests, pathetic rather than tragic. Charlie has matured; he is reliable, sober, patient, tolerant, kind, devoted to his daughter. He is defeated by accident, and by past mistakes over which he no longer has any control. If this interpretation is sound, complaints that the story is sentimental have a certain validity.

But the situation is not really this simple. Charlie has triumphed over his past at the point where Marion Peters agrees to his taking Honoria, and the reversal—the untimely appearance of his drunken friends—cannot be attributed to accident or to past weakness; it is clearly the result of present weakness.

The point of view is Charlie's, and it is easy to read the story only on the level of his understanding; after all he is intelligent and perceptive, and his dilemma arouses our sympathy. But although we see the action through the eyes of the protagonist, and colored by his feelings and opinions, we can at the same time observe the protagonist critically. We are in a position to know everything he knows, and more. The "more" in this case is essential to our full understanding.

The central conflict is not between Charlie past and Charlie present, but between contradictory impulses operating within the latter. Charlie sees that the old, wild, gay way of life was foolish, cruel, and empty; yet it still appeals to him. He feels its temptation despite his firm desire to demonstrate his solid virtues and make a home for his daughter. Thus at the opening we see him inquiring after his old friends—motivated not by morbid curiosity but by nostalgia.

There are two Charlies in the story: Charlie the substantial man of business, the devoted father who wishes to reclaim his child; and Charlie the hedonist, who sees the waste, cruelty and senselessness of his former spree but who still feels somehow that it was gloriously wasteful, gloriously cruel and gloriously senseless—and in spite of the suffering it caused, glorious fun. It is Charlie number two who feels Lorraine Quarrles' "passionate, provocative attraction," when he suddenly encounters her. Next day Charlie number one is in control again, and he remembers her as "trite, blurred, worn away." Were he not pulled in two directions, Charlie could easily make it clear to his old friends, when he first meets them, that he is a changed man. But this he cannot do. He can brag about his moderate drinking to Lincoln Peters; he can speak of it with satisfaction even to the bartender; but he cannot bring himself to admit it to his former playmates.

At the story's climax Duncan Schaeffer and Lorraine Quarrles appear, drunk, at the Peterses' home. "For a moment Charlie was astounded; unable to understand how they ferreted out the Peterses' address." He protests to Lincoln Peters: "They wormed your name out of somebody." The surprise of the respectable Charlie is genuine, but the reader will remember the other Charlie inquiring at the Ritz bar about his old companions in dissipation: "Charlie scribbled an address in his notebook and tore out the page. 'If you see Mr. Schaeffer, give him this,' he said. 'It's my brother-in-law's address.'" And thus, in a passage placed for emphasis at the very opening of the story, Charlie plants the seed of his own destruction.

Charlie has come to dinner at the Peterses' at six, ignoring an invitation to meet Lorraine an hour earlier at the Ritz bar. Apparently Duncan has encountered Lorraine there, and Alix has handed him the note bearing the Peterses' address. Charlie, who has since instructed Alix not to reveal his hotel, has obviously forgotten the note. So the "reformed" Charlie is defeated, not by accident, but by an impulsive act of the other side of his nature.

Charlie's "maturity and knowledge" are still incomplete. He has turned over a new leaf, but it refuses to lie flat. The central symbol of the story is Charlie's one drink a day: he wants to give up the old way of life—almost. But for all this he is likable and admirable, a strong and tragic character wrestling with a weakness he does not completely understand.

[Selected from James M. Harrison. Fitzgerald's "Babylon Revisited". Anna J. Sheets, (ed.). *Short Story Criticism* (Vol. 31). Detroit: Gale Group, 1999.]

3. Ernest Hemingway

3.1 Presentation Topics

(1) Ernest Hemingway's code-heroes, grace under pressure.

(2) Hemingway's Iceberg Theory of Prose.

(3) The influence of "Hemingway Hero" and Hemingway's style on modern American literature.

3.2 Selected Reading

Ⅰ. Central issue of concern

The theme which is typical of Hemingway's work is examining the courage with which men face different kinds of tragedy.

Ⅱ. Text

In Another Country

In the fall the war① was always there, but we did not go to it any more. It was cold in the fall in Milan② and the dark came very early. Then the electric lights came on, and it was pleasant along the streets looking in the windows. There was much game hanging outside the shops, and the snow powdered in the fur of the foxes and the wind blew their tails. The deer hung stiff and heavy and empty, and small birds blew in the wind and the wind turned their feathers. It was a cold fall and the wind came down from the mountains.

We were all at the hospital every afternoon, and there were different ways of walking across the town through the dusk to the hospital. Two of the ways were alongside canals, but they were long. Always, though, you crossed a bridge across a canal to enter the hospital. There was a choice of three bridges. On one of them a woman sold roasted chestnuts. It was warm, standing in front of her charcoal fire, and the chestnuts were warm afterward in your pocket. The hospital was very old and very beautiful, and you entered through a gate and walked across a courtyard and out a gate on the other side. There were usually funerals starting from the courtyard. Beyond the old hospital were the new brick pavilions, and there we met every afternoon and were all very polite and interested in what was the matter③, and sat in the machines④ that were to make so much difference.

---

① The World War Ⅰ.

② A city in Italy.

③ Inquiring politely about one another's wounds.

④ The equipment for treatment.

The doctor came up to the machine where I was sitting and said: "What did you like best to do before the war? Did you practice a sport?"

I said: "Yes, football."

"Good," he said. "You will be able to play football again better than ever."

My knee did not bend and the leg dropped straight from the knee to the ankle without a calf, and the machine was to bend the knee and make it move as in riding a tricycle. But it did not bend yet, and instead the machine lurched when it came to the bending part. The doctor said: "That will all pass. You are a fortunate young man. You will play football again like a champion."

In the next machine was a major who had a little hand like a baby's. He winked at me when the doctor examined his hand, which was between two leather straps that bounced up and down and flapped the stiff fingers, and said: "And will I too play football, captain-doctor?" He had been a very great fencer, and before the war the greatest fencer in Italy.

The doctor went to his office in the back room and brought a photograph which showed a hand that had been withered almost as small as the major's, before it had taken a machine course, and after was a little larger. The major held the photograph with his good hand and looked at it very carefully. "A wound?" he asked.

"An industrial accident," the doctor said.

"Very interesting, very interesting," the major said, and handed it back to the doctor.

"You have confidence?"

"No," said the major.

There were three boys who came each day who were about the same age I was. They were all three from Milan, and one of them was to be a lawyer, and one was to be a painter, and one had intended to be a soldier, and after we were finished with the machines, sometimes we walked back together to the Café Cova, which was next door to the Scala①. We walked the short way through the communist quarter because we were four together. The people hated us because we were

---

① The name of the opera house in Milan, Italy.

officers, and from a wine-shop some one called out "A basso gli ufficiali"① as we passed. Another boy who walked with us sometimes and made us five wore a black silk handkerchief across his face because he had no nose then and his face was to be rebuilt. He had gone out to the front from the military academy and been wounded within an hour after he had gone into the front line for the first time. They rebuilt his face, but he came from a very old family and they could never get the nose exactly right. He went to South America and worked in a bank. But this was a long time ago, and then we did not any of us know how it was going to be afterward. We only knew then that there was always the war, but that we were not going to it any more.

We all had the same medals, except the boy with the black silk bandage across his face, and he had not been at the front long enough to get any medals. The tall boy with a very pale face who was to be a lawyer had been a lieutenant of Arditi② and had three medals of the sort we each had only one of. He had lived a very long time with death and was a little detached③. We were all a little detached, and there was nothing that held us together except that we met every afternoon at the hospital. Although, as we walked to the Cova through the tough part of town, walking in the dark, with light and singing coming out of the wine-shops, and sometimes having to walk into the street when the men and women would crowd together on the sidewalk so that we would have had to jostle them to get by, we felt held together by there being something that had happened that they, the people who disliked us, did not understand.

We ourselves all understood the Cova, where it was rich and warm and not too brightly lighted, and noisy and smoky at certain hours, and there were always girls at the tables and the illustrated papers on a rack on the wall. The girls at the Cova were very patriotic, and I found that the most patriotic people in Italy were the café girls—and I believe they are still patriotic.

The boys at first were very polite about my medals and asked me what I had done to get them. I showed them the papers, which were written in very beautiful

---

① Down with officers!

② Assault troops of the Italian army, 1915—1918.

③ He had faced death and had seen others die so frequently that he could no longer plunge wholeheartedly into life's activities himself.

language and full of fratellanza[①] and abnegazione[②], but which really said, with the adjective removed, that I had been given the medals because I was an American. After that their manner changed a little toward me, although I was their friend against outsiders. I was a friend, but I was never really one of them after they had read the citations, because it had been different with them and they had done very different things to get their medals. I had been wounded, it was true; but we all knew that being wounded, after all, was really an accident. I was never ashamed of ribbons, though, and sometimes, after the cocktail hour, I would imagine myself having done all the things they had done to get their medals; but walking home at night through the empty streets with the cold wind and all the shops closed, trying to keep near the street lights, I knew that I would never have done such things, and I was very much afraid to die, and often lay in bed at night by myself, afraid to die and wondering how I would be when I went back to the front again.

The three with the medals were like hunting hawks; and I was not a hawk, although I might seem a hawk to those who had never hunted; they, the three, knew better and so we drifted apart. But I stayed good friends with the boy who had been wounded his first day at the front, because he would never know now how he would have turned out; so he could never be accepted either, and I liked him because I thought perhaps he would not have turned out to be a hawk either.

The major, who had been the great fencer, did not believe in bravery, and spent much time while we sat in the machines correcting my grammar. He had complimented me on how I spoke Italian, and we talked together very easily. One day I had said that Italian seemed such an easy language to me that I could not take a great interest in it; everything was so easy to say. "Ah, yes," the major said. "Why, then, do you not take up the use of grammar?" So we took up the use of grammar, and soon Italian was such a difficult language that I was afraid to talk to him until I had the grammar straight in my mind.

The major came very regularly to the hospital. I do not think he ever missed a day, although I am sure he did not believe in the machines. There was a time when none of us believed in the machines, and one day the major said it was all nonsense.

---

① Brotherhood.

② Renunciation, self-denial.

The machines were new then and it was we who were to prove them. It was an idiotic idea, he said, *"a theory, like another"*[①]. I had not learned my grammar, and he said I was a stupid impossible disgrace, and he was a fool to have bothered with me. He was a small man and he sat straight up in his chair with his right hand thrust into the machine and looked straight ahead at the wall while the straps thumped up and down with his fingers in them.

"What will you do when the war is over if it is over?" he asked me. "Speak grammatically!"

"I will go to the States."

"Are you married?"

"No, but I hope to be."

"The more of a fool you are," he said. He seemed very angry. "A man must not marry."

"Why, Signor Maggiore[②]?"

"Don't call me 'Signor Maggiore.'"

"Why must not a man marry?"

"He cannot marry. He cannot marry," he said angrily. "If he is to lose everything, he should not place himself in a position to lose. He should find things he cannot lose."

He spoke very angrily and bitterly, and looked straight ahead while he talked.

"But why should he necessarily lose it?"

"He'll lose it," the major said. He was looking at the wall. Then he looked down at the machine and jerked his little hand out from between the straps and slapped it hard against his thigh. "He'll lose it," he almost shouted. "Don't argue with me!" Then he called to the attendant who ran the machines. "Come and turn this damned thing off."

He went back into the other room for the light treatment and the massage. Then I heard him ask the doctor if he might use his telephone and he shut the door. When he came back into the room, I was sitting in another machine. He was

---

① The major knows that the machines are useless to mend his crippled hand, that they are merely "a theory, like another."

② Major (military title).

wearing his cape and had his cap on, and he came directly toward my machine and put his arm on my shoulder.

"I am so sorry," he said, and patted me on the shoulder with his good hand. "I would not be rude. My wife has just died. You must forgive me."

"Oh," I said, feeling sick for him. "I am so sorry."

He stood there biting his lower lip. "It is very difficult," he said. "I cannot resign myself."

He looked straight past me and out through the window. Then he began to cry. "I am utterly unable to resign myself." He said, and choked. And then crying, his head up looking at nothing, carrying himself straight and soldierly, with tears on both his cheeks and biting his lips, he walked past the machines and out the door.

The doctor told me that the major's wife, who was very young and whom he had not married until he was definitely invalided out of the war, had died of pneumonia. She had been sick only a few days. No one expected her to die. The major did not come to the hospital for three days. Then he came at the usual hour, wearing a black band on the sleeve of his uniform. When he came back, there were large framed photographs around the wall, of all sorts of wounds before and after they had been cured by the machines. In front of the machine the major used were three photographs of hands like his that were completely restored. I do not know where the doctor got them. I always understood we were the first to use the machines. The photographs did not make much difference to the major because he only looked out of the window.

[Selected from Walter Blair. *The United States in Literature*. Illinois: Scott, Foresman and Company, 1968.]

Ⅲ. Questions for discussion

(1) Why does Hemingway begin his story with a description of dead animals?

(2) Not only are the soldiers, as a group, shut off from other groups; as individuals, they are separated from one another. How do they happen to be separated? Have their war experiences had anything to do with their loneliness? Explain.

(3) Judging from your knowledge of the characters in Hemingway's stories, to

what extent is the narrator typical of the characters Hemingway admires? Are the other characters typical?

(4) In this story the machines come to symbolize the false hopes and the promises of the modern age. What details convey the symbolic meaning of the machines?

(5) Gertrude Stein wrote, "You are all a lost generation." This epigraph has come to stand for the young people of Hemingway's time. In what way are the young people in this story "lost"? Are there any ways in which they are not lost? And why?

(6) Explain the possible meanings suggested by the title of this story.

(7) World War Ⅰ left many people feeling disillusioned because it caused the death of thousands of men, though it seemed to have no purpose. How does this story reflect this sense of disillusion?

3.3 Assigned Reading

Hemingway and Gender History

Rena Sanderson

A Farewell to Arms is the only book by Hemingway that centers on a fully developed and happy modern love affair. It may be his happiest book because in it he gave fullest expression to his fantasy of paradise on earth. And even here the fantasy is qualified—not only, of course, by Catherine's death, but also by our knowledge that she is the creation of Frederic's bereaved memory. Hemingway said that he rewrote the last chapter over forty times. That it ends with the death of Catherine and the son does not prove, as Judith Fetterley charges, that the book's "message to women readers" is that "the only good woman is a dead one." Rather, the ending sounds the final note of fatalism and Frederic's realization that he cannot avoid losing "the happiness of the Garden that a man must lose."

After the publication of *A Farewell to Arms*, a new and more authoritative Hemingway emerged, a he—man of exaggerated virility and masculine expertise. This Hemingway can best be understood as the author's defensive response to what he saw as a general takeover by women. He found evidence of this takeover both in his personal life and in the culture at large.

His father's suicide in December 1928 bitterly reminded him of the failure of his parents' marriage, a failure Hemingway blamed on his mother's bullying and on his father's inability to stand up to her. Linda Wagner suggests that it was at this point that Hemingway stopped believing in the "mystic ideal of a genuine love" between a man and a woman. By this time, too, his own marriage to Hadley was over, and he was remarried to Pauline. Years later, when he reflected back on these events, Hemingway stated flatly that his mother "forced father to suicide."

The shift in Hemingway's self-definition fitted into a broader contemporary movement, a defensive cultural "re-masculinization" of American society intended to shore up its patriarchal basis. The backlash of the 1930s was a reaction to the growing influence of two groups of women. The first group, which coalesced in the late 19th century, consisted of the traditional female culture-bearers who applied domestic values to the public sphere. The second group was comprised of a diverse range of New Women, including political feminists, flappers, and career women. Within the literary world, Hemingway was only one of several leading male authors whose writings express an anxiety over the power of women in that world. In his correspondence, Hemingway frequently shows defensiveness or hostility toward women who compete with men. Competition from female writers and the female influence in the publishing industry on critical standards and on popular tastes threatened to stigmatize the writing profession as effeminate and to devalue the style and marketability of men's writings.

Although Hemingway has been condemned for depicting women as "bitches," very few such women actually appear in his writings, and almost exclusively during the 1930s. The few times that Hemingway embodies his fears of powerful women in a fictive "bitch," he is attacking not only or primarily the woman but rather male passivity and dependence on women—traits he found in himself.

What we have identified as Hemingway's solution to the confusions of modern life—reciprocity between the sexes, achieved in a natural setting remote from society—is well illustrated by the love between Jordan and Maria in *For Whom the Bell Tolls*. Maria is the female principle that complements Jordan's male nature; her qualities unite with his, and the idyllic love affair blossoms. For all the intensity of the love scenes, however, *For Whom the Bell Tolls* ultimately conveys the failure of romantic love. It is not simply that love will not stop the fascist advance. Blowing up the bridge will not stop the Fascists, either.

One of the features that runs throughout Hemingway's writing is the recurrence of failed communication between men and women. Linguistic studies of gender-linked differences in language that result in miscommunication confirm what we have long known—Hemingway had a great ear for dialogue. In his renderings of common speech, he captures those moments when men and women stop truly hearing each other.

The Old Man and the Sea, then, may be read as Hemingway's acceptance of ultimate failure, a reconciliation with the idea that victory—never to be despised—is temporary, for all, as the Precher reminds us, is vanity. It is therefore no small irony that when the novella was published in *Life* magazine, it was widely hailed as proof that the old master still had his powers. The book won the Pulitzer Prize in 1953 and paved the way for Hemingway's Nobel Prize in 1954. And its popular reception in the conservative Eisenhower 1950s suggests that its essentialist, archetypal presentation of woman was well suited to that decade's prevailing ideology of gender.

Analyzing Hemingway's posthumous publications is a tricky business, because we cannot know with certainty why he left them unpublished in his lifetime, nor, without consulting the original manuscripts, the full extent of the editorial emendations and omissions. It is sufficient to note that the posthumous works show his continuing preoccupation with the motifs we have already discussed. While the critics have mined these works for further evidence of Hemingway's fascination with the writing/gender nexus, their psychological readings should be supplemented by an awareness of historical contexts. Although Hemingway's fictional treatment for gender necessarily proceeded from his personal psychology, that very personality was shaped by, and was reacting to, biographical and historical circumstances that included the increasing influence of women within the literary world and over American culture generally.

One important way to understand Hemingway's depiction of women is as a reassertion of patriarchal power in American literature and culture. Reading his work provides an opportunity to reflect upon the gendered nature of the literary canon and of the American cultural history that canon is supposed to reflect. Although he was far form alone in the attempt to reestablish male domination in the cultural sphere, he stands out as a major figure in that effort, a culture hero (or a villain) whose life and work had a marked effect on the history of gender in the 20th century.

[Selected from Scott Donaldson, (ed.), *The Cambridge Companion to Ernest Hemingway*. Shanghai: Shanghai Foreign Language Education Press, 2000.]

Chapter 3 Southern Literature

1. Introduction

Southern literature refers to literary works about the Southern United States or by writers who were born or spent their formative years in the South, which is basically a type of regional literature reflecting the features of the American South. The American South is a peculiar area in the United States where people there have their own distinctive dialect, ideas, culture and history. Traditionally, it serves as the opposite of the American North: the North is considered to be industrialized, progressive and democratic, while the south is supposed to be agrarian, stable and aristocratic. The peculiar culture and history are the fundamental reason that leads to the difference between Southern literature and the rest of American literature. The troubled history of the South—the American Civil War and the following Reconstruction, the slavery and the racial problems become not only the subject matters, but also themes for its literary works.

Southern literature often has its own features. Southern literary works reveal a strong sense of history. The Southern history, especially the impact of the Civil War on the South, is often described. Also, land plays a vital role in Southern Literature. The characters have a strong sense of belonging to the land, and their personalities are defined by the land. They usually hold fast to the Southern tradition and the family tie. In the setting of a typical Southern novel, the community is important, and people tend to get measured by their relationship to the community. The language in Southern literature is rich and ornamental—fully rhetorically expressed. The Southern dialect is often used in it. The dominant religion in the South (Protestantism), racial problems and conflicts between different social classes are focus of Southern literary works, thus common themes like agrarianism vs. industrialism, black vs. white, past vs. present, chivalry vs. chauvinism, old politics vs. new politics, and aristocracy vs. the people frequently appear in it.

Southern literature can be traced back to Captain John Smith and his memoirs of Virginia, which are records about the early history of the South. The development of Southern literature can be divided into 4 periods: the antebellum era (1783—1965), the post-bellum era (1965—1918), the Southern renaissance (1918—1940) and the present days. Southern literature prior to 1865 revolves around the topic of the defense of slavery. Anti-Tom literature—literature in support of slavery and against *Uncle Tom's Cabin* becomes the major type. The only writer of this period who gained a national and international fame is Edgar Allan Poe. Though his status as a "Southern" writer may be ambiguous, Poe's influence on Southern literature can never be ignored. Poe's use of Gothic elements—the horrible plot, mysterious atmosphere and morbid characters—became a common writing technique of Southern literature. After the Civil War, due to a sense of loss on the battlefield, Southern literature greatly romanticized the old way of life and the Southern writers turned their defeat almost into a legend. There appeared lots of poetry and novels about the "Lost Cause," in which the defeated South and its lost culture were greatly idealized. Writers with this point of view were referred to as Magnolia School. It is worth mentioning that there were still writers, especially the African American writers who dismissed this nostalgia by pointing out the racism and exploitation of blacks that happened during this period in the South. The most prominent writers of this period were two regionalists or local colorists: Mark Twain and Kate Chopin. Twain gained his fame with a typical Southern tall tale "The Notorious Jumping Frog of Calaveras County." *The Adventures of Tom Sawyer* depicted the life of a group of boys living in a small town along Mississippi and the customs and superstition of local people. Its sequel, *The Adventures of Huckleberry Finn*, which Ernest Hemingway commented as "all modern American literature comes from," satirized the out-of-date antebellum South through a southward voyage of Huck and a runaway slave Jim on the Mississippi. Kate Chopin established her literary reputation with the short story collections *Bayou Folk* (1894) and *A Night in Acadie* (1897), which focused on the Acadian communities of Louisiana and described a specific Southern culture. Her second and final novel *The Awakening* (1899) turned out to be not only a fine feminist work, but also paved the way for the Southern novel as a serious genre. Chopin's writing earned her the reputation of an important feminist writer as well as one of the most important chroniclers of the post-Civil War South.

Not until the turn of the 20th century, Southern writers had begun to exhibit a new readiness to examine Southern culture and attitudes with an objective eye. The fiercest criticism came from H. L. Mencken, who called Southern culture the "Sahara of the Bozart" and declared that the intellectual and cultural life in the South had been on the decline since the Civil War. Meanwhile, a group of poets and literary scholars started to gather at Vanderbilt University around 1920. They were called "The Fugitives." Some of them later joined the Southern Agrarians and issued a manifesto "I'll Take My Stand: The South and the Agrarian Tradition," which revealed their pro-Southern agrarian position and their opposition to industrialization. The Southern renaissance started. It is a cultural and intellectual movement in the 1920s reacted to the conflicts between old beliefs and values and the new ones and the expansion of Northern industrialization as mentioned above. Literary works of this period of time discussed two problems: the influence of Southern tradition to the present life and the racial problems.

The writers of the Southern Renaissance denied the Southern literary tradition of the previous generation, undertook a radical reassessment of Southern culture, and re-examined the Southern past in an attempt to define and revalidate their cultural tradition. Two of the most famous ones are William Faulkner (1897—1962) and Robert Penn Warren (1905—1995). Other famous writers include Katherine Anne Porter (1890—1980), Tennessee Williams (1911—1983) and Thomas Wolfe (1900—1938).

Faulkner was born and raised in Mississippi, and he was greatly influenced by this state as well as by the history and culture of the South as a whole. For instance, the fictional town of "Jefferson" in the "Yoknapatawpha County" was basically modeled on his hometown Oxford. He even created various types of inhabitants for this town: the decadent aristocratic Sartoris and Compson families; the emerging uncultured, Bourbon, money-minded Snopes family; and the dispossessed Indians and exploited Negroes in order to present his epic legend of the disintegration of the Old South. His writing style is a combination of techniques from Gothic romance, symbolism, allegory, stream of consciousness and a bold experimentation of complex multiple point of view narration. Faulkner wrote 19 novels and 3 volumes of short stories altogether. His most important novels include *The Sound and the Fury* (1929), *As I Lay Dying* (1930), *Light in August* (1932), *Absalom, Absalom!* (1936), and *Go Down, Moses* (1942). He won the 1949 Nobel Prize in Literature.

Robert Penn Warren was a poet, novelist, and literary critic(he was a founder of New Criticism) and also a charter member of the Fellowship of Southern Writers. He was born in Kentucky and studied at Vanderbilt where he joined the Fugitives. He received the 1947 Pulitzer Prize for Novel for *All the King's Men* (1946) and the 1958 Pulitzer Prize for Poetry for *Promises: Poems 1954—1956* , and in 1979 for *Now and Then*. He is the only person who has won Pulitzer Prizes for both fiction and poetry. A major theme in his writing is the necessity of self-knowledge, and the basic conflict in his works centers upon a character's attempt to create worthy values in the face of a complex and often hostile world.

Katherine Anne Porter was the penname of Callie Russel Porter, who was born in Indian Creek, Texas. When young, she worked briefly as an actress and singer. In 1930, she published her first short story collection, *Flowering Judas and Other Stories*, which received favorable critical acclaim that it alone virtually assured her place in American literature. Her own ill experience provided the background for her short novel *Pale Horse, Pale Rider* in 1939. Her 1962 novel *Ship of Fools* was the best-selling novel in America that year, but her short stories received much more critical acclaim. In 1966 she was awarded the Pulitzer Prize and the National Book Award for *The Collected Stories of Katherine Anne Porter*, and in that year she was also appointed to the American Academy of Arts and Letters. She is known for her penetrating insight and dark themes such as betrayal, death and the origin of human evil.

Tennessee Williams was born Thomas Lanier Williams in Columbus, Mississippi. He moved to New Orleans in 1939 and changed his name to "Tennessee," the state of his father's birth. He was awarded the Pulitzer Prize for Drama for *A Streetcar Named Desire* in 1948 and for *Cat on a Hot Tin Roof* in 1955. Besides, *The Glass Menagerie* (1945) and *The Night of the Iguana* (1961) won New York Drama Critics' Circle Awards. His 1952 play *The Rose Tattoo* received the Tony Award for best play. In 1980 he was presented with the Presidential Medal of Freedom by President Jimmy Carter. Williams set his plays in the South. Much of the pathos in his drama was taken from his own life—alcoholism, depression, thwarted desire, loneliness, and insanity. The "mad heroine" theme appeared in many of his plays while his male characters were often vulgar and irresponsible.

Thomas Wolfe was born to a lower class family in poverty stricken western North Carolina. He witnessed the rebuilding of his hometown, and while he reveled in the growth of Asheville, he feared the loss of values coming with money-grubbing industrialism. Wolfe's most famous works were *Look Homeward, Angel* (1929) and *You Can't Go Home Again* (1940), which chronicled the tourism in Asheville and the conflicts between Northern and Southern values. He is known for mixing highly original, poetic, rhapsodic, and impressionistic prose with autobiographical writing. His books vividly reflect American culture and mores of the period.

From the 1940s onward, Southern literature developed with the social and cultural changes in the South due to the American Civil Rights Movement. More female and African American writers began to be accepted as part of Southern literature, such as Eudora Welty, Flannery O'Connor, Ellen Glasgow, and Carson McCullers among many others.

Key words

Antebellum South

The antebellum period was the period in the United States from after the birth of the U.S. to the start of the American Civil War. The Antebellum South refers to the south of the United States before the Civil War where slavery system developed.

The Southern Renaissance

The Southern Renaissance is the reinvigoration of American Southern literature that began in the 1920s and 1930s with the appearance of writers such as William Faulkner, Caroline Gordon, Tennessee Williams, Katherine Anne Porter, Allen Tate, Thomas Wolfe, and Robert Penn Warren, among others. The

Southern Renaissance is a literary movement as well as a cultural movement, and it has also been regarded as a consequence of the agrarian South's opening up to outside world because of the influence of industrialization that took place in the region during and after World War Ⅰ.

The Fugitives

The Fugitives were a group of poets and literary scholars who came together at Vanderbilt University in Nashville, Tennessee around 1920. They published a small literary magazine called *The Fugitive* from 1922—1925. Although its published life was brief, *The Fugitive* is considered to be one of the most influential publications in the history of American letters. The Fugitives made Vanderbilt a fountainhead of the New Criticism, the dominant mode of textual analysis in English during the first half of the 20th century.

2. William Faulkner

2.1 Presentation Topics

(1) William Faulkner as a novelist and regionalist.

(2) Racial problems and social class conflicts in William Faulkner's novels.

(3) The decadent and even culturally degenerate settings in William Faulkner's novels.

(4) The stream of consciousness technique and multiple point of view in his fiction.

2.2 Selected Reading

Ⅰ. Central issue of concern

William Faulkner's view on the idea of white-superiority in the South and on the sharp class conflicts between the poor white and the landlord.

Ⅱ. Text

Barn Burning

The store in which the justice of the Peace's court was sitting smelled of cheese. The boy, crouched on his nail keg at the back of the crowded room, knew he smelled cheese, and more: from where he sat he could see the ranked shelves close-packed with the solid, squat, dynamic shapes of tin cans whose labels his stomach read, not from the lettering which meant nothing to his mind but from the scarlet devils and the silver curve of fish—this, the cheese which he knew he smelled and the hermetic meat which his intestines believed he smelled coming in intermittent gusts momentary and brief between the other constant one, the smell and sense just a little of fear because mostly of despair and grief, the old fierce pull of blood. He could not see the table where the Justice sat and before which his father and his father's enemy (*our enemy*, he thought in that despair, *ourn*! *mine and his both*! *He's my father*!) stood, but he could hear them, the two of them that is, because his father had said no word yet:

"But what proof have you, Mr. Harris?"

"I told you. The hog got into my corn. I caught it up and sent it back to him, He had no fence that would hold it. I told him so, warned him. The next time I put the hog in my pen. When he came to get it I gave him enough wire to patch tip his pen. The next time I put the hog up and kept it. I rode down to his house and saw the wire I gave him still rolled on to the spool in his yard. I told him he could have the hog when he paid me a dollar pound fee. That evening a nigger came with the dollar and got the hog. He was a strange nigger. He said, 'He say to tell you wood and hay kin burn.' I said, 'What?' 'That whut he say to tell you,' the nigger said. 'Wood and hay kin burn.' That night my barn burned. I got the stock out but I lost the barn."

"Where is the nigger? Have you got him?"

"He was a strange nigger, I tell you. I don't know what became of him."

"But that's not proof. Don't you see that's not proof?"

"Get that boy up here. He knows." For a moment the boy thought too that the man meant his older brother until Harris said, "Not him. The little one. The boy," and, crouching, small for his age, small and wiry like his father, in patched and faded jeans even too small for him, with straight, uncombed, brown hair and eyes gray and wild as storm scud, he saw the men between himself and the table part and become a lane of grim faces, at the end of which he saw the justice, a shabby, collarless, graying man in spectacles, beckoning him, he felt no floor under his bare feet; he seemed to walk beneath the palpable weight of the grim turning faces. His father, stiff in his black Sunday coat donned not for the trial but for the moving, did not even look at him. *He aims for me to lie*, he thought, again with that frantic grief and despair. *And I will have to do hit.*

"What's your name, boy?" the Justice said.

"Colonel Sartoris Snopes," the boy whispered.

"Hey?" the Justice said. "Talk louder. Colonel Sartoris? I reckon anybody named for Colonel Sartoris in this country can't help but tell the truth, can they?" The boy said nothing. *Enemy*! *Enemy*! He thought; for a moment he could not even see, could not see that the justice's face was kindly nor discern that his voice was troubled when he spoke to the man named Harris: "Do you want me to question this boy?" But he could hear, and during those subsequent long seconds while there was absolutely no sound in the crowded little room save that of quiet and intent breathing it was as if he had swung outward at the end of a grape vine, over a ravine, and at the top of the swing had been caught in a prolonged instant of mesmerized gravity, weightless in time.

"No!" Harris said violently, explosively. "Damnation! Send him out of here!" Now time, the fluid world, rushed beneath him again, the voices coming to him again through the smell of cheese and sealèd meat, the fear and despair and the old grief of blood:

"This case is closed. I can't find against you, Snopes, but I can give you advice. Leave this county and don't come back to it."

His father spoke for the first time, his voice cold and harsh, level, without emphasis: "I aim to. I don't figure to stay in a country among people who..." he said something unprintable and vile, addressed to no one.

"That'll do," the justice said. "Take your wagon and get out of this county before dark. Case dismissed."

His father turned, and he followed the stiff black coat, the wiry figure walking a little stiffly from where a Confederate provost's man's musket ball had taken him in the heel on a stolen horse thirty years ago, followed the two backs now, since his older brother had appeared from somewhere in the crowd, no taller than the father but thicker, chewing tobacco steadily, between the two lines of grim-faced men and out of the store and across the worn gallery and down the sagging steps and among the dogs and half-grown boys in the mild May dust, where as he passed a vôice hissed:

"Barn burner!"

Again he could not see, whirling; there was a face in a red haze, moonlike, bigger than the full moon, the owner of it half again his size, he leaping in the red haze toward the face, feeling no blow, feeling no shock when his head struck the earth, scrabbling up and leaping again, feeling no blow this time either and tasting no blood, scrabbling up to see the other boy in full flight and himself already leaping into pursuit as his father's hand jerked him back, the harsh, cold voice speaking above him: "Go get in the wagon."

It stood in a grove of locusts and mulberries across the road. His two hulking sisters in their Sunday dresses and his mother and her sister in calico and sunbonnets were already in it, sitting on and among the sorry residue of the dozen and more movings which even the boy could remember—the battered stove, the broken beds and chairs, the clock inlaid with mother-of-pearl, which would not run, stopped at some fourteen minutes past two o'clock of a dead and forgotten day and time, which had been his mother's dowry. She was crying, though when she saw him she drew her sleeve across her face and began to descend from the wagon. "Get back," the father said.

"He's hurt. I got to get some water and wash his ...."

"Get back in the wagon," his father said, he got in too, over the tail-gate. His father mounted to the seat where the older brother already sat and struck the gaunt mules two savage blows with the peeled willow, but without heat. It was not even sadistic; it was exactly that same quality which in later years would cause his descendants to over-run the engine before putting a motor car into motion, striking and reining back in the same movement. The wagon went on, the store with its quiet crowd of grimly watching men dropped behind; a curve in the road hid it. Forever he thought. Maybe he's done satisfied now, now that he has ... stopping himself, not to say it aloud even to himself. His mother's hand touched his shoulder.

"Does hit hurt?" she said.

"Naw," he said. "Hit don't hurt. Lemme be."

"Can't you wipe some of the blood off before hit dries?"

"I'll wash to night," he said. "Lemme be, I tell you."

The wagon went on. He did not know where they were going. None of them ever did or ever asked, because it was always somewhere, always a house of sorts waiting for them a day or two days or even three days away. Likely, his father bad already arranged to make a crop on another farm before he ... Again he had to stop himself. He (the father) always did. There was something about his wolflike independence and even courage, when the advantage was at least neutral, which impressed strangers, as if they got from his latent ravening ferocity not so much a sense of dependability as a feeling that his ferocious conviction in the rightness of his own actions would be of advantage to all whose interest lay with his.

That night they camped, in a grove of oaks and beeches where a spring ran. The nights were still cool and they had a fire against it, of a rail lifted from a nearby fence and cut into lengths—a small fire, neat, niggard almost, a shrewd fire; such fires were his father's habit and custom always, even in freezing weather. Older, the boy might have remarked this and wondered why not a big one; why should not a man who had not only seen the waste and extravagance of war, but who had in his blood an inherent voracious prodigality with material not his own, have burned everything in sight? Then he might have gone a step farther and thought that was the reason: that niggard blaze was the living fruit of nights passed during those four years in the woods hiding from all men, blue or gray, with his strings of horses (captured horses, he called them). And older still, he might have divined the true reason: that the element of fire spoke to some deep mainspring of his father's being, as the element of steel or of powder spoke to other men, as the one weapon for the preservation of integrity, else breath were not worth the breathing, and hence to be regarded with respect and used with discretion.

But he did not think this now and he had seen those same niggard blazes all his life. He merely ate his supper beside it and was already half asleep over his iron plate when his father called him, and once more he followed the stiff back, the stiff and ruthless limp, up the slope and on to the starlit road where, turning, he could see his father against the stars but without face or depth—a shape black, flat, and bloodless as though cut from tin in the iron folds of the frockcoat which had not been made lot him, the voice harsh like tin and without heat like tin:

"You were fixing to tell them. You would have told him," He didn't answer. His father struck him with the flat of his hand on the side of the head, hard but without heat, exactly as he had struck the two mules at the store, exactly as he would strike either of them with any stick in order to kill a horse fly, his voice still without heat or anger: "You're getting to be a man. You got to learn. You got to learn to stick to your own blood or you ain't going to have any blood to stick to you. Do you think either of them, any man there this morning, would? Don't you know all they wanted was a chance to get at me because they knew I had them beat? Eh?" Later, twenty years later, he was to tell himself, "If I had said they wanted only truth, justice, he would have hit me again." But now he said nothing. He was not crying. He just stood there. "Answer me," his father said.

"Yes," he whispered. His father turned.

"Get on to bed. We'll be there tomorrow."

Tomorrow they were there. In the early afternoon the wagon stopped before a paintless two-room house identical almost with the dozen others it had stopped before even in the boy's ten years, and again, as on the other dozen occasions, his mother and aunt got down and began to unload the wagon, although his two sisters and his father and brother had not moved.

"Likely hit ain't fitten for hawgs," one of the sisters said.

"Nevertheless, fit it will and you'll hog it and like it," his father said. "Get out of the chairs and help your Ma unload."

The two sisters got down, big, bovine, in a flutter of cheap ribbons; one of them drew from the jumbled wagon bed a battered lantern, the other a worn broom. His father handed the reins to the older son and began to climb stiffly over the wheel. "When they get unloaded, take the team to the barn and feed them." Then he said, and at first, the boy thought he was still speaking to his brother:

"Come with me."

"Me?" he said.

"Yes," his father said, "you."

"Abner," his mother said. His father paused and looked back—the harsh level state beneath the shaggy, graying, irascible brows.

"I reckon I'll have a word with the man that aims to begin tomorrow owning me body and soul for the next eight months."

They went back up the road. A week ago—or before last night, that is—he would have asked where they were going, but not now. His father had struck him before last night but never before had he paused afterward to explain why, it was as if the blow and the following calm, outrageous voice still rang, repercussed, divulging nothing to him save the terrible handicap of being young, the light weight of his few years, just heavy enough to prevent his soaring free of the world as it seemed to be ordered but not heavy enough to keep him footed solid in it, to resist it and try to change the course of its events.

Presently he could see the grove of oaks and cedars and the other flowering trees and shrubs where the house would be, though not the house yet. They walked beside a fence massed with honeysuckle and Cherokee roses and came to a gate swinging open between two brick pillars, and now, beyond a sweep of drive, he saw the house for the first time and at that instant he forgot his father and the terror and despair both, and even when he remembered his father again (who had not stopped), the terror and despair did not return. Because, for all the twelve movings, they had sojourned until now in a poor country, a land of small farms and fields and houses, and he had never seen a house like this before. *Hits big as a courthouse*, he thought quietly, with a surge of peace and joy whose reason he could not have thought into words, being too young for that: *They are safe from him. People whose lives are a part of this peace and dignity are beyond his touch, he no more to them than a buzzing wasp: capable of stinging for a little moment but that's all—the spell of this peace and dignity rendering even the barns and stable and cribs which belong to it impervious to the puny flames he might contrive ....* This, the peace and joy, ebbing for an instant as he looked again at the stiff black back, the stiff and implacable limp of the figure which was not dwarfed by the house, for the reason that it had never looked big anywhere and which now, against the serene columned backdrop, had more than ever that impervious quality of something cut ruthlessly from tin, depthless, as though, sidewise to the sun, it would cast no shadow. Watching him, the boy remarked the absolutely undeviating course which his father held and saw the stiff foot come squarely down in a pile of fresh droppings where a horse had stood in the drive and which his father could have avoided by a simple change of stride. But it ebbed only for a moment, though he could not have thought this into words either, walking on in the spell of the house, which he could ever want but without envy, without sorrow, certainly never with that ravening and jealous rage which unknown to him walked in the ironlike black coat before him; Maybe he will feel it too, *Maybe it will even change him now from what maybe be couldn't help but be.*

They crossed the portico. Now he could hear his father's stiff foot as it came down on the boards with clocklike finality, a sound out of all proportion to the displacement of the body it bore and which was not dwarfed either by the white door before it, as though it had attained to a sort of vicious and ravening minimum not to be dwarfed by anything—the flat, wide, black hat, the formal coat of broadcloth which had once been black but which had now that friction-glazed greenish cast of the bodies of old house flies, the lifted sleeve which was too large, the lifted hand like a curled claw. The door opened so promptly that the boy knew the Negro must have been watching them all the time, an old man with neat grizzled hair, in a linen jacket. who stood barring the door with his body, saying, "Wipe yo foots, white man, fo you come in here, Major ain't home nohow."

"Get out of my way, nigger," his father said, without heat too, flinging the door back and the Negro also and entering, his hat still on his head. And now the boy saw the prints of the stiff foot on the doorjamb and saw them appear on the pale rug behind the machinelike deliberation of the foot which seemed to bear (or transmit) twice the weight which the body compassed. The Negro was shouting "Miss Lula! Miss Lula!" somewhere behind them, then the boy, deluged as though by a warm wave by a suave turn of carpeted stair and a pendant glitter of chandeliers and a mute gleam of gold frames, heard the swift feet and saw her too, a lady—perhaps he had never seen her like before either—in a gray, smooth gown with lace at the throat and an apron tied at the waist and the sleeves turned back, wiping cake or biscuit dough from her hands with a towel as she came up the hall, looking not at his father at all but at the tracks on the blond rug with an expression of incredulous amazement.

"I tried," the Negro cried. "I told him to...."

"Will you please go away?" she said in a shaking voice. "Major de Spain is not at home. Will you please go away?"

His father had not spoken again. He did not speak again. He did not even look at her. He just stood stiff in the center of the rug, in his hat, the shaggy iron-gray brows twitching slightly above the pebble-colored eyes as he appeared to examine the house with brief deliberation. Then with the same deliberation he turned; the boy watched him pivot on the good leg and saw the stiff foot drag round the arc of the turning, leaving a final long and fading smear. His father never looked at it, he never once looked down at the rug, The Negro held the door, it closed behind them, upon the hysteric and indistinguishable woman-wail. His father stopped at the top of the steps and scraped his boot clean on the edge of it. At the gate he stopped again. He stood for a moment, planted stiffly on the stiff foot, looking back at the house. "Pretty and white, ain't it?" he said. "That's sweat. Nigger sweat. Maybe it ain't white enough yet to suit him. Maybe he wants to mix some white sweat with it."

Two hours later the boy was chopping wood behind the house within which his mother and aunt and the two sisters (the mother and aunt, not the two girls, he knew that; even at this distance and muffled by walls the flat loud voices of the two girls emanated an incorrigible idle inertia) were setting up the stove to prepare a meal, when he heard the hooves and saw the linen-clad man on a fine sorrel mare, whom he recognized even before he saw the rolled rug in front of the Negro youth following on a fat boy carriage horse—a suffused, angry face vanishing, still at full gallop, beyond the corner of the house where his father and brother were sitting in the two tilted chairs; and a moment later, almost before he could have put the axe down, he heard the hooves again and watched the sorrel mare go back out of the yard, already galloping again. Then his father began to shout one of the sisters' names, who presently emerged backward from the kitchen door dragging the rolled rug along the ground by one end while the other sister walked behind it.

"If you ain't going to tote, go on and set up the wash pot," the first said.

"You, Sarty!" the second shouted. "Set up the wash pot!" His father appeared at the door, framed against that shabbiness, as he had been against that other bland perfection, impervious to either, the mother's anxious face at his shoulder.

"Go on," the father said. "Pick it up." The two sisters stooped, broad, lethargic; stooping, they presented an incredible expanse of pale cloth and a flutter of tawdry ribbons.

"If I thought enough of a rug to have to git hit all the way from France I wouldn't keep hit where folks coming in would have to tromp on hit," the first said. They raised the rug.

"Abner," the mother said. "Let me do it."

"You go back and git dinner," his father said. "I'll tend to this."

From the woodpile through the rest of the afternoon the boy watched them, the rug spread flat in the dust beside the bubbling wash-pot, the two sisters stooping over it with that profound and lethargic reluctance, while the father stood over them in turn, implacable and grim, driving them though never raising his voice again. He could smell the harsh homemade lye they were using; he saw his mother come to the door once and look toward them with an expression not anxious now but very like despair; he saw his father turn, and he fell to with the axe and saw from the corner of his eye his father raise from the ground a flattish fragment of field stone and examine it and return to the pot, and this time his mother actually spoke: "Abner. Abner. Please don't. Please, Abner."

Then he was done too. It was dusk; the whippoorwills had already begun. He could smell coffee from the room where they would presently eat the cold food remaining from the mid-afternoon meal, though when he entered the house he realized they were having coffee again probably because there was a fire on the hearth, before which the rug now lay spread over the backs of the two chairs. The tracks of his father's foot were gone. Where they had been were now long, water-cloudy scoriations resembling the sporadic course of a Lilliputian mowing machine.

It still hung there while they ate the cold food and then went to bed, scattered without order or claim up and down the two rooms, his mother in one bed, where his father would later lie, the older brother in the other, himself, the aunt, and the two sisters on pallets on the floor. But his father was not in bed yet. The last thing the boy remembered was the depthless, harsh silhouette of the hat and coat bending over the rug and it seemed to him that he had not even closed his eyes when the silhouette was standing over him, the fire almost dead behind it, the stiff foot prodding him awake. "Catch up the mule," his father said.

When he returned with the mule his father was standing in the black door, the rolled rug over his shoulder. "Ain't you going to ride?" he said.

"No, Give me your foot."

He bent his knee into his father's hand, the wiry, surprising power flowed smoothly, rising, he rising with it, on to the mule's bare back (they had owned a saddle once; the boy could remember it though not when or where) and with the same effortlessness his father swung the rug up in front of him. Now in the starlight they retraced the afternoon's path, up the dusty road rife with honeysuckle, through the gate and up the black tunnel of the drive to the lightless house, where he sat on the mule and felt the rough warp of the rug drag across his thighs and vanish.

"Don't you want me to help?" he whispered. His father did not answer and now he heard again that stiff foot striking the hollow portico with that wooden and clock like deliberation, that outrageous overstatement of the weight it carried. The rug, hunched, not flung (the boy could tell that even in the darkness) from his father's shoulder struck the angle of wall and floor with a sound unbelievably loud, thunderous, then the foot again, unhurried and enormous; a light came on in the house and the boy sat, tense, breathing steadily and quietly and just a little fast, though the foot itself did not increase its beat at all, descending the steps now; now the boy could see him.

"Don't you want to ride now?" he whispered. "We kin both ride now," the light within the house altering now, flaring up and sinking. He's coming down the stairs now, he thought fie had already ridden the mule up beside the horse block; presently his father was up behind him and he doubled the reins over and slashed the mule across the neck, but before the animal could begin to trot the hard, thin arm came round him, the hard, knotted hand jerking the mule back to a walk.

In the first red rays of the sun they were in the lot, putting plow gear on the mules. This time the sorrel mare was in the lot before he heard it at all, the rider collarless and even bareheaded, trembling, speaking in a shaking voice as the woman in the house had done, his father merely looking up once before stooping again to the hame he was buckling, so that the man on the mare spoke to his stooping back:

"You must realize you have ruined that rug, wasn't there anybody here, any of your women .... " He ceased, shaking, the boy watching him, the older brother leaning now in the stable door, chewing, blinking slowly and steadily at nothing apparently. "It cost a hundred dollars. But you never had a hundred dollars. You never will. So I'm going to charge you twenty bushels of corn against your crop.

I'll add it in your contract and when you come to the commissary you can sign it. That won't keep Mrs. de Spain quiet but maybe it will teach you to wipe your feet off before you enter her house again."

Then he was gone. The boy looked at his father, who still had not spoken or even looked up again, who was now adjusting the logger-head in the hame.

"Pap," he said. His father looked at him—the inscrutable face, the shaggy brows beneath which the gray eyes glinted coldly. Suddenly the boy went toward him, fast, stopping also, suddenly. "You done the best you could!" he cried. "If he wanted hit done different why didn't he wait and tell you how? He won't git no twenty bushels! He won't git none! We'll gether hit and hide hit! I kin watch...."

"Did you put the cutter back in that straight stock like I told you?"

"No, sir," he said.

"Then go do it."

That was Wednesday. During the rest of that week he worked steadily, at what was within his scope and some which was beyond it, with an industry that did not need to be driven nor even commanded twice; he had this from his mother, with the difference that some at least of what he did he liked to do, such as splitting wood with the half-size axe which his mother and aunt had earned; or saved money somehow, to present him with at Christmas. In company with the two older women (and on one afternoon, even one of the sisters), he built pens for the shoat and the cow which were a part of his father's contract with the landlord, and one afternoon, his father being absent, gone somewhere on one of the mules, he went to the field.

They were running a middle buster now, his brother holding the plow straight while he handled the reins, and walking beside the straining mule, the rich black sod shearing cool and damp against his bare ankles, he thought maybe this is the end of it. Maybe even that twenty bushels that seems hard to have to pay for just a rug will be a cheap price for him to stop forever and always from being what he used to be; thinking, dreaming now, so that his brother had to speak sharply to him to mind the mule: Maybe he even won't collect the twenty bushels, Maybe it will all add up and balance and vanish-corn, rug, fire—The terror and grief the being pulled two ways like between two teams of horses-gone, done with for ever and ever.

Then it was Saturday; he looked Lip from beneath the mule he was harnessing and saw his father in the black coat and hat. "Not that," his father said. "The wagon gear. " And then, two hours later, sitting in the wagon bed behind his father and brother on the seat, the wagon accomplished a final curve, and he saw the weathered paintless store with its tattered tobacco and patent-medicine posters and the tethered wagons and saddle animals below the gallery. He mounted the gnawed steps behind his father and brother, and there again was the lane of quiet, watching faces for the three of them to walk through. I le saw the man in spectacles sitting at the plank table and he did not need to be told this was a Justice of the Peace; he sent one glare of fierce, exultant, partisan defiance at the man in collar and cravat now, whom he had seen but twice before in his life, and that on a galloping horse, who now wore on his face an expression riot of rage but of amazed unbelief which the boy could not have known was at the incredible circumstance of being sued by one of his own ten ants, and came and stood against his father and cried at the Justice: "He ain't done it! He ain't burnt.... "

"Go back to the wagon," his father said.

"Burnt?" the Justice said. "Do I understand this rug was burned too?"

"Does anybody here claim it was?" his father said. "Go back to the wagon. " But he did not, he merely retreated to the rear of the room, crowded as that other had been, but not to sit down this time, instead, to stand pressing among the motionless bodies, listening to the voices:

"And you claim twenty bushels of corn is too high for the damage you did to the rug?"

"He brought the rug to me and said he wanted the tracks washed out of it. I washed the tracks out and took the rug back to him,"

"But you didn't carry the rug back to him in the same condition it was in before you made the tracks on it. "

His father did not answer, and now for perhaps half a minute there was no sound at all save that of breathing, the faint, steady suspiration of complete and intent listening.

"You decline to answer that, Mr. Snopes?" Again his father did not answer. "I'm going to find against you, Mr. Snopes. I'm going to find that you were responsible for the injury to Major de Spain's rug and hold you liable for it. But twenty bushels of corn seems a little high for a man in your circumstances to have to pay. Major de Spain claims it cost a hundred dollars. October corn will be worth about fifty cents. I figure that if Major de Spain can stand a ninety-five dollar loss on something he paid cash for, you can stand a five-dollar loss you haven't earned yet. I hold you in damages to Major de Spain to the amount of ten bushels of corn over and above your contract with him, to be paid to him out of your crop at gathering time. Court adjourned."

It had taken no time hardly, the morning was but half begun. He thought they would return home and perhaps back to the field, since they were late, far behind all other farmers. But instead his father passed on behind the wagon, merely indicating with his hand for the older brother to follow with it, and crossed the road toward the blacksmith shop opposite, pressing on after his father, overtaking him, speaking, whispering up at the harsh, calm face beneath the weathered hat: "He won't git no ten bushels neither. I le won't git one. We'll ...." until his father glanced for an instant down at him, the face absolutely calm, the grizzled eyebrows tangled above the cold eyes, the voice almost pleasant, almost gentle:

"You think so? Well, we'll wait till October anyway."

The matter of the wagon—the setting of a spoke or two and the tightening of the tires—did not take long either, the business of the tires accomplished by driving the wagon into the spring branch behind the shop and letting it stand there, the mules nuzzling into the water from time to time, and the boy on the seat with the idle reins, looking up the slope and through the sooty tunnel of the shed where the slow hammer rang and where his father sat on an upended cypress bolt, easily, either talking or listening, still sitting there when the boy brought the dripping wagon up out of the branch and halted it before the door.

"Take them on to the shade and hitch," his father said. He did so and returned. His father and the smith and a third man squatting on his heels inside the door were talking, about crops and animals; the boy, squatting too in the ammoniac dust and hoof parings and scales of rust, heard his father tell a long and unhurried story. Out of the time before the birth of the older brother even when he had been a professional horsetrader. And then his father came lip beside him where he stood before a tattered last year's circus poster on the other side of the store, gazing rapt and quiet it the scarlet horses, the incredible poisings and convolutions of tulle and tights and painted leers of comedians, and said, "It's time to eat."

But not at home. Squatting beside his brother against the front wall, he watched his lather emerge from the store and produce from a paper sack a segment of cheese and divide it carefully and deliberately into three with his pocket knife and produce crackers from the same sack. They all three squatted on the gallery and ate, slowly, without talking; then in the store again, they drank from a tin dipper tepid water smelling of the cedar bucket and of living beech trees. And still they did not go home. It was as a horse lot this time, a tall rail fence upon and along which men stood and sat and out of which one by one horses were led, to be walked and trotted and then cantered back and forth along the road while the slow swapping and buying went on and the sun began to slant westward, they—the three of them—watching and listening, the older brother with his Muddy eyes and his steady, inevitable tobacco, the father commenting now and then on certain of the animals, to no one in particular.

It was after sundown when they reached home. They ate supper by lamplight, then, sitting on the doorstep, the boy watched the night fully accomplish, listening to the whippoorwills and the frogs, when he heard his mother's voice: "Abner! No! No! Oh, God. Oh, God. Abner!" and he rose, whirled, and saw the altered light through the door where a candle stub now burned in a bottle neck on the table and his father, still in the hat and coat, at once formal and burlesque as though dressed carefully for some shabby and ceremonial violence, emptying the reservoir of the lamp back into the five-gallon kerosene can from which it had been filled, while the mother tugged at his arm until he shifted the lamp to the other hand and flung her back, not savagely or viciously, just hard, into the wall, her hands flung out against the wall for balance, her mouth open and in her face the same quality of hopeless despair as had been in her voice. Then his father saw him standing in the door.

"Go to the barn and get that can of oil we were oiling the wagon with," he said. The boy did not move. Then he could speak.

"What..." He cried. "What are you..."

"Go get that oil," his father said. "Go."

Then he was moving, running, outside the house, toward the stable: this the old habit, the old blood which he had not been permitted to choose for himself, which had been bequeathed him willy nilly and which had run for so long (and who knew where, battening on what of outrage and savagery and lust) before it came to him. *I could keep on*, he thought. *I could run on and on and never look back, never need to see his face again. Only I can't, I can't.* The rusted can in his hand now, the liquid sploshing in it as he ran back to the house and into it, into the sound of his mothers weeping in the next room, and handed the can to his father.

"Ain't you going to even send a nigger?" he cried. "At least you sent a nigger before!"

This time his father didn't strike him, the hand came even faster than the blow had, the same hand which had set the can on the table with almost excruciating care flashing from the can toward him too quick for him to follow it, gripping him by the back of his shirt and onto tiptoe before he had seen it quit the can, the face stooping at him in breathless and frozen ferocity, the cold, dead voice speaking over him to the older brother who leaned against the table, chewing with that steady, curious, sidewise motion of cows:

"Empty the can into the big one and go on. I'll catch up with you."

"Better tie him up to the bedpost," the brother said.

"Do like I told you," the father said. Then the boy was moving, his bunched shirt and the hard, bony hand between his shoulder-blades, his toes just touching the floor, across the room and into the other one, past the sisters sitting with spread heavy thighs in the two chairs over the cold hearth, and to where his mother and aunt sat side by side on the bed, the aunt's arms about his mother's shoulders.

"Hold him," the father said. The aunt made a startled movement. "Not you," the father said. "Lennie. Take hold of him. I want to see you do it." His mother took him by the wrist. "You'll hold him better than that. If he gets loose don't you know what he is going to do? He will go up yonder." He jerked his head toward the road, "maybe I'd better tie him."

"I'll hold him," his mother whispered.

"See you do then." Then his father was gone, the stiff foot heavy and measured upon the boards, ceasing at last.

Then he began to struggle. His mother caught him in both arms, he jerking and wrenching at them. He would be stronger in the end, he knew that. Buthe had no time to wait for it. "Lemme go!" he cried. "I don't want to have to hit you!"

"Let him go!" the aunt said. "If he don't go, before God, I am going up there myself!"

"Don't you see I can't?" his mother cried. "Sarty! Sarty! No! No! Help me, Lizzie!"

Then he was free. His aunt grasped at him but it was too late. He whirled, running, his mother stumbled forward on to her knees behind him, crying to the nearer sister: "Catch him, Net! Catch him!" But that was too late too, the sister (the sisters were twins, born at the same time, yet either of them now gave the impression of being, encompassing as much living meat and volume and weight as any other two of the family) not yet having begun to rise from the chair, her head, face, alone merely turned, presenting to him in the flying instant an astonishing expanse of young female features untroubled by any surprise even, wearing only an expression of bovine interest. Then he was out of the room, out of the house, in the mild dust of the starlit road and the heavy ripeness of honeysuckle, the pale ribbon unspooling with terrific slowness under his running feet, reaching the gate at last and turning in, running, his heart and lungs drumming, on up the drive toward the lighted house, the lighted door. *I le did not knock*, he burst in, sobbing for breath, incapable for the moment of speech; he saw the astonished face of the Negro in the linen jacket without knowing when the Negro had appeared.

"De Spain!" he cried, panted. "Where's ..." Then he saw the white man too emerging from a white door down the hall. "Barn!" he cried. "Barn!"

"What?" the white man said. "Barn?"

"Yes!" the boy cried. "Barn!"

"Catch him!" the white man shouted.

But it was too late this time too. The Negro grasped his shirt, but the entire sleeve, rotten with washing, carried away, and he was out that door too and in the drive again, and had actually never ceased to run even while he was screaming into the white man's face.

Behind him the white man was shouting, "My horse! Fetch my horse!" And he thought for an instant of cutting across the park and climbing the fence into the road, but he did not know the park nor how high the vine-massed fence might be and he dared not risk it. So he ran on town the drive, blood and breath roaring; presently he was in the road again though he could not see it. He could not hear either: the galloping mare was almost upon him before he heard her, and even then he held his course, as if the very urgency of his wild grief and need must in a moment more find him wings, waiting until the ultimate instant to hurl himself aside and into the weed-choked roadside ditch as the horse thundered past and on, for an instant in furious silhouette against the stars, the tranquil early summer night sky which, even before the shape of the horse and rider vanished, stained abruptly and violently upward: a long, swirling roar incredible and soundless, blotting the stars, and he springing up and into the road again, running again, knowing it was too late yet still running even after he heard the shot and, an instant later, two shots, pausing now without knowing he had ceased to run, crying "Pap! Pap!" running again before he knew he had begun to run, stumbling, tripping over something and scrabbling Lip again without ceasing to run, looking backward over his shoulder at the glare as he got up, running on among the invisible trees, panting, sobbing, "Father! Father!"

At midnight he was sitting on the crest of a hill. He did not know it was midnight and he did not know how far he had come. But there was no glare behind him now and he sat now, his back toward what he had called home for four days anyhow, his face toward the dark woods which he would enter when breath was strong again, small, shaking steadily in the chili darkness, hugging himself into the remainder of his thin, rotten shirt, the grief and despair now no longer terror and fear but just grief and despair. *Father, My father*, he thought. "He was brave!" he cried suddenly, aloud but not loud, no more than a whisper: "He was! He was in the war! He was in Colonel Sartoris' cav'ry!" not knowing that his father had gone to that war a private in the fine old European sense, wearing no uniform, admitting the authority of and giving fidelity to no man or army or flag, going to war as Malbrouck himself did; for booty—it meant nothing and less than nothing to him if it were enemy booty or his own.

The slow constellations wheeled on. It would be dawn and then sun-up after a while and he would be hungry. But that would be tomorrow and now he was only cold, and walking would cure that. His breathing was easier now, and he decided to get up and go on, and then he found that he bad been asleep because he knew it was almost dawn, the night almost over. He could tell that from the whippoorwills. They were everywhere now among the dark trees below him, constant and inflectioned and ceaseless, so that, as the instant for giving over to the day birds drew nearer and nearer, there was no interval at all between them. He got up. He was a little stiff, but walking would cure that too as it would be cold, and soon there would be the sun. He went on down the hill, toward the dark woods within which the liquid silver voices of the birds, called unceasing—the rapid and urgent beating of the urgent and quiring heart of the late spring night. He did not look back.

[Selected from Nina Baym, et al, (eds.). *The Norton Anthology of American Literature*. (Sixth Edition). New York: W. W. Norton & Company, 2003.]

Ⅲ. Questions for discussion

(1) What are the basic features of Sarty's predicament? What are the major conflicts in the story?

(2) What are the different values to which Sarty seems to be committed? How are these values embodied?

(3) How do you explain Abner Snope's bizarre behavior—having burned the first barn, the rug incident, and going to burn the second barn? What factor is motivating the father to do these things?

(4) How do you interpret the actions of the boy, especially as he seems ready to tell the truth about his father? Examine the boy's interior monologues—the italicized parts of the story. What do these tell us about the boy, about others, about Faulkner's style of narration?

(5) How do you think of the relationship between Abner Snopes and his son?

(6) What is the major theme of this story?

(7) From what perspective is the story narrated? Does the point of view shift in the course of the story?

2.3 Assigned Reading

Art-style and Life-style: The 1920s

Malcolm Bradbury

Dos Passos was an important contributor to American fictional modernism, but perhaps the most crucial and exemplary figure of all was William Faulkner. Not all critics have shared that view of him. To many, he is pre-eminently a novelist of that distinct region of the United States, the South: a complex late product of its romance tradition, its celebrations of heroism and chivalry, its idealisms, its semi-feudal social institutions, its rooted struggle against industrialism, its defeats, pains, and anxieties. To others he is, rather, one of the great figures of international modernist experiment—a writer with the range, capacities, and formal preoccupations we associate with Joyce, Proust, or Virginia Woolf, an experimenter, a symbolist, a witness to modern exile. His own view of himself was as a private man and a farmer, a man of his region, a writer writing of enduring human values, honour, endurance, compassion, sacrifice, in a rhetoric bred, as he put it, "by Oratory out of Solitude." He did have a bohemian phase, but in the Southern capital of New Orleans, and never attended the expatriate feasts of Paris; he did fly in the war, but only as a trainee pilot in Canada. Though his writings draw on the primary methods of modernism—stream of consciousness, collage presentation, time shifts and a chronicity—he never fully explained, in his own aesthetic statements, the impulses that drove him to use those techniques. And, where many modernists probed ever further into experiment, Faulkner's most experimental writing occurs as a "phase" in the middle of his career.

But these two views of Faulkner are not incompatible; indeed they attest to his extraordinary complexity. It is largely when his work grows most Southern and, in that sense, most provincial or localized that his technical experiment emerges in its full force. Certainly Faulkner was very much a writer of the South; born in 1897, he grew up in Oxford, Mississippi, and spent most of his life there. Going early to New Orleans to pursue his ambition to write, he found there Sherwood Anderson, and a bohemian climate; his early work, much influenced by all this, was mostly in poetry, and its debts to the Romantics, especially Keats, but above all to the *fin de siècle* decadent poets, are notable. These early writings are packed with avaricious borrowings, the accumulation of a self-educated provincial catching at certain romantic and new modern texts (like *The Waste Land*) to define his aesthetic preoccupations and find his way. Like Fitzgerald, Faulkner saw himself as a romantic egoist, and knew that beautiful was damned; he saw the world of art hunger crossed with the wasteland of modern life. And he too saw the need for redemptive style, in the new decadent fashion. So, as he moved towards fiction, notions of the failure of history, the decline of the west, the degenerations of modernity, the narcissism of modern existence, the displacement of sexuality, the need to refine sensation, and the claims of bohemia were all part of his push towards a modern definition of art and the discovery of a modern style.

His first two novels, *Soldier's Pay* and *Mosquitoes* (1927), were thus works of the new decadence. The motif is clad in its modern garb, in figures like the death-hungry airman, the epicene new woman, the artist hunting stasis out of time. In *Soldier's Pay* the central figure is the scarred, blinded veteran, Donald Mahon, who comes home to find the malaise of post-war society in the sterility of the people around him, unable to connect desire and fulfillment. In this voided world symbolist spaces and enclosures abound. The virginal and unchaste are ever in contention, while time rots and wastes. *Mosquitoes* is set directly among artists in New Orleans; the Keatsian search in the book is for a timeless beauty that will both capture and transcend present reality, and for a mode of realization that is more than words or euphony, that is wrapped in life. In both these novels, Faulkner seems to adopt the modes of the sophisticated and cosmopolitan writer, though there is much inner unease. But with *Sartoris* (1929), a great change came. Faulkner returned home, discovering that his essential materials were not simply contemporary, but had an extended historical and social dimension, emerging from his familiar Mississippi environment, and its past. This is a far less arch, much more deeply textured novel, fairly conventionally presented; it is a novel of deep social investment, exploring a community at many levels. Out of the book comes Yoknapatawpha County, Faulkner's local, Mississippi version of Hardy's Wessex, a complex invented society overlaying a real one which he was to rearrange, alter, and complicate through most of the rest of his novels. With Jefferson as its county seat, and with its distinctive world of displaced aristocrats, carpet-baggers, sharecroppers and entrepreneurs, its blacks and its standing chorus of town gossips, with its woods, pine-winey afternoons, bear hunts and its own historical "curse," coming from the possession of Indian lands, the history of slavery, and the deep lesion of the Civil War, Yoknapatawpha becomes a totally functional society, a community with its quite distinct class and racial structure, its own inward agonies, its own processes of historical transformation towards commercialism and industrialism.

Faulkner sets the present of *Sartoris* in the post-World War I world, in the uneasy and changing South to which the ex-flyer the young Bayard Satoris returns, uneasy about his manhood and his place, seeking his masculine death recklessly in modern machines. But one world evokes another: Bayard's is a latter-day version of the reckless courage of his Southern aristocrat ancestors. And one story evokes another; the present, in debased form, both releases and re-enacts the past. Two essential contrasts dominate: one between the masculine chivalric cult of the Sartorises, and the feminized world of the Benbows, delicate, intellectual, and finally narcissistic, at odds with action and time; the other between those who have an invested historical and social sense, like the Sartorises, De Spains, and Compsons, and those who act according to entrepreneurial and commercial self-interest, above all the Snopeses. Out of these contrasts arises third, between past and present, a past of action, a present of sterility, a world of men, a world of women. For class barriers now fade, aristocratic manners are superimposed on a commercial world, slaves have been replaced by sharecroppers, the women have learned to turn inward and the men towards inner tragedy, and above all the machine begins to dominate. Thus a special postage stamp of soil, haunted with its own history, institutions, and sense of modern tragedy, now began to be populated, and "I discovered," said Faulkner, "that writing was a mighty fine thing. You could make people stand on their hind legs and cast a shadow. I felt that I had all these people, and as soon as I discovered it I wanted to bring them all back."

But bringing them back seemed to involve a complex aesthetic introversion, as if the very fact of making his own characters part of a larger history and hence part of a pluralized narrative forced this on him. But so did other things; a deep sense of temporal disjunction, an apocalyptic sense of time; and a desire to penetrate the psychic myths underlying the needs and rituals of this society. It is in the work of the end of the Twenties and the Thirties that we can feel Faulkner's experimental power at full force in *The Sound and the Fury* (1929), *As I Lay Dying* (1930), *Light in August* (1932), and *Absalom, Absalom!* (1936). These are works which involve a sense of history, but they are not necessarily historical novels; and they reach, most of them, segmentally, in small selective units, into the Yoknapatawpha experience, yielding it up not as expository narrative but units of perception. The underlying history—reaching from the point of settlement in the new land to the contemporary, dislocated instant—is itself an imaginative fiction, a process where moments of concentration and dissipation occur both collectively and personally, where psychic time strangely crosses historical time, where chiliastic moments in the world and frozen instants of personal perception interweave, where the chance of human innocence is newly offered to the American, but where taint, corruption, and rape re-enact their historical and hereditary cycles. Faulkner's writing contains some of the most powerful moments of modernizing unease in contemporary literature. The intensity arises partly from the facts of Southern history: the South concentrated in a single event, the Civil War, a hundred years of western history, facing a modern exposure, a cultural defeat and deprivation, and the process of industrialization all at once. Hence Faulkner's history is apocalyptic: it exists in the context of a fallen Eden, though its degenerating sequence—as land as spirit yields to land as property, woods to axes, gardens to machines, South to North—none the less contains moments of promise, renewed outside time and process and put into play the contingencies of a careless historical development.

In the books that Faulkner now undertook, modernist pluralization begins to occur, arising from temporal disjunction and the broken relation between "social" and "subjective" consciousness. He displays a remarkable compendium of fictional strategies, structuring his work not through chronological or historical ordering but through alternative radical sequences challenging such orders and generating symbolic resonance. His tactics have very different rationales than do, say, those of Joyce or Proust. One of these is the historical interlocking of the stories; his characters have, so to speak, a reality outside the stories in which they occur. As Faulkner said of them: "These people I figure belong to me and I have the right to move them about in time when I need them." The same applies to the larger history of Yoknapatawpha: Faulkner does not give it to us as really "there," but manifests the conditions under which he is inventing it on this occasion. "Time," the interlocking of present and past, personal public histories, is actually an essential mystery in Faulkner's work. In these central novels and the related stories, there is a recurrent structure of a continuous present behind which are stacked up different layers of time, validated in the story by a variety of justifications. Thus, in the long story "The Bear," in *Go Down, Moses* (1942), there are layers belonging specifically to the evolution of Ike McCaslin, the central figure, dealing with his life at sixteen, eighteen, and so on; and others having to do with a broad apocalyptic historical conspectus (*"Fun 1833 yr stars fell"*). In *The Sound and the Fury*, we have a noncausative or continuous present given us for mimetic reasons, because we are dealing with the perceptions of Benjy, an idiot with the mental age of five; but we also have complicated strata of consciousness relating to the reasons for Quentin Compson's suicide. In *Light in August*, there is a stream of consciousness appropriate to Joe Christmas' present position as it relates to the crises of his childhood, which are there in his consciousness without their actually being "known" to be there, and this helps us comprehend his confused psychic and radical identity. Yet beyond all this there is an experimental author extremely and self-consciously interested in his own rhetoric and structure, his own power to generate form.

These novels of the late Twenties and early Thirties are classics of spatial form, each very different, and generating its own rationale. There are, though, two recurrent paradigms: one is historical or exterior temporal intrusion into personal life; the other is the instant of wonder or personal renewal, or of delocalized vision, of Adamic self-discovery (as experienced, say, by Ike McCaslin in "The Bear"), converted into an eternal moment within time. It is the conversion of this—the flow and the arrest, the process and the transcendence—into art that constitutes the distinct basis of Faulkner's history and his experimentalism. These key novels are modes of penetrating the symbol, the psyche, and the historical continuum. In *The Sound and the Fury*, the central story concerns Quentin's attempt to arrest both historical and subjective time and maintain Candace's virginity from psychic corruption and time's flow; the novel started, Faulkner has told us, from the single image of Caddy's dirty drawers. There are four layers on interlocking response: Benjy's tale told by an idiot in the continuous present holds the story and its images in the form of a timeless memory; Quentin transliterates the image into psychic and historical tragedy, in one form of cause-and-effect; Jason sees it all causally and empirically; and Dilsey offers an enduring continuity. Associative links, like the coincidence between Caddy's name and the caddie at the golf course, generate the process of multiplication. These inward psychic connectives permit Faulkner's primary concern with consciousness to develop; at the same time the story links outward to the larger "objective" history of

Yoknapatawpha, in which Quentin's suicide is a key event. *As I Lay Dying* shows a different experimental tactic. About the six-day funeral journey of the Bundren family, it is told though 59 interior monologues, reflections on movement and stasis, living and death, the moving wagon "with an outward semblance of form and purpose, but with no inference of motion, progress or retrograde," and the complicated and grotesque panorama of life surrounding it.

The early thirties saw a change in Faulkner's preoccupations—a darkening of his themes, an increased concern with a sterile modern evil, with the destruction of men by either the corrupt and dirty sexuality of women, or their fecundity, with the dark outcome of the South's history of Puritanism and miscegenation. *Sanctuary* (1932) creates a figure of modern evil in Popeye, the emptied man who has "the vicious depthless quality of stamped tin," and who revenges his impotence with his corncob rape of Temple Drake, the whore-woman whose decadent sexuality in turn defeats the sentimental sanctuary of innocence sought by Horace Benbow. *Sanctuary* is sensational, and was written largely with commercial intent; *Light in August* draws on similar themes for probably Faulkner's finest novel, a work of extraordinary experiment written through extreme narrative indirections. Here three essential stories interlock. The central narrative is about the black wandering orphan Joe Christmas, whose sexual dislocation brings about the murder of the woman who protects and taunts him, and so his final self-sacrifice to racial lynching. The story of the Revd Gail Hightower shows sterility in another form, as Hightower attempts to lock himself into one timeless Civil War moment when life had meaning, and, unable to relate either to love or violence, now seeks, like Christmas, his own crucifixion. And both these dark stories are enfolded in a third, that of the fertile and abundant Lena Grove, the country woman comes to town to find the father of her child, who lives in a natural timelessness and endurance, a lasting autumn of natural sexuality, opposite to the rigidly puritanic world of the town. Faulkner products in this period one more extraordinary experimental novel, *Absalom, Absalom!*, a work that locks in more directly to his continuous history of Yoknapatawpha. It is the massive, historical, gothic story of Thomas Sutpen's "design," of cursed land, old tragedies and crimes, of the interlocking of history and psychic disorientation and perversion. It is his last truly "modernist" book, but it opens yet another phase of Faulkner's writing.

For by now, Yoknapatawpha County—"William Faulkner, sole owner and proprietor," 2,400 square miles of crossing histories, a web of dynasties and genealogies, taints and crimes, stories and storytellers—was becoming infinitely populous. Much of Faulkner's later work extends that populousness, as in, for example, the extraordinary stories of *Go Down, Moses*, with their complex exploration of the transformation of the virgin American land through taint, crime, and racial exploitation into emptiness and void, but their images of redemptive timelessness. Faulkner found many tones of voice for this—from the bleak tragedy of *Absalom, Absalom!* to the comedy of his late Snopes trilogy (*The Hamlet*, 1940, *The Town*, 1957, and *The Mansion*, 1959) or the spirited note of his last novel *The Reivers* (1962). In his later books, some of his complexity of manner went, or moved towards convention. But that complexity had always come from two visions. One was Faulkner's quarrel with history; his multiples of consciousness seem, like Eliot's fragments, to be of a piece with the loss of meaning and order that he saw in the lapsed Eden of the American South. The other was opposite: Faulkner was interested not just in the disorders of the psyche, but in its plenitude, its sentience and lyricism, its structures and myths. And because consciousness is creative, as indeed it is in the lyrical flow of prose within the author's own mind, then time need not destroy; rather it can be re-lived, passed on from one human being to another. The past is perpetuated, and so renewable; through consciousness itself history may become timeless.

So the artist is central, and style his business. Faulkner came to create a language that worked not through cause and effect, but through processes of imagistic distillation, through symbolist suspensions that work between motion and stillness, coalescing past and present, between the advancing movement and the static centre, perception and the thing perceived. Such moments form the heart of his style, as in this from *Light in August*:

> Though the mules plod on in a steady and unflagging hypnosis, the vehicle does not seem to progress. It seems to hang suspended in the middle distance forever and forever, so infinitesimal is its progress, like a shabby bead upon the mild red string of road. So much is this so that in the watching of it the eye loses it as sight and sense drowsily merge and blend, like the road itself, with all the peaceful and monotonous changes between darkness and day, like already measured thread being rewound on a spool.

Faulkner's sentences repeatedly work like this, producing not the "scrupulous meanness" of modern style that Joyce advocated and Hemingway realized, nor that "fear of abstractions" advanced by imagism, but a complex, prolix, lyrical modern rhetoric. That rhetoric is of a piece with Faulkner's conviction that the modern lapse is temporary, that in human lives there are transcendent powers of endurance, that the curse may be lifted, that history, past or present, retains the potential for becoming timeless myth.

In 1950 Faulkner won the Nobel Prize for Literature, and spoke of his belief in "courage and honor and hope and pride and compassion and pity and sacrifice," the human material of the timelessness in his work. That work originates amid the anxieties of the Twenties, in its decadent despair, its attempt to create the novel as a modern and a modernist genre, a form for encompassing our understanding of the disorientations of, but also the possible artistic recoveries in, twentieth century experience. Faulkner portrays a world in which history goes awry, and his central figures experience extreme disorientation or psychic damage, in which both time and person are grotesque. But, changing through striking switches of genre, from tragedy to comedy, from tales of sound fury to stories of amused narrative loquacity, his work moves towards formal and mythic recovery. Both the regionalism and the modernism of his enterprise made him a central modern influence. The extraordinary line of modern Southern gothic fiction would surely not have been realized without him; he creates the landscape and the historical and moral anxiety that feed the work of major successors like Robert Penn Warren, Eudora Welty, Carson McCullers, and Flannery O'Connor. But his activation of the possibilities of modern form as a new discourse for coping with temporal and psychic disturbance, for the existential dislocation of the modern mind, has made him an international influence, as powerful a force in, for example, modern French fiction as in the Southern tradition. Faulkner's was a major contribution to the key enterprise of the Twenties, the attempt to perceive the modern alike as a historical situation and a new aesthetic condition.

In its hunger for new styles, new mores, new forms, new modes of personal self-realization in time and history, the American Twenties supported one of the most notable generations of modern writers of fiction. Yet, in a repeated fable, their new formal intensity was based on an artistic withdrawal from the American

Twenties, a reaction against Puritanism and materialism, an avant-garde displacement. In fact, these writers shared their age's mixture of progress and nostalgia. They looked on American through the long lens offered by bohemia or Paris or decadent irony, but they also returned to catch the notes of acceleration that made the decade one of modernization and change. It was one of the ironies of the decade that many writers who had thus expatriated themselves, convinced that America would never understand its advanced artists, found themselves, by the decade's end, famous and commercially successful. It was a bigger irony still that the boundless commercialism and possibility that had fed the decade and displaced its writers itself exploded, in the Great Crash of 1929. It was, Fitzgerald saw, not just an economic but a psychic crisis, as a fragile, illusory time laid bare many of its underlying tensions and disorders. This theme had, however, been present in the new novel throughout the decade, as writers explored two histories, one that of what Fitzgerald called "the great gaudy spree" of the modern, the other that of underlying economic, psychic, and formal disorder which, if understood, might lead to national rediscovery.

[Selected from Malcolm Bradbury. *The Modern American Novel*. London: Oxford University Press, 1983.]

3. Robert Penn Warren

3.1 Presentation Topics

(1) Robert Penn Warren as a winner of Pulitzer Prize both for Novel and for Poetry.

(2) Robert Penn Warren as a literary critic and one of the initiators of New Criticism.

(3) The Fugitives.

3.2 Selected Reading

Ⅰ. Central issue of concern

Robert Penn Warren's contemplation over the relation between history and reality.

Ⅱ. Text

Blackberry Winter①

It was getting into June and past eight o'clock in the morning, but there was a fire—even if it wasn't a big fire, just a fire of chunks—on the hearth of the big stone fireplace in the living room. I was standing on the hearth, almost into the chimney, hunched over the fire, working my bare toes slowly on the warm stone. I relished the heat which made the skin of my bare legs warp and creep and tingle, even as I called to my mother, who was somewhere back in the dinning room or kitchen, and said: " But it's June, I don't have to put them on!"

"You put them on if you are going out," she called.

I tried to assess the degree of authority and conviction in the tone, but at that distance it was hard to decide. I tried to analyze the tone, and then I thought what a fool I had been to start out the back door and let her see that I was barefoot. If I had gone out the front door or the side door she would never have known, not till dinner time anyway, and by then the day would have been half gone and I would have been all over the farm to see what the storm had done and down to the creek to see the flood. But it had never crossed my mind that they would try to stop you from going barefoot in June, no matter if there had been a gully-washer② and a cold spell.

Nobody had ever tried to stop me in June as long as I could remember, and when you are nine years old, what you remember seems forever; for you remember everything and everything is important and stands big and full and fills up Time and is so solid that you can walk around and around it like a tree and look at it. You are aware that time passes, that there is a movement in time, but that is not what Time is. Time is not a movement, a flowing, a wind then, but is, rather, a kind of climate in which things are, and when a thing happens it begins to live and keeps on living and stands solid in Time like the tree that you can walk around. And if there is a movement, the movement is not Time itself, no more than a breeze is climate, for all the breeze does is to shake a little the leaves on the tree which is alive and solid. When you are nine, you know that there are things that you don't know, but

---

① A late-spring cold spell that occurs when blackberries are in bloom.

② A heavy rain shower that occurs suddenly, possibly creating a flash flood.

you know that when you know something you know it. You know how a thing has been and you know that you can go barefoot in June. You do not understand that voice from back in the kitchen which says that you cannot go barefoot outdoors and run to see what has happened and rub your feet over the wet shivery grass and make the perfect mark of your foot in the smooth, creamy, red mud and then muse upon it as though you had suddenly come upon that single mark on the glistening auroral beach of the world. You have never seen a beach, but you have read the book① and how the footprint was there.

The voice had said what it had said, and I looked savagely at the black stockings and the strong, scuffed brown shoes which I had brought from my closet as far as the hearth rug. I called once more, "But it's June," and waited.

"It's June," the voice replied from far away, "but it's blackberry winter."

I had lifted my head to reply to that, to make one more test of what was in that tone, when I happened to see the man.

The fireplace in the living room was at the end; for the stone chimney was built, as in so many of the farmhouses in Tennessee, at the end of a gable②, and there was a window on each side of the chimney. Out of the window on the north side of the fireplace I could see the man. When I saw the man I did not call out what I had intended, but, engrossed by the strangeness of the sight, watched him, still far off, come along the path by the edge of the woods.

What was strange was that there should be a man there at all. That path went along the yard fence, between the fence and the woods which came right down to the yard, and then on back past the chicken runs and on by the woods until it was lost to sight where the woods bulged out and cut off the back field. There the path disappeared into the woods. It led on back, I knew, through the woods and to the swamp, skirted the swamp where the big trees gave way to sycamores and water oaks and willows and tangled cane, and then led on to the river. Nobody ever went back there except people who wanted to gig frogs in the swamp or fish in the river or to hunt in the woods, and those people, if they didn't have a standing permission from my father, always stopped to ask permission to cross the farm. But the man

---

① *Robinson Crusoe*.

② Triangular portion of a wall between the edges of a sloping roof.

whom I now saw wasn't, I could tell even at that distance, a sportsman. And what would a sportsman have been doing down there after a storm? Besides, he was coming from the river, and nobody had gone down there that morning. I knew that for a fact, because if anybody had passed, certainly if a stranger had passed, the dogs would have made a racket and would have been out on him. But this man was coming up from the river and had come up through the woods. I suddenly had a vision of him moving up the grassy path in the woods, in the green twilight under the big trees, not making any sound on the path, while now and then, like drops off the leaves, a big drop of water would fall from a leaf or bough and strike a stiff oak leaf lower down with a small, hollow sound like a drop of water hitting tin. That sound, in the silence of the woods, would be very significant.

When you are a boy and stand in the stillness of woods, which can be so still that your heart almost stops beating and makes you want to stand there in the green twilight until you feel your very feet sinking into and clutching the earth like roots and your body breathing slow through its pores like the leaves—when you stand there and wait for the next drop to drop with its small, flat sound to a lower leaf, that sound seems to measure out something, to put an end to something, to begin something, and you cannot wait for it to happen and are afraid it will not happen, and then when it has happened, you are waiting again, almost afraid.

But the man who I saw coming through the woods in my minds' eye did not pause and wait, growing into the ground and breathing with the enormous, soundless breathing of the leaves. Instead, I saw him moving in the green twilight inside my head as he was moving at that very moment along the path by the edge of the woods, coming toward the house. He was moving steadily, but not fast, with his shoulders hunched a little and his head thrust forward, like a man who has come a long way and has a long way to go. I shut my eyes for a couple of seconds, thinking that when I opened them he would not be there at all. There was no place for him to have come from, and there was no reason for him to come where he was coming, toward our house. But I opened my eyes, and there he was, and he was coming steadily along the side of the woods. He was not yet even with the back chicken yard.

"Mama," I called.

"You put them on," the voice said.

"There's a man coming," I called, "out back."

She did not reply to that, and I guessed that she had gone to the kitchen window to look. She would be looking at the man and wondering who he was and what he wanted, the way you always do in the country, and if I went back there now she would not notice right off whether or not I was barefoot. So I went back to the kitchen.

She was standing by the window. "I don't recognize him," she said, not looking around at me.

"Where could he be coming from?" I asked.

"I don't know," she said.

"What would he be doing down at the river? At night? In the storm?"

She studied the figure out the window, then said, "Oh, I reckon maybe he cut across from the Dunbar place."

That was, I realized, a perfectly rational explanation. He had not been down at the river in the storm, at night. He had come over this morning. You could cut across from the Dunbar place if you didn't mind breaking through a lot of elder and sassafras and blackberry bushes which had about taken over the old cross path, which nobody ever used any more. That satisfied me for a moment, but only for a moment. "Mama," I asked, "What would he be doing over at the Dunbar place last night?"

Then she looked at me, and I knew I had made a mistake, for she was looking at my bare feet. "You haven't got your shoes on," she said.

But I was saved by the dogs. That instant there was a bark which I recognized as Sam, the collie①, and then a heavier, churning kind of bark which was Bully, and I saw a streak of white as Bully tore round the corner of the back porch and headed out for the man. Bully was a big, bone-white bull dog, the kind of dog that they used to call a farm bull dog but that you don't see any more, heavy chested and heavy headed, but with pretty long legs. He could take a fence as light as a hound. He had just cleared the white paling fence toward the woods when my mother ran out to the back porch and began calling: "Here you, Bully! Here you!"

Bully stopped in the path, waiting for the man, but he gave a few more of those

① A distinctive type of herding dog.

deep, gargling, savage barks that reminded you of something down a stone-lined well. The red clay mud, I saw, was splashed up over his white chest and looked exciting, like blood.

The man, however, had not stopped walking even when Bully took the fence and started at him. He had kept right on coming. All he had done was to switch a little paper parcel which he carried from the right hand to the left, and then reach into his pants pocket to get something. Then I saw the glitter and knew that he had a knife in his hand, probably the kind of mean knife just made for devilment and nothing else, with a blade as long as the blade of a frog-sticker, which will snap out ready when you press a button in the handle. That knife must have had a button in the handle, or else how could he have had the blade out glittering so quick and with just one hand?

Pulling his knife against the dogs was a funny thing to do, for Bully was a big, powerful brute and fast, and Sam was all right. If those dogs had meant business, they might have knocked him down and ripped him before he got a stroke in. He ought to have picked up a heavy stick, something to take a swipe at them with and something which they could see and respect when they came at him. But he apparently did not know much about dogs. He just held the knife blade close against the right leg, low down, and kept on moving down the path.

Then my mother had called, and Bully had stopped. So the man let the blade of the knife snap back into the handle, and dropped it into his pocket, and kept on coming. Many women would have been afraid with the strange man who they knew had that knife in his pocket. That is, if they were alone in the house with nobody but a nine-year-old boy. And my mother was alone, for my father had gone off, and Dellie, the cook, was down at her cabin because she wasn't feeling well. But my mother wasn't afraid. She wasn't a big woman, but she was clear and brisk about everything she did and looked everybody and everything right in the eye from her own blue eyes in her tanned face. She had been the first woman in the country to ride a horse astride (that was back when she was a girl and long before I was born), and I have seen her snatch up a pump gun and go out and knock a chicken hawk out of the air like a busted skeet when he came over her chicken yard. She was a steady and self-reliant woman, and when I think of her now after all the years she has been dead, I think of her brown hands, not big, but somewhat square for a woman's hands, with square-cut nails. They looked, as a matter of fact, more like a young boy's hands than a grown woman's. But back then it never crossed my mind that she would ever be dead.

She stood on the back porch and watched the man enter the back gate, where the dogs (Bully had leaped back into the yard) were dancing and muttering and giving sidelong glances back to my mother to see if she meant what she had said. The man walked right by the dogs, almost brushing them, and didn't pay them any attention. I could see now that he wore old khaki pants, and a dark wool coat with stripes in it, and a gray felt hat. He had on a gray shirt with blue stripes in it, and on tie. But I could see a tie, blue and reddish, sticking in his side coat-pocket. Everything was wrong about what he wore. He ought to have been wearing blue jeans or overalls, and a straw hat or an old black felt hat, and the coat, granting that he might have been wearing a wool coat and not a jumper, ought not to have had those stripes. Those clothes, despite the fact that they were old enough and dirty enough for any tramp, didn't belong there in our back yard, coming down the path, in Middle Tennessee, miles away from any big town, and even a mile off the pike.

When he got almost to the steps, without having said anything, my mother, very matter-of-factly, said, "Good morning."

"Good morning," he said, and stopped and looked her over. He did not take off his hat, and under the brim you could see the perfectly unmemorable face, which wasn't old and wasn't young, or thick or thin. It was grayish and covered with about three days of stubble. The eyes were a kind of nondescript, muddy hazel, or something like that, rather bloodshot. His teeth, when he opened his mouth, showed yellow and uneven. A couple of them had been knocked out. You knew that they had been knocked out, because there was a scar, not very old, there on the lower lip just beneath the gap.

"Are you hunting work?" my mother asked him.

"Yes," he said—not "yes, mam"—and still did not take off his hat.

"I don't know about my husband, for he isn't here," she said, and didn't mind a bit telling the tramp, or whoever he was, with the mean knife in his pocket, that no man was around, "but I can give you a few things to do. The storm has drowned a lot of chicks. Three coops of them. You can gather them up and bury them. Bury them deep so the dogs won't get at them. In the woods. And fix the coops the wind blew over. And down yonder beyond that pen by the edge of the woods are some drowned poults. They got out and I couldn't get them in. Even after it started to rain hard. Paults haven't got any sense.

"What are them things—poults?" he demanded, and spat on the brick wall. He rubbed his foot over the spot, and I saw that he wore a black, pointed-toe low shoe, all cracked and broken. It was a crazy kind of shoe to be wearing in the country.

"Oh, they're young turkeys," my mother was saying. "And they haven't got any sense. I oughtn't to try to raise them around here with so many chickens, anyway. They don't thrive near chickens, even in separate pens. And I won't give up my chickens." Then she stopped herself and resumed briskly on the note of business. "When you finish that, you can fix my flower beds. A lot of trash and mud and gravel has washed down. Maybe you can save some of my flowers if you are careful."

"Flowers," the man said, in a low, impersonal voice which seemed to have a wealth of meaning, but a meaning which I could not fathom. As I think back on it, it probably was not pure contempt. Rather, it was a kind of impersonal and distant marveling that he should be on the verge of grubbing in a flower bed. He said the word, and then looked off across the yard.

"Yes, flowers," my mother replied with some asperity, as though she would have nothing said or implied against flowers. "And they were very fine this year." Then she stopped and looked at the man. "Are you hungry?" she demanded.

"Yeah," he said.

"I'll fix you something," she said, "before you get started." She turned to me. "Show him where he can wash up," she commanded, and went into the house.

I took the man to the end of the porch where a pump was and where a couple of wash pans sat on a low shelf for people to use before they went into the house. I stood there while he laid down his little parcel wrapped in newspaper and took off his hat and looked around for a nail to hang it on. He poured the water and plunged his hands into it. They were big hands, and strong looking, but they did not have the creases and the earth-color of the hands of men who work outdoors. But they were dirty, with black dirt ground into the skin and under the nails. After he had washed his hands, he poured another basin of water and washed his face. He dried his face, with the towel still dangling in his grasp, stepped over to the mirror on the house wall. He rubbed one hand over the stubble on his face. Then he carefully inspected his face, turning first one side and then the other, and stepped back and settled his striped coat down on his shoulder. He had the movements of a man who had just dressed up to go to church or a party—the way he settled his coat and smoothed it and scanned himself in the mirror.

Then he caught my glance on him. He glared at me for an instant out of the bloodshot eyes, then demanded in a low, harsh voice, "What you looking at?"

"Nothing," I managed to say, and stepped back a step from him.

He flung the towel down, crumple, on the shelf, and went towards the kitchen door and entered without knocking.

My mother said something to him which I could no catch. I started to go in again, then thought about my barefeet, and decided to go back of the chicken yard, where the man would have to come to pick up the dead chicks. I hung around behind the chicken house until he came out.

He moved across the chicken yard with a fastidious, not quite finicking, motion, looking down at the curdled mud flecked with bits of chicken-droppings. The mud curled up over the soles of his black shoes. I stood back from him some six feet and watched him pick up the first of the drowned chicks. He held it up by one foot and inspected it.

There is nothing deader looking than a drowned chick. The feet curl in that feeble, empty way which back when I was a boy, even if I was a country boy who did not mind hog-killing or frog-gigging, made me feel hollow in the stomach. Instead of looking plump and fluffy, the body is stringy and limp with the fluff plastered to it, and the neck is long and loose like a little sting of rag. And the eyes have that bluish membrane over them which makes you think of a very old man who is sick about to die.

The man stood there and inspected the chick. Then he looked all around as though he didn't know what to do with it.

"There's a great big old basket in the shed," I said, and pointed to the shed attached to the chicken house.

He inspected me as though he had just discovered my presence, and moved toward the shed.

"There's a great spade there, too," I added.

He got the basket and began to pick up the other chicks, picking each one up slowly by a foot and then flinging it into the basket with a nasty, snapping motion. Now and then he would look at me out of the bloodshot eyes. Every time he seemed on the verge of saying something, but he did not. Perhaps he was building up to say something to me, but I did not wait that long. His way of looking at me made me so uncomfortable that I left the chicken yard.

Besides, I had just remembered that the creek was in flood, over the bridge, and that people were down there watching it. So I cut across the farm toward the creek. When I got to the big tobacco field I saw that it had not suffered much. The land lay right and not many tobacco plants had washed out of the ground. But I knew that a lot of tobacco round the country had been washed right out. My father had said so at breakfast.

My father was down at the bridge. When I came out of the gap in the osage hedge into the road, I saw him sitting on his mare over the heads of the other men who were standing around, admiring the flood. The creek was big here, even in low water; for only a couple of miles away it ran into the river, and when a real flood came, the red water got over the pike where it dipped down to the bridge, which was an iron bridge, and high over the flood and even the side railings of the bridge. Only the upper iron work would show, with the water boiling and frothing red and white around it. That creek rose so fast and so heavy because a few miles back it came down out of the hills, where the gorges filled up with water in no time when a rain came. The creek ran in a deep bed with limestone bluffs along both sides until it got within three quarters of a mile of the bridge, and when it came out from between those bluffs in flood it was boiling and hissing and steaming like water from a fire hose.

Whenever there was a flood, people from half the country would come down to see the sight. After a gully-washer there would not be any work to do anyway. If it didn't ruin your crop, you couldn't plow and you felt like taking a holiday to celebrate. If it did ruin your crop, there wasn't anything to do except to try to take your mind off the mortgage, if you were rich enough to have a mortgage, and if you couldn't afford a mortgage you needed something to take your mind off how hungry you would be by Christmas. So people would come down to the bridge and look at the flood. It made something different from the run of days.

There would not be much talking after the first few minutes of trying to guess how high the water was this time. The men and kids just stood around, or sat their horses or mules, as the case might be, or stood up in the wagon beds, they looked at the strangeness of the flood for an hour or two, and then somebody would say that he had better be getting on home to dinner and would start walking down the gray, puddle limestone pike, or would touch heel to his mount and start off. Everybody always knew what it would be like when he got down to the bridge, but people always came. It was like church or a funeral. They always came, that is, if it was summer and the flood unexpected. Nobody ever came down in winter to see high water.

When I came out of the gap in the bowdock hedge, I saw the crowd, perhaps fifteen or twenty men and a lot of kids, and saw my father sitting on his mare, Nellie Gray. He was a tall, limber man and carried himself well. I was always proud to see him sit on a horse, he was so quiet and straight, and when I stepped through the gap of the hedge that morning, the first thing that happened was, I remember, the warm feeling I always had when I saw him up on a horse, just sitting. I did not go toward him, but skirted the crowd on the far side, to get a look at the creek. For one thing, I was not sure what he would say about the fact that I was barefoot. But the thing I knew, I heard his voice calling, "Seth!"

I went toward him, moving apologetically past the men, who bent their large, red or thin, sallow faces above me. I knew some of the men and knew their names, but because those I knew were there in a crowd, mixed with the strange faces, they seemed foreign to me, and not friendly. I did not look up at my father until I was almost within touching distance of his heel. Then I looked up and tried to read his face, to see if he was angry about my being barefoot. Before I would decide anything from that impassive, high-boned face, he had leaned over and reached a hand to me. "Grab on," he commanded.

I grabbed on and gave a little jump, and he said, "Up-see-daisy!" and whisked me, light as a feather, up to the pommel of his McClellan saddle.

"You can see better up here," he said, slid back on the cantle a little to make me more comfortable, and then, looking over my head at the swollen, tumbling water, seemed to forget all about me. But his right hand was laid on my side, just above my thigh, to steady me.

I was sitting there as quiet as I could, feeling the faint stir of my father's chest against my shoulders as it rose and fell with his breath, when I saw the cow. At first, looking up the creek, I thought it was just another big piece of driftwood steaming down the creek in the ruck of water, but all at once a pretty good-size boy who had climbed part way up a telephone pole by the pike so that he could see better yelled out, "Gollydamn①, look at that-air cow!"

Everybody looked. It was a cow all right, but it might just as well have been driftwood; for it was dead as a chunk, rolling and rolling down the creek, appearing and disappearing, feet up or head up, it didn't matter which.

The cow started up the talk again. Somebody wondered whether it would hit one of the clear places under the top girder of the bridge and get through or whether it would get tangled in the drift and trash that had piled against the upright girders and braces. Somebody remembered how about ten years before so much driftwood had piled up on the bridge that it was knocked off its foundations. Then the cow hit. It hit the edge of the drift against one of the girders, and hung there. For a few seconds it seemed as though it might tear loose, but then we saw that it was really caught. It bobbed and heaved on its side there in a slow, grinding, uneasy fashion. It had a yoke around its neck, the kind made out of a forked limb to keep a jumper behind fence.

"She shore② jumped one fence," one of the men said.

And another: "Well, she done jumped her last one, fer a fack."

Then they began to wonder about whose cow it might be. They decided it must belong to Milt Alley. They said that he had a cow that was a jumper, and kept her in a fenced-in piece of ground up the creek. I had never seen Milt Alley, but I knew who he was. He was a squatter and lived up the hills a way, on a shirt-tail patch of set-on-edge land, in a cabin. He was pore white trash. He had lots of children. I had seen the children at school, when they came. They were thin-faced, with straight, sticky-looking, dough-colored hair, and they smelled something like old

---

① God-damn.

② Sure.

sour buttermilk, not because they drank so much buttermilk but because that is sort of smell which children out of those cabins tend to have. The big Alley boy drew dirty pictures and showed them to the little boys at school.

That was Milt Alley's cow. It looked like the king of cow he would have, a scrawny, old, sway-backed cow, with a yoke around her neck. I wondered if Milt Alley had anther cow.

"Poppa," I said, "do you think Milt Alley has got another cow?"

"You say 'Mr. Alley'," my father said quietly.

"Do you think he has?"

"No telling," my father said.

Then a big gangly boy, about fifteen, who was sitting on a scraggly little old mule with a piece of croker sack thrown across the saw-tooth spine, and who had been staring at the cow, suddenly said to nobody in particular, "Reckin anybody ever et drownt cow?"①

He was the kind of boy who might just as well as not have been the son of Milt Alley, with his faded and patched overalls ragged at the bottom of the pants and the mud-stiff brogans hanging off his skinny, bare ankles at the level of the mule's belly. He had said what he did, and then looked embarrassed and sullen when all the eyes swung at him. He hadn't meant to say it, I am pretty sure now. He would have been too proud to say it, just as Milt Alley would have been too proud. He had just been thinking out loud, and the words had popped out.

There was an old man standing there on the pike, an old man with a white beard. "Son," he said to the embarrassed and sullen boy on the mule, "you live long enough and you'll find a man will eat anything when the time comes."

"Time gonna come fer some folks this year," another man said.

"Son," the old man said, "in my time I et things a man don't like to think on. I was a sojer② and I rode with Gin'l③ Forrest, and the things we et when the time come. I tell you. I et meat what got up and run when you taken out yore knife to cut a slice to put on the fire. You had to knock it down with a carbeen butt, it was so

① Reckon anybody ever ate drowned cow?
② Soldier.
③ General.

active. That-air meat would jump like a bullfrog, it was so full of skippers."

But nobody was listening to the old man. The boy on the mule turned his sullen sharp face from him, dug a heel into the side of the mule and went off up the pike with a motion which made you think that any scrofulous hide.

"CY Dundee's boy," a man said, and nodded toward the figure going up the pike on the mule.

"Reckin Cy Dundee's young-uns seen times they'd settle fer drownt cow," another man said. The old man with the beard peered at them both from this weak, slow eyes, first at one and then at the other. "Live long enough," he said, "and a man will settle fer what he kin git."

Then there was silence again, with the people looking at the red, foam-flecked water.

My father lifted the bridle rein in his left hand, and the mare turned and walked around the group and up the pike. We rode on up to our big gate, where my father dismounted to open it and let me myself ride Nellie Gray through. When he got to the lane that led off from the drive about two hundred yards from our house, my father said, "Grab on." I grabbed on, and he let me down to the ground. "I'm going to ride down and look at my corn," he said. "You go on." He took the lane, and I stood there on the drive and watched him ride off. He was wearing cowhide boots and an old hunting coat, and I thought that that made him look very military, like a picture. That and the way he rode.

I did not go the house. Instead, I went by the vegetable garden and crossed behind the stables, and headed down for Dellie's cabin. I wanted to go down and play with Jebb, who was Dellie's little boy about two years older than I was. Besides, I was cold. I shivered as I walked, and I had goose-fiesh. The mud which crawled up between my toes with every step I took was like ice. Dellie would have a fire, but she wouldn't make me put on shoes and stockings.

Dellie's cabin was of logs, with one side, because it was on a slope, set on limestone chunks, with a little porch attached to it, and had a little whitewashed fence around it and a gate with plow-points on a wire to clink when somebody came in, and had two big white oaks in the yard and some flowers and a nice privy in the back with some honeysuckle growing over it. Dellie and Old Jebb, who was Jebb's father and who lived with Dellie and had lived with her for twenty-five years even if they never had got married, were careful to keep everything nice around their cabin. They had the name all over the community for being clean and clever negroes. Dellie and Jebb were what they used to call "white-folks' niggers." There was a big difference between their cabin and the other two cabins farther down where the other tenants lived. My father kept the other cabins weatherproof, but he couldn't undertake to go down and pick up after the litter they strewed. They didn't take the trouble to have a vegetable patch like Dellie and Jebb or to make preserves from wild plum, and jelly from crab apple the way Dellie did. They were shiftless, and my father was always threatening to get shed of them. But he never did. When they finally left, they just up and left on their own, for no reason, to go and be shiftless somewhere else. Then some more came. But meanwhile they lived down there, Matt Rawson and his family, and Sid Turner and his, and I played with their children all over the farm when they weren't working. But when I wasn't around they were mean sometimes to Little Jebb. That was because the other tenants down there were jealous of Dellie and Jebb.

I was so cold that I ran the last fifty yards to Dellie's gate. As soon as I had entered the yard, I saw that the storm had been hard on Dellie's flowers. The yard was, as I have said, on a slight slope, and the water running across had gutted the flower beds and washed out all the good black woods-earth which Dellie had brought in. what little grass there was in the yard was plastered sparsely down on the ground, the way the drainage water had left it. It reminded me of the way the fluff was plastered down on the skin of the drowned chicks that the strange man had been picking up, up in my mother's chicken yard.

I took a few steps up the path to the cabin, and then I saw that the drainage water had washed a lot of trash and filth out from under Dellie's house. Up toward the porch, the ground was not clean any more. Old pieces of rag, two or three rusted cans, pieces of rotten rope, some hunks of old dog dung, broken glass, old paper, and all sorts of things like that had washed out from under Dellie's house to foul her clean yard. It looked just as bad as the yards of the other cabins, or worse. It was worse, as a matter of fact, because it was a surprise. I had never thought of all that filth being under Dellie's house. It was not anything against Dellie that the stuff had been under the cabin. Trash will get under any house. But I did not think of that when I saw the foulness which had washed out on the ground which Dellie sometimes used to sweep with a twig broom to make nice and clean.

I picked my way past the filth, being careful not to get my bare feet on it, and mounted to Dellie's door. When I knocked, I heard her voice telling me to come in.

It was dark inside the cabin, after the daylight, but I could make out Dellie piled up in bed under a quilt, and Little Jebb crouched by the hearth, where a low fire simmered. "Howdy," I said to Dellie, "how you feeling?"

Her big eyes, the whites surprising and glaring in the black face, fixed on me as I stood there, but she did not reply. It did not look like Dellie, or act like Dellie, who would grumble and bustle around our kitchen, talking to herself, scolding me or Little Jebb, clanking pans, making all sorts of unnecessary noises and mutterings like an old-fashioned black steam thrasher engine when it has got up an extra head of steam and keeps popping the governor and rumbling and shaking on its wheels. But now Dellie just lay there on the bed, under the patch-work quilt, and turned the black face, which I scarcely recognized, and the glaring white eyes on me.

"How you feeling?" I repeated.

"I'se sick," the voice said croakingly out of the strange black face which was not attached to Dellie's big, squat body, but stuck out from under a pile of tangled bedclothes. Then the voice added: "Mighty sick."

"I'm sorry," I managed to say.

The eyes remained fixed on me for a moment, then they left me and the head rolled back on the pillow. "Sorry," the voice said, in a flat way which wasn't question or statement of anything. It was just the empty word put into the air with no meaning or expression, to float off like a feather or a puff of smoke, while the big eyes, with the whites like the peeled white of hard-boiled eggs, stared at the ceiling.

"Dellie," I said after a minute, "there's a tramp up at the house. He's got a knife."

She was not listening. She closed her eyes.

I tiptoed over to the hearth where Jebb was and crouched beside him. We began to talk in low voices. I was asking him to get out his train and play train. Old Jebb had put spool wheels on three cigar boxes and put wire links between the boxes to make a train for Jebb. The box that was the locomotive had the top closed and a length of broom stick for a smoke stack. Jebb didn't want to get the train out, but I told him I would go home if he didn't. So he got out the train, and the colored rocks, and fossils of crinoids stems, and other junk he used for the load, and we began to push it around, talking the way we thought trainmen talked, making a chuck-chucking sound under the breath for the noise of the locomotive and now and then uttering low, cautious toots for the whistle. We got so interested in playing train that the toots got louder. Then, before he thought, Jebb gave a good, loud *toot-toot*, blowing for a crossing.

"Come here," The voice said from the bed.

Jebb got up slow from his hands and knees, giving me a sudden, naked, inimical look.

"Come here!" The voice said.

Jebb went to the bed. Dellie propped herself weakly up on one arm, muttering, "Come closer."

Jebb stood closer.

"Last thing I do, I'm gonna do it," Dellie said. "Done tole you to be quiet."

Then she slapped him. It was an awful slap, more awful for the kind of weakness which it came from and brought to focus. I had seen her slap Jebb before, but the slapping had always been the kind of easy slap you would expect from a good-natured, grumbling Negro woman like Dellie. But this was different. It was awful. It was so awful that Jebb didn't make a sound. The tears just popped out and ran down his face, and his breath came sharp, like grasps.

Dellie fell back. "Cain't even be sick," she said to the ceiling, "git sick and they won't even let you lay. They tromp all over you. Cain't even be sick." Then she closed her eyes.

I went out of the room. I almost ran getting to the door, and I did run across the porch and down the steps and across the yard, not caring whether or not I stepped on the filth which had washed out from under the cabin. I ran almost all the way home. Then I thought about my mother catching me with the bare feet. So I went down to the stables.

I heard a noise in the crib, and opened the door. There was Big Jebb, sitting on an old nail keg, shelling corn into a bushel basket. I went in, pulling the door shut behind me, and crouched on the floor near him. I crouched there for a couple of minutes before either of us spoke, and watched him shelling the corn.

He had very big hands, knotted and grayish at the joints, with callused palms which seemed to be streaked with the rust coming up between the fingers to show from the back. His hands were so strong and tough that he could take a big ear of corn and rip the grains right off the cob with the palm of his hand, all in one motion, like a machine. "Work long as me," he would say, "and the good Lawd'll give you a hand lak cass ion won't nuthin' hurt." And his hands did look like cast iron, old cast iron streaked with rust.

He was an old man, up in his seventies, thirty years or more older than Dellie, but he was strong as a bull. He was a squat sort of man, heavy in the shoulders, with remarkably long arms, the kind of build they say the river natives have on the Congo from paddling so much in their boats. He had a round bullet-head, set on powerful shoulders. His skin was very black, ant the thin hair on his head was now grizzled like tufts of old cotton batting. He had small eyes and a flat nose, not big, and the kindest and wisest old face in the world, the blunt, sad, wise face of an old animal peering tolerantly on the goings-on of the merely human creatures before him. He was a good man, and I loved him next to my mother and father. I crouched there on the floor of the crib and watched him shell corn with the rusty cast-iron hands, while he looked down at me out of the little eyes in the blunt face.

"Dellie says she's mighty sick," I said.

"Yeah," he said.

"What's she sick from?"

"Woman-mizry," he said.

"What's woman-mizry?"

"Hit comes on 'em," he said. "Hit just comes on 'em when the time comes."

"What is it?"

"Hit is the change," he said. "Hit is the change of life and time."

"What changes?"

"Tell me."

"Time come and you find out everything."

I knew that there was no use in asking him any more. When I asked him things and he said that, I always knew that he would not tell me. So I continued to crouch there and watch him. Now that I had sat there a little while, I was cold again.

"What you shiver fer?" he asked me.

"I am cold. I'm cold because it's blackberry winter," I said.

"Maybe 'tis and maybe 'tain't" he said.

"My mother said it is."

"Ain't sayen Miss Sallie doan know and ain't sayen she do. But folks doan know everything."

"Why isn't it blackberry winter?"

"Too late for blackberry winter. Blackberries done bloomed."

"She said it was."

"Blackberry winter just a leetle cold spell. Hit come and then hit go away, and hit is growed summer of a sudden lak a gunshot. Ain't no tellen hit will go way this time."

"It's June," I said.

"June," he replied with great contempt. "That what folks say. What June mean? Maybe hit is come cold to stay."

"Why?"

"Cause this-here old yearth is tahrd. Hit is tahrd and ain't gonna perduce. Lawd let hit come rain one time forty days and forty nights, 'cause He wus tahrd of sinful folks. Maybe this-here old yearth say to the Lawd, Lawd, I done plum tahrd. Lawd, lemme rest. And Lawd say, Yearth, you done yore best, you give'em cawn and you give'em taters, and all they think on is they gut, and Yearth, you kin take a rest."

"What will happen?"

"Folks will eat up everything. The yearth won't perduce no more. Folks cut down all the trees and burn 'em cause they cold, and the yearth won't grow no more. I been tellen 'em. I been tellen folks. Sayen, maybe this year, hit is the time. But they doan listen to me, how the yearth is tahrd. Maybe this year they find out."

"Will everything die?"

"Everything and everybody, hit will be so."

"This year?"

"Ain't no tellen. Maybe this year."

"My mother said it is blackberry winter," I said confidently, and got up.

"Ain't sayen nuthin'agin Miss Sallie," he said.

I went to the door of the crib. I was really cold. Running, I had got up a sweat and now I was worse.

I hung on the door, looking at Jebb, who was shelling corn again.

"There is a tramp came to the house," I said. I had almost forgotten the tramp.

"Yeah."

"He came by the back way. What was he doing down there in the storm?"

"They comes and they goes," he said, "and ain't no tellen."

"He had a mean knife."

"The good ones and the bad ones, they comes and they goes. Storm or sun, light or dark. They is folks and they comes and goes lak folks."

I hung on the door, shivering.

He studied me a moment, then said, "You git on to the house. You ketch yore death. Then what yore mammy say?"

I hesitated.

"You git," he said.

When I came to the back yard, I saw that my father was standing by the back porch and the tramp was walking toward him. They began talking before I reached them, but I got there just as my father was saying, "I'm sorry, but I haven't got any work. I got all the hands on the place I need now. I won't need extra until wheat thrashing."

The stranger made no reply, just looked at my father.

My father took out his leather coin purse, and got out a half-dollar. He held it toward the man. "That is for half a day," he said.

The man looked at the coin, and then at my father, making no motion to take the money. But that was the right amount. A dollar a day was what you paid them back in 1910. And the man hadn't even worked half a day.

Then the man reached out and took the coin. He dropped it into the right side pocket of his coat. Then he said, very slowly and without feeling: "I didn't want to work on your—farm."

He used the word which they would have frailed me to death for using.

I looked at my father's face and it was streaked white under the sunburn. Then he said, "Get off this place. Get off this place or I won't be responsible."

The man dropped his right hand into his pants pocket. It was the pocket where he kept his knife. I was just about to yell to my father about the knife when the hand came back out with nothing in it. The man gave a kind of twisted grin, showing where the teeth had been knocked out above the new scar. I thought that instant how maybe he had tried before to pull a knife on somebody else and had got his teeth knocked out.

So now he just gave that twisted, sickish grin out of the unmemorable, grayish face, and then spat on the brick path. The glob landed just about six inches from the toe of my father's right boot. My father looked down at it, and so did I. I thought that if that glob had hit my father's boot something would have happened. I looked down and saw the bright glob, and on one side of it my father's strong cowhide boots, with the brass eyelets and the leather thongs, heavy boots splashed with good red mud and set solid on the bricks, and on the other side the pointed-toe, broken, black shoes, on which the mud looked so sad and out of place. Then I saw one of the black shoes move a little, just a twitch first, then a real step backward.

The man moved in a quarter circle to the end of the porch, with my father's steady gaze upon him all the while. At the end of the porch, the man reached up to the shelf where the wash pans were to get his little newspaper-wrapped parcel. Then he disappeared around the corner of the house and my father mounted the porch and went into the kitchen without a word.

I followed around the house to see what the man would do. I wasn't afraid of him now, no matter if he did have the knife. When I got around in front, I saw him going out the yard gate and starting up the drive toward the pike. So I ran to catch up with him. He was sixty yards or so up the drive before I caught up.

I did not walk right up even with him at first, but trailed him, the way a kid will, about seven or eight feet behind, now and then running two or three steps in order to hold my place against his loner stride. When I first came up behind him, he turned to give me a look, just a meaningless look, and then fixed his eyes up the drive and kept on walking.

When we had got around the bend in the drive which cut the house from sight, and were going along by the edge of the wood, I decided to come up even with him. I ran a few steps, and was by his side, or almost, but some feet off to the right. I walked along in this position for a while, and he never noticed me. I walked along until we got within sight of the big gate that let on the pike.

Then I said: "Where did you come from?"

He looked at me then with a look which seemed almost surprised that I was there. Then he said, "It ain't none of yore business."

We went on another fifty feet.

Then I said, "Where are you going?"

He stopped, studied me dispassionately for a moment, then suddenly took a step toward me and leaned his face down at me. The lips jerked back, but not in any grin, to show where the teeth were knocked out and to make the scar on the lower lip come white with the tension.

He said: "Stop following me. You don't stop following me and I cut yore throat, you little son-of-a-bitch."

Then he went on to the gate, and up the pike.

That was thirty-five years ago. Since that time my father and mother have died. I was still a boy, but a big boy, when my father got cut on the blade of a mowing machine and died of lockjaw. My mother sold the place and went to town to live with her sister. But she never took hold after father's death, and she died with three years, right in middle life. My aunt always said, "Sallie just died of a broken heart, she was so devoted." Dellie is dead, too, but she died, I heard, quite a long time after we sold the farm.

As for Little Jebb, he grew up to be a mean and ficey Negro. he killed another Negro in a fight and got sent to the penitentiary, where he is yet, the last I heard tell. He probably grew up to be mean and fiecy from just being picked on so much by the children of the other tenants, who were jealous of Jebb and Dellie for being thrifty and clever and being white-folks' niggers.

Old Jebb lived forever. I saw him ten years ago and he was about a hundred then, and not looking much different. He was living in town then, on relief—that was back in the Depression—when I went to see him. He said to me: "Too strong to die. When I was a young feller just comen on and seen how things wuz, I prayed the Lawd. I said, Oh, Lawd, gimme strength and make me strong fer to do and indure. The Lawd hearkened to my prayer. He give me strength. I was in-duren proud fer being strong and me much man. The Lawd give me my prayer and my strength. But now He done gone off and fergot me and left me alone with my strength. A man doan know what to pray fer, and him mortal."

Jebb is probably living yet, as far as I know.

That is what has happened since the morning when the tramp leaned his face down at me and showed his teeth and said: "Stop following me. You don't stop following me and I cut yore throat, you little son-of-a-bitch." That was what he said, for me not to follow him. But I did follow him, all the years.

[Selected from Cleanth Brooks, Robert Penn Warren, (ed.). *Understanding Fiction*. New York: Prentice, 1979.]

Ⅲ. Questions for discussion

(1) This is a story remembered by Seth. Is it a piece about a nostalgia for his childhood or the country life in the South?

(2) How does the author link the past and the present together? Does the past has anything to do with the present? What is the author's view about time?

(3) The story presents many conflicting ideas about a single thing. For example, Mother, Seth and Big Jebb have different comments on whether it is called Blackberry Winter, and Mother and the tramp in seeing the flowers. What effect do these contrasts achieve?

(4) How do you interpret the image of Big Jebb?

(5) Why do you think Seth was and is still following the tramp? What does this character mean?

(6) How does the story present the boy's growth?

3.3 Assigned Reading

Images of Initiation in Robert Penn Warren's "Blackberry Winter"

Albert E. Wilhelm

(In the following excerpt, Wilhelm explores the rite of passage motif in "Blackberry Winter" as expressed through the imagery of the Tennessee farm and the biblical themes of the Garden of Eden, the Fall, and the Flood.)

In analyzing the initiation motif in Robert Penn Warren's "Blackberry Winter," Richard Allan Davison asserts that in no other story has Warren "better integrated his imagistic patterns." Davison comments further:

> Through this dramatization of a child's rite of passage Warren explores the complications of a nine-year-old farm boy's initiation into the complexities of the adult world largely by centering the most telling imagery on the young protagonist's feet .... The responses of Seth's barefeet serve as indications of his changing awareness of the mystery, uncertainty and evil in the world from which his parents have so long sheltered him. ①

Such imagery is indeed pervasive, but another cluster of images is equally significant in conveying Seth's maturation. These images derive from the topography of the Tennessee farm (which is Seth's home) and include, in particular, references to enclosures, fences, and gates.

Among the most basic images is the white picket fence which surrounds the farmhouse yard and defines the boundary between pastoral security and the ominous unknown. The fence encloses orderly beds of flowers, the warm hearth, and other manifestations of maternal protection, while beyond the fence are a bewildering tangle of cane and, eventually, a dark, cold swamp. Symbolically, this fence has protected Seth both by exclusion and confinement—by keeping out alien forces and by restricting him to the limited world of the farm. As the story begins, however, both functions of the fence are challenged. At the very moment of Seth's rebellion against maternal authority, he sees an interloper coming from the direction of the swamp and toward the back gate. Despite the protests of the farm watch dog (which jumps the fence to challenge the intrusion), the tramp enters the yard bringing with him city clothes, a switchblade knife, scars of past violence, and ultimately a sullen threat to the protective power of Seth's father.

As the protective wall is breached, Seth's curiosity about the outside world is simultaneously stimulated. The watchdog, described initially as "bone-white," serves as an indicator of this change. When he jumps the fence, his white chest is splashed with "red clay mud," which to Seth is exciting, like blood. As the tramp intrudes further into the warm kitchen (normally the realm of maternal care), Seth ironically moves in the opposite direction—to the realm of cold and death within the chicken pen. Soon he is attracted by a more distant and more turbulent sight—the flood at the bridge. Like the dog's stained chest, the muddy, boiling creek also

① Richard Allan Davison. Physical Imagery in Robert Penn Warren's "Blackberry Winter". *Georgia Review* 1968(22). p. 482.

displays the alluring mixture of red and white, and to reach this scene Seth must pass through three successive enclosures (the chicken pen, the picket fence around the yard, and finally the fence-like bodock hedge). In doing so he literally passes beyond the pale of his childlike innocence.

At the bridge Seth confronts the harsh reality of poverty (sharecroppers whose tobacco has been destroyed) and death (the carcass of a drowned cow). Certain images suggest that the dead cow is, to some extent, a symbolic counterpart of Seth himself. Its former home was a "fenced-in piece of ground up the creek," and "it had a yoke around its neck, the kind made out of a forked limb to keep a jumper behind fence"①. Just as these restraints have not insured the cow's safety, Seth himself cannot be protected from the pain of maturation. Furthermore, other references to farm animals emphasize the same point. Seth's mother is adept at shooting hawks if they fly over her chicken yard," but she cannot protect her poultry from the storm. The young turkeys drown because they escape from their pen, and the baby chickens are apparently killed even inside their coops. As in Seth's case the fences do not completely protect either by confinement or exclusion. Only the dog seems able to jump the fence and return with impunity.

After the ominous scene at the bridge, Seth's pattern of advancing beyond the fences is replaced by one of retreat. As in many other initiation stories curiosity about the unknown is transformed to fear or revulsion (compare, for example, Hemingway's "Indian Camp"). First, Seth's father lifts him to the saddle and encloses Seth within his arm to steady him. Later, they ride together to the big gate where his father dismounts to open it and lets Seth ride Nellie Gray through. Within this large enclosure Seth retreats further to Dellie's cabin. Significantly, this cabin has a little whitewashed fence around it and a gate with plow-points on a wire to clink when somebody enters. The plow-points serve then as a warning device but also as a mechanism to keep the gate tightly shut when not in use. In the cabin Seth seeks the warmth of the hearth and an alternative mother figure (since Dellie ordinarily displays the benevolence but not the authority of his real mother). Further evidence of his reversion to a childlike role is his attempt to participate in the train game with Little Jebb. But the forces of change have invaded, and a

① *The Circus in the Attic and Other Stories*. New York: Harcourt, Brace and Company, 1947. p. 67.

return to childhood is not possible. Suffering herself from the change of life, Dellie now displays violence which drives Seth from the cabin and the yard.

Seth's flight leads to one more place of refuge—the crib where Old Jebb is shelling corn. The word "crib" is perhaps intended as a pun since Seth goes there seeking warmth and comforting answers. As he enters he pulls the door shut behind him and notes that Old Jebb has the kindest and wisest old face in the world. But instead of reassurance Jebb offers only predictions of apocalyptic doom, and Seth hangs on the door, shivering.

The story's final images again emphasize Seth's movement beyond the protective fences. After the argument between his father and the tramp, Seth intently watches the tramp going out the yard gate. With some initial hesitation Seth trails him until they get within sight of the big gate that let on the pike. In spite of the tramp's injunction, "Stop following me," Seth can pursue no other course. Like his postlapsarian Biblical namesake he now stands outside the gates of paradise. Pain and evil have been made real, and he cannot return to the protection of the garden.

[Selected from Albert E. Wilhelm. Images of Initiation in Robert Penn Warren's "Blackberry Winter". *Studies in Short Fiction*, 1980(3).]

Chapter 4 Postmodernist Fiction and Avant-Pop Art

1. Introduction

Entering the post-World War Ⅱ era, America accelerated its pace of change in economics, technology, politics, and culture. Similar to the situation after World War Ⅰ, America emerged from World War Ⅱ with a dramatic economic recovery and relatively few casualties. The war, however, brought a tremendous trauma on Americans. The atomic bombs devastated Hiroshima and Nagasaki as well as Americans' belief of human goodness. The subsequent Cold War exerted a further influence on the mentality of Americans. McCarthyism and the Korean War featured growing hostility between the USSR and its satellite states, and the powers of the Western world, and also heightened fears of common people in America. The seemingly endless and hopeless Vietnam War gradually broadened the gap between the government and the people. Furthermore, domestic political upheavals such as the assassination of John F. Kennedy and Martin Luther King, Jr., the blunders of the Johnson administration, the Watergate Scandal, etc., helped institutionalize chaos. Though Americans benefited greatly from new advances in science and technology, the threat of nuclear power, the eco-environmental deterioration, overpopulation, instantaneous changes of knowledge, and unveracity of mass mechanography had all the time weighed on the consciousness of the people. Every American was subjected to a prevailing skepticism, an intensified terror, and a sense of life being absurd. The whole nation was tossed into "an inverted millenarianism in which premonitions of the future, catastrophic or redemptive, have been replaced by senses of the end of this or that (the end of ideology, art, or social class; the 'crisis' of Leninism, social democracy, or the welfare state, etc.); taken together, all of these perhaps constitute what is increasingly called postmodernism"①.

In the wake of World War Ⅱ and out of the postindustrial societies, postmodernist literature, especially postmodernist fiction, dealing with the new experience, acquired an imposing stature. Not necessarily implying a new era as the prefix indicates, postmodernist fiction may be seen as a continuation of modernism's alienated mood, daring experimentation and disorienting techniques (relying heavily, for example, on fragmentation, paradox, questionable narrators, etc.). At the same time, postmodernist fiction subverted modernist traditions. While the practitioners of modernism attempted to develop new ways to represent reality, the postmodernists often questioned the very existence of a reliable reality. With a tendency to present, lament and mourn a fragmented tragedy of human subjectivity and history, many modernist works sought for artistic unity, coherence and meaning which had been lost in modern life. Postmodernist fiction, in contrast, is engaged in deconstructing the "authority, originary status, or supposed unconstructedness of the space outside the fiction." It denied the feasibility of any literary work to represent or bring order to the elusive and uncertain reality. By emphasizing discontinuity and ambiguity, it guided readers to come to terms with absurdity of the world.

Challenging mimetic representation of reality and subjectivity, postmodern writers employed metafiction to undermine the author's univocal control and thus postmodernist fiction turned out to be overtly textual and self-reflexive. In metafiction, the author featured himself as a character and simultaneously foregrounded himself and the craft, the intricacies, and composition were put on display. For example, in the first chapter of *Slaughterhouse Five*, Kurt Vonnegut shared with readers the process of writing the novel. Throughout the following chapters about Billy Pilgrim's experiences during World War Ⅱ, the author

---

① Durham Frederic Jameson. *Postmodernism or, the Cultural Logic of Late Capitalism*. NC: Duke University Press, 1991.

constantly called attention to his own presence and reminded readers of the artificiality. It is characterized by discontinuity of tone, point of view, register and logical sequence, apparently random unexpected intrusions and disruptions in the text, a self-consciousness about language and literary technique. Hence the line between reality and fantasy, fact and fiction was blurred, and chaotic absurdity permeated on all levels of social life.

In addition to self-consciousness and reflexivity, postmodern fiction includes features such as, interrogation of category distinctions, mixing of high and popular cultural forms, pastiche, parody, pluralism and radical experimentation. The proposal by John Barth(1930—) in his article "The Literature of Exhaustion" that the conventional modes of literary representation had been "used up," allied to the philosophical climate of structuralism and deconstruction, encouraged postmodernist fiction to turn to others' works, different genre and popular forms (including detective fiction, science fiction, and fairy tale). Kathy Acker's novel *Don Quixote: Which Was a Dream* is with apparent references to the classic. Equally postmodernistic is the blurring of boundaries between the novel and journalism in Robert Pirsig's *Zen and the Art of Motorcycle Maintenance: An Inquiry into Values* (1974). Postmodernist writers' dissolving the distinctions between high and low culture even resulted in an insertion of typography, photos, color and cartoons, graphic symbols, tape recordings, etc. in the text. Consequently, the intertextuality of postmodernist fiction reveals the chaotic and pluralistic society composed of disparate fragmentary experiences and images, devoid of depth, coherence, or originality.

The general concept of "play" is among the most recognizable aspects of postmodernism. The playfulness of postmodernist works not only is rooted in the features mentioned above but also manifests itself in irony, black humor and wordplay. It was common for postmodernists to treat serious subjects in a playful and bitterly humorous way, which was to be explained in the latter part. Besides this, postmodernists favored to coin some new words to express particular ideas or to achieve ironical effects. They also shifted their linguistic styles from written language to the colloquial, from standard English to the vulgar. Sometimes they disarranged the unity and coherence between discourse. A paragraph of merely one short sentence covers one page or even one page is left entirely blank. Sentences with blanks are made for readers themselves to complete with their own imagination. Disintegrating texts into a form of deliberate unreadability and irrationality, postmodern writers aimed at the meaningless confusion of contemporary existence.

In conclusion, postmodernist fiction is in favor of a sharpened sense of artifice, a delight in games and verbal pyrotechnics, a suspicion of absolute truth and a resulting inclination to stress the fictionality of fiction. All these traits were ushered in America with the publications of *Lolita* (1955) by Vladimir Nabokov (1899—1977), *The Recognition* (1955) by William Gaddis (1922—1988), and *Naked Lunch* (1959) by William Burroughs (1914—1997). *Lolita* chronicles the life of its unreliable narrator and protagonist, Humbert Humbert, centering on his disastrous obession with the young Lolita. Portrayed as both perpetrator and victim of his own erotic desire, Humbert indeed seduced readers to believe in his love story through the power of his artistry. In this dark and comic memoir, Nabokov's self-consciousness of fictionality, brilliant techniques and evocative language produce a poetic textual world within which the boundary between reality and fantasy is erased.

In the 1960s, postmodernist fiction reached its first peak with a group of writers labelled as Black Humor. They tended to treat serious or taboo subject matters in bitter, grotesque, and morbid humor and farce to express the absurdity, insensitivity, paradox, and cruelty of the modern world. The characters in their works are anti-heroes who are self-centered but unimportant minors and ineffectual failures succumbing to the blackness of modern life. In accordance with the indetermincay of meaning and the decenteredness of existence, black humorists constructed the reality in the form of anti-novels from a disordered narrative and played with various linguistic devices. A typical representative is Vladimir Nabokov mentioned above whose fiction make light of the disturbing topic of sex and integrate the memories of a dissolving past with the precariousness of the present. Thomas Pynchon(1937—) in particular provides prime examples of playfulness within a serious context.

Another recognizable spokesman of Black Humor is Joseph Heller (1923—

1999) with his masterpiece *Catch-22* (1961). Set in a United States Air Force base in Italy during World War Ⅱ, the novel accounts a frantic bombardier's desperate efforts to survive. But Yossarian soon discovered that it was impossible to be discharged from military service because of the paradoxical Catch-22 and its circular reasoning. Only the insane could excuse themselves from the perious missions. Yet a man was considered really insane if he willingly continued to fly combat missions. Insane people who asked to be grounded prove themselves sane through a concern for personal safety. Sane or insane, all the characters can never be relieved. A protest novel underscored with dark humor, *Catch-22* satirizes the horrors of war and the power of bureaucratic institutions, to destroy the human spirit. Joseph Heller also attaches a great importance to an absurd linguistic surface to reflect the depth of irrationality. It is noted for its non-chronological style where the timeline is quite disorienting, events are repeatedly described from different characters' points of view, and many of words, phrases, and sentences are circular and repetitive.

Always mentioned in the same breath with Joseph Heller, Kurt Vonnegut (1922—2007) blended satire, black humor, and science fiction in his works. In *Cat's Cradle* (1963), John encountered the family of the deceased father of the nuclear bomb as he gathered background information for his writing on the atomic bomb. The three children divided Ice-nine, another deadly invention by Dr. Felix Hoenikker, for their own advantage, only to bring about the end of the world. Holding a prophetic, satirical and pessimistic vision of mankind's unintentional self-destruction, Vonnegut explored issues of science and religion. In 1969, this author finally finished his most famous semi-autobiographical novel *Slaughterhouse Five*. In the journeys through time of a disoriented and fatalistic American soldier named Billy Pilgrim, Vonnegut described various moments of his life such as the World War Ⅱ firebombing of Dresden and the kidnapping by aliens. More than an anti-war novel, it exactly reflects the mood of American society at the height of the anti-Vietnam War movement through fragmentary scenes and nonlinear frame.

Since the declaration that contemporary writers were confronting the exhaustedness of literature by John Barth in 1967, American postmodernist fiction moved into its second stage of metafiction, literally, fiction about fiction. John

Bath topped metafiction writers. Beginning from *The Sot-Weed Factor*(1960), he made a thorough breakthrough in style. Being a parody of *Tom Jones*(1749) by Henry Fielding(1707—1754), the novel of inverted structure reduces the American history of the colonial period to an absurd farce. And similarly, his next novel *Giles Goat-Boy*(1966) is a pastiche of Nabokov and Jorge Luis Borges(1899—1986). He drew from the ontological rupture between art and life and turned to exploit the impossibility of their reconciliation. His short story collections *Lost in the Funhouse*(1968) and *Chimera*(1972) best exemplify his theory and practice in creative writing which is for disjunction, simultaneity, irrationality, self-reflexiveness, medium-as-message, political dystopianism, and a moral pluralism. And all these traits can be felt in his increasingly experimental novels of later period.

In the mid-1980s, America saw various changes which were different from those of the turbulent 1960s and 1970s. Popular culture flourished apace and the fast development of information industry and mass media unprecedentedly changed the manner how the people observed and faced the reality. Avant-Pop fiction emerged and, along with Postmodern Realism, actually reversed the numbing effects of years of exposure to television, movies, glossy magazines, and commercial bestsellers. Beyond those experimental writers touched upon above and their subversives, Avant-Pop writers payed special attention to pop culture and applied various materials from the mass media to their writings to deconstruct the reality. They are characteristic of heterroglossia, plagiarism and recontextualization. *White Noise*(1985) and *Mao II* (1991) by Don DeLillo (1936—) are regarded as two of the most important avant-pop novels of the last decade of the 20th century. Both explore the excess of signs and meaning in our lives of media and other information technologies and the consequential effacement of reality. Including some postmodernist authors like Kurt Vonnegut and Thomas Pynchon, this category also covers Don DeLillo, Mark Leyner, David Foster Wallace, Lance Olsen, Bret Easton Ellis, Michael Joyce, etc.

All in all, American fiction from Postmodernism to Avant Pop have inherited the critical tradition of American literature and have brought it to a new level. Though it often gave up the world of social and political engagement for the solipsistic pleasures of word play and overestimated the importance of artistic devices, it provided the world with a treasure of established novelists and unique literary heritages.

Key words:

Black Humor

The humor based on the grotesque, morbid, or macabre. It refers primarily to a kind of bitter and often outrageous satire. Black Humor rose in America in the 1950s and 1960s to reveal human follies, the absurdity, insensitivity and cruelty of the modern world and social instiutions including government bureaucracies, the military, and large corporations by depicting them as dehumanizing organizations.

Metafiction

A type of fiction that self-consciously addresses the devices of fiction. It is the literary term describing fictional writing that self-consciously and systematically draws attention to its status as an artifact in posing questions about the relationship between fiction and reality, usually, irony and self-reflection.

Postmodern realism, or Neorealism

A product of both the rediscovery of traditional methods of writing and the importance of the reader and the reader's response and the influence of postmodernism since the 1970s. It inherited the advantage of conventional realism in storytelling and characterization while absorbing the experimentalist methods of postmodernism.

Avant-pop Art

An artistic genre based on the combination of avant-garde and pop art, inheriting the spirit of rebellion, radicalism, subversion and innovation of avant-garde while taking various forms of pop culture as its nutrition of object of expression. It usually takes pop culture as the object of its criticism and deconstruction to reveal the influence of media technology and pop culture on people's everyday life and to free people's mind from the bondage of "the society of the spectacle."

2. Joseph Heller

2.1 Presentation Topics

(1) Black humor.

(2) Joseph Heller as a Black humor novelist.

(3) Joseph Heller's works on the war and on the lives of the middle class.

2.2 Selected Reading

Ⅰ. Central issue of concern

Catch-22 as a masterpiece of Black humor literature.

Ⅱ. Text

Catch-22

Chapter 40

There was, of course, a catch.

"Catch-22?" inquired Yossarian.

"Of course," Colonel Korn answered pleasantly, after he had chased the mighty guard of massive M. P. s out with an insouciant flick of his hand and a slightly contemptuous nod—most relaxed, as always, when he could be most cynical. His rimless square eyeglasses glinted with sly amusement as he gazed at Yossarian. "After all, we can't simply send you home for refusing to fly more missions and keep the rest of the men here, can we? That would hardly be fair to them."

"You're goddam right!" Colonel Cathcart blurted out, lumbering back and forth gracelessly like a winded bull, puffing and pouting angrily. "I'd like to tie him up hand and foot and throw him aboard a plane on every mission. That's what I'd like to do."

Colonel Korn motioned Colonel Cathcart to be silent and smiled at Yossarian. "You know, you really have been making things terribly difficult for Colonel Cathcart," he observed with flip good humor, as though the fact did not displease him at all. "The men are unhappy and morale is beginning to deteriorate. And it's all your fault."

"It's your fault," Yossarian argued, "for raising the number of missions."

"No, it's your fault for refusing to fly them," Colonel Korn retorted. "The men were perfectly content to fly as many missions as we asked as long as they thought they had no alternative. Now you've given them hope, and they're unhappy. So the blame is all yours."

"Doesn't he know there's a war going on?" Colonel Cathcart, still stamping back and forth, demanded morosely without looking at Yossarian.

"I'm quite sure he does," Colonel Korn answered. "That's probably why he refuses to fly them."

"Doesn't it make any difference to him?"

"Will the knowledge that there's a war going on weaken your decision to refuse to participate in it?" Colonel Korn inquired with sarcastic seriousness, mocking Colonel Cathcart.

"No, sir," Yossarian replied, almost returning Colonel Korn's smile.

"I was afraid of that," Colonel Korn remarked with an elaborate sigh, locking his fingers together comfortably on top of his smooth, bald, broad, shiny brown head. "You know, in all fairness, we really haven't treated you too badly, have we? We've fed you and paid you on time. We gave you a medal and even made you a captain."

"I never should have made him a captain," Colonel Cathcart exclaimed bitterly. "I should have given him a court-martial after he loused up that Ferrara mission and went around twice."

"I told you not to promote him," said Colonel Korn, "but you wouldn't listen to me."

"No you didn't. You told me to promote him, didn't you?"

"I told you not to promote him. But you just wouldn't listen."

"I should have listened."

"You never listen to me," Colonel Korn persisted with relish. "That's the reason we're in this spot."

"All right, gee whiz. Stop rubbing it in, will you?"

Colonel Cathcart burrowed his fists down deep inside his pockets and turned away in a slouch. "Instead of picking on me, why don't you figure out what we're going to do about him?"

"We're going to send him home, I'm afraid." Colonel Korn was chuckling triumphantly when he turned away from Colonel Cathcart to face Yossarian. "Yossarian, the war is over for you. We're going to send you home. You really don't deserve it, you know, which is one of the reasons I don't mind doing it. Since there's nothing else we can risk doing to you at this time, we've decided to return you to the States. We've worked out this little deal to—"

"What kind of deal?" Yossarian demanded with defiant mistrust.

Colonel Korn tossed his head back and laughed. "Oh, a thoroughly despicable deal, make no mistake about that. It's absolutely revolting. But you'll accept it quickly enough."

"Don't be too sure."

"I haven't the slightest doubt you will, even though it stinks to high heaven. Oh, by the way. You haven't told any of the men you've refused to fly more missions, have you?"

"No, sir," Yossarian answered promptly.

Colonel Korn nodded approvingly. "That's good. I like the way you lie. You'll go far in this world if you ever acquire some decent ambition."

"Doesn't he know there's a war going on?" Colonel Cathcart yelled out suddenly, and blew with vigorous disbelief into the open end of his cigarette holder.

"I'm quite sure he does," Colonel Korn replied acidly, "since you brought that identical point to his attention just a moment ago." Colonel Korn frowned wearily for Yossarian's benefit, his eyes twinkling swarthily with sly and daring scorn. Gripping the edge of Colonel Cathcart's desk with both hands, he lifted his flaccid haunches far back on the corner to sit with both short legs dangling freely. His shoes kicked lightly against the yellow oak wood, his sludge-brown socks, garterless, collapsed in sagging circles below ankles that were surprisingly small and white. "You know, Yossarian," he mused affably in a manner of casual reflection that seemed both derisive and sincere, "I really do admire you a bit. You're an intelligent person of great moral character who has taken a very courageous stand. I'm an intelligent person with no moral character at all, so I'm in an ideal position to appreciate it."

"These are very critical times," Colonel Cathcart asserted petulantly from a far corner of the office, paying no attention to Colonel Korn.

"Very critical times indeed," Colonel Korn agreed with a placid nod. "We've just had a change of command above, and we can't afford a situation that might put us in a bad light with either General Scheisskopf or General Peckem. Isn't that what you mean, Colonel?"

"Hasn't he got any patriotism?"

"Won't you fight for your country?" Colonel Korn demanded, emulating Colonel Cathcart's harsh, self-righteous tone. "Won't you give up your life for Colonel Cathcart and me?"

Yossarian tensed with alert astonishment when he heard Colonel Korn's concluding words. "What's that?" he exclaimed. "What have you and Colonel Cathcart got to do with my country? You're not the same."

"How can you separate us?" Colonel Korn inquired with ironical tranquility.

"That's right," Colonel Cathcart cried emphatically. "You're either for us or against us. There's no two ways about it."

"I'm afraid he's got you," added Colonel Korn. "You're either for us or against your country. It's as simple as that."

"Oh, no, Colonel. I don't buy that."

Colonel Korn was unruffled. "Neither do I, frankly, but everyone else will. So there you are."

"You're a disgrace to your uniform!" Colonel Cathcart declared with blustering wrath, whirling to confront Yossarian for the first time. "I'd like to know how you ever got to be a captain, anyway."

"You promoted him," Colonel Korn reminded sweetly, stifling a snicker. "Don't you remember?"

"Well, I never should have done it."

"I told you not to do it," Colonel Korn said. "But you just wouldn't listen to me."

"Gee whiz, will you stop rubbing it in?" Colonel Cathcart cried. He furrowed his brow and glowered at Colonel Korn through eyes narrow with suspicion, his fists clenched on his hips. "Say, whose side are you on, anyway?"

"Your side, Colonel. What other side could I be on?"

"Then stop picking on me, will you? Get off my back, will you?"

"I'm on your side, Colonel. I'm just loaded with patriotism."

"Well, just make sure you don't forget that." Colonel Cathcart turned away grudgingly after another moment, incompletely reassured, and began striding the floor, his hands kneading his long cigarette holder. He jerked a thumb toward Yossarian. "Let's settle with him. I know what I'd like to do with him. I'd like to take him outside and shoot him. That's what I'd like to do with him. That's what General Dreedle would do with him."

"But General Dreedle isn't with us any more," said Colonel Korn, "so we can't take him outside and shoot him." Now that his moment of tension with Colonel Cathcart had passed, Colonel Korn relaxed again and resumed kicking softly against Colonel Cathcart's desk. He returned to Yossarian. "So we're going to send you home instead. It took a bit of thinking, but we finally worked out this horrible little plan for sending you home without causing too much dissatisfaction among the friends you'll leave behind. Doesn't that make you happy?"

"What kind of plan? I'm not sure I'm going to like it."

"I know you're not going to like it." Colonel Korn laughed, locking his hands contentedly on top of his head again. "You're going to loathe it. It really is odious and certainly will offend your conscience. But you'll agree to it quickly enough. You'll agree to it because it will send you home safe and sound in two weeks, and because you have no choice. It's that or a court-martial. Take it or leave it."

Yossarian snorted. "Stop bluffing, Colonel. You can't court-martial me for desertion in the face of the enemy. It would make you look bad and you probably couldn't get a conviction."

"But we can court-martial you now for desertion from duty, since you went to Rome without a pass. And we could make it stick. If you think about it a minute, you'll see that you'd leave us no alternative. We can't simply let you keep walking around in open insubordination without punishing you. All the other men would stop flying missions, too. No, you have my word for it. We will court-martial you if you turn our deal down, even though it would raise a lot of questions and be a terrible black eye for Colonel Cathcart."

Colonel Cathcart winced at the words "black eye" and, without any apparent premeditation, hurled his slender onyx-and-ivory cigarette holder down viciously on the wooden surface on his desk. "Jesus Christ!" he shouted unexpectedly. "I hate this goddam cigarette holder!" The cigarette holder bounced off the desk to the wall, ricocheted across the window sill to the floor and came to a stop almost where he was standing. Colonel Cathcart stared down at it with an irascible scowl. "I wonder if it's really doing me any good."

"It's a feather in your cap with General Peckem, but a black eye for you with General Scheisskopf," Colonel Korn informed him with a mischievous look of innocence.

"Well, which one am I supposed to please?"

"Both."

"How can I please them both? They hate each other. How am I ever going to get a feather in my cap from General Scheisskopf without getting a black eye from General Peckem?"

"March."

"Yeah, march. That's the only way to please him. March. March." Colonel Cathcart grimaced sullenly. "Some generals! They're a disgrace to their uniforms. If people like those two can make general, I don't see how I can miss."

"You're going to go far." Colonel Korn assured him with a flat lack of conviction, and turned back chuckling to Yossarian, his disdainful merriment increasing at the sight of Yossarian's unyielding expression of antagonism and distrust. "And there you have the crux of the situation. Colonel Cathcart wants to be a general and I want to be a colonel, and that's why we have to send you home."

"Why does he want to be a general?"

"Why? For the same reason that I want to be a colonel. What else have we got to do? Everyone teaches us to aspire to higher things. A general is higher than a colonel, and a colonel is higher than a lieutenant colonel. So we're both aspiring. And you know, Yossarian, it's a lucky thing for you that we are. Your timing on this is absolutely perfect, but I suppose you took that factor into account in your calculations."

"I haven't been doing any calculating," Yossarian retorted.

"Yes, I really do enjoy the way you lie," Colonel Korn answered. "Won't it make you proud to have your commanding officer promoted to general—to know you served in an outfit that averaged more combat missions per person than any other? Don't you want to earn more unit citations and more oak leaf clusters for your Air Medal? Where's your 'sprit de corps? Don't you want to contribute further to this great record by flying more combat missions? It's your last chance to answer yes."

"No."

"In that case, you have us over a barrel—" said Colonel Korn without rancor.

"He ought to be ashamed of himself!"

"—And we have to send you home. Just do a few little things for us, and—"

"What sort of things?" Yossarian interrupted with belligerent misgiving.

"Oh, tiny, insignificant things. Really, this is a very generous deal we're making with you. We will issue orders returning you to the States—really, we will—and all you have to do in return is..."

"What? What must I do?"

Colonel Korn laughed curtly. "Like us."

Yossarian blinked. "Like you?"

"Like us."

"Like you?"

"That's right," said Colonel Korn, nodding, gratified immeasurably by Yossarian's guileless surprise and bewilderment. "Like us. Join us. Be our pal. Say nice things about us here and back in the States. Become one of the boys. Now, that isn't asking too much, is it?"

"You just want me to like you? Is that all?"

"That's all."

"That's all?"

"Just find it in your heart to like us."

Yossarian wanted to laugh confidently when he saw with amazement that Colonel Korn was telling the truth. "That isn't going to be too easy," he sneered.

"Oh, it will be a lot easier than you think," Colonel Korn taunted in return, undismayed by Yossarian's barb. "You'll be surprised at how easy you'll find it to like us once you begin." Colonel Korn hitched up the waist of his loose, voluminous trousers. The deep black grooves isolating his square chin from his jowls were bent again in a kind of jeering and reprehensible mirth. "You see,

Yossarian, we're going to put you on easy street. We're going to promote you to major and even give you another medal. Captain Flume is already working on glowing press releases describing your valor over Ferrara, your deep and abiding loyalty to your outfit and your consummate dedication to duty. Those phrases are all actual quotations, by the way. We're going to glorify you and send you home a hero, recalled by the Pentagon for morale and public-relations purposes. You'll live like a millionaire. Everyone will lionize you. You'll have parades in your honor and make speeches to raise money for war bonds. A whole new world of luxury awaits you once you become our pal. Isn't it lovely?"

Yossarian found himself listening intently to the fascinating elucidation of details. "I'm not sure I want to make speeches."

"Then we'll forget the speeches. The important thing is what you say to people here." Colonel Korn leaned forward earnestly, no longer smiling. "We don't want any of the men in the group to know that we're sending you home as a result of your refusal to fly more missions. And we don't want General Peckem or General Scheisskopf to get wind of any friction between us, either. That's why we're going to become such good pals."

"What will I say to the men who asked me why I refused to fly more missions?"

"Tell them you had been informed in confidence that you were being returned to the States and that you were unwilling to risk your life for another mission or two. Just a minor disagreement between pals, that's all."

"Will they believe it?"

"Of course they'll believe it, once they see what great friends we've become and when they see the press releases and read the flattering things you have to say about me and Colonel Cathcart. Don't worry about the men. They'll be easy enough to discipline and control when you've gone. It's only while you're still here that they may prove troublesome. You know, one good apple can spoil the rest," Colonel Korn concluded with conscious irony. "You know—this would really be wonderful—you might even serve as an inspiration to them to fly more missions."

"Suppose I denounce you when I get back to the States?"

"After you've accepted our medal and promotion and all the fanfare? No one would believe you, the Army wouldn't let you, and why in the world should you want to? You're going to be one of the boys, remember? You'll enjoy a rich, rewarding, luxurious, privileged existence. You'd have to be a fool to throw it all away just for a moral principle, and you're not a fool. Is it a deal?"

"I don't know."

"It's that or a court-martial."

"That's a pretty scummy trick I'd be playing on the men in the squadron, isn't it?"

"Odious," Colonel Korn agreed amiably, and waited, watching Yossarian patiently with a glimmer of private delight.

"But what the hell!" Yossarian exclaimed. "If they don't want to fly more missions, let them stand up and do something about it the way I did. Right?"

"Of course," said Colonel Korn.

"There's no reason I have to risk my life for them, is there?"

"Of course not."

Yossarian arrived at his decision with a swift grin. "It's a deal!" he announced jubilantly.

"Great," said Colonel Korn with somewhat less cordiality than Yossarian had expected, and he slid himself off Colonel Cathcart's desk to stand on the floor. He tugged the folds of cloth of his pants and undershorts free from his crotch and gave Yossarian a limp hand to shake. "Welcome aboard."

"Thanks, Colonel. I—"

"Call me Blackie, John. We're pals now."

"Sure, Blackie. My friends call me Yo-Yo. Blackie, I—"

"His friends call him Yo-Yo," Colonel Korn sang out to Colonel Cathcart. "Why don't you congratulate Yo-Yo on what a sensible move he's making?"

"That's a real sensible move you're making, Yo-Yo," Colonel Cathcart said, pumping Yossarian's hand with clumsy zeal.

"Thank you, Colonel, I—"

"Call him Chuck," said Colonel Korn.

"Sure, call me Chuck," said Colonel Cathcart with a laugh that was hearty and awkward. "We're all pals now."

"Sure, Chuck."

"Exit smiling," said Colonel Korn, his hands on both their shoulders as the three of them moved to the door.

"Come on over for dinner with us some night, Yo-Yo," Colonel Cathcart invited hospitably. "How about tonight? In the group dining room."

"I'd love to, sir."

"Chuck," Colonel Korn corrected reprovingly.

"I'm sorry, Blackie. Chuck. I can't get used to it."

"That's all right, pal."

"Sure, pal."

"Thanks, pal."

"Don't mention it, pal."

"So long, pal."

Yossarian waved goodbye fondly to his new pals and sauntered out onto the balcony corridor, almost bursting into song the instant he was alone. He was home free; he had pulled it off; his act of rebellion had succeeded; he was safe, and he had nothing to be ashamed of to anyone. He started toward the staircase with a jaunty and exhilarated air. A private in green fatigues saluted him. Yossarian returned the salute happily, staring at the private with curiosity. He looked strangely familiar. When Yossarian returned the salute, the private in green fatigues turned suddenly into Nately's whore and lunged at him murderously with a bone-handled kitchen knife that caught him in the side below his upraised arm. Yossarian sank to the floor with a shriek, shutting his eyes in overwhelming terror as he saw the girl lift the knife to strike at him again. He was already unconscious when Colonel Korn and Colonel Cathcart dashed out of the office and saved his life by frightening her away.

[Selected from Joseph Heller. *Catch-22*. New York: Simon & Schuster Press, 1996.]

Ⅲ. Questions for discussion

(1) How does Heller illustrate the absurdity of war as well as the absurdity of the human condition itself through the analysis of the characters?

(2) Heller's view of war is not that it is crazy because world leaders are corrupt. Discuss the leader characters in this novel, like Colonel Korn and Colonel Cathcart. What are their leadership qualities, methods, and attitudes toward the men?

(3) Instead of making broad statements about ideologies for or against war, Heller focuses on the self-absorption of characters and their twisted relationships. Why does Heller elaborate in this way?

(4) In this novel, Joseph Heller employs devices like "circular conversations," comic, unexpected responses, the "wrenched cliché" to depict his characters. How does he use this absurd linguistic surface to reflect the illogicality and the unpredictability of a crazy world?

(5) As the story progresses, it appears that no one is "normal," how does Heller use black humor to shed light on an otherwise dismal situation?

(6) The idea of *Catch-22* is explained in different ways throughout the novel. Do any of the explanations represent the real *Catch-22* ? How do you understand the "*Catch-22* "?

(7) Take "*Catch-22* " for example and tell how language is manipulated and influences the soldiers. What are the functions and essence of language as revealed in this novel?

(8) Comparing some traditional war stories, how does *Catch-22* differ from them?

2.3 Assigned Reading

Method in Madness, Part Ⅰ

Stephen W. Potts

It is difficult to approach the study of *Catch-22* without first coming to terms with its structure. Anyone who has read beyond the novel's first chapter quickly becomes aware of its lack of a traditional chronological plot. Indeed, one of the most frequent complaints made by early reviewers was that the novel was formless and chaotic, and many blamed Heller for not exercising more artistic control over his materials. For the *New York Times Book Review* the novel "gasps for want of craft and sensibility"; the *New Yorker* agreed that the book was not even a novel and argued, "it doesn't even seem to have been written; instead it gives the impression of having been shouted onto paper." Even sympathetic reviewers gave in on this point, although defending the novel's formlessness on the grounds that it is consistent with the chaotic cosmos and lunatic logic of the story.

When academic critics began to give Heller's book a closer look, the issue of structure arose as an early concern. A close analysis of the narrative revealed that it does in fact have organization of a sort, albeit an intricate one, and that beneath the apparent chaos of the story line exists a coherent sequence of events. Relatively few, however—indeed, a mere handful—have attempted to unravel Heller's complicated chronology, and all so far have fallen victim to some degree to the rhetorical traps Heller sets in the narrative to foil such attempts.

The first such serious endeavor to unravel *Catch-22*'s meticulously snarled skein was Jan Solomon's 1967 article "The Structure of Joseph Heller's *Catch-22*." Solomon maintains that two opposing time lines dominate the novel. One is the cyclical pattern of most of the novel, rooted in Yossarian's psychological perception of events. Yossarian's world is one of increasing moral decay, with suggestions of existentialist absurdism, and the dizzy nature of the narrative reflects this fact. On the other hand, Milo Minderbinder's history progresses in "the solid fashion of nineteenth century fiction"; he begins as an ambitious mess hall officer and ends up dominating the world.

According to Solomon, Milo's linear time line cuts across Yossarian's cyclical time line in a manner patently impossible. For example, he maintains that Milo and Yossarian are introduced only after Yossarian's hospital visit of chapter 1, and thus after Avignon, Snowden, and the Great Big Siege of Bologna. This is of course causally impossible, since Yossarian and Milo appear together in the tree at Snowden's funeral, and a number of Milo's earlier dealings, such as the cornering of the Egyptian cotton market and his subsequent contracts with the Germans, take place when he already knows Yossarian.

Solomon cites these and other examples as evidence that Heller intends Milo and Yossarian to operate on absurdly contradictory time lines, and he argues that it is Heller's intent thus to make a thematic point: Yossarian is trapped within the illogical circles of his world, while Milo, operating successfully according to its mad rules, progresses inexorably to ultimate triumph.

Unfortunately, Solomon reaches his conclusion on a faulty assessment of the chronology, as noted by Doug Gaukroger a few years later in his article "Time Structure in *Catch-22*." Gaukroger dispenses entirely with Solomon's incorrect reading of the narrative and does a reasonably good job of establishing the true sequence of the novel's major events, based on a painstaking analysis of the text. In a long plot summary, he correctly sets in order the main bombing campaigns of the plot—respectively, Ferrara, Bologna, and Avignon—and weaves the careers of Yossarian, Milo, and the other major characters through them. In this way he does discover a couple of errors on Heller's part, which will be noted in their proper place later in this discussion.

Although Gaukroger's time line has proved accurate enough to serve as the basis for most subsequent discussions of chronology, he does make a couple of errors himself. For instance, he has Milo buying the Egyptian cotton crop and arranging his deals with the Germans during the Bologna campaign, instead of before it; he also has the novel beginning when Yossarian has thirty-eight missions instead of forty-four, an assumption picked up by Clinton S. Burhans, Jr. , in his 1973 article.

Burhans' contribution to the discussion of structure is a revised chronology with dates. He begins with Yossarian's entrance into the army sometime in 1941, followed by his transfer to the air corps that same year; his first Thanksgiving in the hospital while a private at Lowery Field, Colorado, thus takes place in November 1941, and his Thanksgiving in bed with Mrs. Scheisskopf, therefore, one year later, in 1942. By this scheme Yossarian reaches Pianosa before September 1943, when Burhans has him at twenty-three missions at the time of Colonel Cathcart's appearance.

The chronology becomes more detailed after April 1944 and the foundation of Milo's syndicate. According to Burhans, Milo arranges the Orvieto deal in April; Ferrara and Bologna both take place in May; Avignon and the death of Snowden transpire in June, and the first chapter opens in July. From there on the major events of the last third of the book unfold, ending with Yossarian's desertion in December 1944.

Utilizing his chronology, Burhans points out what he sees as errors in Heller's planning. He is troubled by the long, six-month gap between September 1943, when he has Cathcart appear, and April 1944, when most of the story begins; he finds it incredible that Yossarian would only fly nine missions in that time and that Cathcart would only raise those required by ten. Also, he notes that according to the narrative Milo bombed the squadron only seven months after Yossarian left cadet training, whereas his chronology shows a gap of couple of years between these events—according to Burhans, a clear error of Heller's part.

Later commentator Robert Merrill, however, correctly notes that Burhans himself errs in at least two places. First of all, the mission of Orvieto, where Milo contracts with both the Allied and Axis forces and where Mudd, the dead man in Yossarian's tent, dies, takes place after Milo's disastrous cornering of the Egyptian cotton market, not before it, as Burhans' chronology shows; Orvieto, like the bombing of the Squadron, is prompted, after all, by Milo's expensive error in judgment. Furthermore, Merrill correctly notes, during Yossarian's visit to the hospital with which the novel opens, he has forty-four missions, not thirty-eight, as Gaukroger and Burhans both allege.

Burhans' problems with the six-month gap can also be explained by errors on his, not Heller's part—errors that Merrill fails to note. This gap exists because Burhans unaccountably places the beginning of Yossarian's World War Ⅱ career early in 1941; thus Burhans has him malingering in the hospital in Lowery Field over Thanksgiving of that year and complaining to Wintergreen and others that the war is not proceeding fast enough to end before his training does. But the United States did not even enter World War Ⅱ until the bombing of Pearl Harbor on 7 December 1941. It is not at all likely that Yossarian would be training for combat months before America even declared war. Far more logical, and historical, would be to begin Yossarian's training in 1942; doing so also matches Heller's real-life wartime history, which was the basis for Yossarian's.

All of the discussions of chronology cited above have worked directly out of Heller's admittedly difficult and convoluted text. Surprisingly, no critic has taken much advantage of one set of evidence that was publicly provided with the publication in 1973 of the essay collection *A "Catch-22" Casebook*, edited by Frederick Kiley and Walter McDonald: facsimiles of the charts that Heller himself created on desk blotter paper in the final stages of *Catch-22*'s composition. Though not every episode of the novel is accounted for in the sections of the charts visible in the book, Heller's intentions are clear for many of the most important characters, and particularly Yossarian. While these charts are not wholly infallible, they do help solve some of the difficulties that the critics have fallen into by trying to tease the chronology out of the text alone, and they do endorse certain interpretations of the chronology over others.

The charts are organized with a time line running vertically along the left edge and a list of characters extending along the top edge at the head of several columns. Yossarian has the first three columns, followed to the right by a column for Dunbar and McWatt, one for Clevinger and Nately, one for Hungry Joe and Dobbs, one for Orr, another for Milo, and so on through the chaplain, the majors, the colonels, the generals, the doctors, the nurses, and others. The time line begins with Yossarian leaving civilian life for basic training at Lowery Field, Colorado, where he meets Wintergreen and discovers the hospital as a refuge from calisthenics. The chart offers no dates at this point, but for the reasons noted above the first hospital stay must take place in 1942; Thanksgiving 1943, therefore, finds him stationed as an air cadet in Santa Ana, California, and arguing about God with Scheisskopf's wife. Heller does date Yossarian's arrival on Pianosa, placing it in "early 1944," well after the September 1943 date set by Burhans. According to the chart, Yossarian flies twenty-three missions before Colonel Cathcart arrives, also in early 1944, and raises the required missions to thirty.

In March, according to Heller's time line, occurs the mission to Ferrara, where Aarfy's incompetence forces Yossarian to go over the bridge twice before destroying it. Milo forms his cartel in April, and Cathcart raises the missions to thirty-five. On 4 June 1944, the Allies enter Rome—a historical fact noted on the chart—and Yossarian accompanies Nately to the Roman whorehouse where Nately falls in love with his whore.

In late June the Great Big Siege of Bologna takes place, with all of its attendant episodes. Immediately thereafter Yossarian takes his rest leave in Rome with thirty-two missions behind him and meets Luciana. He returns to his unit and heads directly for the hospital when Cathcart raises the missions to forty. Here is where some scholars have become confused: no sooner does Yossarian leave the hospital than, according to the chart, Cathcart raises the missions to forty-five and Yossarian, now with only thirty-eight missions, enters the hospital a second time within this narrow interval.

The mission over Avignon, and thus Snowden's death, takes place in July, as do Snowden's funeral and Yossarian's receipt of a medal in the nude. About the time Cathcart orders fifty missions, Clevinger disappears inside a cloud. Yossarian returns to the hospital at the beginning of August, "in despair over Clevinger's death," according to the chart. He has forty-four missions at this point, and it is here, when he meets the chaplain, that the first chapter of the novel takes place. After this stay Yossarian begs Daneeka to ground him, and the chaplain takes Yossarian's case to Cathcart during their discussion of the *Saturday Evening Post*.

In September, according to Heller's chart, the missions required go to fifty-five, and Yossarian, with forty-eight missions, pleads with Daneeka again; he reaches fifty-one just before Cathcart raises the required missions to sixty, at which point Yossarian tackles Major Major. Shortly thereafter Yossarian is wounded in the thigh on the milk run over Parma. While convalescing in the hospital he gooses Nurse Duckett, which begins their affair, and has his interview with the psychiatrist Major Sanderson. Over the following month, Orr disappears, McWatt accidentally chops Kid Sampson in half and commits suicide, and missions are raised to sixty-five and then seventy.

Mid-October finds Yossarian in Rome again, where he helps Nately rescue his whore from the "big shots," at which time she finally falls in love with Nately. The following month Yossarian breaks Nately's nose at the raucous Thanksgiving celebration during which Sergeant Knight sprays the camp with a machine gun. Yossarian and Dunbar lie their way into the hospital to visit Nately, where they are joined by the chaplain. During this stay the soldier in white returns, driving Dunbar crazy, and Dunbar is disappeared.

By early December Yossarian and Nately have flown seventy missions. After Milo expresses his wish to get combat credit, Cathcart boots them up to eighty, and Nately, wishing to remain near his whore, volunteers to continue. After Nately and Dobbs collide mid-air, killing both crews, Yossarian refuses to fly more missions. The remainder of the plot unfolds in December 1944: the chaplain's trial, Peckem's fleeting triumph over Dreedle and Sceisskopf's promotion, Yossarian's AWOL flight to "the Eternal City," Nately's whore's assaults on his life, Korn's deal, and Yossarian's desertion upon hearing of Orr's arrival in Sweden.

For the most part, Heller's charts explain the book's chronology better than do the scholars who have limited themselves to textual evidence. Even using the charts, however, one discovers that Heller did make some errors, though not as many as his critics think. Some errors are the result of apparent last-minute changes, such as the time of Milo's arrival to the squadron. According to the text, Milo is unaware of the incident wherein the mess sergeant, Corporal Snark, poisoned the men with laundry soap during the Ferrara campaign. The charts, however, show Milo arriving well before March, when Ferrara took place. Heller has Yossarian and Milo meet for the first time in the spring of 1944, before Milo sets up his cartel in April. One of the first subjects they discuss, however, is Nately, his whore, and the old man who lives in her brothel in Rome. Since Rome did not fall into Allied hands until June 4, we have a patent impossibility here, inconsistent with the story line.

But the chart helps explain away another "error" noted by Burhans and seconded by Merrill regarding Major—de Coverley's promotion of Milo to mess officer. Both see Heller as erring in having the Major promote Milo upon his triumphal return from Rome in early June after having secured the whore-filled apartments, even though Milo clearly had his cartel going in April. Looking at the relevant text, one can see where they got the idea, since the promotion takes place immediately after a description of the Major's visit to Rome and his new eyepatch. But in Heller's complex narrative, juxtaposition in space does necessarily mean juxtaposition in time; the transitional lines in no way insist that what follows in the text must follow in the story's chronology. Between the description of the Major's Roman excursion and his appointment of Milo stands only the statement, to the men in the squadron, Major—de Coverley was a colossus, though they never dared tell him so. The only one who ever did dare address him was Milo Minderbinder, who approached the horseshoe-pitching pit with a hard-boiled egg his second week in the squadron and held it aloft for Major—de Coverley to see. Nothing in this passage suggests explicitly or implicitly that happens after the fall of Rome described just above it.

Merrill makes a similar mistake when he claims Heller erred because Chapters 2 and 17 refer to the same hospital visits, even though in Chapter 2 Yossarian has forty-four missions, while in Chapter 17 he is rushing into the hospital "determined to remain (there) forever rather than fly one mission more" than thirty-eight. Once more a critical reader has been fooled by a narrative bridge; between this paragraph in Chapter 17 and the reappearance of the soldier in white are nearly two pages that concern hospitals in general and death, with specific reference to Snowden and

Clevinger. In fact, one sees from Heller's chart that Snowden and Clevinger both meet their ends between Yossarian's hospital visit at thirty-eight missions (in late June) and his visit "that last time" at forty-four (in August). These intervening paragraphs thus serve as a transition between the two visits, which Merrill, among others, incorrectly sees as the same visit.

On the other hand, other anomalies that scholars have noted do represent oversights on Heller's part. Beside the impossibility of Yossarian and Milo discussing Nately's whore at their introduction is Appleby's prompt visit to squadron commander Major Major, as soon as he and Yossarian arrive on Pianosa, to report Yossarian's refusal to take his Atabrine tablets. Here Appleby is humiliated when Sergeant Towser, following Major Major's orders, refuses to admit him until Major Major leaves his office. But this episode is impossible within the chronology: Major Major does not go into hiding until after Colonel Cathcart promotes him to squadron commander, and Colonel Cathcart does not arrive on Pianosa until after the death of Colonel Nevers, at which time Appleby and Yossarian have been on the island long enough for Yossarian to have flown twenty-three missions. Major Major is thus simply another pilot at the time Yossarian and Appleby arrive, and not yet a reclusive squadron commander.

It is of course possible that the author tossed in a few such impossibilities to underline the absurdity of his story, though, as his notes and charts demonstrate, he otherwise did a painstaking job of setting the episodes straight. Combining these notes and charts with close textual analysis does iron out most of the chronology; nonetheless, between the difficult texture of the narrative and the few errors, intentional or not, that Heller does make, no time line will perfectly account for every single one of the intersections of character and event in the novel. A substantially accurate chart of the major event in the novel, however, has been appended to the end of this study for ready reference; it is based on Heller's own chart but fine-tuned to eliminate some textual anomalies, particularly in Milo's history.

The main value of this exercise is twofold: it gives us a reliable framework for discussing the important episodes of the story, and it proves that, contrary to the complaints of early critics and new readers, *Catch-22* is not simply chaotic, but meticulously written to appear chaotic, as Heller has insisted in a number of interviews. It is in fact a painstakingly constructed book.

Why, then did Heller go to so much trouble to confuse the time sense of the plot? And are there some overarching principles and patterns of organization behind the apparent chaos?

[Selected from Stephen W. Potts. *Catch-22 Antiheroic Antinovel*. Boston: Twayne Publishers, 1989.]

3. Kurt Vonnegut

3.1 Presentation Topics

(1) War experiences and Kurt Vonnegut's writing.

(2) Multilevel narrative in his works.

(3) The firebombing of Dresdon.

3.2 Selected Reading

Ⅰ. Central issue of concern

A satirical novelist who captures the absurdity of war with the juxtaposition of the world of art and the world of science.

Ⅱ. Text

Slaughterhouse Five

Chapter 5

(*Slaughterhouse Five* is an anti-war science fiction about the fire bombing of Dresden, Germany by the British and American air forces in the February of 1945. In a plot-scrambling display, readers follow Billy Pilgrim simultaneously through all phases of his life, concentrating on his (and Vonnegut's) shattering experience as an American prisoner of war. In the longest chapter of the novel, Billy continues to travel through time between World War Ⅱ, Tralfamadore, the psychiatric ward of a veteran's hospital, and his marriage.)

Billy Pilgrim says that the Universe does not look like a lot of bright little dots to the creatures from Tralfamadore[①]. The creatures can see where each star has been and where it is going, so that the heavens are filled with rarefied, luminous spaghetti. And Tralfamadorians don't see human beings as two-legged creatures, either. They see them as great millipedes—"with babies' legs at one end and old people's legs at the other," says Billy Pilgrim.

Billy asked for something to read on the trip to Tralfamadore. His captors had five million Earthling books on microfilm, but no way to project them in Billy's cabin. They had only one actual book in English, which would be placed in a Tralfamadorian museum. It was *Valley of the Dolls*, by Jacqueline Susann[②].

Billy read it, thought it was pretty good in spots. The people in it certainly had their ups-and-downs, ups-and-downs. But Billy didn't want to read about the same ups-and-downs over and over again. He asked if there wasn't, please, some other reading matters around.

"Only Tralfamadorian novels, which I'm afraid you couldn't begin to understand," said the speaker on the wall.

"Let me look at one anyway."

So they sent him in several. They were little things. A dozen of them might have had the bulk of *Valley of the Dolls*—with all its ups-and-downs, up-and-downs.

Billy couldn't read Tralfamadorian, of course, but he could at least see how the books were laid out—in brief clumps of symbols separated by stars. Billy commented that the clumps might be telegrams.

"Exactly," said the voice.

"They are telegrams?"

"There are no telegrams on Tralfamadore. But you're right: each clump of symbols is a brief, urgent message describing a situation, a scene. We Tralfamadorians read them all at once, not one after the other. There isn't any particular relationship between all the messages, except that the author has chosen them carefully, so that, when seen all at once, they produce an image of life that is

---

① A fictional extraterrestrial planet. The race on it kidnaps Billy Pilgrim and places him in a zoo with Montana Wildhack, an actress in pornographic films.

② An American author noted for *Valley of the Dolls* in 1966. It is reported to be a fiction based on real-life celebrities.

beautiful and surprising and deep. There is no beginning, no middle, no end, no suspense, no moral, no causes, no effects. What we love in our books are the depths of many marvelous moments seen all at one time."

Moments after that, the saucer entered a time warp, and Billy was flung back into his childhood. He was twelve years old, quaking as he stood with his mother and father on Bright Angel Point①, at the rim of Grand Canyon. The little human family was staring at the floor of the canyon, one mile straight down.

"Well," said Billy's father, manfully kicking a pebble into space, "there it is." They had come to this famous place by automobile. They had had several blowouts on the way.

"It was worth the trip," said Billy's mother raptly. "Oh, God was it ever worth it."

Billy hated the canyon. He was sure that he was going to fall in. His mother touched him, and he wet his pants.

There were other tourists looking down into the canyon, too, and a ranger was there to answer questions. A Frenchman who had come all the way from France asked the ranger in broken English if many people committed suicide by jumping in.

"Yes, sir," said the ranger. "About three folks a year." So it goes.

And Billy took a very short trip through time, made a peewee jump of only ten days, so he was still twelve, still touring the West with his family. Now they were down in Carlsbad Caverns②, and Billy was praying to God to get him out of there before the ceiling fell in.

A ranger was explaining that the Caverns had been discovered by a cowboy who saw a huge cloud of bats come out of a hole in the ground. And then he said that he was going to turn out all the lights, and that it would probably be the first time in the lives of most people there that they had ever been in darkness that was total.

Out went the lights. Billy didn't even know whether he was still alive or not. And then something ghostly floated in air to his left. It had numbers on it. His

---

① A hiking trail located on the North Rim of the Grand Canyon National Park in the U. S. state of Arizona.

② A show cave in Carlsbad Caverns National Park in the Guadalupe Mountains in southeastern New Mexico.

father had taken out his pocket watch. The watch had a radium dial.

Billy went from total dark to total light, found himself back in the war, back in the delousing station again. The shower was over. An unseen hand had turned the water off.

When Billy got his clothes back, they weren't any cleaner, but all the little animals that had been living in them were dead. So it goes. And his new overcoat was thawed out and limp now. It was much too small for Billy. It had a fur collar and a lining of crimson silk, and had apparently been made for an impresario about as big as an organ-grinder's monkey. It was full of bullet holes.

Billy Pilgrim dressed himself. He put on the little overcoat, too. It split up the back, and, at the shoulders, the sleeves came entirely free. So the coat became a fur-collared vest. It was meant to flare at its owners waist, but the flaring took place at Billy's armpits. The Germans found him to be one of the most screamingly funny things they had seen in all of the Second World War. They laughed and laughed.

And the Germans told everybody else to form in ranks of five, with Billy as their pivot. Then out of doors went the parade, and through gate after gate again. There were more starving Russians with faces like radium dials. The Americans were livelier than before. The jazzing with hot water had cheered them up. And they came to a shed where a corporal with only one arm and one eye wrote the name and serial number of each prisoner in a big, red ledger. Everybody was legally alive now. Before they got their names and numbers in that book, they were missing in action and probably dead.

So it goes.

As the Americans were waiting to move on, an altercation broke out in their rear-most rank. An American had muttered something which a guard did not like. The guard knew English, and he hauled the American out of ranks knocked him down.

The American was astonished. He stood up shakily, spitting blood. He'd had two teeth knocked out. He had meant no harm by what he'd said, evidently, had no idea that the guard would hear and understand.

"Why me?" he asked the guard.

The guard shoved him back into ranks. "Vy you? Vy anybody?" he said.

When Billy Pilgrim's name was inscribed in the ledger of the prison camp, he was given a number, too, and an iron dogtag in which that number was stamped. A slave laborer from Poland had done the stamping. He was dead now. So it goes.

Billy was told to hang the tag around his neck along with his American dogtags, which he did. The tag was like a salt cracker, perforated down its middle so that a strong man could snap it in two with his bare hands. In case Billy died, which he didn't, half the tag would mark his body and half would mark his grave.

After poor Edgar Derby, the high school teacher, was shot in Dresden later on, a doctor pronounced him dead and snapped his dogtag in two. So it goes.

Properly enrolled and tagged, the Americans were led through gate after gate again. In two days' time now their families would learn from the International Red Cross that they were alive.

Next to Billy was little Paul Lazzaro, who had promised to avenge Roland Weary. Lazzaro wasn't thinking about vengeance. He was thinking about his terrible bellyache. His stomach had shrunk to the size of a walnut. That dry, shriveled pouch was as sore as a boil.

Next to Lazzaro was poor, doomed old Edgar Derby, with his American and German dogs displayed like a necklace, on the outside of his clothes. He had expected to become a captain, a company commander, because of his wisdom and age. Now here he was on the Czechoslovakian border at midnight.

"Halt," said a guard.

The Americans halted. They stood there quietly in the cold. The sheds they were among were outwardly like thousands of other sheds they had passed. There was this difference, though: the sheds had tin chimneys, and out of the chimneys whirled constellations of sparks.

A guard knocked on a door.

The door was flung open from inside. Light leaped out through the door, escaped from prison at 186,000 miles per second. Out marched fifty middle-aged Englishmen. They were singing "Hail, Hail, the Gang's All Here" from *The Pirates of Penzance*①.

---

① A classic comic opera in two acts. Since its debut at the Fifth Avenue Theater in 1879, it was well-received.

These lusty, ruddy vocalists were among the first English-speaking prisoners to be taken in the Second World War. Now they were singing to nearly the last. They had not seen a woman or a child for four years or more. They hadn't seen any birds, either. Not even sparrows would come into the camp.

The Englishmen were officers. Each of them had attempted to escape from another prison at least once. Now they were here, dead-center in a sea of dying Russians.

They could tunnel all they pleased. They would inevitably surface within a rectangle of barbed wire, would find themselves greeted listlessly by dying Russians who spoke no English, who had no food or useful information or escape plans of their own. They could scheme all they pleased to hide aboard a vehicle or steal one, but no vehicle ever came into their compound. They could feign illness, if they liked, but that wouldn't earn them a trip anywhere, either. The only hospital in the camp was a six-bed affair in the British compound itself.

The Englishmen were clean and enthusiastic and decent and strong. They sang boomingly well. They had been singing together every night for years.

The Englishmen had also been lifting weights and chinning themselves for years. Their bellies were like washboards. The muscles of their calves and upper arms were like cannonballs. They were all masters of checkers and chess and bridge and cribbage and dominoes and anagrams and charades and Ping-Pong and billiards, as well.

They were among the wealthiest people in Europe, in terms of food. A clerical error early in the war, when food was still getting through to prisoners, had caused the Red Cross to ship them five hundred parcels every month instead of fifty. The Englishmen had hoarded these so cunningly that now, as the war was ending, they had three tons of sugar, one ton of coffee, eleven hundred pounds of chocolate, seven hundred pounds of tobacco, seventeen hundred pounds of tea, two tons of flour, one ton of canned beef, twelve hundred pounds of canned butter, sixteen hundred pounds of canned cheese, eight hundred pounds of powdered milk, and two tons of orange marmalade.

They kept all this in a room without windows. They had ratproofed it by lining it with flattened tin cans.

They were adored by the Germans, who thought they were exactly what the

Englishmen ought to be. They made war look stylish and reasonable, and fun. So the Germans let them have four sheds, though one shed would have held them all. And, in exchange for coffee or chocolate or tobacco, the Germans gave them paint and lumber and nails and cloth for fixing things up.

The Englishmen had known for twelve hours that American guests were on their way. They had never had guests before, and they went to work like darling elves, sweeping, mopping, cooking, baking—making mattresses of straw and burlap bags, setting tables, putting party favors at each place.

Now they were singing their welcome to their guests in the winter night. Their clothes were aromatic with the feast they had been preparing. They were dressed half for battle, half for tennis or croquet. They were so elated by their own hospitality, and by all the goodies waiting inside, that they did not take a good look at their guests while they sang. And they imagined that they were singing to fellow officers fresh from the fray.

They wrestled the Americans toward the shed door affectionately, filling the night with manly blather and brotherly rodomontades. They called them "Yank," told them "Good show," promised them that "Jerry① was on the run," and so on.

Billy Pilgrim wondered dimly who Jerry was.

Now he was indoors, next to an iron cookstove that was glowing cherry red. Dozens of teapots were boiling there. Some of them had whistles. And there was a witches' cauldron full of golden soup. The soup was thick. Primeval bubbles surfaced it with lethargical majesty as Billy Pilgrim stared.

There were long tables set for a banquet. At each place was a bowl made from a can that had once contained powdered milk. A smaller can was a cup. A taller, more slender can was a tumbler. Each tumbler was filled with warm milk.

At each place was a safety razor, a washcloth, a package of razor blades, a chocolate bar, two cigars, a bar of soap, ten cigarettes, a book of matches, a pencil and a candle.

Only the candles and the soap were of German origin. They had a ghostly, opalescent similarity. The British had no way of knowing it, but the candles and the soap were made from the fat of rendered Jews and Gypsies and fairies and

① The British and American slang term for Germans.

communists, and other enemies of the State.

So it goes.

The banquet hall was illuminated by candlelight. There were heaps of fresh baked white bread on the tables, gobs of butter, pots of marmalade. There were platters of sliced beef from cans. Soup and scrambled eggs and hot marmalade pie were yet to come.

And, at the far end of the shed, Billy saw pink arches with azure draperies hanging between them, and an enormous clock, and two golden thrones, and a bucket and a mop. It was in this setting that the evening's entertainment would take place, a musical version of Cinderella, the most popular story ever told.

Billy Pilgrim was on fire, having stood too close to the glowing stove. The hem of his little coat was burning. It was a quiet, patient sort of fire-like the burning of punk.

Billy wondered if there was a telephone somewhere. He wanted to call his mother, to tell her he was alive and well.

There was silence now, as the Englishmen looked in astonishment at the frowsy creatures they had so lustily waltzed inside. One of the Englishmen saw that Billy was on fire. "You're on fire lad!" he said, and he got Billy away from the stove and beat out the sparks with his hands.

When Billy made no comment on this, the Englishman asked him, "Can you talk? Can you hear?"

Billy nodded.

The Englishman touched him exploratorily here and there, filled with pity. "My God—what have they done to you, lad? This isn't a man. It's a broken kite."

"Are you really an American?" said the Englishman.

"Yes," said Billy.

"And your rank?"

"Private."

"What became of your boots, lad?"

"I don't remember."

"Is that coat a joke?"

"Sir?"

"Where did you get such a thing?"

Billy had to think hard about that. "They gave it to me," he said at last.

"Jerry gave it to you?"

"Who?"

"The Germans gave it to you?"

"Yes."

Billy didn't like the questions. They were fatiguing.

"Ohhhh—Yank, Yank, Yank," said the Englishman, "that coat was an insult."

"Sir?"

"It was a deliberate attempt to humiliate you. You mustn't let Jerry do things like that."

Billy Pilgrim swooned.

Billy came to on a chair facing the stage. He had somehow eaten, and now he was watching Cinderella. Some part of him had evidently been enjoying the performance for quite a while. Billy was laughing hard.

The women in the play were really men, of course. The clock had just struck midnight and Cinderella was lamenting.

"Goodness me, the clock has struck—Alackaday, and fuck my luck."

Billy found the couplet so comical that he not only laughed—he shrieked. He went on shrieking until he was carried out of the shed and into another, where the hospital was. It was a six-bed hospital. There weren't any other patients in there.

Billy was put to bed and tied down, and given a shot of morphine. Another American volunteered to watch over him. This volunteer was Edgar Derby, the high school teacher who would be shot to death in Dresden. So it goes.

Derby sat on a three-legged stool. He was given a book to read. The book was *The Red Badge of Courage*, by Stephen Crane①. Derby had read it before. Now he read it again while Billy Pilgrim entered a morphine paradise.

Under morphine, Billy had a dream of giraffes in a garden. The giraffes were following gravel paths, were pausing to munch sugar pears from treetops. Billy was a giraffe, too. He ate a pear. It was a hard one. It fought back against his

---

① An American novelist, short story writer, poet and journalist of Realism and Naturalism. He won international acclaim for his 1895 Civil War novel *The Red Badge of Courage*.

grinding teeth. It snapped in juicy protest.

The giraffes accepted Billy as one of their own, as a harmless creature as preposterously specialized as themselves. Two approached him from opposite sides, leaned against him. They had long, muscular upper lips which they could shape like the bells of bugles. They kissed him with these. They were female giraffes-cream and lemon yellow. They had horns like doorknobs. The knobs were covered with velvet.

Why?

Night came to the garden of the giraffes, and Billy Pilgrim slept without dreaming for a while, and then he traveled in time. He woke up with his head under a blanket in a ward for nonviolent mental patients in a veterans' hospital near Lake Placid, New York. It was springtime in 1948, three years after the end of the war.

Billy uncovered his head. The windows of the ward were open. Birds were twittering outside. "Poo-tee-weet?" One asked him. The sun was high. There were twenty-nine other patients assigned to the ward, but they were all outdoors now, enjoying the day. They were free to come and go as they pleased, to go home, even, if they liked—and so was Billy Pilgrim. They had come here voluntarily, alarmed by the outside world.

Billy had committed himself in the middle of his final year at the Ilium School of Optometry. Nobody else suspected that he was going crazy. Everybody else thought he looked fine and was acting fine. Now he was in the hospital. The doctors agreed: He was going crazy.

They didn't think it had anything to do with the war. They were sure Billy was going to pieces because his father had thrown him into the deep end of the Y. M. C. A①. swimming pool when he was a little boy, and had then taken him to the rim of the Grand Canyon.

The man assigned to the bed next to Billy's was a former infantry captain named Eliot Rosewater. Rosewater was sick and tired of being drunk all the time.

It was Rosewater who introduced Billy to science fiction, and in particular to

① Young Men's Christian Association.

the writings of Kilgore Trout①. Rosewater had a tremendous collection of science-fiction paperbacks under his bed. He had brought them to the hospital in a steamer trunk. Those beloved, frumpish books gave off a smell that permeated the ward-like flannel pajamas that hadn't been changed for a month, or like Irish stew.

Kilgore Trout became Billy's favorite living author, and science fiction became the only sort of tales he could read.

Rosewater was twice as smart as Billy, but he and Billy were dealing with similar crises in similar ways. They had both found life meaningless, partly because of what they had seen in war. Rosewater, for instance, had shot a fourteen-year-old fireman, mistaking him for a German soldier. So it goes. And Billy had seen the greatest massacre in European history, which was the firebombing of Dresden. So it goes.

So they were trying to re-invent themselves and their universe. Science fiction was a big help.

Rosewater said an interesting thing to Billy one time about a book that wasn't science fiction. He said that everything there was to know about life was in *The Brothers Karamazov*, by Feodor Dostoevsky②. "But that isn't enough any more." said Rosewater.

Another time Billy heard Rosewater say to a psychiatrist, "I think you guys are going to have to come up with a lot of wonderful new lies, or people just aren't going to want to go on living."

There was a still life on Billy's bedside table—two pills, an ashtray with three lipstick stained cigarettes in it, one cigarette still burning, and a glass of water. The water was dead. So it goes. Air was trying to get out of that dead water. Bubbles were clinging to the walls of the glass, too weak to climb out.

The cigarettes belonged to Billy's chain-smoking mother. She had sought the ladies' room, which was off the ward for WACS and WAVES and SPARS and WAFS③ who had gone bananas. She would be back at any moment now.

---

① A fictional character as a science fiction author created by Kurt Vonnegut.

② A Russian writer and essayist, known for his novels *Crime and Punishment* and *The Brothers Karamazov*. The latter novel is a philosophical novel about the ethical debates of God, free will and morality.

③ They refer to the Women's Army Corps, a World War Ⅱ era woman division of the U. S. navy, a divisioin of U. S. Coast Guard, and Women in Air Force respectively.

Billy covered his head with his blanket again. He always covered his head when his mother came to see him in the mental ward—always got much sicker until she went away. It wasn't that she was ugly, or had bad breath or a bad personality. She was a perfectly nice, standard-issue, brown-haired, white woman with a high-school education.

She upset Billy simply by being his mother. She made him feel embarrassed and ungrateful and weak because she had gone to so much trouble to give him life, and to keep that life going, and Billy didn't really like life at all.

Billy heard Eliot Rosewater come in and lie down. Rosewater's bedsprings talked a lot about that. Rosewater was a big man, but not very powerful. He looked as though he might be made out of nose putty.

And then Billy's mother came back from the ladies' room, sat down on a chair between Billy's and Rosewater's bed. Rosewater greeted her with melodious warmth, asked how she was today. He seemed delighted to hear that she was fine. He was experimenting with being ardently sympathetic with everybody he met. He thought that might make the world a slightly more pleasant place to live in. He called Billy's mother "dear." He was experimenting with calling everybody "dear."

Some day she promised Rosewater, "I'm going to come in here, and Billy is going to uncover his head, and do you know what he's going to say?"

"What's he going to say, dear?"

"He's going to say, 'Hello, Mom,' and he's going to smile. He's going to say, 'Gee, it's good to see you, Mom. How have you been?'"

"Today could be the day."

"Every night I pray."

"That's a good thing to do."

"People would be surprised if they knew how much in this world was due to prayers."

"You never said a truer word, dear."

"Does your mother come to see you often?"

"My mother is dead," said Rosewater. So it goes.

"I'm sorry."

"At least she had a happy life as long as it lasted."

"That's a consolation, anyway."

"Yes."

"Billy's father is dead, you know," said Billy's mother. So it goes.

"A boy needs a father."

And on and on it went—that duet between the dumb, praying lady and the big, hollow man so full of loving echoes.

"He was at the top of his class when this happened," said Billy's mother.

"Maybe he was working too hard." said Rosewater. He held a book he wanted to read, but he was much too polite to read and talk, too, easy as it was to give Billy's mother satisfactory answers. The book was *Maniacs in the Fourth Dimension*, by Kilgore Trout. It was about people whose mental diseases couldn't be treated because the causes of the diseases were all in the fourth dimension, and three-dimensional Earthling doctors couldn't see those causes at all, or even imagine them.

One thing Trout said that Rosewater liked very much was that there really were vampires and were wolves and goblins and angels and so on, but that they were in the fourth dimension. So was William Blake, Rosewater's favorite poet, according to Trout. So were heaven and hell.

"He's engaged to a very rich girl," said Billy's mother.

"That's good," said Rosewater. "Money can be a great comfort sometimes."

"It really can."

"Of course it can."

"It isn't much fun if you have to pinch every penny till it screams."

"It's nice to have a little breathing room."

"Her father owns the optometry school where Billy was going. He also owns six offices around our part of the state. He flies his own plane and has a summer place up on Lake George."

"That's a beautiful lake."

Billy fell asleep under his blanket. When he woke up again, he was tied to the bed in the hospital back in prison. He opened one eye, saw poor old Edgar Derby reading *The Red Badge of Courage* by candlelight.

Billy closed that one eye saw in his memory of the future poor old Edgar Derby in front of a firing squad in the ruins of Dresden. There were only four men in that squad. Billy had heard that one man in each firing squad was customarily given a rifle loaded with blank cartridge. Billy didn't think there would be a blank cartridge issued in a squad that small, in a war that old.

Now the head Englishman came into the hospital to check on Billy. He was an infantry colonel captured at Dunkirk①. It was he who had given Billy morphine. There wasn't a real doctor in the compound, so the doctoring was up to him. "How's the patient?" he asked Derby.

"Dead to the world."

"But not actually dead."

"No."

"How nice—to feel nothing, and still get full credit for being alive."

Derby now came to lugubrious attention.

"No, no—please—as you were. With only two men for each officer, and all the men sick, I think we can do without the usual pageantry between officers and men."

Derby remained standing. "You seem older than the rest," said the colonel.

Derby told him he was forty-five, which was two years older than the colonel. The colonel said that the other Americans had all shaved now, that Billy and Derby were the only two still with beards. And he said, "You know we've had to imagine the war here, and we have imagined that it was being fought by aging men like ourselves. We had forgotten that wars were fought by babies. When I saw those freshly shaved faces, it was a shock. My God, my God—" I said to myself. "It's the Children's Crusade."

The colonel asked old Derby how he had been captured, and Derby told a tale of being in a clump of trees with about a hundred other frightened soldiers. The battle had been going on for five days. The hundred had been driven into the trees by tanks.

Derby described the incredible artificial weather that Earthlings sometimes create for other Earthlings when they don't want those other Earthlings to inhabit Earth any more. Shells were bursting in the treetops with terrific bangs, he said, showering down knives and needles and razorblades. Little lumps of lead in copper

① A seaport in Northern France on the North Sea, scene of the evacuation of British forces in 1940 during World War Ⅱ.

jackets were crisscrossing the woods under the shellbursts, zipping along much faster than sound.

A lot of people were being wounded or killed. So it goes.

Then the shelling stopped, and a hidden German with a loudspeaker told the Americans to put their weapons down and come out of the woods with their hands on the top of their heads, or the shelling would start again. It wouldn't stop until everybody in there was dead.

So the Americans put their weapons down, and they came out of the woods with their hands on top of their heads, because they wanted to go on living, if they possibly could.

Billy traveled in time back to the veterans' hospital again. The blanket was over his head. It was quiet outside the blanket. "Is my mother gone?" said Billy.

"Yes."

Billy peeked out from under his blanket. His fiancée was out there now, sitting on the visitor's chair. Her name was Valencia Merble. Valencia was the daughter of the owner of the Ilium School of Optometry. She was rich. She was as big as a house because she couldn't stop eating. She was eating now. She was eating a Three Musketeers Candy Bar. She was wearing trifocal lenses in harlequin frames, and the frames were trimmed with rhinestones. The glitter of the rhinestones was answered by the glitter of the diamond in her engagement ring. The diamond was insured for eighteen hundred dollars. Billy had found that diamond in Germany. It was booty of war.

Billy didn't want to marry ugly Valencia. She was one of the symptoms of his disease. He knew he was going crazy, when he heard himself proposing marriage to her, when he begged her to take the diamond ring and be his companion for life.

Billy said, "Hello," to her, and she asked him if he wanted some candy, and he said, "No, thanks."

She asked him how he was, and he said, "Much better, thanks." She said that everybody at the Optometry School was sorry he was sick and hoped he would be well soon, and Billy said, "When you see 'em, tell 'em, 'Hello.'"

She promised she would.

She asked him if there was anything she could bring him from the outside, and he said, "No. I have just about everything I want."

"What about books?" said Valencia.

"I'm right next to one of the biggest private libraries in the world," said Billy, meaning Eliot Rosewater's collection of science fiction.

Rosewater was on the next bed, reading, and Billy drew him into the conversation, asked him what he was reading this time.

So Rosewater told him. It was *The Gospel from Outer Space*, by Kilgore Trout. It was about a visitor from outer space, shaped very much like a Tralfamadorian by the way. The visitor from outer space made a serious study of Christianity, to learn, if he could, why Christians found it so easy to be cruel. He concluded that at least part of the trouble was slipshod storytelling in the New Testament. He supposed that the intent of the Gospels was to teach people, among other things, to be merciful, even to the lowest of the low.

But the Gospels actually taught this:

Before you kill somebody, make absolutely sure he isn't well connected. So it goes.

The flaw in the Christ stories, said the visitor from outer space, was that Christ, who didn't look like much, was actually the Son of the Most Powerful Being in the Universe. Readers understood that, so, when they came to the crucifixion, they naturally thought, and Rosewater read out loud again:

Oh, boy—they sure picked the wrong guy to lynch that time!

And that thought had a brother: "There are right people to lynch." Who? People not well connected. So it goes.

The visitor from outer space made a gift to Earth of a new Gospel. In it, Jesus really was a nobody, and a pain in the neck to a lot of people with better connections than he had. He still got to say all the lovely and puzzling things he said in the other Gospels.

So the people amused themselves one day by nailing him to a cross and planting the cross in the ground. There couldn't possibly be any repercussions, the lynchers thought. The reader would have to think that, too, since the new Gospel hammered home again and again what a nobody Jesus was.

And then, just before nobody died, the heavens opened up, and there was thunder and lightning. The voice of God came crashing down. He told the people that he was adopting the bum as his son giving him the full powers and privileges of

The Son of the Creator of the Universe throughout all eternity. God said this: From this moment on, He will punish horribly anybody who torments a bum who has no connections!

Billy's fiancée had finished her Three Musketeers Candy Bar. Now she was eating a Milky Way.

"Forget books," said Rosewater, throwing that particular book under his bed. "The hell with 'em."

"That sounded like an interesting one," said Valencia.

"Jesus—if Kilgore Trout could only write!" Rosewater exclaimed. He had a point: Kilgore Trout's unpopularity was deserved. His prose was frightful. Only his ideas were good.

"I don't think Trout has ever been out of the country," Rosewater went on. "My God—he writes about Earthlings all the time, and they're all Americans. Practically nobody on is an American."

"Where does he live?" Valencia asked.

"Nobody knows," Rosewater replied. "I'm the only person who ever heard of him, as far as I can tell. No two books have the same publisher, and every time I write him in care of a publisher, the letter comes back because the publisher has failed."

He changed the subject now, congratulated Valencia on her engagement ring.

"Thank you," she said, and held it out so Rosewater could get a close look. "Billy got that diamond in the war."

"That's the attractive thing about war," said Rosewater. "Absolutely everybody gets a little something."

With regard to the whereabouts of Kilgore Trout: he actually lived in Ilium, Billy's hometown, friendless and despised. Billy would meet him by and by.

"Billy—" said Valencia Merble.

"Hm?"

"You want to talk about our silver pattern?"

"Sure."

"I've got it narrowed down pretty much to either Royal Danish or Rambler Rose."

"Rambler Rose," said Billy.

"It isn't something we should rush into," she said. "I mean whatever we decide on, that's what we're going to have to live with the rest of our lives."

Billy studied the pictures. "Royal Danish," he said at last.

"Colonial Moonlight is nice, too."

"Yes, it is," said Billy Pilgrim.

And Billy traveled in time to the zoo on Tralfamadore. He was forty-four years old, on display under a geodesic dome. He was reclining on the lounge chair which had been his cradle during his trip through space. He was naked. The Tralfamadorians were interested in his body—all of it. There were thousands of them outside, holding up their little hands so that their eyes could see him. Billy had been on Tralfamadore for six Earthling months now. He was used to the crowd.

Escape was out of the question. The atmosphere outside the dome was cyanide, and Earth was 446,120,000,000,000,000 miles away.

Billy was displayed there in the zoo in a simulated Earthling habitat. Most of the furnishings had been stolen from the Sears & Roebuck warehouse in Iowa City, Iowa. There was a color television set and a couch that could be converted into a bed. There were end tables with lamps and ashtrays on them by the couch. There was a home bar and two stools. There was a little pool table. There was wall-to-wall carpeting in federal gold, except in the kitchen and bathroom areas and over the iron manhole cover in the center of the floor. There were magazines arranged in a fan on the coffee table in front of the couch.

There was a stereophonic phonograph. The phonograph worked. The television didn't. There was a picture of one cowboy killing another one pasted to the television tube. So it goes.

There were no wall in the dome, nor place for Billy to hide. The mint green bathroom fixtures were right out in the open. Billy got off his lounge chair now, went into the bathroom and took a leak. The crowd went wild.

Billy brushed his teeth on Tralfamadore, put in his partial denture, and went into his kitchen. His bottled-gas range and his refrigerator and his dishwasher were mint green, too. There was a picture painted on the door of the refrigerator. The refrigerator had come that way. It was a picture of a Gay Nineties couple on a bicycle built for two.

Billy looked at that picture now, tried to think something about the couple. Nothing came to him. There didn't seem to be anything to think about those two people.

Billy ate a good breakfast from cans. He washed his cup and plate and knife and fork and spoon and saucepan, put them away. Then he did exercises he had learned in the Army-straddle jumps, deep knee bends, sit-ups and push-ups. Most Tralfamadorians had no way of knowing Bill's body and face were not beautiful. They supposed that he was a splendid specimen. This had a pleasant effect on Billy, who began to enjoy his body for the first time.

He showered after his exercises and trimmed his toenails. He shaved and sprayed deodorant under his arms, while a zoo guide on a raised platform outside explained what Billy was doing and why. The guide was lecturing telepathically, simply standing there, sending out thought waves to the crowd. On the platform with him was the little keyboard instrument with which he would relay questions to Billy from the crowd.

Now the first question came—from the speaker on the television set: "Are you happy here?"

"About as happy as I was on Earth," said Billy Pilgrim, which was true.

There were fives sexes on Tralfamadore, each of them performing a step necessary in the creation of a new individual. They looked identical to Billy—because their sex differences were all in the fourth dimension.

One of the biggest moral bombshells handed to Billy by the Tralfamadorians, incidentally, had to do with sex on Earth. They said their flying-saucer crews had identified no fewer than seven sexes on Earth, each essential to reproduction. Again: Billy couldn't possibly imagine what five of those seven sexes had to do with the making of a baby, since they were sexually active only in the fourth dimension.

The Tralfamadorians tried to give Billy clues that would help him imagine sex in the invisible dimension. They told him that there could be no Earthling babies without male homosexuals. There could be babies without female homosexuals. There couldn't be babies without women over sixty-five years old. There could be babies without men over sixty-five. There couldn't be babies without other babies who had lived an hour or less after birth. And so on.

It was gibberish to Billy.

There was a lot that Billy said that was gibberish to the Tralfamadorians, too. They couldn't imagine what time looked like to him. Billy had given up on explaining that. The guide outside had to explain as best he could.

The guide invited the crowd to imagine that they were looking across a desert at a mountain range on a day that was twinkling bright and clear. They could look at a peak or a bird or a cloud, at a stone right in front of them, or even down into a canyon behind them. But among them was this poor Earthling, and his head was encased in a steel sphere which he could never take off. There was only one eyehole through which he could look, and welded to that eyehole were six feet of pipe.

This was only the beginning of Billy's miseries in the metaphor. He was also strapped to a steel lattice which was bolted to a flatcar on rails, and there was no way he could turn his head or touch the pipe. The far end of the pipe rested on a bi-pod which was also bolted to the flatcar. All Billy could see was the dot at the end of the pipe. He didn't know he was on a flatcar, didn't even know there was anything peculiar about his situation.

The flatcar sometimes crept, sometimes went extremely fast, often stopped—went uphill, downhill, around curves, along straightaways. Whatever poor Billy saw through the pipe, he had no choice but to say to himself: "That's life."

Billy expected the Tralfamadorians to be baffled and alarmed by all the wars and other forms of murder on Earth. He expected them to fear that the Earthling combination of ferocity and spectacular weaponry might eventually destroy part or maybe all of the innocent Universe. Science fiction had led him to expect that.

But the subject of war never came up until Billy brought it up himself. Somebody in the zoo crowd asked him through the lecturer what the most valuable thing he had learned on Tralfamadore was so far, and Billy replied: "How the inhabitants of a whole planet can live in peace. As you know, I am from a planet that has been engaged in senseless slaughter since the beginning of time. I myself have seen the bodies of schoolgirls who were boiled alive in a water tower by my own countrymen, who were proud of fighting pure evil at the time." This was true. Billy saw the boiled bodies in Dresden. "And I have lit my way in a prison at night with candles from the fat of human beings who were butchered by the brothers and fathers of those school girls who were boiled. Earthlings must be the terrors of the Universe! If other planets aren't now in danger from Earth, they soon will be. So tell me the secret so I can take it back to Earth and save us all: How can a planet live at peace?"

Billy felt that he had spoken soaringly. He was baffled when he saw the Tralfamadorians close their little hands on their eyes. He knew from past experience what this meant: He was being stupid.

"Would—would you mind telling me," he said to the guide, much deflated, "what was so stupid about that?"

"We know how the Universe ends," said the guide, "and Earth has nothing to do with it, except that it gets wiped out, too."

"How—how does the Universe end?" said Billy.

"We blow it up, experimenting with new fuels for our flying saucers. A Tralfamadorian test pilot presses a starter button, and the whole Universe disappears." So it goes.

"If You know this," said Billy, "isn't there some way you can prevent it? Can't you keep the pilot from pressing the button?"

"He has always pressed it, and he always will. We always let him and we always will let him. The moment is structured that way."

"So," said Billy gropingly, "I suppose that the idea of, preventing war on Earth is stupid, too."

"Of course."

"But you do have a peaceful planet here."

"Today we do. On other days we have wars as horrible as any you've ever seen or read about. There isn't anything we can do about them, so we simply don't look at them. We ignore them. We spend eternity looking at pleasant moments—like today at the zoo. Isn't this a nice moment?"

"Yes."

"That's one thing Earthlings might learn to do, if they tried hard enough: Ignore the awful times, and concentrate on the good ones."

"Um," said Billy Pilgrim.

Shortly after he went to sleep that night, Billy traveled in time to another moment which was quite nice, his wedding night with the former Valencia Merble. He had been out of the veterans' hospital for six months. He was all well. He had graduated from the Ilium School of Optometry—third in his class of forty-seven.

[Selected from Kurt Vonnegut. *Slaughterhouse-Five, or The Children's Crusade: A Duty-Dance with Death*. New York: Dell Publishing. Co., 1979.]

Ⅲ. Questions for discussion

(1) How are English prisoners of the war portrayed in this selection? What is the effect of the contrast between the Englishmen and starving, half-dressed and sick Americans?

(2) This novel is cnosidered as an anti-war book. How do the Tralfamadorians and Rosewater view war? What perspective do you think Vonnegut holds?

(3) Support with details from this section that life is meaningless. How might this relate to Billy becoming unstuck in time? How would the Tralfamadorians answer the problem of life having no meaning?

(4) Define your understanding of Vonnegut's term "unstuck in time." Describe how Billy was unstuck in time with specific examples.

(5) Billy is portrayed abnormally detached from reality. Do you think his visit on Tralfamadore is real? What causes Billy's nervous breakdown? Why does science fiction appeal to him and Rosewater?

(6) How are Tralfamadorian books written and laid out? Is there a similarity between the format of Vonnegut's novel and the description of Tralfamadorian novels? Why does Vonnegut write in this style?

(7) Discuss Vonnegut's continuous use of "So it goes." What is his purpose?

3.3 Assigned Reading

The Arbitrary Cycle of *Slaughterhouse-Five*: A Relation of Form to Theme

(An Excerpt)

Wayne D. McGinnis

The poignancy and force of *Slaughterhouse-Five* derive largely from an attitude about art and life that Vonnegut apparently shares with Louis-Ferdinand Celine, whom he quotes in the first chapter as saying two things: "No art is possible without a dance with death" and "the truth is death." Taking *his cue from Celine, Vonnegut calls his novel* A DUTY-DANCE WITH DEATH on the title page. Ultimately, however, *Slaughterhouse-Five* goes beyond the fatalism implied in Celine's statements by stressing survival through the use of the imagination.

Vonnegut has said that the novel "was a therapeutic thing. I'm a different person now. I got rid of a lot of crap." Although strikingly similar to Lawrence's notion that "one sheds one's sicknesses in books," the important thing is to go on, to escape the paralyzing emotional rigidity that can turn one into a pillar of salt. The ability to go on, to escape fixity by motion in time is precisely what *Slaughterhouse-Five* is about, and its success comes from being able to effect a regeneration in reader as well as writer.

In keeping with the theme of regeneration, the form of the novel avoids the climax and denouement typical of linear narration, as indicated by Vonnegut's rejection of the grid-like outline of the story, he proposes in the first chapter, with its climax at Edgar Derby's execution for taking a teapot and its ending in a POW trade made after the destruction of Dresden. Essentially, Vonnegut avoids framing his story in linear narration, choosing a circular structure. Such a view of the art of the novel has much to do with the protagonist of *Slaughterhouse-Five* the author's alter ego, Billy Pilgrim, an optometrist who provides corrective lenses for Earthlings. For Pilgrim, who learns of a new view of life as he becomes "unstuck in time," the lenses are corrective metaphorically as well as physically...

Vonnegut's decision to cast hisDresden experience in a "non-explainable" work of the imagination is a movement away from framing and toward a more unresolved circular structure. Vonnegut supplies strong hints of the circular nature of *Slaughterhouse-Five* in Chapter One. He is reminded, he says, of a particular song when he thinks of "how useless the Dresden part of my memory has been, and yet how tempting Dresden has been to write about":

> My name is Yon Yonson, / I work in Wisconsin, / I work in a lumbermill there. / The people I meet when I walk down the street, / They say, "What's your name?" / And I say, / "my name is Yon Yonson, / I work in Wisconsin..." / And so on to infinity.

The message of the song is that life is cyclical, self-renewable—at least part of the implication of Roethke's "The Waking," the first stanza of which Vonnegut quotes in Chapter One. The paradox of the villanelle is its circularity both in form and content. Vonnegut invokes the same sort of circularity when he begins the fictional part of his novel by writing at the end of the first chapter:

> This book is a failure, and had to be, since it was written by a pillar of salt. It begins like this: Listen: / Billy Pilgrim bas come unstuck in time. / It ends like this: / Poo-tee-weeft.

The rather strange preamble, then, helps to create the essentially cyclical nature of the novel, for here we have beginning and end in one place, the cycle completed in a small space.

The cyclical nature is inextricably bound up with the large themes of *Slaughterhouse-Five*, time, death, and renewal. Once again, the first chapter, the autobiographical one, prepares the reader for the full exploration of these themes in the novel itself. Vonnegut uses Celine to start two of the themes when he writes.... In Celine's novel—and persistently in his other works—time means change and is, obviously, equivalent to death: hence, the title, *Death on the Installment Plan*. What Celine would have as an antidote in the passage Vonnegut quotes is fixity, which would prevent the flow of time and the constant encroachment of death. The agonizing paradox here, of course, is that fixity or rigidity is also associated with death. Lot's wife is punished for looking back on the burning cities of Sodom and Gomorrah with death, the rigidity of a pillar of salt. While Vonnegut loves Lot's wife for looking back "because it was so human," obviously he, like anyone desiring life, wants not to be rigid. Stopping the flow of time is at once a solution and no solution.

The Tralfamadorian answer to the problem is hinted at from the very first page. After telling of the German taxicab driver, Gerhard Mueller, Vonnegut begins what will be a persistent refrain throughout the novel, the phrase "so it goes." The reader does not know until the second chapter, however, that this is what the Tralfamadorians, those mythical creatures who live on a distant planet in Billy Pilgrim's mind, say about dead people. The philosophy of Tralfamadore on time and death, as Billy explains it, is an escape from the concept of linear time, just as their novels are an escape from linear narration.

The Tralfamadorians, then, avoid the "duty-dance with death" by ignoring death as a finality. Their little formula "so it goes," said ritualistically throughout the novel whenever any death, no matter how trivial, is mentioned, is from the human point of view, the height of fatalism. The most important function of "so it goes," however, is its imparting a cyclical quality to the novel, both in form and content. Paradoxically, the expression of fatalism serves as a source of renewal, a situation typical of Vonnegut's works, for it enables the novel to go on despite—even because of the proliferation of deaths. Once again we come upon a paradox:

death keeps life in motion, even the life of the novel, but the movement is essentially unaided in Vonnegut's silent universe. As he emphasizes in *The Sirens of Titan*, beyond man's interior universe is only the emptiness of space eternal. In a world where life must renew itself arbitrarily, the mental construct becomes tremendously important. The phrase "so it goes" is a sign of the human will to survive, and it recurs throughout the novel as an important aid to going on.

Vonnegut's fiction deals heavily with survival by the arbitrary imposition of meaning on meaningless reality, as demonstrated most forcefully in *Cat's Cradle*. Tralfamadore is another mental construct, like Bokononism, that goes beyond the question of true or false. As Eliot Rosewater says in *Slaughterhouse-Five* to the psychiatrists: "I think you guys are going to have to come up with a lot of wonderful new lies, or people just aren't going to want to go on living." The statement is certainly a clue to the meaning of Tralfamadore, since it comes right after the statement that Rosewater and Billy had found life meaningless, partly because of what they had seen in the war: "So they were trying to reinvent themselves and their universe. Science fiction was a big help." Vonnegut lets us know that an act of reinvention is going on within the novel, just as the novel is Vonnegut's own recreation of his past and even of his other novels. Mental constructs like Bokononism and Tralfanmadore, both re-inventive fictions, are models of Vonnegut's own fiction, throughout which one can see the pattern of meaninglessness/reinvention.

That Tralfamadore is ultimately a "supreme fiction," a product of the imagination, and that Vonnegut emphasizes using the imagination as a method of survival are obvious from his preoccupation with the value of works of art, especially in the novels from *Cat's Cradle* on. Especially interesting is Vonnegut's source for his idea of Tralfamadore; evidence shows that, characteristically, Vonnegut was inspired by modern science in creating his fiction. Shortly after *Slaughterhouse-Five* was published, Vonnegut wrote an article in which he quotes from another book arranged along the lines of a trip into space, Guy Murchie's popularization of the great body of science, *Music of the Spheres*. In his article Vonnegut writes, "I had lifted a comment Murchie made about time for a book of my own?" (The book must surely be *Slaughterhouse-Five*.)

Vonnegut, then, is apparently trying to get away from "framing" in

Slaughterhouse-Five by means of circularity. Both the Tralfamadorian concept of time and the Murchie passage from which it is probably lifted imply a kind of cyclical "return," though, of course, Billy Pilgrim's movement in time embodies this return, rather than the Tralfamadorian idea of fixity expressed by the mountain range image....

Time as a circle is eternal, timeless. The location of the circle is in the human mind, which is where Zarathustra's eternal return to the selfsame life ultimately occurs. As Frederick Hoffman has written: "Perhaps the most remarkable of all speculative adventures in the history of man's adjustment to death is his struggle to understand the paradoxical relationship of time to eternity." Circularity is what Billy also affirms when, having "memories of the future," he talks of his own death while preaching his Tralfamadorian gospel: "'If you protest, if you think that death is a terrible thing, then you have not understood a word I've said.' Now he closes his speech as he closes every speech—with these words: 'Farewell, hello, farewell, hello.'" His little ritual manifests the ever present possibility of renewal through the imagination.

The Tralfamadorian concept of time, with the suggestion of cyclical return embodied in Billy's time travels, reflects the fact that timelessness is a product of the irrational, the un-conscious, the imagination itself. Although we might be tempted to see *Slaughterhouse-Five* as a "plotless" novel allied to the stream of consciousness novel, Billy's psyche is not as fully explored as, say, Mrs. Dalloway's or Benjy Compson's, for he is too effaced and manipulated by the author to have the kind of independent being required for the stream of consciousness novel. While *Slaughterhouse-Five* cannot fully employ the stream of consciousness technique because it simply does not deal with the internal psychic processes of a fully developed character, it does make a secondary use of the technique by providing certain signals to help predict time and space shifts in the "durational" world of the novel. Among these images or attitudes are feet of blue and ivory, the black and orange color of a POW train, nestling like spoons, sleeping and waking, and having tears in the eyes. With the use of these signals the reader gets a strong feeling that Billy's time travels are manipulated from outside—by Vonnegut. As the narrator rather mockingly says of Billy's becoming unstuck in time: "He has seen his birth and death many times, he says, and pays random visits to all the events in between. He says. Billy is spastic in time, has no control over where he is going next, and the trips aren't necessarily fun." The idea of being "spastic" captures the immediate quality of Billy's travels in the regenerative cycle.

The novel seems, indeed, allied not so much to stream of consciousness or any novelistic tradition as it is to the Tralfamadorian novel which is invented by Vonnegut-Pilgrim. The Tralfamadorian novel is arranged by space, then, and not by time, a quality that could loosely be called "cinematic." Here again we see that *Slaughterhouse-Five* has at least an affinity with the stream of consciousness novel, which, as Robert Humphrey has noted, often employs cinematic devices, such as montage. Humphrey goes on to explain that the analogy for fictional technique rests in the fact that "montage and the secondary devices have to do with transcending or modifying arbitrary and conventional time and space barriers," and he notes David Daiches' distinction between time-montage (subject remains fixed in space and his consciousness moves in time) and space-montage (time is fixed and the spatial element changes). Montage, then, is one of the things that take the place of plot in the stream of consciousness novel; when viewed from such perspective, *Slaughterhouse-Five* is seen to combine space- and time-montage techniques.

Actually, *Slaughterhouse-Five* is cinematic to a degree, especially in the sense described by Humphrey; it has also been made into a motion picture directed by George Roy Hill and much praised by Vonnegut himself. The montage technique, however, does not fully explain the form of the novel. What is also limiting for the technique—cinematic, kaleidoscopic, or spatial-form—is the fact that at least in reading literature one can never completely experience "the depths of many marvelous moments seen all at one time." Form in literature appears, finally, to be linked with temporality, although attempts have been made to read much modern literature as atemporal. Although Joseph Frank appears to have begun something of a revolution with his ideas of "spatial form," his claim that spatialization in the major works of modern literature "eliminates any feeling of sequence by the very act of juxtaposition" has not gone wholly uncontested.

The rather simple point is that Vonnegut himself cannot really write fully in the Tralfamadorian mode, but Lynen's stress on the sequential nature of literature is relevant to *Slaughterhouse-Five*. The form created in the novel is essentially circular, not spatial or linear; because its "sequence" is that of the circle, *Slaughterhouse-Five* is a novel without climaxes, since its real subject matter and formal arrangement is renewal. In this sense it is like the Tralfamadorian novel, a novel without beginning, middle, and end, without suspense and without a moral. Like the Roethke villanelle, it learns by going where it has to go. While the Tralfamadorian style implies an indirect statement of the novel's aesthetic, the real impression one is left with is based on its form, that of continual self-renewal. That the renewal is arbitrary is the thematic point of the novel, and even the novel's circular form shares the arbitrary quality. Aside from the specific question of how Tralfamadorian *Slaughterhouse-Five* is, its echo of cinematic technique is quite loose and appears especially loose when one considers how closely other novels have reflected their formal references—the echo of the fugue in the Sirens section of *Ulysses* or the echo of musical counterpoint in *Point Counter Point*, for example. The debt of *Slaughterhouse-Five* to cinema is enough to establish a general basis for considering its cinematic technique, but not enough to say that it does more than loosely borrow from the formal pattern that film has to offer the novel. Neither does the form of *Slaughterhouse-Five* share more than a certain affinity with the technique of the stream of consciousness novel. Humphrey states that two of the ways in which stream of consciousness novels supply necessary form or pattern without the help of plot are by the formal patterns of "natural cyclical schemes (seasons, tides, etc.)" and of "theoretical cyclical schemes (musical structures, cycles of history, etc.)." The cyclical scheme of *Slaughterhouse-Five*, however, is "arbitrary" in that its continual self-renewal is essentially unaided by an echo of some general outside form.

What makes self-renewal possible in *Slaughterhouse-Five* is the human imagination, which is what the novel finally celebrates. Many critics have failed to perceive how strongly the novel affirms the value of the mental construct and have attacked it either for urging passivity or being hopelessly ambiguous about the Tralfamadorian ethic—which does, of course, deny free will and support Billy's passivity. Willed action is simply not stressed in Vonnegut's fictional world. In *Breakfast of Champions*, Vonnegut finally stresses that "our awareness is all that is alive and maybe sacred in any of us. Everything else about us is dead machinery." The imagination, then, beholds the immaterial core of every living thing, the "unwavering band of light" that the minimalist artist in that novel paints. Billy Pilgrim is a kind of artist, too, as Howard W. Campbell, Jr., Bokonon, and Eliot Rosewater have been before him. Like Vonnegut's other protagonists-artists, Billy must use an artistic stance to survive in a basically absurd world. As a doer Billy is ineffectual—thus, he simply drives through a burned-out ghetto, for example. Despite his lack of enthusiasm about living, Billy does go on, largely through the aid of his Tralfamadorian fiction. Neither he nor Vonnegut can change the fact of Dresden, but they both can survive it by the use of the imagination.

Finally, the fixity of death at Dresden, which reduces people to "seeming little logs lying around," is overcome in *Slaughterhouse-Five* by the novel's arbitrary cycle. Appropriately, the novel "ends" with a recycling back to the Dresden experience. Billy's liberation from his German captors is described. Vonnegut's "famous Dresden book," then, comes to its open end with the symbol of renewal that had saved the narrator Jonah from suicide in *Cat's Cradle* and had awakened Eliot Rosewater in *God Bless You, Mr. Rosewater* to the potential of living a life of the absurd, the bird that asks, "Poo-tee-weet?" With the faint echo of the cycle of nature, the green and coffin-shaped wagon, we realize that the cycle itself reflects man's own nature as he experiences the regeneration of immortality in his mind. In using the idea of regeneration to integrate both theme and form, Vonnegut has written in *Slaughterhouse-Five* his best and even most hopeful novel to date.

[Selected from Wayne D. McGinnis. The Arbitrary Cycle of *Slaughterhouse-Five*: A Relation of Form to Theme. 1975: 55-67.]

4. John S. Barth

4.1 Presentation Topics

(1) John Barth's literary fiction.

(2) The postmodernist and Metafictive quality of John Barth's works.

(3) John Barth's theoretical ideas in his essays of "The Literature of Exhaustion" and "The Literature of Replenishment."

4.2 Selected Reading

Ⅰ. Central issue of concern

The story examines the art of fiction writing, among other things, and seems to undermine the conventional and predictable nature of fiction.

Ⅱ. Text

Lost in the Funhouse

For whom is the funhouse fun? Perhaps for lovers. For Ambrose it is a *place of fear and confusion*. He has come to the seashore with his family for the holiday, *the occasion of their visit is Independence Day, the most important secular holiday of the United States*. A single straight underline is the manuscript mark for italic type, *which in turn* is the printed equivalent to oral emphasis of words and phrases as well as the customary type for titles of complete works, not to mention. Italics are also employed, in fiction stories especially, for "outside," intrusive, or artificial voices, such as radio announcements, the texts of telegrams and newspaper articles, *et cetera*. They should be used *sparingly*. If passages originally in roman type are italicized by someone repeating them, it's customary to acknowledge the fact. *Italics mine*.

Ambrose was "at that awkward age." His voice came out high-pitched as a child's if he let himself get carried away; to be on the safe side, therefore, he moved and spoke with *deliberate calm and adult gravity*. Talking soberly of unimportant or irrelevant matters and listening consciously to the sound of your own voice are useful habits for maintaining control in this difficult interval. *En route to* Ocean City he sat in the back seat of the family car with his brother Peter, age fifteen, and Magda G—, age fourteen, a pretty girl and exquisite young lady, who lived not far from them on B—Street in the town of D—, Maryland. Initials, blanks, or both were often substituted for proper names in nineteenth century fiction to enhance the *illusion* of reality. It is as if the author felt it necessary to delete the names for reasons of tact or legal liability. Interestingly, as with other aspects of realism, it is an illusion that is being enhanced, by purely artificial means. Is it likely, does it violate the principle of verisimilitude, that a thirteen-year-old boy could make such a sophisticated observation? A girl of fourteen is the *psychological coeval* of a boy of fifteen or sixteen; a thirteen-year-old boy, therefore, even one precocious in some other respects, might be three years *her emotional junior*.

Thrice a year—on Memorial, Independence, and Labor Days—the family visits Ocean City for the afternoon and evening. When Ambrose and Peter's father was at their age, the excursion was made by train, as mentioned in the novel *The 42nd Parallel* by John Dos Passos. Many families from the same neighborhood used to travel together, with dependent relatives and often with Negro servants; schoolfuls of children swarmed through the railway cars; everyone shared everyone else's Maryland fried chicken, Virginia ham, deviled eggs, potato salad, beaten biscuits, iced tea. Nowadays (that is, in 19—, the year of our story) the journey is made by automobile—more comfortably and quickly though without the extra fun though without the *camaraderie of* a general excursion. It's all part of the deterioration of American life, their father declares; Uncle Karl supposes that when the boys take *their* families to Ocean City for the holidays they'll fly in Autogiros. Their mother, sitting in the middle of the front seat like Magda in the second, only with her arms on the seat-back behind the men's shoulders, wouldn't want the good old days back again, the steaming trains and stuffy long dresses; on the other hand, she can do without Autogiros, too, if she has to become a grandmother to fly in them.

Description of physical appearance and mannerisms is one of several standard methods of characterization used by writers of fiction. It is also important to "keep the senses operating"; when a detail from one of the five senses, say visual, is "crossed" with a detail from another, say auditory, the reader's imagination is oriented to the scene, perhaps unconsciously. This procedure may be compared to the way surveyors and navigators determine their positions by two or more compass—bearings, a process known as triangulation. The brown hair on Ambrose's mother's forearms gleamed in the sunlight. Though right-handed, she took her left arm from the seat back to press the dashboard cigar-lighter for Uncle Karl. When the glass bead in its handle glowed red, the lighter was ready for use. The smell of Uncle Karl's cigar—smoke reminded one of. The fragrance of the ocean came strong to the picnic—ground where they always stopped for lunch, two miles inland from Ocean City. Having to pause for a full hour almost within sound of the breakers was difficult for Peter and Ambrose when they were younger; even at their present age it was not easy to keep their anticipation, *stimulated by the briny spume,* from turning into short temper. The Irish author James Joyce, in his unusual novel entitled *Ulysses*, now available in this country, uses the adjectives *snot-green* and *scrotum-tightening* to describe the sea. Visual, auditory, tactile, olfactory, gustatory Peter and Ambrose's father, while steering their black 1936 LaSalle sedan with one hand, could with the other remove the first cigarette from a white pack of Lucky Strikes and, more remarkably, light it with a match forefingered from its book and thumbed against the flint—paper without being detached. The matchbook cover merely advertised U. S. War Bonds and Stamps. A fine metaphor, simile, or other figure of speech, in addition to its obvious "first-order" relevance to the thing it describes, will be seen upon reflection to have a second order of significance: it may be drawn from the *milieu* of the action, for example, or be particularly appropriate to the sensibility of the narrator, even hinting to the reader things of which the narrator is unaware; or it may cast further and subtler lights upon the things it describes, sometimes ironically qualifying the more evident sense of the comparison.

To say that Ambrose's and Peter's mother was *pretty* is to accomplish nothing; the reader may acknowledge the proposition, but his imagination is not engaged. Besides, Magda was also pretty, yet in an altogether different way. Although she lived on B—Street she had very good manners and did better than average in school. Her figure was very well developed for her age. Her right hand lay casually on the plush upholstery of the seat, very near Ambrose's left leg, on which his own hand rested. The space between their legs, between her right and his left leg, was out of the line of sight of anyone sitting on the other side of Magda, as well as anyone glancing into the rear-view mirror. Uncle Karl's face resembled Peter's—rather, vice versa. Both had dark hair and eyes, short husky statures, deep voices. Magda's left hand was probably in a similar position on her left side. The boys' father is difficult to describe; no particular feature of his appearance or manner stood out. He wore glasses and taught English in the T—County High school. Uncle Karl was a masonry contractor.

Although Peter must have known as well as Ambrose that the latter, because of his position in the car, would be first to see the electrical towers of the power plant at V—, the halfway point of their trip, he leaned forward and slightly toward the center of the car and pretended to be looking for them through the flat pinewoods and tuckahoe creeks along the highways. For as long as the boys could remember, "Looking for the Towers" had been a feature of the first half of their excursions to Ocean City, "looking for the standpipe" of the second. Though the game was childish, their mother preserved the tradition of rewarding the first to see the Towers with a candy-bar or piece of fruit. She insisted now that Magda play the game; the prize, she said, was "something hard to get nowadays." Ambrose decided not to join in; he sat far back in his seat. Magda, like Peter, leaned forward. Two sets of straps were discernible through the shoulders of her sundress; the inside right one, a brassiere-strap, was fastened or shortened with a small safety pin. The right armpit of her dress, presumably the left as well, was damp with perspiration. The simple strategy for being first to espy the Towers, which Ambrose had understood by the age of four, was to sit on the right-hand side of the car. Whoever sat there, however, had also to put up with the worst of the sun, and so Ambrose, without mentioning the matter, chose sometimes the one and sometimes the other. Not impossibly Peter had never caught on to the trick, or thought that his brother hadn't simply because Ambrose on occasion preferred shade to a Baby Ruth or tangerine.

The shade-sun situation didn't apply to the front seat, owing to the windshield; if anything the driver got more sun, since the person on the passenger side not only was shadowed below by the door and dashboard but might swing down his sun visor all the way too.

"Is that them?" Magda asked. Ambrose's mother teased the boys for letting Magda win, insinuating that "somebody (had) a girlfriend." Peter and Ambrose's father reached a long thin arm across their mother to butt his cigarette in the dashboard ashtray, under the lighter. The prize this time for seeing the Towers first was a banana. Their mother bestowed it after chiding their father for wasting a half-smoked cigarette when everything was so scarce. Magda, to take the prize, moved her hand from so near Ambrose's that he could have touched it as though accidentally. She offered to share the prize, things like that were so hard to find; but everyone insisted it was hers alone. Ambrose's mother sang an iambic trimeter couplet from a popular song, femininely rhymed:

What's good is in the Army:
What's left will never harm me.

Uncle Karl tapped his cigar-ash out the ventilator window; some particles were sucked by the slipstream back into the car through the rear window on the passenger side. Magda demonstrated her ability to hold a banana in one hand and peel it with her teeth. She still sat forward; Ambrose pushed his glasses back onto the bridge of his nose with his left hand, which he then negligently let fall to the seat cushion immediately behind her. He even permitted the single hair, gold, on the second joint of his thumb to brush the fabric of her skirt. Should she have sat back at that instant, his hand would have been caught under her.

Plush upholstery prickles uncomfortably through gabardine slacks in the July sun. The function of the *beginning* of a story is to introduce the principal characters, establish their initial relationships, set the scene for the main action, expose the background of the situation if necessary, plant motifs and foreshadowings where appropriate, and initiate the first complication or whatever of the "rising action." Actually, if one imagines a story called "The Funhouse," or "Lost in the Funhouse," the details of the drive to Ocean City don't seem especially relevant. The beginning should recount the events between Ambrose's first sight of the funhouse early in the afternoon and his entering it with Magda and Peter in the evening. The *middle* would narrate all relevant events from the time he goes in to the time he loses his way; middles have the double and contradictory function of delaying the climax while at the same time preparing the reader for it and fetching him to it. Then the *ending* would tell what Ambrose does while he's lost, how he finally finds his way out, and what everybody makes of the experience. So far there's been no real dialogue, very little sensory detail, and nothing in the way of a *theme*. And a long time has gone by already without anything happening; it makes a person wonder. We haven't even reached Ocean City yet: we will never get out of the funhouse.

The more closely an author identifies with the narrator, literally or metaphorically, the less advisable it is as a rule to use the first-person narrative viewpoint. Once three years previously the young people *aforementioned* played Niggers and Masters in the backyard; when it was Ambrose's turn to be Master and theirs to be Niggers Peter had to go serve his evening papers; Ambrose was afraid to punish Magda alone, but she led him to the whitewashed Torture Chamber between the woodshed and the privy in the Slaves Quarters; there she knelt sweating among bamboo rakes and dusty Mason jars, pleadingly embraced his knees, and while bees droned in the lattice as if on an ordinary summer afternoon, purchased clemency at a surprising price set by herself. Doubtless she remembered nothing of this event; Ambrose on the other hand seemed unable to forget the least detail of his life. He even recalled how, standing beside himself with awed impersonality in the reeky heat, he'd stared the while at an empty cigar box in which Uncle Karl kept stone-cutting chisels: beneath the words *El Producto*, a laureled, loose-toga'd lady regarded the sea from a marble bench; beside her, forgotten or not yet turned to, was a five-stringed lyre. Her chin reposed on the back of her right hand; her left depended negligently from the bench-arm. The lower half of scene and lady was peeled away; the words EXAMINED BY were inked there into the wood. Nowadays cigar-boxes are made of pasteboard. Ambrose wondered what Magda would have done, Ambrose wondered what Magda would do when she sat back on his hand as he resolved she should. Be angry. Make a teasing joke of it. Give no sign at all. For a long time she leaned forward, playing cow-poker with Peter against Uncle Karl and Mother and watching for the first sign of Ocean City. At nearly the same instant, picnic ground and Ocean City standpipe hove into view; an Amoco filling station on their side of the road cost Mother and Uncle Karl fifty cows and the game; Magda bounced back, clapping her right hand on Mother's right arm; Ambrose moved clear "in the nick of time."

At this rate our hero, at this rate our protagonist will remain in the funhouse forever. Narrative ordinarily consists of alternating dramatization and summarization. One symptom of nervous tension, paradoxically, is repeated and violent yawning; neither Peter nor Magda nor Uncle Karl nor Mother reacted in this manner. Although they were no longer small children, Peter and Ambrose were each given a dollar to spend on boardwalk amusements in addition to what money of their own they'd brought along. Magda too, though she protested she had ample spending money. The boys' mother made a little scene out of distributing the bills; she pretended that her sons and Magda were small children and cautioned them not to spend the sum too quickly or in one place. Magda promised with a merry laugh and, having both hands free, took the bill with her left. Peter laughed also and pledged in a falsetto to be a good boy. His imitation of a child was not clever. The boys' father was tall and thin, balding, fair-complexioned. Assertions of that sort are not effective; the reader may acknowledge the proposition, but we should be much farther along than we are; something has gone wrong; not much of the preliminary rambling seems relevant. Yet everyone begins in the same place; how is it that most go along without difficulty but a few lose their way?

"Stay out from under the boardwalk," Uncle Karl growled from the side of his mouth. The boys' mother pushed his shoulder in *mock annoyance*. They were all standing before Fat May, the Laughing Lady who advertised the funhouse. Larger than life, Fat May mechanically shook, rocked on her heels, slapped her thighs while recorded laughter—uproarious, female—came amplified from a hidden loudspeaker. It chuckled, wheezed, wept; tried in vain to catch its breath; tittered, groaned, exploded raucous and anew. You couldn't hear it without laughing yourself, no matter how you felt. Father came back from talking to a Coast-Guardsman on duty and reported that the surf was spoiled with crude oil from tankers recently torpedoed offshore. Lumps of it, difficult to remove, made tarry tide lines on the beach and stuck on swimmers. Many bathed in the surf nevertheless and came out speckled; others paid to use a municipal pool and only sunbathed on the beach. We would do the latter. We would do the latter. We would do the latter.

Under the boardwalk, cold sand littered with cigar-butts, treasured with cigarette-stubs, Coco-Cola caps, cardboard lollipop-sticks, matchbook-covers warning that A Slip of the Lip Can Sink a Ship, grainy other things. What is the story's point? Ambrose is ill. He perspires in the dark passages, candied apples-on-a-stick, delicious-looking, disappointing to eat. Funhouses need men's and ladies' rooms at intervals. Others perhaps have also vomited in corners and corridors; may even have had bowel movements liable to be stepped in in the dark. The word fuck suggests suction and/or and/or flatulence. Mother and Father; grandmothers and grandfathers on both sides; great-grandmothers and great-grandfathers on four sides, et cetera. Count a generation as thirty years: in approximately the year when Lord Baltimore was granted charter to the province of Maryland by Charles I, five hundred twelve women—English, Welsh, Bavarian, Swiss—of every class and character, received into themselves the penises the intromittent organs of five hundred twelve men, ditto, in every circumstance and posture, to conceive the five hundred twelve ancestors and the two hundred fifty-six ancestors of the et cetera et cetera et cetera et cetera et cetera et cetera et cetera et cetera of the author, of the narrator, of this story, *Lost in the Funhouse*. In alleyways, ditches, canopy beds, pinewoods, bridal suites, ship's cabins, coach-and-fours, coaches and four sultry toolsheds; on the cold sand under boardwalks, littered with El Producto cigar butts, treasured with Lucky Strike cigarette stubs, Coca-Cola caps, gritty turds, cardboard lollipop sticks, matchbook covers warning that A Slip of the Lip Can Sink a Ship. The shluppish whisper, continuous as seawash round the globe, tide like falls and rises with the circuit of dawn and dusk.

Magda's teeth. She was left-handed. Perspiration. They've gone all the way, through, Magda and Peter, they've been waiting for hours with Mother and Uncle Karl while Father searches for his lost son; they draw french-fried potatoes from a paper cup and shake their heads. They've named the children they'll one day have and bring to Ocean City on holidays. Can spermatozoa properly be thought of as male animalcules when there are no female spermatozoa? They grope through hot, dark windings, past Love's Tunnel's fearsome obstacles. Some perhaps lose their way.

Peter suggested then and there that they do the funhouse; he had been through it before, so had Magda, Ambrose hadn't and suggested, his voice cracking on account of Fat May's laughter, that they swim first. All were chuckling, couldn't help it; Ambrose's father, Ambrose's and Peter's father came up grinning like a lunatic with two boxes of syrup-coated popcorn, one for Mother, one for Magda; the men were to help themselves. Ambrose walked on Magda's right; being by nature left-handed, she carried the box in her left hand. Up front the situation was reversed.

"What are you limping for?" Magda inquired of Ambrose. He supposed in a husky tone that his foot had gone to sleep in the car. Her teeth flashed. "Pins and needles?" It was the honeysuckle on the lattice of the former privy that drew the bees, imagine being stung there. How long is this going to take?

The adults decided to forgo the pool; but Uncle Karl insisted they change into swimsuits and do the beach. "He wants to watch the pretty girls," Peter teased, and ducked behind Magda from Uncle Karl's pretended wrath. "You've got all the pretty girls you need right here," Magda declared, and Mother said: "Now that's the gospel truth." Magda scolded Peter, who reached over her shoulder to sneak some popcorn. "Your brother and father aren't getting any," Uncle Karl wondered if they were going to have fireworks that night, what with the shortages. It wasn't the shortages, Mr. M—replied; Ocean City had fireworks from pre-war. But it was too risky on account of the enemy submarines, some people thought.

"Don't seem like Fourth of July without fireworks," said Uncle Karl. The inverted tag in dialogue writing is still considered permissible with proper names or epithets, but sounds old-fashioned with personal pronouns. "We'll have 'em again soon enough," predicted the boys' father. Their mother declared she could do without fireworks: they reminded her too much of the real thing. Their father said all the more reason to shoot off a few now and again. Uncle Karl asked *rhetorically* who needed reminding, just looked at people's hair and skin.

"The oil, yes," said Mrs. M—.

Ambrose had a pain in his stomach and so didn't swim but enjoyed watching the others. He and his father burned red easily. Magda's figure was exceedingly well developed for her age. She too declined to swim, and got mad, and became angry when Peter attempted to drag her into the pool. She always swam, he insisted; what did she mean not swim? Why did a person come to Ocean City?

"Maybe I want to lay here with Ambrose," Magda teased.

Nobody likes a pedant.

"Aha," said Mother. Peter grabbed Magda by one ankle and ordered Ambrose to grab the other. She squealed and rolled over on the beach blanket. Ambrose pretended to help hold her back. Her tan was darker than even Mother's and Peter's. "Help out, Uncle Karl!" Peter cried. Uncle Karl went to seize the other ankle. Inside the top of her swimsuit, however, you could see the line where the sunburn ended and, when she hunched her shoulders and squealed again, one nipple's auburn edge. Mother made them behave themselves. "*You* should certainly know," she said to Uncle Karl, archly, "That when a lady says she doesn't feel like swimming, a gentleman doesn't ask questions." Uncle Karl said excuse *him*; Mother winked at Magda; Ambrose blushed; stupid Peter kept saying "Phooey on *feel like!*" and tugging at Magda's ankle; then even he got the point, and cannon balled with a holler into the pool.

"I swear," Magda said, in mock in *feigned* exasperation.

The diving would make a suitable literary symbol. To go off the high board you had to wait in a line along the poolside and up the ladder. Fellows tickled girls and goosed one another and shouted to the ones at the top to hurry up, or razzed them for belly floppers. Once on the springboard some took a great while posing or clowning or deciding on a dive or getting up their nerve; others ran right off. Especially among the younger fellows the idea was to strike the funniest pose or do the craziest stunt as you fell, a thing that got harder to do as you kept on and kept on. But whether you hollered "*Geronimo!* or *Sieg heil!* ," held your nose or "rode a bicycle," pretended to be shot or did a perfect jackknife or changed your mind halfway down and ended up with nothing, it was over in two seconds, after all that wait. Spring, pose, splash. Spring, neat-o, splash, Spring, aw fooey, splash.

The grown-ups had gone on; Ambrose wanted to converse with Magda; she was remarkably well develcped for her age; it was said that that came from rubbing with a turkish towel, and there were other theories. Ambrose could think of nothing to say except how good a diver Peter was, who was showing off for her benefit. You could pretty well tell by looking at their bathing suits and arm muscles how far along the different fellows were. Ambrose was glad he hadn't gone in swimming, the cold water shrank you up so. Magda pretended to be uninterested in the diving; she probably weighed as much as he did. If you knew your way around in the funhouse like your own bedroom, you could wait until a girl came along and then slip away without ever getting caught, even if her boyfriend was right with her. She'd think *he* did it! It would be better to be the boyfriend, and act outraged, and tear the funhouse apart. Not act; *be.*

"He's a master diver," Ambrose said. In feigned admiration. "You really have to slave away at it to get that good. " What would it matter anyhow if he asked her right out whether she remembered, even teased her with it as Peter would have?

There's no point in going farther; this isn't getting anybody anywhere; they haven't even come to the funhouse yet. Ambrose is off the track, in some new or old part of the place that's not supposed to be used; he strayed into it by some one-in-a-million chance, like the time the roller-coaster car left the tracks in the nineteen-teens against all the laws of physics and sailed over the boardwalk in the dark. And they can't locate him because they don't know where to look. Even the designer and operator have forgotten this other part, that winds around on itself like a whelk shell. That winds around the right part like the snakes on Mercury's caduceus[①]. Some people, perhaps, don't "hit their stride" until their twenties, when the growing-up business is over and women appreciate other things besides wisecracks and teasing and strutting. Peter didn't have one-tenth the imagination *he* had, not one-tenth. Peter did this naming-their-children thing as a joke, making up names like Aloysius and Murgatroyd, but Ambrose knew *exactly* how it would feel to be married and have children of your own, and be a loving husband and father, and go comfortably to work in the mornings and to bed with your wife at night, and wake up with her there. With a breeze coming through the sash and birds and mocking birds singing in the Chinese-cigar trees. His eyes watered, there aren't enough ways to say that. He would be quite famous in his line of work. Whether Magda was his wife or not, one evening when he was wise-lined and gray at the temples he'd smile gravely, at a fashionable dinner party and remind her of his youthful passion. The time they went with his family to Ocean City; the *erotic fantasies* he used to have about her. How long ago it seemed, and childish! Yet tender, too, *n'est-ce pas*[②]? Would she have imagined that the world-famous whatever remembered how many strings were on the lyre on the bench beside the girl on the label of the cigar box he'd stared at in the tool shed at age ten while, she, age eleven. Even then he had felt *wise beyond his years*; he'd stroked her hair and said in his deepest voice and correctest English, as to a dear child: "I shall never forget this moment."

But though he had breathed heavily, groaned as if ecstatic, what he'd really felt throughout was an odd detachment, as though someone else were Master. Strive as he might to be transported, he heard his mind take notes upon the scene: "*This is what they call* passion. *I am experiencing it.*" Many of the digger machines were out of order in the penny arcades and could not be repaired or replaced for the duration. Moreover the prizes, made now in USA, were less interesting than formerly, pasteboard items for the most part, and some of the machines wouldn't work on white pennies. The gypsy fortuneteller machine might

---

① (Greek Mythology) A winged staff with two serpents twined around it, carried by Hermes.

② Isn't it?

have provided a foreshadowing of the climax of this story if Ambrose had operated it. It was even dilapidateder than most: the silver coating was worn off the brown metal handles, the glass windows around the dummy were cracked and taped, her kerchiefs and silks long faded. If a man lived by himself, he could take a department-store mannequin with flexible joints and modify her in certain ways. *However*, by the time he was that old he'd have a real woman. There was a machine that stamped your name around a white-metal coin with a star in the middle: A—. His son would be the second, and when the lad reached thirteen or so he would put a strong arm around his shoulder and tell him calmly: "It is perfectly normal. We have all been through it. It will not last forever." Nobody knew how to be what they were right. He'd smoke a pipe, teach his son how to fish and softcrab, assure him he needn't worry about himself. Magda would certainly give, Magda would certainly yield a great deal of milk, although guilty of occasional solecisms. It don't taste so bad. Suppose the lights came on now!

The day wore on. You think you're yourself, but there are other persons in you. Ambrose gets hard when Ambrose doesn't want to, *and obversely*. Ambrose watches them disagree; Ambrose watches him watch. In the fun-house mirror room you can't see yourself go on forever, because no matter how you stand, your head gets in the way. Even if you had a glass periscope, the image of your eye would cover up the thing you really wanted to see. The police will come; there'll be a story in the papers. That must be where it happened. Unless he can find a surprise exit, an unofficial backdoor or escape hatch opening on an alley, say, and then stroll up to the family in front of the funhouse and ask where everybody's been; *he's* been out of the place for ages. That's just where it happened, in that last lighted room: Peter and Magda found the right exit; he found one that you weren't supposed to find and strayed off into the works somewhere. In a perfect funhouse you'd be able to go only one way, like the divers off the high board; getting lost would be impossible; the doors and halls would work like minnow traps on the valves in veins.

On account of German U-boats, Ocean City was "browned out": streetlights were shaded on the seaward side; shop-windows and boardwalk amusement places were kept dim, not to silhouette tankers and Liberty ships for torpedoing. In a short story about Ocean City, Maryland, during World War Ⅱ, the author could make use of the image of sailors on leave in the penny arcades and shooting galleries, sighting through the crosshairs of toy machine guns at swastika'd[①] subs, while out in the black Atlantic a U-boat skipper squints through his periscope at real ships outlined by the glow of penny arcades. After dinner the family strolled back to the amusement end of the boardwalk. The boys' father had burnt red as always and was masked with Noxzema, a minstrel in reverse. The grown-ups stood at the end of the boardwalk where the Hurricane of '33 had cut an inlet from the ocean to Assawoman Bay.

"Pronounced with a long o," Uncle Karl reminded Magda with a wink. His shirt-sleeves were rolled up; Mother punched his brown biceps with the arrowed heart on it and said his mind was naughty. Fat May's laugh came suddenly from the funhouse, as if she'd just got the joke; the family laughed too at the coincidence. Ambrose went under the boardwalk to search for out-of-town matchbook covers with the aid of his pocket flashlight; he looked out from the edge of the North American continent and wondered how far their laughter carried over the water. Spies in rubber rafts; survivors in lifeboats. If the joke had been beyond his understanding, he could have said: "*The laughter was over his head.*" And let the reader see the serious wordplay on second reading.

He turned the flashlight on and then off at once even before the woman whooped. He sprang away, heart athud, dropping the light. What had the man grunted? Perspiration drenched and chilled him by the time he scrambled up to the family. "See anything?" his father asked. His voice wouldn't come; he shrugged and violently brushed sand from his pants legs.

"Let's ride the old flying horses!" Magda cried. I'll never be an author. It's been forever already, everybody's gone home, Ocean City's deserted, the ghost-crabs are tickling across the beach and down the littered cold streets. And the empty halls of clapboard hotels and abandoned funhouses. A tidal wave; an enemy air raid; a monster-crab swelling like an island from the sea. *The inhabitants fled in terror*. Magda clung to his trouser leg; he alone knew the maze's secret. "He

---

① An ancient cosmic or religious symbol formen by a Greek cross with the ends of the arms bent at right angles in either a clockwise or a counterclockwise direction. Also, the emblem of Nazi Germany, officially adopted in 1935.

gave his life that we might live," said Uncle Karl with a scowl of pain, as he. The fellow's hands had been tattooed; the woman's legs, the woman's fat white legs had. *An astonishing coincidence*. He yearned to tell Peter. He wanted to throw up for excitement. They hadn't even chased him. He wished he were dead.

One possible ending would be to have Ambrose come across another lost person in the dark. They'd match their wits together against the funhouse, struggle like Ulysses past obstacle after obstacle, help and encourage each other. Or a girl. By the time they found the exit they'd be closest friends, sweethearts if it were a girl; they'd know each other's inmost souls, be bound together *by the cement of shared adventure*; then they'd emerge into the light and it would turn out that his friend was a Negro. A blind girl. President Roosevelt's son. Ambrose's former arch-enemy.

Shortly after the mirror-room he'd groped along a musty corridor, his heart already misgiving him at the absence of phosphorescent arrows and other signs. He'd found a crack of light—not a door, it turned out, but a seam between the ply board wall-panels—and squinting up to it, espied a small old man, in appearance not unlike the photographs at home of Ambrose's late grandfather, nodding upon a stool beneath a bare, speckled bulb. A crude panel of toggle-and knife-switches hung beside the open fuse box near his head; elsewhere in the little room were wooden levers and ropes belayed to boat cleats. At the time, Ambrose wasn't lost enough to rap or call; later he couldn't find that crack. Now it seemed to him that he'd possibly dozed off for a few minutes somewhere along the way; certainly he was exhausted from the afternoon's sunshine and the evening's problems; he couldn't be sure he hadn't dreamed part or all of the sight. Had an old black wall fan droned like bumble-bees and shimmied two flypaper streamers? Had the funhouse operator—gentle, somewhat sad and tired-appearing, in expression not unlike the photographs at home of Ambrose's late Uncle Konrad—murmured in his sleep? Is there really such a person as Ambrose, or is he a figment of the author's imagination? Was it Assawoman Bay or Sinepuxent? Are there other errors of fact in this fiction? Was there another sound besides the little slap of thigh on ham, like water sucking at the chine-boards of a skiff?

When you're lost, the smartest thing to do is stay put till you're found hollering if necessary. But to holler guarantees humiliation as well as rescue;

keeping silent permits some saving of face—you can act surprised at the fuss when your rescuers find you and swear you weren't lost, if they do. What's more you might find your own way yet, *however belatedly*.

"Don't tell me your foot's still asleep!" Magda exclaimed as the three young people walked from the inlet to the area set aside for ferris wheels, carrousels, and other carnival rides, they having decided in favor of the vast and ancient merry-go-round instead of the funhouse. What a sentence, everything was wrong from the outset. People don't know what to make of him, he doesn't know what to make of himself, he's only thirteen, *athletically and socially inept*, not astonishingly bright, but there are antennae; he has... some sort of receivers in his head; things speak to him, he understands more than he should, the world winks at him through its objects, grabs grinning at his coat. Everybody else is in on some secret he doesn't know; they've forgotten to tell him. Through simple *procrastination* his mother put off his baptism until this year. Everyone else had it done as a baby; he'd assumed the same of himself, as had his mother, so she claimed, until it was time for him to join Grace Methodist-Protestant and the oversight came out. He was mortified, but pitched sleepless through his private catechizing, intimidated by the ancient mysteries, a thirteen year old would never say that, resolved to experience conversion like St. Augustine. When the water touched his brow and Adam's sin left him, he contrived by a strain like defecation to bring tears into his eyes—but felt nothing. There was some simple, radical difference about him; he hoped it was genius, feared it was madness, devoted himself to amiability and inconspicuousness. Alone on the seawall near his house he was seized by the terrifying transports he'd thought to find in tool shed, in Communion-cup. The grass was alive! The town, the river, himself, were not imaginary; time roared in his ears like wind; the world was *going on*! This part ought to be dramatized. The Irish author James Joyce once wrote. Ambrose M—is going to scream.

There is no *texture of rendered sensory detail*, for one thing. The faded distorting mirrors beside Fat May; the impossibility of choosing a mount when one had but a single ride on the great carrousel; the *vertigo attendant on his recognition* that Ocean City was worn out, the place of fathers and grandfathers, straw-boatered men and parasoled ladies survived by their amusements. Money spent, the three paused at Peter's insistence beside Fat May to watch the girls get their skirts blown up. The object was to tease Magda, who said: "I swear, Peter M—, you've got a one-track mind! Amby and me aren't *interested* in such things." In the tumbling-barrel, too, just inside the Devil's mouth enhance to the funhouse, the girls were upended and their boyfriends and others could see up their dresses if they cared to. Which was the whole point, Ambrose realized. Of the entire funhouse! If you looked around, you noticed that almost all the people on the boardwalk were paired off into Couples except the small children; in a way, that was the whole point of Ocean City! If you had X-ray eyes and could see everything going on at that instant under the boardwalk and in all the hotel rooms and cars and alleyways, you'd realize that all that normally *showed*, like restaurants and dance halls and clothing and test-your-strength machines, was merely preparation and intermission. Fat May screamed.

Because he watched the going-ons from the corner of his eye, it was Ambrose who spied the half-dollar on the boardwalk near the tumbling-barrel. Losers weepers. The first time he'd heard some people moving through a corridor not far away, just after he'd lost sight of the crack of light, he'd decided not to call to them, for fear they'd guess he was scared and poke fun; it sounded like roughnecks; he'd hoped they'd come by and he could follow in the dark without their knowing. Another time he'd heard just one person, unless he imagined it, bumping along as if on the other side of the plywood; perhaps Peter coming back for him, or Father, or Magda lost too. Or the owner and operator of the funhouse. He'd called out once, as though merrily: "Anybody know where the heck we are?" But the query was too stiff, his voice cracked, when the sounds stopped he was terrified: maybe it was a queer who waited for fellows to get lost, or a longhaired filthy monster that lived in some cranny of the funhouse. He stood rigid for hours it seemed like, scarcely respiring. His future was shockingly clear, in outline. He tried holding his breath to the point of unconsciousness. There ought to be a button you could push to end your life absolutely without pain; disappear in a flick, like turning out a light. He would push it instantly! He despised Uncle Karl. But he despised his father too, for not being what he was supposed to be. Perhaps his father hated *his* father, and so on, and his son would hate him, and so on. Instantly!

Naturally he didn't have nerve enough to ask Magda to go through the funhouse with him. With incredible nerve and to everyone's surprise he invited Magda, quietly and politely, to go through the funhouse with him. "I warn you, I've never been through it before," he added, *laughing easily*, "but I reckon we can manage somehow. The important thing to remember, after all, is that it's meant to be a funhouse; that is, a place of amusement. If people really got lost or injured or too badly frightened in it, the owner'd go out of business. There'd even be lawsuits. No character in a work of fiction can make a speech this long without interruption or acknowledgment from the other characters."

Mother teased Uncle Karl: "There's a crowd, I always heard." But actually Ambrose was relieved that Peter now had a quarter too. Nothing was what it looked like. Every instant, under the surface of the Atlantic Ocean, millions of living animals devoured one another. Pilots were falling in flames over Europe; women were being forcibly raped in the South Pacific. His father should have taken him aside and said: "There is a simple secret to getting through the funhouse, as simple as being first to see the Towers. Here it is. Peter does not know it; neither does your Uncle Karl. You and I are different. Not surprisingly, you've often wished you weren't. Don't think I haven't noticed how unhappy your childhood has been! But you'll understand, when I tell you, why it had to be kept secret until now. And you won't regret not being like your brother and your uncle. *On the contrary.*" If you knew all the stories behind all the people on the boardwalk, you'd see that *nothing* was what it looked like. Husbands and wives often hated each other; parents didn't necessarily love their children; et cetera. A child took things for granted because he had nothing to compare his life to and everybody acted as if things were as they should be. Therefore each saw himself as the hero of the story, when the truth might turn out to be that he's the villain, or the coward. And there wasn't one thing you could do about it!

Hunchbacks, fat ladies, fools—that no one chose what he was was unbearable. In the movies he'd meet a beautiful young girl in the funhouse; they'd have hairs-breadth escapes from real dangers; he'd do and say the right things; she also; in the end they'd be lovers; their dialogue lines would match up; he'd be perfectly at ease; she'd not only like him well enough, she'd think he was *marvelous*; she'd lie awake thinking about *him*, instead of vice versa—the way his face looked in different lights and how he stood and exactly what he'd said—and yet that would be only one small episode in his wonderful life, among many many others. Not a *turning point* at all. What had happened in the tool shed was nothing. He hated, he loathed his parents! One reason for not writing a lost-in-the-funhouse story is that either everybody's felt what Ambrose feels, in which case it goes without saying, or else no normal person feels such things, in which case Ambrose is a freak. "Is anything more tiresome, in fiction, than the problems of sensitive adolescents?" And it's all too long and rambling, as if the author. For all a person knows the first time through, the end could be just around any corner; perhaps, *not impossibly* it's been within reach any number of times. On the other hand he may be scarcely past the start, with everything yet to get through, an intolerable idea.

Fill in: His father's raised eyebrows when he announced his decision to do the funhouse with Magda. Ambrose understands now, but didn't then, that his father was wondering whether he knew what the funhouse was for—especially since he didn't object, as he should have, when Peter decided to come along too. The ticket-woman, witchlike, mortifying him when inadvertently he gave her his name-coin instead of the half-dollar, then unkindly calling Magda's attention to the birthmark on his temple: "Watch out for him, girlie, he's a marked man!" She wasn't even cruel, he understood, only vulgar and insensitive. Somewhere in the world there was a young woman with such splendid understanding that she'd see him entirely, like a poem or story, and find his words so valuable after all that when he confessed his apprehensions she would explain why they were in fact the very things that made him precious to her... and to Western Civilization! There was no such girl, the simple truth being. Violent yawns as they approached the mouth. Whispered advice from an old-timer on a bench near the barrel: "Go crabwise and ye'll get an eyeful without upsetting!" Composure vanished at the first pitch: Peter hollered joyously, Magda tumbled, shrieked, clutched her skirt; Ambrose scrambled crabwise, tight-lipped with terror, was soon out, watched his dropped name-coin slide among the couples. Shame-faced he saw that to get through expeditiously was not the point; Peter feigned assistance in order to trip Magda up, shouted "I see Christmas!" when her legs went flying. The old man, his latest betrayer, cackled approval. A dim hall then of black-thread cobwebs and recorded gibber: he took Magda's elbow to steady her against revolving discs set in the slanted floor to throw your feet out from under, and explained to her in a calm, deep voice his theory that each phase of the funhouse was triggered either automatically, by a series of photoelectric devices, or else manually by operators stationed at peepholes. But he lost his voice thrice as the discs unbalanced him; Magda was anyhow squealing; but at one point she clutched him about the waist to keep from falling, and her right cheek pressed for a moment against his belt-buckle. Heroically he drew her up, it was his chance to clutch her close as if for support and say: "I love you." He even put an arm lightly about the small of her back before a sailor-and-girl pitched into them from behind, sorely treading his left big toe and knocking Magda asprawl with them. The sailor's girl was a string-haired hussy with a loud laugh and light blue drawers; Ambrose realized that he wouldn't have said "I love you" anyhow, and was smitten with self-contempt. How much better it would be to be that common sailor! A wiry little Seaman 3rd, the fellow squeezed a girl to each side and stumbled hilarious into the mirror room, closer to Magda in thirty seconds than Ambrose had got in thirteen years. She giggled at something the fellow said to Peter; she drew her hair from her eyes with a movement so womanly it struck Ambrose's heart; Peter's smacking her backside then seemed particularly coarse. But Magda made a pleased indignant face and cried, "All right for *you*, mister!" and pursued Peter into the maze without a backward glance. The sailor followed after, leisurely, drawing his girl against his hip; Ambrose understood not only that they were all so relieved to be rid of his burdensome company that they didn't even notice his absence, but that he himself shared their relief. Stepping from the treacherous passage at last into the mirror-maze, he saw once again, more clearly than ever, how readily he deceived himself into supposing he was a person. He even foresaw, wincing at his dreadful self-knowledge, that he would repeat the deception, at ever-rarer intervals, all his wretched life, so fearful were the alternatives. Fame, madness, suicide; perhaps all three. It's not believable that so young a boy could articulate that reflection, and in fiction the merely true must always yield to the plausible. Yet Ambrose M—understood, as few adults do, that the famous loneliness of the great was no popular myth but a general truth—and moreover, that it was as much cause as effect.

All the preceding except the last few sentences is exposition that should've been done earlier or interspersed with the present action instead of lumped together. No reader would put up with so much with such *prolixity*. It's interesting that Ambrose's father, though presumably an intelligent man (as indicated by his role as grade-school principal), neither encouraged nor discouraged his sons at all in any way—as if he either didn't care about them or cared all right but didn't know how to act. If this fact should contribute to one of them's becoming a celebrated but wretchedly unhappy scientist, was it a good thing or not? He too might someday face the question; it would be useful to know whether it had tortured his father for years, for example, or never once crossed his mind.

In the mirror-maze two important things happened. First, our hero found a name-coin someone else had lost or discarded: *AMBROSE*, suggestive of the famous lightship and of his father's favorite dessert, which his mother prepared on special occasions out of coconut, oranges, grapes, and what else. Second, as he wondered at the endless replication of his image in the mirrors—second, as he *lost himself in the reflection* that the necessity for an observer makes perfect observation impossible, better make him eighteen at least, yet that would render other things unlikely, he heard Peter and Magda chuckling somewhere together in the maze. "Here!" "No, here!" they shouted to each other. Peter said, "Where's Amby?" Magda murmured "Amb?" Peter called, in a pleased, friendly voice. He didn't reply. The truth was, his brother was a *happy-go-lucky* youngster who'd've been better off with a regular brother of his own, but who seldom complained of his lot and was generally cordial. Ambrose's throat ached; there aren't enough different ways to say that. He stood quietly while the two young people giggled and thumped through the glittering maze, hurrah'd their discovery of its exit, cried out in joyful alarm at what next beset them. Then he set his mouth and followed after, as he supposed, took a wrong turn, strayed into the pass *wherein he lingers yet*.

The action of conventional dramatic narrative may be represented by a diagram called *Freitag's Triangle*①:

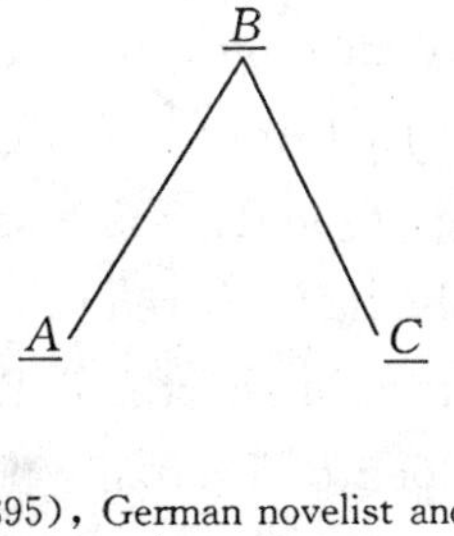

① After Gustave Freytag (1816—1895), German novelist and critic who analyzed dramatic structure in his *Technique of Drama*.

or more accurately by a variant of that diagram:

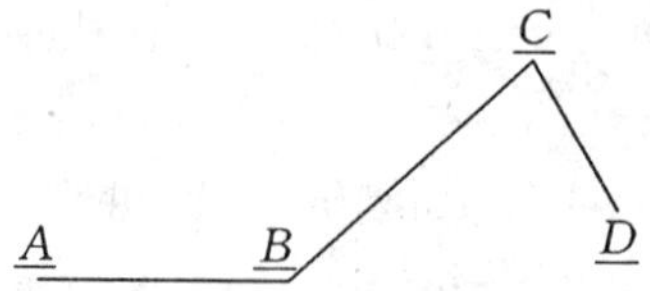

in which AB represents the exposition, B the introduction of conflict, BC the "rising action," complication, or development of the conflict, C the climax, or turn of the action, CD the *dénouement*, or resolution of the conflict. While there is no reason to regard this pattern as an absolute necessity, like many other conventions it became conventional because great numbers of people over many years learned by trial and error that it was effective; one ought not to forsake it, therefore, unless one wishes to forsake as well the effect of drama or has clear cause to feel that deliberate violation of the "normal" pattern can better effect that effect. This can't go on much longer; it can go on forever. He died telling stories to himself in the dark; years later, when that vast unsuspected area of the funhouse came to light, the first expedition found his skeleton in one of its labyrinthine corridors and mistook it for part of the entertainment. He died of starvation telling himself stories in the dark; but unbeknownst to him, an assistant operator of the funhouse, happening to overhear him, crouched just behind the ply board partition and wrote down his every word. The operator's daughter, an exquisite young woman with a figure unusually well developed for her age, crouched just behind the partition and transcribed his every word. Though she had never laid eyes on him, she recognized that here was one of Western Culture's truly great imaginations, the eloquence of whose suffering would be an inspiration to unnumbered. And her heart was torn between her love for the misfortunate young man (yes, she loved him, though she had never laid though she knew him only—but how well! —through his words, and the deep, calm voice in which he spoke them) between her love et cetera and her womanly intuition that only in suffering and isolation could he give voice et cetera. Lone dark dying. Quietly she kissed the rough ply board, and a tear fell upon the page. Where she had written in shorthand *Where she had written in shorthand* Where she had written in shorthand *Where she* et cetera. A long time ago we should have passed the apex of Freitag's Triangle and made brief work of the *dénouement*; the plot doesn't rise by meaningful steps but winds upon itself, digresses, retreats, hesitates, sighs, collapses, expires. The climax of the story must be its protagonist's discovery of a way to get through the funhouse. But he had found none, may have ceased to search.

What relevance does the war have to the story? Should there be fireworks outside or not?

Ambrose wandered, languished, dozed. Now and then he fell into his habit of rehearsing to himself the unadventurous story of his life, narrated from the third-person point of view, from his earliest memory parenthesis of maple leaves stirring in the summer breath of tidewater Maryland end of parenthesis to the present moment. Its principal events, on this telling, would appear to have been *A*, *B*, *C*, and *D*.

He imagined himself years hence, successful, married, at ease in the world, the trials of his adolescence far behind him. He has come to the seashore with his family for the holiday: how Ocean City has changed! But at one seldom at one ill-frequented end of the boardwalk a few derelict amusements survive from times gone by: the great carrousel from the turn of the century, with its monstrous griffins and mechanical concert band; the roller coaster rumored since 1916 to have been condemned; the mechanical shooting gallery in which only the image of our enemies changed: His own son laughs with Fat May and wants to know what a funhouse is; Ambrose hugs the sturdy lad close and smiles around his pipe stem at his wife.

The family's going home. Mother sits between Father and Uncle Karl, who teases him good-naturedly who chuckles over the fact that the comrade with whom he'd fought his way shoulder to shoulder through the funhouse had turned out to be a colored boy to their mutual discomfort, as they'd opened their souls. But such are the walls of custom, which even. Whose arm is there? How must it feel? He dreams of a funhouse vaster by far than any vet constructed; but by then they may be out of fashion, like steamboats and excursion—trains. Already quaint and seedy: the draperied ladies on the frieze of the carrousel are his father's mooncheeked dreams; if he thinks of it more he will vomit his apple-on-a-stick.

He wonders: will he become a regular person? Something has gone wrong; his vaccination didn't take; at the Boy-Scout initiation campfire he only pretended to be deeply moved, as he pretends to this hour that it is not so bad after all in the funhouse, and that he has a little limp. How long will it last? He envisions a truly astonishing funhouse, incredibly complex yet utterly controlled from a great central switchboard like the console of a pipe organ. Nobody had enough imagination. He could design such a place himself, wiring and all, and he's only thirteen years old. He would be its operator: panel lights would show what was up in every cranny of its cunning of its multifarious vastness; a switch-flick would ease this fellow's was, complicate that's, to balance things out; if anyone seemed lost or frightened, all the operator had to do was.

He wishes he had never entered the funhouse. No: he wishes he had never been born. But he was. Then he wishes he were dead. But he's not. Therefore he will construct funhouses for others and be their secret operator—though he would rather be among the lovers for whom funhouses are designed.

[Selected from John Barth. *Lost in the Funhouse*. New York: Anchor, 1988.]

Ⅲ. Questions for discussion

(1) How is the virtual world related to the real world in this story?

(2) What features of metafiction does this story carry?

(3) This story is much devoted to the revelation of Ambrose's consciousness of sex and how to write. What is the relationship between them?

(4) The "funhouse" obviously carries its metaphorical meanings. How to understand it?

(5) What is the symbolic meaning of the fact that Ambrose is left alone in the end of the story?

(6) Do you think the author tried to demonstrate the exhaustion of literature while replenishing it in this very story? If yes, how?

4.3 Assigned Reading

"Lost in the Funhouse": Overview

Dennis Vannatta

John Barth is no doubt best known as a novelist, but his one collection of short stories, "Lost in the Funhouse: Fiction for Print, Tape, Live Voice," is so startling in its virtuosity that Barth's place in the history of short fiction is also assured.

"Lost in the Funhouse" is the pivotal story in a collection of related fictions that trace the conception, youth, maturity, decline, and renewal of not only a writer (Ambrose) but also life and fiction in general. In "Lost in the Funhouse," Ambrose travels to an amusement park on the Maryland shore with his parents, brother Peter, and Peter's girlfriend Magda. As the title suggests, Ambrose gets lost in the funhouse. More important, by the end he realizes the direction he will henceforth take in reference to art (being a writer) and life (specifically in terms of sex and love). The tragic implications are felt through the realization that the choice between art and life of necessity excludes thereafter the one not chosen. Ambrose, a good deal reluctantly, chooses art.

The story is an example of metafiction—as are most others in the collection—because it is not only about Ambrose's trip to the park but also about writing a story about Ambrose's trip to the park. The narrator (Barth? An older Ambrose?) frequently steps in and comments on the writing strategy he is at that moment using. For example, after the introductory section the narrator observes, "The function of the beginning of a story is to introduce the principal characters, establish their initial relationships, set the scene for the main action," etc. The narrator seems to be trying not so much to instruct his reader but to keep straight in his own mind what he should be doing. Indeed, the narrator is having as much trouble with his story as Ambrose is with puberty. At the end of the same paragraph in which the narrator summarizes the purposes of the beginning, he suddenly realizes that he is five pages into his story without having gotten past the beginning: "And a long time has gone by already without anything happening; it makes a person wonder. We haven't even reached ocean city yet: we will never get out of the funhouse."

Already we can see the funhouse taking on at least two connotations. It is the physical structure in which Ambrose gets lost; it is also the story that we are reading and with which the narrator is struggling, constantly getting bogged down or lost, introducing events out of sequence, jumping ahead to the funhouse before the family even reaches the park, offering more than one ending, and so on.

The funhouse is also sex and love, as the opening lines suggest: "For whom is the funhouse fun? Perhaps for lovers. For Ambrose it is a place of fear and confusion" (emphasis Barth's). Why cannot Ambrose simply relax and have fun? For one thing, Ambrose is just entering adolescence, and the funhouse has clear sexual connotations for him and the narrator (a confused adolescent of a writer): "If you knew your way around in the funhouse like your own bedroom, you could wait until a girl came along and then slip away without ever getting caught, even if her boyfriend was right with her. She'd think he did it! It would be better to be the boyfriend, and act outraged, and tear the funhouse apart ... Not act; be." The direction the thought takes in this passage is from furtiveness (the phantom molester) and dissimilation (act outraged) to actual passion (be outraged). It is a path Ambrose would like to take, but cannot.

His problem is not simply that he is an adolescent, typically confused about sex and wary of the future, but that he is a budding writer, a calling that will set him apart from life-beyond-art. His recollection of an earlier sex game with Magda indicates his problem. He recalls during the sex act, "standing beside himself with awed impersonality"; and recalling the same scene later in the story: "But though he'd breathed heavily, groaned as if ecstatic, what he'd really felt throughout was an odd detachment, as though someone else were Master. Strive as he might to be transported, he heard his mind take notes upon the scene: This is what they call passion. I am experiencing it." What Ambrose is already doing, obviously, is distancing himself from experience, taking notes, preparing to write. Later, fantasizing about finding his great love, he imagines her as someone who will appreciate him as a writer.

The end of the story finds Ambrose lost in the funhouse of fiction, committed to it, but committed with a sense of resignation and loss: "He wishes he had never entered the funhouse. But he has. Then he wishes he were dead. But he's not. Therefore he will construct funhouses for others and be their secret operator—though he'd rather be among the lovers for whom funhouses are designed."

One of the most provocative short stories of the post-World War Ⅱ period, "Lost in the Funhouse" shows Barth at the top of his form: as a great innovator whose fictions would be worth the reader's time for their technical virtuosity alone but also as a writer with a profound grasp of the human spirit in conflict with itself, its world, and its art.

[Selected from Dennis Vannatta. Lost in the Funhouse: Overview. *Reference Guide to Short Fiction*. Noelle Watson, (ed.). Detroit: St. James Press, 1994.]

5. Don DeLillo

5.1 Presentation Topics

(1) Avant-Pop Art.

(2) Jean Baudrillard's notion of simulacra.

(3) Don DeLillo's writing career.

5.2 Selected-Reading

Ⅰ. Central issue of concern

Don DeLillo's concern about rampant consumerism and media saturation during the late 20th century.

Ⅱ. Text

White Noise

(An Excerpt)

(*White Noise* is the eighth novel by Don DeLillo. Published in 1985, it won the writer the National Book Award and a wide acclaim. Set at bucolic midwestern college named The-College-on-the-Hill, the novel follows the life of Jack Gladney's. The first part from Chapter 1 to 20, entitled as "Waves and Radiation," is of little plot and describes a variety of daily tasks of the family. Chapter 21 "The Airborne Toxic Event" focuses on the mortality of the characters after a chemical spill from a rail car. And then in the third part "Dylarama," Jack discovers that his wife has been cheating on him for experimental pills to block out her fear of death. In the process of Jack's killing the drug inventor, the novel ends with a meditation of death. Being a typical postmodern fiction, White Noise explores several themes of American magic and dread.)

9

They had to evacuate the grade school on Tuesday. Kids were getting headaches and eye irritations, tasting metal in their mouths. A teacher rolled on the floor and spoke foreign languages. No one knew what was wrong. Investigators said it could be the ventilating system, the paint or varnish, the foam insulation, the electrical insulation, the cafeteria food, the rays emitted by microcomputers, the asbestos fireproofing, the adhesive on shipping containers, the fumes from the chlorinated pool, or perhaps something deeper, finer-grained, more closely woven into the basic state of things.

Denise and Steffie stayed home that week as men in Mylex suits and respirator masks made systematic sweeps of the building with infrared detecting and measuring equipment. Because Mylex is itself a suspect material, the results tended to be ambiguous and a second round of more rigorous detection had to be scheduled.

The two girls and Babette, Wilder and I went to the supermarket. Minutes after we entered, we ran into Murray. This was the fourth or fifth time I'd seen him in the supermarket, which was roughly the number of times I'd seen him on campus. He clutched Babette by the left bicep and sidled around her, appearing to smell her hair.

"A lovely dinner," he said, standing directly behind her. "I like to cook myself, which doubles my appreciation of someone who does it well."

"Come any time," she said, turning in an effort to find him.

We moved together into the ultra-cool interior. Wilder sat in the shopping cart trying to grab items off the shelves as we went by. It occurred to me that he was too old and too big to be sitting in supermarket carts. I also wondered why his vocabulary seemed to be stalled at twenty-five words.

"I'm happy to be here," Murray said.

"In Blacksmith?"

"In Blacksmith, in the supermarket, in the rooming house, on the Hill. I feel I'm learning important things every day. Death, disease, afterlife, outer space. It's all much clearer here. I can think and see."

We moved into the generic food area and Murray paused with his plastic basket to probe among the white cartons and jars. I wasn't sure I understood what he was talking about. What did he mean, much clearer? He could think and see what?

Steffie took my hand and we walked past the fruit bins, an area that extended about forty-five yards along one wall. The bins were arranged diagonally and backed by mirrors that people accidentally punched when reaching for fruit in the upper rows. A voice on the loudspeaker said: "Kleenex Softique, your truck's blocking the entrance." Apples and lemons tumbled in twos and threes to the floor when someone took a fruit from certain places in the stacked array. There were six kinds of apples, there were exotic melons in several pastels. Everything seemed to be in season, sprayed, burnished, bright. People tore filmy bags off racks and tried to figure out which end opened. I realized the place was awash in noise. The toneless systems, the jangle and skid of carts, the loudspeaker and coffee-making machines, the cries of children. And over it all, or under it all, a dull and unlocatable roar, as of some form of swarming life just outside the range of human apprehension.

"Did you tell Denise you were sorry?"

"Maybe later," Steffie said. "Remind me."

"She's a sweet girl and she wants to be your older sister and your friend if you'll let her."

"I don't know about friend. She's a little bossy, don't you think?"

"Aside from telling her you're sorry, be sure to give her back her *Physicians' Desk Reference*①."

"She reads that thing all the time. Don't you think that's weird?"

"At least she reads something."

"Sure, lists of drugs and medicines. And do you want to know why?"

"Why?"

"Because she's trying to find out the side effects of the stuff that Baba uses."

"What does Baba use?"

"Don't ask me. Ask Denise."

"How do you know she uses anything?"

"Ask Denise."

"Why don't I ask Baba?"

"Ask Baba," she said.

Murray came out of an aisle and walked alongside Babette, just ahead of us. He took a twin roll of paper towels out of her cart and smelled it. Denise had found

---

① A commercially published compilation of manufacturers' prescribing information on prescription drugs, updated annually.

some friends and they went up front to look at the paperback books in spindly racks, the books with shiny metallic print, raised letters, vivid illustrations of cult violence and windswept romance. Denise was wearing a green visor. I heard Babette tell Murray she'd been wearing it fourteen hours a day for three weeks now. She would not go out without it, would not even leave her room. She wore it in school, when there was school, wore it to the toilet, the dentist's chair, the dinner table. Something about the visor seemed to speak to her, to offer wholeness and identity.

"It's her interface with the world," Murray said.

He helped Babette push her loaded cart. I heard him say to her, "Tibetans believe there is a transitional state between death and rebirth. Death is a waiting period, basically. Soon a fresh womb will receive the soul. In the meantime the soul restores to itself some of the divinity lost at birth." He studied her profile as if to detect a reaction. "That's what I think of whenever I come in here. This place recharges us spiritually, it prepares us, it's a gateway or pathway. Look how bright. It's full of psychic data."

My wife smiled at him.

"Everything is concealed in symbolism, hidden by veils of mystery and layers of cultural material. But it is psychic data, absolutely. The large doors slide open, they close unbidden. Energy waves, incident radiation. All the letters and numbers are here, all the colors of the spectrum, all the voices and sounds, all the code words and ceremonial phrases. It is just a question of deciphering, rearranging, peeling off the layers of unspeakability. Not that we would want to, not that any useful purpose would be served. This is not Tibet. Even Tibet is not Tibet anymore."

He studied her profile. She put some yogurt in her cart.

"Tibetans try to see death for what it is. It is the end of attachment to things. This simple truth is hard to fathom. But once we stop denying death, we can proceed calmly to die and then go on to experience uterine rebirth or Judeo-Christian afterlife or out-of-body experience or a trip on a UFO or whatever we wish to call it. We can do so with clear vision, without awe or terror. We don't have to cling to life artificially, or to death for that matter. We simply walk toward the sliding doors. Waves and radiation. Look how well-lighted everything is. The place is sealed off, self-contained. It is timeless. Another reason why I think of Tibet. Dying is an art in Tibet. A priest walks in, sits down, tells the weeping relatives to get out and has the room sealed. Doors, windows sealed. He has serious business to see to. Chants, numerology, horoscopes, recitations. Here we don't die, we shop. But the difference is less marked than you think."

He was almost whispering now and I tried to get up closer without ramming my cart into Babette's. I wanted to hear everything.

"Supermarkets of this large and clean and modern are a revelation to me. I spent my life in small steamy delicatessens with slanted display cabinets full of trays that hold soft wet lumpy matter in pale colors. High enough cabinets so you had to stand on tiptoes to give your order. Shouts, accents. In cities no one notices specific dying. Dying is a quality of the air. It's everywhere and nowhere. Men shout as they die, to be noticed, remembered for a second or two. To die in an apartment instead of a house can depress the soul, I would imagine, for several lives to come. In a town there are houses, plants in bay windows. People notice dying better. The dead have faces, automobiles. If you don't know a name, you know a street name, a dog's name. 'He drove an orange Mazda.'"

"You know a couple of useless things about a person that become major facts of identification and cosmic placement when he dies suddenly, after a short illness, in his own bed, with a comforter and matching pillows, on a rainy Wednesday afternoon, feverish, a little congested in the sinuses and chest, thinking about his dry cleaning."

Babette said, "where is Wilder?" and turned to stare at me in a way that suggested ten minutes had passed since she'd last seen him. Other looks, less pensive and less guilty, indicated greater time spans, deeper seas of inattention. Like: "I didn't know whales were mammals." The greater the time span, the blanker the look, the more dangerous the situation. It was as if guilt were a luxury she allowed herself only when the danger was minimal.

"How could he get out of the cart without my noticing?"

The three adults each stood at the head of an aisle and peered into the traffic of carts and gliding bodies. Then we did three more aisles, heads set forward, weaving slightly as we changed our sightlines. I kept seeing colored spots off to the right but when I turned there was nothing there. I'd been seeing colored spots for years but never so many, so gaily animated. Murray saw Wilder in another woman's cart. The woman waved at Babette and headed toward us. She lived on our street with a teenage daughter and an Asian baby, Chun Duc. Everyone referred to the baby by name, almost in a tone of proud proprietorship, but no one knew who Chun belonged to or where he or she had come from.

"Kleenex Softique, Kleenex Softique①."

Steffie was holding my hand in a way I'd come to realize, over a period of time, was not meant to be gently possessive, as I'd thought at first, but reassuring. I was a little astonished. A firm grip that would help me restore confidence in myself, keep me from becoming resigned to whatever melancholy moods she thought she detected hovering about my person.

Before Murray went to the express line he invited us to dinner, a week from Saturday.

"You don't have to let me know till the last minute."

"We'll be there," Babette said.

"I'm not preparing anything major, so just call beforehand and tell me if something else came up. You don't even have to call. If you don't show up, I'll know that something came up and you couldn't let me know."

"Murray, we'll be there."

"Bring the kids."

"No."

"Great. But if you decide to bring them, no problem. I don't want you to feel I'm holding you to something. Don't feel you've made an ironclad commitment. You'll show up or you won't. I have to eat anyway, so there's no major catastrophe if something comes up and you have to cancel. I just want you to know I'll be there if you decide to drop by, with or without kids. We have till next May or June to do this thing so there's no special mystique about a week from Saturday."

"Are you coming back next semester?" I said.

"They want me to teach a course in the cinema of car crashes."

"Do it."

"I will."

---

① The brand of tissues.

I rubbed against Babette in the checkout line. She backed into me and I reached around her and put my hands on her breasts. She rotated her hips and I nuzzled her hair and murmured, "Dirty blond." People wrote checks, tall boys bagged the merchandise. Not everyone spoke English at the cash terminals, or near the fruit bins and frozen foods, or out among the cars in the lot. More and more I heard languages I could not identify much less understand, although the tall boys were American-born and the checkout women as well, short, fattish in blue tunics, wearing stretch slacks and tiny white espadrilles. I tried to fit my hands into Babette's skirt, over her belly, as the slowly moving line edged toward the last purchase point, the breath mints and nasal inhalers.

It was out in the parking lot that we heard the first of the rumors about a man dying during the inspection of the grade school, one of the masked and Mylex-suited men, heavy-booted and bulky. Collapsed and died, went the story that was going around, in a classroom on the second floor.

10

Tuition at the College-on-the-Hill is fourteen thousand dollars, Sunday brunch included. I sense there is a connection between this powerful number and the way the students arrange themselves physically in the reading areas of the library. They sit on broad cushioned seats in various kinds of ungainly posture, clearly calculated to be the identifying signs of some kinship group or secret organization. They are fetal, splayed, knock-kneed, arched, square-knotted, sometimes almost upside-down. The positions are so studied they amount to a classical mime. There is an element of overrefinement and inbreeding. Sometimes I feel I've wandered into a Far Eastern dream, too remote to be interpreted. But it is only the language of economic class they are speaking, in one of its allowable outward forms, like the convocation of station wagons at the start of the year.

Denise watched her mother pull the little cellophane ribbon on a bonus pack of sixteen individually wrapped units of chewing gum. Her eyes narrowed as she turned back to the address books on the kitchen table before her. The eleven-year-old face was an expert mask of restrained exasperation.

She waited a long moment, then said evenly, "That stuff causes cancer in laboratory animals in case you didn't know."

"You wanted me to chew sugarless gum, Denise. It was your idea."

"There was no warning on the pack then. They put a warning, which I would have a hard time believing you didn't see."

She was transcribing names and phone numbers from an old book to a new one. There were no addresses. Her friends had phone numbers only, a race of people with a seven-bit analog consciousness.

"I'm happy to do it either way," Babette said. "It's totally up to you. Either I chew gum with sugar and artificial coloring or I chew sugarless and colorless gum that's harmful to rats."

Steffie got off the phone. "Don't chew at all," she said. "Did you ever think of that?"

Babette was breaking eggs into a wooden salad bowl. She gave me a look that wondered how the girl could talk on the phone and listen to us at the same time. I wanted to say because she finds us interesting.

Babette said to the girls, "Look, either I chew gum or I smoke. If you want me to start smoking again, take away my chewing gum and my Mentho-Lyptus①."

"Why do you have to do one or the other?" Steffie said. "Why not do neither one?"

"Why not do both?" Denise said, the face carefully emptying itself of expression. "That's what you want, isn't it? We all get to do what we want, don't we? Except if we want to go to school tomorrow we can't because they're fumigating the place or whatever."

The phone rang; Steffie grabbed it.

"I'm not a criminal," Babette said. "All I want to do is chew a pathetic little tasteless chunk of gum now and then."

"Well it's not that simple," Denise said.

"It's not a crime either. I chew about two of those little chunks a day."

"Well you can't anymore."

"Well I can, Denise. I want to. Chewing happens to relax me. You're making a fuss over nothing."

Steffie managed to get our attention by the sheer pleading force of the look on her face. Her hand was over the mouthpiece of the phone. She did not speak but

---

① The brand for cough drops.

only formed the words.

The Stovers wanted to come over.

"Parents or children?" Babette said.

My daughter shrugged.

"We don't want them," Babette said.

"Keep them out," Denise said.

"What do I say?"

"Say anything you want."

"Just keep them out of here."

"They're boring."

"Tell them to stay home."

Steffie retreated with the phone, appearing to shield it with her body, her eyes full of fear and excitement.

"A little gum can't possibly hurt," Babette said.

"I guess you're right. Never mind. Just a warning on the pack."

Steffie hung up. "Just hazardous to your health," she said.

"Just rats," Denise said. "I guess you're right. Never mind."

"Maybe she thinks they died in their sleep."

"Just useless rodents, so what's the difference?"

"What's the difference, what's the fuss?" Steffie said.

"Plus I'd like to believe she chews only two pieces a day, the way she forgets things."

"What do I forget?" Babette said.

"It's all right," Denise said. "Never mind."

"What do I forget?"

"Go ahead and chew. Never mind the warning. I don't care."

I scooped Wilder off a chair and gave him a noisy kiss on the ear and he shrank away in delight. Then I put him on the counter and went upstairs to find Heinrich. He was in his room studying the deployment of plastic chessmen.

"Still playing with the fellow in prison? How's it going?"

"Pretty good. I think I got him cornered."

"What do you know about this fellow? I've been meaning to ask."

"Like who did he kill? That's the big thing today. Concern for the victim."

"You've been playing chess with the man for months. What do you know about him except that he's in jail for life, for murder? Is he young, old, black, white? Do you communicate at all except for chess moves?"

"We send notes sometimes."

"Who did he kill?"

"He was under pressure."

"And what happened?"

"It kept building and building."

"So he went out and shot someone. Who did he shoot?"

"Some people in Iron City."

"How many?"

"Five."

"Five people."

"Not counting the state trooper, which was later."

"Six people. Did he care for his weapons obsessively? Did he have an arsenal stashed in his shabby little room off a six-story concrete car park?"

"Some handguns and a bolt-action rifle with a scope."

"A telescopic sight. Did he fire from a highway overpass, a rented room? Did he walk into a bar, a washette, his former place of employment and start firing indiscriminately? People scattering, taking cover under tables. People out on the street thinking they heard firecrackers. 'I was just waiting for the bus when I heard this little popping noise like firecrackers going off.'"

"He went up to a roof."

"A rooftop sniper. Did he write in his diary before he went up to the roof? Did he make tapes of his voice, go to the movies, read books about other mass murderers to refresh his memory?"

"Made tapes."

"Made tapes. What did he do with them?"

"Sent them to people he loved, asking for forgiveness."

"'I can't help myself, folks.' Were the victims total strangers? Was it a grudge killing? Did he get fired from his job? Had he been hearing voices?"

"Total strangers."

"Had he been hearing voices?"

"On TV."

"Talking just to him? Singling him out?"

"Telling him to go down in history. He was twenty-seven, out of work, divorced, with his car up on blocks. Time was running out on him."

"Insistent pressuring voices. How did he deal with the media? Give lots of interviews, write letters to the editor of the local paper, try to make a book deal?"

"There is no media in Iron City. He didn't think of that till it was too late. He says if he had to do it all over again, he wouldn't do it as an ordinary murder, he would do it as an assassination."

"He would select more carefully, kill one famous person, get noticed, make it stick."

"He now knows he won't go down in history."

"Neither will I."

"But you've got Hitler."

"Yes, I have, haven't I?"

"What's Tommy Roy Foster got?"

"All right, he's told you all these things in the letters he sends. What do you say when you respond?"

"I'm losing my hair."

I looked at him. He wore a warmup suit, a towel around his neck, sweatbands on both wrists.

"You know what your mother would say about this chess by mail relationship."

"I know what you would say. You're saying it."

"How is your mother? Hear from her lately?"

"She wants me to go out to the ashram this summer."

"Do you want to go?"

"Who knows what I want to do? Who knows what anyone wants to do? How can you be sure about something like that? Isn't it all a question of brain chemistry, signals going back and forth, electrical energy in the cortex? How do you know whether something is really what you want to do or just some kind of nerve impulse in the brain? Some minor little activity takes place somewhere in this unimportant place in one of the brain hemispheres and suddenly I want to go to Montana or I don't want to go to Montana. How do I know I really want to go and it isn't just some neurons firing or something? Maybe it's just an accidental flash in the medulla and suddenly there I am in Montana and I find out I really didn't want to go there in the first place. I can't control what happens in my brain, so how can I be sure what I want to do ten seconds from now, much less Montana next summer? It's all this activity in the brain and you don't know what's you as a person and what's some neuron that just happens to fire or just happens to misfire. Isn't that why Tommy Roy killed those people?"

In the morning I walked to the bank. I went to the automated teller machine to check my balance. I inserted my card, entered my secret code, tapped out my request. The figure on the screen roughly corresponded to my independent estimate, feebly arrived at after long searches through documents, tormented arithmetic. Waves of relief and gratitude flowed over me. The system had blessed my life. I felt its support and approval. The system hardware, the mainframe sitting in a locked room in some distant city. What a pleasing interaction. I sensed that something of deep personal value, but not money, not that at all, had been authenticated and confirmed. A deranged person was escorted from the bank by two armed guards. The system was invisible, which made it all the more impressive, all the more disquieting to deal with. But we were in accord, at least for now. The networks, the circuits, the streams, the harmonies.

11

I woke in the grip of a death sweat. Defenseless against my own racking fears. A pause at the center of my being. I lacked the will and physical strength to get out of bed and move through the dark house, clutching walls and stair rails. To feel my way, reinhabit my body, re-enter the world. Sweat trickled down my ribs. The digital reading on the clock-radio was 3:51. Always odd numbers at times like this. What does it mean? Is death odd-numbered? Are there life-enhancing numbers, other numbers charged with menace? Babette murmured in her sleep and I moved close, breathing her heat.

Finally I slept, to be awakened by the smell of burning toast. That would be Steffie. She burns toast often, at any hour, intentionally. She loves the smell, she is addicted; it's her treasured scent. It satisfies her in ways wood smoke cannot, or snuffed candles, or the odor of explosive powder drifting down the street from firecrackers set off on the Fourth. She has evolved orders of preference. Burnt rye, burnt white, so on.

I put on my robe and went downstairs. I was always putting on a bathrobe and going somewhere to talk seriously to a child. Babette was with her in the kitchen. It startled me. I thought she was still in bed.

"Want some toast?" Steffie said.

"I'll be fifty-one next week."

"That's not old, is it?"

"I've felt the same for twenty-five years."

"Bad. How old is my mother?"

"She's still young. She was only twenty when we were married the first time."

"Is she younger than Baba?"

"About the same. Just so you don't think I'm one of those men who keeps finding younger women."

I wasn't sure whether my replies were meant for Steffie or Babette. This happens in the kitchen, where the levels of data are numerous and deep, as Murray might say.

"Is she still in the CIA?" Steffie said.

"We're not supposed to talk about that. She's just a contract agent anyway."

"What's that?"

"That's what people do today for a second income."

"What exactly does she do?" Babette said.

"She gets a phone call from Brazil. That activates her."

"Then what?"

"She carries money in a suitcase the length and breadth of Latin America."

"That's all? I could do that."

"Sometimes they send her books to review."

"Have I met her?" Babette said.

"No."

"Do I know her name?"

"Dana Breedlove."

Steffie's lips formed the words as I spoke them.

"You're not planning to eat that, are you?" I said to her.

"I always eat my toast."

The phone rang and I picked it up. A woman's voice delivered a high-performance hello. It said it was computer-generated, part of a marketing survey aimed at determining current levels of consumer desire. It said it would ask a series of questions, pausing after each to give me a chance to reply.

I gave the phone to Steffie. When it became clear that she was occupied with the synthesized voice, I spoke to Babette in low tones.

"She liked to plot."

"Who?"

"Dana. She liked to get me involved in things."

"What kind of things?"

"Factions. Playing certain friends against other friends. Household plots, faculty plots."

"Sounds like ordinary stuff."

"She spoke English to me, Spanish or Portuguese to the telephone."

Steffie twisted around, used her free hand to pull her sweater away from her body, enabling her to read the label.

"Virgin acrylic," she said into the phone.

Babette checked the label on her sweater. A soft rain began to fall.

"How does it feel being nearly fifty-one?" she said.

"No different from fifty."

"Except one is even, one is odd," she pointed out.

That night, in Murray's off-white room, after a spectacular meal of Cornish hen in the shape of a frog, prepared on a two-burner hot plate, we moved from our metal folding chairs to the bunk bed for coffee.

"When I was a sportswriter," Murray said, "I traveled constantly, lived in planes and hotels and stadium smoke, never got to feel at home in my own apartment. Now I have a place."

"You've done wonders," Babette said, her gaze sweeping desperately across the room.

"It's small, it's dark, it's plain," he said in a self-satisfied way. "A container for thought."

I gestured toward the old four-story building on several acres across the street.

"Do you get any noise from the insane asylum?"

"You mean beatings and shrieks? It's interesting that people still call it the insane asylum. It must be the striking architecture, the high steep roof, the tall chimneys, the columns, the little flourishes here and there that are either quaint or sinister—I can't make up my mind. It doesn't look like a rest home or psychiatric facility. It looks like an insane asylum."

His trousers were going shiny at the knees.

"I'm sorry you didn't bring the kids. I want to get to know small kids. This is the society of kids. I tell my students they're already too old to figure importantly in the making of society. Minute by minute they're beginning to diverge from each other. 'Even as we sit here,' I tell them, 'you are spinning out from the core, becoming less recognizable as a group, less targetable by advertisers and mass-producers of culture. Kids are a true universal. But you're well beyond that, already beginning to drift, to feel estranged from the products you consume. Who are they designed for? What is your place in the marketing scheme? Once you're out of school, it is only a matter of time before you experience the vast loneliness and dissatisfaction of consumers who have lost their group identity.' Then I tap my pencil on the table to indicate time passing ominously."

Because we were seated on the bed, Murray had to lean well forward, looking past the coffee cup poised in my hand, in order to address Babette.

"How many children do you have, all told?"

She appeared to pause.

"There's Wilder, of course. There's Denise."

Murray sipped his coffee, trying to look at her, sideways, with the cup at his lower lip.

"There's Eugene, who's living with his daddy this year in Western Australia. Eugene is eight. His daddy does research in the outback. His daddy is also Wilder's daddy."

"The boy is growing up without television," I said, "which may make him worth talking to, Murray, as a sort of wild child, a savage plucked from the bush, intelligent and literate but deprived of the deeper codes and messages that mark his species as unique."

"TV is a problem only if you've forgotten how to look and listen," Murray said. "My students and I discuss this all the time. They're beginning to feel they ought to turn against the medium, exactly as an earlier generation turned against their parents and their country. I tell them they have to learn to look as children again. Root out content. Find the codes and messages, to use your phrase, Jack."

"What do they say to that?"

"Television is just another name for junk mail. But I tell them I can't accept that. I tell them I've been sitting in this room for more than two months, watching TV into the early hours, listening carefully, taking notes. A great and humbling experience, let me tell you. Close to mystical."

"What's your conclusion?"

He crossed his legs primly and sat with the cup in his lap, smiling straight ahead.

"Waves and radiation," he said. "I've come to understand that the medium is a primal force in the American home. Sealed-off, timeless, self-contained, self-referring. It's like a myth being born right there in our living room, like something we know in a dreamlike and preconscious way. I'm very enthused, Jack."

He looked at me, still smiling in a half sneaky way.

"You have to learn how to look. You have to open yourself to the data. TV offers incredible amounts of psychic data. It opens ancient memories of world birth, it welcomes us into the grid, the network of little buzzing dots that make up the picture pattern. There is light, there is sound. I ask my students, 'What more do you want?' Look at the wealth of data concealed in the grid, in the bright packaging, the jingles, the slice-of-life commercials, the products hurtling out of darkness, the coded messages and endless repetitions, like chants, like mantras. 'Coke is it, Coke is it, Coke is it.' The medium practically overflows with sacred formulas if we can remember how to respond innocently and get past our irritation, weariness and disgust."

"But your students don't agree."

"Worse than junk mail. Television is the death throes of human consciousness, according to them. They're ashamed of their television past. They want to talk about movies."

He got up and refilled our cups.

"How do you know so much?" Babette said.

"I'm from New York."

"The more you talk, the sneakier you look, as if you're trying to put something over on us."

"The best talk is seductive."

"Have you ever been married?" she said.

"Once, briefly. I was covering the Jets, the Mets and the Nets①."

"How odd a figure I must seem to you now, a solitary crank who maroons himself with a TV set and dozens of stacks of dust-jacketed comic books. Don't think I wouldn't appreciate a dramatic visit between two and three in the morning," he told her, "from an intelligent woman in spike heels and a slit skirt, with high-impact accessories."

It was drizzling as we walked home, my arm around her waist. The streets were empty. Along Elm all the stores were dark, the two banks were dimly lit, the neon spectacles in the window of the optical shop cast a gimmicky light on the sidewalk.

Dacron, Orion, Lycra Spandex②.

"I know I forget things," she said, "but I didn't know it was so obvious."

"It isn't."

"Did you hear Denise? When was it, last week?"

"Denise is smart and tough. No one else notices."

"I dial a number on the phone and forget who I'm calling. I go to the store and forget what to buy. Someone will tell me something, I'll forget it, they'll tell me again, I'll forget it, they'll tell me again, showing a funny-looking smile."

"We all forget," I said.

"I forget names, faces, phone numbers, addresses, appointments, instructions, directions."

"It's something that's just been happening, more or less to everyone."

"I forget that Steffie doesn't like to be called Stephanie. Sometimes I call her Denise. I forget where I've parked the car and then for a long, long moment I forget what the car looks like."

---

① Three sports teams in New York City.

② Brand-name items.

"Forgetfulness has gotten into the air and water. It's entered the food chain."

"Maybe it's the gum I chew. Is that too farfetched?"

"Maybe it's something else."

"What do you mean?"

"You're taking something besides chewing gum."

"Where did you get that idea?"

"I got it secondhand from Steffie."

"Who did Steffie get it from?"

"Denise."

She paused, conceding the possibility that if Denise is the source of a rumor or theory, it could very well be true.

"What does Denise say I'm taking?"

"I wanted to ask you before I asked her."

"To the best of my knowledge, Jack, I'm not taking anything that could account for my memory lapses. On the other hand I'm not old, I haven't suffered an injury to the head and there's nothing in my family background except tipped uteruses."

"You're saying maybe Denise is right."

"We can't rule it out."

"You're saying maybe you're taking something that has the side effect of impairing memory."

"Either I'm taking something and I don't remember or I'm not taking something and I don't remember. My life is either/or. Either I chew regular gum or I chew sugarless gum. Either I chew gum or I smoke. Either I smoke or I gain weight. Either I gain weight or I run up the stadium steps."

"Sounds like a boring life."

"I hope it lasts forever," she said.

Soon the streets were covered with leaves. Leaves came tumbling and scraping down the pitched roofs. There were periods in every day when a stiff wind blew, baring the trees further, and retired men appeared in the backyards, on the small lawns out front, carrying rakes with curved teeth. Black bags were arrayed at the curbstone in lopsided rows.

A series of frightened children appeared at our door for their Halloween treats.

[Selected from Don DeLillo. *White Noise*. New York: Penguin, 1998.]

Ⅲ. Questions for discussion

(1) How is the supermarket described? What role does the supermarket play in characters' life?

(2) How does Denise treat the visor? What view does Jack hold about the ATM system? What is revealed about identity in the consumer world?

(3) Explain your understanding of Heinrich's chess playing by mail relationship.

(4) Is Murray Jay Siskind right that the world is full of "psychic data"? What kind of data does it present? Is it a coding and decoding world? What data does Jack notice in this selection?

(5) What are those various forms of white noise in the excerpt? How can a reader interpret the novel from the perspective of ecocriticism?

(6) Death is a major concern of this novel. How does death hang like a cloud over the events of Chapter 9? How does Murray Jay Siskind view death?

(7) Frank Lentricchia, one of DeLillo's most avid critical commentators, once wrote, "Like Melville's Ishmael, Twain's Huck, and Fitzgerald's Nick Carraway, DeLillo's Jack Gladney is a sharp observer and commentator who at the same time participates—often to the reader's bewilderment—in an action which fatally shapes him, so that he will not understand with total lucidity what it is he observes, or who he himself really is, or the extent to which he, Jack Gladney, is the less than self-possessed voice of a culture that he would subject to criticism and satire." How does the writer employ the postmodern narrative technique of movement from a first-person subjectivity to a third-person objectivity as integral to the American experience?

5.3 Assigned Reading

Whole Families Shopping at Night!

(An Excerpt)

Thomas J. Ferraro

In the seminal criticism on television and postmodernity, the representation of the family in television has begun to be discussed persuasively. The question of how television works within the family has not moved much beyond extrapolations from the formal content. DeLillo's fiction lies at the cutting edge of mass-culture theory because he struggles to imagine how television as a medium functions within the home as the foremost site for what sociologists call our "primary" social relations. As DeLillo envisions it, television menaces the home with an omnipresent temptation to substitute the communal experience of the image for the ties that no longer bind.

Murray Jay Siskind, an ex-sportswriter from New York City, is a visiting lecturer in the American Environments Department at the College-on-the-Hill, a colleague of Jack who wants "to do for Elvis" what Jack "has done for Hitler." As a participant-observer in the Gladney household, Murray says he has come to feel vindicated in an ongoing argument he has been having with his students at the university, which focuses on the inherent worth of television. "TV offers incredible amounts of psychic data," he proselytizes. "It opens ancient memories of world birth, it welcomes us into the grid, the network of little buzzing dots that make up the picture pattern." His students resist with equal conviction. For them, television is "worse than junk mail. Television is the death throes of human consciousness.... They're ashamed of their television past. They want to talk about movies."

The students are identifying with both the antimodernization of culture critics since the turn of the century and the increasing tendency as the century has passed to treat film as a form of high modernism. According to Murray, his students are also rebelling against what we can safely take to have been their own childhoods, "exactly as an earlier generation turned against their parents and their country." Thus Murray's urgent plea to the students can be taken literally: "I tell them they have to look as children again."

While Murray contends that his students have rejected television, Jack listens intently, then returns to the subject. It is no coincidence that Murray has been taking notes in the Gladneys' home; and it is no coincidence that all of the Gladney children are under the age of fifteen. Heinrich, Denise, and Stettie are each thoroughly, unselfconsciously immersed: they vie for control over the TV set (which therefore moves from room to room); when not actually watching, they talk TV trivia of one sort or another (contributing to the family as "cradle of the world's misinformation"); above all, they murmur things like "Toyota Celica" in their dreams. "If our complaints have a focal point, it would have to be the TV set, where the outer torment lurks, causing fears and secret desires." Jack's fingering of television reflects a modernist sense of alienation that is also, perhaps first and foremost, a parent's lament for his children; his rapt interest in Murray's students reflects a resparking of hope for their futures.

Both Jack and Babette fear the "narcotic undertow and eerie diseased brain-sucking power" of television. Babette has designed the principal strategy with which they try to defeat television's invasive presence, which is "de-glamorize" it as "wholesome domestic sport." She has made it a rule to watch TV en famlile on Friday nights. The evenings themselves tend to be disliked: Heinrich pouts, Jack fidgets in boredom and in anticipation of reading Hitler, Steffie irritates the others by her sentimentalism. The children are made wary of group television sessions, especially preplanned, but are by no means discouraged from television itself.

At worst, the Friday night sessions backfire, for instance, on "the night of the catastrophes." Uncannily anticipating the rise of TV staples such as Geraldo Rivera, DeLillo portrays an evening in which the programming resembles the supermarket tabloid. The entire family is transfixed in grotesque voyeurism: "We were otherwise silent, watching houses slide into the ocean, whole villages crackle and ignite in a mass of advance lava. Every disaster made us wish for more, for something bigger, grander, more sweeping." Beyond the ethical dimension of taking pleasure in the sufferings of others that attends this particular evening is a more general point about the nature of television's threat: the specter here of group addiction, fascistic cultism in and of the family. "Heinrich was not sullen. I was not bored. Steffie... appeared totally absorbed." Killing the capacity for individual response, television unites families in an orgy of sensationalism that leaves its participants, like any powerful narcotic, thirsty (in this case, bloodthirsty) for more.

One evening, when Babette is teaching her posture class at a local church, the rest of the family discovers that her class is being broadcast on local access cable. Compelled beyond volition, they gather around the television and watch Babette's instruction without raising the sound, a detail fraught with Platonic terror. "It was the picture that mattered." Babette appears as if in a state of constant becoming—

"endlessly being formed and reformed"—yet it is not her that is acting and reacting but, of course, a swarm of "electronic dots." The "Babette of electrons and photons" touches each of them ("her image was projected on our bodies, swam in us and through us"), like a physical commingling, a joining with her and a cojoining with each other under the aegis of her radiated presence. The rhetoric of light's physicality suggests that the screen's ultimate strategy is to destroy the distinction between flesh and image, re-presenting the image-in-all-its-fleshiness as the thing-in-itself: If the vehicle that generates perception is to replace the object perceived, then television can be said to seduce us with a major reconstruction of the nature of reality itself. Jack feels "a certain disquiet" as the kids grow flush with excitement. Murray is there, too, undifferentiated from the others except for taking notes.

"It was but wasn't her." In his foreboding, Jack speaks out of a stubborn effort to preserve the distinction between Babette-in-the-flesh and Babette-as-image despite the fact that he feels and understands its narcotic allure. "I tried to tell myself it was only television—whatever that was, however it worked—and not some journey out of life or death, not some mysterious separation." Each of the children responds with unselfconscious zest and the equally innocent assumption that the others are elated too. Throughout the novel, the children give themselves over whole-heartedly to energizing rituals of familial consumerism: the lunch of "crumpled tinfoil" and "shiny bags," the Christmas-in-September shopping spree at the Mid-Village Mall, the night of watching natural disasters on TV. For them, the unannounced appearance of Babette on TV raises familial consumerism to a higher power. They feel exhilaration in the crossing of the boundary between substance and illusion, between their actual mother and her mediated likeness. They participate in something like a secular Mass: what is circulated as the transcendent is Babette's image made holy by the power of the medium, a postmodern communion of the commodified illusion.

Daniel Aaron has written of DeLillo's crafted separation from his characters: "I think he does care about their ideas, although he is professedly indifferent to them as 'persons,' and he isn't always so detached as he claims to be." Of course, it is DeLillo who has crafted this scene to push beyond Murray's seemingly uncritical celebration of the medium, and it is DeLillo who, in giving the scene its final wrinkles, in effect confirms Jack's uneasiness. When Denise decides at last to raise the volume of the TV, she gets "no sound, no voice, nothing," yielding a silence that even the children experience as frightening. "She turned to look at me, a moment of renewed confusion." Of course, Jack could tell Denise and the others that it is only a problem with the transmission, but that does not address the fear that in making of Babette an image the media has robbed her of her inner self, a process that by their rapturous passivity they have approved, supported, exploited. Heinrich, the technological wizard of the house and also the last to take the concerns of his fellow family members seriously, adjusts knobs to no avail; when he flips the tuning dial, sound booms out on the other channels, which the group finds only more disturbing. Again, one could tell them that obviously the trouble is back at the cable-television studio, surely an amateur operation prone to this sort of thing, but such doesn't allay the sense that it is their mother who has been lost, their appetite for her image that is under supernatural censure. "As we watched Babette finish the lesson, we were in a mood of odd misgiving." DeLillo has, it seems to me, pulled the plug on the proceedings.

Although the children are shocked momentarily into sharing Jack's disquiet, at the close of the program "the two girls get excited" and await Babette's return, to complete the adventure by sharing it with her. Babette's projection has not been so spellbinding that the reappearance of the woman in the flesh, with experiences to relate and a capacity to listen, would be a disappointment; at least the girls are not going to be disappointed, though Heinrich is conspicuously absent from the sentence. What DeLillo understands the family to have negotiated is signified by Wilder, whose youthful innocence is meant to augur the next stage of human experience. Throughout the viewing, Wilder alone has remained calm, alone has acted as if nothing out of the ordinary has occurred: for in the naivete that signifies the advance of postmodernity itself, Wilder has simply taken the image to be Babette. "The small boy remained at the TV set, within inches of the dark screen, crying softly, uncertainly, in low heaves and swells." Wilder's anxiety that Babette has "disappeared"—which is in developmental terms merely the common experience of toddlers when adults are no longer in sight—signifies here the danger of television mediating all experience: one day the transmission lines will go down and leave us staring before a blank screen, perhaps infantilized, no doubt helpless without our image-fix. If the chapter had concluded with the reappearance of Babette, Jack might have left us with a sense that the danger has been averted and regeneration is at hand. Leaving us with Wilder's tears, he issues a warning that our acts of recovery against image narcosis may (one day soon) come too late.

Jack invests his hope—even if he is too intimidated to say so—in the maturing of his children into "postpostmodernist" alienation. I take Jack to be gladdened by the fact that the children share his "odd misgiving" when the volume cannot be raised, a sign for him that he is not going crazy and that the kids may yet as they grow older follow in the way of Murray's students. The signs have to be gathered from scattered moments, acts, habits. Ritualistically burning toast, young Steffie cuts a pungent swath in the buzz and blur of household white noise—a defiant effort to stir the senses that television has numbed, first for herself and then for the others. Prone these days to wearing a dark green visor, Denise has since early girlhood preserved and surrounded herself with similar commodity-relecs of her own past—"from cartoon clocks to werewolf posters"; in a world of displacements, she rescues "remembering objects" from the trash compactor of capitalism "as a way of fastening herself to a life." Finally, there is Heinrich's appetite for science, particularly the sciences of the environment. One day in the car, Heinrich tells his father that the weather is unknowable without the confirming testimony of the weather personalities on the radio. "You're so sure that's rain. How do you know it's not sulfuric acid from factories across the river?" On the one hand, Heinrich is behaving like any other precocious fourteen-year-old boy, what my mother called being "disagreeable" (she meant it literally), and what Jack calls taking a "critical-observer" position. On the other hand, by his facetiousness (he knows it is really raining), and quite unlike Murray and the other avatars of postmodernity, he both distances himself from a medium that wills to displace his senses with its word and counts the cost of consumer capitalism's march to power in terms of chemical and nuclear fallout that would be no (Friday) night's entertainment to undergo.

[Selected from Frank Lentricchia, (ed.). *New Essays on White Noise*. Beijing: Peking University Press, 2007.]

Chapter 5 Realistic Literature After 1945

1. Introduction

"Realism" is the term used to describe the type of writing which characterizes American literature between the end of the Civil War and the beginning of World War Ⅰ (1865—1914). Yet, realism never dies. In spite of the seemingly dominance of the modernistic literature in post-war America, there are still many writers who cling to traditional realism: Saul Bellow, John O'Hara, Norman Mailer, John Cheever, John Updike, J. D. Salinger, Raymond Carver, Joyce Carol Oates, Alice Walker and Toni Morrison, to name just a few. Of course, it can no longer be what it was. It is now extremely various and multifaceted. It has been vitalized by international currents such as Black Humor, European Existentialism and Latin American Magical Realism. It tends to be more and more ironic, which is heightened by means of intensifying violence, amassing documentation, or resorting to fantasy. Writers have become highly innovative, self-aware or reflexive and they have borrowed various experimental forms and techniques in probing the inner world in detail. Oral genre, media, and popular culture have increasingly influenced it. To put it another way, American realistic literature, in the decades after 1945, has developed a post-modern sensibility: old-fashioned realism is combined with modernism.

The short stories and novels of John O'Hara (1905—1970) show a tendency to "documentary realism." They are tough, realistic descriptions of the changing American scene from World War Ⅰ to the Vietnam War. He was influenced by Theodore Dreiser and Sinclair Lewis in his descriptions of the minutiae, the status seekers and ragged class divisions of the town from whence he came. His dominant theme is described as "the imagination of society as some strange sentient organism which acts by laws of its own being which are not to be understood." His important works include *Appointment in Samarra* (1934), *Butterfield 8* (1935), *A Rage to Live* (1949), *From the Terrace* (1958), *Ourselves to Know* (1960), *Elizabeth Appleton* (1963), *The Lockwood Concern* (1965).

Norman Mailer (1923—2007) became an international celebrity at the age of 25 thanks to *The Naked and the Dead*, which is hailed by many as one of the best American wartime novels. It is based on his military service in World War Ⅱ and employs realism verging on grim naturalism. His other novels include *An American Dream* (1965), *Harlot's Ghost* (1991) and *The Castle in the Forest* (2007). He is also known for using a form of journalism—called New Journalism—that combines the imaginative subjectivity of literature with more objective qualities of journalism. Such works include *The Armies of the Night* (1968), *Miami and the Siege of Chicago* (1968), *Of a Fire on the Moon* (1970), and *The Executioner's Song* (1979). Both Mailer's fiction and nonfiction make a radical critique of the totalitarianism he believed inherent in the centralized power structure of the 20th and 21st century America.

John Cheever (1912—1982) has been called "the Chekhov of the suburbs," for his ability to capture the drama and sadness of the lives of his characters by revealing the undercurrents of apparently insignificant events. His elegant, suggestive short stories documented and scrutinized the anxieties of the New York middle-class suburban world in the relatively tranquil years after World War Ⅱ. While Cheever is perhaps best remembered for his short stories (including "The Enormous Radio," "Goodbye, My Brother," "The Five-Forty-Eight," "The Country Husband," and "The Swimmer"), he also wrote a number of novels, such as *The Wapshot Chronicle* (1958), *The Wapshot Scandal* (1965), *Bullet Park* (1969), and *Falconer* (1977). His main theme is the duality of human nature. Many of his works also express a nostalgia for a vanishing way of life, characterized by abiding cultural traditions and a profound sense of community, as opposed to the alienating nomadism of modern suburbia.

Louis Auchincloss (1917—2010) is a prolific novelist who took the world of the New York wealthy as his subject. His dry, ironic fiction continued the tradition of Henry James and Edith Wharton. Like Wharton, Auchincloss was interested in class and morality and in the corrosive effects of money on both. His famous novels include *The House of Five Talents* (1960), *Portrait in Brownstone* (1962), *The Rector of Justin* (1964), *The Embezzler* (1966), and *East Side Story* (2004).

J. D. Salinger (1919—2010) is best known for his 1951 novel *The Catcher in the Rye*, as well as his reclusive nature. Energetic, realistically sparse dialogue features in his writing style and he used techniques such as interior monologue, letters, and extended telephone calls to display his gift for dialogue. The recurring theme in his stories is the disconnect between teenagers and phony adult world. Adolescents are featured or appear in all of Salinger's work. Salinger identified closely with his characters.

John Cheever and John Updike (1932—2009) have frequently been called "novelists of manners" in the sense that they both wrote stories that reflected and criticized a certain kind of society that they knew well. John Updike described his subject as "the American small town, Protestant middle class." He populated his fiction with characters who "frequently experience personal turmoil and must respond to crises relating to religion, family obligations, and marital infidelity." Updike is famous for his Rabbit series (the novels *Rabbit, Run*; *Rabbit Redux*; *Rabbit Is Rich*; *Rabbit At Rest*; and the novella "Rabbit Remembered") which chronicled the life of Harry "Rabbit" Angstrom over the course of several decades, from young adulthood to his death. This remarkably prolific author's other works include the novels *The Poorhouse Fair* (1959), *The Centaur* (1962), *Couples* (1968), *The Coup* (1978), *The Witches of Eastwick* (1984), *In the Beauty of the Lilies* (1995), *Seek My Face* (2002), and *Terrorist* (2006). Among his many short-story collections are *The Same Door* in 1959, *Pigeon Fathers* in 1962, *Olinger Stories* in 1964, *The Music School* in 1966, *Bech* in 1970, *Museums and Women* in 1972, *Too Far to Go* in 1979, *Problems* in 1979, *Trust Me* in 1984, *The Afterlife* in 1994, *Licks of Love* in 2000, *The Early Stories* in 2003 and *My Father's Tears* in 2009.

Raymond Carver (1938—1988) specializes in short stories set in the Pacific Northwest. Rejecting the more experimental fiction of the 1960s and 1970s, he pioneered a precisionist realism, heading the line of so-called "minimalists," "dirty realists" or "Kmart realists." His careful, sparely written, usually bleak stories are about working-class life that often resembles and parallels his own. He tends to meditate upon the humor and tragedy in the everyday lives of working class people, presents his characters with compassion and doesn't place judgement on them or their actions. Raymond Carver's major short-story collections include: *Will You Please Be Quiet, Please?* (1976), *What We Talk About When We Talk About Love* (1981), *Cathedral* (1983), *Where I'm Calling From: New and Selected Stories* (1988).

Joyce Carol Oates (1938), with a reputation for prolificity, has been one of the leading American novelists since the 1960s. She writes about contemporary American life, which she sees as often defined by violence. She is particularly concerned with the connection between violence and love. Her characters are mainly ordinary, inarticulate people who sublimate the terrible things that happen to them. Her works often mix Gothic estrangement with high social observation. Her best-known novels include *Them* (1969), *Black Water* (1992), *What I Lived For* (1994), and *Blonde* (2000). Some of her finest stories are in collections such as *The Wheel of Love* (1970) and *Where Are You Going, Where Have You Been?* (1974).

American literature in the late 20th and early 21st century has increasingly expressed the cultural pluralism, regional variety, and historical and ethnic range of American life. Within such contemporary writings, realism has intensified, with the rise of "reality" television programs and photo-realism in art. This artistic strategy is suitable for a mass audience, since the artistic form is more accessible.

Key Words

Magic Realism

Fiction which displays a mingling of the mundane with the fantastic, giving the narrative dual dimensions of realism and fantasy. The technique is mainly associated with South American writers such as Gabriel García Márquez, but has also been widely used by some American minority writers such as Toni Morrison, Amy Tan, Maxine Hong Kingston, etc.

New Journalism

A type of American writing in the 1960s and 1970s in which the journalist presents factual information in a form usually used in fiction. New Journalism emphasizes description, narration, and character development to bring readers closer to the human element of the story, and is often used in personality profiles and in-depth feature articles. The term was codified with its current meaning by Tom Wolfe in a 1973 collection of journalism articles he published as *The New Journalism*, which included works by himself, Truman Capote, Hunter S. Thompson, Norman Mailer, Joan Didion, Robert Christgau, and others.

Literary Minimalism

Literary Minimalism is characterized by an economy with words and a focus on surface description. Minimalist authors eschew adverbs and prefer allowing context to dictate meaning. Readers are expected to take an active role in the creation of a story, to "choose sides" based on oblique hints and innuendo, rather than reacting to directions from the author. Minimalist authors, or those who are identified with minimalism during certain periods of their writing careers, include Raymond Carver, Ernest Hemingway, Richard Ford and so on.

Dirty Realism or Kmart Realism

It is a derivative of minimalism in the 1970s—1980s. Found in American short fiction, it is defined as "a literary genre characterized by a spare, terse style that features struggling, working-class characters in sterile, bleak environments." These short stories "represent and reproduce the disintegration of public life; they also represent the colonization of private life by consumer capitalism."

2. John Updike

2.1 Presentation Topics

(1) John Updike's "Rabbit" pentalogy.

(2) Themes in John Updike's works.

(3) Writing style of his works.

2.2 Selected Reading

Ⅰ. Central issue of concern

John Updike's idea about contemporary American middle-class family life: the characters "frequently experience personal turmoil and must respond to crises relating to religion, family obligations, and marital infidelity."

Ⅱ. Text

Separating

The day was fair. Brilliant. All that June the weather had mocked the Maples' internal misery with solid sunlight—golden shafts and cascades of green in which their conversations had wormed unseeing, their sad murmuring selves the only stain in Nature. Usually by this time of the year they had acquired tans; but when they met their elder daughter's plane on her return from a year in England they were almost as pale as she, though Judith was too dazzled by the sunny opulent jumble of her native land to notice. They did not spoil her homecoming by telling her immediately. Wait a few days, let her recover from jet lag, had been one of their formulations, in that string of gray dialogues—over coffee, over cocktails, over Cointreau①—that had shaped the strategy of their dissolution, while the earth performed its annual stunt of renewal unnoticed beyond their closed windows. Richard had thought to leave at Easter; Joan had insisted they wait until the four children were at last assembled, with all exams passed and ceremonies attended, and the bauble of summer to console them. So he had dredged away, in love, in dread, repairing screens, getting the mowers sharpened, rolling and patching their new tennis court.

The court, clay, had come through its first winter pitted and windswept bare of redcoat. Years ago the Maples had observed how often, among their friends, divorce followed a dramatic home improvement, as if the marriage were making one last twitchy effort to live; their own worst crisis had come amid the plaster dust and exposed plumbing of a kitchen renovation. Yet, a summer ago, as canary-yellow bulldozers gaily churned a grassy, daisy-dotted knoll into a muddy plateau, and a crew of pigtailed young men raked and tamped clay into a plane, this transformation did not strike them as ominous, but festive in its impudence; their marriage could rend the earth for fun. The next spring, waking each day at dawn to a sliding sensation as if the bed were being tipped, Richard found the barren tennis

① A strong sweet alcoholic drink made with oranges, from France.

court, its net and tapes still rolled in the barn, an environment congruous with his mood of purposeful desolation, and the crumbling of handfuls of clay into cracks and holes (dogs had frolicked on the court in a thaw; rivulets had evolved trenches), an activity suitably elemental and interminable. In his sealed heart he hoped the day would never come.

Now it was here. A Friday. Judith was reacclimated; all four children were assembled, before jobs and camps and visits again scattered them. Joan thought they should be told one by one. Richard was for making an announcement at the table. She said, "I think just making an announcement is a cop-out. They'll start quarrelling and playing to each other instead of focussing. They're each individuals, you know, not just some corporate obstacle to your freedom."

"O. K., O. K. I agree." Joan's plan was exact. That evening, they were giving Judith a belated welcome-home dinner, of lobster and champagne. Then, the party over, they, the two of them, who nineteen years before would push her in a baby carriage along Tenth Street to Washington Square, were to walk her out of the house, to the bridge across the salt creek, and tell her, swearing her to secrecy. Then Richard Jr., who was going directly from work to a rock concert in Boston, would be told, either late when he returned on the train or early Saturday morning before he went off to his jobs; he was seventeen and employed as one of golf-course maintenance crew. Then the two younger children, John and Margaret, could, as the morning wore on, be informed.

"Mopped up, as it were," Richard said.

"Do you have any better plan? That leaves you the rest of Saturday to answer any questions, pack, and make your wonderful departure."

"No," he said, meaning he had no better plan, and agreed to hers, though it had an edge of false order, a plea for control in the semblance of its achievement, like Joan's long chore lists and financial accountings and, in the days when he first knew her, her too copious lecture notes. Her plan turned one hurdle for him into four—four knife-sharp walls, each with a sheer blind drop on the other side.

All spring he had been morbidly conscious of insides and outsides, of barriers and partitions. He and Joan stood as a thin barrier between the children and the troth. Each moment was a partition, with the past on one side and the future on the other, a future containing this unthinkable now. Beyond four knifelike walls a new life for him waited vaguely. His skull cupped a secret, a white face, a face both frightened and soothing, both strange and known, that he wanted to shield from tears, which he felt all about him, solid as the sunlight. So haunted, he had become obsessed with battening down the house against his absence, replacing screens and sash cords, hinges and latches—a Houdini① making things snug before his escape.

The lock. He had still to replace a lock on one of the doors of the screened porch. The task, like most such, proved more difficult than he had imagined. The old lock, aluminum frozen by corrosion, had been deliberately rendered obsolete by manufacturers. Three hardware stores had nothing that even approximately matched the mortised hole its removal (surprisingly easy) left. Another hole had to be gouged, with bits too small and saws too big, and the old hole fitted with a block of wood—the chisels dull, the saw rusty, his fingers thick with lack of sleep. The sun poured down, beyond the porch, on a world of neglect. The bushes already needed pruning, the windward side of the house was shedding flakes of paint, rain would get in when he was gone, insects, rot, death. His family, all those he would lose, filtered through the edges of his awareness as he struggled with screw holes, splinters, opaque instructions, minutiae of metal.

Judith sat on the porch, a princess returned from exile. She regaled them with stories of fuel shortages, of bomb scares in the Underground, of Pakistani workmen loudly lusting after her as she walked past on her way to dance school. Joan came and went, in and out of the house, calmer than she should have been, praising his straggles with the lock as if this were one more and not the last of their chain of shared chores. The younger of his sons, John, now at fifteen suddenly, unwittingly handsome, for a few minutes held the rickety screen door while his father clumsily hammered and chiselled, each blow a kind of sob in Richard' s ears. His younger daughter, having been at a slumber party, slept on the porch hammock through all the noise—heavy and pink, trusting and forsaken. Time, like

① Harry Houdini (1874—1926), a Hungarian American magician and escapologist. His speciality is escapes: slipping out of ropes, chains and handcuffs while locked in trunks or milk cans or submerged underwater.

the sunlight, continued relentlessly; the sunlight slowly slanted. Today was one of the longest days. The lock clicked, worked. He was through. He had a drink; he drank it on the porch, listening to his daughter. "It was so sweet," she was saying, "during the worst of it, how all the butcher's and bakery shops kept open by candlelight. They're all so plucky and cute. From the papers, things sounded so much worse here—people shooting people in gas lines, and everybody freezing."

Richard asked her, "Do you still want to live in England forever?" Forever: the concept, now a reality upon him, pressed and scratched at the back of his throat.

"No," Judith confessed, turning her oval face to him, its eyes still childishly far apart, but the lips set as over something succulent and satisfactory. "I was anxious to come home. I'm an American." She was a woman. They had raised her; he and Joan had endured together to raise her, alone of the four. The others had still some raising left in them. Yet it was the thought of telling Judith—the image of her, their first baby, walking between them arm in arm, to the bridge—that broke him. The partition between himself and the tears broke. Richard sat down to the celebratory meal with the back of his throat aching; the champagne, the lobster seemed phases of sunshine; he saw them and tasted them through tears. He blinked, swallowed, croakily joked about hay fever. The tears would not stop leaking through; they came not through a hole that could be plugged but through a permeable spot in a membrane, steadily, purely, endlessly, fruitfully. They became, his tears, a shield for himself against these others—their faces, the fact of their assembly, a last time as innocents, at a table where he sat the last time as head. Tears dropped from his nose as he broke the lobster' s back; salt flavored his champagne as he sipped it; the raw clench at the back of his throat was delicious. He could not help himself.

His children tried to ignore his tears. Judith on his right, lit a cigarette, gazed upward in the direction of her too energetic, too sophisticated exhalation; on her other side, John earnestly bent his face to the extraction of the last morsels—legs, tail segments—from the scarlet corpse. Joan, at the opposite end of the table, glanced at him surprised, her reproach displaced by a quick grimace, of forgiveness, or of salute to his superior girl of strategy. Between them, Margaret, no longer called Bean, thirteen and large for her age, gazed from the other side of his pane of tears as if into a shop-window at something she coveted—at her father, a crystalline heap of splinters and memories. It was not she, however, but John who, in the kitchen, as they cleared the plates and carapaces away, asked Joan the question: "Why is Daddy crying?"

Richard heard the question but not the murmured answer. Then he heard Bean cry, "Oh, no-oh!"—the faintly dramatized exclamation of one who had long expected it.

John returned to the table carrying a bowl of salad. He nodded tersely at his father and his lips shaped the conspiratorial words: "She told."

"Told what?" Richard asked aloud, insanely.

The boy sat down as if to rebuke his father's distraction with the example of his own good manners and said quietly, "The separation."

Joan and Margaret returned; the child, in Richard's twisted vision, seemed diminished in size, and relieved, relieved to have had the boogeyman① at last proved real. He called out to her—the distances at the table had grown immense—"you knew, you always knew," but the clenching at the back of his throat prevented him from making sense of it. From afar he heard Joan talking, levelly, sensibly, reciting what they had prepared: it was a separation for the summer, and experiment. She and Daddy both agreed it would be good for them; they needed space and time to think; they liked each other but did not make each other happy enough, somehow.

Judith, imitating her mother's factual tone, but in her youth off-key, too cool, said, "I think it's silly. You should either live together or get divorced."

Richard's crying, like a wave that has crested and crashed, had become tumultuous, but it was overtopped by another tumult, for John, who had been so reserved, now grew larger and larger at the table. Perhaps his younger sister's being credited with knowing set him off. "Why didn't you tell us?" he asked, in a large round voice quite unlike his own. "You should have told us you weren't getting along."

Richard was startled into attempting to force words through his tears. "We do

① Boogeyman: bogeyman. A bogeyman is an imaginary evil spirit. Some parents tell their children that the bogeyman will catch them if they behave badly.

get along, that's the trouble, so it doesn' t show even to us—" "That we do not love each other" was the rest of the sentence; he couldn't finish it.

Joan finished for him, in her style. "And we' ve always, especially, loved our children."

John was not mollified. "What do you care about us?" he boomed. "We're just little things you had." His sister's laughing forced a laugh from him, which he turned hard and parodistic: "Ha ha ha." Richard and Joan realized simultaneously that the child was drank, on Judith's homecoming champagne. Feeling bound to keep the center of the stage, John took a cigarette from Judith's pack, poked it into his mouth, let it hang from his lower lip, and squinted like a gangster.

"You're not little things we had," Richard called to him. "You're the whole point. But you're grown. Or almost."

The boy was lighting matches. Instead of holding them to his cigarette (for they had never seen him smoke; being "good" had been his way of setting himself apart), he held them to his mother's face, closer and closer, for her to blow out. Then he lit the whole folder—a hiss and then a torch, held against his mother's face. Prismed by tears, the flame filled Richard's vision; he didn't know how it was extinguished. He heard Margaret say, "Oh stop showing off," and saw John, in response, break the cigarette in two and put the halves entirely into his mouth and chew, sticking out his tongue to display the shreds to his sister.

Joan talked to him, reasoning—a fountain of reason, unintelligible. "Talked about it for year.... Our children must help us.... Daddy and I both want..." As the boy listened, he carefully wadded a paper napkin into the leaves of his salad, fashioned a ball of paper and lettuce, and popped it into his mouth, looking around the table for the expected laughter. None came. Judith said, "Be mature," and dismissed a plume of smoke.

Richard got up from this stifling table and led the boy outside. Though the house was in twilight, the outdoors still brimmed with light, the long waste light of high summer. Both laughing, he supervised John' s spitting out the lettuce and paper and tobacco into the pachysandra①. He took him by the hand—a square gritty hand, but for its softness a man's. Yet, it held on. They ran together up

① Low-growing evergreen herbs or subshrubs having dentate leaves and used as ground cover.

into the field, past the tennis court. The raw banking left by the bulldozers was dotted with daisies. Past the court and a flat stretch where they used to play family baseball stood a soft green rise glorious in the sun, each weed and species of grass distinct as illumination on parchment. "I'm sorry, so sorry," Richard cried. "You were the only one who ever tried to help me with all the goddam jobs around this place."

Sobbing, safe within his tears and the champagne, John explained, "It's not just the separation, it' s the whole crummy year, I hate that school, you can't make any friends, the history teacher's a scud."

They sat on the crest of the rise, shaking and warm from their tears but easier in their voices, and Richard tried to focus on the child's sad year—the weekdays long with homework, the weekends spent in his room with model airplanes, while his parents murmured down below, nursing their separation. How selfish, how blind, Richard thought; his eyes felt scoured. He told his son, "We'll think about getting you transferred. Life's too short to be miserable."

They had said what they could, but did not want the moment to heal, and talked on, about the school, about the tennis court, whether it would ever again be as good as it had been that first summer. They walked to inspect it and pressed a few more tapes more firmly down. A little stiltedly, perhaps trying to make too much of the moment, to prolong it, Richard led the boy to the spot in the field where the view was best, of the metallic blue river, the emerald marsh, the scattered islands velvet with shadow in the low light, the white bits of beach far away. "See," he said. "It goes on being beautiful. It'll be here tomorrow."

"I know," John answered, impatiently. The moment had closed.

Back in the house, the others had opened some white wine, the champagne being drank, and still sat at the table, the three females, gossiping. Where Joan sat had become the head. She turned, showing him a tearless face, and asked, "All right?"

"We're fine," he said, resenting it, though relieved, that the party went on without him.

In bed she explained, "I couldn't cry I guess because I cried so much all spring. It really wasn't fair, It's your idea, and you made it look as though I was kicking you out."

"I'm sorry," he said. "I couldn't stop. I wanted to but couldn't."

"You didn't want to. You loved it. You were having your way, making a general announcement."

"I love having it over," he admitted. "God, those kids were great. So brave and funny." John, returned to the house, had settled to a model airplane in his room, and kept shouting down to them, "I'm O. K. No sweat." "And the way," Richard went on, cozy in his relief, "they never questioned the reasons we gave. Not thought of a third person. Not even Judith."

"That was touching," Joan said.

He gave her a hug. "You were great too. Thank you." Guiltily, he realized he did not feel separated.

"You still have Dickie to do," she told him. These words set before him a black mountain in the darkness; its cold breath, its near weight affected his chest. Of the four children Dickie was most nearly his conscience. Joan did not need to add, "That's one piece of your dirty work I won't do for you."

"I know. I'll do it. You go to sleep."

Within minutes, her breathing slowed, became oblivious and deep. It was a quarter to midnight. Dickie's train from the concert would come in at one-fourteen. Richard set the alarm for one. He had slept atrociously for weeks. But whenever he closed his lids some glimpse of the last hours scorched them—Judith exhaling toward the ceiling in a kind of aversion, Bean's mute staring, the sunstruck growth of the field where he and John had rested. The mountain before him moved closer, moved within him; he was huge, momentous. The ache at the back of his throat felt stale. His wife slept as if slain beside him. When, exasperated by his hot lids, his crowded heart, he rose from bed and dressed, she awoke enough to mm over. He told her then, "If I could undo it all, I would."

"Where would you begin?" she asked. There was no place. Giving him courage, she was always giving him courage. He put on shoes without socks in the dark. The children were breathing in their rooms, the downstairs was hollow. In their confusion they had left lights burning. He turned off all but one, the kitchen overhead. The car started. He had hoped it wouldn't. He met only moonlight on the road; it seemed a diaphanous companion, flickering in the leaves along the roadside, haunting his rearview mirror like a pursuer, melting under his headlights. The center of town, not quite deserted, was eerie at this hour. A young cop in uniform kept company with a gang of T-shirted kids on the steps of the bank. Across from the railroad station, several bars kept open. Customers, mostly young, passed in and out of the warm night, savoring summer's novelty. Voices shouted from cars as they passed; an immense conversation seemed in progress. Richard parked and in his weariness put his head on the passenger seat, out of the commotion and wheeling lights. It was as when, in the movies, an assassin grimly carries his mission through the jostle of a carnival—except the movies cannot show the precipitous, palpable slope you cling to within. You cannot climb back down; you can only fall. The synthetic fabric of the car seat, warmed by his cheek, confided to him an ancient, distant scent of vanilla.

A train whistle caused him to lift his head. It was on time; he had hoped it would be late. The slender drawgates descended. The bell of approach tingled happily. The great metal body, horizontally fluted, rocked to a stop, and sleepy teenagers disembarked, his son among them. Dickie did not show surprise that his father was meeting him at this terrible hour. He sauntered to the car with two friends, both taller than he. He said "Hi" to his father and took the passenger's seat with an exhausted promptness that expressed gratitude. The friends got into the back, and Richard was grateful; a few more minutes' postponement would be won by driving them home.

He asked, "How was the concert?"

"Groovy," one boy said from the back seat.

"It bit," the other said.

"It was O. K.," Dickie said, moderate by nature, so reasonable that in his childhood the unreason of the world had given him headaches, stomach aches, nausea. When the second friend had been dropped off at his dark house, the boy blurted, "Dad, my eyes are killing me with hay fever! I'm out there cutting that mothering grass all day!"

"Do we still have those drops?"

"They didn't do any good last summer."

"They might this." Richard swung a U-tum on the empty street. The drive home took a few minutes. The mountain was here, in his throat. "Richard," he said, and felt the boy, slumped and rubbing his eyes, go tense at his tone, "I didn't come to meet you just to make your life easier. I came because your mother and I have some news for you, and you're a hard man to get ahold of these days. It's sad news."

"That's O. K." The reassurance came out softly, but quickly, as if released from the tip of a spring.

Richard had feared that his tears would return and choke him, but the boy's manliness set an example, and his voice issued forth steady and dry. "It's sad news, but it needn't be tragic news, at least for you. It should have no practical effect on your life, though it's bound to have an emotional effect. You'll work at your job, and go back to school in September. Your mother and I are really proud of what you're making of your life; we don't want that to change at all."

"Yeah," the boy said lightly, on the intake of his breath, holding himself up. They turned the corner; the church they went to loomed like a gutted fort. The home of the woman Richard hoped to marry stood across the green. Her bedroom light burned.

"Your mother and I," he said, "have decided to separate. For the summer. Nothing legal, no divorce yet. We want to see how it feels. For some years now, we haven't been doing enough for each other, making each other as happy as we should be. Have you sensed that?"

"No," the boy said. It was an honest, unemotional answer: true or false in a quiz.

Glad for the factual basis, Richard pursued, even garrulously, the details. His apartment across town, his utter accessibility, the split vacation arrangements, the advantages to the children, the added mobility and variety of the summer. Dickie listened, absorbing. "Do the others know?"

Richard described how they had been told.

"How did they take it?"

"The girls pretty calmly. John flipped out; he shouted and ate a cigarette and made a salad out of his napkin and told us how much he hated school."

His brother chuckled. "He did?"

"Yeah. The school issue was more upsetting for him than Mom and me. He seemed to feel better for having exploded."

"He did?" The repetition was the first sign that he was stunned.

"Yes. Dickie, I want to tell you something, This last hour, waiting for your train to get in, has been about the worst of my life. I hate this. Hate it. My father would have died before doing it to me." He felt immensely lighter, saying this. He had dumped the mountain on the boy. They were home. Moving swiftly as a shadow, Dickie was out of the car, through the bright kitchen. Richard called after him, "Want a glass of milk or anything?"

"No thanks."

"Want us to call the course tomorrow and say you're too sick to work?"

"No, that's all right." The answer was faint, delivered at the door to his room; Richard listened for the lam of a tantrum. The door closed normally. The sound was sickening.

Joan had sunk into the first deep trough of sleep and was slow to awake. Richard had to repeat, "I told him."

"What did he say?"

"Nothing much. Could you go say good night to him? Please."

She left their room, without putting on a bathrobe. He sluggishly changed back into his pajamas and walked down the hall. Dickie was already in bed, Joan was sitting beside him, and the boy's bedside clock radio was murmuring music. When she stood, an inexplicable light—the moon? —outlined her body through the nightie. Richard sat on the warm place she had indented on the child's narrow mattress. He asked him, "Do you want the radio on like that?"

"It always is."

"Doesn't it keep you awake? It would be me."

"No."

"Are you sleepy?"

"Yeah."

"Good. Sure you want to get up and go to work? You've had a big night."

"I want to."

Away at school this winter he had learned for the first time that you can go short of sleep and live. As an infant he had slept with an immobile, sweating intensity that had alarmed his babysitters. As the children aged, he became the first to go to bed, earlier for a time than his younger brother and sister. Even now, he would go slack in the middle of a television show, his sprawled legs hairy and brown. "O. K. Good boy, Dickie, listen. I love you so much, I never knew how much until now. No matter how this works out, I'll always be with you. Really."

Richard bent to kiss an averted face but his son, sinewy, turned and with wet cheeks embraced him and gave him a kiss, on the lips, passionate as a woman's. In his father's ear he moaned one word, the crucial, intelligent word: "Why?"

Why. It was a whistle of wind in a crack, a knife thrust, a window thrown open on emptiness. The white face was gone, the darkness was featureless. Richard had forgotten why.

[Selected from John Updike. *Too Far to Go: The Maples Stories*. New York: Fawcett Books, 1979.]

Ⅲ. Questions for discussion

(1) What is the story line of this short story? Please make a comparison between this story and a traditional short story in the light of plot, characterization, climax, etc.

(2) How do the protagonist Richard and his wife Joan feel about their separating? Do you think they are both responsible for their family? How to understand their sense of familial responsibility and their plan of separating?

(3) How do the couple expect their children to react to the news about their separating? What are the four children's reactions after they are told their parents' separation? How to understand the difference between their expectation and the children's reactions?

(4) Why are the couple separating? What is the effect of making this reason so difficult to discover?

(5) What is the theme in this story?

(6) How is the protagonist's psychology reflected through the author's detailed description of the physical world? What does "four—four knife-sharp walls, each with a sheer blind drop on the other side" symbolize?

(7) Many contrasts are employed like those between nature and feelings, appearance and inner mind, and even the home improvement and the marital separation. What do you think is the effect of these contrasts?

(8) What are the effects of Updike's sentence structure including his use of short periodic sentences and his occasional use of fragments? Do you think this

story demonstrates the author's efforts to employ techniques of graphic arts in his story-telling?

2.3 Assigned Reading

On John Updike

Ian McEwan

In his autobiography *Self-Consciousness*, a "big-bellied Lutheran God" within the young John Updike looked on in contempt as he struggled to give up cigarettes. Many years later the older Updike, now giving up on alcohol, coffee, and salt, put into the mouth of that God the words of Frederick the Great excoriating his battle-shy soldiers—"Dogs, would you live forever?" But all the life-enhancing substances were set aside, and writing became Updike's "sole remaining vice. It is an addiction, an illusory release, a presumptuous taming of reality." In the mornings, he could write "breezily" of what he could not "contemplate in the dark without turning in panic to God." The plain facts of life were "unbearably heavy, weighted as they are with our personal death. Writing, in making the world light—in codifying, distorting, prettifying, verbalizing it—approaches blasphemy." And now this masterly blasphemer, whose literary schemes and pretty conceits touched at points on the Shakespearean, is gone, and American letters, deprived in recent years of its giants, Bellow and Mailer, is a leveled plain, with one solitary peak guarded by Roth. We are coming to the end of the golden age of the American novel in the twentieth century's second half. Henry Bech, Updike's remote Jewish other, never immune to an attack of status anxiety, mused on the teeming hordes of his gifted and despised contemporaries: "Those that didn't appear, like John Irving and John Fowles, garrulously, Dickensianly reactionary in method seemed, like John Hawkes and John Barth, smugly, hermetically experimental. O'Hara, Hersey, Cheever, Updike—suburbanites all living safe while art's inner city disintegrated. And that was just the Johns." This most Lutheran of writers, driven by intellectual curiosity all his life, was troubled by science as others are troubled by God. When it suited him, he could easily absorb and be impressed by physics, biology, astronomy, but he was constitutionally unable to "make the leap of unfaith." The "weight" of personal death did not allow it, and much seriousness and dark humor derive from this tension between intellectual reach and metaphysical dread.

In a short story from 1985, "The Wallet," Mr. Fulham (who, we are told in the first line, "had assembled a nice life") experiences death terrors when he takes his grandchildren to a local cinema. While "starships did special-effects battle," Fulham's "true situation in time and space" was revealed: "a speck of consciousness now into its seventh decade, a mortal body poised to rejoin the minerals, a member of a lost civilization that once existed on a sliding continent." This "lonely possession" of his own existence, he concludes, is "sickeningly serious."

God makes no appearance in this story, but it is unlikely that an atheist could have conjured so much from the minor domestic disturbance that follows. First, a large check "in the low six figures," a return on canny investments, fails to show up in the post. Fulham makes many phone calls to the company in Houston; the matter begins to loom too large—"He slept poorly, agitated by the injustice of it." He suspects a thief, a "perpetrator," or that there is a flaw in the mindless system. He is tormented by "outrageous cosmic unanswerableness."

Then, the "perpetrator" strikes again. His wallet—"a friendly adjunct to his person"—vanishes. This being Updike, its contents are minutely, satirically listed, the credit, membership, and hospital cards, the priceless clippings, photographs of family and one of a long-ago lover, the obsolete receipts. Who has not searched in vain, like Fulham, returning superstitiously to the same places, trying to recreate the movements of the careless self of yesterday? But "the wallet's non-existence rang out through the rooms like a pistol shot which leaves deafness in its wake." In despair, Fulham exclaims to his wife, "Without that wallet, I'm nothing." His tongue had outraced his brain, but once he said he realized this to be true: without the wallet, he was a phantom, flitting about in a house without walls. At last, the check shows up, only after it has been canceled; the granddaughter finds the wallet, but only after the accounts have been frozen. The nights are cooler now and something has shifted in Fulham. He has had a near-death experience, a rehearsal, and now is reconciled to his end.

Like much that appears secular in Updike, this story is suffused with his religious seriousness—the very spirit that Philip Larkin, an atheist, famously acknowledged in his description of a church as being "a serious house on serious earth...." It is no accident that Fulham's moments of dread come upon him in a movie house. In the opening of the major novel *In the Beauty of the Lilies*, Mary Pickford faints on the set of a D. W. Griffith movie, *The Call to Arms*, while elsewhere a clergyman is painfully losing his faith after reading a book by the atheist Robert Ingersoll and realizing "what he had long suspected, that the universe was utterly indifferent to his states of mind and as empty of divine content as a corroded kettle." He confronts "the blood-soaked selfishness of a cosmic mayhem" and leaves the ministry to become an encyclopedia salesman. And so they are linked, cinema and religion, two grand designs conjuring light out of darkness. For Updike, cinema and its brattish child television "became our religion." This was not a disapproving observation—in his youth, "it was the movies that moved me, and gave me something to live for, to live toward."

And cinema was above all, for the young Updike, an education in sexual manners, in modes of seduction, in the codes of glances and touch and all that business with cigarettes. It was there from the very beginning, in his writing, that celebrated or infamous capacity for fastidious, clinical, visually intense, painfully and hilariously honest descriptions of men and women making love. However fleeting or disastrous the coupling, the metaphysical shadows are always on the wall—the same seriousness is in play. "Nature dangles sex to keep us walking toward the cliff," Piet reflects in *Couples*. When he makes love outdoors to Georgene—"A lip of resistance, then an easeful deepness, a slipping by steps"—he is troubled that he is "under the eye of God."

The ruthless recording eye made Updike unpopular with some women readers, especially back in the salad days of Theory, when talk of the "male gaze" was the fashion. Piet notes in Foxy's nakedness "the goosebumped roughness of her buttocks, the gray unpleasantness of her shaved armpits ...." But in Updike as in life, bodies are rarely perfect, unlike in the movies; this is fictional realism and goosebumps do not stand in the way of the lovers' transcendent pleasure. While she fellates him "lazily," he combs her lovely hair and reflects on her "coral cunt, coral into burgundy, with its pansy-shaped M, or W, of fur"; then it comes to him that mouths are noble. "They move in the brain's court. We set our genitals mating down below like peasants, but when the mouth condescends, mind and body marry."

In his last novel, *The Widows of Eastwick*, Updike engaged playfully with his female critics through his character Sukie, the romantic novelist. She erases from a work in progress a passage about carefully buffed fingernails digging deep "into Hercule's broad, heaving back." She reminds herself that a proper romance never dwells on sexual details, for it might lose its "targeted demographic of dreamy, dissatisfied women.... Women know the facts but don't want them spelled out."

In fact, Updike's level unblinking gaze is not only on women, and is not confined to the physical. In *Roger's Version*, when Lambert lies to his wife to conceal an infidelity, he does so, "trusting my face, that thin-skinned traitor, to back me up." And there was never a more fallible and exposed character in modern fiction than Harry "Rabbit" Angstrom. The Rabbit tetralogy not only describes from the inside a modern man's major and minor dishonesties, self-deceptions, special pleadings, and lumpish passivity, it also charts over four novels and more than thirty years a slow physical and mental deterioration accelerated by laziness, junk food, and American prosperity.

The tetralogy is Updike's masterpiece and will surely be his monument. In all its detail, homely or hard-edged, and all its arenas—work, politics, retirement, and above all sex—the metaphysical is always there, sometimes a mere gleam buried in the fold of a sentence, at other times overtly, comically. In the first of the novels, *Rabbit Run*, when youngish Harry, the typesetter and ex-basketball player, makes love to Ruth, a small-town prostitute, their sessions are interrupted by a gut-level theological dispute about God's existence, prompted by Sunday churchgoers in the street below. Harry, naturally, is on the side of God—"The idea of making it while the churches are full excites him."

Many years later, he is on the operating table, watching his own insides on a screen ("the Rabbit Angstrom Show"), surrounded by machines and technocratic doctors and their satellites who "murmurously crouch over Harry's sheeted, strategically exposed body," conducting a three-and-a-half-hour angioplasty following his heart attack. The scene is rich in Updike's strengths. "The mechanically precise dark ghost of the catheter is the worm of death within him. Godless technology is fucking the pulsing wet tubes we inherited from the squid, the boneless sea-cunts." The experience is intensely unpleasant—"like his chest is being cooked in a microwave. Jesus." He closes his eyes a few times and attempts to pray—"but it feels like a wrong occasion, there is too much crowding in, of the actual material world. No old wispy Biblical God would dare interfere." The one consolation is that his doctor is Jewish, for Harry has a "gentile prejudice that Jews do everything a little better than other people, something about all those generations crouched over the Talmud and watch-repair tables, they aren't as distracted as other persuasions, they don't expect to have as much fun. They stay off the booze and dope and have a weakness only ... for broads." Like Bellow, his only equal in this, Updike is a master of effortless motion—between third and first person, from the metaphorical density of literary prose to the demotic, from specific detail to wide generalization, from the actual to the numinous, from the scary to the comic. For his own particular purposes, Updike devised for himself a style of narration, an intense, present tense, free indirect style, that can leap up, whenever it wants, to a God's eye view of Harry, or the view of his put-upon wife, Janice, or his victimized son, Nelson.. This carefully crafted artifice permits here assumptions about evolutionary theory, which are more Updike than Harry, and comically sweeping notions of Jewry, which are more Harry than Updike.

This at the heart of the tetralogy's achievement. Updike once said of the Rabbit books that they were an exercise in point of view. This was typically self-deprecating, but contains an important grain of truth. Harry's education extends no further than high school, his view is further limited by a range of prejudices and a stubborn, combative spirit, and yet he is the vehicle for a half-million-word meditation on postwar American anxiety, failure, and prosperity. A mode had to be devised to make this possible, and that involved pushing beyond the bounds of realism. In a novel like this, Updike insisted, you have to be generous and allow your characters eloquence, "and not chop them down to what you think is the right size." He was clear too that we all sense more than we can ever put into words, and was mindful of the example of Joyce and his "great attempt to capture the way we move through life."

The three Bech books, which Updike always listed with his short stories, have alliterative titles, like the tetralogy, and read now like a trilogy of a distinctive comic genius. Henry Bech is a Jewish-American writer whose career rises, fades horribly, and rises again to embrace the Nobel Prize denied his creator. In one of the final episodes, *Bech Noir*, Henry takes, rather implausibly, to murdering the critics who have offended him over a lifetime. A poisoned self-addressed envelope and a discreet shove on a crowded subway platform dispose of two with little bother. To reach another, Bech done up in cape and mask, armed with gun and silencer, climbs a fire escape with an accomplice, his current lover in a catsuit, to take the life of Orlando Cohen, an old man with emphysema, whose chaste ambition was to be "the ultimate adjudicator" of American literature and who had "refused to grant Bech a place, even a minor place, in the canon."

They find an emaciated, enfeebled Cohen breathing oxygen through a mask with a volume of Walter Benjamin's *Selected Writings* on his lap. This is comedy, high and dark, but it does not prevent the critic, minutes before his death, delivering a sharp dismissal of Bech's work for its failure to understand America. Its core, Bech had failed to grasp, was essentially Protestant. The first settlers thought the Holy Ghost had led them to a Promised Land. Fighting for air, Cohen pronounces: "The Holy Ghost ... who the hell is that? Some pigeon, that's all ... but that God-awful faith ... Bech ... when it burns out ... it leaves a dead spot. Love it or leave it ... a dead spot. That's where America is ... in that dead spot." Bech failed to find that spot, but his creator had long ago made it his subject. That dead spot was the ruined inner city of *Roger's Version*, a spoiled landscape through which a divinity professor takes a thirty-page stroll—one of the great set pieces of the entire body of work; the dead spot was the shadowy center of scores of novels and stories, in the freeways, malls, TV-addicted children, junk food, the boundless suburbs and their heartless intrigues and pursuit of ecstasy in restless, hopeful couplings, the messy divorces and their wounded children, the racial divide, the rackety politics filtered through TV screens, the national bafflement as manufacturing industries declined and the Japanese moved in with their cheaper cars.

That dead spot is probed and palpated in the ever-present metaphysics, the thwarted religious sense, or in moments when a denatured suburbanite glances up beyond the telegraph poles and wires and notices that spring is coming on and experiences a jolt of indistinct excitement that is quickly smothered; or when Harry Angstrom, waiting to receive a serve in a game of social tennis, thinks of the mounting numbers of dead in his life, and feels camaraderie for his friends, and loves the treetops around him—but cannot name a single tree, never reads a book, knows nothing, and feels his life to be threadbare.

There is in Updike always comedy or mischief in these moments of frustrated entitlement. A great writer cannot help showing us that there is something strangely comic, or antic, about the perfectly turned phrase; the precise insight into a human moment carries with it generosity and warmth, and prompts a smile of recognition. A baby "corkscrews" in its father's arms; a newly married couple look "self-cherished, like gladioli"; when gales of Sixties social mayhem sweep through Harry's marital home and the house has unwanted visitors and, in the dead of night, he must make love quietly to his new mistress, Updike notes that "the rooms are quadrants of one rustling heart"—a sweetly pitched observation that finds expression in an iambic pentameter.

The Updike opus is so vast, so varied and rich, that we will not have its full measure for years to come. We have lived with the expectation of his new novel or story or essay so long, all our lives, that it does not seem possible that this flow of invention should suddenly cease. We are truly bereft, that this reticent, kindly man with the ferocious work ethic and superhuman facility will write for us no more. He was intensely private, learned, generous, courtly, the kind of man who could apologize for replying to one's letter by return mail because it was the only way he could keep his desk clear.

Contrary to what his work might suggest to a literal reader, John Updike was in actual life devoted to his large family that sprawled across the generations, so why not let one of his youngest characters take the parting bow on his behalf? When Henry Bech goes up on stage in Stockholm to make his Nobel acceptance speech, he takes with him on his hip his one-year-old daughter. She wriggles impatiently through his lecture and when at last he has finished, she reaches out for the microphone "with the curly, be slobbered fingers of one hand as if to pluck the fat metallic bud." Bech feels the warmth of her skull, he inhales "her scalp's powdery scent... Then she lifted her right hand, where all could see, and made the gentle clasping and unclasping that signifies bye-bye."

[Selected from *New York Review of Books*, 2009(4).]

3. Raymond Carver

3.1 Presentation Topics

(1) Raymond Carver as a leading short fiction writer and poet in the late 20th century.

(2) Raymond Carver's contribution to the revitalization of American short stories in the 1980s.

(3) Literary minimalism.

3.2 Selected Reading

Ⅰ. Central issue of concern

Raymond Carver's inheriting realistic tradition in writing to convey and communicate with the reader about the common concern with the human beings while adopting some postmodern techniques.

Ⅱ. Text

What We Talk About When We Talk About Love

My friend Mel McGinnis was talking. Mel McGinnis is a cardiologist, and sometimes that gives him the right.

The four of us were sitting around his kitchen table drinking gin. Sunlight filled the kitchen from the big window behind the sink. There were Mel and me and his second wife, Teresa—Terri, we called her—and my wife, Laura. We lived in Albuquerque then. But we were all from somewhere else.

There was an ice bucket on the table. The gin and the tonic water kept going around, and we somehow got on the subject of love. Mel thought real love was nothing less than spiritual love. He said he'd spent five years in a seminary before quitting to go to medical school. He said he still looked back on those years in the seminary as the most important in his life.

Terri said the man she lived with before she lived with Mel loved her so much he tried to kill her. Then Terri said, "He beat me up one night. He dragged me around the living room by my ankles. He kept saying, 'I love you, I love you, you bitch.' He went on dragging me around the living room. My head kept knocking on things." Terri looked around the table. "What do you do with love like that?"

She was a bone-thin woman with a pretty face, dark eyes, and brown hair that hung down her back. She liked necklaces made of turquoise, and long pendant earrings.

"My God, don't be silly. That's not love, and you know it," Mel said. "I don't know what you'd call it, but I sure know you wouldn't call it love."

"Say what you want to, but I know it was," Terri said. "It may sound crazy to you, but it's true just the same. People are different, Mel. Sure, sometimes he may have acted crazy. Okay. But he loved me. In his own way, maybe, but he loved me. There was love there, Mel. Don't say there wasn't."

Mel let out his breath. He held his glass and turned to Laura and me. "The man threatened to kill me," Mel said. He finished his drink and reached for the gin bottle. "Terri's a romantic. Terri's of the 'Kick-me-so-I'll-know-you-love-me' school. Terri hon, don't look that way." Mel reached across the table and touched Terri's cheek with his fingers. He grinned at her.

"Now he wants to make up," Terri said.

"Make up what?" Mel said. "What is there to make up? I know what I know. That's all."

"How'd we get started on this subject anyway?" Terri said. She raised her glass and drank from it. "Herb always has love on his mind," she said. "Don't you, honey?" She smiled, and I thought that was the last of it.

"I just wouldn't call Ed's behavior love. That's all I'm saying, honey," Mel said. "What about you guys?" Mel said to Laura and me. "Does that sound like love to you?"

"I'm the wrong person to ask," I said. "I didn't even know the man. I've only heard his name mentioned in passing. I wouldn't know. You'd have to know all the particulars. But I think what you're saying is that love is an absolute."

Mel said, "The kind of love I'm talking about is. The kind of love I'm talking about, you don't try to kill people."

Laura said, "I don't know anything about Ed, or anything about the situation. But who can judge anyone else's situation?"

I touched the back of Laura's hand. She gave me a quick smile. I picked up Laura's hand. It was warm, the nails polished, perfectly manicured. I encircled the broad wrist with my fingers, and I held her.

"When I left he drank rat poison," Terri said. She clasped her arms with her hands. "They took him to the hospital in Santa Fe. That's where we lived then, about ten miles out. They saved his life. But his gums went crazy from it. I mean they pulled away from his teeth. After that his teeth stood out like fangs. My God," Terri said. She waited a minute, then let go of her arms and picked up her glass.

"What people won't do!" Laura said.

"He's out of the action now," Mel said. "He's dead."

Mel handed me the saucer of limes. I took a section, squeezed it over my drink, and stirred the ice cubes with my finger.

"It gets worse," Terri said. "He shot himself in the mouth. But he bungled that too. Poor Ed," she said. Terri shook her head.

"Poor Ed nothing," Mel said. "He was dangerous."

Mel was forty-five years old. He was tall and rangy with curly soft hair. His face and arms were brown from the tennis he played. When he was sober, his gestures, all his movements, were precise, very careful.

"He did love me though, Mel. Grant me that," Terri said. "That's all I'm asking. He didn't love me the way you love me. I'm not saying that. But he loved me. You can grant me that, can't you?"

"What do you mean, He bungled it?" I said.

Laura leaned forward with her glass. She put her elbows on the table and held her glass in both hands. She glanced from Mel to Terri and waited with a look of bewilderment on her open face, as if amazed that such things happened to people you were friendly with.

"How'd he bungle it when he killed himself?" I said.

"I'll tell you what happened," Mel said. "He took this twenty-two pistol he'd bought to threaten Terri and me with. Oh, I'm serious, the man was always threatening. You should have seen the way we lived in those days. Like fugitives. I even bought a gun myself. Can you believe it? A guy like me? But I did. I bought one for self-defense and carried it in the glove compartment. Sometimes I'd have to leave the apartment in the middle of the night. To go to the hospital, you know? Terri and I weren't married then, and my first wife had the house and kids, the dog, everything, and Terri and I were living in this apartment here. Sometimes, as I say, I'd get a call in the middle of the night and have to go in to the hospital at two or three in the morning. It'd be dark out there in the parking lot and I'd break into a sweat before I could even get to my car. I never knew if he was going to come up out of the shrubbery or from behind a car and start shooting. I mean, the man was crazy. He was capable of wiring a bomb, anything. He used to call my service at all hours and say he needed to talk to the doctor, and when I'd return the call he'd say, 'Son of a bitch, your days are numbered.' Little things like that. It was scary, I'm telling you."

"I still feel sorry for him," Terri said.

"It sounds like a nightmare," Laura said. "But what exactly happened after he shot himself?"

Laura is a legal secretary. We'd met in a professional capacity. Before we knew it, it was a courtship. She's thirty-five, three years younger than I am. In addition to being in love, we like each other and enjoy one another's company. She's easy to be with.

"What happened?" Laura asked again.

Mel said, "He shot himself in the mouth in his room. Someone heard the shot and told the manager. They came in with a passkey, saw what had happened, and called an ambulance. I happened to be there when they brought him, alive, but past recall. The man lived for three days. His head swelled up to twice the size of a normal head. I'd never seen anything like it, and I hope I never do again. Terri wanted to go in and sit with him when she found out about it. We had a fight over it. I didn't think she should see him like that. I didn't think she should see him, and I still don't."

"Who won the fight?" Laura said.

"I was in the room with him when he died," Terri said. "He never came up out of it. But I sat with him. He didn't have anyone else."

"He was dangerous," Mel said. "If you call that love, you can have it."

"It was love," Terri said. "Sure it was abnormal in most people's eyes. But he was willing to die for it. He did die for it."

"I sure as hell wouldn't call it love," Mel said. "I mean, no one knows what he did it for. I've seen a lot of suicides, and I couldn't say anyone ever knew what they did it for."

Mel put his hands behind his neck and tilted his chair back. "I'm not interested in that kind of love," he said. "If that's love, you can have it."

Terri said, "We were afraid. Mel even made a will out and wrote to his brother in California who used to be a Green Beret. Mel told him who to look for if something happened to him."

Terri drank from her glass. She said, "But Mel's right—we lived like fugitives. We were afraid. Mel was, weren't you, honey? I even called the police at one point, but they were no help. They said they couldn't do anything until Ed actually did something. Isn't that a laugh?" Terri said.

She poured the last of the gin into her glass and waggled the bottle. Mel got up from the table and went to the cupboard. He took down another bottle.

"Well, Nick and I know what love is," Laura said. "For us, I mean," Laura said. She bumped my knee with her knee. "You're supposed to say something now," Laura said, and turned her smile on me.

For an answer, I took Laura's hand and raised it to my lips. I made a big production out of kissing her hand. Everyone was amused.

"We're lucky," I said.

"You guys," Terri said. "Stop that now. You're making me sick. You're still on a honeymoon, for God's sake. You're still gaga, for crying out loud. Just wait. How long have you been together now? How long has it been? A year? Longer than a year?"

"Going on a year and a half," Laura said, flushed and smiling. "Oh, now," Terri said. "Wait a while."

She held her drink and gazed at Laura.

"I'm only kidding," Terri said.

Mel opened the gin and went around the table with the bottle.

"Here, you guys," he said. "Let's have a toast. I want to propose a toast. Toast to love. To true love," Mel said.

We touched glasses.

"To love," we said.

Outside in the backyard, one of the dogs began to bark. The leaves of the aspen that leaned past the window ticked against the glass. The afternoon sunlight was like a presence in this room, the spacious light of ease and generosity. We could have been anywhere, somewhere enchanted. We raised our glasses again and grinned at each other like children who had agreed on something forbidden.

"I'll tell you what real love is," Mel said. "I mean, I'll give you a good example. And then you can draw your own conclusions." He poured more gin into his glass. He added an ice cube and a sliver of lime. We waited and sipped our drinks. Laura and I touched knees again. I put a hand on her warm thigh and left it there.

"What do any of us really know about love?" Mel said. "It seems to me we're just beginners at love. We say we love each other and we do, I don't doubt it. I love Terri and Terri loves me, and you guys love each other too. You know the kind of love I'm talking about now. Physical love, that impulse that drives you to someone special, as well as love of the other person's being, his or her essence, as it were. Carnal love and, well, call it sentimental love, the day-to-day caring about the other person. But sometimes I have a hard time accounting for the fact that I must have loved my first wife too. But I did, I know I did. So I suppose I am like Terri in that regard. Terri and Ed." He thought about it and then he went on. "There was a time when I thought I loved my first wife more than life itself. But now I hate her guts. I do. How do you explain that? What happened to that love? What happened to it, is what I'd like to know. I wish someone could tell me. Then there's Ed. Okay, we're back to Ed. He loves Terri so much he tries to kill her and he winds up killing himself." Mel stopped talking and swallowed from his glass. "You guys have been together eighteen months and you love each other. It shows all over you. You glow with it. But you both loved other people before you met each other. You've both been married before, just like us. And you probably loved other people before that too, even. Terri and I have been together five years, been married for four. And the terrible thing, the terrible thing is, but the good thing, too, the saving grace, you might say, is that if something happened to one of us—excuse me for saying this—but if something happened to one of us tomorrow, I think the other one, the other person, would grieve for a while, you know, but then the surviving party would go out and love again, have someone else soon enough. All this, all of this love we're talking about it would just be a memory. Maybe not even a memory. Am I wrong? Am I way off base? Because I want you to set me straight if you think I'm wrong. I want to know. I mean, I don't know anything, and I'm the first one to admit it."

"Mel, for God's sake," Terri said. She reached out and took hold of his wrist. "Are you getting drunk? Honey? Are you drunk?"

"Honey, I'm just talking," Mel said. "All right? I don't have to be drunk to say what I think. I mean, we're all just talking, right?" Mel said. He fixed his eyes on her.

"Sweetie, I'm not criticizing," Terri said.

She picked up her glass.

"I'm not on call today," Mel said. "Let me remind you of that. I am not on call."

"Mel, we love you," Laura said.

Mel looked at Laura. He looked at her as if he couldn't place her, as if she was not the woman she was.

"Love you too, Laura," Mel said. "And you, Nick, love you too. You know something?" Mel said. "You guys are our pals," Mel said.

He picked up his glass.

Mel said, "I was going to tell you about something. I mean, I was going to prove a point. You see, this happened a few months ago, but it's still going on right now, and it ought to make us feel ashamed when we talk like we know what we' re talking about when we talk about love."

"Come on now," Terri said. "Don't talk like you're drunk if you're not drunk."

"Just shut up for once in your life," Mel said very quietly. "Will you do me a favor and do that for a minute? So as I was saying, there's this old couple who had this car wreck out on the interstate? A kid hit them and they were all torn to shit and nobody was giving them much chance to pull through."

Terri looked at us and then back at Mel. She seemed anxious, or maybe that's too strong a word.

Mel was handing the bottle around the table.

"I was on call that night," Mel said. "It was in May or maybe it was June.

Terri and I had just sat down to dinner when the hospital called. There'd been this thing out on the interstate. Drunk kid, teenager, plowed his dad's pickup into this camper with this old couple in it. They were up in their mid-seventies, that couple. The kid—eighteen, nineteen, something—he was DOA. Take the steering wheel through his sternum. The old couple, they were alive, you understand. I mean, just barely. But they had everything. Multiple fractures, internal injuries, hemorrhaging, contusions, lacerations, the works, and they each of them had themselves concussions. They were in a bad way, believe me. And, of course, their age was two strikes against them. I'd say she was worse off than he was. Ruptured spleen along with everything else. Both kneecaps broken. But they'd been wearing their seatbelts and, God knows, that's what saved them for the time being."

"Folks, this is an advertisement for the National Safety Council," Terri said. "This is your spokesman, Doctor Melvin R. McGinnis, talking." Terri laughed. "Mel," she said, "sometimes you're just too much sometimes. But I love you, hon," She said.

"Honey, I love you," Mel said.

He leaned across the table. Terri met him halfway. They kissed.

"Terri's right," Mel said as he settled himself again. "Get those seatbelts on. But seriously, they were in some shape, those oldsters. By the time I got down there, the kid was dead, as I said. He was off in a corner, laid out on a gurney. I took one look at the old couple and told the ER nurse to get me a neurologist and an orthopedic man and a couple of surgeons down there right away."

He drank from his glass. "I'll try to keep this short," he said. "So we took the two of them up to the OR and worked like fuck on them most of the night. They had these incredible reserves, those two. You see that once in a while. So we did everything that could be done, and toward morning we're giving them a fifty-fifty chance, maybe less than that for her. So here they are, still alive the next morning. So, okay, we move them into the ICU, which is where they both kept plugging away at it for two weeks, hitting it better and better on all the scopes. So we transfer them out to their own room."

Mel stopped talking. "Here," he said, "let's drink this cheap gin the hell up. Then we're going to dinner, right? Terri and I know a new place. That's where we'll go, to this new place we know about. But we're not going until we finish up this cut-rate, lousy gin."

Terri said, "We haven't actually eaten there yet. But it looks good. From the outside, you know."

"I like food," Mel said. "If I had it to do all over again, I'd be a chef, you know? Right, Terri?" Mel said.

He laughed. He fingered the ice in his glass.

"Terri knows. Terri can tell you. But let me say this. If I could come back again in a different life, a different time and all, you know what? I'd like to come back as a knight. You were pretty safe wearing all that armor. It was all right being a knight until gunpowder and muskets and pistols came along."

"Mel would like to ride a horse and carry a lance," Terri said, "Carry a woman's scarf with you everywhere," Laura said.

"Or just a woman," Mel said.

"Shame on you," Laura said.

Terri said,"Suppose you came back as a serf. The serfs didn't have it so good in those days," Terri said.

"The serfs never had it good,"Mel said. "But I guess even the knights were vessels to someone. Isn't that the way it worked? But then everyone is always a vessel to someone else. Isn't that right? Terri? But what I liked about knights, besides their ladies, was that they had that suit of armor, you know, and they couldn't get hurt very easy. No cars in those days, you know? No drunk teenagers to tear into your ass."

"Vassals," Terri said.

"What?" Mel said.

"Vassals," Mel said. "They were called vassals, not vessels."

"Vassals,vessels," Mel said, "what the fuck's the difference? You knew what I meant anyway. All right," Mel said. "So I'm not educated. I learned my stuff. I'm a heart surgeon, sure, but I'm just a mechanic. I go in and I fuck around and I fix things. Shit," Mel said.

"Modesty doesn't become you,"Terri said.

"He's just a humble sawbones," I said. "But sometimes they suffocated in all that armor, Mel. They'd even have heart attacks if it got too hot and they were too tired and worn out. I read somewhere that they'd fall off their horses and not be able to get up because they were too tired to stand with all that armor on them. They got trampled by their own horses sometimes."

"That's terrible,"Mel said. "That's a terrible image, Nicky. I guess they'd just lay there and wait until somebody came along and made a shish kebab out of them."

"Some other vessel," Terri said.

"That's right," Mel said. "Some vassal would come along and spear the bastard in the name of love. Or whatever the fuck it was they fought over in those days."

"Same things we fight over these days," Mel said.

Laura said, "Nothing's changed."

The color was still high in Laura's cheeks. Her eyes were bright. She brought her glass to her lips.

Mel poured himself another drink. He looked at the label closely as if studying a long row of numbers. Then he slowly put the bottle down on the table and reached for the tonic water.

"What about the old couple?" Laura said. "You didn't finish that story you started."

Laura was having a hard time lighting her cigarette. Her matches kept going out.

The sunshine inside the room was different now, changing, getting thinner. But the leaves outside the window were still shimmering, and I stared at the pattern they made on the panes and on the Formica counter. They weren't the same patterns, of course.

"What about that old couple?" I said.

"Older but wiser," Terri said.

Mel stared at her.

Terri said, "Go on with your story, hon. I was only kidding. Then what happened?"

"Terri, sometimes," Mel said.

"Please, Mel," Terri said. "Don't always be so serious, sweetie. Can't you take a joke?"

"Where's the joke?" Mel said.

He held his glass and gazed steadily at his wife.

"What happened?" Laura said.

Mel fastened his eyes on Laura. He said, "Laura, if I didn't have Terri and if I didn't love her so much, and if Nick wasn't my best friend, I'd fall in love with you. I'd carry you off, honey," He said.

"Tell your story," Terri said. "Then we'll go to that new place, okay?"

"Okay?" Mel said. "Where was I?" he said. He stared at the table and then he began again.

"I dropped in to see each of them every day, sometimes twice a day if I was up doing other calls anyway. Casts and bandages, head to foot, the both of them. You know, you've seen it in the movies. That's just the way they looked, just like in the movies. Little eye-holes and nose-holes and mouth-holes. And she had to have her legs slung up on top of it. Well, the husband was very depressed for the longest while. Even after he found out that his wife was going to pull through, he was still very depressed. Not about the accident, though. I mean, the accident was one thing, but it wasn't everything. I'd get up to his mouth-hole, you know, and he'd say no, it wasn't the accident exactly but it was because he couldn't see her through his eye-holes. He said that was what was making him feel so bad. Can you imagine? I'm telling you, the man's heart was breaking because he couldn't turn his goddamn head and see his goddamn wife."

Mel looked around the table and shook his head at what he was going to say.

"I mean, it was killing the old fart just because he couldn't look at the fucking woman."

We all looked at Mel.

"Do you see what I'm saying?"

Maybe we were a little drunk by then. I know it was hard keeping things in focus. The light was draining out of the room, going back through the window where it had come from. Yet nobody made a move to get up from the table to turn on the overhead light.

"Listen," Mel said. "Let's finish this fucking gin. There's about enough left here for one shooter all around. Then let's go eat. Let's go to the new place."

"He's depressed," Terri said. "Mel, why don't you take a pill?" Mel shook his head. "I've taken everything there is."

"We all need a pill now and then," I said.

"Some people are born needing them," Terri said.

She was using her finger to rub at something on the table. Then she stopped rubbing.

"I think I want to call my kids," Mel said. "Is that all right with everybody? I'll call my kids," He said.

Terri said, "What if Marjorie answers the phone? You guys, you've heard us on the subject of Marjorie. Honey, you know you don't want to talk to Marjorie. It'll make you feel even worse."

"I don't want to talk to Marjorie," Mel said. "But I want to talk to my kids."

"There isn't a day goes by that Mel doesn't say he wishes she'd get married again. Or else die," Terri said. "For one thing," Terri said, "she's bankrupting us. Mel says it's just to spite him that she won't get married again. She has a boyfriend who lives with her and the kids, so Mel is supporting the boyfriend too."

"She's allergic to bees," Mel said. "If I'm not praying she'll get married again, I'm praying she'll get herself stung to death by a swarm of fucking bees."

"Shame on you," Laura said.

"Bzzzzzz," Mel said, turning his fingers into bees and buzzing them at Terri's throat. Then he let his hands drop all the way to his sides.

"She's vicious," Mel said. "Sometimes I think I'll go up there dressed like a beekeeper. You know, that hat that's like a helmet with the plate that comes down over your face, the big gloves, and the padded coat? I'll knock on the door and let loose a hive of bees in the house. But first I'd make sure the kids were out, of course."

He crossed one leg over the other. Then he put both feet on the floor and leaned forward, elbows on the table, his chin cupped in his hands.

"Maybe I won't call the kids, after all. Maybe it isn't such a hot idea. Maybe we'll just go eat. How does that sound?"

"Sounds fine to me," I said. "Eat or not eat. Or keep drinking. I could head right on out into the sunset."

"What does that mean, honey?" Laura said.

"It just means what I said," I said. "It means I could just keep going. That's all it means."

"I could eat something myself," Laura said. "I don't think I've ever been so hungry in my life. Is there something to nibble on?"

"I'll put out some cheese and crackers," Terri said.

But Terri just sat there. She did not get up to get anything.

Mel turned his glass over. He spilled it out on the table.

"Gin's gone," Mel said.

Terri said, "Now what?"

I could hear my heart beating. I could hear everyone's heart. I could hear the human noise we sat there making, not one of us moving, not even when the room went dark.

[Selected from Raymond Carver. *What We Talk About When We Talk About Love*. New York: Vintage, 1981.]

Ⅲ. Questions for discussion

(1) How many marriages are dealt with in this story? What are they?

(2) What are they talking about when the two couples are talking about love? What are their attitudes towards love?

(3) How are Minimalistic techniques employed in this story?

(4) How to understand this genre in the social-cultural context of the 20th century America?

3.3 Assigned Reading

What We Write About When We Write About Love

Sharon Oard Warner

"What do any of us really know about love?" So asks Mel McGinnis, the main character in one of Raymond Carver's finest stories, "What We Talk About When We Talk About Love."

Mel's question is rhetorical, of course, simply his way of introducing the subject to the three other people at the table. Like the rest of us, Mel considers himself an expert. As Scottish novelist and poet George MacDonald said, "There is no feeling in the human heart which exists in that heart alone which is not, in some form or degree, in every heart." We all recognize love when we see it, know it when we feel it, cherish its presence and grieve its loss.

No wonder writers come to the subject with a certain degree of confidence. Write about what you know, we're admonished. Well, we all know about love, don't we? Sure we do. Since all of us are experts, then why is it so damned difficult to write a good love story? Why do stories about love and the lovelorn so often leave us cold?

In my quest for answers, I reread Carver's famous story. Right off the bat, the author establishes a number of facts. By the end of the second sentence we learn that Mel McGinnis is a cardiologist, and in the following three sentences we discover the immediate setting of the story—Mel's kitchen—and the city in which the story takes place, Albuquerque, N. M. The other characters are introduced as well: Mel's second wife, Terri; the narrator, Nick; and Nick's wife, Laura. But that's not all. Carver also tells us that the four are drinking gin and that "sunlight filled the kitchen from the big window behind the sink." Because I live in Albuquerque, I know the quality of this sunlight, its clarity and brilliance. Those of you in Cleveland or Minneapolis or elsewhere don't have this advantage, but that's OK. The story's only a little less glorious for your not knowing the vivid blue of an Albuquerque sky.

So, what's the sky got to do with it? Actually, a lot more than you might think. In order to establish characters, Carver has to place them in a particular location, and the sooner the better. For Carver, it isn't enough to let us into Mel's kitchen, ice bucket and bottle of gin on the table. He also puts Mel's kitchen in a specific city, Albuquerque. In so doing, he allows readers to relax. We don't have to be casting about for clues to set up this scene. It's all there, in the first five sentences, which allows us to focus on the people, what they're saying and doing.

Early on, Nick, the narrator, gives us a dear physical description of his best friend: "Mel was 45 years old. He was tall and rangy with curly soft hair. His face and arms were brown from all the tennis he played. When he was sober, his gestures, all his movements, were precise, very careful." He also tells us a little something about Mel's past—that he spent five years in the seminary before going to medical school, which explains why he believes that real love is "nothing less than spiritual love."

Even sooner, in the middle of the first page, we get a description of Mel's wife, Terri: "She was a bone-thin woman with a pretty face, dark eyes, and brown hair that hung down her back. She liked necklaces made of turquoise, and long pendant earrings." Note that the details about Terri's jewelry reinforce our sense of place—New Mexico, where lots of women wear silver and turquoise.

Terri's description comes before Mel's because she's the first to speak, and the reader must visualize her first. What she says is a bit shocking: she regales those at the table with the story of her ex-lover, a man who beat her and dragged her around the room by her ankles. "What do you do with love like that?" she asks those at the table (and us). It's another rhetorical question, and one that provokes an argument. "My God, don't be silly. That's not love, and you know it," Mel responds. "I don't know what you'd call it, but I sure know you wouldn't call it love." Plenty of readers are sure to agree with him. They may even be relieved that someone in this story has his head on straight. (But keep in mind they haven't yet finished the story.)

"People are different, Mel," Terri replies. "Sure, sometimes he may have acted crazy. Okay. But he loved me. In his own way, maybe, but he loved me." And there we have it, the essential catalyst of fiction: conflict. It unfolds quite naturally in the first two pages—so naturally we hardly notice—and it deepens and darkens, like the light from the kitchen window as day gives way to night.

Like everything else that matters, love is in the details. Human beings believe they're loved because others act in loving ways. Words and words alone don't convince us, not for long, anyway. And it's the same in fiction. We believe in these people—Mel and Terri and, to a lesser degree, Nick and Laura—because Carver has done the behind-the-scenes work. Either before he began writing, or else in successive drafts, he presented the relevant details that bring his characters to life: physical descriptions, personal histories, temperments, quirks and mannerisms. We note, for instance, that the newly marrieds repeatedly reach out to one another for reassurance; early on, Nick touches Laura's hand, then encircles her broad wrist with his fingers, holding her. Their body language alone speaks volumes.

To write convincingly, fiction writers must hold two complementary but seemingly opposing ideas in mind: People are both entirely similar and utterly different. We all walk, yes, but we all walk differently. Some of us skim along the surface of the sidewalk; others scuff, sidle, swagger or schlump. A few of us make our way in wheelchairs, and if we're small enough or sick enough, we crawl. We all love, yes (well, all but sociopaths, my husband the psychologist would remind me), but we all love differently. Defending her ex-lover, Terri says, "It was love. Sure it was abnormal in most people's eyes. But he was willing to die for it." Mel scoffs at this notion. His preference is for chivalrous love, ethereal and everlasting. Late in the story, he admits that if he could be born in another day and time, he'd come back as a knight in shining armor. While our similarities bind us to the rest of humanity, our differences define us.

We writers have our theories on love. Southern writer Carson McCullers believed in what she called "the lover and the beloved." According to her, two people rarely have the good sense to love one another. Rather, she maintained that "love is a solitary thing," that we are destined to be either the lover or the beloved. My own theory has to do with childhood experience. As I see it, the way we make our way through this word is determined in large part by our pasts and, particularly, by what we experienced as children. Our definitions of love, our capacity for love whom we love and why—are all strongly influenced by what we learned of love when we were young. Thus, I come to my characters through their childhoods. In developing them, I want to learn as much as possible about their formative experiences—for good and for ill.

Over the last seven years, I've written a novel called Deep in the Heart. Central to the story is a couple married 17 years, Carl and Hannah Solace. While composing the first few drafts, I took great pains to discover the childhood histories of the two. I knew, for instance, about the death of Hannah's mother and the aftermath of that death, which turns out to be critical to Hannah's decision not to have children. I also learned/discovered/made up all I could about Cad's early life in Terrell, Texas; about his mother's job at the state hospital; about his father's retreat to a fishing cabin at Lake Texoma; and about his bullying brother, Buddy.

I wrote whole chapters that have long since disappeared from the actual book. But the lost chapters were not a waste of time. Far from it. This sort of "research" is absolutely critical to my understanding of the characters' motivations. Because I did this work, I know that Carl yearns for unequivocal love, the sort that most of us get from our children. When he learns that his wife is pregnant for the first time, he is dumbstruck and overcome by an immense happiness he's desperate to convey to his miserable wife.

Needless to say, I felt fairly secure in my knowledge of these characters. It wasn't until after I sold the novel and made a trip to New York to meet my editors that I learned differently. During a two-hour meeting, I woke up to the limitations of my own process. Although I knew a great deal about some things, it turned out that I was entirely ignorant about others. "How did Hannah and Cad meet?" My editors asked. "How were the early years of their marriage? When did they stop being happy together?" I didn't have the faintest idea and had to admit it. A few days later, when the flush of embarrassment finally left me, I went over the notes of the meeting, then spent a month or so filling in the gaps. To do this, I turned to an exercise I've recommended to students over the years but had never completed myself.

It comes from "Chronology in the Short Story" in The Passionate, Accurate Story by Carol Bly. She brings up a story by Richard Brautigan, "The World War I Los Angeles Airplane," a three-page wonder that's nothing more than a list of 33 items from one man's life. Upon reading that story, I immediately saw Bly's point: "We can learn a chronology lesson from Brautigan," she writes. "It is that if a meaningful scene, no matter how short, is set next to another meaningful scene, feeling and value multiply."

I called my list "Story of a Marriage." It begins when Hannah and Cad met and concludes some 20 years later, after they divorce and remarry. In that way, I discovered what becomes of them in the years after the book ends, and this, too, has been useful because it has granted me a sort of omniscience. Once, I happened to mention Cad's remarriage to my editor, Carla Riccio. "He gets married again!" She exclaimed. "Oh, I'm so glad to hear that, Sharon? Somewhere along the way, Carl had ceased to be a collection of characteristics and had become—for us, anyway—a real human being."

Perhaps you've heard the truism that the only people who can understand a marriage are the two living inside it. Accurate as this may be in real life, it's wrong when it comes to fiction. Writers interested in the vagaries of love must inhabit a relationship in the same way the couple does, from the inside out. Only then will they know enough to convince the rest of us to care.

At the end of "What We Talk About When We Talk About Love," Mel—

thoroughly drunk and waxing nostalgic—says he wants to call his kids. Terri discourages him, pointing out that Mel's ex-wife, Marjorie, might answer. Terri knows all about Marjorie: "There isn't a day goes by that Mel doesn't say he wishes she'd get married again. Or else die," she explains. While some readers (and delicate little Laura) may be surprised by this harsh comment, Terri isn't and neither is Carver. Even knights in shining armor have their soft spots—even knights miss their children and grieve over their failures. Losing love, they may turn to hate. We begin to understand what Mel knows about love, and yes, our hearts go out to him.

[Selected from Sharon Oard Warner. What We Write About When We Write About Love. *Writer*, 2002(11).]

4. Joyce Carol Oates

4.1 Presentation Topics

(1)Joyce Carol Oates as a prolific writer, known as the "dark lady of American letters."

(2)Postmodern techniques in Oates' works.

(3)Women characters and feminist overtones in her works.

4.2 Selected Reading

Ⅰ. Central issue of concern

Oates' ongoing interest in adolescence, her preoccupation with the psychological and social turmoil, and her keen sense of the teenager pressures as well as her constant concern about violence, rural poverty, female issues, sexual abuse, class tension, and desire for power, as mostly reflected in "Where Are You Going, Where Have You Been?".

Ⅱ. Text

Where Are You Going, Where Have You Been?①

For Bob Dylan

Her name was Connie. She was fifteen and she had a quick, nervous giggling habit of craning her neck to glance into mirrors or checking other people's faces to make sure her own was all right. Her mother, who noticed everything and knew everything and who hadn't much reason any longer to look at her own face, always scolded Connie about it. "Stop gawking② at yourself. Who are you? You think you're so pretty?" She would say. Connie would raise her eyebrows at these familiar old complaints and look right through her mother, into a shadowy vision of herself as she was right at that moment: she knew she was pretty and that was everything. Her mother had been pretty once too, if you could believe those old snapshots in the album, but now her looks were gone and that was why she was always after Connie.

"Why don't you keep your room clean like your sister? How've you got your hair fixed—what the hell stinks? Hair spray? You don't see your sister using that junk."

Her sister June was twenty-four and still lived at home. She was a secretary in the high school Connie attended, and if that wasn't bad enough—with her in the same building—she was so plain and chunky③ and steady that Connie had to hear her praised all the time by her mother and her mother's sisters. June did this, June did that, she saved money and helped clean the house and cooked and Connie couldn't do a thing, her mind was all filled with trashy daydreams. Their father was away at work most of the time and when he came home he wanted supper and he read the newspaper at supper and after supper he went to bed. He didn't bother talking much to them, but around his bent head Connie's mother kept picking at

---

① Oates was inspired to write "Where Are You Going, Where Have You Been?" after reading an account in *Life* magazine of a charismatic but insecure young man who had enticed and then killed several girls in Tucson, Arizona, during the early 1960s. This story was first published by the literary journal *Epoch* in 1966 and was included in Oates' 1970 short story collection *The Wheel of Love*. Oates said that she dedicated the story to Bob Dylan because she had been inspired to write it after listening to his song "It's All Over Now, Baby Blue."

② Staring or gaping stupidly.

③ Short and thick; stocky.

her until Connie wished her mother was dead and she herself was dead and it was all over. "She makes me want to throw up sometimes," she complained to her friends. She had a high, breathless, amused voice that made everything she said sound a little forced, whether it was sincere or not.

There was one good thing: June went places with girl friends of hers, girls who were just as plain and steady as she, and so when Connie wanted to do that her mother had no objections. The father of Connie's best girl friend drove the girls the three miles to town and left them at a shopping plaza so they could walk through the stores or go to a movie, and when he came to pick them up again at eleven he never bothered to ask what they had done.

They must have been familiar sights, walking around the shopping plaza in their shorts and flat ballerina slippers that always scuffed① the sidewalk, with charm bracelets jingling on their thin wrists; they would lean together to whisper and laugh secretly if someone passed who amused or interested them. Connie had long dark blond hair that drew anyone's eye to it, and she wore part of it pulled up on her head and puffed out and the rest of it she let fall down her back. She wore a pull-over jersey blouse that looked one way when she was at home and another way when she was away from home. Everything about her had two sides to it, one for home and one for anywhere that was not home: her walk, which could be childlike and bobbing, or languid enough to make anyone think she was hearing music in her head; her mouth, which was pale and smirking② most of the time, but bright and pink on these evenings out; her laugh, which was cynical and drawling at home—"Ha, ha, very funny,"—but high pitched and nervous anywhere else, like the jingling of the charms on her bracelet.

Sometimes they did go shopping or to a movie, but sometimes they went across the highway, ducking fast across the busy road, to a drive-in restaurant where older kids hung out. The restaurant was shaped like a big bottle, though squatter than a real bottle, and on its cap was a revolving figure of a grinning boy holding a hamburger aloft. One night in midsummer they ran across, breathless with daring, and right away someone leaned out a car window and invited them over, but it was

---

① To scrape the feet while walking; shuffle.

② Smiling in an affected, often offensively self-satisfied manner.

just a boy from high school they didn't like. It made them feel good to be able to ignore him. They went up through the maze of parked and cruising cars to the bright-lit, fly-infested restaurant, their faces pleased and expectant as if they were entering a sacred building that loomed up out of the night to give them what haven and blessing they yearned for. They sat at the counter and crossed their legs at the ankles, their thin shoulders rigid with excitement, and listened to the music that made everything so good: the music was always in the background, like music at a church service; it was something to depend upon.

A boy named Eddie came in to talk with them. He sat backwards on his stool, turning himself jerkily around in semicircles and then stopping and turning back again, and after a while he asked Connie if she would like something to eat. She said she would and so she tapped her friend's arm on her way out—her friend pulled her face up into a brave, droll① look—and Connie said she would meet her at eleven, across the way. "I just hate to leave her like that," Connie said earnestly, but the boy said that she wouldn't be alone for long. So they went out to his car, and on the way Connie couldn't help but let her eyes wander over the windshields and faces all around her, her face gleaming with a joy that had nothing to do with Eddie or even this place; it might have been the music. She drew her shoulders up and sucked in her breath with the pure pleasure of being alive, and just at that moment she happened to glance at a face just a few feet from hers. It was a boy with shaggy black hair, in a convertible jalopy② painted gold. He stared at her and then his lips widened into a grin. Connie slit her eyes at him and turned away, but she couldn't help glancing back and there he was, still watching her. He wagged a finger and laughed and said, "Gonna get you, baby," and Connie turned away again without Eddie noticing anything.

She spent three hours with him, at the restaurant where they ate hamburgers and drank Cokes in wax cups that were always sweating, and then down an alley a mile or so away, and when he left her off at five to eleven only the movie house was still open at the plaza. Her girl friend was there, talking with a boy. When Connie came up, the two girls smiled at each other and Connie said, "How was the

① Amusingly odd or whimsically comical.

② An old, dilapidated motor vehicle, especially an automobile.

movie?" And the girl said, "You should know." They rode off with the girl's father, sleepy and pleased, and Connie couldn't help but look back at the darkened shopping plaza with its big empty parking lot and its signs that were faded and ghostly now, and over at the drive-in restaurant where cars were still circling tirelessly. She couldn't hear the music at this distance.

Next morning June asked her how the movie was and Connie said, "So-so."

She and that girl and occasionally another girl went out several times a week, and the rest of the time Connie spent around the house—it was summer vacation—getting in her mother's way and thinking, dreaming about the boys she met. But all the boys fell back and dissolved into a single face that was not even a face but an idea, a feeling, mixed up with the urgent insistent pounding of the music and the humid night air of July. Connie's mother kept dragging her back to the daylight by finding things for her to do or saying suddenly, "What's this about the Pettinger girl?"

And Connie would say nervously, "Oh, her. That dope." She always drew thick clear lines between herself and such girls, and her mother was simple and kind enough to believe it. Her mother was so simple, Connie thought, that it was maybe cruel to fool her so much. Her mother went scuffling around the house in old bedroom slippers and complained over the telephone to one sister about the other, then the other called up and the two of them complained about the third one. If June's name was mentioned her mother's tone was approving, and if Connie's name was mentioned it was disapproving. This did not really mean she disliked Connie, and actually Connie thought that her mother preferred her to June just because she was prettier, but the two of them kept up a pretense of exasperation, a sense that they were tugging and struggling over something of little value to either of them. Sometimes, over coffee, they were almost friends, but something would come up—some vexation that was like a fly buzzing suddenly around their heads—and their faces went hard with contempt.

One Sunday Connie got up at eleven—none of them bothered with church—and washed her hair so that it could dry all day long in the sun. Her parents and sister were going to a barbecue at an aunt's house and Connie said no, she wasn't interested, rolling her eyes to let her mother know just what she thought of it. "Stay home alone then," her mother said sharply. Connie sat out back in a lawn chair and watched them drive away, her father quiet and bald, hunched around so that he could back the car out, her mother with a look that was still angry and not at all softened through the windshield, and in the back seat poor old June, all dressed up as if she didn't know what a barbecue was, with all the running yelling kids and the flies. Connie sat with her eyes closed in the sun, dreaming and dazed with the warmth about her as if this were a kind of love, the caresses of love, and her mind slipped over onto thoughts of the boy she had been with the night before and how nice he had been, how sweet it always was, not the way someone like June would suppose but sweet, gentle, the way it was in movies and promised in songs; and when she opened her eyes she hardly knew where she was, the back yard ran off into weeds and a fence-like line of trees and behind it the sky was perfectly blue and still. The asbestos ranch house that was now three years old startled her—it looked small. She shook her head as if to get awake.

It was too hot. She went inside the house and turned on the radio to drown out the quiet. She sat on the edge of her bed, barefoot, and listened for an hour and a half to a program called XYZ Sunday Jamboree, record after record of hard, fast, shrieking songs she sang along with, interspersed by exclamations from "Bobby King": "An' look here, you girls at Napoleon's—Son and Charley want you to pay real close attention to this song coming up!"

And Connie paid close attention to herself, bathed in a glow of slow-pulsed joy that seemed to rise mysteriously out of the music itself and lay languidly about the airless little room, breathed in and breathed out with each gentle rise and fall of her chest.

After a while she heard a car coming up the drive. She sat up at once, startled, because it couldn't be her father so soon. The gravel kept crunching all the way from the road—the driveway was long—and Connie ran to the window. It was a car she didn't know. It was an open jalopy, painted a bright gold that caught the sunlight opaquely①. Her heart began to pound and her fingers snatched at her hair, checking it, and she whispered, "Christ. Christ," wondering how bad she looked. The car came to a stop at the side door and the horn sounded four short taps, as if this were a signal Connie knew.

---

① Not allowing light to pass through; not transparent.

She went into the kitchen and approached the door slowly, then hung out the screen door, her bare toes curling down off the step. There were two boys in the car and now she recognized the driver: he had shaggy, shabby black hair that looked crazy as a wig and he was grinning at her.

"I ain't late, am I?" he said.

"Who the hell do you think you are?" Connie said.

"Toldja I'd be out, didn't I?"

"I don't even know who you are."

She spoke sullenly, careful to show no interest or pleasure, and he spoke in a fast, bright monotone. Connie looked past him to the other boy, taking her time. He had fair brown hair, with a lock that fell onto his forehead. His sideburns gave him a fierce, embarrassed look, but so far he hadn't even bothered to glance at her. Both boys wore sunglasses. The driver's glasses were metallic and mirrored everything in miniature.

"You wanta come for a ride?" he said.

Connie smirked and let her hair fall loose over one shoulder.

"Don'tcha like my car? New paint job," he said. "Hey."

"What?"

"You're cute."

She pretended to fidget①, chasing flies away from the door.

"Don'tcha believe me, or what?" he said.

"Look, I don't even know who you are," Connie said in disgust.

"Hey, Ellie's got a radio, see. Mine broke down." He lifted his friend's arm and showed her the little transistor radio the boy was holding, and now Connie began to hear the music. It was the same program that was playing inside the house.

"Bobby King?" she said.

"I listen to him all the time. I think he's great."

"He's kind of great," Connie said reluctantly.

"Listen, that guy's great. He knows where the action is."

Connie blushed a little, because the glasses made it impossible for her to see

---

① To behave or move nervously or restlessly.

just what this boy was looking at. She couldn't decide if she liked him or if he was just a jerk, and so she dawdled① in the doorway and wouldn't come down or go back inside. She said, "What's all that stuff painted on your car?"

"Can'tcha read it?" He opened the door very carefully, as if he were afraid it might fall off. He slid out just as carefully, planting his feet firmly on the ground, the tiny metallic world in his glasses slowing down like gelatin hardening, and in the midst of it Connie's bright green blouse. "This here is my name, to begin with, he said. ARNOLD FRIEND was written in tarlike black letters on the side, with a drawing of a round, grinning face that reminded Connie of a pumpkin, except it wore sunglasses. "I wanta introduce myself, I'm Arnold Friend and that's my real name and I'm gonna be your friend, honey, and inside the car's Ellie Oscar, he's kinda shy." Ellie brought his transistor radio up to his shoulder and balanced it there. "Now, these numbers are a secret code, honey," Arnold Friend explained. He read off the numbers 33, 19, 17 and raised his eyebrows at her to see what she thought of that, but she didn't think much of it. The left rear fender had been smashed and around it was written, on the gleaming gold background: DONE BY CRAZY WOMAN DRIVER. Connie had to laugh at that. Arnold Friend was pleased at her laughter and looked up at her. "Around the other side's a lot more—you wanta come and see them?"

"No."

"Why not?"

"Why should I?"

"Don'tcha wanta see what's on the car? Don'tcha wanta go for a ride?"

"I don't know."

"Why not?"

"I got things to do."

"Like what?"

"Things."

He laughed as if she had said something funny. He slapped his thighs. He was standing in a strange way, leaning back against the car as if he were balancing himself. He wasn't tall, only an inch or so taller than she would be if she came

① To take more time than necessary.

down to him. Connie liked the way he was dressed, which was the way all of them dressed: tight faded jeans stuffed into black, scuffed boots, a belt that pulled his waist in and showed how lean he was, and a white pull-over shirt that was a little soiled and showed the hard small muscles of his arms and shoulders. He looked as if he probably did hard work, lifting and carrying things. Even his neck looked muscular. And his face was a familiar face, somehow: the jaw and chin and cheeks slightly darkened because he hadn't shaved for a day or two, and the nose long and hawklike, sniffing as if she were a treat he was going to gobble① up and it was all a joke.

"Connie, you ain't telling the truth. This is your day set aside for a ride with me and you know it," he said, still laughing. The way he straightened and recovered from his fit of laughing showed that it had been all fake.

"How do you know what my name is?" she said suspiciously.

"It's Connie."

"Maybe and maybe not."

"I know my Connie," he said, wagging his finger. Now she remembered him even better, back at the restaurant, and her cheeks warmed at the thought of how she had sucked in her breath just at the moment she passed him—how she must have looked to him. And he had remembered her. "Ellie and I come out here especially for you," he said. "Ellie can sit in back. How about it?"

"Where?"

"Where what?"

"Where're we going?"

He looked at her. He took off the sunglasses and she saw how pale the skin around his eyes was, like holes that were not in shadow but instead in light. His eyes were like chips of broken glass that catch the light in an amiable way. He smiled. It was as if the idea of going for a ride somewhere, to someplace, was a new idea to him.

"Just for a ride, Connie sweetheart."

"I never said my name was Connie," she said.

"But I know what it is. I know your name and all about you, lots of things,"

---

① To devour in large, greedy gulps.

Arnold Friend said. He had not moved yet but stood still leaning back against the side of his jalopy. "I took a special interest in you, such a pretty girl, and found out all about you—like I know your parents and sister are gone somewhere and I know where and how long they're going to be gone, and I know who you were with last night, and your best girl friend's name is Betty. Right?"

He spoke in a simple lilting① voice, exactly as if he were reciting the words to a song. His smile assured her that everything was fine. In the car Ellie turned up the volume on his radio and did not bother to look around at them.

"Ellie can sit in the back seat," Arnold Friend said. He indicated his friend with a casual jerk of his chin, as if Ellie did not count and she should not bother with him.

"How'd you find out all that stuff?" Connie said.

"Listen: Betty Schultz and Tony Fitch and Jimmy Pettinger and Nancy Pettinger," he said in a chant. "Raymond Stanley and Bob Hutter—"

"Do you know all those kids?"

"I know everybody."

"Look, you're kidding. You're not from around here."

"Sure."

"But—how come we never saw you before?"

"Sure you saw me before," he said. He looked down at his boots, as if he were a little offended. "You just don't remember."

"I guess I'd remember you," Connie said.

"Yeah?" He looked up at this, beaming. He was pleased. He began to mark time with the music from Ellie's radio, tapping his fists lightly together. Connie looked away from his smile to the car, which was painted so bright it almost hurt her eyes to look at it. She looked at that name, ARNOLD FRIEND. And up at the front fender was an expression that was familiar—MAN THE FLYING SAUCERS. It was an expression kids had used the year before but didn't use this year. She looked at it for a while as if the words meant something to her that she did not yet know.

"What're you thinking about? Huh?" Arnold Friend demanded. "Not worried

---

① To say, sing, or play (something) in a cheerful, rhythmic manner.

about your hair blowing around in the car, are you?"

"No."

"Think I maybe can't drive good?"

"How do I know?"

"You're a hard girl to handle. How come?" he said. "Don't you know I'm your friend? Didn't you see me put my sign in the air when you walked by?"

"What sign?"

"My sign." And he drew an X in the air, leaning out toward her. They were maybe ten feet apart. After his hand fell back to his side the X was still in the air, almost visible. Connie let the screen door close and stood perfectly still inside it, listening to the music from her radio and the boy's blend together. She stared at Arnold Friend. He stood there so stiffly relaxed, pretending to be relaxed, with one hand idly on the door handle as if he were keeping himself up that way and had no intention of ever moving again. She recognized most things about him, the tight jeans that showed his thighs and buttocks and the greasy leather boots and the tight shirt, and even that slippery friendly smile of his, that sleepy dreamy smile that all the boys used to get across ideas they didn't want to put into words. She recognized all this and also the singsong way he talked, slightly mocking, kidding, but serious and a little melancholy, and she recognized the way he tapped one fist against the other in homage to the perpetual music behind him. But all these things did not come together.

She said suddenly, "Hey, how old are you?"

His smile faded. She could see then that he wasn't a kid, he was much older—thirty, maybe more. At this knowledge her heart began to pound faster.

"That's a crazy thing to ask. Can't cha see I'm your own age?"

"Like hell you are."

"Or maybe a couple years older. I'm eighteen."

"Eighteen?" she said doubtfully.

He grinned to reassure her and lines appeared at the corners of his mouth. His teeth were big and white. He grinned so broadly his eyes became slits and she saw how thick the lashes were, thick and black as if painted with a black tarlike material. Then, abruptly, he seemed to become embarrassed and looked over his shoulder at Ellie. "Him, he's crazy," he said. "Ain't he a riot? He's a nut, a real character." Ellie was still listening to the music. His sunglasses told nothing about what he was thinking. He wore a bright orange shirt unbuttoned halfway to show his chest, which was a pale, bluish chest and not muscular like Arnold Friend's. His shirt collar was turned up all around and the very tips of the collar pointed out past his chin as if they were protecting him. He was pressing the transistor radio up against his ear and sat there in a kind of daze, right in the sun.

"He's kinda strange," Connie said.

"Hey, she says you're kinda strange! Kinda strange!" Arnold Friend cried. He pounded on the car to get Ellie's attention. Ellie turned for the first time and Connie saw with shock that he wasn't a kid either—he had a fair, hairless face, cheeks reddened slightly as if the veins grew too close to the surface of his skin, the face of a forty-year-old baby. Connie felt a wave of dizziness rise in her at this sight and she stared at him as if waiting for something to change the shock of the moment, make it all right again. Ellie's lips kept shaping words, mumbling along with the words blasting in his ear.

"Maybe you two better go away," Connie said faintly.

"What? How come?" Arnold Friend cried. "We come out here to take you for a ride. It's Sunday." He had the voice of the man on the radio now. It was the same voice, Connie thought. "Don'tcha know it's Sunday all day? And honey, no matter who you were with last night, today you're with Arnold Friend and don't you forget it! Maybe you better step out here," he said, and this last was in a different voice. It was a little flatter, as if the heat was finally getting to him.

"No. I got things to do."

"Hey."

"You two better leave."

"We ain't leaving until you come with us."

"Like hell I am—"

"Connie, don't fool around with me. I mean—I mean, don't fool around," he said, shaking his head. He laughed incredulously. He placed his sunglasses on top of his head, carefully, as if he were indeed wearing a wig, and brought the stems down behind his ears. Connie stared at him, another wave of dizziness and fear rising in her so that for a moment he wasn't even in focus but was just a blur standing there against his gold car, and she had the idea that he had driven up the driveway all right but had come from nowhere before that and belonged nowhere and that everything about him and even about the music that was so familiar to her was only half real.

"If my father comes and sees you—"

"He ain't coming. He's at a barbecue."

"How do you know that?"

"Aunt Tillie's. Right now they're uh—they're drinking. Sitting around," he said vaguely, squinting① as if he were staring all the way to town and over to Aunt Tillie's back yard. Then the vision seemed to get clear and he nodded energetically. "Yeah. Sitting around. There's your sister in a blue dress, huh? And high heels, the poor sad bitch—nothing like you, sweetheart! And your mother's helping some fat woman with the corn, they're cleaning the corn—husking the corn—"

"What fat woman?" Connie cried.

"How do I know what fat woman, I don't know every goddamn fat woman in the world!" Arnold Friend laughed.

"Oh, that's Mrs. Hornsby... Who invited her?" Connie said. She felt a little lightheaded. Her breath was coming quickly.

"She's too fat. I don't like them fat. I like them the way you are, honey," he said, smiling sleepily at her. They stared at each other for a while through the screen door. He said softly, "Now, what you're going to do is this: you're going to come out that door. You're going to sit up front with me and Ellie's going to sit in the back, the hell with Ellie, right? This isn't Ellie's date. You're my date. I'm your lover, honey."

"What? You're crazy—"

"Yes, I'm your lover. You don't know what that is but you will," he said. "I know that too. I know all about you. But look: it's real nice and you couldn't ask for nobody better than me, or more polite. I always keep my word. I'll tell you how it is, I'm always nice at first, the first time. I'll hold you so tight you won't think you have to try to get away or pretend anything because you'll know you can't. And I'll come inside you where it's all secret and you'll give in to me and you'll love me."

---

① Looking with the eyes partly closed, as in bright sunlight.

"Shut up! You're crazy!" Connie said. She backed away from the door. She put her hands up against her ears as if she'd heard something terrible, something not meant for her. "People don't talk like that, you're crazy," she muttered. Her heart was almost too big now for her chest and its pumping made sweat break out all over her. She looked out to see Arnold Friend pause and then take a step toward the porch, lurching①. He almost fell. But, like a clever drunken man, he managed to catch his balance. He wobbled② in his high boots and grabbed hold of one of the porch posts.

"Honey?" he said. "You still listening?"

"Get the hell out of here!"

"Be nice, honey. Listen."

"I'm going to call the police—"

He wobbled again and out of the side of his mouth came a fast spat curse, an aside not meant for her to hear. But even this "Christ!" sounded forced. Then he began to smile again. She watched this smile come, awkward as if he were smiling from inside a mask. His whole face was a mask, she thought wildly, tanned down to his throat but then running out as if he had plastered make-up on his face but had forgotten about his throat.

"Honey—? Listen, here's how it is. I always tell the truth and I promise you this: I ain't coming in that house after you."

"You better not! I'm going to call the police if you—if you don't—"

"Honey," he said, talking right through her voice, "honey, I'm not coming in there but you are coming out here. You know why?"

She was panting. The kitchen looked like a place she had never seen before, some room she had run inside but that wasn't good enough, wasn't going to help her. The kitchen window had never had a curtain, after three years, and there were dishes in the sink for her to do—probably—and if you ran your hand across the table you'd probably feel something sticky there.

"You listening, honey? Hey?" "—going to call the police—"

"Soon as you touch the phone I don't need to keep my promise and can come

---

① Leaning or rolling suddenly.

② To move or rotate with an uneven or rocking motion or unsteadily from side to side.

inside. You won't want that."

She rushed forward and tried to lock the door. Her fingers were shaking. "But why lock it," Arnold Friend said gently, talking right into her face. "It's just a screen door. It's just nothing." One of his boots was at a strange angle, as if his foot wasn't in it. It pointed out to the left, bent at the ankle. "I mean, anybody can break through a screen door and glass and wood and iron or anything else if he needs to, anybody at all, and specially Arnold Friend. If the place got lit up with a fire, honey, you'd come runnin' out into my arms, right into my arms an' safe at home—like you knew I was your lover and'd stopped fooling around. I don't mind a nice shy girl but I don't like no fooling around." Part of those words were spoken with a slight rhythmic lilt, and Connie somehow recognized them—the echo of a song from last year, about a girl rushing into her boy friend's arms and coming home again—

Connie stood barefoot on the linoleum floor, staring at him. "What do you want?" she whispered.

"I want you," he said.

"What?"

"Seen you that night and thought, that's the one, yes sir. I never needed to look anymore."

"But my father's coming back. He's coming to get me. I had to wash my hair first—" She spoke in a dry, rapid voice, hardly raising it for him to hear.

"No, your daddy is not coming and yes, you had to wash your hair and you washed it for me. It's nice and shining and all for me. I thank you sweetheart," he said with a mock bow, but again he almost lost his balance. He had to bend and adjust his boots. Evidently his feet did not go all the way down; the boots must have been stuffed with something so that he would seem taller. Connie stared out at him and behind him at Ellie in the car, who seemed to be looking off toward Connie's right, into nothing. This Ellie said, pulling the words out of the air one after another as if he were just discovering them, "You want me to pull out the phone?"

"Shut your mouth and keep it shut," Arnold Friend said, his face red from bending over or maybe from embarrassment because Connie had seen his boots. "This ain't none of your business."

"What—what are you doing? What do you want?" Connie said. "If I call the police they'll get you, they'll arrest you—"

"Promise was not to come in unless you touch that phone, and I'll keep that promise," he said. He resumed his erect position and tried to force his shoulders back. He sounded like a hero in a movie, declaring something important. But he spoke too loudly and it was as if he were speaking to someone behind Connie. "I ain't made plans for coming in that house where I don't belong but just for you to come out to me, the way you should. Don't you know who I am?"

"You're crazy," she whispered. She backed away from the door but did not want to go into another part of the house, as if this would give him permission to come through the door. "What do you... you're crazy, you..."

"Huh? What're you saying, honey?"

Her eyes darted everywhere in the kitchen. She could not remember what it was, this room.

"This is how it is, honey: you come out and we'll drive away, have a nice ride. But if you don't come out we're gonna wait till your people come home and then they're all going to get it."

"You want that telephone pulled out?" Ellie said. He held the radio away from his ear and grimaced, as if without the radio the air was too much for him.

"I toldja shut up, Ellie," Arnold Friend said, "you're deaf, get a hearing aid, right? Fix yourself up. This little girl's no trouble and's gonna be nice to me, so Ellie, keep to yourself, this ain't your date right? Don't hem in on me, don't hog, don't crush, don't bird dog, don't trail me," he said in a rapid, meaningless voice, as if he were running through all the expressions he'd learned but was no longer sure which of them was in style, then rushing on to new ones, making them up with his eyes closed. "Don't crawl under my fence, don't squeeze in my chipmunk hole, don't sniff my glue, suck my popsicle, keep your own greasy fingers on yourself!" He shaded his eyes and peered in at Connie, who was backed against the kitchen table. "Don't mind him, honey, he's just a creep. He's a dope. Right? I'm the boy for you, and like I said, you come out here nice like a lady and give me your hand, and nobody else gets hurt, I mean, your nice old bald-headed daddy and your mummy and your sister in her high heels. Because listen: why bring them in this?"

"Leave me alone," Connie whispered.

"Hey, you know that old woman down the road, the one with the chickens and stuff—you know her?"

"She's dead!"

"Dead? What? You know her?" Arnold Friend said.

"She's dead—"

"Don't you like her?"

"She's dead—she's—she isn't here any more—"

"But don't you like her, I mean, you got something against her? Some grudge or something?" Then his voice dipped as if he were conscious of a rudeness. He touched the sunglasses perched up on top of his head as if to make sure they were still there. "Now, you be a good girl."

"What are you going to do?"

"Just two things, or maybe three," Arnold Friend said. "But I promise it won't last long and you'll like me the way you get to like people you're close to. You will. It's all over for you here, so come on out. You don't want your people in any trouble, do you?"

She turned and bumped against a chair or something, hurting her leg, but she ran into the back room and picked up the telephone. Something roared in her ear, a tiny roaring, and she was so sick with fear that she could do nothing but listen to it—the telephone was clammy and very heavy and her fingers groped down to the dial but were too weak to touch it. She began to scream into the phone, into the roaring. She cried out, she cried for her mother, she felt her breath start jerking back and forth in her lungs as if it were something Arnold Friend was stabbing her with again and again with no tenderness. A noisy sorrowful wailing rose all about her and she was locked inside it the way she was locked inside this house.

After a while she could hear again. She was sitting on the floor with her wet back against the wall.

Arnold Friend was saying from the door, "That's a good girl. Put the phone back."

She kicked the phone away from her.

"No, honey. Pick it up. Put it back right."

She picked it up and put it back. The dial tone stopped.

"That's a good girl. Now, you come outside."

She was hollow with what had been fear but what was now just an emptiness. All that screaming had blasted it out of her. She sat, one leg cramped under her, and deep inside her brain was something like a pinpoint of light that kept going and would not let her relax. She thought, I'm not going to see my mother again. She thought, I'm not going to sleep in my bed again. Her bright green blouse was all wet.

Arnold Friend said, in a gentle-loud voice that was like a stage voice, "The place where you came from ain't there any more, and where you had in mind to go is cancelled out. This place you are now—inside your daddy's house—is nothing but a cardboard box I can knock down any time. You know that and always did know it. You hear me?"

She thought, I have got to think. I have got to know what to do.

"We'll go out to a nice field, out in the country here where it smells so nice and it's sunny," Arnold Friend said. "I'll have my arms tight around you so you won't need to try to get away and I'll show you what love is like, what it does. The hell with this house! It looks solid all right," he said. He ran a fingernail down the screen and the noise did not make Connie shiver, as it would have the day before. "Now, put your hand on your heart, honey. Feel that? That feels solid too but we know better. Be nice to me, be sweet like you can because what else is there for a girl like you but to be sweet and pretty and give in? —And get away before her people come back?"

She felt her pounding heart. Her hand seemed to enclose it. She thought for the first time in her life that it was nothing that was hers, that belonged to her, but just a pounding, living thing inside this body that wasn't really hers either.

"You don't want them to get hurt," Arnold Friend went on. "Now, get up, honey. Get up all by yourself."

She stood.

"Now, turn this way. That's right. Come over here to me. —Ellie, put that away, didn't I tell you? You dope. You miserable creepy dope," Arnold Friend said. His words were not angry but only part of an incantation①. The incantation was kindly. "Now come out through the kitchen to me, honey, and let's see a

① Ritual recitation of verbal charms or spells to produce a magic effect.

smile, try it, you're a brave, sweet little girl and now they're eating corn and hot dogs cooked to bursting over an outdoor fire, and they don't know one thing about you and never did and honey, you're better than them because not a one of them would have done this for you."

Connie felt the linoleum under her feet; it was cool. She brushed her hair back out of her eyes. Arnold Friend let go of the post tentatively and opened his arms for her, his elbows pointing in toward each other and his wrists limp, to show that this was an embarrassed embrace and a little mocking, he didn't want to make her self-conscious.

She put out her hand against the screen. She watched herself push the door slowly open as if she were back safe somewhere in the other doorway, watching this body and this head of long hair moving out into the sunlight where Arnold Friend waited.

"My sweet little blue-eyed girl," he said in a half-sung sigh that had nothing to do with her brown eyes but was taken up just the same by the vast sunlit reaches of the land behind him and on all sides of him—so much land that Connie had never seen before and did not recognize except to know that she was going to it.

[Selected from Joyce Carol Oates. *The Wheel of Love and Other Stories*. New York: Vanguard, 1970.]

Ⅲ. Questions for Discussion

(1) How is the relationship between Connie and her family members? Any problem existed? What kind of girl is Connie?

(2) Who is Arnold Friend? Do you think he is a friend-like figure as his name suggested? Or, is he a friend? What is the significance of his car? His clothing? His language?

(3) When and why does Connie begin to question Arnold's identity? What impact does her confusion have on her own personality?

(4) What do you think of the ending of the story? What may happen next?

(5) Think of and interpret the symbols used in the story, such as the house, the screen door, the telephone, Arnold's high boots, his "X" sign, the numbers on his car, etc.

(6) This story is published in 1966. How much do you know about the 1960s'

in the United States? How to understand Oates' view of the demonic aspect of that time in America?

(7) How to understand the title of the story? Why is it dedicated to Bob Dylan?

4.3 Assigned Reading

The Shadow of a Satyr in Oates'

"Where Are You Going, Where Have You Been?"

Joan Easterly

The sinister Arnold Friend in Joyce Carol Oates' most anthologized short story has been accepted as the personification of Satan ever since Joyce M. Wegs skillfully identified his traits as being those of the Devil. However, a devil and a satyr cast similar shadows, and the complex allusive patterning of "Where Are You Going, Where Have You Been?" becomes more significant when Friend is interpreted as representing a satyr, a demi-god from Greek and Roman mythology. In *The Edge of Impossibility*, Oates states that "the abstract parody of human life as acted out by gods, has a profound and magical value, inexplicable." She further elaborates that tragedies should return to the figures of ancient Greek mythology for artistic expression that will be meaningful today:

If communal belief in God has diminished so that, as writers we can no longer presume upon it, then a redefinition of God in terms of the furthest reaches of man's hallucinations can provide us with a new basis for tragedy. The abyss will always open for us, though it begins as a pencil mark, the parody of a crack; the shapes of human beasts—centaurs and satyrs and their remarkable companions—will always be returning with nostalgia to our great cities.

In "Where Are You Going, Where Have You Been?", a satyr does come into the city, in the form of Arnold Friend. Dressed like a teenager, Friend first coaxes then intimidates fifteen-year-old Connie out of her house for a date that will clearly involve her sexual initiation. Although Wegs perceives Connie's words, "Christ, Christ" and "Who the hell do you think you are?" as clues to Friend's Satanic identity, these terms may also be interpreted as mere examples of current teenage speech as well as part of Oates' realistic packaging of a story with a mythological—not a Judeo-Christian—focus. The ambiguous power this stranger has over Connie, the depth of his deceptiveness, and the danger the ensuing adventure holds for her become more understandable when Friend is viewed as the manifestation of a satyr in modern dress, the story's expanding itself in the adumbration of a myth with universal implications.

Oates emphasizes the major themes of deception and identity by ironically contrasting Connie's adolescent perception of intriguing hints concerning Arnold Friend with the discerning reader's more sophisticated recognition of who or what he is. The theme of deception first occurs in the names. Friend assures Connie that he is her "friend," but the dropping of the two r's transforms the name into "an old fiend," the first warning that this dangerous character may have been around since antiquity. In contrast, Connie's name suggests one who is "conned," but, in typical teenage fashion, she believes she can control most situations. It is only at the story's end that Connie realizes she is a victim of a nefarious power beyond her experience. Similarly, Ellie Oscar is a parody of the name of the Greek god of mercy, Elios, yet this character's psychopathic behavior gives no hint of succor.

Many of the clues regarding Friend's appearance suggest both Satan or a satyr since the physiognomy of both beings developed from the same source: the goat god, Pan. Thus, one can hypothesize that Friend wears a wig to hide his pointed ears and horns. His feet do not go all the way down into his boots (one of which is described as bending over and twisting to a strange angle) because they are really hooves. He wears sunglasses because his eyes, "like chips of broken glass" reflect direct light like those of an animal. He is short, with the muscular upper body, black hair, and long, hawklike nose often depicted on satyrs. Although he does not have a beard, his face is covered with stubble. To complete the physical details usually associated with such creatures, Friend could be hiding a satyr's hairy tail in his tight jeans "that showed his thighs and buttocks" whereas a devil's long, forked appendage would be more difficult to conceal.

Connie naively assumes that Friend has merely stuffed his boots in an effort to appear taller, and she also notices three other subterfuges he has used to make himself seem younger. But these details are qualified as suppositions, emphasizing Connie's ignorance of the dangerous power Friend represents. Oates describes him "as if he were indeed wearing a wig," "as if he had plastered makeup on his face," "as if his eyelashes were ... painted with a black tarlike material." Wigs and makeup usually being associated with actors, satyrs were not only some of the earliest characters in Greek plays, but they were also the first to wear disguises. In addition, Friend looks "as if he were smiling from inside a mask. His whole face was a mask," another element suggestive of Greek drama. However, the irony inherent in Oates' characterization is that Friend is not a man acting like a satyr, but a satyr pretending to be a man.

Friend's superhuman ability to tell precisely what Connie's absent parents are doing and the sinister capacity for evil demonstrated by his threats to harm her family suggest a Satanic identity. However, the Devil is usually presented as interested in possessing human souls, and as deceitfully tempting his victims to their fate, which is hell. Friend, on the other hand, clearly desires a physical relationship with Connie, he threatens rather than tempts, and he wants to take her "out in the country here where it smells so nice and it's sunny." His motives echo those of satyrs, notorious for their lechery, aggressive in their pursuit, and pastoral in their habitat. Friend's domain, as described in the last line of the story, is the natural setting for a satyr: "The vast sunlit reaches of the land behind him and on all sides of him—so much land that Connie had never seen before and did not recognize except to know that she was going to it." Hell, the realm of the Prince of Darkness, is not usually described as sunny.

Another argument for satyr symbolism is the function of music in the story, for it always accompanies Friend as a leitmotif to his almost supernatural ability to dominate Connie. Noting that satyrs were feared in ancient myths for their power to seduce unwary women through music, Kaufmann devotes an entire chapter to "music-making, the satyr's most consistent and typical activity." When Connie first glimpses Friend at the drive-in restaurant, her face is beaming with "a joy that ... might have been the music." Later, when he and Ellie arrive unannounced at her house, Connie has been listening to "hard, fast shrieking songs," and she is "bathed in a glow of slow-pulsed joy that seemed to rise mysteriously out of the music itself." The music enchants Connie, and Arnold Friend uses it both to deceive and entice her. Connie resists talking to him until she realizes that he and Ellie are playing the same station that is on her radio. The music works like a charm to make Connie lower her defenses because it is familiar and reminds her of the drive-in where "the music was always in the background" and of the pleasant "caresses of love" she experiences with boys she meets there, caresses that are "sweet, gentle, the way it was ... promised in songs." When Connie does not immediately agree to come for a ride, Ellie turns up the volume on the radio in an effort to influence her. Music is also an important part of Friend's camouflage, for he speaks "in a simple lilting voice, exactly as if he were reciting the words to a song." At one point lyrics serve as an incantation to seduce her as Connie recognizes in Friend's words "the echo of a song from last year about a girl rushing into her boy friend's arms." Eventually she realizes that "the singsong way" he talks and the way he taps "one fist against another in homage to the perpetual music behind him" are only a pose, part of his teenage guise, yet she senses something supernatural about Friend vaguely associated with the music: "She had the idea that he had driven up the driveway all right but had come from nowhere before that and belonged nowhere and that everything about him and even about the music that was so familiar to her was only half-real." "Half-real" succinctly describes the satyr, half-man and half-beast, and the music that evokes intense feelings of pleasure in Connie becomes in his hands a snare and sortilege. Arnold Friend's attempting to enchant Connie is also suggested by the fact that he makes his sign in the air as if to claim her on the two occasions when he sees her, and that his words to her and Ellie are described as "part of an incantation" at the end of the story. By then, Connie is the reluctant but spellbound nymph whose will is completely destroyed, a more sympathetic interpretation of Connie as an inexperienced and unprotected adolescent rather than as a sinner corrupted by Satan.

The theme of sexual initiation in "Where Are You Going, Where Have You Been?" is also enhanced when the antagonist is seen as a satyr—the personification of lechery. Arnold Friend bluntly tells Connie: "I'm your lover. You don't know what that is but you will." He then reassures her that the experience is "real nice and you couldn't ask for nobody better than me or more polite," but he qualifies this promise by saying, "I'm always nice at first, the first time." These words point to subsequent cruelty, especially when he adds: "I'll hold you so tight you won't think you have to get away or pretend anything because you'll know you can't." This foreshadowing that Connie will be repelled and disillusioned by the experience becomes more ominous when the figure of Friend is interpreted as a satyr, for the lovemaking of these creatures was historically excessive and uncontrolled as the word satyriasis suggests. "I'll show you what love is like, what it does," Friend assures Connie, but his version of love, considered in the context of the satyr myths, is certain to be perverted. The "secret code" on his car, "33, 19, 17" consists of three prime numbers whose sum forms a sexual symbol commonly used by teenagers. (Jerseys printed with the words "class of" in tiny letters and the numbers "69" in bold foot-high numerals were popular with the more risque youths of the sixties.) C. Harold Hurley sees Friend's code and certain expressions in his tirade to Ellie Oscar as indicating Friend's propensity for sexual deviation, which would be consistent with the bestial nature of the satyr. Thus, Oates' use of imagery suggesting the satyr provides a deeper insight into Connie's fate, a repulsive mockery of the gentle, romantic lovemaking of her daydreams.

Arnold Friend's confidence in his ability to manipulate Connie also parallels the relationship of the satyr and the nymph. In Greek mythology, nymphs were inferior divinities frequently mentioned as attending a superior deity, and Friend, who speaks quietly in direct commands by the end of the story, never questions his right to Connie's subservience. When he unexpectedly arrives at her house, his words, "I ain't late, am I? Toldja I'd be out didn't I?" are the first of a series of questions that confuse and intimidate her. Young, inexperienced Connie's lack of self-identity is the pivot on which the story turns and the reason she becomes Friend's prey. In the opening lines she is presented as looking into mirrors and other people's faces to define and reassure herself. "She knew she was pretty and that was everything," and Friend uses her shallow self-concept to trap her: "Be nice to me, be sweet like you can because what else is there for a girl like you but to be sweet and pretty and give in ..." Connie helplessly allows Friend to direct her because she has no foundation upon which to base a resistance: no role models, no strong relationships with her family, no religious convictions, no values except those of popular music. Because Connie has no clear concept of herself or of what the predacious Friend represents, she allows him to define her—and for Arnold, the satyr, this means that Connie is to become a nymph.

The dangerous implications of this relationship become clear in the light of classical myths, for these half-animals were brutal in their pursuit of feminine prey. "Satyrs habitually raped nymphs, their companions of the woodlands," states Kaufmann; the satyr "raped more often than he seduced and inevitably evoked fear and rejection from women." Certainly Connie becomes terrified of Friend, and the extreme fear that destroys what is left of her will and leaves her screaming into the dial tone of the telephone suggests the "panic" that is the spell of the demi-god Pan who led the satyrs. Satyrs also pursued women in pairs, and Ellie Oscar, Arnold's forty-year-old sidekick whose baby face is lined with broken bloodveins suggesting the satyr's devotion to Dionysus, expresses the violence that is an undercurrent in Friend's character. Ellie speaks only twice, casually asking both times if Friend wants Connie's telephone ripped out. Friend rejects his offers, but Ellie's apparent indifference becomes threatening when Friend has to tell him to put away an unnamed weapon. Satyrs are not usually considered dangerous creatures since music is their most potent weapon. Several critics have noted, however, that these two men probably killed the old woman who lived down the road from Connie, and the threats to Connie's family are direct. Connie's suspicion that Friend may harm her is suggested by her eerie sensation of "something Arnold Friend was stabbing her with again and again with no tenderness," and she realizes by the end of the story that she will never see her mother again or sleep in her own bed. The image of Friend as a savage, insatiable, feral creature is reinforced by the shadow of the satyr in him, and this, along with the menacing presence of Ellie, implies that he is a predator who will kill his prey.

Other interpretations of the story's symbolism are also supported and strengthened when Friend is seen as Oates' reincarnation of a satyr. From a feminist point of view, Connie then becomes the stereotypical passive, submissive, emotional, ignorant female—the nymph—the extreme of feminine sensuality, dependence, and intemperance. From a psychological standpoint, the arguments that Friend represents the unconscious are substantiated by the half-beast satyr's symbolism of the animal, uncontrolled, irrational side of human nature. If, as critics have noted, he is the personification of the adolescent Connie's unconscious erotic feelings, then the lecherous satyr, whose music makes men and women mad with desire, is a more obvious and appropriate image than the Devil, who is interested in all excesses. When Arnold's seemingly inexplicable power over Connie is seen as the extraordinary power of a supernatural being, then he becomes representative of the mysterious and dangerous forces present in our world since antiquity that prey on those who are vulnerable.

Joyce Carol Oates herself once described Friend as "a fantastic figure: he is Death, he is the 'elf-Knight' of the ballads, he is the Imagination, he is a Dream, he is a Lover, a Demon, and all that." The satyr, too, is a figure of fantasy, powerful enough to represent, Death and, like the elf-Knight, a magical being who can take on human disguise. Half-man and half-animal, this wild creature symbolizes the freedom of Imagination as opposed to the discipline of culture and intellect. He is surely the fabulous embodiment of a Dream. The satyr also traditionally personifies the insatiable and ungoverned Lover, but his appearance's semi-divine status, and evil intentions combine to suggest the Demon as well. The interpretations of Arnold Friend are complex and diverse, a tribute to Oates' skill in creating allusive patterns, but the shadow of a satyr, flute in hand, lurks behind them all.

[Selected from Joyce Carol Oates. *The Wheel of Love and Other Stories*. *Studies in Short Fiction*, 1990(4).]

Chapter 6 Ethnic Literature

1. Introduction

A premise of ethnic American literature is that American culture and history should be defined by Americans of all ethnic groups. It is a fact that the immense cultural diversity has become a great strength of American literature, and multi-cultures provide the greatest variety of literary expression in American literature. This chapter could only cover a small number of representative ethnic writers who utter the most distinctive voices in Native American, African American, Jewish American and Asian American literatures.

Native literature's first recognition, the so-called "Native American Renaissance" is generally believed to begin with Kiowa writer N. Scott Momaday's publication of *House Made of Dawn* in 1968 and its reception of Pulitzer Prize in the next year. Momaday's Pulitzer success heralded a bourgeoning of Native American literature. *House Made of Dawn* tells the story of a Walatowa Indian, Abel, whose sense of alienation and quest for identity forms the major plot. The form of this novel is clearly influenced by modernist writing. So the most important result of Momaday's Pulitzer Prize is mainstream culture's recognition of Native Literature as "recognizably modernist," and thus Native cultures as recognizably modern.

The influence of Momaday's theme and form can be detected in a host of subsequent Native writers, including James Welch (blackfoot), Leslie Marmon Silko (Laguna), Gerald Vizenor (Ojibwe / Chippewa), Simon Ortiz (Acoma), Louis Owens (Choctaw/Cherokee), Louise Erdrich (German / Ojibwe), Anna Lee Walters (Pawnee/Otoe-Missouria). Among those writers, Laguna woman writer Leslie Marmon Silko is a leading voice. Her novel *Ceremony* (1977) describes

Tayo, a mixed blood Native American and a returning World War II veteran. Younger than Silko, Louise Erdrich is as prominent as, and perhaps, with broader horizon. Less political and more polished, Erdrich is one of the most popular and international successful contemporary Native American writers. The success of Erdrich's writing lies in her focus upon what she is familiar with: the world of the mixed-blood Ojibwe. The publication of the 1984 novel *Love Medicine* ensured Erdrich's popular appeal and her critical acclaim. And along with *Love Medicine*, three other novels are identified as her "tetralogy": *The Beat Queen* (1986), *Tracks* (1988) and *The Bingo Palace* (1994). All volumes of the tetralogy trace the lives and experiences of the same four families throughout the 20th century, emphasizing the complex problems that are derived from five hundred of assimilative pressure on Native communities.

Although African American literature has a long history, it was not until the Harlem Renaissance that African American literature as "the first body of ethnic writing (began) to emerge"①. In the early 1920s, a few African American writers and artists congregated in Harlem, an African American ghetto in New York City, started magazines, published anthologies, and promoted the creativity of the "New Negro." Their works made Harlem the hub of black life and center for African Americans. This movement was known as "Harlem Renaissance," which is the great movement in the cultural and intellectual history of the African Americans. Many African American writers, including Langston Hughes(1902—1967), Jean Toomer (1894—1967), Countee Cullen (1903—1946), made great contribution to this movement. Langston Hughes was one of the most talented and original black writers in the 20th century. He is best known for his poetry, but he was good at all literary genres, including plays, short stories, and novels. African American heritage is the rich fund from which Hughes drew his nutrition. In his poetry, Hughes employed a hybrid free verse with interspersed rhymes and dialect. He frequently turns to jazz, blues, behop, and rap for poetic inspiration and artistic experiment in form and rhythm.

Richard Wright(1908—1960) is a major figure to appear in the 1940s whose

① John R. Maitino, David R. Peck, (ed.). *Teaching American Ethnic Literatures*. Albuquerque: University of New Mexico Press, 1996. p. 10.

great achievement in fiction established him as pioneer in African American novel. His masterpiece *Native Son* is a novel exploring the complex social, racial and psychological problems involved in the protagonist—Bigger Thomas, a black boy's violent crime. Bigger is an embodiment of the black revolt against the racial injustices, and his revolt takes the form of horrendous crimes against the white society. African American literature got to a higher degree of maturity in the 1950s with the publication of *Invisible Man* by Ralph Ellison. Ralph Ellison did not follow the lead of Richard Wright to devote himself to the social protest novels about the tragedy of black ghetto life. Instead, he intended to write the novel to represent an "American theme," to make everyone, black or white, to identify with the protagonist. By so doing, Ellison successfully transformed the story about a young black boy's life into an odyssey of modern man's quest for self-identification, self-evaluation and self-realization. Compared with *Native Son*, *Invisible Man* dedicates to the broader range of life and richer sense of art. James Baldwin has been known as Richard Wright's successor in quite a few respects. His first novel, *Go Tell It on the Mountain* (1954) is closely autobiographical. The protagonist, John Grimes, a black boy of 14 years old tried to define himself against his harsh religious preacher stepfather.

When Leroi Jones (1934—) changed his name to the Bantuized Muslim name Amiri Baraka (meaning Prince, a Blessed One) in 1967, he was undergoing another spiritual and artistic growth in his progression as a maker of African American literature. Baraka is one of the principal figures of Black Arts Movement and his dedication to this movement was great. Just as William W. Cook put it, "if movements can be dated by the appearance of a single book, Black Arts poetry can date its birth from the appearance of (Baraka's) *Black Magic* in 1969"①. To Baraka, poetry is a vehicle of popular encouragement. More definitely, as an art form, poetry is not separate from the violent struggles of the people and it must be a weapon in that struggle.

Black woman writers are the key figures during the era of the new black consciousness movement of the late 20th century. Gwendolyn Brooks(1917—2000),

---

① Jay Parini, Brett C. Millier, (ed.). *The Columbia History of American Poetry*. Beijing: Foreign Language Teaching and Research Press, 2005. p. 687.

the first black person to win Pulitzer Prize and poet laureate of Illinois, had established her fame as a poet before the Black Arts Movement. But the rise of Black Arts Movement changed her poetic creation greatly. So she is a good exemplar of the changes in black poetry that Black Arts Movement wrought. Brooks once said that her poetry written before 1967 was the product of a "Negro" fraction. The Black Arts Movement made her redefine herself and her poetry. Brooks' 1968 volume *In the Mecca* is a good example of the changes wrought by this movement, which showed a sharp turn to militant nationalist poetics.

Rita Dove (1952—) was the Poet Laureate of the United States from 1993 to 1995, the youngest person and the first African-American to be so named. Dove's international insight, her woman's vision of events in everyday life, and the elegance of her language signal a dramatic shift in African-American woman poetry from the work of Gwendolyn Brooks in the 1960s. After a long time of emphasis on the expression of distinct African-American experiences, Rita Dove returns to an expression of the common ancestry of women of all races and times. And after nearly half century of experiment on free verse forms and harsh language, African American women poets begin to write of their lives in very disciplined and technically-polished language and forms. Dove is a prolific poet. From her first book, *The Yellow House on the Corner* (1980) to her most recent volume, *American Smooth* (2006), Dove published eight poem collections, two novels and one verse drama. She won Pulitzer Prize for *Thomas and Beulah* (1986) which was an extended sequence based on her grandparents' lives.

Black women's great achievements in fiction are mainly found in Toni Morrison and Alice Walker. Toni Morrison (1931—) is the central figure who helped to put African American woman fiction at the forefront of contemporary American canon. Morrison won Nobel Prize in Literature in 1993. Morrison is praised for her intriguing plots, powerful style, complex narrative techniques and poetic language. Morrison is adept at using modernist techniques of stream of consciousness, multiple perspectives, and deliberate fragmentation. But she knows profoundly that her works are more fundamentally as part of a black cultural tradition. Drawing upon her personal experience as black and woman, Morrison explores the terror and trauma of racial oppression and black people's complex psychological factors for survival. Her smooth prose is inflected with black musical traditions, such as Jazz and Blues. The important novels by Morrison include *The Blues Eyes* (1970), *Sula* (1972), *Beloved* (1987), *Song of Solomon* (1977), *Tar Baby* (1981), *Jazz* (1992), *Love*(2003) and her latest work *A Mercy*(2008). *Beloved* is Morrison's best-known novel. Set in the middle 1870s, this novel tells a story of a mother (Sethe) being haunted by the ghost of a daughter (Beloved). Eighteen years ago, Sethe killed her baby daughter rather than let her be taken by a slave master. This novel is told in a style of magical realism that combines the historical, the gothic and psychological all in one.

Alice Walker (1944—) is a feminist African American writer. A recurrent theme in her novel is black woman's struggle towards self-identity and self-realization. Many of her women characters are adept in the new cultural language of black arts and black power to which Walker contributed as a younger writer. Walker's female characters with strength and wisdom are usually admirably portrayed, while the black men characters are often brutal and irresponsible. Walker writes both poetry and fiction. Her first collection of poem *Once* was published in 1968. From *Once* to her first collection in the new millennium *Absolute Trust in the Goodness of the Earth* (2003) to her latest poem volume *Why War Is Never a Good Idea* (2007), Walker has published several collections of poetry. But she is best known as the author of the novel *The Color Purple* (1982), for which Walker was awarded both American Book Award and the Pulitzer Prize. This book is written from a "womanist" perspective which is formulated by Walker as opposed to strictly feminist.

The history of the Jews in America is characterized by discrete waves of immigration and different tales of assimilation and resistance. As a "dehistoricized and culturally vacant category of 'whiteness'" ①, American Jews have no clearly defined place on America's multicultural map. They dangle between the dominant position of the white majority and the marginal position of peoples of color. For this reason, the quest for self-identity is always a central theme to Jewish American writers. To the diasporic Jews, language and story might be the best ways to cling to their tradition and culture. Ruth Wisse said, "modern Jewish literature is the repository of modern Jewish experience," and as such, "the most complete way of

① David Hollinger. *Postethnic America*. New York: Basic Books, 1995. p. 30.

knowing the inner life of the Jews"①.

There are a few gifted Jewish American writers in American literary history. In the 1970s, Jewish American novelists, Saul Bellow (1915—2005) and Isaac Bashevis Singer (1904—1991) were awarded the Nobel Prize in Literature(1976 and 1978 respectively), which added a brand new chapter to Jewish American literature. Bernard Malamud (1914—1986) won the Pulitzer Prize for *The Fixer* written in 1976. Philip Roth (1933—), the younger contemporary Jewish American, is right now the most significant Jewish voice and presents the new development at the new millennium.

Saul Bellow was born in a Russian-Jewish family and grew up in the Jewish ghetto of Montreal. He attended University of Chicago and majored in anthropology. So Bellow inherited many gifts from many sources. In terms of cultural heritage, Bellow was Jewish, and the Jewish condition offered a valid metaphor for Bellow to meditate on human condition in the modern world in general. The themes central to Bellow's novels are the relationships between modern civilization and human life and human integrity and man's quest for truth and values in personal and social senses. Bellow's characters, Herzog or Mr. Sammler or Humboldt, always find themselves in rootless and homeless situations. Bellow's works are versatile in terms of style. His *Dangling Man* (1944) is a comic existentialist tale in the wartime America; his *The Adventures of Augie March* (1953) is a coming of age novel of Augie; his *Henderson the Rain King* (1958) is a mythic adventure of an American millionaire; His *Herzog* (1964) is a psychological record of the inner life of Jewish intellectual; *Humboldt's Gift* (1975) is about a tragic and desperate life of Jewish writer.

Philip Roth's novels represent the postmodern variety and complexity of Jewish life at the turn of the millennium. From his first collection of stories *Goodbye, Columbus* (1959) to his novels at the new millennium *The Human Stain* (2000), *The Dying Animal* (2001) and *Everyman* (2007), Roth increasingly weaves European texts, American myth and Jewish cultural preoccupations with time, memory, loss and history into his novels. For contemporary Jewish writers,

① Ruth R. Wisse. *The Modern Jewish Canon: A Journey Through Language and Culture*. New York: The Free Press, 2000. p. 4.

metaphors of exile have been replaced by images that accept America as the emotional and literary homeland. And that is the case in Roth's *American Pastoral* (1997), his critical acclaimed masterpiece. The narrator Zuckerman in *American Pastoral* left his Jewish background behind like an old coat he discovered no longer fit. Everyone in this novel has his own pastoral dream and everyone is free to realize it in his own way.

Asian American literature can be traced back to the first years of the 20th century, but it was not until the 1970s that Asian American literature began to make its presence felt as a category. Some anthologies of Asian American writings came out, such as Kai-yu Hsu and Helen Palumobinskas' *Asian American Authors* (1972) and Jeffrey Paul Chan's *Aiiieeeee! An Anthology of Asian American Writers* (1974). Chinese American writers, in recent years, utter the most distinct voice. The most famous of them is Maxine Hong Kingston (1940—). The publication of her *The Woman Warrior* in 1976 was a great event in Chinese American literature, as it means that Asian American literature, and Chinese American literature in particular, eventually enters into the mainstream. This book won the National Book Critics Circe Award in 1976 and established Kingston's position as an important American writer. *The Woman Warrior* is a fictional autobiography, mixing memories, tales and stories together. It tells a story of a Chinese American girl's growing up with a dream of becoming a woman warrior like Chinese woman hero—Hua Mulan. Amy Tan (1952—) is another famous Chinese American woman writer. Her best-known novel is *The Joy Luck Club* (1989). Four Chinese form a club to play mah-jongg, a traditional Chinese game. This is what the title of the novel means. Forty years later, the founder of the club dies, and her daughter comes to take her place at the mah-jongg table. Only then does the misunderstanding between mother and daughter dissolve. Thematically, it is about the lives of four Chinese women and their relationships with their four daughters. Structurally, the novel is written in the form of a short story cycle. It consists of four parts, each of which begins with a brief statement narrated by one of the four mothers, indicating the theme of the section. Frank Chin (1940—) has played an important role in the development of Asian American literature. His well-known novel *Donald Duk* (1991) tells the story of twelve-year-old Donald Duk, who, on the eve of the Chinese New Year in San Francisco's Chinatown, attempts to deal with his comical name and his feelings for his cultural heritage. However, Frank Chin is recognized by both popular media as well as serious academic circle for his fierce criticism, especially his Criticism of Maxine Hong Kingston. In 1991, Frank Chin published his famous essay, "Come All Ye Asian American Writer of the Real and the Fake," criticizing Kingston's *The Woman Warrior*. Chin believes that Kingston's novel embodies an inaccurate, inauthentic sensibility. He wrote, "Maxine Hong Kingston has defended her revision of Chinese history, culture, and childhood literature and myth by restating a white racist stereotype"①. To Frank Chin's criticism, Kingston responsed, "After all, I am not writing history or sociology but a 'memoir' like Proust"②. The literary feud between Frank Chin and Maxine Hong Kingston represents Chinese American writer's different attitude towards "authenticity" of presentation of Chinese culture and tradition, but it is also a debate over the quest to validate the humanity of various peoples. And most readers are interested in whether there is a way to synthesize two different traditions and settle their debate.

Key Words

Harlem Renaissance

Harlem Renaissance is also known as the "New Negro Renaissance." In the early 1920s, a group of talented African-American writers, painters and musicians congregated in Harlem, an African American neighborhood in New York, started magazines, published anthologies, and promoted the creativity of the "New Negro." Their works transformed Harlem into an intellectual and cultural center for African Americans. Harlem Renaissance was the period of the meteoric rise of such talents as Claude McKay, Jean Toomer, Countee Cullen, Langston Hughes. It was the second birth of African American culture. It was also another phase of the complex struggle against white "colonial" rule and cultural domination of nonwhite peoples in American and Africa.

---

① Jeffery Paul Chan, et al. *The Big Aiieeeee!*. New York: Meridian, 1991. p. 29.

② King-Kok Chueung. *Articulate Silences: Hisaye Yamamoto, Maxine Hong Kingston, Joy Kogawa*. NY: Cornell University Press, 1993. p. 79.

Black Arts Movement

The Black Arts Movement spans the period from the mid 1960s to the mid 1970s. It was the artistic branch of the Black Power movement. It was started in Harlem by writer and activist Amiri Baraka. Other well-known writers that were involved with this movement included Nikki Giovanni, Sonia Sanchez, Maya Angelou, and Rosa Grey. In a 1968 essay, "The Black Arts Movement," Larry Neal proclaimed Black Arts Movement the "aesthetic and spiritual sister of the Black Power concept." The Black Arts Repertory Theatre is a key institution of the Black Arts Movement.

Womanist

Womanist first appeared in Alice Walker's *In Search of Our Mothers' Gardens*. Walker states that a womanist is a black feminist or feminist of color. The proposal of womanism brings new demands and different perspectives to feminism, and compels the expansion of feminist horizons in theory and practice.

2. Leslie Marmon Silko

2.1 Presentation Topics

(1) Leslie Marmon Silko as a Native American woman writer.

(2) Oral traditions in Silko's works.

(3) Typical themes, concerns, and narrative forms in Silko's works.

2.2 Selected Reading

Ⅰ. Central issue of concern

Silko's use of traditional Native American elements.

Ⅱ. Text

Ceremony①

*Ts'its'tsi'nako*②, Thought-Woman,
is sitting in her room
and whatever she thinks about
appears.

She thought of her sisters,
Nau'ts'ity'i and I'tcts'ity'i,
and together they created the Universe
this world
and the four worlds below.

Thought-Woman, the spider,
named things and
as she named them
they appeared.

She is sitting in her room
thinking of a story now

I'm telling you the story
she is thinking.

Ceremony
I will tell you something about stories,
[he said]

---

① Silko's *Ceremony* employs both tribal and western elements to tell the story. She intersperses portions of an allegorical poem throughout the novel, which is characteristic of tribal literature. This poem myth is important in two respects. First, it explains the Pueblo belief that the universe consists of our world, which is the earth, and the "four worlds below," where the spirits of the dead go. Second, it reveals the crucial function that storytelling serves in the Pueblo culture. Storytelling is more than entertainment or even the passing on of history and religious beliefs to the next generation; it is also a ceremony that acts as a link between the mythical deities and the people themselves, whose ritual life is based on the myths.

② Thought woman or spider woman, a creator figure in Laguna Native American myth.

They aren't just entertainment.
Don't be fooled.
They are all we have, you see,
all we have to fight off
illness and death.

You don't have anything
if you don't have the stories.

Their evil is mighty
But it can't stand up to our stories.
So they try to destroy the stories
let the stories be confused or forgotten.
They would like that
They would be happy
Because we would be defenseless then.

He rubbed his belly.
I keep them here
[he said]
Here, put your hand on it
See, it is moving.
There is life here
for the people.

And in the belly of this story
the rituals and the ceremony
are still growing.

What She Said:

The lonely cure
I know
is a good ceremony,

that's what she said.

Sunrise.

Tayo didn't sleep well that night. He tossed in the old iron bed, and the coiled springs kept squeaking even after he lay still again, calling up humid dreams of black night and loud voices rolling him over and over again like debris caught in a flood. Tonight the singing had come first, squeaking out of the iron bed, a man singing in Spanish, the melody of a familiar love song, two words again and again, "Y volveré." Sometimes the Japanese voices came first, angry and loud, pushing the song far away, and then he could hear the shift in his dreaming, like a slight afternoon wind changing its direction, coming less and less from the south, moving into the west, and voices would become Laguna voices, and he could hear Uncle Josiah calling him, Josiah bought him the fever medicine when he had been sick of a long time ago. But before Josiah could come, the fever voices would drift and whirl and emerge again—Japanese soldiers shouting orders to him, suffocating damp voices that drifted out in the jungle steam, and he heard the women's voices then; they faded in and out until he was frantic because he thought the Laguna words were his mother's, but when he was about to make out the meaning of the words, the voice suddenly broke into a language he could not understand; and it was then that all the voices were drowned by the music—loud, loud music from a big juke box, its flashing red and blue lights pulling the darkness closer.

He lay there early in the morning and watched the high small window above the bed; dark gray gradually became lighter until it cast a white square on the opposite wall at dawn. He watched the room grow brighter then, as the square of light grew steadily warmer, more yellow with the climbing sun. He had not able to sleep for a long time—for as long as all things had become tied together like colts in single file when he and Josiah had taken them to the mountain, with the halter rope of one colt tied to the tail of the colt ahead of it, and the lead colt's rope tied to the wide horn on Josiah's Mexican saddle. He could still see them now—the creamy sorrel, the bright red bay, and the gray roan—their slick summer coats reflecting the sunlight as it came up from behind the yellow mesas, shining on them, strung out behind Josiah's horse like an old-time pack train. He could get no rest as long as the memories were tangled with the present, tangled up like colored threads from old Grandma's wicker sewing basket when he was a child, and he had carried them outside to play and they had spilled out of his arms into the summer weeds and rolled away in all directions, and them he had hurried to pick them up before Auntie found him. He could feel it inside his skull—the tension of little threads being pulled and how it was with tangled things, things tied together, and as he tried to pull them apart and rewind them into their places, they snagged and tangled even more. So Tayo had to sweat through those nights when thoughts became entangled; he had to sweat to think of something that wasn't unraveled or tied in knots to the past—something that existed by itself standing alone like a deer. And if he could hold that image of the deer in his mind long enough, his stomach might shiver less and let him sleep for a while. It worked as long as the deer was alone, as long as he could keep it a gray buck on an unrecognized hill; but if he did not hold it tight, it would spin away from him and become the deer he and Rocky had hunted. That memory would unwind into the last day when they had sat together, oiling their rifles in the jungle of some nameless Pacific island. While they used up the last of the oil in Rocky's pack, they talked about the deer that Rocky had hunted, and the corporal next to them shook his head, and kept saying he had dreamed the Japs would get them that day.

The humid air turned into sweat that had run down the corporal's face while he repeated his dream to them. That was the first time Tayo had realized that the man's skin was not much different from his own. The skin. He saw the skin of the corpses again and again, in ditches on either side of the long muddy road—skin that was stretched shiny and dark over bloated hands; even white men were darker after death. There was no difference when they were swollen and covered with flies. That had become the worst thing for Tayo: they looked too familiar even when they were alive. When the sergeant told them to kill all the Japanese soldiers lines up in front of the cave with their hands on their heads, Tayo could not pull the trigger. The fever made him shiver, and the sweat was stinging his eyes and he couldn't see clearly; in that instant he saw Josiah standing there; the face was dark from the sun, and the eyes were squinting as thought he were about to smile at Tayo. So Tayo stood there, stiff with nausea, while they fired at the soldiers, and he watched his uncle fall, and he knew it was Josiah; and even after Rocky started shaking him by the shoulders and telling him to stop crying, it was still Josiah lying there. They forced medicine into Tayo's mouth, and Rocky pushed him toward the corpses and told him to look, look past the blood that was already dark like the jungle mud, with only flecks of bright red still shimmering in it. Rocky made him at the corpse and said, "Tayo, this is a *Jap*! This is a *Jap* uniform!" And then he rolled the body over with his boot and said, "Look, Tayo, look at the face," and that was when Tayo started screaming because it wasn't a Jap, it was Josiah, eyes shrinking back into the skull and all their shining black light glazed over by death.

The sergeant had called for a medic and somebody rolled up Tayo's sleeve; they told him to sleep, and the next day they all acted as though nothing had happed. They called it battle fatigue, and they said hallucinations were common with malarial fever.

Rocky had reasoned it out with him; it was impossible for the dead man to be Josiah, because Josiah was an old Laguna man, thousands of miles from the Philippine jungles and Japanese armies. "He's probably up on some mesa right now, chopping wood," Rocky said. He smiled and shook Tayo's shoulders. "Hey, I know you're homesick. But, Tayo, we're supposed to be here. This is what we're supposed to do."

Tayo nodded, slapped at the insects mechanically and staring straight ahead, past the smothering dampness of the green jungle leaves. He examined the facts and logic again and again, the way Rocky had explained it to him; the facts made what he had seen an impossibility. He felt the shivering then; it began at the tips of his fingers and pulsed into his arms. He shivered because all the facts, all the reasons made no difference any more; he could hear Rocky's words, and he could follow the logic of what Rocky said, but he could not feel anything except a swelling in his belly, a great swollen grief that was pushing into his throat.

He had to keep busy; he had to keep moving so that the sinews connected behind his eyes did not slip loose and spin his eyes to the interior of his skull where the scenes waited for him. He got out of the bed quickly while he could still see the square of yellow sunshine on the wall opposite the bed, and he pulled on his jeans and the scuffed brown boots he had worn before the war, and the red plaid western shirt old Grandma gave him the day he had come home after the war.

The air outside was still cool; it smelled like night dampness, faintly of rain.

He washed his face in the steel-cold water of the iron trough by the windmill. The yellow striped cat purred and wrapped herself around his legs while he combed his hair. She ran ahead of him to the goat pen and shoved her head under his left arm when he knelt down to milk the black goat. He poured mild for her in the lid of an old enamel coffeepot, and then he opened the pen and let them run, greedy for the tender green shoots of tumbleweeds pushing through the sand. The kid was almost too big to nurse any more, and it knelt by the doe and hunched down to reach the tits, butting her to make the milk come faster, wiggling its tail violently until the nanny jumped away and turned on the kid, butting it away from her. The process of weaning had gone on like this for weeks, but the nanny was more intent on weeds than the lesson, and when Tayo left them, the kid goat was back at the tits, a little more careful this time.

The sun was climbing then, and it looked small in that empty morning sky. He knew he should eat, but he wasn't hungry any more. He sat down in the kitchen, at the small square table with the remains of a white candle melted to a nub on the lid of a coffee can; he wondered how long the candle had been there, he wondered if Josiah had been the one to light it last. He thought he would cry then, thinking of Josiah and how he had been here and touched all these things, sat in the chair. So he jerked his head away from the candle, and looked at the soot around the base of the coffeepot. He wouldn't waste firewood to heat up yesterday's coffee of maybe it was day-before-yesterday's coffee. He had lost track of the days there.

The drought years had returned again, as they had after the First World War and in the twenties, when he was a child and they had to haul water to the sheep in big wooden barrels in the old wagon. The windmill near the sheep camp had gone dry, so the gray mules pulled the wagon from the springs, moving slowly so that the water would not splash over the rims. He sat close to his uncle then, on the wagon seat, above the bony gray rumps of the mules. After they had dumped water for the sheep, they went to burn the spines from the cholla and prickly pear. They stood back by the wagon and watched the cows walk up to the cactus cautiously, sneezing at the smoldering ashes. The cows were patient while the scorched green pulp cooled, and then they brought out their wide spotted tongues and ate those strange remains because the hills were barren those years and only the cactus could grow.

Now there was no wagon or wooden barrels. One of the gray mules had eaten a poison weed near Acoma, and the other one was blind; it stayed close to the windmill at the ranch, grazing on the yellow rice grass that grew in the blow sand. It walked a skinny trail, winding in blind circles from the grass to the water trough, where it dipped its mouth in the water and let the water dribble out again, rinsing its mouth four or five times a day to make sure the water was still there. The dry air shrank the wooden staves of the barrels' they pulled loose, and now the rusty steel hoops were scattered on the ground behind the corral in the crazy patterns of some flashy Kiowa hoop dancer at the Gallup Ceremonials, throwing his hoops along the ground where he would hook and flip them into the air again and they would skim over his head and shoulders down to his dancing feet, like magic. Tayo stepped inside one that was half buried in the reddish blow sand; he hooked an edge with the toe of his boot, and then he let it slip into the sand again.

[Selected from Leslie Marmon Silko. *Ceremony*. New York: Penguin Group, 1986.]

Ⅲ. Questions for discussion

(1) As the novel begins, why is Tayo so miserable?

(2) What part does World War Ⅱ play in Silko's *Ceremony*?

(3) How are time and space represented in the novel? How does Silko suggest characteristics of a "ceremonial" time and space, as opposed to the everyday European American senses of time and space?

(4) *The Boston Globe* once commented, "The novel is very deliberately a ceremony itself—demanding but confident and beautifully written." Then in what sense is the novel a "ceremony" for the reader as well as for Tayo?

(5) What are the elements of the "oral tradition" in the beginning poem in this novel? What is the role of the oral tradition in general in *Ceremony*? In which ways traditional Native American and European storytellers might differ?

(6) What social issue appears in Silko's *Ceremony*?

(7) As Native American author N. Scott Momaday wrote, "The voices are all around us, the three voices. You have the mythic and the historical and the personal and then they become a wheel, they revolve, they alternate.... Myth becomes history becomes memoir becomes myth." Could you identify the three voices from Silko's *Ceremony*?

(8)In her book *The Sacred Hoop*, author and critic (and cousin of Silko) Paula Gunn Allen made a rather bold statement about the position of women in American Indian cultures: she argued that "traditional [Indian] tribal lifestyles are more often gynocratic [governed by women] than not, and they are never patriarchal." Could you find the similar expression in "The Feminine Landscape of Leslie Marmon Silko's *Ceremony*"? What do you think of this idea?

2.3 Assigned Reading

The Feminine Landscape of Leslie Marmon Silko's *Ceremony*

Paula Gunn Allen

Whenever one sets out to read or analyze a novel or tale by an Indian writer, one must bear in mind that the basic reality experienced by tribal peoples and by Western peoples is not the same, and therefore Indian American literature will reflect basic assumptions and beliefs about the Universe which the western reader may not identify or be familiar with. As a matter of fact, western cultures tend to separate the material from the spiritual and supernatural, while for the American Indians the material and spiritual are different expressions of the same reality.

To put it more explicitly, in American Indian thought their god/goddess is the All Spirit, but other beings are also spirit, in fact more spirit than body, more spirit than intellect, more spirit than mind. Once the natural state of existence is whole, beauty, health and goodness are regarded as wholeness while disease is seen as a condition of division and separation from the harmony of the Whole. Therefore, the tribes seek—through song, ceremony, legend, sacred stories (myths) and tales—to embody, articulate and share reality, in order to bring the isolated, private self into harmony and balance with this reality.

The structure of American Indian literature reflects this egalitarian view of Nature/Life, and for that reason does not rely on conflict, crisis and resolution for its organization. Instead its significance is determined by its reflection of tribal understanding, and its relation to the unitary nature of reality.

The assumption that the Universe is Whole and unitary implies that all phenomena are perceived as intelligent manifestations of the intelligent universe from which they arise and is supported by the way most Indians believe Creation to have taken place.

In fact, according to Keres/Laguna religion—and for the purposes of this essay we will be concerned particularly with the worldview of the Keres Laguna Pueblo from New Mexico, once Silko is of Pueblo descent—in the beginning existed Thought Woman and her dormant sisters. Thought Woman thinks Creation and sings her dormant sisters (Uretsete and Naotsete) into life. After they are vital she instructs them to sing over the items in their baskets (medicine bundles) in such a way that those items will have life, and will take on the power of reproducing other creatures of their kind.

Thought Woman and her sisters are not related on account of having parents in common. Uretsete and Naotsete are in fact Thought Woman's equals, who have the power to vitalize the creatures who will inhabit the Earth. In short, the Indian goddess acknowledges her limited power (as well as a sense of proportion and respect for the other creatures). Actually, this rejection of the idea of Omnipotence is common to most Indian cultures as it is suggested by the following passage from a Cheyenne tale:

> "How beautiful their wings are in the light," Maheo said to his Power, as the birds wheeled and turned and became living patterns against the sky.
>
> The loon was the first to drop back to the surface of the lake. "Maheo," he said, looking around, for he knew that Maheo was all about him "You have made us sky and light to fly in, and you have made us water to swim in. It sounds ungrateful to want something else, yet still we do. When we are tired of swimming and tired of flying, we should like a dry solid place where we could walk and rest. Give us a place to build our nests, please, Maheo."
>
> "So be it," answered Maheo, "but to make such a place I must have your help, all of you. By myself, I have made four things... Now I must have your help if I am to create more, for my Power will only let me make four things by myself."

The American-Indian Universe is therefore based on dynamic self-esteem, whereas the Christian Universe is, on the other hand, based on a sense of separation and loss. It follows then that individuals brought up in a Christian environment are inclined to perceive events and phenomena in hierarchical and dualistic terms, while those reared in traditional American Indian societies tend to believe events and experiences are related to one another, in a process of reciprocal interdependence.

This way of perceiving reality implies that the American Indians view space as spherical and time as cyclical. The circular concept requires all "points" that make up the sphere of being to have a significant identity and function, while the linear model assumes that some "points" are more significant than others. At the center of all is Woman, and no thing is sacred without her blessing and her thinking. This spirit, this power of intelligence appears on the plains, in the forests, in the great canyons, on the mesas, beneath the seas, and her variety and multiplicity testify to her complexity. She is the true Creatix, for she is thought itself, from which all else is born. She is the necessary precondition for material creation, and she, like all of her creation, is fundamentally female.

It is within this framework that Leslie Marmon Silko's novel *Ceremony* acquires significance. As a matter of fact, in her novel there is not one single symbol that is not in one way or another connected with womanhood, and does not, in some way, relate back to Ts'eh and through her to the universal feminine principle of Creation. In this sense, it would not be inappropriate to assume that although *Ceremony* is ostensibly a tale about a man, Tayo, it is as much (or even more), a tale about two forces: on the one hand, the feminine life force of the Universe, represented by the female figures of Ts'eh, Laura, Night Swan, Grandmother, Betonie's grandmother, and by the male figures of Josiah, the Mountain Spirit, Betonie's grandfather, Betonie, Robert and Tayo, and on the other hand, the mechanistic death force of witchery, symbolized by Auntie and Betonie's grandfather's wives, Rocky or Emo, to mention only a few.

While Rocky or Emo, who embody the forces of witchery (evil) appear to believe that the Earth is separate from themselves, a place (no more than a place) where they act out the drama of their isolate destinies, Betonie, in consonance with Josiah or the Mountain Spirit assume that the Earth is in fact being, and that it is aware, palpable, intelligent and alive as all other creatures are. Thus, one might consider Tayo's illness as a result of the disruption of an ancient balance and unity of person, ceremony and land. Because he was a half-breed, Tayo had not been taught Laguna traditions, and did not share the arcane knowledge of his Laguna people.

Before the war, he had been treated as an outsider, mocked and despised on account of the circumstances of his birth. The only two people who in a certain way cared for him, had been his uncle Josiah and his cousin Rocky. Unfortunately,

Josiah died while Tayo was in the Philippines, and Rocky was killed during the war. With Josiah and Rocky dead, Tayo's sense of where he fits in disappears, only to be recovered with the help of Betonie. Because he is comfortable with his integrated cultures and familiar with ceremonialism, Betonie is able to help Tayo find the mission he is supposed to undertake. Betonie's magic propels Tayo along his ceremonial journey, which takes him to Ts'eh, the mountain spirit woman, whom Tayo had loved, without knowing, from "time immemorial." Before he knew her name, he had already pledged his love to her, and she had answered him with rain:

So that last summer, before the war, he got up before dawn and rode the bay mare south to the spring in the narrow canyon. The water oozed out from the dark orange sandstone at the base of the long mesa. He waited for the sun to come over the hills .... The canyon was full of shadows when he reached the pool. He had picked the flowers along the path, flowers with long yellow petals the color of the sunlight. He shook the pollen from them gently and sprinkled it over the water; he laid blossoms beside the pool and waited. He heard the water, flowing into the pool, drop by drop from the big crack in the side of the cliff. The things he did seemed right, as he imagined with his heart the rituals the cloud priests performed during the drought. Here the dust and heat began to recede; the short grass and stunted corn seemed distant.

As Tayo finishes his prayers and starts climbing down the mountain, he sees a bright green hummingbird and watches it as it disappears: "but it left something with him; as long as the hummingbird had not abandoned the land, somewhere there were still flowers, and they could all go on."

Forty eight hours after Tayo makes his prayer, heavy rains pour down upon the earth. The rain comes from the west, and the thunder which precedes it comes from Mount Taylor (a mountain that is blue against the sky) called Tse-pi'na in Laguna, which means Woman Veiled in Clouds. Having prayed this rain in, Tayo must experience its power personally as the next step in the ceremony. The rain makes it necessary for Josiah to miss his date with Night Swan, so he sends Tayo to the nearby village of Cubero with a message for her.

Night Swan is a mysterious and powerful woman. We know that she is related to Ts'eh by her circumstances and the colors with which she surrounds herself. Many signs indicate that she is associated with the ceremony of which Tayo is an integral part: the color of her eyes (hazel brown like Tayo's own), her implication in the matter of the spotted (half-breed) cattle, Auntie's dislike of her, and her mysterious words to Tayo when he leaves her. Moreover, her room is filled with blue: a blue armchair, blue sheets, a cup made of blue pottery... she is dressed in a blue kimono when Tayo enters her room, and she wears blue slippers. Most importantly, she is imbued with a mysterious power that Tayo relates with whatever lies beyond the white curtain:

> He could feel something back there, something of her life which he could not explain. The room pulsed with feeling, the feeling flowing with the music and the breeze from the curtains, feeling colored by the blue flowers painted in a border around the walls. He could feel it everywhere, even in the blue sheets that were stretched tightly across the bed.

Night Swan takes Tayo to bed, and through her body the love that Ts'eh bears for him is transmitted: "She moved under him, her rhythm merging into the sound of the rain in the tree. And he was lost somewhere, deep beneath the surface of his own body and consciousness, swimming away from all his life before that hour." She is aware of the significance of her act and tells Tayo: "You don't have to understand what is happening. But remember this day. You will recognize it later."

These passages tell of the ceremonial nature of man and woman, and embody the meaning of the relation between the characters and Thought Woman, that is the basis of Laguna life: "In the beginning Tse che nako, Thought Woman, finished everything, thoughts, and the names of all things ... and then our mothers, Uretsete and Naotsete, said they would make names and they would make thoughts. Thus they said. Thus they did." After Tayo completes the first steps of the ceremony, he is ready to enter into the central rituals connected with a ceremony of cosmic significance, for only a cosmic ceremony can simultaneously heal a wounded man, a stricken landscape, and a disorganized, discouraged society.

Within a peace-centered culture, having been a warrior meant that Tayo would inevitably have to experience total separation from the tribe, a role he had been predestined to fulfil, on account of the very circumstances of his birth and upbringing. It is in fact his status as an outcast who, at the same time is one of the Laguna people in his heart, which enables him to suffer the ritual of war and dissolution, the annihilation of the mundane self likely to produce a magic man of sufficient power to carry out the ceremony Tayo is embroiled in.

At the beginning of the story Tayo is still experiencing this stage of the ceremony. He is formless, an empty space, a mere outline. He has no voice: "He can't talk to you. He is invisible. His words are formed with an invisible tongue, they have no sound," he tells the army psychiatrist. Like rainless clouds, he seeks fulfillment—a story, a ceremony about his life that will make him whole. In fact, the purpose of the ceremony is to integrate: to fuse the individual with his or her fellows, the community of people with that of the other kingdoms, and this larger communal group with the worlds below this one. A raising or expansion of individual consciousness accompanies this process. The person sheds the isolated, individual personality and is restored to conscious harmony with the universe. We are entitled to assume, then, that a ceremony such as Betonie performs with Tayo as the active participant is intended to restore (to Tayo as much as to his people) the sense of belonging, of being part of a harmonious Whole.

After Tayo walks through Betonie's ceremony, finds the cattle and puts them in a safe pasture, after he has confronted the witchery and abandoned all thought of retaliating against it, after he has been transformed by these efforts and his meeting with Ts'eh from isolated warrior to a spiritually integrated person, after he has taken on the aspect of unity termed naiya (mother) in Laguna, he is free to understand the whole thing: "He would go back there now, where she had shown him the plant. He would gather the seeds for her and plant them with great care in places near sandy hills ... The plants would grow there like the story, strong and translucent as stars." "But you know, grandson, this world is fragile," old Ku'oosh had told Tayo, and having entered the ways of unification of a fragmented ego, Tayo is able to experience that fragility directly:

> He dreamed with his eyes open that he was wrapped in a blanket in the back of Josiah's wagon, crossing the sandy flat below Paguate Hill ... the rumps of the two grey mules were twin moons in front of him. Josiah was driving the wagon, old Grandma was holding him, and Rocky whispered "my brother." They were taking him home.

The fragility of the world is a result of its nature as thought. Both land and human beings participate in the same kind of being, for both are thoughts in the mind of Thought Woman. Tayo's illness is a corollary of disordered thinking—his own, that of those around him, and that of the forces which thrust them all into the tragic circumstances of World War Ⅱ. Witchery had put this disordered thinking into motion long ago and had distorted human beings' perceptions so that they believed that other creatures (insects and beasts and half-breeds and whites and Indians and Japanese) were enemies—rather than part of the one being we all share—and thus should be destroyed. The cure for that misunderstanding, for Tayo, was a reorientation of perception so that he could realize that the proper duty of the creatures, the land and the human beings is to live in harmony with what is. For Tayo, wholeness consists of sowing plants and nurturing them, caring for the spotted cattle, and especially acknowledging that he belongs exactly where he is, that he is and always has been home. The story that is capable of healing his mind, is the story that the land has always had meaning attached to it:

> The transition was completed. In the west and in the south too, the clouds with round heavy bellies had gathered for the dawn. It was not necessary, but it was right, even if the sky had been cloudless the end was the same. The ear for the story and the eye for the pattern were theirs; the feeling was theirs; we came out of this land and we are hers [. . .] they had always been loved. He thought of her then; she had always loved him, she had never left him; she had always been there. He crossed the river at sunrise.

Tayo bridges the distance between his isolated consciousness and the universe of being because he has loved the Spirit Woman who brings all things into being, and because he is aware at last that she has always loved them, his people as well as himself. He is finally able to take his normal place in the life of the Laguna. When he returns from the Paguate Hills, even Grandmother realizes that he is no longer special that he has become a pattern of Laguna life. She comments: "these goings-on around Laguna don't excite me any more." Perhaps she is also implying that ordinariness can successfully replace the extraordinary nature of life. Tayo has come home, ordinary in his being, and they can get on with serious business, the day-to-day life of a village, which is what the land, the ceremony, the story and time immemorial are all about.

In conclusion, underlying its apparent complexity, Leslie Marmon Silko's novel *Ceremony* possesses a unity and harmony of symbol, structure and articulation that relates back to the American-Indian world. This harmony is based on the perceived harmony of the Universe and on thousands of years of refinement. This essential sense of unity among all things flows like a clear stream through the songs and stories of the peoples of the western hemisphere, and is embodied in the words of an old man, Hiamove, at the close of this essay:

There are birds of many colors—red, blue, green, yellow—yet it is all one bird. There are horses of many colors—brown, black, yellow, white—yet it is all one horse. So cattle, so all living things—animals, flowers trees. So men: in this land there once were only Indians are now men of every color—white, black, yellow, red—yet all one people. That this should come to pass was in the heart of the Great Mystery. It is right thus. And everywhere there shall be peace.

[Selected from Paula Gunn Allen, (ed.). *Studies in American Indian Literature: Critical Essays and Course Designs*. NY: MLA, 1983.]

3. Maxine Hong Kingston

3.1 Presentation Topics

(1) Maxine Hong Kingston as a Chinese American writer.

(2) *The Woman Warrior*, a unique blend of folklore, myth, feminism and autobiography.

(3) Women in China and women in America in Kingston's works.

3.2 Selected Reading

I. Central issueof concern

The Woman Warrior: Memoirs of a Girlhood Among Ghosts as a personal narrative that represents Kingston's effort "to reconcile American and Chinese female identities" by handling themes relating to immigrant communities and cross-cultural conflicts.

II. Text

Shaman①

(Excerpt from *The Woman Warrior: Memoirs of a Girlhood Among Ghosts*)

My mother left China in the winter of 1939, almost six months after the stoning, and arrived in New York Harbor in January 1940. She carried the same

① "Shaman" tells the story of Brave Orchid (Kingston's mother) in China and America. This excerpt begins from her life in America.

suitcase she had taken to Canton, this time filled with seeds and bulbs. On Ellis Island the officials asked her, "What year did your husband cut off his pigtail?" And it terrified her when she could not remember. But later she told us perhaps this lapse was for the best: what if they were trying to trap him politically? The men had cut their pigtails to defy the Manchus and to help Sun Yat-sen, fellow Cantonese.

I was born in the middle of World War Ⅱ. From earliest awareness, my mother's stories always timely, I watched for three airplanes parting. Much as I dream recurringly about shrinking babies, I dream that the sky is covered from horizon to horizon with rows of airplanes, dirigibles, rocket ships, flying bombs, their formations as even as stitches. When the sky seems clear in my dreams and I would fly, if I look too closely, there so silent, far away, and faint in the daylight that people who do not know about them do not see them, are shiny silver machines, some not yet invented, being moved, fleets always being moved from one continent to another, one planet to another. I must figure out a way to fly between them.

But America has been full of machines and ghosts—Taxi Ghosts, Bus Ghosts, Police Ghosts, Fire Ghosts, Meter Reader Ghosts, Tree Trimming Ghosts, Five-and-Dime Ghosts. Once upon a time the world was so thick with ghosts, I could hardly breathe; I could hardly walk, limping my way around the White Ghosts and their cars. There were Black Ghosts too, but they were open eyed and full of laughter, more distinct than White Ghosts.

What frightened me most was the Newsboy Ghost, who came out from between the cars parked in the evening light. Carrying a newspaper pouch instead of a baby brother, he walked right out in the middle of the street without his parents. He shouted ghost words to the empty streets. His voice reached children inside the houses, reached inside the children's chests. They would come running out of their yards with their dimes. They would follow him just a corner too far. And when they went to the nearest house to ask directions home, the Gypsy Ghosts would lure them inside with gold rings and then boil them alive and bottle them. The ointment thus made was good for rubbing on children's bruises.

We used to pretend we were Newsboy Ghosts. We collected old Chinese newspapers (the Newsboy Ghost not giving us his ghost newspapers) and trekked about the house and yard. We waved them over our heads, chanting a chant: "Newspapers for sale. Buy a newspaper." But those who could hear the insides of words heard that we were selling a miracle salve made from boiled children. The newspapers covered up green medicine bottles. We made up our own English, which I wrote down and now looks like "eeeeeeeee." When we heard the real newsboy calling, we hid, dragging our newspapers under the stairs or into the cellar, where the Well Ghost lived in the black water under a lid. We crouched on our newspapers, the San Francisco *Gold Mountain News*, and plugged up our ears with our knuckles until he went away.

For our very food we had to traffic with the Grocery Ghosts, the supermarket aisles full of ghost customers. The Milk Ghost drove his white truck from house to house every other day. We hid watching until his truck turned the corner, bottles rattling in their frames. Then we unlocked the front door and the screen door and reached for the milk. We were regularly visited by the Mail Ghost, Meter Reader Ghost, Garbage Ghost. Staying off the streets did no good. They came nosing at windows—Social Worker Ghosts, Public Health Nurse Ghosts, Factory Ghosts recruiting workers during the war (they promised free child care, which our mother turned down), two Jesus Ghosts who had formerly worked in China. We hid directly under the windows, pressed against the baseboard until the ghost, calling us in the ghost language so that we'd almost answer to stop its voice, gave up. They did not try to break in, except for a few Burglar Ghosts. The Hobo Ghosts and Wino Ghosts took peaches off our trees and drank from the hose when nobody answered their knocks.

It seemed as if ghosts could not hear or see very well. Momentarily lulled by the useful chores they did for whatever ghostly purpose, we did not bother to lower the windows one morning when the Garbage Ghost came. We talked loudly about him through the fly screen, pointed at his hairy arms, and laughed at how he pulled up his dirty pants before swinging his hoard on to his shoulders. "Come see the Garbage Ghost get its food," we children called. "The Garbage Ghost," we told each other, nodding our heads. The ghost looked directly at us. Steadying the load on his back with one hand, the Garbage Ghost walked up to the window. He had cavernous nostrils with yellow and brown hair. Slowly he opened his red mouth. "The...Gar...bage...Ghost," he said, copying human language. "Gar... bage...

Ghost?" We ran, screaming to our mother, who efficiently shut the window. "Now we know," she told us, "the White Ghosts can hear Chinese. They have learned it. You mustn't talk in front of them again. Someday, very soon, we're going home, where there are Han people everywhere. We'll buy furniture then, real tables and chairs. You children will smell flowers for the first time."

"Mother! Mother! It's happening again. I taste something in my mouth, but I'm not eating anything."

"Me too, Mother. Me too. There's nothing there. Just my spit. My spit tastes like sugar."

"Your grandmother in China is sending you candy again," said my mother. Human beings do not need Mail Ghosts to send messages.

I must have tinkered too much wondering how my invisible grandmother, illiterate and dependent on letter writers, could give us candy free. When I got older and more scientific, I received no more gifts from her. She died, and I did not get "home" to ask her how she did it. Whenever my parents said "home," they suspended America. They suspended enjoyment, but I did not want to go to China. In China my parents would sell my sisters and me. My father would marry two or three more wives, who would spatter cooking oil on our bare toes and lie that we were crying for naughtiness. They would give food to their own children and rocks to us. I did not want to go where the ghosts took shapes nothing like our own.

As a child I feared the size of the world. The farther away the sound of howling dogs, the farther away the sound of the trains, the tighter I curled myself under the quilt. The trains sounded deeper and deeper into the night. They had not reached the end of the world before I stopped hearing them, the last long moan diminishing towards China. How large the world must be to make my grandmother only a taste by the time she reaches me.

When I last visited my parents, I had trouble falling asleep, too big for the hills and valleys scooped in the mattress by child-bodies. I heard my mother come in. I stopped moving. What did she want? Eyes shut, I pictured my mother, her white hair frizzy in the dark-and-light doorway, my hair white now too, Mother. I could hear her move furniture about. Then she dragged a third quilt, the thick, homemade Chinese kind, across me. After that I lost track of her location. I spied from underneath my eyelids and had to hold back a jump. She had pulled up a chair and was sitting by the bed next to my head. I could see her strong hands in her lap, not working fourteen pairs of needles. She is very proud of her hands, which can make anything and stay pink and soft while my father's became like carved wood. Her palm lines do not branch into head, heart, and life lines like other people's but crease with just one atavistic fold. That night she was a sad bear; a great sheep in a wool shawl. She recently took to wearing shawls and granny glasses, American fashions. What did she want, sitting there so large next to my head? I could feel her stare—her eyes two lights warm on my greying hair, then on the creases at the sides of my mouth, my thin neck, my thin cheeks, my thin arms. I felt her sight warm each of my bony elbows, and I flopped about in my fake sleep to hide them from her criticism. She sent light at full brightness beaming through my eyelids, her eyes at my eyes, and I had to open them.

"What's the matter, Mama? Why are you sitting there?"

She reached over and switched on a lamp she had placed on the floor beside her. "I swallowed the LSD pill you left on the kitchen counter," she announced.

"That wasn't LSD, Mama. It was just a cold pill. I have a cold."

"You're always catching colds when you come home. You must be eating too much yin. Let me get you another quilt."

"No, no more quilts. You shouldn't take pills that aren't prescribed for you. 'Don't eat pills you find on the kerb,' you always told us."

"You children never tell me what you're really up to. How else am I going to find out what you're really up to?" As if her head hurt, she closed her eyes behind the gold wire rims. "Aiaa," she sighed, "how can I bear to have you leave me again?"

How can I bear to leave her again? She would close up this room, open temporarily for me, and wander about cleaning and cleaning the shrunken house, so tidy since our leaving. Each chair has its place now. And the sinks in the bedrooms work, their alcoves no longer stuffed with laundry right up to the ceiling. My mother has put the clothes and shoes into boxes, stored against hard times. The sinks had been built of grey marble for the old Chinese men who boarded here before we came. I used to picture modest little old men washing in the mornings and dressing before they shuffled out of these bedrooms. I would have to leave and go again into the world out there which has no marble ledges for my clothes, no quilts made from our own ducks and turkeys, no ghosts of neat little old men.

The lamp gave off the sort of light that comes from a television, which made the high ceiling disappear and then suddenly drop back into place. I could feel that clamping down and see how my mother had pulled the blinds down so low that the bare rollers were showing. No passer-by would detect a daughter in this house. My mother would sometimes be a large animal, barely real in the dark; then she would become a mother again. I could see the wrinkles around her big eyes, and I could see her cheeks sunken without her top teeth.

"I'll be back again soon," I said. "You know that I come back. I think of you when I'm not here."

"Yes, I know you. I know you now. I've always known you. You're the one with the charming words. You have never come back. 'I'll be back on Turkeyday,' you said. Huh."

I shut my teeth together, vocal shords cut, they hurt so. I would not speak words to give her pain. All her children gnash their teeth.

"The last time I saw you, you were still young," she said. "Now you're old."

"It's only been a year since I visited you."

"That's the year you turned old. Look at you, hair gone grey, and you haven't even fattened up yet. I know how the Chinese talk about us. 'They're so poor,' they say, 'they can't afford to fatten up any of their daughters.' 'Years in America,' they say, 'and they don't eat.' Oh, the shame of it—a whole family of skinny children. And your father—he's so skinny, he's disappearing."

"Don't worry about him, Mama. Doctors are saying that skinny people live longer. Papa's going to live a long time."

"So! I knew I didn't have too many years left. Do you know how I got all this fat? Eating your leftovers. Aiaa, I'm getting so old. Soon you will have no more mother."

"Mama, you've been saying that all my life."

"This time it's true. I'm almost eighty."

"I thought you were only seventy-six."

"My papers are wrong. I'm eighty."

"But I thought your papers are wrong, and you're seventy-two, seventy-three in Chinese years."

"My papers are wrong, and I'm eighty, eighty-one in Chinese years. Seventy. Eighty. What do numbers matter? I'm dropping dead any day now. The aunt down the street was resting on her porch steps, dinner all cooked, waiting for her husband and son to come home and eat it. She closed her eyes for a moment and died. Isn't that a wonderful way to go?"

"But our family lives to be ninety-nine."

"That's your father's family. My mother and father died very young. My youngest sister was an orphan at ten. Our parents were not even fifty."

"Then you should feel grateful you've lived so many extra years."

"I was so sure you were going to be an orphan too. In fact, I'm amazed you've lived to have white hair. Why don't you dye it?"

"Hair color doesn't measure age, Mother. White is just another pigment, like black and brown."

"You're always listening to Teacher Ghosts, those Scientist Ghosts, Doctor Ghosts."

"I have to make a living."

"I never do call you Oldest Daughter. Have you noticed that? I always tell people, 'This is my Biggest Daughter.'"

"Is it true then that Oldest Daughter and Oldest Son died in China? Didn't you tell me when I was ten that she'd have been twenty; when I was twenty, she'd be thirty?" Is that why you've denied me my title?

"No, you must have been dreaming. You must have been making up stories. You are all the children there are."

Who was that story about—the one where the parents are throwing money at the children, but the children don't pick it up because they're crying too hard? They're writhing on the floor covered with coins. Their parents are going out the door for America, hurling handfuls of change behind them.

She leaned forward, eyes brimming with what she was about to say: "I work so hard," she said. She was doing her stare—at what? My feet began rubbing together as if to tear each other's skin off. She started talking again, "The tomato vines prickle my hands; I can feel their little stubble hairs right through my gloves. My feet squish-squish in the rotten tomatoes, squish-squish in the tomato mud the feet ahead of me have sucked. And do you know the best way to stop the itch from the tomato hairs? You break open a fresh tomato and wash yourself with it. You cool your face in tomato juice. Oh, but it's the potatoes that will ruin my hands. I'll get rheumatism washing potatoes, squatting over potatoes."

She had taken off the Ace bandages around her legs for the night. The varicose veins stood out.

"Mama, why don't you stop working? You don't have to work any more. Do you? Do you really have to work like that? Scabbing in the tomato fields?" Her black hair seems filleted with the band of white at its roots. She dyed her hair so that the farmers would hire her. She would walk to Skid Row and stand in line with hobos, the winos, the junkies, and the Mexicans until the farm buses came and the farmers picked out the workers they wanted. "You have the house," I said. "For food you have Social Security. And urban renewal must have given you something. It was good in a way when they tore down the laundry. Really, Mama, it was. Otherwise Papa would never have retired. You ought to retire too."

"Do you think your father wanted to stop work? Look at his eyes; the brown is going out of his eyes. He has stopped talking. When I go to work, he eats leftovers. He doesn't cook new food," she said, confessing, me maddened at confessions. "Those Urban Renewal Ghosts gave us moving money. It took us seventeen years to get our customers. How could we start all over on moving money, as if we two old people had another seventeen years in us? Aa"—she flipped something aside with her hand—"White Ghosts can't tell Chinese age."

I closed my eyes and breathed evenly, but she could tell I wasn't asleep.

"This is terrible ghost country, where a human being works her life away," she said. "Even the ghosts work, no time for acrobatics. I have not stopped working since the day the ship landed. I was on my feet the moment the babies were out. In China I never even had to hang up my own clothes. I shouldn't have left, but your father couldn't have supported you without me. I'm the one with the big muscles."

"If you hadn't left, there wouldn't have been a me for you two to support. Mama, I'm really sleepy. Do you mind letting me sleep?" I do not believe in old age. I do not believe in getting tired.

"I didn't need muscles in China. I was small in China." She was. The silk dresses she gave me are tiny. You would not think the same person wore them. This mother can carry a hundred pounds of Texas rice up-and-downstairs. She could work at the laundry from six thirty a. m. until midnight, shifting a baby from an ironing table to a shelf between packages, to the display window, where the ghosts tapped on the glass. "I put you babies in the clean places at the laundry, as far away from the germs that fumed out of the ghosts' clothes as I could. Aa, their socks and handkerchiefs choked me. I cough now because of these seventeen years of breathing dust. Tubercular handkerchiefs. Lepers' socks." I thought she had wanted to show off my baby sister in the display window.

In the midnight unsteadiness we were back at the laundry, and my mother was sitting on an orange crate sorting dirty clothes into mountains—a sheet mountain, a white shirt mountain, a dark shirt mountain, a work-pants mountain, a long underwear mountain, a short underwear mountain, a little hill of socks pinned together in pairs, a little hill of handkerchiefs pinned to tags. Surrounding her were candles she burned in daylight, clean yellow diamonds, footlights that ringed her, mysterious masked mother, nose and mouth veiled with a cowboy handkerchief. Before undoing the bundles, my mother would light a tall new candle, which was a luxury, and the pie pans full of old wax and wicks that sometimes sputtered blue, a noise I thought was the germs getting seared.

"No tickee, no washee, mama-san?" a ghost would say, so embarrassing.

"Noisy Red-Mouth Ghost," she'd write on its package, naming it, marking its clothes with its name.

Back in the bedroom I said, "The candles must have helped. It was a good idea of yours to use candles."

"They didn't do much good. All I have to do is think about dust sifting out of clothes or peat dirt blowing across a field or chick mash falling from a scoop, and I start coughing." She coughed deeply. "See what I mean? I have worked too much. Human beings don't work like this in China. Time goes slower there. Here we have to hurry, feed the hungry children before we're too old to work. I feel like a mother cat hunting for its kittens. She has to find them fast because in a few hours she will forget how to count or that she had any kittens at all. I can't sleep in this country because it doesn't shut down for the night. Factories, canneries, restaurants—always somebody somewhere working through the night. It never gets done all at once here. Time was different in China. One year lasted as long as my total time here; one evening so long, you could visit your women friends, drink tea, and play cards at each house, and it would still be twilight. It even got boring, nothing to do but fan ourselves. Here midnight comes and the floor's not swept, the ironing's not ready, the money's not made. I would still be young if we lived in China."

"Time is the same from place to place," I said unfeelingly. "There is only the eternal present, and biology. The reason you feel time pushing is that you had six children after you were forty-five and you worried about raising us. You shouldn't worry any more, though, Mama. You should feel good you had so many babies around you in middle age. Not many mothers have that. Wasn't it like prolonging youth? Now wasn't it? You mustn't worry now. All of us have grown up. And you can stop working."

"I can't stop working. When I stop working, I hurt. My head, my back, my legs hurt. I get dizzy. I can't stop."

"I'm like that too, Mama. I work all the time. Don't worry about me starving. I won't starve. I know how to work. I work all the time. I know how to kill food, how to skin and pluck it. I know how to keep warm by sweeping and mopping. I know how to work when things get bad."

[Selected from Maxine Hong Kingston. *The Woman Warrior*. New York: Picador, 1981.]

Ⅲ. Questions for discussion

(1) Who are the ghosts Kingston describes in "Shaman," and why does she call them in that way? Why do ghosts play such an important role in this section and in the book as a whole?

(2) How does Kingston depict her mother (Brave Orchid) in this section? In what ways does this depiction fit in some of the book's larger themes?

(3) Are there any ambiguity of Brave Orchid's talk-stories? What, in these stories, is factual and what resides merely in the imagination of either Kingston or Brave Orchid?

(4) Why does Kingston include so much information about food?

(5) How would you describe Kingston's relationship with her mother?

(6) "Shaman" depicts the conflicts and paradoxes of Brave Orchid's life and of the mother-daughter relationship she has with Kingston. On one hand, Kingston seems to gain intelligence who escapes her traditional role as housewife and mother.

As a ghost destroyer, Brave Orchid is a woman warrior in her own right, not unlike Hua Mulan. On the other hand, Brave Orchid reinforces many of the negative stereotypes that Chinese women are useless and disappointing. How do you understand this paradox?

(7) Read the following interview as assigned reading. The interview which followed Maxine Hong Kingston's reading at the University of California, Santa Barbara on February 22, 2006 is framed to cover the thirty years of Kingston's production. Why and how has she become a multi-genre author in the past thirty years? What is Kingston's opinion of the emergence of a global novel?

3.3 Assigned Reading

Reading Back, Looking Forward: A Retrospective Interview with Maxine Hong Kingston

Shirley Geok-lin Lim①

Shirley Lim: When *The Woman Warrior* appeared in 1976, you were about thirty-five or thirty-six years old. It brought you tremendous recognition, not only from Asian American readers but also from a mainstream U.S. literary and cultural intelligentsia. How did such immediate and widespread success affect you and your writing, if at all?

Maxine Hong Kingston: Well, publishing big when you are thirty-five years old doesn't really change your life that much. If I had been younger—if I were in my twenties—I might have gotten really excited and wild and let it all go to my head. At thirty-five, I'm settled. I'm living the life that I want, and so emotionally, psychologically, it did not change me at all. But for the practicalities of the writer's life, it made a difference in that I did not have to do any other work for money.

What happened was that I was teaching at a boarding school in Honolulu and it meant I was on duty twenty-four hours a day. You're always on call at a boarding school. I had been teaching there exactly six years during which time I wrote *The Woman Warrior*. When it was published and I got an advance, it just so happened that I was there for six years so I got a sabbatical. I had made up my mind that

① Shirley Geok-lin Lim (1944—) was born in Malaysia. She is an American writer of poetry, fiction, and criticism and also a professor in the English Department at the University of California, Santa Barbara.

during the sabbatical I would write the next book. The conditions of the sabbatical are you have to come back to teach for an additional two years. I got my advance for *The Woman Warrior* and paid off my sabbatical, so I did not have to come back, and I quit teaching. At that time I got a \$5000 advance, enough to pay for one year's salary of my teaching. I thought of it as buying my freedom and then I could write without doing any other (work), no more moonlighting, I could concentrate on writing.

SL: That's really productive for all of us (to hear). Could you reflect on some of the changes or transformations that characterize your work as a writer in the thirty years since *The Woman Warrior* appeared?

MHK: All my writing is different from all my other writing. I think the progression or the evolution is such that first *The Woman Warrior* is an I-book; it is very self-centered. I got that out of the way. It's very necessary, at least for me, to write that book in which I can establish who I am. As a writer, it seems to me that growth takes place when I can put it into words. If I can say who I am, if I can say what powers I want, then I can have them. That was the function of *The Woman Warrior*: self-understanding, understanding myself in relation to my family, to my mother, my place in my community, in my society, and in the world.

Then, (in) the next book I felt I didn't want to concentrate on me anymore. My growth is that I would understand the other, no more self, but I need to get into the point of view of people who are very unlike myself. I wrote about men, *China Men*. My concerns were larger than just myself or even my gender but to write about the other gender and a larger history. I saw *China Men* as a history book, and it would be a story that has been left out of history, the migrations coming from China, the migrations to America that came from the east and not from Europe.

Then the next book... actually there is another book in-between. While I was writing *China Men*, it was so large and it included the story of the Chinese coming here to build the railroads. I was myself having to build a railroad, but it's done in words. I thought the physical exertion of it was just as hard as if I were building a railroad, building a transcontinental railroad. I needed a break or something easier, so I started writing a column for the *New York Times*, a weekly column that came out every Thursday. Every column is only 800 words. It's so manageable. I could see the end right at the beginning, whereas with *The Women Warrior* and *China Men* I never could see the end. *China Men* was endless. I mean these guys were digging the tunnels through the Sierras, and I felt like that too, that I was never going to see the end of the tunnel, the light. I couldn't even conceive of that book ever ending. It went on year after year.

So I wrote these 800-word columns. It was an interesting feat because I was writing in Honolulu, (while) my point of view was supposed to be from New York, and that really stretched me. I saw myself as spanning not only the continent but the Pacific Ocean. The editors quite often would make little tinkering changes because New York really does have its own provincial viewpoint. They don't quite understand or like it when you write from the West, not only California but Hawaii. I did about a dozen columns which I then published in a book called *Hawaii: One Summer*. It gave me a good chance to use the Hawaiian language and the image (of Hawaii) with all of its Polynesian and Asian influences. That book is so interesting because it began as a column in the *New York Times*, which is the most disposable thing on earth. But then a fine book artist wanted to collect those columns, and she honored my writing with a book that she hand-sewed and she dyed the cover. It was created with woodprint blocks by (San Francisco book designer) Mark Stuart Ong (who is Jade Snow Wong's son).

She bought the paper from Korea. That book cost, without the slipcover, $400. With the slipcover, it's a $500 book. It went all the way from the *New York Times* to the $500 book, which, when it came out, I realized (was) for collectors, not for readers. I got the University of Hawaii Press to do a paperback, so that book has all its different incarnations. I just kind of squeezed that in while I was doing *China Men*, which I finally finished.

Every time I write a book I try to tell everything I know. I got to the end of *China Men*, and I thought, "Wait a minute. There's still some more stuff I know that didn't make it into that book," and (I thought) also that the book is not good enough because it is based on fact. What about fiction? What about the whole life of the imagination? I have not written a novel, a real fiction novel. Nor have I written a story that went cover to cover. In both *The Woman Warrior* and *China Men*, I didn't think I was able to write a long form such as the novel. I would write a short story and then I would write another short story, and all the short stories interwove and I kind of fool people into thinking that it's a long form. It's like when you make a quilt and you just make it out of little squares. You know that's really cheating. The great quit is when you make the whole thing.

So I thought, "Okay, that's what I'm going to do: a book that goes from cover to cover and it's one long story, and those are really chapter headings; they are not a series of little short stories." (*Tripmaster Monkey*) is the first book that does not have an "I" narrator; I made an omniscient narrator. I got to that point, a big breakthrough, because you are looking at the world from the point of view of God. But in my case I was thinking from the point of view of the Goddess. I hope it's a feminine voice but I don't tell you what it is.

After that I started *The Fifth Book of Peace*, and it burned (in a house fire in 1991), and I started (again). And again I had that feeling, "Oh, this is endless. I'm never going to get to write the end," so, just for fun, why don't I write again the short form? But this time I did poems, which give you that instant gratification.

One thing that really alarmed me in my life—*The Woman Warrior* took three years to write. At the time I was doing my twenty-four hours a day job at the school, and yet I was able to write *The Woman Warrior* in three years. Then I had all the time in the world. No more teaching. I could devote full-time to my writing. Then *China Men* took four years. And *Tripmaster Monkey*, I don't know, eight years. Every one took longer and longer. And then *The Fifth Book of Peace* burns, and I had to rewrite it again, so it ends up being twelve years. Every time I write something it takes longer. It is very alarming to me. So I think, "Well, I'm going to do haiku. I'm going to write poems and get some instant gratification."

SL: Thank you for this exposition on your texts. A major distinction between you and some other well known Asian American women authors is that you did not see your first book and its success as a formula to be repeated. That's clear in your exposition. In fact, you appear deliberately to avoid such repetition in your book of memoirs, your (second) memoir, a history of sorts, *China Men*, an epic novel *Tripmaster Monkey*, your book of poems, and your fifth book, appropriately titled also *The Fifth Book of Peace*, which is a mixed genre work or creative nonfiction. Could you tell us something about these choices, why you seem to work on very divergent genres? Are you conscious of genre when you are writing a book? Have you thought about why and how you have become a multi-genre author?

MHK: When I am writing I am always exploring, and I'm always going into the new. I have to find new life, new understandings. I'm living life, and I am looking for its meaning or I'm looking for the wonderful that is existence and I take great joy in describing it. I cannot find a formula and then re-do the formula because then I'm doing the same thing over again. I'm not interested in doing anything over again. I have to try something that I've never tried before. When I learn something and I write it down, then I go on to write the new thing.

I do think about genre. Part of it is, okay, I am experimenting with genre. I think that *The Woman Warrior* is a mix of ... it's got myth and nonfiction, autobiography. I am writing about people who have wild imaginations, so I also have to use fictional techniques, and I am mixing genres. But I'm also aware (that) I've written a couple of nonfiction books but I haven't done the fiction, so let's try that genre.

I think of poetry as the highest, hardest thing to do. And then of course I need to try it, and I need to try all its different forms. Doing essay forms is what the *New York Times* columns were. I can feel the intellectual work that is going on. It seems to come from my head, and sometimes I have to try. There's this feeling of: where does it come from? Is it the stomach or is it my heart? Or is it coming from my toe or what? There's a physicality.

The way I work is that at the beginning all is formless. We all learn that early in our spiritual lives: at first there is no form. As a writer what that translates into is, first, I don't know what I'm doing. I don't know what I'm writing about. I don't know what my opening is. I don't know where this story is going. I don't even know if it's going to be a story. But there is something that grabs me. And so I start connecting sounds and notes, and it's like I'm gathering clay. I'm gathering dirt and rocks and mud. I think of it as mud. I'm putting all this ur-draft together.

Or I think of a character. And I keep following this character to see what the character will do. I keep writing any old thing. At first it is a mess; it is a pile of dirt. I rewrite it again and again, and pretty soon it starts to take a shape. Then I say, Oh, I know, I think I start recognizing this shape. Oh, I think this looks like an epic novel. This looks like an autobiography, but it is an autobiography that hasn't been done before. Of course, it's an autobiography that hasn't been done before because nobody ever did my autobiography before.

It's like searching to shape this thing and I have a sort of faith that it will coalesce into a form, and that maybe forms are elemental and platonic. That, there is, you know, the sonnet. You can go off in all sorts of directions, but maybe what you have to say when you finally get that thing organized is a sonnet. It does come across as a recognizable form once you pull it together.

SL: On a slightly different subject, I was re-reading your books prior to this interview and became much more aware that your texts very often indicate the presence of at least two languages: Chinese and English. What are some of the challenges you face in your attempt to describe the presence of Chinese in an English-language narrative? It seems to me that you work with forms of plurality or re-heard speech, either Chinese or Chinese-inflected English. Could you expand on what I might call "translinguistic stylistics" that I see emerging in your texts?

MHK: I'm so glad that you asked me that because I want to correct something I said last night. Someone from the audience had asked about the use of Chinese in my English. I gave this example that it seems to me there is language that seems to come from the very depth of our human bodies. The example I gave was this. China brought about yearning, and I noticed that there is an English word for longing, for yearning, which is to long, and I said it really fits my theory because there is a Chinese word that is also long. But it's a mistake. There is not a Chinese word that also is the same as long. The word is mong. So we are mong-ing, we are longing, we are yearning. When I come across a linguistic coincidence like that I think, "Oh that is so right." When I say long, when I say mong, I just feel it. You know, you can just feel it in your body, what that feeling of yearning is.

I write from the language that I hear. This is an old American tradition from the very first writings of the Transcendentalists. They tried to distinguish themselves from the British. So we are going to write the new American language. And you've got that during the Beat generation. William Carlos Williams, too. Find the American language. Edgar Allan Poe was working on the American language, and this is what I'm trying to do too.

But my American language is spoken by Chinese speakers. Williams said that poetry is going to come from hearing, that you walk among your people, among everyone. Go out on the streets. You interact with everyone; a writer tunes her ear. You tune your ear the same way that a musician tunes your ear and the ears for language.

It was such a linguistic adventure for me to travel to the British Isles and to hear English, and then to travel through China and to hear Chinese. Karen Yamashita talked about the DNA; there are the stories that are in your DNA. I think there are the sounds that are in our DNA. We hear words—the Word—words—and they come into our bodies, into our ears, and then we find a way to transmit it into the written word. I want everything that I hear to get into the way that I write, oh, like the way I become poetry, oral. Everything that I write I say it aloud.

SL: Every word in *Tripmaster Monkey*?

MHK: Every word. Every word in everything, including academic papers, I read it aloud. Because you can feel in your mouth, whether it is pleasant or unpleasant, angry or leering or whatever, and then you also hear it in your ear. The whole body goes into this composition.

SL: To go back to another point you made earlier, another difference between you and some other Asian American writers is the pace at which your books have appeared. I tell my students that it took you about, as you say, eight to ten years between the publication of *China Men* and *Tripmaster Monkey*. So if they wish to understand the novel they might anticipate spending at least ten years on it. This is not of course to say that you are a slow writer.

MHK: I am a slow writer.

SL: Could you maybe talk a bit about the question of your pace of writing, perhaps in reference to some other authors?

MHK: I was just thinking lately, or it was pointed out to me, or I read somewhere that Jane Austen only wrote six books in her whole life; and I thought, "Oh, I wrote six books. I did that, too. I already wrote six books, and can I quit now?" And if I died, is it okay because I've got six, and she got six? It's all right.

But actually it's not all right. I'm always nagging myself. I'm always so worried and, oh, I go so slow. I can't pick up the pace and I'm always feeling bad if I take some time off, but I can't do it any faster. I don't know how. If I had some tricks I would do it. Maybe it has to do with this idea that I always have to come up with something new and every book is harder and every book is longer both in time and the length of the book and maybe that just has to do with my always wanting to discover a new thing.

SL: Well, your books are so dense I think it's remarkable you've written this many books in one lifetime. With *Tripmaster Monkey*, at 340 pages, it is clearly an epic text, an epic novel, and it is quite overt about its epic status. My colleague, Richard Helgerson, says that he displays your novel in talking about seventeenth century epics and Milton's *Paradise Lost*, to demonstrate how flexible and continuous the epic form has been. My question is taken from his discussion with me, where he observes that any author writing an epic has both to reproduce a tradition which goes back all the way to Homer up to James Joyce and Walt Whitman (whom you reference in *Tripmaster Monkey*) and also to change that tradition. How conscious were you about shaping *Tripmaster Monkey* as an epic novel and what were some of the conscious and quasi-conscious strategies that you undertook in order to author your own Chinese American epic?

MHK: I was very conscious of writing an epic because I was thinking that in order to build a life it must take long distances of travel. I was thinking about Homer, but I was mostly thinking about Homer and *The Odyssey* and the big epics when I was writing *The Fifth Book of Peace* because that would be kind of more like a war book. (With *Tripmaster Monkey*) I thought about James Joyce's *Ulysses* (which covers) only about one day can be epic. I certainly feel that from my own experience of what a day is that it is epic. For *Tripmaster Monkey* my model was the monkey stories, Sun Wukong, the Monkey King. I like the form of the saga because (in) this oral tradition every night the theater, or the storyteller, can tell one episode or two episodes or maybe three or four. No more than that. But then the next night or the next time you encounter the monkey story, you could hear another episode. These episodes are all out of order; there isn't a linear sequence. You can go to the theater and maybe you'll see an episode that you never saw before and then you can figure where it might belong in the sequence in which you heard it. The listener or the reader, you, can put them into a sequence that you experience.

I love the long epic novel because it makes the reader participate in a long life. I remember reading *War and Peace* when I was a teenager. It took me all summer. Well, of course, I lived with that novel for a whole summer. I would love it if my readers could live with one of my books for a week of their lives, or a month of their lives, so we could participate in this adventure together. I liked the way that this trippy monkey form allowed me to experiment. Sometimes I will start a story and I don't know if it's going to pay off and whether it will be very exciting or what. Sometimes it pays off and sometimes it doesn't, but it allows me to experiment with a lot of different stories and see whether they will come together or not.

SL: You said, "I'd like my reader to spend a week or a month with me." Many of my graduate students studying your work usually spend more than a month with you! But let's move to the question of the ethnic author's responsibility or at least relationship to his or her ethnic community, the community that she is representing in her work. This question has been really fraught and continues to divide many Asian American writers. Amy Tan, for example, has argued that the expectation that Asian American writers should have some responsibility to their communities, and that the American readers believed their works represent this community, is politically correct and should be rejected. What's your position on this matter?

MHK: Oh, my position goes back and forth, back and forth. But what I start with is that in order to create and in order to compose, I have to not let any critics or any readers or anybody be breathing down my back or looking over my shoulder. Or any editors, I just don't like anybody with any expectations because I need to really get deep within whatever journey I need to make: journeys within and also thinking about the world and life. I don't want any constraints on that. I want to be free to write whatever I want. I need to be free, to be socially irresponsible with no allegiances to anybody. I have to have that. I think every creative person needs that freedom, and so there are times when I will say, "Okay, I don't represent anybody."

But then also I am a political person. I am a citizen of this country and of this world, and I also have political concerns and social concerns. At the same time I'm thinking I don't want to write propaganda because that's no good. Also our Asian American, Chinese American communities claim you whether you like it or not. I mean, there is no escape. People will come and say, why aren't you writing about this and this and this? Why aren't you writing about ... You should be writing about the International Hotel. You've got to be writing about ... I even hear from

Asian Americans who will come and say, "You're always writing about the poor people. There are some very good rich people, too. Why don't you write about them?"

There's always these demands, and I just have to work out my own politics and decide what part I want to bring in and what parts I don't want to bring in, and write well enough so I can convince everybody that my politics are the correct ones and they should be happy to be represented by me.

SL: In a 1995 published interview in *Weber Studies*, Neila C. Seshachari noted that in the *Mother Jones* piece you wrote in 1987 you talked about the emergence of a global novel. Could you elaborate on this foresight, which you talked about in 1987, nearly twenty years ago? What are some of the dynamics you think are moving the novel from a national toward a global identity?

MHK: I think I was working on *Tripmaster Monkey* when I was talking to Neila and seeing how everything connects with everything. Here was the monkey, a Chinese monkey, but he might have been an Indonesian monkey too. I try to find out where the Chinese monkey and the Indonesian monkey were connected. During the 1960s the hippies were trying to stop the war by being monkeys, by clowning and trying to levitate the Pentagon and using monkey magic to try to stop the war. Then I was thinking, "Oh, so the monkey flew all the way from China to America, and I see monkey antics right here in American culture." Then I noticed that wherever we go—any city I've ever been to—is a global city. There are people from all over the world in every city. What I was telling Neila was the time of the great American novel is over. If you were going to write a great American novel, then it is also the global novel. At the same time Salman Rushdie was writing, and I could see he was writing a global novel. It breaks across borders and boundaries. *The Satanic Verse* starts with an airplane crashing, and I said, "Oh yes, that's the monkey and it's flying across and crashes and the monkey falls to earth." It's breaking across boundaries. The references are from all cultures; the language has the accents of every culture. Any good writing has to have elements of all of our backgrounds.

SL: This question is prompted by Eric Martinsen who is writing his dissertation on the global novel, and I want to thank him for it. Did you find this global novel concept twenty years ago a full emergent form? You mentioned Rushdie. Do you have some other authors in mind besides Rushdie and yourself, with *Tripmaster Monkey*?

MHK: I think that Bharati Mukherjee has been doing a lot of work. She lived in Canada for a long time and in India, and then she's writing here. She actually has said she is writing across borders and characters have to be global, that an author has to be able to write characters that come from everywhere and with all their different accents.

Right now I'm a judge for the Kuriyama Prize and we have had seventy-five novels nominated or that have been submitted for the prize. And I notice, yes, they are global. What they have in common, I think, a lot of novels are about a village somewhere in India, Sri Lanka, Burma, Vietnam, Singapore, China. It's about little villages somewhere, and then come crashing into this village is modernity. It could be tanks, guns, airplanes, chemicals. All of a sudden this village is part of whatever affects the whole world. The whole world comes to this village. A lot of writers from everywhere are writing that story.

SL: Let's talk about *The Fifth Book of Peace*, which you read from last night. It appeared in 2003, two years after the World Trade Towers fell. The opening chapter raises the loss of your manuscript and your home in the 1991 Oakland-Berkeley fires, and it also refers to the killing of Iraqi children and women. Obviously in the chronology (of the book), that is a reference to the first Bush presidency, the first Gulf War. So *The Fifth Book of Peace* was in many ways an evolving text, because you had to rewrite, because you had lost the ur-draft, the first manuscript; and it is interestingly a self-referential text because it talks about how it is being composed as it is being composed. Did world events, particularly in the Middle East with the second Gulf War, overtake the text? Did you have to take time to rewrite sections of that first chapter as you see the United States become even more militaristic while pacifist sympathizers have been largely overwhelmed?

MKH: In all my writing I am constantly worried about life events overtaking my text. The way I answer to myself is that I must write in such a universal, forever, way. That what I need to write is a vision that is always true. It's immovable. If I can find a truth or a story that will be relevant to readers a hundred years from now, a thousand years from now, then the text will still be alive no matter what temporary conditions are. I had that goal.

But at the same time I did keep noticing, "Oh now I haven't even finished the book yet and the planes went into the World Trade Center and everybody is saying it's new world." In fact here's what actually happened. I had delivered the last draft of *The Fifth Book of Peace* to my publisher in New York. My editor is Deborah Garrison, the poet, and she was reading my book—it was on her desk—when the planes went into the World Trade Center, and she phoned me and said, "Well, now your book is outdated." And anyway, what a thing to say to me. And then she said that we all need to be more sensitive now. We need to be more sensitive to patriotic feelings, more sensitive to people who have had their losses. More sensitive to the political climate. More sensitive, maybe, you know, a book that gets too pacifist, maybe it won't sell. We've got to be sensitive. She told me that I need to be more sensitive.

I thought, "Oh, god. This is terrible." What she said, too, is that I get the chance to kind of tweak it or something. My first solution was that, "Oh well, I have to write an introduction, to make it more up to date." I did write that introduction, and in it I give my obeisance to the World Trade Center and to everything. But I found that my introduction took away suspense. The whole book is about suspense. Will I find the three lost books of peace? Will I make it alive out of that fire? Will pacifists have their say? When I made my very sensitive introduction I felt that it took away...I was giving people answers already.

So I decided, "Okay, no introduction." But I did write an epilogue. In the epilogue I am able to say, "Here is the attack on the World Trade Center and on the Pentagon." I found a wonderful form for the epilogue. Sometimes you see a movie, and at the end of the movie they tell you what happened to these people when they got older. I got to tell what had happened to all those veterans, and then I got to tell about demonstrating in front of the White House and getting arrested. I thought that's a really nice ending.

SL: So that was your answer to Deborah.

MHK: Yeah.

[Selected from Maxine Hong Kingston. *The Woman Warrior*. *MELUS* (Vol. 33). 2008(1).]

4. Frank Chin

4.1 Presentation Topics

(1) Frank Chin as a playwright and essayist.

(2) The traditional Chinese folklore in Frank Chin's works

(3) Frank Chin's debate with Maxine Hong Kingston.

4.2 Selected Reading

Ⅰ. Central issue of concern

Frank Chin's determination to remake or reconfigure the Chinese American male, to restore the masculinity, sexuality, voice and power that were stripped away by white Americans and Western culture.

Ⅱ. Text

Donald Duk and the White Monsters

Who would believe anyone named Donald Duk dances like Fred Astaire? Donald Duk does not like his name. Donald Duk never liked his name. He is not a duck. He is not a cartoon character. He does not go home to sleep in Disneyland every night. The kids that laugh at him are very smart. Everyone at his private school is smart. Donald Duk is smart. He is a gifted one, they say.

No one in school knows he takes tap dance lessons from a man who calls himself "The Chinese Fred Astaire." Mom talks Dad into paying for the lesson and tap shoes.

Fred Astaire. Everybody everywhere likes Fred Astaire in the old black-and-white movies. Late at night on TV, even Dad smiles when Fred Astaire dances. Mom hums along. Donald Duk wants to live the late night life in old black-and-white movies and talk with his feet like Fred Astaire, and smile Fred Astaire's sweet lemonade smile.

The music teacher and English teacher in school go dreamy eyed when they talk about seeing Fred Astaire and Ginger Rogers on the late-night TV.

"Remember when he danced with Barbara Stanwyck? What was the name of that move?"

"Barbara Stanwyck?"

"Did you see the one where he dances with Rita Hayworth?"

"Oooh, Rita Hayworth!"

Donald Duk enjoys the books he reads in school. The math is a curious game. He is not the only Chinese in the private school. But he is the only Donald Duk. He avoids the other Chinese here. And the Chinese seem to avoid him. This school is a place where the Chinese are comfortable hating Chinese. "Only the Chinese are stupid enough to give a kid a stupid name like Donald Duk," Donald Duk says to himself. "And if the Chinese were that smart, why didn't they invent tap dancing?"

Donald Duk's father's name is King. King Duk. Donald hates his father's name. He hates being introduced with his father. "This is King Duk, and his son Donald Duk." Mom's name is Daisy. "That's Daisy Duk, and her son Donald." Venus Duk and Penny Duk are Donald's sisters. The girls are twins and a couple of years older than Donald.

His own name is driving him crazy! Looking Chinese is driving him crazy! All his teachers are making a big deal about Chinese stuff in their classes because of Chinese. New Year coming on soon. The teacher of California History is so happy to be reading about the Chinese. "The man studied history under at Berkeley authored this book. He was a spellbinding lecturer," the teacher throbs. Then he reads, "The Chinese in America were made passive and nonassertive by centuries of Confucian thought and Zen mysticism. They were totally unprepared for the violently individualistic and democratic Americans. From their first step on American soil to the middle of the 20th century, the timid, introverted Chinese have been helpless against the relentless victimization by aggressive, highly competitive Americans."

"One of the Confucian concepts that lends the Chinese vulnerable to the assertive ways of the West is 'the mandate of heaven.' As the European kings of old ruled by divine right, so the emperors of China ruled by the mandate of heaven." The teacher takes a breath and looks over his spellbound class. Donald wants to barf pink and green stuff all over the teacher's teacher's book.

"What's he saying?" Donald Duk's pal Arnold Azalea asks in a whisper.

"Same thing as everybody-Chinese are artsy, cutesy and chickendick." Donald Duk whispers back.

Oh, no! Here comes Chinese New Year again! It is Donald Duk's worst time of year. Here come the stupid questions about the funny things Chinese believe in. The funny things Chinese do. The funny things Chinese eat. And, "Where can I buy some Chinese firecrackers?"

And in Chinatown it's Goong hay fot choy everywhere. And some gang kids do sell firecrackers. And some gang kids rob other kids looking for firecrackers. He doesn't like the gang kids. He doesn't like speaking their Chinese. He doesn't have to—this is America. He doesn't like Chinatown. But he lives here.

The gang kids know him. They call him by name. One day the Frog Twins wobble onto the scene with their load of full shopping bags. There is Donald Duk. And there are five gang boys and two girlfriends chewing gum, swearing and smirking. The gang kids wear black tanker Jackets, white tee shirts and baggy black denim jeans. It is the alley in front of the Chinese Historical Society Museum. There are fish markets on each side of the Chinatown end of the alley. Lawrence Ferlinghetti's famous City Lights Bookstore is at the end that opens on Columbus Street. Suddenly there are the Frog Twins in their heavy black overcoats. They seem to be wearing all the clothes they own under their coats. Their coats bulge. Under their skirts they wear several pairs of trousers and slacks. They wear one knit cap over the other. They wear scarves tied over their heads and shawls over their shoulders.

That night, after he is asleep, Dad comes home from the restaurant and wakes him up. "You walk like a sad softie," Dad says. "You look like you want everyone to beat you up."

"I do not!" Donald Duk says.

"You look at yourself in the mirror," Dad says, and Donald Duk looks at himself in his full-length dressing mirror. "Look at those slouching shoulders, that pouty face. Look at those hands holding onto each other. You look scared!" Dad's voice booms and Donald hears everyone's feet hit the floor. Mom and the twins are out in the hall looking into his open door.

"I am scared!" Donald Duk says.

"I don't care if you are scared," Dad says. His eyes sizzle into Donald Duk's frightened pie-eyed stare. "Be as scared as you want to be, but don't look scared. Especially ought when you walk through Chinatown."

"How do I look like I'm not scared if I am scared?" Donald Duk asks.

"You walk with your back straight. You keep your hands out of your pockets. Don't hunch your shoulders. Think of them as being down. Keep your head up. Look like you know where you're going. Walk like you know where you're going. And you say, 'Don't mess with me, horsepuckie! Don't mess with me!' But you don't say it with your mouth. You say it with your eyes. You say it with your hands where everybody can see them. Anybody get two steps in front of you, you zap them with your eyes, and they had better nod at you or look away. When they nod, you nod. When you walk like nobody better mess with you, nobody will mess with you. When you walk around like you're walking now, all rolled up in a little ball and hiding out form everything, they'll get you for sure."

Donald does not like his dad waking him up like that and yelling at him. But what the old man says works. Outside among the cold San Francisco shadows and the early morning shoppers, Donald Duk hears his father's voice and straightens his back, takes his hands out of his pockets, says "Don't mess with me!" with his eyes and every move of his body. And, yes, he's talking with his body the way Fred Astaire talks, and shoots every gang kid who walks toward him in the eye with a look that says, "Don't mess with me." And no one messes with him. Dad never talks his about it again.

Later, gang kids laugh at his name and try to pick fights with him during the afternoon rush hour, Dad's busy time in the kitchen. Donald is smarter than these lowbrow beady-eyed goons. He has to beat them without fighting them because he doesn't know how to fight. Donald Duk gets the twins to talk about it with Dad while they are all at the dining room table working on their model airplanes.

Dad laughs. "So he has a choice. He does not like people laughing at his name. He does not want the gangsters laughing at his name to beat him up. He mostly doesn't want to look like a sissy in front of them, so what can he do?"

"He can pay them to leave him alone," Venus says.

"He can not! That is so chicken it's disgusting!" Penelope says.

"So, our little brother is doomed."

"He can agree with them and laugh at his name," Dad says. "He can tell them lots of Donald Duk jokes. Maybe he can learn to talk that quack-quack Donald Duk talk."

"Whaaat?" the twins ask in one voice.

"If he keeps them laughing," Dad says, "even if he can just keep them listening, they are not beating him up, right? And they are not calling him a sissy. He does not want to fight? He does not have to fight. He has to use his smarts, okay? If he's smart enough, he makes up some Donald Duk jokes to surprise them and make them laugh. They laugh three times, he can walk away. Leave them there laughing, thinking Donald Duk is one terrific fella."

"So says King Duk," Venus Duk flips. The twins often talk as if everything they hear everybody say and see everybody do is dialog in a memoir they're writing or action in a play they're directing. This makes Mom feel like she's on stage and drives Donald Duk crazy.

"Is that Chinese psychology, dear?" Daisy Duk asks.

"Daisy Duk inquires," says Penelope Duk.

"And little Donnie Duk says, 'Oh, Mom' and sighs."

"I do not!" Donald Duk yelps at the twins.

"Well, then, say it," Penelope Duk says. "It's a good line. So you, you, you know."

"Thank you," Venus says.

"Oh goshes, you all, your sympathy is so ... so ... so literary. So dramatic," Donald Duk says. "It is truly depressing."

"I thought it was narrative," Venus says.

"Listen up for some Chinese psychology, girls and boys," Daisy Duk says.

"No, that's not psychology, that's Bugs Bunny," Dad says.

"You don't mean, Bugs Bunny, dear. You always make that mistake."

"Br'er Rabbit!" Dad says.

"What does that mean?" Donald Duk asks the twins. They shrug their shoulders. Nobody knows what Br'er Rabbit has to do with Dad's way of avoiding a fight and not being a fool, but it works.

One bright and sunny afternoon, a gang boy stops Donald and talks to him in the quacking voice of Walt Disney's Donald Duk. The voice breaks Donald Duk's mind for a flash, and he is afraid to turn on his own Donald Duk voice. He tries telling a joke about Donald Duk not wearing trousers or shoes, when the gangster-in black jeans, black tee shirt, black jacket, black shades-says in a perfect Donad Duk voice, "Let's take the pants off Donald Duk!"

"Oh oh! I stepped in it now!" Donald Duk says in his Donald Duk voice and stuns the gangster and his two gangster friends and their three girlfriends. Everything is seen and understood very fast. Without missing a beat, his own perfect Donald Duk voice cries for help in perfect Cantonese "Gow meng ahhh!" And they all laugh. Old women pulling little wire shopping carts full of fresh vegetables stop and stare at him. Passing children recognize the voice and say Donald Duk talks Chinese.

"Don't let these monsters take off my pants. I may be Donald Duk, but I am as human as you," he says in Chinese, in his Donald Duk voice, "I known how to use chopsticks. I use flush toilets. Why shouldn't I wear pants on Grant Street in China-town?" They all laugh more than three times. Their laughter roars three times on the comer of Grant and Jackson, and Donald Duk walks away, leaving them laughing, just the way Dad says he can. He feels great. Just great!

Donald Duk does not want to laugh about his name forever. There has to be an end to this. There is an end to all kidstuff for a kid. An end to diapers. An end to nursery rhymes and fairy tales. There has to be an end to laughing about his name to get out of a fight. Chinese New Year. Everyone will be laughing. He is twelve years old. Twelve years old is special to the Chinese. There are twelve years in the Asian lunar zodiac. For each year there is an animal. This year Donald will complete his first twelve-year cycle of his life. To celebrate, Donald Duk's father's old operamentor, Uncle Donald Duk, is coming to San Francisco to perform a Cantonese opera. Donald Duk does not want Chinese New Year. He does not want his uncle Donald Duk to tell him again how Daddy was a terrible man to name his little boy Donald Duk, because all the bok gwai, the white monsters, will think he is named after that bare-butt cartoon duck in the top half of a sailor suit and no shoes.

[Selected from Frank Chin. *Donald Duk*. Minneapolis: Coffee House Press, 1991.]

Ⅲ. Questions for discussion

(1) Do you think Frank Chin's choice of the name Donald Duk has any

particular value in this novel?

(2) What is Donald Duk's attitude toward the American popular culture and Chinese culture?

(3) What picture of Donald Duk's father does the novel convey? How does he teach the son to show masculinity?

(4) In what way does the setting help to characterize Donald Duk? Why does Frank Chin use a comic voice to tell this story?

(5) Read the following essay by Frank Chin as assigned reading. Think about the questions on culture, identity and racism. How is Frank Chin different from Maxine Hong Kingston in the way they treat their culture?

4.3 Assigned Reading

Preface to *The Big AIIIEEEEE !*

Frank Chin

ASIAN-AMERICANS are not one people but several—Chinese-Americans, Japanese-Americans, and Filipino-Americans. Chinese- and Japanese-Americans have been separated by geography, culture, and history from China and Japan for seven and four generations respectively. They have evolved cultures and sensibilities distinctly not Chinese or Japanese and distinctly not white American. Even the Asian languages as they exist today in America have been adjusted and developed to express a sensitivity created by a new experience. In America, Chinese- and Japanese-American culture and history have been inextricably linked by confusion, the popularization of their hatred for each other, and World War Ⅱ.

Filipino America differs greatly from Chinese and Japanese America in its history, the continuity of culture between the Philippines and America, and the influence of western European and American culture on the Philippines. The difference is definable only in its own terms, and therefore must be discussed separately.

Our anthology is exclusively Asian-American. That means Pilipino-, Chinese-, and Japanese-Americans, American born and raised, who got their China and Japan from the radio, off the silver screen, from television, out of comic books, from the pushers of white American culture that pictured the yellow man as something that when wounded, sad, or angry, or swearing, or wondering whined, shouted, or screamed "aiiieeeee!" Asian America, so long ignored and forcibly excluded from creative participation in American culture, is wounded, sad, angry, swearing, and wondering, and this is his AIIIEEEEE!!! It is more than a whine, shout, or scream. It is fifty years of our whole voice.

Seven generations of suppression under legislative racism and euphemized white racist love have left today's Asian-Americans in a state of self-contempt, self-rejection, and disintegration. We have been encouraged to believe that we have no cultural integrity as Chinese- or Japanese-Americans, that we are either Asian (Chinese or Japanese) or American (white), or are measurably both. This myth of being either / or and the equally goofy concept of the dual personality haunted our lobes while our rejection by both Asia and white America proved we were neither one nor the other. Nor were we half and half or more one than the other. Neither Asian culture nor American culture was equipped to define us except in the most superficial terms. However, American culture, equipped to deny us the legitimacy of our uniqueness as American minorities, did so, and in the process contributed to the effect of stunting self-contempt on the development and expression of our sensibility that in turn has contributed to a mass rejection of Chinese and Japanese America by Chinese- and Japanese-Americans. The Japanese-American Citizens League (JACL) weekly, the *Pacific Citizen*, in February, 1972, reported that more than 50 percent of Japanese-American women were marrying outside their race and that the figure was rising annually. Available statistics indicate a similar trend among Chinese-American women, though the 50 percent mark may not have been topped yet. These figures say something about our sensibility, our concept of Chinese-America and Japanese-America, our self-esteem, as does our partly real and partly mythical silence in American culture.

The age, variety, depth, and quality of the writing collected here proves the existence of Asian-American sensibilities and cultures that might be related to but are distinct from Asia and white America. American culture, protecting the sanctity of its whiteness, still patronizes us as foreigners and refuses to recognize Asian-American literature as "American" literature. America does not recognize Asian America as a presence, though Asian-Americans have been here seven generations. For seven generations we have been aware of that refusal, and internalized it, with disastrous effects.

Asian-American sensibility is so delicate at this point that the fact of Chinese or Japanese birth is enough to distinguish you from being American-born, in spite of the fact that you may have not actual memories of life in Asia. However, between the writer's actual birth and birth of the sensibility, we have used the birth of sensibility as the measure of being an Asian-American. Victor Nee was born in China and came to the United States when he was five. Novelist Louis Chu came when he was nine. For both, Chinese culture and China are not so much matters of experience as they are of hearsay and study. Victor and his wife Brett have written the first Chinese-American history of Chinese America, *Longtime Californ': A Documentary Study of an American Chinatown* (1973). Louis Chu's *Eat a Bowl of Tea* (1961) is the first Chinese-American novel set in Chinese America. Here we get sticky, however, for the first novel published by an American-born Chinese-American is the *Frontiers of Love* (1956), by Diana Chang, a Eurasian. She was born in America but moved to China before her first birthday, to be raised in the "European Compound" of Shanghai as an American in China. She writes of that experience, while Chu writes of Chinatown, New York. Between them so many questions are raised as to what is or is not Chinese-American that to save, and in another sense encourage, confusion (our criterion of Asian-American literature and identity is not a matter of dogma or party line), we have included them both. Chu's book honestly and accurately dramatizes the Chinese-American experience from a Chinese-American point of view, and not from an exclusively "Chinese or Chinese-according-to-white" point of view. Diana Chang in her protagonists of mixed blood and their single-blooded parents provides us with a logical dramatic metaphor for the conflict of cultures. Her protagonist, Sylvia, cannot choose between her parents or identify her blood as one thing or the other. The question of choice is shown to be a phony one imposed on her by outside forces.

Sensibility and the ability to choose differentiate the Asian-American writers in this collection from the Americanized Chinese writers Lin Yutang and C. Y. Lee. They were intimate with and secure in their Chinese cultural identity in an experiential sense, in a way we American-born can never be. Again, unlike us, they are American by choice. They consciously set out to become American, in the white sense of the word, and succeeded in becoming "Chinese-American" in the stereotypical sense of the good, loyal, obedient, passive, law-abiding, cultured sense of the word. It is no surprise that their writing is from whiteness, not from Chinese America. Becoming white supremacist was part of their consciously and voluntarily becoming "American." Lin Yutang's *A Chinatown Family* (1948) and C. Y. Lee's *Flower Drum Song* affected our sensibility but did not express it. They come from a white tradition of Chinese novelty literature, would-be Chinese writing about America for the entertainment of Americans in books like *As a Chinaman Sees Us*, *Chinaman's Chance*, and *A Chinaman Looks at America*. These travel books were in the tradition not so much of de Tocqueville as of *Gulliver's Travels*. Their attraction was comic. The humor derived from the Chinese mangling of the English language and from their comic explanations of American customs and psychology. These books appeared in the early 20th century after almost fifty years of travel books on China written by Christian missionaries and "world travelers" who cited missionaries as authorities on China. The reversal of the form, books of American adventures by Chinese travelers, was a comic inevitability. During this period the exploitation of the comic potential of Asian dialect became, forever, a part of popular American culture, giving rise to Earl Derr Biggers' series of Charlie Chan novels and Wallace Irwin's Hashimura Togo stories. The Hashimura Togo stories were featured in *Good Housekeeping* Magazine and described the adventures of a Japanese house servant who is both unintelligible and indispensible in an American household. A sample of the wit and wisdom of Hshimura Togo, from "Togo Assists in a Great Diamond Robbery"①:

> With occasional oftenness she approached up to me and report with frogged voice, "Togo where did you put my diamond broach and Mother Hubbard chamois ring when you stole it?"

The substance and imagery of these books and stories were reinforced by the whining, apologetic tone of books done by Chinese government officials giving the official explanations of Chinese culture and the nonthreatening, beneficial, humble motivations of the Chinese presence and immigration to America. Books were written as *The Real Chinese in America* (1923) by J. S. Tow, secretary of the Chinese Consulate at New York, with the rank of Consul-Eleven. The subservient character of the Chinese and inferiority of China were major themes in the works by

① *Good Housekeeping*, 1917(3).

Chinese converts to white supremacy and Christianity. Yung Wing's *My Life in China and America* (1909) is the outstanding example of early yellow white supremacy.

In 1925 Earl Derr Biggers, a distinctly non-Chinese, non-Chinese-American, and subtly racist writer, created the modern Chinese-American: Charlie Chan, the Chinese detective, who first appears in "The House Without a Key" walking with "the light dainty step of a woman." The travel format, going from one nation to another, became in Biggers' immensely popular Charlie Chan novels, an interior journey from one culture to another. Thus, the form evolved into the Chinatown book itself reinforced, and clearly articulated today's popular notion of being an Asian-American. The concept of the dual personality, of going from one culture to another, emerged.

Eleven years after the appearance of the fat, inscrutable, flowery but flub-tongued effeminate little detective, the first book by a Chinese-American about Chinese America was published. Leong Gor Yun's *Chinatown Inside Out* (1938) was a direct descendant of the Charlie Chan novels and became the prototype of what was to become the "Chinatown Book." The essence of the formula was, "I'm an American because I eat spaghetti and Chinese because I eat chow mein." The Charlic Chan model of Chinese-Americans was developed in books like Pardee Lowe's *Father And Glorious Descendant*, Lin Yutang's novel *A Chinatown Family*, Jade Snow Wong's *Fifth Chinese Daughter*, *Inside Chinatown*, by Garding Lui, and two books titled *Chinatown, U. S. A.*, one by Calvin Lee and the other by a white, Elizabeth Coleman.

Chinatown Inside Out was obviously a fraud. The author's name, "Leong Gor Yun," means "two men" in Cantonese. The book consists of items cribbed and translated from the Chinese-language newspapers of Chinatowns in San Francisco and New York tied together with Charlie Chan /Fu Manchu imaginings and the precise logic of a paranoid schizophrenic. Part expose, part cookbook, the book was supremacist in its overlooking of the effect of racism on our psychology and its never missing a chance to brown-nose the white man with Charlie Chan-like observations, i. e.:

Like chop-suey, this (unofficial Chinatown) government is an American product. It uses racketeer methods and ingenuity but it depends for its continued and prosperous existence on Chinese psychology, in this connection more precisely called passivity.

Far from giving America a big yuk, and celebrated as a classic of American humor, *Chinatown Inside Out* was accepted by everyone as the first book about Chinese America by a Chinese-American. No one, not even the scholars of Chinese America, noticed the awkward changes of voice and style, the differences between the outright lies and the rare facts. The clue of the author's pen name "two men" escaped all. *Chinatown Inside Out* was the source of Lin Yutang's 1948 novel *A Chinatown Family*. In 1962 S. W. Kung from China published *Chinese in American Life* and cited the work of another foreigner to Chinese America, Lin Yutang's *A Chinatown Family*. In 1965 Calvin Lee, a former assistant dean at Columbia University and the author of Chinese cookbooks, saw the light and testified to his successful conversion to utter white supremacy in *Chinatown U. S. A.* in which he cited Leong Gor Yun and S. W. Kung. Betty Lee Sung loosed *Mountain of Gold* in 1967. She praised the "Chinese in America" for never being "overly bitter about prejudice." In this book, she told us, "If you make yourself obnoxious ... that is a hindrance to acceptance." *Mountain of Gold* cited the gospel according to S. W. Kung, Lin Yutang, and Calvin Lee. In 1971 the gospel of Leong Gor Yun became hilarious sef-parody in Francis L. K. Hsu's *The Challenge of the American Dream*:

> The Chinese in America, in common with other minority groups, will have a continuing problem of double identity. But the effective way of dealing with it is not to deny its existence but to face it squarely. The first step is to realize that the double identity of a minority group is not dissimilar to that of the professional woman. She is a woman and a professional. Some American professional women have tended to forget their sex identity but most have kept some sort of balance between it and their profession. In the latter case, their sex identity sometimes becomes an advantage rather a disability.

Hsu's work may or may not give us insight into the mind of the first-generation upper-middle-class Chinese immigrant scholar, but in terms of the native Chinese-American sensibility, we can only note that, in the great tradition of Charlie Chan and Leong Gor Yun, his vision of Chinese America reinforces white racist stereotypes and falls short of the vision Malcolm X and other blacks had for their "minority."

The period from the late twenties through the thirties that spawned Charlie Chan, Fu Manchu, and Leong Gor Yun also produced a rash of popular songs,

Charlestons, and fox trots about "China boys" being stranded in America without their women. Such a song was "So Long Oolong (How Long You Gonna Be Gone)," that tells of a girl, "Ming Toy," pining for her sweetheart, "Oolong," stranded in America. Songs with titles like "Little Chinky Butterfly," "Hong Kong Dream Girl," and dozens of others appeared to be Tin Pan Alley's way of celebrating America's closing of the last loopholes in the Chinese Exclusion Act of 1923 by finding ways to exclude entry to Chinese women into the country. Also, a series of popular novels and movies involving passive Chinese men, worshiping white women and being afraid to touch them, appeared in *Son of the Gods*, *East is West*, and the Fu Manchu and Charlie Chan series.

In the meantime Japanese-Americans cranked up an underground press and literary movement in English, publishing their own poetry magazines, literary quarterlies, and newspapers that featured, as they still do, creative writing supplements in their holiday issues.

The "Inside Chinatown" books were done by American-born Chinese for the most part, but Chinese from China capitalized on the formula, and played it for bucks and popularity. Secure in their Chinese identities and Chinese cultural values—both of which were respectable in America, in the Mandarin versions—these books were not as significant or personally affecting to them as they were to the American-born, for whom these books represented manifestoes of Chinese-American identity and assimilation. The Chinese (not Chinese-American) writers Lin Yutang and C. Y. Lee refined the "spaghetti-chow-mein" form. In Arthur T. S. Chu's *We Are Going to Make the Lousiest Chop Suey in Town* (1966), the form takes its most ridiculous shape.

During World War Ⅱ the inside books became more personal and more manipulated. Patriotic Chinese-Americans wrote anti-Japanese propaganda disguised as autobiography. Pardee Lowe's *Father and Glorious Descendant* was the first. Though *Fifth Chinese Daughter* was published in 1950, it fits the propaganda-as-autobiography mold perfectly. There is reason to believe work on it actually began during the war. Chapters of it appeared in magazines in 1947. America's "anti-Jap" prejudice, as indicated by the release of new anti-Japanese war movies, continued strong until the mid-fifties, when the first sign of a change in white attitude was an announcement disclaiming prejudice against loyal Japanese-Americans before the airing of World War Ⅱ "anti-Jap" movies on television.

In travel books and in music, Japanese America was indiscriminately linked in confusion with Chinese America. In America's pop mind, Japan and China, as well as Japanese America and Chinese America, were one in exotica. China and Japan and Japanese America became distinguished from each other by hatred. That hatred was not explained in the terms of culture and politics, but in the terms of the Hatfields and McCoys—we were all some kind of silly, but civilized hillbillies feuding in the hills of jade. Chinese-Americans became America's pets, were kept and groomed in kennels, while Japanese-Americans were the mad dogs who had to be locked up in pounds. The editors and writers of the Japanese-American community papers were thrown ever closer to Japanese-American artists, poets, and storytellers. The Japanese-American writing in English that had been an activity was now welded into a movement.

The tradition of Japanese-American verse as being quaint and foreign in English, established by Yone Noguchi and Sadakichi Hartman, momentarily influenced American writing with the quaintness of the Orient but said nothing about Asian America, because, in fact, these writers weren't Asian-Americans but Americanized Asians like Lin Yutang and C. Y. Lee.

The first serious creative writing by an Asian-American to hit the streets was Mine Okubo's *Citizen* 13660, an autobiographical narrative in drawings and words, describing the relocation and camp experience from an artist's point of view. It was a remarkable book given the time of its appearance, 1946, when anti-Japanese sentiment was still high. Toshio Mori's collection of stories, *Yokohama, California*, appeared in 1949. It had been scheduled for release in 1941, but World War Ⅱ "anti-Jap" prejudice worked against Japanese-Americans appearing in print; however, it also spared their being shaped, used, and manipulated as Chinese-Americans.

After the war, the best way to rehabilitate Japanese America, from the white point of view, was to link it up and get it inextricably confused with Chinese America again, so from *Fifth Chinese Daughter* came son of *Fifth Chinese Daughter*, Monica Sone's *Nisei Daughter*, a book remarkable for maintaining its Japanese-American integrity in spite of its being, in the publisher's eyes, blatantly modeled on Wong's snow job.

None of the Chinese-, Japanese-, and Filipino-American works in this volume are snow jobs pushing Asian-Americans as the miracle synthetic white people that America's proprietors of white liberal pop, like Tom Wolfe, ABC television ("If Tomorrow Comes," "Kung Fu," "Madame Sin"), and such racist henchmen passing for scholars as Gunther Barth and Stuart Miller, make us out to be.

The Asian-American writers here are elegant or repulsive, angry and bitter, militantly anti-white or not, not out of any sense of perversity or revenge but of honesty. America's dishonesty—its racist white supremacy passed off as love and acceptance—has kept seven generations of Asian-American voices off the air, off the streets, and praised us for being Asiatically no-show. A lot is lost forever. But from the few decades of writing we have recovered from seven generations, it is clear that we have a lot of elegant, angry, and bitter life to show. We know how to show it. We are showing off. If the reader is shocked, it is due to his own ignorance of Asian-America. We're not new here. Aiiieeeee!!

[Selected from Frank Chin. *The Big AIIIEEEEE! : An Anthology of Chinese American and Japanese American Literature*. New York: Meridian, 1991.]

5. Saul Bellow

5.1 Presentation Topics

(1) Saul Bellow as a Jewish novelist in America.

(2) Artistic features of his works.

(3) Humanism in Bellow's works.

5.2 Selected Reading

Ⅰ. Central issue of concern

The search for meaning, the notion of an existence rendered absurd (in the philosophical as well as the more general sense) by the omnipresence of mortality, the relation of esoteric philosophy with practical action, and the need for transcendence.

Ⅱ. Text

Henderson the Rain King

(1)

What made me take this trip to Africa? There is no quick explanation. Things got worse and worse and worse and pretty soon they were too complicated.

When I think of my condition at the age of fifty-five when I bought the ticket, all is grief. The facts begin to crowd me and soon I get a pressure in the chest. A disorderly rush begins—my parents, my wives, my girls, my children, my farm, my animals, my habits, my money, my music lessons, my drunkenness, my prejudices, my brutality, my teeth, my face, my soul! I have to cry, "No, no, get back, curse you, let me alone!"But how can they let me alone? They belong to me. They are mine. And they pile into me from all sides. It turns into chaos.

However, the world which I thought so mighty an oppressor has removed its wrath from me. But if I am to make sense to you people and explain why I went to Africa I must face up to the facts. I might as well start with the money. I am rich. From my old man I inherited three million dollars after taxes, but I thought myself a bum and had my reasons, the main reason being that I behaved like a bum. But privately when things got very bad I often looked into books to see whether I could find some helpful words, and one day I read, "The forgiveness of sins is perpetual and righteousness first is not required," This impressed me so deeply that I went around saying it to myself. But then I forgot which book it was. It was one of thousands left by my father, who had also written a number of them. And I searched through dozens of volumes but all that turned up was money, for my father had used currency for bookmarks—whatever he happened to have in his pockets—fives, tens, or twenties. Some of the discontinued bills of thirty years ago turned up, the big yellowbacks. For old times' sake I was glad to see them and locking the library door to keep out the children. I spent the afternoon on a ladder shaking out books and the money spun to the floor. But I never found that statement about forgiveness.

Next order of business: I am a graduate of an Ivy League university—I see no reason to embarrass my alma mater by naming her. If I hadn't been a Henderson and my father's son, they would have thrown me out. At birth I weighed fourteen pounds, and it was a tough delivery. Then I grew up. Six feet four inches tall. Two hundred and thirty pounds. An enormous head, rugged, with hair like Persian lambs' fur. Suspicious eyes, usually narrowed. Blustering ways. A great nose, I was one of three children and the only survivor. It took all my father's charity to forgive me and I don't think he ever made it altogether. When it came time to marry I tried to please him and chose a girl of our own social class. A remarkable person, handsome, tall, elegant, sinewy, with long arms and golden hair, private, fertile, and quiet. None of her family can quarrel with me if I add that she is a schizophrenic, for she certainly is that. I, too, am considered crazy, and with good reason—moody, rough, tyrannical, and probably mad. To go by the ages of the kids, we were married for about twenty years. There are Edward, Ricey, Alice, and two more—Christ, I've got plenty of children. God bless the whole bunch of them.

In my own way I worked very hard. Violent suffering is labor, and often I was drunk before lunch. Soon after I came back from the war (I was too old for combat duty but nothing could keep me from it; I went down to Washington and pressured people until I was allowed to join the fight), Frances and I were divorced. This happened after V-E Day. Or was it so soon? No, it must have been in 1948. Anyway, she's now in Switzerland and has one of our kids with her. What she wants with a child I can't tell you, but she has one, and that's all right. I wish her well.

I was delighted with the divorce. It offered me a new start in life. I had a new wife already picked out and we were soon married. My second wife is called Lily (maiden name, Simmons). We have twin boys,

Now I feel the disorderly rush—I gave Lily a terrible time, worse than Frances. Frances was withdrawn, which protected her, but Lily caught it. Maybe a change for the better threw me; I was adjusted to a bad life. Whenever Frances didn't like what I was doing, and that was often, she turned away from me. She was Like Shelley's moon, wandering companionless. Not so Lily; and I raved at her in public and swore at her in private. I got into brawls in the country saloons near my farm and the troopers locked me up, I offered to take them all on, and they would have worked me over if I hadn't been so prominent in the county. Lily came and bailed me out. Then I had a fight with the vet over one of my pigs, and another with the driver of a snowplow on U. S. 7 when he tried to force me off the road. Then about two years ago I fell off a tractor while drunk and ran myself over and broke my leg. For months I was on crutches, hitting everyone who crossed my path, man or beast, and giving Lily hell. With the bulk of a football player and the color of a gipsy, swearing and crying out and showing my teeth and shaking my head—no wonder people got out of my way. But this wasn't all.

Lily is, for instance, entertaining ladies and I come in with my filthy plaster cast, in sweat socks; I am wearing a red velvet dressing gown which I bought at Sulka's in Paris in a mood of celebration when Frances said she wanted a divorce. In addition I have on a red wool hunting cap. And I wipe my nose and mustache on my fingers and then shake hands with the guests, saying, "I'm Mr. Henderson, how do you do?" And I go to Lily and shake her hand, too, as if she were merely another lady guest, a stranger like the rest. And I say, "How do you do?" I imagine the ladies are telling themselves, "He doesn't know her. In his mind he's still married to the first. Isn't that awful?" This imaginary fidelity thrills them.

But they are all wrong. As Lily knows, it was done on purpose, when we're alone she cries out to me, "Gene, what's the big idea? What are you trying to do?"

All belted up with the red braid curd, I stand up to her in my velvet bathrobe, sticking out behind, and the foot-shaped cast scraping hard on the floor, and I wag my head and say, "Tchu-tchu-tchu!"

Because when I was brought home from the hospital in this same bloody heavy cast, I heard her saying on the telephone, "It was just another one of his accidents. He has them all the time but oh, he's so strong. He's unkillable." Unkillable! How do you like that! It made me very bitter.

Now maybe Lily said this jokingly. She loves to joke on the telephone. She is a large, lively woman. Her face is sweet, and her character mostly is consistent with it. We've had some pretty good times, too. And, come to think of it, some of the very best occurred during her pregnancy, when it was far advanced. Before we went to sleep, I would rub her belly with baby oil to counteract the stretch marks. Her nipples had turned from pink to glowing brown, and the children moved inside her belly and changed the round shape.

I rubbed lightly and with greatest care lest my big thick fingers do the slightest harm. And then before I put out the light I wiped my fingers on my hair and Lily and I kissed good night, and in the scent of the baby oil we went to sleep.

But later we were at wax again, and when I heard her say I was unkillable I put an antagonistic interpretation on it, even though I knew better. No, I treated her like a stranger before the guests because I didn't like to see her behave and carry on like the lady of the house; because I, the sole heir of this famous name and estate, am a bum, and she is not a lady but merely my wife—merely my wife.

As the winters seemed to make me worse, she decided that we should go to a resort hotel on the Gulf, where I could do some fishing. A thoughtful friend had given each of the little twins a slingshot made of plywood, and one of these slingshots I found in my suitcase as I was unpacking, and I took to shooting with it. I gave up fishing and sat on the beach shooting stones at bottles. So that people might say, "Do you see that great big fellow with the enormous nose, and the mustache? Well, his great-grandfather was Secretary of State, his great-uncles were ambassadors to England and France, and his father was the famous scholar Willard Henderson who wrote that book on the Albigensians①, a friend of William James② and Henry Adams③." Didn't they say this? You bet they did. There I was at that resort with my sweet-faced anxious second wife who was only a little under six feet herself, and our twin boys. In the dining room I was putting bourbon④ in my morning coffee from a big flask and on the beach I was smashing bottles. The guests complained to the manager about the broken glass and the manager took it up with Lily; me they weren't willing to confront. An elegant establishment, they accept no Jews, and then they get me, E. H. Henderson, The other kids stopped playing with our twins, while the wives avoided Lily.

Lily tried to reason with me. We were in our suite, and I was in swimming trunks, and she opened the discussion on the slingshot and the broken glass and my attitude toward the other guests. Now Lily is a very intelligent woman. She doesn't

---

① The members of a Catharist religious sect of southern France in the 12th and 13th centuries, exterminated for heresy during the Inquisition.

② William James (1842—1910), a pioneering American psychologist and philosopher trained as a medical doctor. He was the brother of novelist Henry James.

③ Hanry Adams(1838—1918), American novelist, journalist, and historian.

④ A strong whiskey, made primarily from corn and named for Bourbon County, Kentucky.

scold, but she does moralize; she is very much given to this, and when it happens she turns white and starts to speak under her breath. The reason is not that she is afraid of me, but that it starts some crisis in her own mind.

But as it got her nowhere to discuss it with me she started to cry, and when I saw tears I lost my head and yelled, "I'm going to blow my brains out! I'm shooting myself. I didn't forget to pack the pistol. I've got it on me now."

"Oh, Gene!" she cried, and covered up her face and run away.

I'll tell you why.

(2)

Because her father had committed suicide in that same way, with a pistol.

One of the bonds between Lily and me is that we both suffer with our teeth. She is twenty years my junior but we wear bridges, each of us. Mine are at the sides, hers are in front. She has lost the four upper indoors. It happened while she was still in high school, out playing golf with her father, whom she adored. The poor old guy was a lush, and far too drunk to be out on a golf course that day. Without looking or giving warning, he drove from the first tee and on the backswing struck his daughter. It always kills me to think of that cursed hot July golf course, and this drunk from the plumbing supply business, and the girl of fifteen bleeding. Damn these weak drunks! Damn these unsteady men! I can't stand these clowns who go out in public as soon as they get swacked to show how broken-hearted they are. But Lily would never hear a single word against him and wept for him sooner than for herself. She carries his photo in her wallet.

Personally I never knew the old guy. When we met he had already been dead for ten or twelve years. Soon after he died she married a man from Baltimore, of pretty good standing, I have been told—though come to think of it it was Lily herself who told me. However, they could not become adjusted and during the war she got her divorce (I was then fighting in Italy). Anyway, when we met she was at home again, living with her mother. The family is from Danbury, the hatters' capital. It happened that Frances and I went to a party in Danbury one winter night, and Frances was only half willing because she was in correspondence with some intellectual or other over in Europe. Frances is a very deep reader and an intense letter-writer and a heavy smoker, and when she got on one of her kicks of philosophy or something I would see very little of her. I'd know she was up in her room smoking Sobranie cigarettes and coughing and making notes, working things out. Well, she was in one of these mental crises when we went to that party, and in the middle of it she recalled something she had to do at once and so she took the car and left, forgetting all about me. That night I had gotten mixed up too, and was the only man there in black tie. Midnight blue. I must have been the first fellow in that part of the state with a blue tuxedo. It felt as though I were wearing a whole acre of this blue cloth, while Lily, to whom I had been introduced about ten minutes before, had on a red and green Christmas-striped dress and we were talking.

When she saw what had happened, Lily offered me a ride, and I said, "Okay." We trod the snow out to her car.

It was a sparkling night and the snow was ringing. She was parked on a hill about three hundred yards long and smooth as iron. As soon as she drove away from the curb the car went into a skid and she lost her head and screamed, "Eugene!" She threw her arms about me. There was no other soul on that hill or on the shoveled walks, nor, so far as I could see, in the entire neighborhood. The car turned completely around. Her bare arms came out of the short fur sleeves and held my head while her large eyes watched through the windshield and the car went over the ice and hoarfrost. It was not even in gear and I reached the key and switched off the ignition. We slid into a snowdrift, but not far, and I took the wheel from her. The moonlight was very keen.

"How did you know my name?" I said, and she said, "Why, everybody knows you are Eugene Henderson."

After we had spoken some more she said to me, "You ought to divorce your wife."

I said to her, "What are you talking about? Is that a thing to say? Besides, I'm old enough to be your father."

We didn't meet again until the summer. This time she was shopping and was wearing a hat and a white piqué dress, with white shoes. It looked like rain and she didn't want to be caught in those clothes (which I noticed were soiled already) and she asked me for a lift. I had been in Danbury buying some lumber for the barn and the station wagon was loaded with it. Lily started to direct me to her house and lost the way in her nervousness; she was very beautiful, but wildly nervous. It was sultry and then it began to rain. She told me to take a right turn and that brought us to a gray cyclone fence around the quarry filled with water—a dead-end street. The air had grown so dark that the mesh of the fence looked white. Lily began to cry out, "Oh, turn around, please! Oh, quick, turn around! I can't remember the streets and I have to go home."

Finally we got there, a small house filled with the odor of closed rooms in hot weather, just as the storm was beginning,

"My mother is playing bridge," said Lily. "I have to phone her and tell her not to come home. There is a phone in my bedroom." So we went up. There was nothing loose or promiscuous about Lily, I assure you. When she took off her clothes she started to speak out in a trembling voice, "I love you! I love you!" And I said to myself as we embraced, "Oh, how can she love you—you—you!" There was a huge knot of thunder, and then a burst of rain on the streets, trees, roofs, screens, and lightning as well. Everything got filled and blinded. But a warm odor like fresh baking arose from her as we lay in her sheets which were darkened by the warm darkness of the storm. From start to finish she had not stopped saying "I love you!" Thus we lay quietly, and the early hours of the evening began without the sun's returning.

Her mother was waiting in the living room. I didn't care too much for that. Lily had phoned her and said, "Don't come home for a while," and therefore her mother bad immediately left the bridge party through one of the worst summer storms in many years. No, I didn't like it. Not that the old lady scared me, but I read the signs. Lily had made sure she would be found out. I was the first down the stairs and saw a light beside the chesterfield. And when I got to the foot of the stairs, face to face with her, I said, "Henderson's the name." Her mother was a stout pretty woman, made up for the bridge party in a china-doll face. She wore a hat, and had a patent-leather pocketbook on her stout knees when she sat down. I realized that she was mentally listing accounts against Lily. "In my own house. With a married man." And so on. Indifferent, I sat in the living room, unshaved, my lumber in the station wagon outside. Lily's odor, that baking odor, must have been noticeable about me. And Lily, extremely beautiful, came down the stairs to show her mama what she had accomplished. Acting oblivious, I kept my big boots apart on the carpet and frisked my mustache once in a while. Between them I sensed the important presence of Simmons, Lily's papa, the plumbing supply wholesaler who had committed suicide. In fact he had killed himself in the bedroom adjoining Lily's, the master bedroom. Lily blamed her mother for her father's death. And what was I, the instrument of her anger? "Oh no, pal," I said to myself, "this is not for you. Be no party to this."

I looked as though the mother had decided to behave well. She was going to be big about it and beat Lily at this game. Perhaps it was natural. Anyway, she was highly ladylike to me, but there came a moment when she couldn't check herself, and she said, "I have met your son."

"Oh yes, a slender fellow? Edward? He drives a red MG. You see him around Danbury sometimes."

Presently I left, saying to Lily, "You're a fine-looking big girl, but you oughtn't to have done that to your mother."

The stout old lady was sitting there on the sofa with her hands clasped and her eyes making a continuous line under her brows from tears or vexation.

"Good-by, Eugene," said Lily.

"So long, Miss Simmons," I said.

We didn't part friends exactly.

Nevertheless we soon met again, but in New York City, for Lily had separated from her mother, quitted Danbury, and bad a cold-water flat on Hudson Street where the drunks hid from the weather on the staircase. I came, a great weight, a huge shadow on those stairs, with my face full of country color and booze, and yellow pigskin gloves on my hands, and a ceaseless voice in my heart that said, *I want, I want, / want, oh, I want—yes, go on*, I said to myself, *Strike, strike, strike, strike*! And I kept going on the staircase in my thick padded coat, in pigskin gloves and pigskin shoes, a pigskin wallet in my pocket, seething with lust and seething with trouble, and realizing how my gaze glittered up to the top banister where Lily had opened the door and was waiting. Her face was round, white, and full, her eyes clear and narrowed.

"Hell! How can you live in this stinking joint? It stinks here," I said. The building had hall toilets; the chain pulls had turned green and there were panes of plum-colored glass in the doors.

She was a friend of the slum people, the old and the mothers in particular. She said she understood why they had television sets though on relief, and she let them keep their milk and butter in her refrigerator and filled out their social-security forms for them. I think she felt she did them good and showed these immigrants and Italians how nice an American could be. However, she genuinely tried to help them and ran around with her impulsive looks and said a lot of disconnected things.

The odors of this building clutched at your face, and I was coming up the stairs and said, "Whew, I am out of condition!"

We went into her apartment on the lop floor. It was dirty, too, but there was light in it at least. We sat down to talk and Lily said to me, "Are you going lo waste the rest of your life?"

With Frances the case was hopeless. Only once after I came back from the Army did anything of a personal nature take place between us, and after that it was no soap, so I let her be, more or less. Except that one morning in the kitchen we had a conversation that set us apart for good and all. Just a few words. They went like this:

"And what would you like to do now?"

(I was then losing interest in the farm.)

"I wonder," I said, "if it's too late for me to become a doctor—if I could enter medical school."

Frances opened her mouth, usually so sober, not to say dismal and straight, and laughed at me; and as she laughed I saw nothing but her dark open mouth, and not even teeth, which is certainly strange, for she has teeth, white ones. What had happened to them?

"Okay, okay, okay," I said.

Thus I realized that Lily was perfectly right about Frances. Nevertheless the rest did not follow.

"I need to have a child. I can't wait much longer," said Lily. "In a few years I'll be thirty."

"Am I responsible?" I said. "What's the matter with you?"

"You and I have got to be together," she said.

"Who says so?"

"We'll die if we're not," she said.

A year or so went by, and she failed to convince me. I didn't believe the thing could be so simple. So she suddenly married a man from New Jersey, a fellow named Hazard, a broker. Come to think of it she had spoken of him a few times, but I thought it was only more of her blackmail. Because she was a blackmailer. Anyway, she married him. This was her second marriage. Then I took Frances and the two girls and went to Europe, to France, for a year.

Several years of my boyhood were spent in the south of the country, near the town of Albi, where my old man was busy with his research. Fifty years ago I used to taunt a kid across the way, "François, oh Fronçois, ta soeur est constipée," My father was a big man, solid and clean. His long underwear was made of Irish linen and his hatboxes were lined with red velvet and he ordered his shoes from England and his gloves from Vitale Milano, Rome. He played pretty well on the violin. My mother used to write poems in the brick cathedral of Albi. She had a favorite story about a lady from Paris who was very affected. They met in a narrow doorway of the church and the lady said, "Voulez-vous queje passasse?" So my mother said, "Passassez, Madame." She told everyone this joke and for many years would sometimes laugh and say in a whisper, "Passassassez." Gone, those times. Closed, sealed, and gone.

But Frances and I did not go to Albi with the children. She was attending the Collège de France, where all the philosophers were. Apartments were hard to get but I rented a good one from a Russian prince. De Vogüé mentions his grandfather, who was minister under Nicolas I. He was a tall, gentle creature; his wife was Spanish and his Spanish mother-in-law, Señora Guirlandes, rode him continually. The guy was suffering from her. His wife and kids lived with the old woman while he moved into the maid's room in the attic. About three million bucks, I have. I suppose I might have done something to help him. But at this time my heart was consumed with the demand I have mentioned—*I want*, *I want!* Poor prince, upstairs! His children were sick, and he said to me that if his condition didn't improve he would throw himself out of the window.

I said, "Don't be nuts, Prince."

Guiltily, I lived in his apartment, slept in his bed, and bathed in his bath twice a day. Instead of helping, those two hot baths only aggravated my melancholy. After Frances laughed at my dream of a medical career I never discussed another thing with her. Around and around the city of Paris I walked every day; all the way to the Gobelin factories and the Père Lachaise Cemetery and St. Cloud I went on foot. The only person who considered what my life was like was Lily, now Lily Hazard. At the American Express I received a note from her written on one of the wedding announcements long after the date of the marriage. I was bursting with trouble, and as there are a lot of whores who cruise that neighborhood near the Madeleine, I looked some of them over, but this terrible repetition within—*I want, I want!* —was not stopped by any face I saw. I saw quite some faces.

"Lily may arrive," I thought. And she did. She cruised the city in a taxi looking for me and caught up with me near the Metro Vavin. Big and shining, she cried out to me from the cab. She opened the antique door and tried lo stand on the runningboard. Yes, she was beautiful—a good face, a clear, pure face, hot and white. Her neck as she stretched forward from the door of the cab was big and shapely. Her upper lip was trembling with joy. But, stirred as she was, she remembered those front teeth and kept them covered. What did I care then about new porcelain teeth! Blessed be God for the mercies. He continually sends me!

"Lily! How are you, kid? Where did you come from?"

I was terribly pleased. She thought I was a big slob but of substantial value just the same, and that I should live and not die (one more year like this one in Paris and something in me would have rusted forever), and that something good might even come of me. She loved me.

"What have you done with your husband?" I said.

On the way back to her hotel, down Boulevard Raspail, she told me, "I thought I should have children. I was getting old. (Lily was then twenty-seven.) But on the way to the wedding I saw it was a mistake. I tried to get out of the car at a stoplight in my wedding dress, but he caught me and pulled me back. He punched me in the eye," she said, "and it was a good thing I had a veil because the eye turned black, and I cried all the way through the ceremony. Also, my mother is dead."

"What! He gave you a shiner?" I said, furious. "If I ever come across him again I will break him in pieces. Say, I'm sorry about your mother."

I kissed her on the eyes, and then we arrived at her hotel on the Quai Voltaire and were on top of the world, in each other's arms. A happy week followed; we went everywhere, and Hazard's private detective followed us. Therefore I rented a car and we began a tour of the cathedral towns. And Lily in her marvelous way—always marvelously—began to make me suffer. "You think you can live without me but you can't," she said, "any more than I can live without you. The sadness just drowns me. Why do you think I left Hazard? Because of the sadness. When he kissed me I felt saddest of all. I felt all alone. And when he—"

"That's enough. Don't tell me," I said.

"It was better when he punched me in the eye. There was some truth in that. Then I didn't feel like drowning."

And I began to drink, harder than ever, and was drunk in every one of the great cathedrals—Amiens, Chartres, Vézelay, and so on. She often had to do the driving. The car was a little one (a Deux Cent Deux décapotable or convertible) and the two of us, of grand size, towered out of the seats, fair and dark, beautiful and drunk. Because of me she had come all the way from America, and I wouldn't let her accomplish her mission. Thus we traveled all the way up to Belgium and back again to the Massif, and if you loved France that would have been fine, but I didn't love it. From start to finish Lily had just this one topic, moralizing: one can't live for this but has to live for that; not evil but good; not death but life; not illusion but reality. Lily does not speak clearly; I guess she was taught is boarding school that a lady speaks softly, and consequently she mumbles, and I am hard of bearing on the right side, and the wind and the tires and the little engine also joined their noise. All the same, from the joyous excitement of her great pure white face I knew she was still at it. With lighted face and joyous eyes she persecuted me. I learned she had many negligent and even dirty habits. She forgot to wash her underthings until, drunk as I was, I ordered her to. This may have been because she was such a moralist and thinker, for when I said, "Wash out your things," she began to argue with me. "The pigs on my farm are cleaner than you are," I told her; and this led to a debate. The earth itself is like that, corrupt. Yes, but it transforms itself. "A single individual can't do the nitrogen cycle all by herself," I said to her; and she said, "Yes, but did I know what love could do?" I yelled at her, "Shut up." It didn't make her angry. She was sorry for me.

The tour continued and I was a double captive—one, of the religion and beauty of the churches which I was not too drunk to see, and two, of Lily, and her glowing and mumbling and her embraces. She said a hundred times if she said it once, "Come back lo the States with me. I've come to take you back."

"No," I said finally. "If there was any heart in you at all you wouldn't torture me, Lily. Damn you, don't forget I'm a Purple Heart① veteran. I've served my country. I'm over fifty, and I've had my bellyful of trouble."

"All the more reason why you should do something now," she said.

Finally I told her at Chartres, "If you don't quit it I'm going to blow my brains out."

This was cruel of me, as I knew what her father had done. Drunk as I was. I could hardly bear the cruelty myself. The old man had shot himself after a family quarrel. He was a charming man, weak, heartbroken, affectionate, and sentimental. He came home full of whisky and would sing old-time songs for Lily and the cook; he told jokes and tap-danced and did corny vaudeville routines in the kitchen, joking with a catch in his throat—a dirty thing to do to your child. Lily told me all about it until her father became so actual to me that I loved and detested the old bastard myself. "Here, you old clog-dancer, you old heart-breaker, you pitiful joker—you cornball!" I said to his ghost. "What do you mean by doing this to your daughter and then leaving her on my hands?" And when I threatened suicide in Chartres cathedral, in the very face of this holy beauty, Lily caught her breath. The light in her face turned fine as pearl. She silently forgave me.

"It's all the same to me whether you forgive me or not," I told her.

We broke up at Vézelay. From the start our visit there was a strange one. The décapotable Deux Cent Deux had a flat when we came down in the morning. It being fine June weather, I had refused to put the car in a garage and in my opinion the management had let out the air. I accused the hotel and stood shouting until the office closed its iron shutter. I changed the tire quickly, using no jack but in my anger heaving up the little car and pushing a rock under the axle. After fighting with the hotel manager (both of us saying, "Pneu, pneu"), my mood was better, and we walked around the cathedral, bought a kilo of strawberries in a paper funnel, and went out on the ramparts to lie in the sun. Yellow dust was dropping

① A United States military decoration awarded in the name of the President to those who have been wounded or killed while serving on or after April 5, 1917 with the U.S. military.

from the lime tree, and wild roses grew on the trunks of the apple trees. Pale red, gorged red, fiery, aching, harsh as anger, sweet as drugs. Lily took off her blouse to get the sun on her shoulders. Presently she took off her slip, too, and after a time her brassiere, and she by in my lap. Annoyed, I said to her, "How do you know what I want?" And then more gently, because of the roses on all the tree trunks, piercing and twining and flaming, I said, "Can't you just enjoy this beautiful churchyard?"

"It isn't a churchyard, it's an orchard," she said.

I said, "Your period just began yesterday. So what are you after?"

She said I had never objected before, and that was true. "But I do object now," I said, and we began to quarrel and the quarrel got so fierce I told her she was going back to Paris alone on the next train.

She was silent. I had her, I thought. But no, it only seemed to prove how much I loved her. Her crazy face darkened with the intensity of love and joy.

"You'll never kill me, I'm too rugged!" I cried at her. And then I began to weep from all the unbearable complications in my heart, I cried and sobbed.

"Get in there, you mad bitch," I said, weeping. And I rolled back the roof of the décapotable. It has rods which come out, and then you reef back the canvas.

Under her breath, pale with terror but consumed also with her damned exalted glory, she mumbled as I was sobbing at the wheel about pride and strength and soul and love, and all of that.

I told her, "Curse you, you're nuts!"

"Without you, maybe it's true. Maybe I'm not all there and I don't understand," she said. "But when we're together, I know."

"Hell you know. How come I don't know anything! Stay the bell away from me. You tear me to pieces."

I dumped her foolish suitcase with the unwashed clothes in it on the platform. Still sobbing, I turned around in the station, which was twenty kilometers or so from Vézelay, and I headed for the south of France. I drove to a place on the Vermilion Coast called Banyules. They keep a marine station there, and I had a strange experience in the aquarium. It was twilight . I looked in at an octopus, and the creature seemed also to look at me and press its soft head to the glass, flat, the flesh becoming pale and granular—blanched, speckled. The eyes spoke to me coldly. But even more speaking, even more cold, was the soft head with its speckles, and the Brownian motion in those speckles, a cosmic coldness in which I felt I was dying. The tentacles throbbed and motioned through the glass, the bubbles sped upward, and I thought, "This is my last day. Death is giving me notice."

So much for my suicide threat to Lily.

(3)

And now a few words about my reasons for going to Africa.

When I came back from the war it was with the thought of becoming a pig farmer, which maybe illustrates what I thought of life in general.

Monte Cassino should never have been bombed; some blame it on the dumbness of the generals. But after that bloody murder, where so many Texans were wiped out, and my outfit also took a shellacking later, there were only Nicky Goldstein and myself left out of the original bunch, and this was odd because we were the two largest men in the outfit and offered the best targets. Later I was wounded too, by a land mine. But at that time, Goldstein and I were lying down under the olive trees—some of those gnarls open out like lace and let the light through—and I asked him what he aimed to do after the war. He said, "Why, me and my brother, if we live and be well, we're going to have a mink ranch in the Catskills①." So I said, or my demon said for me, "I'm going to start breeding pigs." And after these words were spoken I knew that if Goldstein had not been a Jew I might have said cattle and not pigs. So then it was too late to retract. So for all I know Goldstein and his brother have a mink business while I have-something else. I took all the handsome old farm buildings, the carriage house with paneled stalls-in the old days a rich man's horses were handled like opera singers-and the fine old barn with the belvedere above the hayloft, a beautiful piece of architecture, and I filled them up with pigs, a pig kingdom, with pig houses on the lawn and in the flower garden. The greenhouse, too—I let them root out the old bulbs. Statues from Florence and Salzburg were turned over. The place stank of swill and pigs and the mashes cooking, and dung. Furious, my neighbors got the health officer after

① A natural area in New York State northwest of New York City.

me. I dared him to take me to law. "Hendersons have been on this property over two hundred years," I said to this man, a certain Dr. Bullock.

By my then wife, Frances, no word was said except, "Please keep them off the driveway."

"You'd better not hurt any of them," I said to her, "Those animals have become a part of me." And I told this Dr. Bullock, "All those civilians and 4Fs have put you up to this. Those twerps. Don't they ever eat pork?"

Have you seen, coming from New Jersey to New York, the gabled pens and runways that look like model of German villages from the Black forest①? Have you smelled them (before the train enters the tunnel to go under the Hudson)? These are pigfattening stations. Lean and bony after their trip from Iowa and Nebraska, the swine are fed here. Anyway, I was a pig man. And as the prophet Daniel warned King Nebuchadnezzar, "They shall drive thee from among men, and thy dwelling shall be with the beasts of the field"②. Sows eat their young because they need the phosphorous. Goiter attacks them as it dose women. Oh, I made a considerable study of these clever doomed animals. For all pig breeders know how clever they are. The discovery that they were so intelligent gave me a kind of trauma. But if I had not lied to Frances and those animals had actually become a part of me, then it was curious that I lost interest in them.

But I see I haven't got any closer to giving my reasons for going to Africa, and I'd better begin somewhere else.

Shall I start with my father? He was a well-know man. He had a beard and played the violin, and he...

No, not that.

Well, then, here: My ancestors stole land from the Indians. They got more from the government and cheated other settlers too, so I became heir to a great estate.

No, that won't do either. What has that got to do with it?

Still, an explanation is necessary, for living proof of something of the highest

---

① A wooded mountain range in southwestern Germany.

② A ruler of Babylon in the Chaldean Dynasty, who reigned 605 BC—562 BC. According to the Bible, he conquered Judah and Jerusalem, and sent the Jews into exile. Once he had a dream. Daniel interpreted, the king would lose his sanity and live in the wild like an animal for seven years. It really came true finally.

importance has been presented to me so I am obliged to communicate it. And not the least of the difficulties is that it happened as in a dream.

Well, then, it must have been about eight years after the war ended. I was divorced from Frances and married to Lily, and I felt that something had to be done. I went to Africa with a friend of mine, Charlie Albert. He, too, is a millionaire.

I have always had a soldierly rather than a civilian temperament. When I was in the Army and caught the crabs, I went to get some powder. But when I reported what I had, four medics grabbed me, right at the crossroads, in the open they stripped me naked and they soaped and lathered me and shaved every hair from my body, back and front, armpits, pubic hair, mustache, eyebrows, and all. This was right near the waterfront at Salerno. Trucks filled with troops were passing, and fishermen and paisanos and kids and girls and women were looking on. The GIs were cheering and laughing and the paisanos laughed, the whole coast laughed, and even I was laughing as I tried to kill all four. They ran away and left me bald and shivering, ugly, naked, prickling between the legs and under the arms, raging, laughing, and swearing revenge. These are things a man never forgets and afterward truly values. That beautiful sky, and the mad itch and the razors; and the Mediterranean, which is the cradle of mankind; the towering softness of the air; the sinking softness of the water, where Ulysses① got lost, where he, too, was naked as the sirens sang.

In passing the crabs found refuge in a crevice; I had dealings afterward with these cunning animals.

The war meant much to me. I was wounded when I stepped on the land of mine and got the Purple Heart, and I was in the hospital in Naples quite a while. Believe me, I was grateful that my life was spared. The whole experience gave my heart a large and real emotion. Which I continually require.

Beside my cellar door last winter I was chopping wood for the fire—the tree surgeon had left some pine limbs for me—and a chunk of wood flew up from the block and hit me in the nose. Owing to the extreme cold I didn't realize what had happened until I saw the blood on my mackinaw. Lily cried out, "You broke your

---

① The hero in Roman Epic *The Odyssey*.

nose." No, it wasn't broken. I have a lot of protective flesh over it but I carried a bruise there for some time. However as I felt the blow my only thought was truth. Does truth come in blows? That's a military idea if there ever was one. I tried to say something about it to Lily; she, too, had felt the force of truth when her second husband, Hazard, punched her in the eye.

Well, I've always been like this, strong and healthy, rude and aggressive, and something of a bully in boyhood; at college I wore gold earrings to provoke fights, and while I got an M. A. to please my father I always behaved like an ignorant man and a bum. When engaged to France I went to Coney Island and had her name tattooed on my ribs in purple letters. Not that this cut any ice with her. Already forty-six or forty-seven when I got back from Europe after V-E Day (Thursday, May 8) I went in for pigs, and then I confided to France that I was drawn to medicine; and she laughed at me; she remembered how enthusiastic I had been at eighteen over Sir Wilfred Grenfell① and afterward over Albert Schweitzer②.

What do you do with yourself if you have a temperament like mine? A student of the mind once explained to me that if you inflict your anger on inanimate things, you not only spare the living, as a civilized man ought to do, but you get rid of the bad stuff in you. This seemed to make good sense, and I tried it out. I tried with all my heart, chopping wood, lifting, plowing, laying cement blocks, pouring concert, and cooking mask for the pigs. On my own place, stripped to the waist like a convict, I broke stones with a sledgehammer. It helped, but not enough. Rude begets rude, and blows, blows; at least in my case; it not only begot but it increased. Wrath increased with wrath. So what do you do with yourself? More than three million bucks. After taxes, after alimony and all expenses I still have one hundred and ten thousand dollars in income absolutely clear. What do I need it for, a soldierly character like me! Taxwise, even the pigs were profitable. I couldn't lose money, but they were killed and they were eaten. They made ham and gloves and gelatin and fertilizer. What did I make? Why, I made a sort of trophy, I suppose. A man like me may become something like a trophy. Washed, clean, and

---

① Sir Wilfred Grenfell(1865—1940), a medical missionary to Newfoundland and Labrador.

② Albert Schweitzer(1875—1965), an Alsatian German-French theologian, musician, philosopher, and physician, who won the Nobel Peace Prize in 1952.

dressed in expensive garments. Under the roof is insulation: on the windows thermopane; on the floors carpeting; and on the carpets furniture, and on the furniture covers, and on the cloth covers plastic covers; and wallpaper and drapes! All is swept and garnished. And who is in the midst of this? Who is sitting there? Man! That's who it is, man!

But there comes a day, there always comes a day of tears and madness.

Now I have already mentioned that there was disturbance in my heart, a voice that spoke there and said, *I want, I want, I want!* It happened every afternoon, and when I tried to suppress it, it got even stronger. It only said one thing, *I want, I want!*

And I would ask, "What do you want?"

But this was all it would ever tell me. It never said a thing except *I want, I want, I want!*

At times I would treat it like an ailing child whom you offer rhymes or candy. I would walk it, I would trot it. I would sing to it or read to it. No use. I would change into overalls and go up on the ladder and spackle cracks in the ceiling; I would chop wood, go out and drive a tractor, work in the barn among the pigs. No, no! Though fights and drunkenness and labor it went right on, in the country, in the city. No purchase, no matter how expensive, would lessen it. Then I would say, "Come on, tell me. What is the complaint, is it Lily herself? Do you want some nasty whore? It has to be some lust? "But this was no better a guess than the others. The demand came louder, *I want, I want, I want, I want, I want!* And I would cry, begging at last, "Oh, tell me then. Tell me what you want!" And finally I would say, "Okay, then. One of these days, stupid. You wait!"

This was what made me behave as I did. By three o'clock I was in despair. Only toward sunset the voice would let up. And sometimes I thought maybe this was my occupation because it would knock off at five o'clock of itself. America is so big, and everybody is working, making, digging, bulldozing, trucking, loading, and so on, and I guess the sufferers suffer at the same rate. Everybody wanting to pull together. I tried every cure you can think of. Of course, in an age of madness, to expect to be untouched by madness is a form of madness. But the pursuit of sanity can be a form of madness, too.

Among other remedies I took up the violin. One day as I was poking around in a storeroom I found the dusty case and I opened it, and there lay the instrument my father used to play, inside that little sarcophagus, with its narrow scrolled neck and incurved waist and the hair of the bow undone and loose all around it. I tightened the bow screw and scrubbed on the strings. Harsh cries awoke. It was like a feeling creature that had been neglected too long. Then I began to recall my old man. Maybe he would deny it with anger, but we are much alike. He could not settle into a quiet life either. Sometimes he was very hard on Mama; once he made her lie prostrate in her nightgown at the door of his room for two weeks before he would forgive her some silly words, perhaps like Lily's on the telephone when she said I was unkillable.

He was a very strong man, too, but as he declined in strength, especially after the death of my brother Dick (which made me the heir), he shut himself away and fiddled more and more. So I began to recall his bent back and the flatness or lameness of his hips, and his beard like a protest that gushed from his very soul-washed white by the trembling weak blood of old age. Powerful once, his whiskers lost their curl and were pushed back on his collarbone by the instrument while he sighted with the left eye along the fingerboard and his big hollow elbow came and went, and the fiddle trembled and cried.

So right then I decided, "I'll try it too." I banged down the cover and shut the clasps and drove straight to New York to a repair shop on 57th Street to have the violin reconditioned. As soon as it was ready I started to take lessons from an old Hungarian fellow named Haponyi who lived near the Barbizon-Plaza.

At this time I was alone in the country, divorced. An old lady, Miss Lenox from across the way, came in and fixed my breakfast and this was my only need at the time. Frances had stayed behind in Europe. And so one day as I was rushing to my lesson on 57th Street with the case under my arm, I met Lily. "Well!" I said. I hadn't seen her in more than a year, not since I put her on that train for Paris, but we were immediately on the old terms of familiarity just as before. Her large, pure face was the same as ever. It would never be steady, but it was beautiful. Only she had dyed her hair. It was now orange, which was not necessary, and it was parted from the middle of her forehead like the two panels of a curtain. It's the curse of these big beauties sometimes that they are short on taste. Also she had done something with mascara to her eyes so that they were no longer of equal length.

What are you supposed to do if such a person is "the same as ever?" And what are you supposed to think when this tall woman, nearly six feet, in a kind of green plush suit like the stuff they used to have in Pullman cars and high heels, sways; sturdy as her legs are, great as her knees are, she sways; and in one look she throws away all the principles of behavior observed on 57th Street—as if throwing off the plush suit and hat and blouse and stocking and girdle to the winds and crying, "Gene! My life is misery without you"?

However, the first thing she actually said was, "I am engaged."

"What, again?" I said.

"Well, I could use your advice. We are friends. You are my friend, you know. I think we're each other's only friends in the world, after all. Are you studying music?"

"Well, if isn't music then I'm in a game war," I said. "Because this case holds either a fiddle or a tommy gun." I guess I must have felt embarrassed. Then she began to tell me about the new fiancé, mumbling. "Don't talk like that," I said. "What's the matter with you? Blow your nose. Why do you give me this Ivy League jive? This soft-spoken stuff? It's just done to take advantage of common people and make them bend over so as to hear you. You know I'm a little deaf," I said. "Raise your voice. Don't be such a snob. So tell me, did your fiancé go to Choate or St. Paul's? Your last husband went to President Roosevelt's prep school—whatchumajigger."

Lily now spoke more clearly and said, "My mother is dead."

"Dead?" I said. "Hey, that's terrible. But wait just one minute, didn't you tell me in France that she was dead?"

"Yes," she said.

"Then when did she die?"

"Just two months ago. It wasn't true then."

"Then why did you say it? That's a hell of a way. You can't do that. Are you playing chicken-funeral with your own mother? You were trying to con me."

"Oh, that was very bad of me, Gene. I didn't mean any harm. But this time it is true." And I saw the warm shadows of tears in her eyes. "She is gone now. I had to hire a plane to scatter her ashes over Lake George as she wanted."

"Did you? God, I'm sorry about it." I said.

"I fought her too much," said Lily. "Like that time I brought you home. But she was a fighter, and I am one, too. You were right about my fiancé. He did go to Groton."

"Ha, ha, I hit it, didn't I?"

"He's a nice man. He's not what you think. He's very decent and he supports his parents. But when I ask myself whether I could live without him, I guess the answer is yes. But I am learning to get along alone. There's always the universe. A woman doesn't have to marry, and there are perfectly good reasons why people should be lonely."

You know, compassion is useless, too, sometimes I feel. It just lasts long enough to get you in dutch. My heart ached for Lily, and then she tried to con me.

"All right, kid, what are you going to do now?"

"I sold the house in Danbury. I'm living in an apartment. But there was one thing I wanted you to have, and I sent it to you."

"I don't want anything."

"It's a rug," she said. "Hasn't it come yet?"

"Hell, what do I want with your Christly rug! Was it from your room?"

"NO."

"You are a liar. It's the rug from your bedroom."

She denied it, and when it arrived at the farm I accepted it from the delivery man; I felt I should. It was creepy-looking and faded, a Baghdad mustard color, the threads surrendering to time and springs of blue all over it. It was so ugly I had to laugh. This crummy rug! It ticked me. So I put it on the fool of my violin studio, which was down in the basement. I had poured the concrete there myself but not thick enough, for the damp comes through. Anyway, I thought this rug might improve the acoustics.

All right, then, I'd come in to the city for my lesson with that fat Hungarian Haponyi, and I'd see Lily too. We courted for about eighteen months, and then we got married, and then the children were born. As for the violin, I was no Heifetz① but I keep at it. Presently the daily voice, *I want*, *I want*, arose again. Family life with Lily was not all that might have been predicted by an optimist; but I'm sure

① Heifetz(1901—1987), a violin virtuoso born in Lithuania.

that she got more than she had bargained for, too. One of first decisions she made after looking over the whole place as lady of the house was to get her portrait painted and hung with the rest of the family. This portrait business was very important to her and it went on until about six months before I took off for Africa.

So let's look at a typical morning of my married life with Lily. Not inside the house but outside, for inside it is filthy. Let's say it's one of those velvety days of early autumn when the sun is shining on the pines and the air has a spice of cold and stings your lungs with pleasure. I see a large pine tree on my property, and in the green darkness underneath, which somehow the pigs never got into, red tuberous begonias grow, and a broken stone inscription put in by my mother says, "Goe happy rose ...." That's all it says. There must be more fragments beneath the needles. The sun is like a great roller and flattens the grass. Beneath this grass the earth may be filled with carcasses, yet that detracts nothing from a day like this, for they have become humus and the grass is thriving. When the air moves the brilliant flowers move too in the dark green beneath the trees. They brush against my open spirit because I am in the midst of this in the red velvet dressing grown from the Rue de Rivoli bought on the day that Frances spoke the word divorce. I am there and am looking for trouble. The crimson begonias, and the dark green and the radiant green and the spice that pierces and the sweet gold and the dead transformed, the brushing of the flowers on my undersurface are just misery to me. They make me crazy with misery. To somebody these things may have been given, but that somebody is not me in the red velvet robe. So what am I doing here?

Then Lily comes up with the two kids, our twins, twenty-six months old, tender, in their short pants and neat green jerseys, the dark hair brushed down on their foreheads. And here come Lily with that pure face of hers going to sit for the portrait. And I am standing on one foot in the red velvet robe, heavy, wearing dirty farm boots, those Wellingtons which I favor when at home because they are so easy to put on and take off.

She starts to get into the station wagon and I say, "Use the convertible. I am going to Danbury later to look for some stuff, and I need this." My face is black and angry. My gums are aching. The joint is in disorder, but she is going and the kids will be playing indoors at the studio while she sits for the portrait. So she puts them in the back seat of the convertible and drives away.

Then I go down to the basement studio and take the fiddle and start warming up on my Sevcik① exercises. Ottokar Sevcik invented a technique for the quick and accurate change of position on the violin. The student learns by dragging or sliding his fingers along the strings from first position to third and from third to fifth and from fifth to second, on and on, until the ear and fingers are trained and find the notes with precision. You don't even start with scales, but with phrases, and go up and down the strings, crawling. It is frightful: but Haponyi says it is the only way, this fat Hungarian. He knows about fifty words of English, the main one being "dear." He says, "Dear, take de bow like dis vun, not like dis vun, so. Und so, so, so. Not to kill vid de bow. Make nice. Do not stick. Yo, yo, yo. Seretlek! Nice."

And after all, I am a commando, you know. And with these hands I've pushed around the pigs; I've thrown down boars and pinned them and gelded them. So now these same fingers are courting the music of the violin and gripping its neck and toiling up and down on the Sevcik. The noise is like smashing egg crates. Nevertheless, I thought, if I discipline myself eventually the voice of angels may come out. But anyway I didn't hope to perfect myself as an article. My main purpose was to reach my father by playing on his violin.

Down in the basement of the house, I worked very hard as I do at everything. I had felt I was pursuing my father's spirit, whispering, "Oh, Father, Pa. Do you recognize the sounds? This is me, Gene, on your violin, trying to reach you." For it so happens that I have never been able to convince myself the dead are utterly dead. I admire rational people and envy their clear heads, but what's the use of kidding? I played in the basement to my father and my mother, and when I learned a few pieces I would whisper, "Ma, this is 'Humoresque' for you." Or, "Pa, listen—'Meditation' from *Thais*." I played with dedication, with feeling, with longing, love-played to the point of emotional collapse. Also down there in my studio I sang as I played, "Rispondi! Anima bella." (Mozart) "He was despised and rejected, a man of sorrows and acquainted with grief." (Handel) Clutching the peck of the little instrument as if there were strangulation in my heart, I got cramps in my neck and shoulders.

① Sevcik(1852—1934), a Czech violinist.

Over the years I had fixed up the little basement for myself, paneled it with chestnut and put in a dehumidifier. There I keep my little safe and my files and war souvenirs; and there also I have a pistol range. Under foot was now Lily's rug. At her insistence I had got rid of most of the pigs. But she herself was not very cleanly, and for one reason or another we couldn't get anyone from the neighborhood to do the cleaning. Yes, she swept up once in a while, but toward the door and not out of it, so there were mounds of dust in the doorway. Then she went to sit for her portrait, running away from the house altogether while I was playing Sevcik and pieces of opera and oratorio, keeping time with the voice within.
[Selected from Saul Bellow. *Henderson the Rain King*. New York: Penguin Books, 1986.]

Ⅲ. Questions for discussion

(1) What does Henderson look like? What is his family background?

(2) Is he satisfied with the life he lives? Is it peaceful or chaotic?

(3) What does his married life show?

(4) What do you think of the inner voice "*I want*, *I want*, *I want*, *I want*, *I want*"?

(5) What is the structure of the story? Is it narrated in accordance with the plot?

(6) What is the tone of the story? Can you cite some examples to illustrate it?

(7) What narrative techniques are used to enhance the theme?

5.3 Assigned Reading

The Fifties Novels: *The Adventures of Augie March*, *Seize the Day* and *Henderson the Rain King*

Malcolm Bradbury

The comment applies well to *Henderson the Rain King*, a book that steps out of the social and historical world and at the same time evokes many the romance of the past (it has appropriately been compared with Melville's *Moby-Dick*), where Ishmael likewise leaves the dull, land-based life of debasement and irritability to begin his quest into nature; and with Mark twain's *A Connecticut Yankee at King Arthur's Court* (1889), where that romantic quest soon turns toward destruction.

Henderson the Rain King likewise leaves realism behind in order to guest for "reality"—Henderson describes himself as a man who, learning that T. S. Eliot's nightingale tells us that humankind cannot stand very much reality, asks how much unreality it can stand ("I fired that question right back of the nightingale. So what if reality may be terrible? It is better than what we have got.") The difference between classic American romance and Henderson's quest is that his is certainly comic and to a considerable degree parodic, and so needs reading very differently.

Bellow's achievement in the book is that, without ponderousness or over-assertion, he can provide the elaborate constituents of a modern journey into spirit, nature and culture, and so create a texture of contemporary mythography; at the same time he can ironize such a romantic and self-vaunting enterprise. Henderson is thus conceived-by Bellow and by himself, as first-person narrator-in the grand manner. He suffers none of the outward victimzations of Bellow's earlier heroes, being his first non-Jewish central figure, a millionaire of Anglo-Saxon Protestant stock who is recipient to a large heritage of wealth, historical responsibility and social service, a massive access to the history of American and western culture. His utterance is a vaunt, and extravagance is the functional state of his being. He has an excess of body, with a height of 6 ft 4 ins, a weight of 230 lbs; his face is, as he says, like Grand Central Station, or an unfinished church; he has "the bulk of a football player and the colour of a gypsy"; he clothes himself in the clothes of farce. His inward life matches; he is, he says, to suffering what Gary is to smoke. He is a man of excess over-stated in nature:

> The sun is like a great roller and flattens the grass. Beneath this grass the earth may be filled with carcasses, yet that distracts nothing from a day like this, for they have become human and the grass is thriving. When the air moves the brilliant flowers move too in the dark green beneath the trees. They burst against my open spirit because I am in the midst of this in the red violet dressing gown from the Rue de Rivoli bought on the day when Frances spoke the word divorce. I am there and am looking for trouble.

Disconcertingly positioned in relation to others, to society, objects and the natural world, rough, violent, physical, powerful, disoriented and soul-searching, Henderson is a metaphysical comedian, a supernatural bumbler with aspirations for his soul, a psycho-braggart speaking the great romantic vaunt of the Self.

So his wealth and scale, his violence and his frantic and grandiose marrying, loving and soul-searching, his heavy hand holding the delicate violin he wishes to play, all translate into a discourse that moves freely from vernacular confession to biblical incantation, and is the most marvellous quality of the book. His soul as readily to hand as his clothes, Henderson's language becomes a remarkable device for mediating an action that is equally extravagant and giving it intellectual and mythic possibilities and pretensions. His character is deliberately intended to call forth an analogous world of absurdity in experience: as he says, "a damned fool going out into the world is bound and fated to encounter damned fool phenomena." And so, in Africa, he does, for Bellow invents a continent bereft of its more familiar contents and replaced by two contrasting states of history, culture, and psychic relation to nature, and these likewise function both mythically and comically.

Henderson is indeed, as Bellow once said, "an absurd seeker after high qualities"; his adventures both evoke basic myths or archetypes and present themselves as the stuff of eclectic anthropological and cosmic farce. Like all first-person narrators, Henderson is hard to measure, and the book has been very various read. But Henderson's egocentric story of spiritual hunger, his endless *I want*, *I want*, his drive to burst his spirit's sleep, is clearly a central part of Bellow's own mythic world. It is a world that starts in society, departs it, and returns to it; where *Henderson the Rain King* most differs from the other novels is in the scale granted to the hero and the degree to which the novel is created as an outward map of his inward psychic terrain.

Above all Henderson is a comic imperial hero appropriate to his time, that of the Eisenhower regnum, the season of material superpowerdom. He recognizes that it is the destiny of his generation of Americans to get out into the world to try to find life's wisdoms, and this means a step from his present material condition, which is that of a trophy:

> A man like me may become something like a trophy. Washed, clean, and dressed in expensive garments. Under the roof is insulation; on the windows thermopane; on the floors carpeting; and on the carpets furniture, and on the furniture covers, and on the cloth covers plastic covers; and wallpaper and drapes! All is swept and garnished. And who is in the midst of this? Who is sitting there? Man! That's who it is, man!

He belongs to a world stuffed to excess with materials and goods, but feels detached from his antecedents and culture, heir to a meaningless inheritance, "a displaced person," "Nobody truly occupies a station in life any more," he reflects. "There are mostly people who feel they occupy the place that belongs to another by rights."

Society is again a lunatic contemporary prison, a place of chaotic rush and inhuman madness, creating a dislocated or debased image of the self: so, as an act of deliberate cultural sacrilege, he farms pigs, making great profits while feeling powerful but dissipating power, moving toward entropy. Like previous Bellow heroes, if on characteristically larger scale, he finds that social existence generates depression and rage. His marriage is a disaster, and whenever he goes among people there is, he says, "the devil to pay." He accepts that he lives in an age of madness, and that "to expect to be untouched by madness is a form of madness." But the pursuit of sanity can be a form of madness, too. And it is his rage that brings about his break with society; losing his temper with his family one morning at breakfast, he rages so loudly that it frightens and kills the old lady who comes in to cook his meals. He reads this as the final lesson in his debasement, evidence of the way he disturbs and is disturbed by the surrounding environment, is unfit to live among men. So, threatened too with pointless death, he leaves a note on the corpse (do not disturb), and sets out, a men who has ruined "the original piece of goods issued to me and was travelling to find a remedy," from the social to the pre-social world.

The Africa he travels to is of course classic mythic ground for the western mind; his journey calls up the history of safari, exploration and buried treasure; Livingstone, Hemingway, Tarzan and She, the heart of darkness, the waste land of barbarism secreted in civilization, "Mr Kurtz—he dead." But a damned fool indeed encounters damned fool phenomena, and Bellow's is a mock-Africa, anthropologically dense and allusive but populated with African absurdists and Dr. Tamkins, black gurus in pursuit themselves of much the same natural, anthropological and determinist lore that preoccupies Henderson's own abundant mind. Africa promptly looks to Henderson like the ancient bed of mankind; the land is all simplified and splendid, and I felt I was entering the past—the real past, no history or junk like that. In fact history is not so easily escaped; the two tribes he presently encounters represent two fundamental versions of the relationship between man and nature, myth and history. He travels through the desert with a Christian African guide, Romilayu, who takes him first to the Arnewi, a peaceable tribe of cattle-raisers who appear to live in a prehistoric Golden Age. Their language contains no oppositions, and they live by an unambitious goodness, removed from Henderson's desire to burst his spirit's sleep. Even so, Henderson has little trouble making his metaphysical hungers understood, and most of those he meets are in some fashion conspirators in his soul-searching; even the animals conspire with his psychic needs and ambitions. So, too, does the weather; he arrives in a time of drought, when the cattle are dying from the pollution of their water tank by frogs; the Arnewi's religion of acceptance forbids them to intervene.

As with Mark Twain's Hank Morgan (in *A Connecticut Yankee At King Arthur's Court*), Henderson's innocent American desire for service is aroused: "I thought, this will be one of those mutual aid deals; where the Arnewi are irrational I'll help them; and where I'm irrational they'll help me. "Custom first demands he wrestle with the chief, whom he defeats with his strength, and meet the queen, Willatale, blind in one eye, as Bellow's Sammler (*Mr Sammler's Planet*) will be, and similarly a repository of transhistorical wisdom. She accepts Henderson and tells him that he possesses grun-tu-molani, "man wants to live," the life-force. Feeling he is on the right track, he decides to use Yankee technology and blow the frogs out of the tank with home-made explosives; he blows up both frogs and tank. The drought has already been recognized as internal ("As we turned away I felt as though that cistern of problem water with its algae and its frogs had entered me, occupying a square space in my interior, and sloshing around as I moved") and the disaster is Henderson's too. Unable to acquiesce in the given, able to counter stagnation only with excess vitality and technique, he has to leave in disgrace and humiliation, "having demolished both the water and my hopes. From now I'd never learn more about the grun-tu-molani. "

But his unwilling Vergil, Romilayu, leads him to a second tribe, the Wariri ("chillun darkness," says Romilayu), who were once linked to the Arnewi but now live in a different historical and psychological stage, belonging to the fallen timebound world, an age of violence, action and change. Where the Arnewi manifest a "female" peacefulness and acceptance, the Wariri manifest a "male" energy and force. The Arnewi are associated with cattle; the Wariri beast is the lion, and culture and nature are in endless psychic struggle.

This is more appropriate territory for Henderson, and the place of his chief adventures. The Wariri—who have a more complex social system, carry guns, and have a kind of police and immigration service-capture and interrogate him and place him in a room with a corpse, confronting him with his deepest anxiety, that of death; he copes by disposing of the body in a ravine. This is a test of strength; the Wariri have a use for Henderson's excessive, undirected energy. Instead of accepting the drought, they have a rain-making ritual to break it—to "prime the pumps of the firmament," as their king, Dahfu, puts it. Part of the ritual involves lifting a heavy wooden goddess, Mummah, from one spot to another; after the tribal strongman fails, Henderson, feeling use for his strength at last, asks permission to undertake the task and, in what is effectively a moment of sexual mastery over the idol, he succeed and feels renewed:

> I was so gladdened by what I had done that my whole body was filled with soft heat, with soft and sacred light ... My spirit was awake and welcomed life anew. Damn the whole thing! Life anew! I was still alive and kicking and I had the old grun-tu-molani.

Spirit and world seem to meet in a function; part of Henderson's quest is over. But there is the question of social service: Henderson now becomes Sungo, the tribal rain king, being stripped, thrown into a water tank and made part of a shrieking dance as the rain obligingly falls. Above all he must become concerned with the political position of King Dahfu, educated in Syria, and "a genius of my own mental type." Dahfu is one of Bellow's richest versions of the wise if sometimes dangerous instruction, who often appears to Bellovian heroes, a man of though, learning and extreme applications; and, like other heroes of legend, Henderson now has tasks to perform.

Dahfu has evolutionist psychological theories, a compound of Lamarck and Wilhelm Reich, believing that the body originates in the brain, so that man may create his physiology, or change it:

> What he was engrossed by was a belief in the transformation of human materials, that you could work either way, either from the rind to the core or from the rind; the flesh influencing the mind, the mind influencing the flesh, back again to the mind, back once more to the flesh .... For him it was not enough that there might be disorders of the body that originated in the brain. Everything originated

there. "Although I do not wish to reduce the stature of our discussion, " he said, "yet for the sake of example the pimple on a lady's nose may be her own idea, accomplished by a conversion at the solemn command of her psyche; even more fundamentally the nose itself, though part hereditary, is part also her own idea. "

And he urges Henderson to adapt the "exceptional amalgam of violent forces" in him by introducing him to a lioness he keeps in the palace, a figurative equivalent of "the noble" which will have its turn in the world. He explains that Henderson, in isolating himself, become self-conscious, has grown contracted, whereas the lioness "does not take issue with the inherent. Is one hundred per cent within the given. " Henderson's experience of instruction with the lioness, the killing beast totally unified and in itself, generates scenes of wonderful invention within a remarkable inventive book; a book which metaphorically turns on the legendary equivalence between animal life and human states of being. But before the lessons are complete, accident dissolves the apparently profitable instruction; Dahfu is killed by a ritual lion hunt, and reveals finally that Henderson is his successor and that when he loses the power to carry Mummah and satisfy the harem of being mastered but involves lasting violence. Henderson's situation returns to extremity; he see that Dahfu too has not resolved the problem of relating energy to communal task.

Henderson escapes from the Wariri, taking with him the lion cub though to be Dahfu's soul, and a concept of human nobility drawn from him, which he utters to Romilayu:

We're supposed to think nobility is unreal. But that's just it. The illusion is on the other foot. They make us think we crave more and more illusions. Why, I don't crave illusions at all. They say, Think big. Well, that's baloney of course, another business slogan. But greatness! That's another thing altogether. Oh, God! Romilayu, I don't mean inflated, swollen, false greatness . . . . But the universe itself being put into us, it calls out for scope. The eternal is bonded onto us. It calls out for its share.

And, in what is to be a characteristic ending, the path of instruction has itself to be amended: the lessons taken have been to a degree mock lessons. Flying home across the Atlantic, accompanied by the lion cub, reminder of nobility sacrificed to society, and an orphan boy he has met on the flight, his final twin, he realizes that he must settle for his own nature, closer to the fairground bear, that sad humorist, than the lion.

Thus, as before, the novel ends on a contained and measured possibility; Henderson is now no longer matched to the pigs with which he began, nor no the cattle or the lion, but to his own comic shambling largeness. Warrior and female principle, violence and gentleness reconcile; the world contains lasting traces that are more than single occasions. Henderson has found a print in nature to attach himself to:

> If corporeal things are an image of the spiritual and visible objects are renderings of invisible ones, then Smolak (the fairground bear he had once worked with) and I were outcasts together, two humorists before the crowd, but brothers in our souls—I embeared by me ... something deep was already inscribed on me.

Landing in Newfoundland, Henderson, knowing his imprint, runs with bear and child round the plane, "leaping, leaping, pounding and tingling over the pure white lining of the grey Arctic silence." It closes on a sense of freedom, a celebration of stark created nature; but also a sense of the conditioned and the bonded. Like Angie before him and Herzog after, Henderson enters the kingdom of knowledge which contains both process and biology and those eternal traces—the limits and the possibilities of self-creation.

Henderson in fact concludes the book as Bellow's most affirmative hero, to the end the abundant comedian of his own self-assertion. Bellow once spoke of Henderson's quest as "a remedy for his anxiety over death ... the indeterminate and indefinite anxiety, which most of us accept as the condition of life which he is foolhardy enough to resist." His struggle has been against "cosmic coldness," yet, in the Newfoundland cold, he finds a state of joy in which he can run freely.

It is an ending that Leslie Fiedler has called one of "unearned euphoria," and it promotes certain doubts. What, though, sustains the lyric note to the end is Bellow's own note of comic metaphysics, which conducts Henderson—with his sense that one must live a thing before one knows it, and that visible objects are the rendering of invisible ones—into a new and promising state of living to know. It is this engaged space between the lyric and the comic, manifesting itself both as metaphysics and wit, that gives Bellow the tones of a major novelist. Henderson's progress through the kingdom of nature, through a world where animals measure out the stuff of human potential, where single instances leave lasting traces, where a commanding biology can be transliterated into an endless becoming, is an

extraordinary conceit. The mythic intent makes it very much a book of the fifties: a decade obsessed with the hope that the imagination might generate at last the saving fable, the table of the waste land redeemed, the desert of civilization watered by some humanist or metaphysical discovery. But the myth both asserts and mocks itself, takes on a neo-parodic form; and it is the method of comic fabulation, of expansive and pyrotechnic farce, of absurdity finding a path to human measurement, that makes *Henderson the Rain King* so strangely notable a novel.
[Selected from Malcolm Bradbury, (ed.). *Saul Bellow*. London: Methuen, 1982.]

6. Philip Roth

6.1 Presentation Topics

(1) Philip Roth as a novelist.

(2) Sheer playfulness and deadly seriousness in his works.

(3) Roth's concern with Jewish American people.

6.2 Selected Reading

Ⅰ. Central issue of concern

The most prominent features of Philip Roth's sensibility, the solicitude about the possibilities for selfhood and the attention to the moral and psychological crises experienced by the Self and perpetuated by American life.

Ⅱ. Text

Eli, the Fanatic

Leo Tzuref stepped out from back of a white column to welcome Eli Peck. Eli jumped back, surprised; then they shook hands and Tzuref gestured him into the sagging old mansion. At the door Eli turned, and down the slope of lawn, past the jungle of hedges, beyond the dark, untrampled horse path, he saw the street lights blink on in Woodenton. The stores along Coach House Road tossed up a burst of yellow—it came to Eli as a secret signal from his townsmen: "Tell this Tzuref where we stand, Eli. This is a modern community, Eli, we have our families, we pay taxes.... " Eli, burdened by the message, gave Tzuref a dumb, weary stare.

"You must work a full day," Tzuref said, steering the attorney and his briefcase into the chilly hall.

Eli's heels made a racket on the cracked marble floor, and he spoke above it. "It's the commuting that's killing," he said, and entered the dim room Tzuref waved open for him. "Three hours a day ... I came right from the train." He dwindled down into a harp-backed chair. He expected it would be deeper than it was and consequently jarred himself on the sharp bones of his seat. It woke him, this shiver of the behind, to his business. Tzuref, a bald shaggy-browed man who looked as if he'd once been very fat, sat back of an empty desk, halfway hidden, as though he were settled on the floor. Everything around him was empty. There were no books in the bookshelves, no rugs on the floor, no draperies in the big casement windows. As Eli began to speak Tzuref got up and swung a window back on one noisy hinge. "May and it's like August," he said, and with his back to Eli, he revealed the black circle on the back of his head. The crown of his head was missing! He returned through the dimness—the lamps had no bulbs—and Eli realized all he'd seen was a skullcap①. Tzuref struck a match and lit a candle, just as the half-dying shouts of children at play rolled in through the open window. It was as though Tzuref had opened it so Eli could hear them.

"Aah, now," he said. "I received your letter."

Eli poised, waiting for Tzuref to swish open a drawer and remove the letter from his file. Instead the old man leaned forward onto his stomach, worked his hand into his pants pocket, and withdrew what appeared to be a week-old handkerchief. He uncrumpled it; he unfolded it; he ironed it on the desk with the side of his hand. "So," he said.

Eli pointed to the grimy sheet which he'd gone over word-by-word with his partners, Lewis and McDonnell. "I expected an answer," Eli said. "It's a week."

"It was so important. Mr. Peck, I knew you would come."

Some children ran under the open window and their mysterious babble—not mysterious to Tzuref, who smiled—entered the room like a third person. Their noise caught up against Eli's flesh and he was unable to restrain a shudder. He

① A small cloth headgear worn by observant Jewish men and some Jewish women.

wished he had gone home, showered and eaten dinner, before calling on Tzuref. He was not feeling as professional as usual—the plate was too dim, it was too late. But down in Woodenton they would be waiting, his clients and neighbors. He spoke for the Jews of Woodenton, not just himself and his wife.

"Yon understood?" Eli said.

"It's not hard."

"It's a matter of zoning ..." and when Tzuref did not answer, but only drummed his fingers on his lips, Eli said, "We didn't make the laws...."

"You respect them."

"They protect us... the community."

"The law is the law," Tzuref said.

"Exactly!" Eli had the urge to rise and walk about the room.

"And then of course"—Tzuref made a pair of scales in the air with his hands—"the law is not the law. When is the law that is the law not the law?" He jiggled the scales. "And... vice versa."

"Simply," Eli said sharply. "You can't have a boarding school in a residential area." He would not allow Tzuref to cloud the issue with issues. "We thought it better to tell you before any action is undertaken."

"But a house in a residential area?"

"Yes. That's what residential means." The DP's English was perhaps not as good as it seemed at first. Tzuref spoke slowly, but till then Eli had mistaken it for craft—or even wisdom. "Residence means home," he added.

"So this is my residence."

"But the children?"

"It is their residence."

"Seventeen children?"

"Eighteen," Tzuref said.

"But you teach them here."

"The Talmud①. That's illegal?"

"That makes it school."

① A central text of mainstream Judaism, in the form of a record of rabbinic discussions pertaining to Jewish law, ethics, customs and history.

Tzuref hung the scales again, tipping slowly the balance.

"Look. Mr. Tzuref, in America we call such a place a boarding school."

"Where they teach the Talmud?"

"Where they teach period. You are the headmaster, they are the students."

Tzuref placed his scales on the desk. "Mr. Peck," he said, "I don't believe it..." but he did not seem to be referring to anything Eli had said.

"Mr, Tzuref, that is the law. I came to ask what you intend to do."

"What I must do?"

"I hope they are the same."

"They are." Tzuref brought his stomach into the desk. "We stay." He smiled. "We are tired. The headmaster is tired. The students are tired."

Eli rose and lifted his briefcase. It felt so heavy packed with the grievances, vengeances, and schemes of his clients. There were days when he carried it like a feather—in Tzuref's office it weighed a ton.

"Goodbye, Mr. Tzuref."

"Sholom①," Tzuref said.

Eli opened the door to the office and walked carefully down the dark tomb of a corridor to the door. He stepped out on the porch and, leaning against a pillar, looked down across the lawn to the children at play. Their voices whooped and rose and dropped as they chased each other round the old house. The dusk made the children's game look like a tribal dance. Eli straightened up, started off the porch, and suddenly the dance was ended. A long piercing scream trailed after. It was the first time in his life anyone had run at the sight of him. Keeping his eyes on the lights of Woodenton, he headed down the path.

And then, seated on a bench beneath a tree, Eli saw him. At first it seemed only a deep hollow of blackness—then the figure emerged. Eli recognized him from the description. There he was, wearing the hat, that hat which was the very cause of Eli's mission, the source of Woodenton's upset. The town's lights flashed their message once again: "Get the one with the hat. What a nerve, what a nerve...."

Eli started towards the man. Perhaps he was less stubborn than Tzuref, more

---

① A Hebrew word meaning peace, completeness, and welfare and can be used idiomatically to mean both hello and goodbye.

reasonable. After all, it was the law. But when he was close enough to call out, he didn't. He was stopped by the sight of the black coat that fell down below the man's knees, and the hands which held each other in his lap. By the round-topped, wide-brimmed Talmudio hat, pushed onto the back of his head. And by the beard, which hid his neck and was so soft and thin it fluttered away and back again with each heavy breath he took. He was asleep, his sidelocks curled loose on his cheeks. His face was no older than Eli's.

Eli hurried towards the lights.

The note on the kitchen table unsettled him. Scribblings on bits of paper had made history this past week. This one, however, was unsigned. "Sweetie," it said, "I went to sleep. I had a sort of Oedipal experience with the baby today. Call Ted Heller."

She had left him a cold soggy dinner in the refrigerator. He hated cold soggy dinners, but would take one gladly in place of Miriam's presence. He was ruffled, and she never helped that, not with her infernal analytic powers. He loved her when life was proceeding smoothly—and that was when she loved him. But sometimes Eli found being a lawyer surrounded him like quicksand—he couldn't get his breath. Too often he wished he were pleading for the other side; though if he were on the other side, then he'd wish he were on the side he was. The trouble was that sometimes the law didn't seem to be the answer, law didn't seem to have anything to do with what was aggravating everybody. And that, of course, made him feel foolish and unnecessary .... Though that was not the situation here—the townsmen had a case. But not exactly, and if Miriam were awake to see Eli's upset, she would set about explaining his distress to him, understanding him, forgiving him, so as to get things back to Normal, for Normal was where they loved one another. The difficulty with Miriam's efforts was they only upset him more; not only did they explain little to him about himself or his predicament, but they convinced him of her weakness. Neither Eli nor Miriam, it turned out, was terribly strong. Twice before he'd faced this fact, and on both occasions had found solace in what his neighbors forgivingly referred to as "a nervous breakdown."

Eli ate his dinner with his briefcase beside him. Halfway through, he gave in to himself, removed Tzuref's notes, and put them on the table, beside Miriam's. From time to time he flipped through the notes, which had been carried into town by the one in the black hat. The first note, the incendiary:

To whom it may concern:

Please give this gentleman the following: Boys shoes with rubber heels and soles.

5 prs size 6c

3 prs size 5c

3 prs size 5b

2 prs size 4a

2 prs size 4c

1 pr size 7b

1 pr size 7c

Total 18 prs boys shoes. This gentleman has a check already signed. Please fill in correct amount.

L. TZUREF

Director, Yeshivah of Woodenton, N. Y.

(5/8/48)

"Eli, a regular greenhorn," Ted Heller had said. "He didn't say a word. Just handed me the note and stood there, like in the Bronx the old guys who used to come around selling Hebrew trinkets."

"A Yeshivah①!" Artie Berg had said. "Eli, in Woodenton, a Yeshivah! If I want to live in Brownsville, Eli, I'll live in Brownsville."

"Eli," Harry Shaw speaking now, "the old Puddington place. Old man Puddington'll roll over in his grave. Eli, when I left the city, Eli, I didn't plan the city should come to me."

Note number two:

Dear Grocer:

Please give this gentleman ten pounds of sugar. Charge it to our account, Yeshivah of Woodenton, NY—which we will now open with you and expect a bill each month. The gentleman will be in to see you once or twice a week.

L. TZUREF, Director

(5/10/48)

P. S. Do you carry kosher meat?

"He walked right by my window, the greenie," Ted had said, "and he

① An elementary or secondary Judaism school with a curriculum that includes religion and culture as well as general education.

nodded, Eli. He's my friend now."

"Eli," Artie Berg had said, "he handed the damn thing to a clerk at Stop N' Shop—and in that hat yet!"

"Eli," Harry Shaw again, "it's not funny. Someday, Eli, it's going to be a hundred little kids with little yamalkahs chanting their Hebrew lessons on Coach House Road, and then it's not going to strike you funny."

"Eli, what goes on up there—my kids hear strange sounds."

"Eli, this is a modern community."

"Eli, we pay taxes."

"Eli."

"Eli!"

"Eli!"

At first it was only another townsman crying in his ear; but when he turned he saw Miriam, standing in the doorway, behind her belly.

"Eli, sweetheart, how was it?"

"He said no."

"Did you see the other one?" she asked.

"Sleeping, under a tree."

"Did you let him know how people feel?"

"He was sleeping."

"Why didn't you wake him up? Eli, this isn't an everyday thing."

"He was tired!"

"Don't shout, please," Miriam said.

"Don't shout. I'm pregnant. The baby is heavy." Eli found he was getting angry at nothing she'd said yet; it was what she was going tosay.

"He's a very heavy baby the doctor says," Miriam told him.

"Then sit down and make my dinner." Now he found himself angry about her not being present at the dinner which he'd just been relieved that she wasn't present at. It was as though he had a raw nerve for a tail, that he kept stepping on. At last Miriam herself stepped on it.

"Eli, you're upset. I understand."

"You don't understand."

She left the room. From the stairs she called, "I do, sweetheart."

It was a trap! He would grow angry knowing she would be "understanding." She would in turn grow more understanding seeing his anger. He would in turn grow angrier.... The phone rang.

"Hello," Eli said.

"Eli, Ted. So?"

"So nothing."

"Who is Tzuref ? He's an American guy?"

"No. ADP①. German."

"And the kids?"

"DP's too. He teaches them."

"What? What subjects?" Ted asked.

"I don't know."

"And the guy with the hat, you saw the guy with the hat?"

"Yes. He was sleeping."

"Eli, he sleeps with the hat?"

"He sleeps with the hat."

"Goddam fanatics," Ted said. "This is the 20th century, Eli. Now it's the guy with the hat. Pretty soon all the little Yeshivah boys'll be spilling down into town."

"Next thing they'll be alter our daughters."

"Michele and Debbie wouldn't look at them."

"Then," Eli mumbled, "you've got nothing to worry about, Teddie," and he hung up.

In a moment the phone rang. "Eli? We got cut off. We've got nothing to worry about? You worked it out?"

"I have to see him again tomorrow. We can work something out."

"That's fine, Eli. I'll call Artie and Harry."

Eli hung up.

"I thought you said nothing worked out." It was Miriam.

"I did."

---

① The term stands for Displaced Person. It referred originally to those millions of non-Germans who were found by the Allied armies when they liberated German territory.

"Then why did you tell Ted something worked out?"

"It did."

"Eli, maybe you should get a little more therapy."

"That's enough of that, Miriam."

"You can't function as a lawyer by being neurotic. That's no answer."

"You're ingenious, Miriam."

She turned, frowning, and took her heavy baby to bed.

The phone rang.

"Eli, Artie. Ted called. You worked it out? No trouble?"

"Yes."

"When are they going?"

"Leave it to me, will you, Artie? I'm tired. I'm going to sleep."

In bed Eli kissed his wife's belly and laid his head upon it to think. He laid it lightly, for she was that day entering the second week of her ninth month. Still, when she slept, it was a good plate to rest, to rise and fall with her breathing and figure things out. "If that guy would take off that crazy hat. I know it, what eats them. If he'd take off that crazy hat everything would be all right."

"What?" Miriam said.

"I'm talking to the baby."

Miriam, pushed herself up in bed. "Eli, please, baby, shouldn't you maybe stop in to see Dr. Eckman, just for a little conversation?"

"I'm fine."

"Oh, sweetie!" she said, and put her head back on the pillow.

"You know what your mother brought to this marriage—a sling chair and a goddam New School enthusiasm for Sigmund Freud."

Miriam feigned sleep, he could tell by the breathing.

"I'm telling the kid the truth, aren't I, Miriam? A sling chair, three months to go on a *New Yorker* subscription, and An *Introduction to Psychoanalysis*. Isn't that right?"

"Eli, must you be aggressive?"

"That's all you worry about, is your insides. You stand in front of the mirror all day and look at yourself being pregnant."

"Pregnant mothers have a relationship with the fetus that fathers can't understand."

"Relationship my ass. What is my liver doing now? What is my small intestine doing now? Is my island of Langerhans on the blink?"

"Don't be jealous of a little fetus, Eli."

"I'm jealous of your island of Langerhans!"

"Eli, I can't argue with you when I know it's not me you're really angry with. Don't you see, sweetie, you're angry with yourself."

"You and Eckman."

"Maybe he could help, Eli."

"Maybe he could help you. You're practically lovers as it is."

"You're being hostile again." Miriam said.

"What do you tart—it's only me I'm being hostile towards."

"Eli, we're going to have a beautiful baby, and I'm going to have a perfectly simple delivery, and you're going to make a fine father, and there's absolutely no reason to be obsessed with whatever is on your mind. All we have to worry about—" she smiled at him "—is a name."

Eli got out of bed and slid into his slippers. "We'll name the kid Eckman if it's a boy and Eckman if it's a girl."

"Eckman Peck sounds terrible."

"He'll have to live with it," Eli said, and he went down to his study where the latch on his briefcase glinted in the moonlight that came through the window.

He removed the Tzuref notes and read through them all again. It unnerved him to think of all the flashy reasons his wife could come up with for his reading and rereading the notes. "Eli, why are you so preoccupied with Tzuref?" "Eli, stop getting involved. Why do you think you're getting involved. Eli?" Sooner or later, everybody's wife finds their weak spot. His goddam luck he had to be neurotic! Why couldn't he have been born with a short leg.

He removed the cover from his typewriter, hating Miriam for the edge she had. All the time he wrote the letter, he could hear what she would be saying about his not being able to let the matter drop. Well, her trouble was that she wasn't able to face the matter. But he could hear her answer already: clearly, he was guilty of "a reaction formation." Still, all the fancy phrases didn't fool Eli: all she wanted really was for Eli to send Tzuref and family on their way, so that the community's temper would quiet, and the calm circumstances of their domestic happiness return. All she wanted were order and love in her private world. Was she so wrong? Let the world bat its brains out—in Woodenton there should be peace. He wrote the letter anyway:

Dear Mr. Tzuref:

Our meeting this evening seems to me inconclusive. I don't think there's any reason for us not to be able to come up with some sort of compromise that will satisfy the Jewish community of Woodenton and the Yeshivah and yourself. It seems to me that what most disturbs my neighbors are the visits to town by the gentleman in the black hat, suit, etc. Woodenton is a progressive suburban community whose members, both Jewish and Gentile, are anxious that their families live in comfort and beauty and serenity. This is, after all, the twentieth, century, and we do not think it too much to ask that the members of our community dress in a manner appropriate to the time and place.

Woodenton, as you may not know, has long been the home of well-to-do Protestants. It is only since the war that Jews have been able to buy property hero, and for Jews and Gentile to live beside each other in amity. For this adjustment to be made, both Jews and Gentiles alike have had to give up some of their more extreme practices in order not to threaten or offend the other. Certainly such amity is to be desired. Perhaps if such conditions had existed in prewar Europe, the persecution of the Jewish people, of which you and those 18 children have been victims, could not have been carried out with such success—in fact, might not have been carried out at all.

Therefore, Mr. Tzuref, will you accept the following conditions? If you can, we will see fit not to carry out legal action against the Yeshivah for failure to comply with township Zoning ordinances No. 18 and No. 23. The conditions are simply:

1. The religious, educational, and social activities of the Yeshivah of Woodenton will be confined to the Yeshivah grounds.

2. Yeshivah personnel are welcomed in the streets and stores of Woodenton provided they are attired in clothing usually associated with American life in the 20th century.

If these conditions are met, we see no reason why the Yeshivah of Woodenton cannot live peacefully and satisfactorily with the Jews of Woodenton—as the Jews of Woodenton have come to live with the Gentiles of Woodenton. I would appreciate an immediate reply.

Sincerely,

Eli Peck, Attorney

Two days later Eli received his immediate reply:

Mr. Peck:

The suit the gentleman wears is all he's got.

Sincerely,

Leo Tzuref, Headmaster

Once again, as Eli swung around the dark trees and onto the lawn, the children fled. He reached out with his briefcase as if to stop them, but they were gone so fast all he saw moving was a flock of skullcaps.

"Come, come..." a voice called from the porch. Tzuref appeared from behind a pillar. Did he live behind those pillars? Was he just watching the children at play? Either way, when Eli appeared, Tzuref was ready, with no forewarning,

"Hello," Eli said.

"Sholom."

"I didn't mean to frighten them."

"They're scared, so they run."

"I didn't do anything."

Tzuref shrugged. The little movement seemed to Eli strong as an accusation. What he didn't get at home, he got here.

Inside the house they took their seats. Though it was lighter than a few evenings before, a bulb or two would have helped. Eli had to hold his briefcase towards the window for the last gleamings. He removed Tzuref's letter from a manila folder. Tzuref removed Eli's letter from his pants pocket. Eli removed the carbon of his own letter from another manila folder. Tzuref removed Eli's first letter from his back pocket. Eli removed the carbon from his briefcase. Tzuref raised his palms. "... It's all I've got ...."

Those upraised palms, the mocking tone—another accusation. It was a crime to keep carbons! Everybody had an edge on him—Eli could do no right.

"I offered a compromise, Mr. Tzuref. You refused."

"Refused, Mr. Peck? What is, is."

"The man could get a new suit."

"That's all he's got."

"So you told me," Eli said.

"So I told you, so you know."

"It's not an insurmountable obstacle, Mr. Tzuref. We have stores."

"For that too?"

"On Route 12, a Robert Hall—"

"To take away the one thing a man's got?"

"Not take away, replace?"

"But I tell you he has nothing. Nothing, You have that word in English? Nicht? Gornisht?"

"Yes, Mr. Tzuref, we have the word."

"A mother and a father?" Tzuref said. "No. A wife? No. A baby? A little ten-month-old baby? No! A village full of friends? A synagogue where you knew the feel of every seat under your pants? Where with your eyes closed you could smell the cloth of the Torah?" Tzuref pushed out of his chair, stirring a breeze that swept Eli's letter to the floor. At the window he leaned out, and looked, beyond Woodenton. When he turned he was shaking a finger at Eli, "And a medical experiment they performed on him yet! That leaves nothing, Mr. Peck. Absolutely nothing!"

"I misunderstood."

"No news reached Woodenton?"

"About the suit, Mr. Tzuref. I thought he couldn't afford another."

"He can't."

They were right where they'd begun. "Mr. Tzuref!" Eli demanded. "Here?" He smacked his hand to his billfold.

"Exactly!" Tzuref said, smacking his own breast.

"Then we'll buy him one!" Eli crossed to the window and taking Tzuref by the shoulders, pronounced each word slowly. "We-will-pay-for-it. All right?"

"Pay? What, diamonds!"

Eli raised a hand to his inside pocket, then let it drop. Oh stupid! Tzuref, father to eighteen, had smacked not what lay under his coat, but deeper, under the ribs.

"Oh..." Eli said. He moved away along the wall. "The suit is all he's got then."

"You got my letter," Tzuref said.

Eli stayed back in the shadow, and Tzuref turned to his chair. He swished Eli's letter from the floor, and held it up. "You say too much... all this reasoning ... all these conditions..."

"What can I do?"

"You have the word 'suffer' in English?"

"We have the word 'suffer'. We have the word 'law' too."

"Stop with the 'law'! You have the word 'suffer'. Then try it. It's a little thing."

"They won't," Eli said.

"But you, Mr. Peck, how about you?"

"I am them, they are me, Mr. Tzuref."

"Aach! You are us, we are you!"

Eli shook and shook his head. In the dark he suddenly felt that Tzuref might put him under a spell. "Mr. Tzuref, a little light?"

Tzuref lit what tallow was left in the holders. Eli was afraid to ask if they couldn't afford electricity. Maybe candles were all they had left.

"Mr. Peck, who made the law, may I ask you that?"

"The people."

"No."

"Yes."

"Before the people."

"No one. Before the people there was no law." Eli didn't care for the conversation, but with only candlelight, he was being lulled into it.

"Wrong," Tzuref said.

"We make the law, Mr. Tzuref. It is our community. These are my neighbors. I am their attorney. They pay me. Without law there is chaos."

"What you call law, I call shame. The heart, Mr. Peck, the heart is law! God!" he announced.

"Look, Mr. Tzuref, I didn't come here to talk metaphysics. People use the law, it's a flexible thing. They protect what they value, their property, their well-being, their happiness—"

"Happiness? They hide their shame. And you, Mr. Peck, you are shameless?"

"We do it," Eli said, wearily, "for our children. This is the 20th century...."

"For the goyim maybe. For me the Fifty-eighth." He pointed at Eli. "That is too old for shame."

Eli felt squashed. Everybody in the world had evil reasons for his actions. Everybody! With reasons so cheap, who buys bulbs. "Enough wisdom, Mr. Tzuref, Please. I'm exhausted."

"Who isn't?" Tzuref said.

He picked Eli's papers from his desk and reached up with them. "What do you intend for us to do?"

"What you must," Eli said. "I made the offer."

"So he must give up his suit?"

"Tzuref, Tzuref, leave me be with that suit! I'm not the only lawyer in the world. I'll drop the case, and you'll get somebody who won't talk compromise. Then you'll have no home, no children, nothing. Only a lousy black suit! Sacrifice what you want. I know what I would do."

To that Tzuref made no answer, but only handed Eli his letters.

"It's not me, Mr. Tzuref, it's them."

"They are you."

"No," Eli intoned, "I am me. They are them. You are you."

"You talk about leaves and branches. I'm dealing with under the dirt."

"Mr. Tzuref, you're driving me crazy with Talmudic wisdom. This is that, that is the other thing. Give me a straight answer."

"Only for straight questions."

"Oh, God!"

Eli returned to his chair and plunged his belongings into his case. "Then, that's all," he said angrily.

Tzuref gave him the shrug.

"Remember, Tzuref, you called this down on yourself."

"I did?"

Eli refused to be his victim again. Double-talk proved nothing.

"Goodbye," he said.

But as he opened the door leading to the hall, he heard Tzuref.

"And your wife, how is she?"

"Fine, just fine." Eli kept going.

"And the baby is due when, any day?"

Eli turned. "That's right."

"Well," Tzuref said, rising. "Good luck."

"You know?"

Tzuref pointed out the window—then, with his hands, he drew upon himself a beard, a hat, a long, long coat. When his fingers formed the hem they touched the floor. "He shops two, three times a week, he gets to know them."

"He talks to them?"

"He sees them."

"And he can tell which is my wife?"

"They shop at the same stores. He says she is beautiful. She has a kind face. A woman capable of love… though who can be sure."

"He talks about us, to you?" demanded Eli.

"You talk about us, to her?"

"Goodbye, Mr. Tzuref."

Tzuref said, "Sholom. And good luck—I know what it is to have children. Sholom," Tzuref whispered, and with the whisper the candles went out. But the instant before, the flames leaped into Tzuref eyes, and Eli saw it was not luck Tzuref wished him at all.

Outside the door, Eli waited. Down the lawn the children were holding hands and whirling around in a circle. At first he did not move. But he could not hide in the shadows all night. Slowly he began to slip along the front of the house. Under his hands he felt where bricks were out. He moved in the shadows until he reached the side. And then, clutching his briefcase to his chest, he broke across the darkest spots of the lawn. He aimed for a distant glade of woods, and when he reached it he did not stop, but ran through until he was so dizzied that the trees seemed to be running beside him, fleeing not towards Woodenton but away. His lungs were nearly ripping their seams as he burst into the yellow glow of the Gulf station at the edge of town.

[Selected from Philip Roth. *Goodbye, Columbus and Five Short Stories*. New York: Bantam Books, 1968.]

Ⅲ. Questions for discussion

(1) What is in the name Tzuref?

(2) Why has Eli Peck made himself into a commuter? What is he running from or to?

(3) Why does Eli urge the "man in the suit" to take off his black one and put

on Eli's green, lawyer suit?

(4) Why is Eli disoriented around his wife, career and surroundings?

(5) What are the symbols in the story? What do they show?

(6) How does Roth understand the difference between residence and home? Is America a home?

6.3 Assigned Reading

"Nathan Dedalus": Jewish Sons, Jewish Novelists, Jewish Jokes

Hermione Lee

In *Goodbye, Columbus* (1959), his first collection, containing the title novella and five short stories, the revolts are more circumscribed, the net of family and community more closely drawn around the central figure. The distinction of these stories is their attentive, comical display of social detail-army talk in "Defender of the Faith," suburban Jewish life in "Goodbye, Columbus" and "Eli, the Fanatic," schoolboy behavior in "The Conversion of the Jews" and "You Can't Tell a Man by the Song he Sings." In "Goodbye, Columbus," Neil Klugman describes the park outside the Newark public library with a charmed devotion to local minutiae which springs, as he says, from "a deep knowledge of Newark, an attachment so rooted that it could not help but branch out into affection." That, of course, is his and the author's predicament: like Stephen Dedalus, he is emotionally and aesthetically bound to the environment he wants, urgently, to resist. In fact Neil Klugman, as indecisive as Prufrock ("I haven't planned a thing in five yeas"), does not go far in his revolt-just from his surrogate mother's kitchen and the Newark library to the household of the Patimkins, wealthy suburbanized Jews. "Since when do Jewish people live in Short Hills? They couldn't be real Jews believe me," says his Aunt Gladys, and then back again. Even so, the short journey from his ethnic roots in the "Jewish ghetto" to the world of the secularized, Americanized Patimkin wealth is enough to disturb Neil's sense of identity. The newly rich Patimkins have moved up from Newark into gentility on the back of the wartime kitchen-sink boom and now represent the 1950s American dream of affluence. They are "real" enough in terms of goods and clothes and games: "Oh Patimkin! Fruit grew in their refrigerator and sporting goods dropped from their trees." The family is caught in unforgiving detail, from little Julie's cheating ("Mr. Patimkin had taught his daughters that free throws were theirs for the asking") to the neurotic mother's synagogue snobbery, and the son Ron's mindlessly assimilated dedication to the all-American campus (the appropriately chosen university at Columbus, Ohio) and to all American gamesmanship.

Neil's gravitation towards the "prize" of material goods, and his half-baked attempts to liberate the attractive Patimkin daughter Brenda from her family by making her get a diaphragm, are compared (rather mawkishly) to the escapist dreams of the small black boy who comes into the library every day to look at a book of Gauguin's paintings ("Ain't that the fuckin' *life*?"). But "Goodbye, Columbus" doesn't get beyond being a satire on the alternative family lives that are observed by the Jewish boy discovering America. That Neil is missing a sense of self ("I sat down in my Brooks Brothers shirt and pronounced my own name out loud")is just touched on at the end when, the affair over, he gazes into the window of Harvard's Lamont Library ("Patimkin sinks in the rest rooms")and lets his gaze "push through" his own image in the glass to "a broken wall of books, imperfectly shelved." Then, in time for the Jewish New Year, he catches the train back to Newark and his job. A faint suggestion has been made, which will be taken up in later books, that an alternative to the disappointing "American dream" of material wealth and sexual liberation may be found in the "useful fiction" of books and art.

In some of the other stories in *Goodbye, Columbus*, the attempt to "push through" into a real choice of "selfhood" is more powerfully made. Though these are comic dilemmas, with an eye for absurd disruptions of normal life—the boy up on the roof of the shul making everyone kneel down like Gentiles, the guilty married man caught with his trousers down by the entire family—in each case a serious, self-made crisis faces the central character. Little Ozzie Freedman, in "The Conversion of the Jews," chooses to resist orthodoxy by refusing to accept Rabbi Binder's statement that the virgin birth is an impossibility ("You don't know anything about God!"). Sergeant Marx in "Defender of the Faith" refuses to be compromised by Private Grossbart's self-interested appeals for Jewish solidarity in a Gentile world ("Let the goyim clean the floors!"). Moved at first by natural sympathies arising from his "deep memory" of a Bronx childhood, Marx negotiates awkwardly between the Jews and the army officers, in some comical interchanges

("Jewish parents, sir—they're apt to be more protective than you expect"... "Marx, here, tells me Jews have a tendency to be pushy"). But Grossbart and his cronies make a fool of him, and he realizes that he must free himself from what is, in effect, racial persecution "by another Jew." Epstein, in a less interesting story, tries, farcically, to spring the family trapdead son, fat nagging wife, grimly "politicized" daughter—by having an affair with the window next door. An embarrassing infection and a badly timed heart attack put paid to this bid for freedom: "Lou, you'll live normal, won't you?" His wife cries in the ambulance.

In "Eli, the Fanatic" the lawyer (like Sergeant Marx, a negotiator) is "burdened by the message" he has to take from the secularized Jews of suburban Woodenton to Mr. Tzuref (the name means "troubles") who has opened a yeshivah (Orthodox elementary school) in this "assimilated," "progressive" community. Both Eli the lawyer and Sergeant Marx are challenged by potential "doubles," who may be persecutors or saviors. In Roth these "doubles," who will recur, are always Jewish-like Susskind, the Jew in Bernard Malmamud's story "Last Mohican," who makes Fidelman responsible for him "because you are a man. Because you are a Jew," and unlike the more usual situation in Saul Bellow's *The Victim*, where Asa Leventhal is persecuted by the Gentile Allbee. Pulling at Eli on one side are his secularized neighbors. ("This Abraham in the Bible was going to kill his own kid for a sacrifice... Today a guy like that they'd lock him up!") and his pregnant wife, who reads Freud and wants things to be "normal." Pushing at him from the other side is the insistent presence of Mr. Tzuref ("Aach! You are us, we are you!") and his unassimilated, black-robed "greenhorn" assistant, The satire on wealthy suburban Jewish life is more complex here than in "Goodbye, Columbus." Eli knows that this community is peaceful and safe, "a place for families, even Jewish families," "It was what his parents had asked for in the Bronx, and his grandparents in Poland, and theirs in Russia or Austria, or wherever else they'd fled to or from. He half shares its rejection of the yeshivah and the greenie, reminders of the victimized, suffering Jewish past. But that orthodoxy (which others of Roth's characters, like Ozzie Freedman, resist)" goes deeper than anything in the safe suburban landscape of the "Stop'n Shop," the "Bit-in-Teeth Restaurant" and "Roger's Beauty Shoppe." Eli begins to identify with the poor greenie, exchanges clothes with him and, bearing "the terrible weight of the stranger's strange hat," is carted off, after visiting his newborn son, to the community's asylum, feeling a "deep blackness" in his soul.

The story, like Flannery O'Connor's "Revelation" or "The Enduring Chill," works towards a moment of visionary acceptance; it also invokes Hawthorne's tales of the true man's social ostracism (such as "The Minister's Black Veil"). Ozzie races to the edge of the roof, asking himself "Is it me? Is it me Me Me Me Me! It has to be me—but is it?" and longs, like a juvenile Jewish Ahab, to "rip open the sky, plunge his hands through." Sergeant Marx "accepts" his fate when he rejects Grossbart. Similarly, Eli remakes his self against the will of the community, and in so doing lets go of "normality." These are not dignified or triumphant choices: Ozzie has to plummet down from his moment of hubris into the "net" glowing below "like an overgrown halo," and Eli's struggle to decide what kind of Jew he is ends in madness.

These stories aroused enormous controversy among conservative and orthodox Jewish circles, especially when *Goodbye, Columbus* won the National Book Award in 1960. The attacks on Roth by rabbis ("a distorted image of the basic values of Orthodox Judaism"), angry correspondents ("will do irreparable damage to the Jewish people") and Jewish literary critics ("Roth's characters are coarse, crafty, ugly, crude, common, brutish and low-minded precisely because they are Jews") were at once put to use as literary material. "Because recognition—and, with it, opposition—came to me almost immediately, I seem ... to have felt called upon both to assert a literary position and to defend my moral flank the instant after I had managed to take my first steps," he noted. *Portnoy's Complaint* is a form of assertion and defence. The Israeli girl who kicks and derides Portony and takes exception to his beastliness, his "self-hate" and his obscenities is one of Roth's literary critics. Before that, he had defended himself rather solemnly, in the 1963 essay "Writing About Jews," where he argues that the time for living in fear of Gentile persecution is over:

> The cry "Watch out for the goyim!" at times seems more the expression of an unconscious wish than of a warning: "Oh that they were out there, so that we could be together in here!" A rumour of persecution, a taste of exile, might even bring with it that old world of feelings and habits-something to replace the new world of social accessibility and moral indifference, the world which tempts all our promiscuous instincts, and where one cannot always figure out what a Jew is that a Christian is not.

His own fiction, he claims, does for the Jewish image what Ralph Ellison's *Invisible Man* does for the blacks. It is "an expression of moral consciousness."

To have been attacked by the Jewish establishment was nothing unusual for a Jewish writer if he was not Leon Uris or Harry Golden. Leslie Fiedler, reviewing *Goodbye, Columbus*, called "the accusation of anti-Semitism" "the young Jewish writer's initial accolade" and was later to describe the "anti-conformism" of the contemporary Jewish writer as having become, in its turn, a brand of conformity. Roth recognizes that "the opposition was instuctive," and by now it has become essential to his treatment of the Jewish son and writer. The last two novels, *The Ghost Writer*(1956) and *Zuckerman Unbound* (1969), are both, retrospectively, about the son's need to revolt from the community in order to master it as material. Both turn on a comic confrontation between the writer's need for secrecy, aloofness and self-determination and the threatening, importunate criticisms of family, fans, reviewers and nuts on the sidewalk. Both give comic (but probably not much exaggerated) versions of those angry letters of the sixties: "Can you honestly say that there is anything in your short story that would not warm the heart of a Julius Streicher or a Joseph Goebbels?" "Dear Mr Zuckerman: It is hardly possible to write of Jews with more bile and contempt and hatred." In *The Ghost Writer* the parallel predicaments of son and writer merge: it is Nathan's father, furious and heartbroken at Nathan's first story (which draws on the same sort of neighborhood folklore as did Roth's "Epstein"), who speaks, though tenderly, in the voice of Roth's early critics: "It's not your fault that you don't know what Gentiles think when they read something like this.... I wonder if you fully understand just how very little love there is in this world for Jewish people."

Nathan's sad father closes the circle that begins with Rabbi Binder. Those figures of authority—Jewish fathers, teachers, critics—whom Roth had, in life, to resist from the earliest stages of his profession, have since then played a consistent part in his fictions. In all his works so far, Roth's Jewish families, like the Dedalus family in Joyce's *Portrait of the Artist as a Young Man*, are the material for, and the obstacles to, the fully adult writer who can master and describe himself and his world. In order to be a writer one must cease to be a son. The Jewish son who grows up to be the novelist is "in possession" of his material, but he is also "unbound," dispossessed, "no longer any man's son."

Between *Goodbye, Columbus* and *Portnoy's Complaint*, The Jewish son's struggle for freedom and self-possession takes the form of a long, "realist" narrative, *Letting Go* (1962), in which his predicament is split between two central characters. *Letting Go* begins with a dying mother's letter to her son ("I was always doing things for another's good. The rest of my life I could push and pull people with a clear conscience") and then divides itself between two Jewish sons' attempts to get free of all that pushing and pulling. Both Gabe Wallach and Paul Herz are teachers of literature, both are involved with Gentile girls, but Gabe, well-off, confused, unable to commit himself, trails a wreckage of relationships foundered on bad faith, while Paul struggles grimly to be a real mensch, "a man of duty," and to make his marriage to the neurotic Libby (a Jewish convert) work and last. This, Roth's first long novel, has not found a structure to suit it. Like its stultified characters, the narrative gets bogged down in long, detailed set-pieces-Martha Reganhart's messy Gentile household, campus "characters," the Herz family in Brooklyn-strong in themselves, but clogging up the essential idea of Gabe and Paul as alter egos. By the time Gabe begins to act decisively (in getting a child for Paul and Libby to adopt), the shape of the novel has been submerged. But Gabe's resistance to the "overwhelming love" showered on him by his widowed dentist father, a weeper and wise cracker whose "passions ached him" and who spent his married life, like Mr. Portnoy, "constipating himself," is strongly felt as an alternative to Paul's painful choice between being a good husband and being a good son to his anxious father, a failed small businessman sitting in his BarcaLounger in Brooklyn expecting a heart attack. Both Families are surrounded with a mass of half-ironic, half-tender details, lavished on Mr. Wallach's Thanksgiving party, or the Herzes' neighbors, or Paul's uncle Asher—in all of which the two young humanities teachers struggle on their hooks. Paul's cynical, shabbily hedonistic uncle tells him:

> "Listen to Uncle Shmuck, will you? Things come and go, and you have got to be a receptacle, let them pass right through. Otherwise death will be a misery for you, boy; I'd hate to see it .... Wait and accept and learn to pull the hand away. Don't clutch! What is marriage, what is it but a pissy form of greed, a terrible, disgusting ambitiousness."

Whether the Jewish son is trying to escape the clutch of family and marriage, or is conscious that he is himself desperately clutching—whether he is trying to be let go or to let go—he must suffer. The punishment may be sprung on the complaining victim in bizarre, surreal form, like Novotny's undiagnosable back pain, which comes upon him after he has been drafted into the army and is waiting to go to Korea("What had he done in life to deserve this? What had he done, from the day he had grown out of short pants, but everything that was asked of him?"), or David Kepesh's transformation into a breast ("HOW COULD IT HAVE HAPPENED? IN THE ENTIRE HISTORY OF THE HUMEN RACE, WHY PROFESSOR KEPESH?"). Its causes may be pursued through a profusion of realistic detail, or turned into exhaustive, agonized jokes. But the version and descriptions have to be unremittingly regurgitated.

In *My Life as a Man* (1974), the sufferings of the Jewish son, husband and novelist are compulsively reworked in a series of "Useful Fictions," alternative versions of the novelist Peter Tarnopol's "true story," in which he attempts to describe himself and to exorcize his obsession with his destructive marriage. In the fragmentary narratives of *My Life as a Man* the novelist is at once victim and analyst, confessor and interpreter of his own sufferings. Tarnopol's struggle to describe himself beings with the comic narrative "Salad Days," in which Nathan Zuckerman is the protected, petted son of a "bewildering dynamo of a protector" (like Mr. Herz, a repeatedly failing small businessman) and an over-encouraging mother, with a brother whose teenage boasting collapses into domesticity with "flatchested Sheila, the dental technician." The family dream of financial security comes true in 1949 "just as the family was falling apart." Nathan's humanities course at college teaches him a new set of terms ("'irony' and 'values' and 'fate,' 'will and vision' and 'authenticity,' and, of course, 'human'") which make him scornful of his parents and of Sharon Shatsky, the sexy daughter of "the Zipper King" Shatsky, whose mind he despises but whom he debauches in earshot of their mothers: "I want to be your whore," she whispered to him (without prompting too), while on the back terrace her mother told his mother how adorable Sharon looked in the winter coat they'd bought for her that afternoon. In "Courting Disaster," the second "fiction," the father is a book-keeper and Nathan's childhood is taken up with arithmetical problems and luxurious illnesses, but the ingredients of the complaint are the same: the over-protective, anxious-making Jewish childhood leads to a painful split between conscience and libido. Nathan, whose professional life as a teacher is orderly but whose migraines signify repression, "courts disaster" by seeking out Lydia, a goy who has had the most cruel, untender childhood imaginable. He likes her because she has suffered. The marriage (like the marriages of his sister, who twice marries "no-good" boys) ends with his running off to Italy with his stepdaughter and with Lydia's suicide, and is as disastrous (in soap-opera style) as anyone in search of punishment could desire.

The true story of Tarnopol works as a critique on these versions. His real brother and sister are highly successful, one as a rich West Coast society hostess, the other as a bighearted New York radical. In his fictions Tarnopol had wished on them versions of the mess he creates for himself by trying to match "I want' with 'I am horrified.' Tarnopol wants to be 'good,' to be 'humanish: manly, a man,' like Bellow's hero trying to be a marvellous Herzog, a Herzog who, perhaps clumsily, tried to live out marvellous qualities vaguely comprehended." In fact, he is childish, hysterical, narcissistic, at the mercy of desire, fear and loathing. His marriage to Maureen, who defiles all the childhood taboos and destroys the order of his life, plunges him into an "unmanning frenzy." Later heroes may be less frantic than Portnoy or Tarnonl, but they are still guilty about their parents, still divided between wanting to be good, even "marvellous," and plunging into the messy world of unprotected sensations. In *The Professor of Desire* (1977), the spilt is imaged by Kepesh's relationship with the libidinous Baumgarten: "I am Baumgarten... caged in the kennels... while he is a Kepesh, oh, what a Kepesh! with his mouth frothing and his tongue lolling, leash slipped and running wild." In *The Ghost Writer* (1979), the aspiring Jewish writer, looking for a literary father to replace the Newark foot doctor, chooses between the "good," highminded, conscientious, reclusive Lonoff and the "bad," sensual, jet-setting, self-publicizing Abranavel. In *Zuckerman Unbound* (1981), the successful unhappy Nathan, now the notorious author of Carnovsky, is called "bastard" by his dying father. It is only in *The Breast* (1972, revised 1980) that the Jewish parents help their son towards fully adult selfhood. Kepesh, trying to come to terms with himself as a large mammary gland, realizes that his father's nobility and his late mother's determination have helped his acceptance of his fate. But this Jewish hero is allowed to exist only in an absurd, surrealist context: he is the hero of a joke.

[Selected from Hermione Lee. *Philip Roth*. London: Methuen, 1982.]

7. Langston Hughes

7.1 Presentation Topics

(1) Harlem Renaissance.

(2) The spokesman of the black race and a democratic poet.

(3) Hughes' influence on African American literature.

7.2 Selected Reading

Ⅰ. Central issue of concern

Langston Hughes' literary creation based on national culture and racial pride.

Ⅱ. Text

The Negro Speaks of Rivers

I've known rivers:
I've known rivers ancient as the world and older than the
　　flow of human blood in human veins.

My soul has grown deep like the rivers.

I bathed in the Euphrates when dawns were young.
I built my hut near the Congo and it lulled me to sleep.
I looked upon the Nile and raised the pyramids above it.
I heard the singing of the Mississippi when Abe Lincoln
　　went down to New Orleans, and I've seen its muddy
　　bosom turn all golden in the sunset.

I've known rivers:
Ancient, dusky rivers.

My soul has grown up deep like the rivers.

The Weary Blues

Droning a drowsy syncopated tune,

Rocking back and forth to a mellow croon,
    I heard a Negro play.
Down on Lenox Avenue the other night
By the pale dull pallor of an old gas light
    He did a lazy sway...
    He did a lazy sway...
To the tune o' those Weary Blues.
With his ebony hands on each ivory key
He made that poor piano moan with melody.
    O Blues!
Swaying to and fro on his rickety stool
He played that sad raggy tune like a musical fool.
    Sweet Blues!
Coming from a black man's soul.
    O Blues!
In a deep song voice with a melancholy tone
I heard that Negro sing, that old piano moan—
    "Ain't got nobody in all this world,
    Ain't got nobody but ma self.
    I's gwine to quit ma frownin'
    And put ma troubles on the shelf."

    Thump, thump, thump, went his foot on the floor.
He played a few chords then he sang some more—
    "I got the Weary Blues
    And I can't be satisfied.
    Got the Weary Blues
    And can't be satisfied—
    I ain't happy no mo'
    And I wish that I had died."
And far into the night he crooned that tune.
The stars went out and so did the moon.
The singer stopped playing and went to bed

While the Weary Blues echoed through his head.
He slept like a rock or a man that's dead.

A Dream Deferred

What happens to a dream deferred?
Does it dry up
like a raisin in the sun?
Or fester like a sore—
And then run?
Does it stink like rotten meat?
Or crust and sugar over—
like a syrupy sweet?
Maybe it just sags
like a heavy load.

Or does it explode?

[Selected from Langston Hughes. *The Complete Poems of Langston Hughes*. New York: Vintage, 1994.]

Ⅲ. Questions for discussion

(1) Make a comparison between "The Negro Speaks of Rivers" and Walt Whitman's poems. Are there any similarities?

(2) What effect is achieved by juxtaposing the various rivers in the first poem? What kind of tone does the speaker use in his speaking of the rivers?

(3) How is the blues dealt with in the second poem?

(4) Is the speaker in the second poem an outsider for the blues? What is his attitude towards the blues?

(5) What kind of life or inner world of the blues player is revealed in the second poem?

(6) Why is the last line italicized while the previous lines are not?

(7) A striking contrast is achieved between the last line and the others. What meaning does this contrast convey?

7.3. Assigned Reading

The Negro Artist and the Racial Mountain

Langston Hughes

One of the most promising of the young Negro poets said to me once, "I want to be a poet—not a Negro poet," meaning, I believe, "I want to write like a white poet"; meaning subconsciously, "I would like to be a white poet"; meaning behind that, "I would like to be white." And I was sorry the young man said that, for no great poet has ever been afraid of being himself. And I doubted then that, with his desire to run away spiritually from his race, this boy would ever be a great poet. But this is the mountain standing in the way of any true Negro art in America—this urge within the race toward whiteness, the desire to pour racial individuality into the mold of American standardization, and to be as little Negro and as much American as possible.

But let us look at the immediate background of this young poet. His family is of what I suppose one would call the Negro middle-class: people who are by no means rich yet never uncomfortable nor hungry—smug, contented, respectable folk, members of the Baptist church. The father goes to work every morning. He is a chief steward at a large white club. The mother sometimes does fancy sewing or supervises parties for the rich families of the town. The children go to a mixed school. In the home they read white papers and magazines. And the mother often says "Don't be like niggers" when the children are bad. A frequent phrase from the father is, "Look how well a white man does things." And so the word white comes to be unconsciously a symbol of all virtues. It holds for the children beauty, morality, and money. The whisper of "I want to be white" runs silently through their minds. This young poet's home is, I believe, a fairly typical home of the colored middle-class. One sees immediately how difficult it would be for an artist born in such a home to interest himself in interpreting the beauty of his own people. He is never taught to see that beauty. He is taught rather not to see it, or if he does, to be ashamed of it when it is not according to Caucasian patterns.

For racial culture the home of a self-styled "high-class" Negro has nothing better to offer. Instead there will perhaps be more aping of things white than in a less cultured or less wealthy home. The father is perhaps a doctor, lawyer, landowner, or politician. The mother may be a social worker, or a teacher, or she may do nothing and have a maid. Father is often dark but he has usually married the lightest woman he could find. The family attend a fashionable church where few really colored faces are to be found. And they themselves draw a color line. In the North they go to white theaters and white movies. And in the South they have at least two cars and house "like white folks." Nordic manners, Nordic faces, Nordic hair, Nordic art (if any), and an Episcopal heaven. A very high mountain indeed for the would-be racial artist to climb in order to discover himself and his people.

But then there are the low-down folks, the so-called common element, and they are the majority—may the Lord be praised! The people who have their hip of gin on Saturday nights and are not too important to themselves or the community, or too well fed, or too learned to watch the lazy world go round. They live on Seventh Street in Washington or State Street in Chicago and they do not particularly care whether they are like white folks or anybody else. Their joy runs, "Bang!" into ecstasy. Their religion soars to a shout. Work maybe a little today, rest a little tomorrow. Play awhile. Sing awhile. O, let's dance! These common people are not afraid of spirituals, as for a long time their more intellectual brethren were, and jazz is their child. They furnish a wealth of colorful, distinctive material for any artist because they still hold their own individuality in the face of American standardizations. And perhaps these common people will give to the world its truly great Negro artist, the one who is not afraid to be himself. Whereas the better-class Negro would tell the artist what to do, the people at least let him alone when he does appear. And they are not ashamed of him—if they know he exists at all. And they accept what beauty is their own without question.

Certainly there is, for the American Negro artist who can escape the restrictions the more advanced among his own group would put upon him, a great field of unused material ready for his art. Without going outside his race, and even among the better classes with their "white" culture and conscious American manners, but still Negro enough to be different, there is sufficient matter to furnish a black artist with a lifetime of creative work. And when he chooses to touch on the relations between Negroes and whites in this country, with their innumerable overtones and undertones surely, and especially for literature and the drama, there is an inexhaustible supply of themes at hand. To these the Negro artist can give his racial individuality, his heritage of rhythm and warmth, and his incongruous humor that so often, as in the Blues, becomes ironic laughter mixed with tears. But let us look again at the mountain.

A prominent Negro clubwoman in Philadelphia paid eleven dollars to hear Raquel Meller sing Andalusian popular songs. But she told me a few weeks before she would not think of going to hear "that woman," Clara Smith, a great black artist, sing Negro folksongs. And many an upper-class Negro church, even now, would not dream of employing a spiritual in its services. The drab melodies in white folks' hymnbooks are much to be preferred. "We want to worship the Lord correctly and quietly. We don't believe in 'shouting.' Let's be dull like the Nordics," they say, in effect.

The road for the serious black artist, then, who would produce a racial art is most certainly rocky and the mountain is high. Until recently he received almost no encouragement for his work from either white or colored people. The fine novels of Chesnutt's go out of print with neither race noticing their passing. The quaint charm and humor of Dunbar's dialect verse brought to him, in his day, largely the same kind of encouragement one would give a sideshow freak (A colored man writing poetry! How odd!) or a clown (How amusing!).

The present vogue in things Negro, although it may do as much harm as good for the budding artist, has at least done this: it has brought him forcibly to the attention of his own people among whom for so long, unless the other race had noticed him beforehand, he was a prophet with little honor.

The Negro artist works against an undertow of sharp criticism and misunderstanding from his own group and unintentional bribes from the whites. "Oh, be respectable, write about nice people, show how good we are," say the Negroes. "Be stereotyped, don't go too far, don't shatter our illusions about you, don't amuse us too seriously. We will pay you," say the whites. Both would have told Jean Toomer not to write *Cane*. The colored people did not praise it. The white people did not buy it. Most of the colored people who did read *Cane* hate it. They are afraid of it. Although the critics gave it good reviews the public remained indifferent. Yet (excepting the work of Du Bois) *Cane* contains the finest prose written by a Negro in America. And like the singing of Robeson, it is truly racial.

But in spite of the Nordicized Negro intelligentsia and the desires of some white editors we have an honest American Negro literature already with us. Now I await the rise of the Negro theater. Our folk music, having achieved world-wide fame, offers itself to the genius of the great individual American composer who is to come. And within the next decade I expect to see the work of a growing school of colored artists who paint and model the beauty of dark faces and create with new technique the expressions of their own soul-world. And the Negro dancers who will dance like flame and the singers who will continue to carry our songs to all who listen—they will be with us in even greater numbers tomorrow.

Most of my own poems are racial in theme and treatment, derived from the life I know. In many of them I try to grasp and hold some of the meanings and rhythms of jazz. I am as sincere as I know how to be in these poems and yet after every reading I answer questions like these from my own people: Do you think Negroes should always write about Negroes? I wish you wouldn't read some of your poems to white folks. How do you find anything interesting in a place like a cabaret? Why do you write about black people? You aren't black. What makes you do so many jazz poems?

But jazz to me is one of the inherent expressions of Negro life in America; the eternal tom-tom beating in the Negro soul—the tom-tom of revolt against weariness in a white world, a world of subway trains, and work, work, work; the tom-tom of joy and laughter, and pain swallowed in a smile. Yet the Philadelphia clubwoman is ashamed to say that her race created it and she does not like me to write about it, The old subconscious "white is best" runs through her mind. Years of study under white teachers, a lifetime of white books, pictures, and papers, and white manners, morals, and Puritan standards made her dislike the spirituals. And now she turns up her nose at jazz and all its manifestations—likewise almost everything else distinctly racial. She doesn't care for the Winold Reiss' portraits of Negroes because they are "too Negro." She does not want a true picture of herself from anybody. She wants the artist to flatter her, to make the white world believe that all negroes are as smug and as near white in soul as she wants to be. But, to my mind, it is the duty of the younger Negro artist, if he accepts any duties at all from outsiders, to change through the force of his art that old whispering "I want to be white," hidden in the aspirations of his people, to "Why should I want to be white? I am a Negro—and beautiful?"

So I am ashamed for the black poet who says, "I want to be a poet, not a Negro poet," as though his own racial world were not as interesting as any other world. I am ashamed, too, for the colored artist who runs from the painting of Negro faces to the painting of sunsets after the manner of the academicians because he fears the strange unwhiteness of his own features. An artist must be free to choose what he does, certainly, but he must also never be afraid to do what he must choose.

Let the blare of Negro jazz bands and the bellowing voice of Bessie Smith singing the Blues penetrate the closed ears of the colored near intellectuals until they listen and perhaps understand. Let Paul Robeson singing "Water Boy," and Rudolph Fisher writing about the streets of Harlem, and Jean Toomer holding the heart of Georgia in his hands, and Aaron Douglas' drawing strange black fantasies cause the smug Negro middle-class to turn from their white, respectable, ordinary books and papers to catch a glimmer of their own beauty. We younger Negro artists who create now intend to express our individual dark-skinned selves without fear or shame. If white people are pleased we are glad. If they are not, it doesn't matter. We know we are beautiful. And ugly too. The tom-tom cries and the tom-tom laughs. If colored people are pleased we are glad. If they are not, their displeasure doesn't matter either. We build our temples for tomorrow, strong as we know how, and we stand on top of the mountain, free within ourselves.

[Selected from Christopher De Santis, (ed.). *The Collected Works of Langston Hughes* (Vol. 9). Columbia and London: Missouri University Press, 2002.]

8. Gwendolyn Brooks

8.1 Presentation Topics

(1) Gwendolyn Brooks as the first African American author to win the Pulitzer Prize for Poetry.

(2) Her consistant commitment to racial identity and equality.

8.2 Selected Reading

Ⅰ. Central issue of concern

Gwendolyn Brooks' mastery of poetic techniques of both western modernism and black culture.

Ⅱ. Text

The Bean Eaters

They eat beans mostly, this old yellow pair.
Dinner is a casual affair.
Plain chipware on a plain and creaking wood,
Tin flatware.
Two who are Mostly Good.
Two who have lived their day,
But keep on putting on their clothes
And putting things away.
And remembering...
Remembering, with twinklings and twinges,
As they lean over the beans in their rented back room that
is full of beads and receipts and dolls and cloths,
tobacco crumbs, vases and fringes.

Kitchenette Building

We are things of dry hours and the involuntary plan,
Grayed in, and gray. "Dream" mate, a giddy sound, not strong
Like "rent," "feeding a wife," "satisfying a man."

But could a dream sent up through onion fumes
Its white and violet, fight with fried potatoes
And yesterday's garbage ripening in the hall,
Flutter, or sing an aria down these rooms,

Even if we were willing to let it in,

Had time to warm it, keep it very clean,
Anticipate a message, let it begin?

We wonder. But not well! Not for a minute!
Since Number Five is out of the bathroom now,
We think of lukewarm water, hope to get in it.

[Selected from Gwendolyn Brooks. *Selected Poems*. New York: Harper Perennial Mordern Classic, 1994.]

Ⅲ. Questions for discussion

(1) Repetition of words and sounds are frequently used in the prose-like, ordinary speech of the first poem. What function does it perform?

(2) In "Kitchenette Building," how does the "Dream" conflict with reality? What is their attitude toward their dream or the reality?

(3) What do the words like "things" in the 1st line and "Number Five" in the 12th line suggest about black women's life?

(4) Brooks often suggests using "ordinary speech" and "tell a little less" to make "every word work" in a poem. Do you think she followed these principles in these two poems?

8.3 Assigned Reading

Brooks' Life and Career

Kenny Jackson Williams

Although she was born on 7 June 1917 in Topeka, Kansas—the first child of David and Keziah Brooks—Gwendolyn Brooks is "a Chicagoan." The family moved to Chicago shortly after her birth, and despite her extensive travels and periods in some of the major universities of the country, she has remained associated with the city's South Side. What her strong family unit lacked in material wealth was made bearable by the wealth of human capital that resulted from warm interpersonal relationships. When she writes about families that—despite their daily adversities—are not dysfunctional, Gwendolyn Brooks writes from an intimate knowledge reinforced by her own life. [...]

Her profound interest in poetry informed much of her early life. "Eventide," her first poem, was published in *American Childhood Magazine* in 1930. A few years later she met James Weldon Johnson and Langston Hughes, who urged her to read modern poetry—especially the work of Ezra Pound, T. S. Eliot, and E. E. Cummings—and who emphasized the need to write as much and as frequently as she possibly could. By 1934 Brooks had become an adjunct member of the staff of the *Chicago Defender* and had published almost one hundred of her poems in a weekly poetry column.

In 1938 she married Henry Blakely and moved to a kitchenette apartment on Chicago's South Side. Between the birth of her first child, Henry, Jr., in 1940 and the birth of Nora in 1951, she became associated with the group of writers involved in Harriet Monroe's still-extant *Poetry: A Magazine of Verse*. From this group she received further encouragement, and by 1943 she had won the Midwestern Writers Conference Poetry Award.

In 1945 her first book of poetry, *A Street in Bronzeville* (published by Harper and Row), brought her instant critical acclaim. She was selected one of *Mademoiselle* magazine's "Ten Young Women of the Year," she won her first Guggenheim Fellowship, and she became a fellow of the American Academy of Arts and Letters. Her second book of poems, *Annie Allen* (1949), won *Poetry* magazine's Eunice Tietjens Prize. In 1950 Gwendolyn Brooks became the first African American to win a Pulitzer Prize. From that time to the present, she has seen the recipient of a number of awards, fellowships, and honorary degrees usually designated as Doctor of Humane Letters.

President John Kennedy invited her to read at a Library of Congress poetry festival in 1962. In 1985 she was appointed poetry consultant to the Library of Congress. Just as receiving a Pulitzer Prize for Poetry marked a milestone in her career, so also did her selection by the National Endowment for the Humanities as the 1994 Jefferson Lecturer, the highest award in the humanities given by the federal government.

Her first teaching job was a poetry workshop at Columbia College (Chicago) in 1963. She went on to teach creative writing at a number of institutions including Northeastern Illinois University, Elmhurst College, Columbia University, Clay College of New York, and the University of Wisconsin.

A turning point in her career came in 1967 when she attended the Fisk

University Second Black Writers' Conference and decided to become more involved in the Black Arts Movement. She became one of the most visible articulators of "the black aesthetic." Her "awakening" led to a shift away from a major publishing house to smaller black ones. While some critics found an angrier tone in her work, elements of protest had always been present in her writings and her awareness of social issues did not result in diatribes at the expense of her clear commitment to aesthetic principles. Consequently, becoming the leader of one phase of the Black Arts movement in Chicago did not drastically alter her poetry, but there were some subtle changes that become more noticeable when one examines her total canon to date.

The ambiguity of her role as a black poet can be illustrated by her participation in two events in Chicago. In 1967 Brooks, who wrote the commemorative ode for the "Chicago Picasso," attended the unveiling ceremony along with social and business dignitaries. The poem was well received even though such lines as "Art hurts. Art urges voyages ..." made some uncomfortable. Less than two weeks later there was the dedication of the mural known as "The Wall of Respect" at 43rd and Langley streets, in the heart of the black neighborhood. The social and business elites of Chicago were not present, but for this event Gwendolyn Brooks wrote "The Wall." In a measure these two poems illustrate the dichotomy of a divided city, but they also exemplify Brooks' ability both to bridge those divisions and to utilize nonstrident protest.

Gwendolyn Brooks has been a prolific writer. In addition to individual poems, essays, and reviews that have appeared in numerous publications, she has issued a number of books in rapid succession, including *Maud Martha* (1953), *Bronzeville Boys and Girls* (1956), and *In the Mecca* (1968). Her poetry moves from traditional forms including ballads, sonnets, variations of the Chaucerian and Spenserian stanzas as well as the rhythm of the blues to the most unrestricted free verse. In short, the popular forms of English poetry appear in her work; yet there is a strong sense of experimentation as she juxtaposes lyric, narrative, and dramatic poetic forms. In her lyrics there is an affirmation of life that rises above the stench of urban kitchenette buildings. In her narrative poetry the stories are simple but usually transcend the restrictions of place; in her dramatic poetry, the characters are often memorable not because of any heroism on their part but merely because they are trying to survive from day to day.

Brooks' poetry is marked by some unforgettable characters who are drawn from the underclass of the nation's black neighborhoods. Like many urban writers, Brooks has recorded the impact of city life. But unlike the most committed naturalists, she does not hold the city completely responsible for what happens to people. The city is simply an existing force with which people must cope.

While they are generally insignificant in the great urban universe, her characters gain importance—at least to themselves—in their tiny worlds, whether it be Annie Allen trying on a hat in a milliner's shop or DeWitt Williams "on his way to Lincoln Cemetery" or Satin-Legs Smith trying to decide what outlandish outfit to wear on Sundays. Just as there is not a strong naturalistic sense of victimization, neither are there great plans for an unpromised future nor is there some great divine spirit that will rescue them. Brooks is content to describe a moment in the lives of very ordinary people whose only goal is to exist from day to day and perhaps have a nice funeral when they die. Sometimes these ordinary people seem to have a control that is out of keeping with their own insignificance.

Although her poetic voice is objective, there is a strong sense that she—as an observer—is never far from her action. On one level, of course, Brooks is a protest poet; yet her protest evolves through suggestion rather than through a bludgeon. She sets forth the facts without embellishment or interpretation, but the simplicity of the facts makes it impossible for readers to come away unconvinced—despite whatever discomfort they may feel—whether she is writing about suburban ladies who go into the ghetto to give occasional aid or a black mother who has had an abortion.

Trying to determine clear lines of influence from the work of earlier writers to later ones is always a risky business; however, knowing some identifiable poetic traditions can aid in understanding the work of Gwendolyn Brooks. On one level there is the English metaphysical tradition perhaps best exemplified by John Donne. From 19th century American poetry one can detect elements of Walt Whitman, Emily Dickinson, and Paul Laurence Dunbar. From twentieth century American poetry there are many strains, most notably the compact style of T. S. Eliot, the frequent use of the lower-case for titles in the manner of E. E. Cummings, and the racial consciousness of the Harlem Renaissance, especially as found in the work of Countee Cullen and Langston Hughes; but, of perhaps greater importance, she seems to be a direct descendant of the urban commitment and attitude of the "Chicago School" of writing. For Brooks, setting goes beyond the Midwest with a focus on Chicago and concentrates on a small neglected comer of the city. Consequently, in the final analysis, she is not a carbon copy of any of the Chicago writers.

She was appointed poet laureate of Illinois in 1968 and has been perhaps more active than many laureates. She has done much to bring poetry to the people through accessibility and public readings. In fact, she is one of our most visible American poets. Not only is she extremely active in the poetry workshop movement, but her classes and contests for young people are attempts to help inner-city children see "the poetry" in their lives. She has taught audiences that poetry is not some formal activity closed to all but the most perceptive. Rather, it is an art form within the reach and understanding of everybody—including the lowliest among us.

[Selected from William Andrews, Frances Foster, Trudier Harris, (ed). *The Oxford Companion to African-American Literature*. New York: Oxford University Press, 1997.]

9. Amiri Baraka

9.1 Presentation Topics

(1) Amiri Baraka is the soul of the Black Arts Movement.

(2) Baraka is poet, playwright, essayist and social activist with a very radical and controversial political commitment.

9.2 Selected Reading

Ⅰ. Central issue of concern

Amiri Baraka's works characterized by the oral tradition and artistic experimentation based on national culture.

Ⅱ. Text

Preface to a Twenty Volume Suicide Note

Lately, I've become accustomed to the way

The ground opens up and envelopes me
Each time I go out to walk the dog.
Or the broad edged silly music the wind
Makes when I run for a bus...

Things have come to that.

And now, each night I count the stars.
And each night I get the same number.
And when they will not come to be counted,
I count the holes they leave.

Nobody sings anymore.

And then last night I tiptoed up
To my daughter's room and heard her
Talking to someone, and when I opened
The door, there was no one there...
Only she on her knees, peeking into

Her own clasped hands.

Black Art

Poems are bullshit unless they are
teeth or trees or lemons piled
on a step. Or black ladies dying
of men leaving nickel hearts
beating them down. Fuck poems
and they are useful, wd they shoot
come at you, love what you are,
breathe like wrestlers, or shudder
strangely after pissing. We want live
words of the hip world live flesh &

coursing blood. Hearts Brains
Souls splintering fire. We want poems
like fists beating niggers out of Jocks
or dagger poems in the slimy bellies
of the owner-jews. Black poems to
smear on girdlemamma mulatto bitches
whose brains are red jelly stuck
between 'lizabethtaylor's toes. Stinking
Whores! we want "poems that kill."
Assassin poems, Poems that shoot
guns. Poems that wrestle cops into alleys
and take their weapons leaving them dead
with tongues pulled out and sent to Ireland. Knockoff
poems for dope selling wops or slick halfwhite
politicians Airplane poems, rrrrrrrrrrrrrrr
rrrrrrrrrrrrrr... tuhtuhtuhtuhtuhtuhtuhtuhtuhtuh
...rrrrrrrrrrrrrrr... Setting fire and death to
whities ass. Look at the Liberal
Spokesman for the jews clutch his throat
& puke himself into eternity... rrrrrrrr
There's a negroleader pinned to
a bar stool in Sardi's eyeballs melting
in hot flame Another negroleader
on the steps of the white house one
kneeling between the sheriff's thighs
negotiating coolly for his people.
Aggh... stumbles across the room...
Put it on him, poem. Strip him naked
to the world! Another bad poem cracking
steel knuckles in a jewlady's mouth
Poem scream poison gas on beasts in green berets
Clean out the world for virtue and love,
Let there be no love poems written

until love can exist freely and
cleanly. Let Black people understand
that they are the lovers and the sons
of warriors and sons
of warriors Are poems & poets &
all the loveliness here in the world
We want a black poem. And a
Black World.
Let the world be a Black Poem
And Let All Black People Speak This Poem
Silently
or LOUD

[Selected from William M. Harris, (ed.). *The LeRoi Jones/ Amiri Baraka Reader*. New York: Thunder's Mouth Press, 1995.]

Ⅲ. Questions for discussion

(1) In the poem "Preface to a Twenty Volume Suicide Note," what does the title suggest? Does it receive response from the text of the poem itself?

(2) What do the last two stanzas of the first poem suggest by mentioning the daughter and her behavior?

(3) The poem "Black Art" is usually regarded as a manifesto of the "Black Arts Movement." What poetics does it convey?

(4) Does the language and the way the language is used in the second poem respond to the call for the Black Poem? How?

(5) What are the differences between the two poems? Try to give an explanation of this change in the social-cultural context and Baraka's change from a beat poet to a nationalist.

9.3 Assigned Reading

Historical Overview of The Black Arts Movement

Reginald Martin

A central problem in the paradigmatic development of art and literary "history" has always been whose ideas of art and literature will be empowered and, thus, whose ideas will be used to judge what is "good" or "bad" art. The question of who empowers and validates certain literary critical trends is beyond the scope of my inquiry here. But such battles are historically frequent in the sometimes purposely stagnated progression of art "theory." The problems that the progenitors of the Black Arts Movement faced were merely synecdochal of the many traditional and frequent battles in art and literary history fought to decide whose ideas will be censored and whose ideas will be validated and propagated. In other words, stipulative skirmishes have always been fought within the larger battleground of general censorship to decide whose ideas will be codified as a part of the taught canon of art history and criticism. [...] Those whose art triumphs over others' art know that the spoils of that war are certificates of deposit and cold hard cash, not whether one songwriter's love-making lyrics are more acceptable than another's, nor whether nude heterosexual images should preclude nude homosexual images.

The precursors to what is now called the Black Arts Movement (1962—1971) are many and interwoven. One could reasonably argue that there had been a call for a separate black letters in the American literary mainstream since Frederick Douglass' "What the Negro Wants" (1868). But the literary events that took place in the 1960s, influenced by social events from the 1950s and 1960s, overshadowed all work in black letters that had gone on before.

During this volatile period, LeRoi Jones (later Amiri Baraka) wrote in his essay "The Myth of a 'Negro Literature'" (1962) that "a Negro literature, to be a legitimate product of the Negro experience in America, must get at that experience in exactly the terms America has proposed for it in its most ruthless identity," and that the Negro, as an element of American culture, was "completely misunderstood by Americans." In discussing why, in his opinion, there was so little black literature of merit, Jones wrote,

> ... in most cases the Negroes who found themselves in a position to pursue some art, especially the art of literature, have been members of the Negro middle—class, a group that has always gone out of its way to cultivate any mediocrity, as long as that mediocrity was guaranteed to prove to America, and recently to the world at large, that they were not really who they were, ie., Negroes.

Further, Jones wrote that as long as the Negro writer was obsessed with being accepted, middle—class, he would never be able to "tell it like it is," and, thus, would always be a failure, because America made room only for white obfuscators, not black ones. It was from such thoughts by Jones and the thoughts of many like-minded theoreticians such as Hoyt Fuller, that the Black Arts Movement (BAM) took its origins.

In 1969, during his black nationalist period, Baraka laid concrete boundaries for a "nationalistic art." Baraka wrote in "Nationalism vs. Pimpart":

The Art is the National Spirit. That manifestation of it. Black Art must be the Nationalist's vision given more form and feeling, as a razor to cut away what is not central to National Liberation. To show that which is. As a humanistic expression it is itself raised. And these are the poles, out of which we create, to raise, or as raised.

In this difficult passage, Baraka was proposing (in typical 1960s rhetoric) specific and limited boundaries for acceptable art. Though a writer on all aspects of the BAM, Baraka's areas of greatest interest were the related arts of literatures and literary criticism, and it was, indeed, the debate on the content of black letters that would fuel the heat of the BAM from 1969 to its last official flickerings in 1974, when Baraka wrote his amazing essay "Why I Changed My Ideology." After Baraka formally announced that he was a socialist, no longer a black nationalist, his guidelines for "valid" black writing changed, but his new requirements, with slightly different emphases (liberation of an classes, races, genders) and a slightly different First Cause (Monopoly Capitalism), were as rigid as his prior requirements. And at this time, Baraka was powerful enough to influence others to codify his vision of acceptable art.

Baraka saw certain black writers as disrupting the essential and beautiful Black Arts Movement of the 1960s and early 1970s. Baraka called these writers "capitulationists," and said their movement was simultaneous with and counter to the Black Arts Movement. Baraka felt that the simultaneity was no accident. In his long essay "Afro-American Literature and the Class Struggle" in *Black American Literature Forum* (1980), Baraka, for the first time, made several strong, personal attacks on Ishmael Reed, the fiction writer and poet, and also attacked several black female writers whom he felt fit into the capitulationist mold. And, again, Baraka reiterated that he believes that the groundbreakers in the Black Arts Movement (among them, the new black aesthetic literary wing, including Addison Gayle, Houston Baker, and Clarence Major) were doing something that was new, needed, useful, and black, and those who did not want to see such a flourishing of black expression were "appointed" to the scene to damage the movement.

Naming Reed and Calvin Hernton as "conservatives," Baraka wrote:

Yes, the tide was so strong that even some of the "conservatives" wrote work that took the people's side. The metaphysical slide (sic) of the BAM even allowed Reed to adopt a rebellious tone with his "Black power poem" and "sermonette" in *catechism of d neoamerican hoodoo church*, 1970, in which he saw the struggle of Blacks against national oppression as a struggle between two churches, e. g.: "may the best church win. shake hands now and come/out-conjuring." But even during the heat and heart of the BAM, Reed would call that very upsurge and the BAM "a goon squad aesthetic" and say that the revolutionary writers were "fascists" or that the taking up of African culture by Black artists indicated such artists were "tribalists."

Much of the labeling of Reed as a conservative and a "house nigger" began with the publication of *The Last Days of Louisiana Red*, in which a group of characters Reed labeled as "moochers" loiter around Ed Yellings, a small black business owner who is making active efforts to earn a living and who, through practicing voodoo, finds a cure for cancer. Critics interpreted "the moochers" as being stipulative of some of the BAM group. Supposedly, *The Last Days of Louisiana Red* contains autocratic figures who do little more than emphasize Reed's definition of moochers, and who continually reenact negative, black stereotypes. Ed Yellings, the industrious black, is killed by black moocher conspirators. Does this mean blacks will turn against what Reed believes to be the good in their own communities? Ed Yellings is a business and property owner. Baraka wrote,

Ishmael Reed and Stanley Crouch both make the same kind of rah-rah speeches for the Black middle—class. Reed, in fact, says that those of us who uphold Black working people are backwards .... Focus on the middle—class, the property owners and music teachers, not the black masses (Ralph) Ellison tells us. This is the *Roots* crowd giving us a history of the BLM (Black Liberation Movement) as a rags-to-riches, Horatio Alger tale in brown face, going off into the sunset and straight for Carter's cabinet or the National Book Award ...

Baraka also set up a dichotomy for a "white arts movement" and a "black arts movement," but while defining the two—one would assume toward the end of endorsing one or the other—Baraka shows only the failings of each and discusses his points of divergence from the "Black Aesthetic Crowd."

In Baraka's dichotomy, the "white aesthetic is bourgeois art—like the 'national interests' of the U. S. at this late date when the U. S. is an imperialistic superpower." Immediately following this passage, Baraka seemed to defend the black aesthetic group over Ellison's negative criticism of them. Baraka wrote that Ellison said of the black aesthetic crowd that they "buy the idea of total cultural separation between blacks and whites, suggesting that we've been left out of the mainstream. But when we examine American music and literature in terms of its themes, symbolism, rhythms, tonalities, idioms, and images it is obvious that those rejected 'Negroes' have been a vital part of the mainstream and were from the beginning." Baraka responded, "We know we have been exploited, Mr. Ralph, sir; what we's arguing about is that we's been exploited! To use us is the term of stay in this joint ..." Baraka's point is that it makes no difference if the corrupt personage is black; the issue is still corruption, and it is a double insult to the oppressed when that corrupt person turns out to be black. But it is at that point that Baraka separated himself from others in the new black aesthetic movement:

> Where I differ with the bourgeois nationalists who are identified with the "Black Aesthetic" is illuminated by a statement of Addison Gayle's: "An aesthetic based upon economic and class determinism is one which has minimal value for Black people. For Black writers and critics the starting point must be the proposition that the history of Black people in America is the history of the struggle against racism." But what is the basis for racism; ie., exploitation because of one's physical characteristics? Does it drop out of the sky?... Black people suffer from national oppression: We are an oppressed nation, a nation oppressed by U. S. imperialism. Racism is an even more demonic aspect of this national oppression, since the oppressed nationality is identifiable anywhere as that regardless of class.

Baraka reminded the reader that his disagreement with the new black aesthetic elite was not to say that there was no such thing as a black aesthetic, but that his conception of a black aesthetic manifested itself in his definition of it differently than it did for others. For him it was "a nation within a nation" that was brought about by the "big bourgeoisie on Wall Street, who after the Civil War completely dominated U. S. politics and economics, controlled the ex-planters, and turned them into their compradors." Further, black aesthetic ideas had to be subsumed under the larger category of the Black Arts Movement so that its ideas would be in concert with those black ideas from drama, dance, and graphic arts.

Baraka claimed that several women writers, among them Michelle Wallace and Ntozake Shange, like Reed, had their own "Hollywood" aesthetic, one of "capitulation" and "garbage." Toward the end of his article, Baraka said that the "main line" of his argument bad been that "class struggle is as much a part of the arts as it is any place else." His pleas and support were reserved for those artists who were "struggle oriented," those who were trying to "get even clearer on the meaning of class stand, attitude, audience, and study, and their relationship to our work."

And, thus, Baraka's argument is epanaleptic, as it turns back for support upon the same core of arguments of the other black aestheticians with whom he has said he is in disagreement; those arguments form a complete circle with Baraka's stated premise that black literature, black art must do something materially positive to help black people. Art must be socially functional.

The heat and heart really left the BAM after Baraka changed from black nationalist to Leninist/Socialist (1974) and after the death of Hoyt Fuller (1971). Baraka was by far the strongest voice in the movement, and when he changed his ideas and said that before he had been absolutely wrong about his views on black art and that now his Leninist/Marxist vision was absolutely correct, many of his adherents lost faith. The basic tenets of the movement included the ideas that art by black Americans could never be accepted by white Americans, and separate criteria needed to be developed by black artists to appraise properly the talent of black artists. Also, all art should be toward a political/humanistic end that would elevate all people—but especially black people—to a higher consciousness and a better life. In a retrospective on this artist/censor exchange, W. Lawrence Hogue wrote in "Literary Production: A Silence in Afro-American Critical Practice" from his book *Discourse and the Other: The Production of the Afro-American Literary Text* (1986) that the writers of the BAM:

> In using literature to further their political ends ... understand the political function of literature. Their strategy is to promote those Afro-American texts that present an aesthetic theory of literature. But that strategy is silent completely on how established literary institutions and apparatuses, throughout American literary history, have affected the production of Afro-American literature ... Of course, such a discussion would cause these black aestheticians to confront openly the ideological nature and function, and therefore the constraints and exclusions, of their own cultural nationalist critical practices.

Thus, at least in theoretical discussion, an expansive, stylistically, thematically, and racially absorptive and syncretic "aesthetic" would put itself arguably above what Hogue calls the "nationalistic criteria" of the BAM regimen. In theory, a racially syncretic aesthetic would even absorb any facets of the BAM platform it could find useful, transform them, an produce new "discursive formations" (Foucault) that helped to explain itself or explain any kind of art text it chose. It is partly the syncretic idea that the proponents of the BAM fought against. For them, the only way to artistic purity was through separation from the mainstream.

Most recently, Baraka has reassessed Leninist/Marxist theory as an applicable filter for African-American literature. He now finds that, while perhaps a Leninist/Marxist grid is not the best way to assess and form the black arts, he still feels that at the root of any authentic black art endeavor must be the love of black people and the love of self-affirmation.

[Selected from Cathy N. Davidson, Linda Wagner Martin, et al, (ed.). *The Oxford Companion to Women's Writing in the United States*. New York: Oxford University Press, 1995.]

10. Rita Dove

10.1 Presentation Topics

(1) Rita Dove as African-American woman poet laureate of the United States.

(2) Rita Dove as a "cultural mulatto."

(3) Artistic features of Rita Dove's poetry.

10.2 Selected Reading

Ⅰ. Central issue of concern

Dove's negotiations of white and black cultural affiliation, art coalesce and the new trend of African-American poetry represented by Dove.

Ⅱ. Text

Upon Meeting Don L. Lee, In a Dream

He comes toward me with lashless eyes,
Always moving in the yellow half-shadows.

From his mouth I know he has never made love
To thin white boys in toilet stalls...

Among the trees, the black trees,
Women in robes stand, watching. They begin
To chant, stamping their feet in wooden cadences
As they stretch their beaded arms to him;

Moments slip by like worms.
"Seven years ago..." he begins; but
I cut him off: "Those years are gone—
What is there now?" He starts to cry; his eyeballs

Burst into flame. I can see caviar
Imbedded like buckshot between his teeth.
His hair falls out in clumps of burned-out wire.
The music grows like branches in the wind.

I lie down, chuckling as the grass curls around me.
He can only stand, fists clenched, and weep
Tears of iodine, while the singers float away,
Rustling on brown paper wings.

[Selected from Rita Dove. *Selected Poems by Rita Dove*. New York: Random House, Inc., 1993.]

Geometry

I prove a theorem and the house expands:
the windows jerk free to hover near the ceiling,
the ceiling floats away with a sigh.

As the walls clear themselves of everything
but transparency, the scent of carnations
leaves with them. I am out in the open

and above the windows have hinged into butterflies,

sunlight glinting where they've intersected.
They are going to some point true and unproven.

[Selected from Rita Dove. *Selected Poems by Rita Dove*. New York: Random House, Inc. ,1993.]

The Island Women of Paris

Skim from curb to curb like regatta.
from Pont Neuf to the Qual de la Rappe
in cool negotiation with traffic,
each a country to herself
transposed to this city
by a fluke called "imperial courtesy."

The island women glide past held aloft
by a wire running straight to heaven.
Who can ignore their ornamental bearing.
turbans haughty as parrots,
or deft braids carved into airy cages
transfixed on their manifest brows?

The island women move through parts
as if they had just finished inventing
their destinations. It's better
not to get in their way. And better
not look an island woman in the eye—
unless you like feeling unnecessary.

[Selected from Rita Dove. *Grace Notes*. New York: W. W. Norton & Company, Inc. ,1989.]

Rhumba

yo wengo aqui	I come here
para cantar	to sing
la rumba	the rumba
de mi adoración	of my adoration

Wait.

Here comes

At his touch

the music:

(just under the tricep)

lean back, look at me—

lock your knees,

the straighter your legs

look, straight up

the easier to fall,

into him, his hand stroking

to descend

your cheek...

lightly.

Don't close your eyes.

Don't bend your knees.

Let the body lift you

Sigh upwards—trust me!

back on your feet.

Wait. Now

A touch again:

dip down

this time, twist

but spread your arms;

in the knees,

give me some tone

but soft, follow (soft)

(more tone)

the reach, that last yearning

& connect...

to his left wrist.

Where's the audience?

Step forward.

Find them.

Rondé hook-turn

Let them see your face;

& reach again,

now look for the stars,

reach, reach then

yes, keep

snap back—

your elbow straight!

back to him,

Here I am, &

always back to him...

here's your basic walk:

Ah, hips.

Enjoy it.

Quick-&-quick-

Hear the music? Enjoy it.

& slow...

Remember,

snake the right arm up,

after every turn

rock back &

find me &

dive, a swan,

shape,

head in the clouds

shoulders down—

then drop left,

keep going,

he'll catch you,

I've got you—

(good) to a right foot

quick quick now

slow:

relax.

...

[Selected from Rita Dove. *American Smooth*. New York: W. W. Norton & Company, Inc., 2004.]

Ⅲ. Questions for discussion

(1) Don L. Lee is one of the leading figures in Black Arts Movement, while in Dove's "Upon Meeting Don L. Lee," he is an aggressive, intimidating and funny figure. So what do you think of Dove's depiction of Don L. Lee? And from this depiction can you learn Dove's attitude towards Black Arts Movement?

(2) Dove's refusal of accepting Don L. Lee as a poetic black father constitute a swerve in the Bloomian sense of anxiety about influence. Why do Dove and her generation of African-American poets have this anxiety? And what new trend of African-American poetry do they create and represent?

(3) What does geometry in "Geometry" symbolize in this poem? What are the functions of the images in shaping Dove's cultural space?

(4) In "The Island Women of Paris," the island women wandering in Paris form a strong contrast with this cosmopolitan city. What are the functions of this contrast in terms of postcolonial space theory?

(5) Emily Nussbaum once commented, "For Dove, dance is an implicit parallel to poetry." How do you understand this comment? Take "Rhumba" as an example.

(6) According to Malin Pereira, what is Dove's position as a cultural mulatto? And what does "negotiating blackness" mean?

10.3 Assigned Reading

Negotiating Blackness:

Dove and the African American Poetic Tradition

Malin Pereira

African American poetry has exhibited the tension between Afro-Modernism and black nationalism, also seen as mainstream integrationism versus black separatism, since the mid-1940s. Ross Posnock would explain these poles in the context of the ongoing struggle between cosmopolitanism and racial purism within the tradition. Following the modernist, craft-focused poems of the early Gwendolyn Brooks, Robert Hayden, and Melvin B. Tolson after World War Ⅱ and continuing into the 1960s, black arts movement poets such as Amiri Baraka (formerly LeRoi Jones), Haki Madhibuti (formerly Don L. Lee), Maulana Karenga, Etheridge Knight, Nikki Giovanni, and Sonia Sanchez rejected the values of literary formalism—the use of European-derived forms and techniques—in favor of an aesthetic centered on black culture and self-empowerment.

During the 1950s and 1960s white critics often read the formalism and modernist experimentation of Afro-Modernists as their becoming "universal," whereas black audiences—especially during the black arts movement—sometimes read such experimentation as a capitulation to the master's aesthetics. And white critics often perceived the revolutionary thrust of much black arts movement poetry, along with its emphasis on specifically African and African American cultural sources for content, as more political than poetic. Black audiences usually perceived it as engaging in black cultural pride and celebrating specifically black aesthetic forms and techniques. The two movements—Afro-Modernist and black arts—set the terms of the conversation for 1970s and 1980s' black poets who owed debts to the insights of each yet often tended to affiliate more with one than the other. Critics of Dove's poetry have sometimes oscillated between these poles of universalism and nationalism in their appraisals.

Dove's awareness of the points of conflict is conveyed in several of her early writings, including a poem about the black arts movement, "Upon Meeting Don L. Lee, in a Dream." Her 1980s' literary criticism on predecessors in the tradition also relays her anxieties about being perceived as a cultural mulatto and in the figures of Melvin B. Tolson and Gwendolyn Brooks establishes a cosmopolitan literary genealogy for her work. Dove's critical genealogy represses Amiri Baraka as a black literary father, although her early short story "The Spray Paint King," read as a *künstlerroman*, scripts a thematic place for his political legacy in the family romance of the cultural mulatto.

A feeling of navigating between Scylla and Charybdis may explain why so little critical attention had been paid Dove's wide array of work until the mid-1990s, especially attention to the relationship between her poetry and her African American identity. Early criticism on Dove was established in articles by Helen Vendler, Arnold Rampersad, and Ekaterini Georgoudaki, who address how her poetry might reflect, express, or deny her African American personal or literary heritage. In the late 1990s, essays by Peter Erickson and Susan Van Dyne attempted to account for Dove's handling of race.

Vendler argues in a 1994 essay in the *Times Literary Supplement*, unfortunately entitled "Blackness and Beyond Blackness," that a black writer "composes both with and against racial identity." Despite Vendler's enormous powers as a poetry critic, her attempt to account for blackness in Dove's poetry reprises the false universalizing many black writers fought throughout the 20th century, the same moving "beyond" blackness against which Langston Hughes argued in "The Negro Artist and the Racial Mountain" and the same misreadings to which craft-oriented modernists such as early Brooks, Tolson, and Hayden were subjected. Focusing her praise on *Thomas and Beulah*, Vendler claims "it represents Dove's re-thinking of the lyric poet's relationship to the history of blackness." Vendler asserts, Dove makes an important discovery: "Blackness need not be one's central subject, but equally need not be omitted."

In all of these statements Vendler seems to think that there is some discrete area in a black writer's psyche that is exclusively black; beyond that is a vast territory of neutral topics, perceptions, and reactions ripe for poetic plucking. She applauds going into that "beyond" in "color-neutral" poems. Although Vendler probably did not intend for her argument to convey such segregated psychic geography, her either-or formulation fails to recognize that one can be black and have a wide array of subject matter, ideas, and emotions, which, although they are not "marked" black (especially to a white observer), reflect one's core identity and experiences as a black person. [...]

Arnold Rampersad, in an essay modestly entitled "The Poems of Rita Dove" (1986), does not try to move Dove beyond her blackness at all but rather places her squarely within the African American poetic tradition while acknowledging her primary affiliation with the Afro-Modernists. Rampersad grounds Dove's work in the black arts movement of the 1960s and 1970s "as a point of radical departure for her in the development of her own aesthetic." Of her aesthetic oppositioning her notes:

> In many ways, (Dove's) poems are exactly the opposite of those that have come to be quintessentially black verse in recent years. Instead of looseness of structure, one finds in her poems remarkably tight control; instead of reliance on reckless inspiration, one recognizes discipline and practice, and long, taxing hours in competitive university poetry workshops and in her study; instead of a range of reference limited to personal confession, one finds personal reference disciplined by a measuring of distance and a prizing of objectivity; instead of an obsession with the theme of race, one

finds an eagerness, perhaps even an anxiety, to transcend—if not actually to repudiate—black cultural nationalism in the name of a more inclusive sensibility.

That Rampersad positions Dove against the black arts movement is an important and necessary step in understanding her relationship to the African American poetic tradition; it helps us see how to qualify Vendler's overstatements about Dove moving "beyond" race. What Dove's work moves beyond (although it is, of course, an impossibility without) are the aesthetics and black cultural nationalism of the black arts movement, not blackness. As Rampersad makes clear, that does not entail moving beyond racial identification or cultural heritage. In reading of *The Yellow House on the Corner* and *Museum*, Rampersad demonstrates that "[a]s a poet, Dove is well aware of black history." He acknowledges (at the time of his writing only those two volumes had been published) that Dove seems to publish little on "racism today" and places that issue in the context of "the trap set by race for the black writer." Such a conjecture is borne out by a 1985 interview with Dove by Richard Peabody and Gretchen Johnsen in which Dove reveals that she deliberately avoided publishing in black markets early in her career because she did not want to be typecast as a "Black Poet." What Dove wants, Rampersad argues, is "the complete freedom of her imagination." Thus, while Vendler sees Dove as either black or universal Rampersad presents her as both African American and universal.

That Rampersad leans a little more toward the black nationalist pole of the conversation, away from Vendler's false universalizing and emphasis on craft, is not only clear in his discussion of Dove in the context of African American poetry but also in two quasi-black arts movement suggestions he makes near the end of the essay. He encourages her to loosen the technical control and also to return "to her old neighborhood" in her future work. That advice anticipates Dove's emerging nomadic blues subject, whose signifying poetic responses to ideas about home and identity constitute an ongoing journey through *Thomas and Beulah*, *Grace Notes*, *Mother Love*, and *On the Bus with Rosa Parks*.

A third critic, Ekaterini Georgoudaki, in an essay entitled "Rita Dove: Crossing Boundaries" (1991), tries to move beyond the universalism/black nationalism binary. Georgoudaki adopts the "world citizen" view that Rampersad rightly ascertains in Dove's values and that Posnock argues lies behind black cosmopolitanism. She articulates Dove's positioning in the literary tradition as an African American woman in the concept of "crossing boundaries." Perhaps because of her non-American vantage point (Georgoudaki is a Greek scholar who trained in the United States and has since returned to Greece as a professor), she contextualizes Dove's work as follows: "As a black person living in the predominantly white societies of the Old and New World, having entered an inter-racial and inter-cultural marriage (her husband is a German writer), and trying to forge an autonomous female poetic voice against the background of a male-dominated Euro-and Afro-American literary tradition, Dove has often crossed social and literary boundaries, violated taboos, and experienced displacement, i. e. living 'in two different worlds, seeing things with double vision,' wherever she has stayed." Furthermore, Georgoudaki argues that Dove's crossing of literary boundaries "overcomes" the feelings of displacement that divisions and boundaries cause. Offering readings of Dove's poetry through *Thomas and Beulah*, Georgoudaki convincingly demonstrates the wide range of boundaries Dove crosses in her work, thus providing a usable metaphor for her poetic sensibility.

Although Georoudaki's perspective is useful, it is also important not to lose sight of the specifically black elements in Dove's work in addition to its breadth. Not seeking to limit her work to an African American context nor wanting to move her beyond it, this book seeks to establish how Dove's poetry articulates one of the most prominent aesthetics of the contemporary period in African American letters. She leads a new phase in African American poetic history that continues the tradition's thread of cosmopolitanism and brings it out of repression and into full expression. She thus joins the list of late-twentieth-century intellectuals Posnock identifies as rejecting cultural purism in favor of universalism, including Anthony Appiah, Julia Kristeva, Edward Said, and Martha Nussbaum, who "have chosen cosmopolitanism."

This prominent aesthetic in the contemporary phase of African American poetry specifically is anticipated by the work of such Afro-Modernist poets of the 1940s and 1950s as the early Gwendolyn Brooks, Robert Hayden, and Melvin B. Tolson. It is also enabled by the racial and decolonizing cultural pride of the black arts movement, a phase that affirmed cultural particularity and gave lie to white culture's refusal to acknowledge America's indebtedness to African American cultural forms. In this sense, the contemporary period's cosmopolitanism is a revisionist universalism that values racial and cultural particulars. Finally, as a movement, the "new black aesthetic" (NBA) is irretrievably associated with the 50 percent of black Americans who are middle-class or above.

The NBA's relationship to the black arts movement deserves further scrutiny. In his essay, Ellis figures the NBA in Lisa and Kellie Jones, the racially mixed daughters of Amiri Baraka (then LeRoi Jones) and his first wife, Hettie Cohen. In doing so, he emphasizes not only the idea of the cultural malatto—"says Lisa, 'I had a lot of options but I chose (blackness)' "—but also the NBA's debt to the black arts movement.

Little of the aesthetic Ellis describes, however, reflects Maulana (formerly Ron) Karenga's basic prescription that black art must be functional, collective, and committing (1973—1974). Ellis' eagerness to claim not opposition but solidarity with black nationalism shows a filial stance unsupported by aesthetics that enact Karenga's prescriptions. In actuality, the relationship Ellis claims between the NBA and the black arts movement is solely one of the black arts movement providing a foundation of black cultural pride from which NBA artists can grow. NBA artists do not follow in the black arts movement's aesthetic footsteps. This is revealed by the new black aesthetic practice of "parodying ... the black nationalist movement ... NBA artists aren't afraid to flout publicly the official, positivist black party line." Ellis offers such examples as Eddie Murphy's prison poet Tyrone Greene with the poem "Cill (*sic*) My Landlord" and George Wolfe's play *The Colored Museum* with the character "Walter-Lee-Beau-Willie-Jones," whose "brow is heavy from three hundred years of oppression." This parodic relationship suggests the black arts movement's power and influence over contemporary black artists. As Tony Jackson notes, you do not parody a failure.

Such parody of the movement's excesses is reminiscent of Dove's early poem "Upon Meeting Don L. Lee, in a Dream," published in *The Yellow House in the Corner* (Lee, a key figure in the black arts movement, later changed his name to Haki Madhibuti). Although Rampersad finds this poem "astonishing" in its hostility to the black arts movement, from Ellis' perspective it seems merely parodic, perhaps at most satiric, in its depiction of a key black arts movement poet as corrupt, decayed, and outmoded. It can be argued, however, that Ellis underplays the rejection of the black arts movement by NBA artists in characterizing it as parody and that such underplaying might indicate anxiety about affiliation. To use Baraka's arts-scene daughters as figures of the NBA, as Ellis does, supports a more psychoanalytic reading of his African American aesthetic genealogy, one which, as Harold Bloom would frame it, sees "intra-poetic relationships as parallels of family romance." Thus Dove's "hostile" poem on Lee can be read as exhibiting Bloom's classic "anxiety of influence," and Ellis' emphasis on the NBA parody of the black arts movement can be seen as denial of the true weight of NBA artists' "mis-readings" of black arts movement.

The idea of a literary genealogy—inflected by race, culture, class, gender, and aesthetics—becomes critical for the cultural mulatto of the NBA and is apparent particularly in Dove's early work. In the absence of an articulated black cosmopolitan genealogy at the time (Penstock's book was published in 1998), the idea of a cultural mulatto black artist would seem to have been newly born from some interracial cultural miscegenation and thus might be of concern both to the artists and their audiences. The "hipness" of Ellis' formulation and essay—with its coffee-shop interviews, musician's gigs, and avant-garde art scene gossip—covers the pervasive anxiety just under the surface of the term *cultural mulatto*, an anxiety about "Where did I come from?" "Who are my parents?" "How did I become who I am?" "Will anyone understand me?" "How and where do I fit in?" and "Is there anyone else like me?" Although inflammatory, using the image of the cultural mulatto in this early phase of the contemporary period accurately embodies the suppressed fears of culturally mixed mulatto artists and intellectuals after the black essentialism and racial-cultural purism of the black arts movement who are concerned about being perceived as "half-white."

Dove's nonfiction prose especially reveals these anxieties about her position as a cultural mulatto articulating a genealogy for her work in African American poetry. Constructing such a literary lineage—a typical early stage for many artists—is complicated for Dove by race and gender. Hortense Spillers' essay "Mama's Baby, Papa's Maybe: An American Grammar Book" shows how African American genealogy has been shaped by the miscegenous rape of black slave women by their white masters—and thus can help reveal the complexity of, and anxiety behind, Dove's genealogy constructions. As Spillers points out, for many African

American the father was often the white master; a denied paternity was paralleled by an undenied ownership of a child. Even when children were fathered by black men, paternal rights were dissolved in favor of the white master's property rights. Thus "a dual fatherhood is set in motion, comprised of the African father's banished name and body and the captor father's mocking presence." Citing the work of Claude Meillassoux, Spillers observes, "(T)he offspring of the female does not 'belong' to the Mother, nor is she/he 'related' to the 'owner,' though the latter 'possesses' it, and in the African-American instance, often fathered it, and, as often, without whatever benefit of patrimony. In the social outline Meillassoux is pursuing, the offspring of the enslaved, 'being unrelated both to their begetters and to their owners... find themselves in the situation of being orphans.'" Spillers argues that in the United States this situation created not orphans but black men and women "in the boundary, whose human and familial status, by the very nature of the case, had yet to be defined." Dove's search to find and name her literary genealogy traverses this terrain of racial affiliation and white control and ultimately makes a place for herself and her work in African American letters.

Dove's criticism on other African American poets operates as a genealogy for her own poetry. Two particular pieces of nonfiction prose, "Telling It Like It I-S *IS*: Narrative Techniques in Melvin Tolson's *Harlem Gallery*" (1985) and "A Black Rainbow: Modern Afro-American Poetry" (coauthored with Marilyn Nelson Waniek and published in 1991), demonstrate her explicit recuperation of African American poetic forbears, what Sandra Gilbert would term her "literary father and mother." The two essays focus on Melvin B. Tolson and Gwendolyn Brooks and treat the black arts movement in black literary history as having more black psychological impact than aesthetic import. A third essay, a review of Derek Walcott's *collected poems* entitled "Either I'm Nobody, or I'm a Nation," discusses Dove's poetic negotiations in the figure of Derek Walcott, another cultural mulatto and thus a figure for many of her concerns. In Dove's literary genealogy, Walcott is a sort of elder brother whose work confirms that there is someone else like her. Together, these critical writings help in constructing the "family romance" explaining Dove's early self-imaging as a cultural mulatto, a role ultimately figured in her short story "The Spray Paint King."

The essay on Tolson is a remarkable defense of him as a black poet. Dove places his work firmly in the African American poetic tradition and bemoans its censure by black nationalists. Thus she claims an African American paternity for herself and her work, an important step in light of Spillers' articulation of the "maybe" role of black paternity in the United States as a result of slavery. The black male parent with whom she affiliates, however, is one whom some jeered as a sellout to white versions of high-modernist technique. In the essay, Dove delineates the vastly differing black and white reactions to *Harlem Gallery* as indicative of the "crossfire" in which a black artist can be caught. Published in 1965, part one of *Harlem Gallery* met with "enthusiastic" response from the mainstream white audience and often angry dismissal by black critics excited by the burgeoning black aesthetic of the 1960s, which Dove defines as extolling "literature for the common people, a literature that was distinctly oral, using the language patterns and vocabulary of the street to arouse feelings of solidarity and pride among Afro-American." Dove cites Paul Bremen's assessment as typical of African American response to *Harlem Gallery*: "(Tolson) postured for a white audience, and... gave it just what it wanted: an entertaining darkey using almost comically big words as the best wasp tradition demands of its educated house-niggers." Such views, Dove argues, are unfair to Tolson's "virtuoso use of folk talk and street jive," which, as the balance of the essay shows, is central to his narrative technique in *Harlem Gallery*. Dove makes the poem relatively accessible by explaining its literary allusions and focusing on the "storytelling 'riffs' which are rooted in the Afro-American tradition." She also demonstrates how, in the "controversy over racial loyalties," few were able to see that Tolson's poem drew on the complexities of the black oral tradition, just as the black aesthetic group was urging. At the end of a series of examples Dove finally breaks out with, "Can I get a Witness? Because what Tolson has been doing all along is testifying, which is nothing more than to 'tell the truth through story.'" She is testifying to the African American cultural, specifically oral, roots of Tolson's art.

Such a move makes a place for herself in African American literary history by establishing Tolson as a predecessor (she has also indicated his influence in *Thomas and Beulah*, in which she uses his *Harlem Gallery* line "Black boy, O Black boy, / is the port worth the cruise?" as the epigraph to Thomas' section). Having located Tolson firmly in the African American poetic tradition, Dove then accounts for the cultural mix of references in his work that so infuriated black arts movement arbiters: "His references range from Balaam's ass to the game cock who thought he was chicken, from Byzantine texts to eggaroni. If anything, Tolson is deliberately complicating our preconceived notions of cultural—and by further implication, existential—order." Dove could be explaining her own work in *Museum*. Her project, then, is a simple but very necessary one: In order for her work not to suffer the same rejection or dismissal as Tolson's, she must "correct" literary history in such a way that Tolson's work is made clear and its wide cultural milieu affirmed. She is "telling it like it I-S *IS*" so readers can see her work for what it is.

Dove's reading of the poem emphasizes its thematizing of the dilemma of the black artist in white America, which we can read as a mirror of her own early concerns. She sees the roles of the narrator (who, she reminds us, is a mulatto, an ex-professor of art, and the curator of Harlem Gallery) and his alter-ego Dr. Nkomo (whom she describes as "his stronger, more prideful counterpart") as playing out in their observations "a dialectic of the position of blacks—most specifically, the black artist—in white America." Dove concludes her essay by reading "the lives of John Laugart, Hideho Heights and Mister Starks ... as illustrations of the three possibilities/alternatives for the black artist." These three characters from *Harlem Gallery* are emblems of the choices available to Tolson—and, by implication, to Dove herself. One can sell out to the (white) mainstream like Starks, be the "Poet Laureate of Harlem" like Hideho, or "remain uncompromising and be spurned by one's own" like Laugart. Dove believes that "it is John Laugart, the artist given least space in *Harlem Gallery*, who most exemplifies Tolson's own sense of artistic responsibility." Like Laugart, Tolson "was misunderstood by many of those he loved most, by those to whom he dedicated his energies on the creation of his last work—the black intellectuals. No one understood this predicament better than Tolson himself." In closing, she quotes Tolson's highly ironic summation of this theme in *Harlem Gallery*:

> the Afroamerican dilemma in the Arts—
> the dialectic of
> to be or not to be
> a Negro.

Such a dialectic echoes Du Bois' cosmopolitan insistence on a dialectic between "the racial particular and the unraced universal." What Dove's reading of *Harlem Gallery accomplishes is a moving beyond this dialectic to a synthesis that allows Tolson's work to transcend the debate over racial affiliation in art.* In so doing, she makes a place for her own work.

[Selected from Malin Pereira. *Rita Dove's Cosmopolitanism.* Urbama & Chicago: University of Illinois Press, 2003.]

11. Toni Morrison

11.1 Presentation Topics

(1) Toni Morrison as a novelist in African American literature.

(2) History and political concern in Toni Morrison's works.

(3) Artistic features of her works.

11.2 Selected Reading

Ⅰ. Central issue of concern

Toni Morrison's idea about African-American culture and women's identity displayed in her works.

Ⅱ. Text

Beloved

Chapter 5

A fully dressed woman walked out of the water. She barely gained the dry bank of the stream before she sat down and leaned against a mulberry tree. All day and all night she sat there, her head resting on the trunk in a position abandoned enough to crack the brim in her straw hat. Everything hurt but her lungs most of all. Sopping wet and breathing shallow she spent those hours trying to negotiate the weight of her eyelids. The day breeze blew her dress dry; the night wind wrinkled it. Nobody saw her emerge or came accidentally by. If they had, chances are they would have hesitated before approaching her. Not because she was wet, or dozing or had what sounded like asthma, but because amid all that she was smiling.

It took her the whole of the next morning to lift herself from the ground and make her way through the woods past a giant temple of boxwood to the field and then the yard of the slate-gray house. Exhausted again, she sat down on the first handy place—a stump not far from the steps of 124. By then keeping her eyes open was less of an effort. She could manage it for a full two minutes or more. Her neck, its circumference no wider than a parlor-service saucer, kept bending and her chin brushed the bit of lace edging her dress.

Women who drink champagne when there is nothing to celebrate can look like that: their straw hats with broken brims are often askew; they nod in public places; their shoes are undone. But their skin is not like that of the woman breathing near the steps of 124. She had new skin, lineless and smooth, including the knuckles of her hands.

By late afternoon when the carnival was over, and the Negroes were hitching rides home if they were lucky—walking if they were not—the woman had fallen asleep again. The rays of the sun struck her full in the face, so that when Sethe, Denver and Paul D rounded the curve in the road all they saw was a black dress, two unlaced shoes below it, and Here Boy nowhere in sight.

"Look," said Denver. "What is that?"

And, for some reason she could not immediately account for, the moment she got close enough to see the face, Sethe's bladder filled to capacity. She said, "Oh, excuse me," and ran around to the back of 124. Not since she was a baby girl, being cared for by the eight year-old girl who pointed out her mother to her, had she had an emergency that unmanageable. She never made the outhouse. Right in front of its door she had to lift her skirts, and the water she voided was endless. Like a horse, she thought, but as it went on and on she thought, No, more like flooding the boat when Denver was born. So much water Amy said, "Hold on, Lu. You going to sink us you keep that up." But there was no stopping water breaking from a breaking womb and there was no stopping now. She hoped Paul D wouldn't take it upon himself to come looking for her and be obliged to see her squatting in front of her own privy making a mudhole too deep to be witnessed without shame. Just about the time she started wondering if the carnival would accept another freak, it stopped. She tidied herself and ran around to the porch. No one was there. All three were inside Paul D and Denver standing before the stranger, watching her drink cup after cup of water.

"She said she was thirsty," said Paul D. He took off his cap.

"Mighty thirsty look like."

The woman gulped water from a speckled tin cup and held it out for more. Four times Denver filled it, and four times the woman drank as though she had crossed a desert. When she was finished a little water was on her chin, but she did not wipe it away. Instead she gazed at Sethe with sleepy eyes. Poorly fed, thought Sethe, and younger than her clothes suggested—good lace at the throat, and a rich woman's hat. Her skin was flawless except for three vertical scratches on her forehead so fine and thin they seemed at first like hair, baby hair before it bloomed and roped into the masses of black yarn under her hat.

"You from around here?" Sethe asked her.

She shook her head no and reached down to take off her shoes.

She pulled her dress up to the knees and rolled down her stockings. When the hosiery was tucked into the shoes, Sethe saw that her feet were like her hands, soft and new. She must have hitched a wagon ride, thought Sethe. Probably one of those West Virginia girls looking for something to beat a life of tobacco and sorghum. Sethe bent to pick up the shoes.

"What might your name be?" asked Paul D.

"Beloved," she said, and her voice was so low and rough each one looked at the other two. They heard the voice first—later the name.

"Beloved. You use a last name, Beloved?" Paul D asked her.

"Last?" She seemed puzzled. Then "No," and she spelled it for them, slowly as though the letters were being formed as she spoke them.

Sethe dropped the shoes; Denver sat down and Paul D smiled. He recognized the careful enunciation of letters by those, like himself, who could not read but had memorized the letters of their name. He was about to ask who her people were but thought better of it. A young colored woman drifting was drifting from ruin. He had been in Rochester four years ago and seen five women arriving with fourteen female children. All their men—brothers, uncles, fathers, husbands, sons—had been picked off one by one by one. They had a single piece of paper directing them to a preacher on DeVore Street. The War had been over four or five years then, but nobody white or black seemed to know it. Odd clusters and strays of Negroes wandered the back roads and cowpaths from Schenectady to Jackson. Dazed but insistent, they searched each other out for word of a cousin, an aunt, a friend who once said, "Call on me. Anytime you get near Chicago, just call on me." Some of them were running from family that could not support them, some to family; some were running from dead crops, dead kin, life threats, and took-over land. Boys younger than Buglar and Howard; configurations and blends of families of women and children, while elsewhere, solitary, hunted and hunting for, were men, men, men. Forbidden public transportation, chased by debt and filthy "talking sheets," they followed secondary routes, scanned the horizon for signs and counted heavily on each other. Silent, except for social courtesies, when they met one another they neither described nor asked about the sorrow that drove them from one place to another. The whites didn't bear speaking on. Everybody knew.

So he did not press the young woman with the broken hat about where from or how come. If she wanted them to know and was strong enough to get through the telling, she would. What occupied them at the moment was what it might be that she needed. Underneath the major question, each harbored another. Paul D wondered at the newness of her shoes. Sethe was deeply touched by her sweet name; the remembrance of glittering headstone made her feel especially kindly toward her. Denver, however, was shaking. She looked at this sleepy beauty and wanted more.

Sethe hung her hat on a peg and turned graciously toward the girl. "That's a pretty name, Beloved. Take off your hat, why don't you, and I'll make us something. We just got back from the carnival over near Cincinnati. Everything in there is something to see."

Bolt upright in the chair, in the middle of Sethe's welcome, Beloved had fallen asleep again.

"Miss. Miss." Paul D shook her gently. "You want to lay down a spell?"

She opened her eyes to slits and stood up on her soft new feet which, barely capable of their job, slowly bore her to the keeping room. Once there, she collapsed on Baby Suggs' bed. Denver removed her hat and put the quilt with two squares of color over her feet. She was breathing like a steam engine.

"Sounds like croup," said Paul D, closing the door.

"Is she feverish? Denver, could you tell?"

"No. She's cold."

"Then she is. Fever goes from hot to cold."

"Could have the cholera," said Paul D.

"Reckon ?"

"All that water. Sure sign."

"Poor thing. And nothing in this house to give her for it. She'll just have to ride it out. That's a hateful sickness if ever there was one."

"She's not sick!" said Denver, and the passion in her voice made them smile.

Four days she slept, waking and sitting up only for water. Denver tended her, watched her sound sleep, listened to her labored breathing and, out of love and a breakneck possessiveness that charged her, hid like a personal blemish Beloved's incontinence. She rinsed the sheets secretly, after Sethe went to the restaurant and Paul D went scrounging for barges to help unload. She boiled the underwear and soaked it in bluing, praying the fever would pass without damage. So intent was her nursing, she forgot to eat or visit the emerald closet.

"Beloved?" Denver would whisper. "Beloved?" And when the black eyes opened a slice all she could say was "I'm here. I'm still here."

Sometimes, when Beloved lay dreamy-eyed for a very long time, saying nothing, licking her lips and heaving deep sighs, Denver panicked. "What is it?" she would ask.

"Heavy," murmured Beloved. "This place is heavy."

"Would you like to sit up?"

"No," said the raspy voice.

It took three days for Beloved to notice the orange patches in the darkness of the quilt. Denver was pleased because it kept her patient awake longer. She seemed totally taken with those faded scraps of orange, even made the effort to lean on her elbow and stroke them. An effort that quickly exhausted her, so Denver rearranged the quilt so its cheeriest part was in the sick girl's sight line.

Patience, something Denver had never known, overtook her. As long as her mother did not interfere, she was a model of compassion, turning waspish, though, when Sethe tried to help.

"Did she take a spoonful of anything today?" Sethe inquired.

"She shouldn't eat with cholera."

"You sure that's it? Was just a hunch of Paul D's."

"I don't know, but she shouldn't eat anyway just yet."

"I think cholera people puke all the time."

"That's even more reason, ain't it?"

"Well she shouldn't starve to death either, Denver."

"Leave us alone, Ma'am. I'm taking care of her."

"She say anything?"

"I'd let you know if she did."

Sethe looked at her daughter and thought, Yes, she has been lonesome. Very lonesome.

"Wonder where Here Boy got off to?" Sethe thought a change of subject was needed.

"He won't be back," said Denver.

"How you know?"

"I just know." Denver took a square of sweet bread off the plate.

Back in the keeping room, Denver was about to sit down when Beloved's eyes flew wide open. Denver felt her heart race. It wasn't that she was looking at that face for the first time with no trace of sleep in it, or that the eyes were big and black. Nor was it that the whites of them were much too white—blue-white. It was that deep down in those big black eyes there was no expression at all.

"Can I get you something?"

Beloved looked at the sweet bread in Denver's hands and Denver held it out to her. She smiled then and Denver's heart stopped bouncing and sat down—relieved and easeful like a traveler who had made it home.

From that moment and through everything that followed, sugar could always be counted on to please her. It was as though sweet things were what she was born for. Honey as well as the wax it came in, sugar sandwiches, the sludgy molasses gone hard and brutal in the can, lemonade, taffy and any type of dessert Sethe brought home from the restaurant. She gnawed a cane stick to flax and kept the strings in her mouth long after the syrup had been sucked away. Denver laughed, Sethe smiled and Paul D said it made him sick to his stomach.

Sethe believed it was a recovering body's need—after an illness—for quick strength. But it was a need that went on and on into glowing health because

Beloved didn't go anywhere. There didn't seem any place for her to go. She didn't mention one, or have much of an idea of what she was doing in that part of the country or where she had been. They believed the fever had caused her memory to fail just as it kept her slow-moving. A young woman, about nineteen or twenty, and slender, she moved like a heavier one or an older one, holding on to furniture, resting her head in the palm of her hand as though it was too heavy for a neck alone.

"You just gonna feed her? From now on?" Paul D, feeling ungenerous, and surprised by it, heard the irritability in his voice.

"Denver likes her. She's no real trouble. I thought we'd wait till her breath was better. She still sounds a little lumbar to me."

"Something funny 'bout that gal," Paul D said, mostly to himself.

"Funny how?"

"Acts sick, sounds sick, but she doesn't look sick. Good skin, bright eyes and strong as a bull."

"She's not strong. She can hardly walk without holding on to something."

"That's what I mean. Can't walk, but I seen her pick up the rocker with one hand."

"You didn't."

"Don't tell me. Ask Denver. She was right there with her."

"Denver! Come in here a minute."

Denver stopped rinsing the porch and stuck her head in the window.

"Paul D says you and him saw Beloved pick up the rocking chair single-handed. That so?"

Long, heavy lashes made Denver's eyes seem busier than they were; deceptive, even when she held a steady gaze as she did now on Paul D. "No," she said. "I didn't see, no such thing."

Paul D frowned but said nothing. If there had been an open latch between them, it would have close.

...

BELOVED, she my daughter. She mine. See. She come back to me of her own free will and I don't have to explain a thing. I didn't have time to explain before because it had to be done quick. Quick. She had to be safe and I put her where she would be. But my love was tough and she back now. I knew she would be. Paul D ran her off so she had no choice but to come back to me in the flesh. I bet you Baby Suggs, on the other side, helped. I won't never let her go. I'll explain to her, even though I don't have to. Why I did it. How if I hadn't killed her she would have died and that is something I could not bear to happen to her. When I explain it she'll understand, because she understands everything already. I'll tend her as no mother ever tended a child, a daughter. Nobody will ever get my milk no more except my own children. I never had to give it to nobody else—and the one time I did it was took from me—they held me down and took it. Milk that belonged to my baby. Nan had to nurse whitebabies and me too because Ma'am was in the rice. The little white babies got it first and I got what was left. Or none. There was no nursing milk to call my own. I know what it is to be without the milk that belongs to you; to have to fight and holler for it, and to have so little left. I'll tell Beloved about that; she'll understand. She my daughter. The one I managed to have milk for and to get it to her even after they stole it; after they handled me like I was the cow, no, the goat, back behind the stable because it was too nasty to stay in with the horses. But I wasn't too nasty to cook their food or take care of Mrs. Garner. I tended her like I would have tended my own mother if she needed me. If they had let her out the rice field, because I was the one she didn't throw away. I couldn't have done more for that woman than I would my own ma'am if she was to take sick and need me and I'd have stayed with her till she got well or died. And I would have stayed after that except Nan snatched me back. Before I could check for the sign. It was her all right, but for a long time I didn't believe it. I looked everywhere for that hat. Stuttered after that. Didn't stop it till I saw Halle. Oh, but that's all over now. I'm here. I lasted. And my girl come home. Now I can look at things again because she's here to see them too. After the shed, I stopped. Now, in the morning, when I light the fire I mean to look out the window to see what the sun is doing to the day. Does it hit the pump handle first or the spigot? See if the grass is gray-green or brown or what. Now I know why Baby Suggs pondered color her last years. She never had time to see, let alone enjoy it before. Took her a long time to finish with blue, then yellow, then green. She was well into pink when she died. I don't believe she wanted to get to red and I understand why because me and Beloved outdid ourselves with it. Matter of fact, that and her pinkish headstone was the last color I recall. Now I'll be on the lookout. Think what spring will he for us! I'll plant carrots just so she can see them, and turnips. Have you ever seen one, baby? A prettier thing God never made. White and purple with a tender tail and a hard head. Feels good when you hold it in your hand and smells like the creek when it floods, bitter but happy. We'll smell them together, Beloved. Beloved. Because you mine and I have to show you these things, and teach you what a mother should. Funny how you lose sight of some things and memory others. I never will forget that white girl's hands. Amy. But I forget the color of all that hair on her head. Eyes must have been gray, though. Seem like I do rememory that. Mrs. Garner's was light brown—while she was well. Got dark when she took sick. A strong woman, used to be. And when she talked off her head, she'd say it. "I used to be strong as a mule, Jenny." Called me "Jenny" when she was babbling, and I can bear witness to that. Tall and strong. The two of us on a cord of wood was as good as two men. Hurt her like the devil not to be able to raise her head off the pillow. Still can't figure why she thought she needed schoolteacher, though. I wonder if she lasted, like I did. Last time I saw her she couldn't do nothing but cry, and I couldn't do a thing for her but wipe her face when I told her what they done to me. Somebody had to know it. Hear it. Somebody. Maybe she lasted. Schoolteacher wouldn't treat her the way he treated me. First beating I took was the last. Nobody going to keep me from my children. Hadn't been for me taking care of her maybe I would have known what happened. Maybe Halle was trying to get to me. I stood by her bed waiting for her to finish with the slop jar. Then I got her back in the bed she said she was cold. Hot as blazes and she wanted quilts. Said to shut the window. I told her no. She needed the cover; I needed the breeze. Long as those yellow curtains flapped, I was all right. Should have heeded her. Maybe what sounded like shots really was. Maybe I would have seen somebody or something. Maybe. Anyhow I took my babies to the corn, Halle or no. Jesus. then I heard that woman's rattle. She said, Any more? I told her I didn't know. She said, I been here all night. Can't wait. I tried to make her. She said, Can't do it. Come on. Hoo! Not a man around. Boys scared. You asleep on my back. Denver sleep in my stomach. Felt like I was split in two. I told her to take you all; I had to go back. In case. She just looked at me. Said, Woman? Bit a piece of my tongue off when they opened my back. It was hanging by a shred. I didn't mean to. Clamped down on it, it come right off. I thought, Good God, I'm going to eat myself up. They dug a hole for my stomach so as not to hurt the baby. Denver don't like for me to talk about it. She hates anything about Sweet Home except how she was born. But you was there and even if you too young to memory it, I can tell it to you. The grape arbor. You memory that? I ran so fast. Flies beat me to you. I would have known right away who you was when the sun blotted out your face the way it did when I took you to the grape arbor. I would have known at once when my water broke. The minute I saw you sitting on the stump, it broke. And when I did see your face it had more than a hint of what you would look like after all these years. I would have known who you were right away because the cup after cup of water you drank proved and connected to the fact that you dribbled clear spit on my face the day I got to 124. I would have known right off, but Paul D distracted me. Otherwise I would have seen my fingernail prints right there on your forehead for all the world to see. From when I held your head up, out in the shed. And later on, when you asked me about the earrings I used to dangle for you to play with, I would have recognized you right off, except for Paul D. Seems to me he wanted you out from the beginning, but I wouldn't let him. What you think? And look how he ran when he found out about me and you in the shed. Too rough for him to listen to. Too thick, he said. My love was too thick. What he know about it? Who in the world is he willing to die for? Would he give his privates to a stranger in return for a carving? Some other way, he said. There must have been some other way. Let schoolteacher haul us away, I guess, to measure your behind before he tore it up? I have felt what it felt like and nobody walking or stretched out is going to make you feel it too. Not you, not none of mine, and when I tell you you mine, I also mean I'm yours I wouldn't draw breath without my children. I told Baby Suggs that and she got down on her knees to beg God's pardon for me. Still, it's so. My plan was to take us all to the other side where my own ma'am is. They stopped me from getting us there, but they didn't stop you from getting here. Ha ha. You came right on back like a good girl, like a daughter which is what I wanted to be and would have been if my ma'am had been able to get out of the rice long enough before they hanged her and let me be one. You know what? She'd had the bit so many times she smiled. When she wasn't smiling she smiled, and I never saw her own smile. I wonder what they was doing when they was caught. Running, you think? No. Not that. Because she was my ma'am and nobody's ma'am would run off and leave her daughter, would she? Would she, now? Leave her in the yard with a one-armed woman? Even if she hadn't been able to suckle the daughter for more than a week or two and had to turn her over to another woman's tit that never had enough for all. They said it was the bit that made her smile when she didn't want to. Like the Saturday girls working the slaughterhouse yard. When I came out of jail I saw them plain. They came when the shift changed on Saturday when the men got paid and worked behind the fences, back of the outhouse. Some worked standing up, leaning on the toolhouse door. They gave some of their nickels and dimes to the foreman as they left but by then their smiles was over. Some of them drank liquor to keep from feeling what they felt. Some didn't drink a drop—just beat it on over to Phelps to pay for what their children needed, or their ma'ammies. Working a pig yard. That has got to be something for a woman to do, and I got close to it myself when I got out of jail and bought, so to speak, your name. But the Bodwins got me the cooking job at Sawyer's and left me able to smile on my own like now when I think about you.

But you know all that because you smart like everybody said because when I got here you was crawling already. Trying to get up the stairs. Baby Suggs had them painted white so you could see your way to the top in the dark where lamplight didn't reach. Lord, you loved the stairsteps.

I got close. I got close. To being a Saturday girl. I had already worked a stone mason's shop. A step to the slaughterhouse would have been a short one. When I put that headstone up I wanted to lay in there with you, put your head on my shoulder and keep you warm, and I would have if Buglar and Howard and Denver didn't need me, because my mind was homeless then. I couldn't lay down with you then. No matter how much I wanted to. I couldn't lay down nowhere in peace, back then. Now I can. I can sleep like the drowned, have mercy. She come back to me, my daughter, and she is mine.

[Selected from Toni Morrison. *Beloved*. New Tork: Alfred A. Knopf, 2006.]

Ⅲ. Questions for discussion

(1) The novel centers on mother and daughter relationships. Between the mother and daughter, who is more in the focus of attention?

(2) What characters or behaviors indicate that Beloved is just like an infant?

(3) What does each of the other characters think Beloved is?

(4) Why does Denver deny seeing Beloved pick up the rocker with one hand?

(5) What symbolic circumstances attend Beloved's return to Bluestone 124?

(6) Analyze the artistic features of the second chapter selected from Beloved.

(7) Read Marilyn Mobley Mckenzie's essay "Spaces for Readers: the novels of Toni Morrison" in assigned reading. How do you understand Morrison's statement that "to have the reader feel the narrator without identifying that narrator, or hearing him or her knock about, and to have the reader work with the author in the construction of the book—is what's important. What is left out is as important as what is there"? How does it explain to us her construction of the space and time in her novels?

11.3 Assigned Reading

Spaces for Readers: the novels of Toni Morrison

Marilyn Mobley Mckenzie

In the introduction to one of Toni Morrison's often-cited interviews, critic Claudia Tate observed that "while her stories seem to unfold with natural ease, the readers can discern the great care Morrison has taken in constructing them"①. Over the span of nearly thirty years, from *The Bluest Eye* in 1970 to *Paradise* in 1998, The Nobel Laureate has not only continued to take great care in the construction of each novel, but she has also commented on the role of the reader in the construction of meaning, In fact, in one interview, Morrison says, to" make the story appear oral, meandering, effortless, spoken to have the reader feel the narrator without identifying that narrator, or hearing him or her knock about, and to have the reader work with the author in the construction of the book—is what's important. What is left out is as important as what is there" ②. Indeed, as readers have attempted to explicate, analyze, critique, and evaluate Toni Morrison's writing, some have lamented about the challenges her novels pose for the reader, while others take

① Claudia Tate. *Black Women Writers at Work*. New York: Contunuum, 1984. p. 119.

② Toni Morrison. Rootedness: The Ancestor as Foundation *Mari Evans*, (ed.) *Black Women Writers 1950—1980: A Critical Evaluation*. New York: Anchor Books, 1984. p. 341.

pride in filling in the hermeneutic gaps with the historical, cultural, and political meanings they believe her stories invoke. To assess the significance of Morrison's novels, it is critical to interrogate how her narrative aesthetic and cultural politics have shaped spaces for readers to enter her texts and how an even larger, diverse body of interpretations have emerged from the community of readers than she might have ever anticipated. An examination of the seven novels published between 1970 and 1998 reveals that the narrative and literal spaces of her texts are a window into her narrative poetics, her cultural politics, and many of her ideas on the meaning of life itself.

Morrison's first novel, *the Bluest Eye* (1970), actually focuses the reader on domestic space as represented in an elementary school primer. The meanings of house and home circulate throughout all of her novels, but in the first novel of her literary career, the house has some particular meanings that foreshadow the story inside the body of the novel. First, it frames the story of how racial difference affects the social dynamics of the community where the Macteers and Breedloves live. Most readers recall Dick and Jane primers with pictures of blond-haired white people and no people of color whatsoever. The novel can be read as an exploration of the psychic consequences, particularly for black girls, of being marginalized, not only in the earliest textbooks used in elementary schools, but also in their everyday lives both in and outside school. The domestic space of their home, therefore, was a possible refuge, unless, of course, the inhabitants of the household had internalized the racial and racist views of larger society, as the Breedloves did. Second, the references to house and home in the opening passage inscribe, through the literal spacing of words on the page, the ways in which language shapes, mirrors, and defies reality. Third, references to house and home in Morrison's first novel focus on the space in which a black girl's identity first comes into manifestation. Ironically, *The Bluest Eye* directs the reader's attention to the act of reading itself; and the elementary primer suggests the schoolhouse as the space second to home where language takes on meaning, where a child must connect the signs and symbols with what they mean for her life. Thus, the movement from a perfectly grammatical passage, with appropriately placed spaces and punctuation, gives way to less and with appropriate punctuation, to no space between words. The order and apparent logic of the primer gives way to chaos, total disorder, and a loss of meaning that foreshadow Pecola Breedlove's descent into madness after she endures incest, rape, pregnancy, and the illusion that blue eyes will make her beautiful.

Yet we enter the novel through the narrative voice of Claudia MacTeer, and it is through this narrator and her retrospective reading of Pecola's demise, and the community's complicity in that demise, that the reader learns the layers of meaning inscribed in this novel. The narrator's ability to assess the fate of Pocola and the community, to tell the story in all its complex beauty and tragic ugliness, creates a new space for her to go on with her own life based on her illumined perspective, in sharp contradistinction to Pocola, whose descent into madness represents a freedom in her own mind, but a tragic enclosure inside the narrow spaces of disconnection from community and the larger society forever. By the time readers finish the novel, they have ventured into domestic spaces where economic depravity dictates when and how people love, where taboos of rape and incest traumatizes and sabotage black girlhood, where racism in the larger world shapes and constrains the options men and women have to imagine themselves as whole, acceptable human beings, and where people both in and outside the community exploit the moist vulnerable. But Morrison's readers are not permitted the luxury of venturing into Claudia and Pecola's respective worlds unscathed, as disinterested spectators or as mere eavesdroppers on someone else's tragic story. Morrison deftly creates an intimacy between the narrator and the reader that she then disrupts with the plural pronouns, "we" and "our." Of course, Claudia understands, at the end of the narrative, how she and her community are implicated in what happened to Pecola, but the repetitious, insistent use of the plural pronoun in the final paragraphs of the novel suggest that the reader may too be implicated:

> All our waste which we dumped on her and which she absorbed. And all of our beauty, which was hers first and which she gave to us. All of us—all who knew her-felt so wholesome after we cleaned ourselves on her. We were so beautiful when we stood astride her ugliness. Her simplicity decorated us, her guilty sanctifies us, her pain made us glow with health, her awkwardness made us think we had a sense of humor. Her inarticulateness made us believe we were eloquent. Her poverty kept us generous. Even her waking dreams we used—to silence our own nightmares. And she let us and thereby deserved out contempt. We honed our egos on her, padded our characters with her

frailty, and yawned in the fantasy of our strength. ①

By the time the reader comes to the end of the passage, she discovers how she may also be complicit on the condemnation and demise of an innocent child who has internalized the racial gaze into what Morrison calls "racial self-loathing"②. In many regards, the novel lulls the reader into Pocola's story only to shift, in the final pages, into exposing how the familiar phenomenon of scapegoating operates in the society at large. In other words, the reader is not allowed to get off the hook as a mere voyeur. Instead Morrison writes the conclusion of the novel in such a way as to invite the reader to come to terms with his or her own "complicity in the demonization process Pecola was subjected to"③. Nevertheless, the beauty of the prose and the clarity of the narrator's understanding in retrospect what she did not understand as child, all point to Morrison's ability, even in her first novel, to help readers discern how art could be both "unquestionably political and irrevocably beautiful at the same time"④.

In Morrison's second novel *Sula* (1973), she creates a different kind of time and space. She leaves the world of children, literacy, and the complications that racism and poverty create for young people and moves onto the adult world of female friendship. But even this novel begins with an aesthetically riveting description of a place called the Bottom and illustrates how spaces gets racialized and shapes our understanding of our identify and the options available to us. Even before the reader meets Nel and Sula, the two protagonists, she learns about the social space that has transformed a black community into an exclusive country club. In a passage that describes a familiar form of regentrification, in which less economically able citizens are displaced by those who can afford to buy the land and force those who once claimed it as their own to relocate. Morrison seems almost prophetic in anticipating how urban phenomena are changing public and private spaces. Indeed, the text mirrors how many communities have had to grapple with the implications of such relocations of people and the attendant redistribution of resources throughout much of the last three decades of the 20th century and the

① Morrison. *The Bluest Eye*. New York: Plume, 1994. p. 205.
② Morrison. Afterword. *The Bluest Eye*. New York: Plume, 1994. p. 210.
③ Morrison. Afterword. *The Bluest Eye*. New York: Plume, 1994. p. 211.
④ Morrison. Rootedness. *The Bluest Eye*. New York: Plume, 1994. p. 345.

early months of the twenty-first century as well. The novel introduces the "nigger joke," and the black people who were the brunt of it, to provide a historical and geographical context for the narrative that will follow. Having established this racialized context, however, she writes that the people had little time to be preoccupied with the racism that contributed to their fate or their location. Instead:

They were mightily preoccupied with earthly things and each other, wondering, even as early as 1920 what Shadrack was all about, what that little girl Sula who grew into a woman in their town was all about, and what themselves were all about, tucked up there in the Bottom. ①

With these words, Morrison creates two different spaces at once for her readers. On one hand, the readers get a window into how black people in Medallion were reading the text of their own lives; on the other hand, readers learn that the text of their lives is much more complex than any racialized reading of it could contain. Thus, as early as her second novel, Morrison was already creating a space for her readers to consider simultaneously how race does and does not matter for the stories she needs to retell.

Once she introduces her readers to Medallion and to Shadrack, its most eccentric citizen, a shell-shocked World War Ⅱ veteran who, when he returns from war, institutes a National Suicide Day, she then reintroduces Nel Wright, the friend of the woman for whom the novel is named. Morrison organizes this novel, therefore, by gradually moving the reader in from the neighborhood and its history into the particular story of two households and the daughters that emerge from them respectively. The reader learns about Nel's oppressive household through her mother, through the layers of meaning available in how Helene treats her daughter, teaches her to conform, and contains her emergent sense of her identity. Morrison introduces the Peace household as one that is the antithesis of the order and containment of the Wright home. Sula's wild and chaotic household with its seemingly endless stream of boarders and male lovers taught her virtually nothing about intimacy and love, but a great deal about sex and using men for entertainment purposes. While Nel is described as a girl whose strict mother "drover her imagination underground," Sula's personality is best summed up in the following description:

---

① Morrison. *Sula*. New York: Bantam Books, 1973. p. 5.

In a way, her strangeness, her naiveté, her craving for the other half of her equation was the consequence of idle imagination. Had she paints, or clay, or knew the disciple of the dance, or strings had she anything to engage her tremendous curiosity and her gift for metaphor. She might have exchanged the restlessness and preoccupation with whim for activity that provided her with all she yearned for. And like any artist with no art form, she became dangerous①.

[Selected from Maryemma Graham, (ed.). *The Cambridge Companion to The African American Novel*. Cambridge: Cambridge University Press, 2004.]

① Morrison. *Sula*. New York: Bantam Books, 1973. p. 16.

Chapter 7 Poetry Before 1945

1. Introduction

American Poetry began to utter the voice of its own in the mid-19th century through the remarkable works of Emerson, Whitman, Dickinson and Poe. In the 20th century, it has become one of the greatest literary achievements of the nation. Although at the very beginning of the 20th century, American poetry was overshadowed by novels for a while, the second decade of the century, however, began to witness a poetry renaissance. American poets of the 20th century who had always felt a compulsion "to justify his existence as poet"①, began to come to terms with the significant social, economic and political changes of the modern era.

When Chris Baldick tried to give a definition to modernist poetry, he used Ezra Pound and T. S. Eliot as models and said that the two "replaced the logical exposition of thoughts with collages of fragmentary images and complex allusions"②. And for this reason, for a while, critics and readers assume that modern poetry means the combination of a forlorn waste-land view of existence and a bold stylistic experimentation. The typical spirit of modern poets is Ezra Pound's repeated injunction: "Make it new!" The typical paradigm for modern poetry is T. S. Eliot's *The Waste Land*. But in fact, American modern poetry is diverse in style, theme as well as poetics. It is almost impossible to make a coherent survey of American poetry in the first half of the 20th century, as American poetry before

---

① Roy Harvey Pearce. *The Continuity of American Poetry*. Princeton: Princeton University Press, 1961. p. 4.

② Chris Baldick. *Oxford Concise Dictionary of literary Terms*. Shanghai: Shanghai Foreign Language Education Press, 2000. p. 140.

1945 went in "different and often more esoteric direction"①. All we can attempt to do is to sum up some of the major developments and to list some of the leading figures who were active during this period of time.

The first generation of American poets who responded in various ways to the modern era included Ezra Pound, T. S. Eliot, Robert Frost, Wallace Stevens, William Carlos Williams, Hart Crane, E. E. Cummings, H. D., and Marianne Moore, Ezra Pound and T. S. Eliot are unanimously acclaimed leaders of modernist American poetry. They are in the same boat in rejecting the 19th century literary traditions and innovating new experimental and avant-garde poetic forms. Nevertheless, the two are innovative in different ways, which leads to two divergent ranges of modern poetic styles. One is represented by Pound, William Carlos Williams and H. D.; the other is led by Eliot, followed by Ransom and Allen Tate. The conflict of these two poetic lines threads through the whole development of modern American poetry. In addition, there is a group of traditional poets who developed an increasing popularity in this period, such as Robert Frost and Edwin Arlington Robinson.

T. S. Eliot (1888—1965), the Nobel Prize winner in 1948, is the most influential poet of all time. He exerted great impact on modern poetry through his insightful critical essays as well as accomplished poems. Eliot had a profound and fresh understanding of civilization, poetry and poet. He believed that poet must become more comprehensive, more allusive, more indirect, in order to force language into its meaning. He wanted to communicate the predicament of modern man, and in accordance with this aim, he led an intellectual reaction against the 19th century romantic English poets, insisting that poetry should be impersonal and that the poet's private life as well as the world was totally irrelevant to poetry itself. Besides, Eliot expressed the idea that no emotion could be expressed accurately in art without an "objective correlative," which he defined as "a set of objects , a situation, a chain of events which shall be the formula of that particular emotion such that, when the external facts, which must terminate in sensory

---

① Jay Parini. Introduction. Jay Parini, Brett C. Millier, (ed.). *The Columbia History of American Poetry*. Beijing: Foreign Language Teaching and Research Press, 2005. p. 18.

experience, are given, the emotion is immediately evoked"①. Eliot's poetry is often narrative and dramatic, yet he seldom unfolded a situation in a straightforward manner.

Eliot's new understanding of poetry is best illustrated in his most important early poem "The Love Song of J. Alfred Prufrock" he wrote in 1910—1911. This poem is a complete departure from the genteel tradition of 19th century American poetry and the most original American poem since the works of Walt Whitman and Emily Dickinson. The protagonist in this poem is Prufrock who is a "cultured cosmopolitan dilettante," longing for a true love and a meaningful life②. However, he hesitated all the way whenever he made up his mind to break through the inhibitions in which he was accustomed to, and eventually withdrew himself to continuing his superficial life. This poem in many ways serves as an example of Eliot's "objective correlative."

Eliot's real innovation in this poem as well as in his masterpiece *The Waste Land* is his deliberate elimination of all connective and transitional passages. He built up the meaning of the poem through the immediate juxtaposition of images without overt interpretation of what they meant, and he employed oblique references to other woks of literature. *The Waste Land* serves a good example. This 459 line poem shocked the literary world of 1922. This long poem is a series of scenes and images, depicting the emotional and spiritual sterility of modern Western man. Five sections of the poem are entitled "The Burial of the Dead," "A Game of Chess," "The Fire Sermon," "Death by Water," and "What the Thunder Said." A serious difficulty for the critics and the readers is the apparent lack of any relation between the five sections in the poem. The organization of this poem is like a series of photographs taken in different places. But just like the title indicates, the theme of the poem is clear and consistent. It epitomizes the plight of modern civilization.

Pound is undoubtedly the most persistent voice for modernistic poetry. As the self-appointed leader of Imagism, Pound laid down three Imagist Poetic principles

---

① T. S. Eliot. *Selected Essays*. London: Faber and Faber Limited, 1951. p. 145.

② Annette T. Rubistein. *American Literature Root and Flower*. Beijing: Foreign Language Teaching and Research Press, 1998. p. 572.

and wrote the much anthologized exemplary imagist poem "In a Station of the Metro." But if we confine Pound to Imagism, we are guilty of underestimating his contribution to Modernist poetry. Pound believed that poet is "a hero bearing the task of cultural salvation on his shoulders"①. And Pound is such a figure. He not only modernized poetry in his own work, but also encouraged the works of other poets—Eliot, William Carlos Williams, and H. D., to name just a few.

William Carlos Williams and Wallace Stevens are two giants in modern American poetry who are directly opposed to Eliot's poetic approach. Both were deeply impressed by Pound and felt that their poetry should serve a serious social purpose. William Carlos Williams began writing as an Imagist in the early twenties, but he gradually developed his own effective style of free verse. The themes in his poetry are broad ranging, with a wide capacity for the emergence of new life, the rich flavor of everyday experience and the realities of industrial America. Williams was concerned with human involvement, which made him differ from Eliot greatly. Williams once said, American poetry "staggered to a halt for a moment under the blast of Eliot's genius which gave the poem back to the academics." So it is clear that Williams walked in an opposite direction in his poetics.

Wallace Stevens is another great modernist poet who is opposed to Eliot's poetic principles. Similar to Williams' complaint about Eliot, Stevens once made this comment on Eliot: "I don't know what there is any longer to say about. His prodigious reputation is a great difficulty."② Stevens differs from Eliot in his religious outlook. Eliot is Christian in his outlook, while Stevens embraces the Hellenic spirit of life affirmation, the cyclical forces of life in the universe. However, religious difference is not the primary disagreement between Stevens and Eliot. A significant contrast between Eliot and Stevens lies in the fact that Eliot follows the moralistic principle, while Stevens follows the naturalistic principle. So in the eyes of Eliot, the modern world is a waste land where the moral values declined; while in the eyes of Stevens, the world might be a waste land but

---

① M. L. Rosenthal. *The Modern Poets: A Critical Introduction.* Beijing: Foreign Language Teaching and Research Press, 2004. p. 50.

② Sacvan Bercovitch. *The Cambridge History of American Literature.* Cambridge: Cambridge University Press, 2003. p. 636.

revocable and full of possibilities for new creativity. And in the eyes of Stevens, poetry has to be renewed through creation. That can explain the reason why Stevens is against Eliot who clings to a tradition simply because it is traditional.

However, it is worthwhile to note that Stevens' aesthetics is also opposing to Pound's, which is neatly posed by Marjorie Perloff in her essay "Pound/ Stevens: Whose Era." Perloff proposed that the aesthetic represented by Stevens traced back to Romantic and Symbolist modes, emphasizing "visionary humanism" and the inwardness of the lyric imagination. The Poundian aesthetic, on the other hand, radically severs its ties with the 19th century and reclaims the external world by way of collage, fragmentation and parataxis. Stevens differs from Pound not only in technique, but with the concept and status of self in the poem, the perspective of history, the role of the poetic imagination in a social and political context.

Louis Zukofsky (1904—1978) is the most formally radical poet to emerge among the second-wave modernists. He was co-founder and primary theorist of the Objectivist group of poets and was to be an important influence on subsequent generations of poets in America and abroad. He was born in New York of Lithuanian Jewish parents and grew up speaking Yiddish. However, he is Pound's "beloved son" in terms of literary parentage. Zukofsky stood at the centre of the Objectivist tradition. Editing the "Objectivists 1931" issue of poetry was a turning point for Zukofsky. He developed and revised Pound's Imagist principles to derive his own Objectivist program. The essence of Zukofsky's Objectivism is "sincerity" resulting in writing "which is the detail, not mirage, of seeing, of thinking with the things as they exist, and of directing them along a line of melody"①. He preferred minor chords to major keys and particulars to universals. Accordingly, the features of Objectivist poetry are precisely arranged detail, accurate reportage, and historical analysis②. Though Zukofsky was influenced by Pound and Anglo-American modernism greatly, he was still haunted by the problem of his Jewish identity. The question of resistance and accommodation to American culture among the Jewish American modernists can be examined both in his first important poem

① Louis Zukofsky. *Prepositions: The Collected Critical Essays*. Berkeley: U of California P, 1981. pp. 12-18.

② Norman Finkelstein. *Not One of Them in Place: Modern Poetry and Jewish American Identity*. Albany: State University of New York Press, 2001. p. 7.

"Poem beginning 'The'" and epic *A*.

In parallel with the development of the two different lines of modernist poetry is the increasing popularity of relatively traditional poetry represented by Robert Frost and Edwin Arlington Robinson. Frost and Robinson are usually considered transitional figures from traditional poetry to modernist poetry. The two share many things in common. They both are New England poets. Both use fixed forms and conventional poetic meters in surprising ways to express a new realistic content and describe a modern world. Both have their roots in the 19th century and are ignored by both the avant-garde and the New Critics. Robinson is best known for his poems about a fictional New England "Tilbury Town" and the residents there. He is good at exploring the psychology of the alienated characters in his poems. His subject matter is often some characters whose fate and inner life are presented in a complex and ambiguous way.

Compared with Robinson, Robert Frost is more detached by standing a perceptible distance away from his characters. Unlike Robinson's concern with townspeople, Frost was more interested in nature and man's relations to the natural world. He enjoyed a higher and longer reputation than Robinson and was the unofficial poet laureate of the nation. Frost preferred traditional poetic forms and familiar subjects, and on the surface his poetry is simple and direct. But critics reach an agreement that his poetry is deceptively simple, and beneath the surface appeal there lurks a further and terrifying implication. The thoughts and principles at work in his poetry are no that of a plain New England farmer, but a modern mind in search of its own meanings.

Modern American poets have been more experimental and more radical in form than their British fellows. Marianne Moore (1887—1972) and E. E. Cummings are two representatives of radical American experimentalism. Moore put a high value on making a vivid, moving design out of precise factual information, and she preferred to presenting her subjects from many juxtaposed angles, just like Picasso in his painting. She fragmented an object into its component parts, and then rearranged those parts into a new object which is more abstract and more multifaceted. She liked to employ all kind of sources and quotations in her poems, a *Times* sports column, a laboratory report, a telephone company leaflet, all find their ways into her poems. The readers are forced to think and see the world and the objects with new eyes through her dissecting of syntax and odd positionings.

E. E. Cummings (1894—1962) shares with Moore a reputation for intriguing poetic experiment. Cummings was born in Cambridge, Massachusetts. Although critical opinions are divided about E. E. Cummings, they reach an agreement that Cummings is the symbol of the modern pioneering spirit in modern American literary, a "juggler with syntax, grammar and diction." Every unorthodoxy of punctuation, spacing and noncapitalization can be read functionally in Cummings' poem. Cummings is extremely concerned with the auditory impact of language, and his verse is meant to impress both the ear and the eye.

There are a few women poets who continued the literary heritage of Emily Dickinson and made great contribution to American poetry. However, with the exception of Marianne Moore and H. D., women poets of the modernist era have often been overlooked. In recent years, fortunately, women poets of the modernist era have begun to receive a more appropriate share of critical attention. Moore and H. D. have been canonized and the work of once neglected women poets such as Louise Bogan, Amy Lowell, Edna St. Vincent Millay, Laura Riding Jackson, Sara Teasdale, Elinor Wylie has been rediscovered.

Marianne Moore and Elizabeth Bishop are constantly linked by literary criticism. Bishop is Moore's close friend, correspondent and primary woman descendent. Her work, with its complex "negotiation of formal and historical imperatives" aligns her with Moore①. But this alignment will overlook their individual poetic features and their respective influences on younger American poets. Moore tended to rely on a special linguistic and formal allotment to convey special meanings. But this is not the case for Bishop. She avoided Moore's formal and syntactic eccentricities and never strayed too far from the traditional meters. In Bishop's words, "the choice is never wide and never free"②. As for Bishop, poetry is not a matter of "creating one's subjectivity" but of choosing how to

① Mutlu Konuk Blasing. *Politics and Form in Postmodern Poetry*. Cambridge: Cambridge University Press, 1995. p. 68.

② Elizabeth Bishop. *The Complete Poems*, 1927—1979. New York: Farrar, Straus and Girous, 1983. p. 94.

"reappropriate an already overdetermined subjectivity"①. Bishop differs from the two main lines of modernist poetry represented by Eliot and Pound respectively. On one hand, though she tried to deal with in the mid-1930s with questions raised by modern poets and philosophers about the materiality of poetic language, her poetry stayed far away from the moderns' stylistic experimentation, tonal impersonality, and the Poundian effort to "make it new." On the other hand, she never accepted the New Criticism and never wrote like the Fugitives. Her poetic language is colloquial, her settings local and her address direct and personal.

Key Words

Objective Correlative

The term "objective correlative" was first used by poet and painter Washington Allston, describing the process by which the external world produces pleasurable emotion. In 1919, T. S. Eliot gave the term a new meaning. For Eliot, the "objective correlative" is pattern of objects, events, or actions, or a situation that can serve effectively to awaken in the reader the emotional response without being a direct statement of that subjective emotion. It is a means of communicating feeling, giving the "internal world" a correlative relation in the "external world," and doing so in a way that was definite, impersonal, and concrete.

Imagism

Imagism was a movement in early 20th-century Anglo-American poetry. It originated in 1912 and represented by Ezra Pound, Amy Lowell, and others, aiming at clarity of expression through the use of precise visual images. Pound defined an image as that which presented an intellectual and emotional complex in an instant of time. He also laid down three Imagist poetic principles: (1) direct treatment of the "thing," whether subjective or objective; (2) to use absolutely no word that does not contribute to the presentation; (3) as regarding rhythm, to compose in the sequence of the musical phrase, not in the sequence of a metronome.

---

① Mutlu Konuk Blasing. *Politics and Form in Postmodern Poetry*. Cambridge: Cambridge University Press, 1995. p. 69.

2. Ezra Pound

2.1 Presentation Topics

(1)Pound as the poet most responsible for defining and promoting a modernist aesthetic in poetry.

(2)Pound's promulgation of Imagism.

(3)Pound and classical Chinese and Japanese poetry.

2.2 Selected Reading

Ⅰ. Central issue of concern

A central figure of the 20th century American modernist poetry.

Ⅱ. Text

The Return

See, they return; ah see the tentative
Movements, and the slow feet,
The trouble in the pace and the
    uncertain
Wavering!

See, they return, one, and by one,
With fear, as half-awakened;
As if the snow should hesitate
And murmur in the wind,
    and half turn back;
These were the "Wing'd-with-Awe,"
    Inviolable.

Gods of the wingèd shoe!
With them the silver hounds,

sniffing the trace of air!

Haie! Haie!
These were the swift to harry;
These were the keen-scented;
These were the souls of blood.

Slow on the leash,
Pallid the leash-men!

[Selected from Jahan Ramazani, Richard Ellmann, (ed.). *The Norton Anthology of American Modern and Contemporary Poetry* Robert O'Clair, W. W. Norton & Co., 2003.]

Ⅲ. Questions for discussion

(1) What is the theme of the poem?
(2) What are the functions of the images and movements contained in the poem?
(3) How can you interpret the line "See, they return, one, and by one?"
(4) What does the image"dog" symbolize?
(5) Please explain the poem from the perspective of musicality.

2.3 Assigned Reading

Introduction to Ezra Pound

Charles Bernstein

Ezra Pound is one of the most ambitious, influential, and innovative poets of the modernist period (the first half of the 20th century). Pound made significant contributions to American poetry not only as poet but also as a translator, editor, polemicist, and essayist.

Pound's poetics had a profound influence on both the poets and readers of his generation. He was a primary proponent of other modernist writers, including Yeats (who served as a model for him), Eliot (with whom he edited "The Waste Land"), James Joyce, William Carlos Williams, and H. D., and poets of the next generation, such as Louis Zukofsky and Basil Bunting. Pound strenuously attacked the prevailing verse styles of his time, which he found flabby and vague. Such verse, he said, had lost its musicality because of its lock-step adherence to metrical structures that substituted the regularity of the metronome for the intricate patterning of composition by ear. As a leading proponent of what came to be known, somewhat problematically, as "free verse," Pound said that poetry could be divided according to three essential elements: phanopoeia, melopoeia, and logopoeia—the play of image, music, and meaning. In his manifestos for Imagism and Vorticism he advanced a poetry stripped of all nonessential elements, where every word makes a necessary contribution to the poem, "which presents an intellectual and emotional complex in an instant of time."

Pound's "In a Station of the Metro" (1911), exemplary of the condensation and obliqueness of the imagist aesthetic, also reflects the influence of classical Chinese poetry:

IN A STATION OF THE METRO

The apparition of these faces in the crowd;
Petals on a wet black bough.

A second approach that Pound took to poetry, early in his career, was the use of masks or personae (Personae is the title he gave to his collection of shorter poems). Rather than the poem representing the voice of the author, as in much lyric poetry, the speaker in Pound's persona poems is a made-up character with whom Pound did not completely identify. This allowed Pound to be satiric, even sarcastic, not only about the subject of the poems but about their speaker, although he sometimes appeared to share the sentiments of the poem's persona, making for an interesting ambiguity. Section Ⅱ of "Hugh Selwyn Mauberly" (on the accompanying CD) lampoons what "the age" (the period just before World War Ⅰ) "demanded"—the superficial hit of "plaster" rather than the richer pleasures of "alabaster." Section Ⅴ (also on the CD) is a bitter (and anti-patriotic) comment on the futility of the World War Ⅰ, in which so many young men died for a "botched civilization."

"Cantico del Sole" (also on the CD) is a particularly funny example of Pound's critique of the contemporary American culture's rejection of art. The poem is based on a judge's ruling that obscenity is okay in the classics because the audience for the classics is so small. In his poem, Pound mockingly repeated a sentiment that might be said by the advocates of censorship, but he substituted "classics" for "pornography": "The thought of what America would be like / If the Classics had a wide circulation / Troubles my sleep." Hearing Pound draw out "America" and "wide circulation" adds a strikingly perfomative element to his send-up.

The third, and most important, approach Pound took to poetic composition is reflected in his "epic" poem *The Cantos*, a series of long poems on which he worked from his mid-thirties until the end of his life. Pound defined an epic as a "poem including history." By calling his poem an "epic," Pound brought to mind such works as Homer's *Odyssey*, Dante's *Divine Comedy*, and Virgil's *Aenead.* Unlike these narrative poems, however, *The Cantos* uses collage or what now might be called "sampling"—the juxtaposition of quotations from a carefully selected range of Eastern and Western cultures, including a fair amount of American history and current events. Quoted material forms only a small part of the overall text, however, since the entire poem is shot through with Pound's own interventions, interpolations, and compositional extensions. Pound's quotations were often in Chinese, Italian, French and other languages and he usually left them untranslated. This was because Pound was interested in an opaque texture for the poem; he once commented that if you didn't understand something you should just push on. In the later *The Cantos*, Pound organized the words spatially on the page, decisively breaking with the flush left orientation of much Western poetry up until that time, though following the lead of Stephane Mallarmé's *Un Coup de Dés*. The result is a poem of immense sweep, often gorgeous lyricism, with a sometimes baffling range of references and many infuriatingly didactic passages. For this poetry of ideas, Pound maximized discontinuity, what some would call fragmentation. At the same time, he tried to maintain strong authorial control over the intended meaning to be derived from the juxtaposition of what he called "luminous details."

Over the course of *The Cantos*, and in his essays, Pound became increasingly obsessed with economics and, in particular, his belief that charging interest on money lent—in other words, the whole system of monetary credit—was destroying Western civilization. In Canto XLV (on the CD), he attacked "usury"—lending money at exorbitant interest rates, which for Pound was any interest rate. Pound believed interest eroded the rock-solid value of things.

Pound's economic views became increasing rabid over time. He associated Jews with money lending and usury (a common stereotype with genocidal implications), insisting that Jews, not being grounded in the land they own, contributed to a waste land of modern fragmentation (an unintentionally ironic view for one of the greatest progenitors of modernist fragmentation in poetry and one who lived most of life in exile). In World War Ⅱ, while living in Italy, Pound sided with the fascist cause, writing poems and speeches extolling Mussolini and excoriating Roosevelt.

Pound's troubling politics are interwoven, throughout his work, with his poetics and aesthetics, making for a useful, albeit sometimes distasteful, study of the unavoidable relation of poetry to politics. Pound's work reflects, like much of the century in which he wrote, both the best and worst of Western civilization.

[Selected from Elise Paschen, Rebekah Presson Mosby, (ed.). *Poetry Speaks*. Naperville, IL: Sourcebooks, 2001.]

3. Robert Frost

3.1 Presentation Topics

(1) Robert Frost as a great poet outside major poetry schools.

(2) What are the common subjects and settings in his poetry?

(3) How is Robert Frost different from his contemporary poets in form?

3.2 Selected Reading

Ⅰ. Central issue of concern

Robert Frost as a philosophical poet who always fills his poetry with a thought.

Ⅱ. Text

Bereft

Where had I heard this wind before
Change like this to a deeper roar?
What would it take my standing there for,
Holding open a restive door,
Looking down hill to a frothy shore?

Summer was past and the day was past.
Sombre clouds in the west were massed.
Out on the porch's sagging floor,
Leaves got up in a coil and hissed,
Blindly striking at my knee and missed.
Something sinister in the tone
Told me my secret my be known:
Word I was in the house alone
Somehow must have gotten abroad,
Word I was in my life alone,
Word I had no one left but God.

The Oven Bird

There is a singer everyone has heard,
Loud, a mid-summer and a mid-wood bird,
Who makes the solid tree trunks sound again.
He says that leaves are old and that for flowers
Mid-summer is to spring as one to ten.
He says the early petal-fall is past
When pear and cherry bloom went down in showers
On sunny days a moment overcast;
And comes that other fall we name the fall.
He says the highway dust is over all.
The bird would cease and be as other birds
But that he knows in singing not to sing.
The question that he frames in all but words
Is what to make of a diminished thing.

[Selected from Edward Connery Lathem, (ed.). *The Poetry of Robert Frost: The Collected Poems*. New York: Henry Holt, 2002.]

Ⅲ. Questions for discussion

(1) The poem "Bereft" was written when Frost lost his relatives. What tone do you think the poet takes in this poem?

(2) What does the spatial indicator "the porch" mean metaphorically?

(3) What does the image of "Leaves got up in a coil and hissed" remind us of? How is this related with the forthcoming "something sinister?"

(4) What does the Word mean respectively in different lines? Is it possible that these Words mean differently in different lines? Why?

(5) What do you think is the theme of the poem "The Oven Bird?"

(6) How to understand Frost's contemplation over life and the universe?

3.3 Assigned Reading

A Close Look at Robert Frost

John Hollander

I'm going to talk this afternoon about Frost as a myth-maker, which is usually not how we think of him. I'm going to look closely at that poem of Frost's called "The Oven Bird," which I think very easy and very difficult at once.

Mythologizing any construction of nature, an animal, plant, a geological formation, a moment of process—this could be seen both as a desecration and a celebration of pragmatically considered fact. When this goes on in poetry—what Frost himself called "the renewal of words forever and ever"—it is accompanied and invigorated by a reciprocal mythologizing of the very words used in the poetic process. Literature is full of mythological, mostly composite creatures: phoenix, unicorn, basilisk, chimera, hydra, centaur. As nature is even more full of creatures totally innocent of interpretation: woodchuck, anteater, turbot, Shetland pony, jellyfish, and quail. But then, there are the fallen creatures, the intermediate ones: lion, eagle, ant, grasshopper, barracuda, fox, hyena ... who have been infected with signification from Aesop on. It is one of the tasks of poetry to keep renewing the taxonomic class of such creatures, by luring them unwittingly into a cage of metaphor, which of course they are not aware of inhabiting. Such new reconstructions of animals are almost a post-Romantic cottage industry, even as the rehearsal, again and again, of the traditional ones, used to characterize pre-Romantic emblematic poetry. I want to look at a well-known instance of such reconstruction, in the case of Frost's "The Oven Bird."

We'll start with the unpoetic ornithology from *The Field Guide to North*

American Birds: "*Sayerus Oricopilus* is a ground-walking warbler. It is common in deciduous woods. It builds a domed nest on the ground and sings from an exposed perch on the understory of the trees." That an American poem addressing this thrush-like bird might consider its ground-built, oven-shaped nest would seem obvious, with interpretations of some sort of pragmatical sublime, being well-grounded instead of lofty, immediately offering themselves. But the poem we are to consider does not.

Frost's sonnet was started in New Hampshire around 1906, but probably finished in England around 1914, far from the shared habitat of bird and poet. Its ending leaves us with a kind of riddle. The opening puzzles us also, slightly, but in a different way. It starts out with a couplet (and sonnets don't start out with a couplet, unless they intend to continue, as they rarely do, with six more of them). But both octave and sestet of this one are initiated by couplets. And in the case of the sestet, or the last six lines, somewhat strangely for other reasons as well.

From the outset, too, we notice at once how casual and how problematic its rhetoric is. "A singer everyone has heard?" Come now, people in London have no more heard that singer than a New Englander would hear a nightingale. There aren't any nightingales in this country. No, this is the conventional palaver of nature writing, of a newspaper verse of the sort you might still find in a rural newspaper in England. But the low literary prosaic tone is modulated with a jolt, as the second line declares its ulterior agenda with a "Loud, a mid-summer and a mid-wood bird." Because of the contrast of stress marking the new coinage, "mid-wood"—we say "mid-summer"; we never say "mid-wood"—the spatial reciprocal of the ordinary, temporal mid-summer, the line ends with three stresses. You might call it two overlapping spondees, confirming the opening, intrusive, almost self-descriptive, "Loud!" "Loud, a mid-summer and a mid-wood bird." The bird makes the solid tree trunks sound again, but in a first reading this always itself sounds strange. It's not just the densely alliterative pattern, first pointed out by Reuben Brower. "Sound again"—have they been unsound? No, not Germanic sound as in the German gesund, but French and Latin sonorous sound. Still, why do we pause momentarily? Do we mistake this bird for a kind of woodpecker, hitting the trunks directly and thus making them less gesund as they make them resound? But it's this purely English and non-Latin way of putting resound that then allows the matter of an echo of a prior sounding, that of the earlier, and perhaps in this poem, ordinary—and despite literary cliché, unpoetic—spring birds since silent.

Then come the first of the three reiterated assertions of his asserting. It will be apparent later why it's not the seventeenth or eighteenth century locution, the transitive "he sings" or its version in the 19th century and later, "he sings of (whatever it is)." What he says first is hardly celebratory, but pragmatically observational, quite this side of sounding dirge-like. The next thing he says is more interpretive, at first reminding us of the dropping of spring blossoms and of how we tend to read these as nothing more dire than the end of a particularly gorgeous overture or prelude, but then letting the resonance of the term "petal-fall" linger on, as if to make us think, "Yes, they do fall too, don't they?"

We half-notice, too, the patterning in which one dactylic foot, embracing a hyphenated compound, is echoed by another unhyphenated one: "... early (petal-fall) is past, when pear and (cherry bloom)...." Petal-fall and cherry bloom have the same compound effect, though he hyphenates one and not the other. But woven across this is an alliterative pattern, in which "petal, past, pear" enact a different kind of connection, followed by the analogous, but more potently expressive, assonance of "went down in showers." Yet this line is not end-stopped here, but flows into the plain "On sunny days a moment overcast."

There's another moment of resonance at work, one of word, rather than of word-sound. The leaves are cast under, in, and for, a moment, even as the sky is momentarily overcast. The point isn't loudly made nor brandished triumphantly, but allowed wonderfully, subtly to happen. But then things get problematic again. Who says, "And comes that other fall we name the fall"? This line is all the more complex here because it initiates the sestet, and we want the full stop at the end to be a comma, as if to say, when fall—that other fall—comes, he says, (with respect to that), that the highway dust is covering everything. The normal grammar would be that of "come the fall" as in "come Sunday," etc. The present, third-person singular verb form here suggests a counter-thrusting inversion: "And then, comes that other fall," etc. But a first reading would also reaffirm a linkage that the couplet-rhyme (again, in an anomalous place for a sonnet) is implying. Yet the couplet is broken— "And comes that other fall we name the fall." Period. "He says the highway dust is over all." Period. We are reminded by the disjunction that the covering of highway dust—the stasis in between petal-fall which initiates the fullness of leaf—and leaf-fall, which initiates the bareness of branch—spring-fall and fall-fall—this is mid-summer stuff, and we can't have the syntax go the way we'd like to. As for the coming of the real fall—the early petal-fall is the other—we needed the oven bird to point out to us that it was a version of the primary one, a shadowy type of the truth of autumn. And by an almost Milton-like extension, the autumnal fall as type of the fall from Paradise—the original one we name the fall—which brought about the remodeling of Paradise into nature, fracturing spring from fall, promise from conditional fulfillment, because they were both there in Milton's Paradise. There were no seasons. The world was a lemon tree, which of course has blossoms and fruit at the same time.

Relations between literal and figurative falling are made even more interesting by the fact that in the Romance language that's part of English, "cause" and "case" are based ultimately on cadere, the Latin word for "fall." As in the Germanic part we still have residues of the earlier usage: "it fell" or "it happened." There are all those other falls too. I'm not sure whether the poem's relative reticence on this question keeps them at a safe distance or not. Or if there's any safe distance from The Fall. Richard Poirier remarked once of this poem that any falling of leaves, of snow, of man can be redeemed by loving. And the sign of this redemption is, for Frost, the sound of the voice working within the sounds of poetry. Certainly, the cadential full stop at the end of this line—"that other fall we name the fall"—makes us momentarily more aware of the working of the poet's voice. But in any case, the peculiar one-line sentence, which we keep wanting to open out into a dependent clause and a full couplet with a comma, gives us a meditative pause. Perhaps it works as something of a springboard, the better to jump into a final quatrain, which in sonnet form can seem itself to initiate a moment of renewal.

Some of that last quatrain's complexity emerges in a straightforward paradox. What does it mean not to sing in singing? Well, if the singing birds do herald and celebrate spring in the morning, or—as with swallows—fills the sky with skitterish evening hymns, then the oven bird's repeated disyllabic utterance is not that. "He says." "He says." "He says." "He knows." "He frames." And here another kind of construction is fed to us by the way in the metaphor of material construction. Here's the question he frames: "We call the sounds birds make 'singing,' but this bird demands that we suspend the overtones of the word 'sing.'" His are not songs but propositions. The very subtle rhythm of the line makes this clear, for in order for the rhyming syllables to be sufficiently stretched, it can't go "... that he knows in singing not to sing" because 'sing' has to rhyme with 'thing,' which means it's got to be more stressed, which, unless you can't write verse, you know you've got to account for in the syntax." The relation of syntax to meter is absolutely crucial. And so, it can't go "in singing not to sing" as the intoning of the paradox seems to demand, but rather "that he knows in singing not to sing," i. e., not to be claimed by allegorizing human intention as music, but instead as speculative discourse.

By this point in the poem, the casual older fiction of birdsong, like that of the wind in the trees sighing and the brook babbling, can't be acknowledged. Those are the stuff of poetry from Hellenistic times on. So it is that he frames a question in all but words, a formulation which is quite reticent (birds don't really talk, of course, but ...). The very grammar of the phrase "knows in singing" is unusually resonant: (1) (as has been suggested) the bird knows—while singing not "sing," but rather discursively to raise questions; (2) the bird knows not to sing (literally) in-and-by singing (figuratively); (3) knowing-in-singing: like Sidney's "loving in truth," a kind of knowing in singing or as if singing were itself a kind of mental process here? In any event, this song is a matter of knowledge, not of charm, of sense making a claim on tra-la-la. I think here, regarding the issue, always crucial for Frost, of the sound of making sense (what he talks about very often—he has a marvelous phrase when he talks about the "sentence sound"). It's the kind of thing which may be being undermined today by one technological habit. You notice how the air-headed cutter-out of sound bites on television news and that sort of thing will invariably cut at the end of a dependent clause, thus giving generations of poor wretched schoolchildren and others the sense that the end of a declarative sentence ends up in the air like this .... I think that's the reason that so many young women produce all declarative sentences as if they were questions. This may have to do with a lack of sense of authenticity about themselves. "I work for J. C. Penney?" ("Well, do you?") We have amazing resources of the sound of syntax in English by enunciating properly, and that's one of the things that Frost talks about when he says "the sentence sound." It isn't just the way this falls into a line of verse.

This matter, as I said, is of the sound of making sense. How great jazz musicians would often play their purely instrumental solos to the words, singing the texts with a complex system of rhythms all intoned internally in order properly to inform the inventions of the melody. Charlie Parker always used to have the words of the tune he was improvising on in his head. This was crucial.

It could also be observed that this sonnet, itself, like so many other poems in *Mountain Interval*, which is the book it comes from, knows in singing not to sing. This is not in the way of Yeats' "words for music perhaps," a phrase which he used to designate a lot of his lyrical poems that, in its way, defines all lyric poetry in English from Wyatt and Surrey on. This is more of an implicit, revisionary take on the lyrical mode of high modernism, and may in some ways anticipate the rejection in another poem of his, called "Come In," with the sound of a thrush singing in the middle of a wood asking him to come into the dark, etc. Frost answered the thrush by saying, "But no, I was out for stars." So the dark wood is tragedy, or it's a whole other construction of what poetry is; for somebody who's not a poet, it better be about more than just poetry; otherwise it wouldn't be about much. It's about intellectual and moral seductions into a whole mode of experience which are probably inappropriate. Which some weird sense of oneself might demand that one confront. And his wonderful last lines of that poem say:

I would not come in.
I meant not even if asked,
And I hadn't been.

And of course a lot of the times that we make a fuss about an invitation and decide we probably have to reject it, we have to remember that we probably really haven't been invited: we've been inviting ourselves. Be that as may be, we come to the oven bird's question itself, which indeed may be two questions. Our colloquial phrase, "to make something of x" can mean to reshape it, use it as material for some new y, etc. But to ask, "What do you make of x?" means "How do you explain, analyze, interpret x?" "What's with x?" "What do you make of it?" These strangely paired meanings are those of "to construct" and "to construe." They both come from the same Latin verb, and are, indeed, with unfortunate consequences for serious academic discourse in the study of literature, starting about fifteen or twenty years ago, both designated by the same French word, construire. And we still use this in English—to "put a false construction on something" doesn't mean to make something sort of jerry-built and place it on top of something else. "To put a false construction on" means to lay a false interpretation over it. And that's the reason we get that unfortunate word, "deconstruction," which also simply means "interpretation." But through not paying attention, the French-speaking promulgators of that term didn't realize what they were doing with the fabric of English when they did that. Anyway, "what to make of"—those meanings are both present, complicatedly, for Frost in relation to each other.

This poem—this bird—talks neither of beginnings nor of endings, but a time that is both, in a Janus-like July, looking backward and forward at once, from an original, and to a final, fall. Midpoints are strange. They tend not to generate the ceremonies that beginnings and endings do. Midsummer in England tends to mean the solstice, June 21st or thereabouts. But this is not what the bird celebrates. We tend to think of our northeastern, American midsummer as somewhere around July 30th or so, and this is the Oven Bird's time: the somewhat indiscernible middle rather than a clearly marked center.

And thus, the bird's other possible question points toward and away from this matter. "What to make of"—how to construe, understand, interpret—the residual. Is the bottle of summer half-full or half-empty? The invitation to consider the question is not that of the ordinary, crack-pot realist, cynical put-down of epistemology. I think the invited discourse on the question, and what it would mean about you and summer to answer it either way, would lie along the pragmatic approaches to questioning in modern philosophy, is somewhere between William James and the later Wittgenstein. But another way of putting this suggests that one of these diminishings might be thought of as that of the whole tradition of talking about birds having something to say. Richard Wilbur uses the phrase "Winged words going round a stable." And in that kind of subsequent allegorizing that strong poems tend to exude, one thing to make of that diminished thing is, by means of newly animated words, the poem "The Oven Bird" itself. And then, as is the case with very powerful and deep poetic ambiguities, the invitation extends to consider the relation between the two kinds of "making of": between constructing and construing, in which representation is creation, and understandings are imagined. This relation is poetry's realm, as it may not be philosophy's. And, as *The Field Guide to North American Birds* reminds us, the Oven Bird's call is characterized as "a loud and clear teacher."

[Selected from John Hollander. Robert Frost and the Renewal of Birds. Bridget Gellert Lyons, (ed.). *Reading in an Age of Theory*. Newark, New Jersey: Rutgers University Press, 1997.]

4. William Carlos Williams

4.1 Presentation Topics

(1) William Carlos Williams as a poet.

(2) Williams' aesthetic principle of "no idea but in things."

(3) Williams' *Paterson* as an American epic.

4.2 Selected Reading

Ⅰ. Central issue of concern

William Carlos Williams' "new mode"—his American measure, American idiom and American experience.

Ⅱ. Text

The Red Wheelbarrow

so much depends
upon

a red wheel
barrow

glazed with rain
water

beside the white
chickens

Spring and All

By the road to the contagious hospital
under the surge of the blue

mottled clouds driven from the
northeast—a cold wind. Beyond, the
waste of broad, muddy fields
brown with dried weeds, standing and fallen

patches of standing water
the scattering of tall trees

All along the road the reddish
purplish, forked, upstanding, twiggy
stuff of bushes and small trees
with dead, brown leaves under them
leafless vines—

Lifeless in appearance, sluggish
dazed spring approaches—

They enter the new world naked,
cold, uncertain of all
save that they enter. All about them
the cold, familiar wind—

Now the grass, tomorrow
the stiff curl of wild carrot leaf

One by one objects are defined—
It quickens: clarity, outline of leaf

But now the stark dignity of
entrance—Still, the profound change
has come upon them: rooted, they
grip down and begin to awaken

This Is Just to Say

I have eaten
the plums
that were in

the icebox

and which
you were probably
saving
for breakfast

Forgive me
they were delicious
so sweet
and so cold

[Selected from Nina Baym, (ed.). *The Norton Anthology of American Literature* (Sixth Edition, Vol. D). New York: W. W. Norton & Company, 2003.]

Burning the Christmas Greens

Their time past, pulled down
cracked and flung to the fire
—go up in a roar
All recognition lost, burnt clean
clean in the flame, the green
dispersed, a living red,
flame red, red as blood wakes
on the ash—

and ebbs to a steady burning
the rekindled bed become
a landscape of flame

At the winter's midnight
we went to the trees, the coarse
holly, the balsam and
the hemlock for their green

At the thick of the dark
the moment of the cold's
deepest plunge we brought branches

cut from the green trees

to fill our need, and over
doorways, about paper Christmas
bells covered with tinfoil
and fastened by red ribbons

we stuck the green prongs
in the windows hung
woven wreaths and above pictures
the living green. On the

mantle we built a green forest
and among those hemlock
sprays put a herd of small
white deer as if they

were walking there. All this!
and it seemed gentle and good
to us. Their time past,
relief! The room bare. We
stuffed the dead grate
with them upon the half burnt out
log's smoldering eye, opening
red and closing under them

and we stood there looking down.
Green is a solace
a promise of peace, a fort
against the cold (though we

did not say so) a challenge
above the snow's
hard shell. Green (we might
have said) that, where

small birds hide and dodge

and lift their plaintive
rallying cries, blocks for them
and knocks down

the unseeing bullets of
the storm. Green spruce boughs
pulled down by a weight of
snow—Transformed!

Violence leaped and appeared.
Recreant! Roared to life
as the flame rose through and
our eyes recoiled from it.

In the jagged flames green
to red, instant and alive. Green!
Those sure abutments... Gone!
Lost to mind

and quick in the contracting
tunnel of the grate ·
appeared a world! Black
mountains, black and red—as

yet uncolored—and ash white,
an infant landscape of shimmering
ash and flame and we, in
that instant, lost,

breathless to be witnesses,
as if we stood
ourselves refreshed among
the shining fauna of that fire.

[Selected from *The Norton Anthology of American Literature* (Sixth Edition, Vol. D). New York: W. W. Norton & Company, 2003: 1275-1276.]

Ⅲ. Questions for discussion

(1) What is the thing that "so much depends upon?"

(2) What image do you see of the wheelbarrow?

(3) Why are"Wheelbarrow" and "rainwater" cut into their constitutes?

(4) What special effect do the enjambments have in "The Red Wheelbarrow?"

(5) As to"This Is Just to Say," Stephen Matterson points out: "Any thematic interpretation is made self-consciously and somewhat uncertainly. As with the found poem, Williams' poem allows the reader a wide range of possibilities." Do you agree with this comment? What is your interpretation of the meaning of this poem?

(6) What are the striking formal and linguistic features of "Spring and All?"

(7) In some senses, Williams' poetic taste is guided and confirmed by painting, and "Spring and All" is a good example. Albert Gelpi points out, "The poem ("Spring and All") is a fine example of Williams' verbal cubist Realism." Then in what way is the poem cubistic?

(8) Could you make a thematic analysis of"Burning the Christmas Greens?"

(9) T. S. Eliot is a figure against whom Williams came to define many of his own poetic concern. Williams said in his *Autobiography*, *The Waste Land* struck him like a "sardonic bullet." Why?

4.3 Assigned Reading

Williams and the "New Mode"

Roy Harvey Pearce

In 1922, two years after Williams Carlos Williams'*Kora* in Hell was published, there had come "The Waste Land" and Eliot's rise to power. Williams has again and again said what he thought about Eliot's work in comparison to his own and his hopes for it. This is the account he gives in his *Autobiography* (1951):

> Then out if the blue *The Dial* brought out *The Waste Land* and all our hilarity ended. It wiped out our world as if an atom bomb had been dropped upon it and our brave sallies into the unknown were turned to dust.

To me especially it struck like a sardonic bullet. I felt at once that it had set me back twenty years, and I'm sure it did. Critically Eliot returned us to the classroom just at the moment when I felt that we were on the point of an escape to matters much closer to the essence of a new art form itself — rooted in the locality which should give it fruit. I knew at once that in certain ways I was most defeated.

Eliot had turned his back on the possibility of reviving my world. And being an accomplished craftsman, better skilled in some ways than I could ever hope to be, I had to watch him carry my world off with him, the fool, to the enemy.

The "our," "we," and "us" here are all aspects of the first person singular. As the lesson of *Paterson* has it, "our" world is validly "ours" only as is "my." Williams spelled out the lesson to a correspondent in 1950:

I believe that all the old academic values hold today as always. Basically I am a most conventional person. But the TERMS in which we must parallel the past are entirely new and peculiar to ourselves.

The poem to me (until I go broke) is an attempt, an experiment, a failing experiment, toward assertion with broken means but an assertion, always, of a new and total culture, the lifting of an environment to expression. Thus it is social, the poem is a social instrument—accepted or not accepted seems to be of no material importance. It embraces everything we are.

How, against Eliot's claims for the power of myth and religion and Pound's for the power of "Kulchur," lift the environment into expression, and oneself with it? This was the question answered by the first four parts of *Paterson*. Moreover, *Paterson* demonstrated a means, a technique, a mode, appropriate to the poet who would carry on Whitman's work. In the letter just quoted, Williams went on to say: "Whitman to me was an instrument, one thing: he started us on the course of our researches into the nature of the line by breaking finally with English prosody. After him there has been for us no line. There will be none until we invent it. Almost everything I do is of no more interest to me than the technical addition it makes toward the discovery of a workable metric in the new mode." The new mode was a reconstitution of the old—that of Whitman and his peers—under the pressure of a kind of poetry—Eliot's—which would deny its relevance and worth.

Paterson represents only a mid-point, however, climactic, in Williams' poetry. For the "line" toward which he worded came to be nothing less than the poet's means of taking absolute control over his world and of baptizing it in his own name. The strictly historical materials in *Paterson* are presented as so much *disjecta membra* and are allowed to have meaning only as they fit into the poet's scheme of things. (Which is the opposite situation to that of the "Wasteland. ") In this poem everything must be present; not even in imagination can we be elsewhere than where we actually are. Yet in Williams' later poetry the historical is not present, having been eliminated altogether and restored to the process of nature from which it must have at one time been precipitated. It is the line which, as he refines it in the poems after *Paterson*, enables Williams to make such a restoration. It is also the line which brings him perilously close to the loss of his own identity. For the line of the later poems works primarily as a means of imitating the rhythms of perception and cognition, not of discrimination among and organizing what is perceived and cognized. It tends to minimize our need to separate an object perceived from its surroundings, a concept held from antecedents and consequences—as though the reality principle itself, no longer having any function, had withered away. The road away from *Paterson* has been even more dangerous than the road to it. One of the rewards in the great abundance of Williams' poetry and in the record of his compulsively public career is the perspective they give us on the affiliations of his poetry and the kind it represents with major American poetry of the 19th century. He has taken it upon himself to be a prophet among 20th century American poets.

One of Williams' earliest poems, "Pastoral," describe first some sparrows which "hop ingenuously / about the pavement," then " we who are wiser / (and) shut ourselves in," and finally the old man who goes about "without looking up," yet with "tread /... more majestic than / that of the Episcopal minister. " In the poem Williams quite consciously risks being "insignificant" so that he can all the more powerfully say at the end: "These things / astonish me beyond words. " It is that hard-earned right to say "astonish" which makes all the difference. The poem in its entirety goes thus:

The little sparrows
hop ingenuously
about the pavement
quarreling
with sharp voices
over those things
that interest them.

But we who are wiser
shut ourselves in
on either hand
and no one knows
whether we think good
or evil.
  Meanwhile,
the old man who goes about
gathering dog-lime
walks in the gutter
without looking up
  and his tread
is more majestic than
that of the Episcopal minister
approaching the pulpit
of a Sunday
  These things
astonishing me beyond words.

Williams' subject here is that aspect of the human condition so fascinating to the poet in the Adamic mode: the separateness of men from one another and from the things of their world. But the things are not objects for him, nor are the men dramatis personae. His perceptions enable him to impute to each man and each thing that he sees a vital sense of its own existence, a fateful self-consciousness; and in turn he is astonished, beyond the very words which have been his means to the imputation, with what he has discovered: Just think—there is a world like this, like me! The dividing line between what he sees and what he knows, between perception and cognition, is thus difficult to draw, except theoretically. "Astonish," as Williams uses it here, can only be defined by referring to the things which draw the word out from him. This is precisely the effect that Williams wants. His so-called "naturalism," his fascination with the "antipoetic" (which his friend Stevens early pointed out) derives from a compulsion to define separateness (or alienation) in terms of the insignificant (or "anti-poetic").

In "Pastoral" the simple, separate things upon which the imagination feeds have an integrity and vitality so marked as to convince the poet that he cannot relate them coherently one to another. He cannot quite "understand" the world in which he lives. He can almost understand it, and accordingly is quite willing to point up his predicament with appropriate pathos and sentimentalism:

so much depends
upon

a red wheel
barrow

glazes with rain
water

beside the white
chickens.

In this notably sentimental piece, Williams can only dimly specify "what" depends—himself in his vocation as poet. He assures himself that he is what is by virtue of his power to collocate such objects into sharply annotated images like these. He must feel himself into the things of his world; for he is as dependent on them as occasions to be himself—as poet. Perhaps—and herein lies the pathos—they depend on him as much as he depends on them, "So much depends" too upon a poet's being there to make them what, at their best, they can be: objects in a poem. At its worst this is togetherness in a chicken-yard. At its best it is an exercise in the creation of the poetic out of the anti-poetic. Not the least significant characteristic of Williams' work is that the best in it cannot but bring out the worst. Like his friend and enemy Pound, he has had the courage to go all the way with his convictions.

Some of the poems before *Paterson*—so many as to form a definable group and to evince a "theme"—are about persons, quite often the person of the poet. "Danse Russe" for example:

If I when my wife is sleeping
and the baby and Kathleen
are sleeping
and the sun is a flame-white disc
in silken mists
above shining trees—
if I in my north room

dance naked, grotesquely
before mymirror
waving my shirt round my head
and singing softly to myself:
"I am lonely, lonely.
I was born to be lonely,
I am best so!"
If I admire my arms, my face,
My shoulders, flanks, buttocks
against the yellow drawn shades—

Who shall say I am not
the happy genius of my household?

Poems like "Danse Ruess" are essentially "talking" poems. Other examples are "Smell," "Impromptu: The Suckers," "Death," and "The Widow's Lament in Springtime," which begins marvelously:

Sorrow is my own yard
where the mew grass
flames as it has flamed
often before but not
with the cold fire
that closes round me this year.

In such a poem the speaker is made quite self-consciously to ask what he is doing in our world. If the poem works, what is for him a question is for us an answer. The difference between this sort of poem and the traditional dramatic monologue is that whereas in the latter the speaker is talking to us, in the former he is talking to himself. Talking becomes a necessary means not so much of communicating as of creating one's self.

And there are poems primarily of "seeing." Here is the most famous example, the first poem from the group called "Spring and All":

By the road to the contagious hospital
under the surge of the blue
mottled clouds driven from the
northeast—a cold wind. Beyond, the
waste of broad, muddy fields
brown with dried weeds, standing and fallen

patches of standing water
the scattering of tall trees

All along the road the reddish
purplish, forked, upstanding, twiggy
stuff of bushes and small trees
with dead, brown leaves under them
leafless vines—

Lifeless in appearance, sluggish
dazes spring approaches—

They enter the new world naked,
cold, uncertain of all
save that they enter. All about them
the cold, familiar wind—

Now the grass, tomorrow
the stiff curl of wild carrot leaf
One by one objects are defined—
It quickens: clarity, outline of leaf

But now the stark dignity of
entrance—Still, the profound change
has come upon them: rooted, they
grip down and begin to awaken.

Here (other examples are "Spring Strains," "Queen-Ann's-Lace," "Young Sycamore," and "Nantucket") the procedure is to discover "things" and to view what has been discovered sharply and precisely and separately; yet at the same time (since the seeing is a continuous process) through the creative force of seeing, to realize the paradox of continuity in change, relatedness in non relatedness. In the poem I have just quoted a perception of a series of objects is made to blend into a thought ("It quickness"), so that it is the thought. The implicit claim is not that one sees objects and then express their meaning, but rather that they are there, ready to express themselves for one's seeing. The poet sees their meaning, as he hears the meaning of those who populate his "talking" poems. His role as a poet is to recognize, by a kind of affinity, their vital principle and to find the words whereby it might be expressed.

No ideas but in things, as Williams says in *Paterson*—where, writing in both modes at once, he most fully realizes the possibilities of his kind of poem. This is what he called "the new mode." The role of the "lines" here is to control and modulated revelation according to the nature and needs of poet and reader, and of the language they share. Both precision of speech and sharpness of vision are subordinated to the movement toward that awareness which is for the poet antecedent to them—their occasion, in fact. Yet we can distinguish between that of which we become aware and ourselves in the act of becoming aware. Mediating between us and the world of the poem, between subject and object, is the poem itself. This should be enough.

Yet Williams has come to want more than this. He would have the poem be the means whereby subject and object are fused. Toward this purpose he has directed the bulk of his poems since *Paterson*. He was, in fact, moving toward it at the time he was working on *Paterson*. There is "Choral: The Pink Church," in which we read:

> Sing!
> transparent to the light
> through which the light
> shines, through the stone,
> until
> the stone-light glows,
> pink jade
> —that is the light and is
> a stone
> and is a church—if the image
> hold...

"The Pink Church" is the poet's world, and all the persons, places, and things is contains; much of the poem runs, Whitmanlike, over their names, so attempting to absorb them into that ultimate pinkness, that ultimate light, that ultimate revelation, into which a full sense of their presence must issue. Likewise, there is "Burning the Christmas Greens," which begins:

> Their time past, pulled down
> cracked and flung to the fire

—go up in a roar

All recognition lost, burnt clean
clean in the flame, the green
dispersed, a living red,
flame red, red as blood wades
on the ash—

Again, that light which moves as the blood moves. The theme of the poem is put explicitly toward the end:

Transformed!
Violence leaped and appeared.
Recreant! Roared to life
as the flame rose through and
our eyes recoiled from it.

The poem is intended to manifest a resurrection—all the more marvelous because it is made up of words, which are death. "The pink Church" is nominally what I have called a "talking" poem; "Burning the Christmas Greens" is nominally a "seeing" poem. Yet how easily, for Williams, the one becomes the other! How easily that creative awareness toward which they lead becomes ritual! How naturally it takes its substance from matters associated traditionally with ritual—churches and Christmas greens! The poem has become a prayer; but he who prays, prays only to himself and that part of himself he can discover in his world.

Because Williams has wanted so much from poetry, he has pro-claimed from the rooftops of the world the necessity of reconceiving its technique. Technique has meant for him only the "line" and a "workable metric"—as though the sole necessary condition for a poem were an adequate prosody. In the poems from which I have just quoted the incantatory overrides logic, structure, and the disposition of meaning. The millennialist expectation is that out of poems written in this "new mode" there will come a "new language." "The measurement of the poetic line of the future," he wrote in 1955, "has to be expanded so as to take a larger grip of its material." Pound had almost seen this, Williams declared, but not quite. And he continued:

The grammar of the term, variable foot, is simply what is describes itself to be: a poetic foot that is not fixed but varies with the demands of the language, keeping the measured emphasis as it may occur in the line. Its characteristic, where it differs from the fixed foot with which we are familiar, is that it ignores the counting of the number of syllables in the line, which is the mark of the usual scansion, for a measure of the ear, a more sensory counting ...

The advantage of the practice over the old mode of measuring is that without inversion it permits the poet to use the language he naturally speaks, provided he has it well under control and does not lose the measured order of the words.

Behind this theorizing about prosody, there lies the mystique of the new mode:

The only measured form of language ... is its poetry. Therefore ineffective as it may appear to be as a weapon, in the public eye, it is only by attacking there ... that our actions can have a lasting effect.

"On that basis alone will a new language, let us presume it to be the American language, be fit to trust its organization."

Again: Barlow's hopes for a universal language, at base presumably American. "Without measure, we are lost," Williams had written in 1954. In this radically alternative version of the theory of Eliot's "Music of Poetry," man is measure of all things; but the essence of man, and thus the ground of the measure, is expressed not in what he has done or what he is doing, but rather in the way his language bids him do it. The theory of the variable foot is simple—just as a magical formula is simple when compared to the wonders it will work. To be true it has to be simple. Like Eliot's theory, Williams' looks toward its own kind of mirage, beyond mere language. Yielding to the demands of language, the poet yields to that which is essential in his sense of himself in his world. This is the extreme formulation of the "new mode," in which, as Wallace Stevens was to say, "the poem is the cry of its occasion." At its best—in the first four parts of *Paterson*, above all—the new mode is Williams' means, in a phrase from "A Sort of a Song," "through metaphor to reconcile / the people and the stones."

"Reconcile" is the key term. Reconciliation requires a balance between people and stones, with the poem as fulcrum, which after the first four parts of *Paterson* Williams has more and more disclaimed. In his later poetry the measure-as-movement has increasingly come to override the measure-as-gauge. The variety of the foot tends to refer back to the potentiality for variety in the poet, not in his relations with his world. Explicitly rejecting an orthodox Christian world, "a woman's world, / of crossed sticks, stopping/ thought," he decides that "A new world / is only a new mind" ("To Daphne and Virginia"). The mind is the poet's,

its activity. "invention" (a word of which, since *Paterson*, he has grown increasingly fond) according to the principles of the "measured form of language."
[Selected from Roy Harvey Pearce, Middletown. *The Continuity of American Poetry*. Connecticut: Wesleyan University Press, 1987.]

5. Louis Zukofsky

5.1 Presentation Topics

(1) Louis Zukofsky as a Jewish American poet.

(2) Louis Zukofsky as a principal spokesperson for the Objectivists.

(3) The aesthetic features in Zukofsky' *Poem Beginning "The"* and *A*.

5.2 Selected Reading

Ⅰ. Central issue of concern

Zukofsky's negotiation between modernism and Jewishness and the effect of his resistance and accommodation to American culture.

Ⅱ. Text

Poem Beginning "The"

First Movement: "*And out of olde bokes, in good feith*"[1]

The
Voice of Jesus I. Rush singing
                                        in the wilderness
A boy's best friend is his mother[2],
It's your mother all the time.
Residue of Oedipus-faced wrecks
Creating out of the dead—

---

[1] From Geoffrey Chaucer (1343—1400), the Poem "Parliament of Fowls":
And out of olde bokes, in good feith,
Cometh al this newe science that men lere.

[2] There are numerous versions of a popular song with this title and refrain going back to the 1880s.

8 From the candle flames of the souls of dead mothers①
9 Vide the legend of thin Christ sending her
out of the temple—
10 Books from the stony heart, flames rapping
the stone,
11 Residue of self-exiled men
12 By the Tyrrhenian②.
13 Paris.

14 But everywhere only the South Wind③, the
sirocco, the broken Earth-face.
15 The broken Earth-face, the age demands an
image of its life and contacts④,
16 Lord, lord, not that we pray, are sure of
the question,
17 But why are our finest always dead?
18 And why, Lord, this time, is it Mauberly's
Luini in porcelain⑤, why is it Chelifer⑥,

---

① Louis Zukofsky notes D. H. Lawrence here, which could refer to any number of works, but perhaps most likely his first novel, *Sons and Lovers* (1913).

② Sea bounded by the western coast of Italy, Sicily, Sardinia and Corsica. LZ notes Aldous Huxley's *Those Barren Leaves* (1925), a satirical novel set at an Italian Renaissance palace owned by a wealthy Englishwoman near the coast of the Tyrrhenian Sea where she gathers artists and intellectuals who carry on lengthy discussions.

③ Novel by Norman Douglas (1868—1952) set on the imaginary island of Nepenthe (based on Capri) in the Tyrrhenian Sea where a cast of curious characters converse at length on various, often hedonistic topics. The novel was immensely successful on its publication during the war. The South Wind is a constant physical presence in the novel and would be identified with the sirocco, hot dry winds that blow up from North Africa into parts of southern Europe.

④ From Ezra Pound, "Hugh Selwyn Mauberley: Life and Contacts": "The age demanded an image / Of its accelerated grimace, / Something for the modern stage, / Not, at any rate, an Attic grace."

⑤ From Ezra Pound, "Hugh Selwyn Mauberley" (misspelled or misprinted in Louis Zukofsky's poem). Bernardino Luini (1480—1532), Milanese painter and follower of Leonardo da Vinci; this line is usually understood as alluding to a refined but superficial artist.

⑥ Francis Chelifer is a disillusioned poet in Aldous Huxley's *Those Barren Leaves*.

Why is it Lovat who killed Kangaroo[1],
Why Stephen Daedalus with the cane of
ash[2],
But why les neiges[3]?
And why, if all of Mary's Observations[4]
have been made
Have not the lambs become more sapient
drinking of the spring;
Kerith is long dry, and the ravens that
brought the prophet bread[5]
Are dust in the waste land of a raven—
winged evening.
And why if the waste land has been explored,
traveled over, circumscribed,
Are there only wrathless skeletons exhumed
new planted in its sacred wood[6],
Why—heir, long dead—Odysseus, wandering of ten years[7]
Out-journeyed only by our Stephen, bibbing[8]

---

① In D. H. Lawrence, *Kangaroo* (1923), Richard Lovat Somers is the Lawrence character who does not literally kill Kangaroo, a charismatic political figure, but does so in the sense of refusing to carry on the latter's work as he is dying in the chapter "Kangaroo Is Killed."

② From James Joyce, *The Portrait of the Artist as a Young Man* (1915) but especially in *Ulysses* (1922), Stephen Daedalus rarely appears without mention of his ashplant cane.

③ From François Villon's most famous line, "Mais où sont les neiges d'antan?" (Where are the snows of yesteryear?), from the ballade, "Des dames du temps jadis."

④ Marianne Moore (1887—1972), *Observations* (1924) was her second book and includes many of her best-known poems.

⑤ Louis Zukofsky notes here the Irish novelist George Moore (1852—1933), the novel *The Brook Kerith: A Syrian Story* (1916): "Get thee hence, and turn thee eastward, and hide thyself by the brook Cherith, that is before Jordan. And it shall be, that thou shalt drink of the brook; and I have commanded the ravens to feed thee there. So he went and did according unto the word of the Lord: for he went and dwelt by the brook Cherith, that is before Jordan. And the ravens brought him bread and flesh in the morning, and bread and flesh in the evening; and he drank of the brook. And it came to pass after a while, that the brook dried up, because there had been no rain in the land."

⑥ T. S. Eliot's first volume of essays, *The Sacred Wood* (1920).

⑦ Alluding to Homer and Odysseus' ten years of wandering on his journey home.

⑧ James Joyce, *Ulysses* (1922), which takes place in a single day and involves Stephen Daedalus from *The Portrait of an Artist as a Young Man*, moderate but regular drinking, to tipple.

of a day,
30 O why is that to Hecuba as Hecuba to he[1]!
31 You are cra-a-zee on the subject of babies,
says she,
32 That is because somehow our authors have been
given a woman's intuition.
33 Il y a un peu trop de femme[2] in this South Wind.
34 And on the Cobblestones, bang, bang, bang,
myself like the wheels—
35 The tram passes singing
36 O do you take this life as your lawful wife,
37 I do!
38 O the Time is 5
39 I do!
40 O the Time is 5
41 I do!
42 O do you take these friends as your loves
to wive,
43 O the Time is 5
44 I do![3]
45 For it's the hoo-doos, the somethin' voo-does[4]
46 And not Kings onelie, but the wisest men
47 Graue Socrates, what says Marlowe?

---

① From Shakespeare, *Hamlet*:

For Hecuba!
What's Hecuba to him or he to Hecuba,
That he should weep for her? What would he do
Had he the motive and cue for passion
That I have?

② There is a bit too much of the female (*French*).

③ This passage echoes the pub closing section of T. S. Eliot, *The Waste Land* notes E. E. Cummings' is 5 (1926)—is Louis Zukofsky or an editor responsible for the (mis)punctuation of this title in the notes?

④ Echoes Vachel Lindsay's performative poem, "The Congo (A Study of the Negro Race)" (1914), which includes variations on the chorus, "Mumbo-Jumbo will hoo-doo you," as well as mentioning "voo-doo."

For it was myself seemed held
Beating—beating—

Body trembling as over an hors d'oeuvres—①

And the dream ending—Dalloway! Dalloway—②
The blind portals opening, and I awoke!③

Let me be
Not by art have we lived,
Not by graven images forbidden to us④
Not by letters I fancy,
Do we dare say
With Spinoza grinding lenses⑤, Rabbaisi,
After living on Cathedral Parkway⑥?

[Selected from Louis Zukofsky. *Complete Short Poetry*. Baltimore and London: The Johns Hopkins University Press, 1991.]

---

① From Christopher Marlowe. *Edward II*:

The mightiest kings have had their minions,
Great Alexander loved Ephestion,
The conquering Hercules for Hilas wept,
And for Patroclus sterne Achillis droopt:
And not kings onelie, but the wisest men,
The Romaine Tullie loved Octavius,
Grave Socrates, wilde Alcibiades:
Then let his grace, whose youth is flexible,
And promiseth as much as we can wish,
Freely enjoy that vaine light-headed earle,
For riper yeares will weane him from such toyes.

② *Mrs. Dalloway* (1925), novel by Virginia Woolf.

③ Possibly echoing John Keats, "Ode to a Nightingale."

④ Referring to the prohibition among the Jews against creating images of Jehovah: "Thou shalt not make unto thee any graven image, or any likeness of any thing that is in heaven above, or that is in the earth beneath, or that is in the water under the earth."

⑤ The Dutch Jewish philosopher Baruch Spinoza (1632—1677) was excommunicated from the Jewish community of Amsterdam because of his views and made his living grinding lenses.

⑥ Runs east-west along the upper end of Central Park, a few blocks from Columbia University, and becomes 110th Street on the east side.

Ⅲ. Questions for discussion

(1) This poem begins with the idea of memory. What are the features of Zukofsky's concept of time and space in the time? In what way is this concept connected with his Jewish identity?

(2) As a Jewish American poet, one of the central concerns of Zukofsky in this poem is his Jewishness. What is Zukofsky's attitude towards his identity?

(3) Structurally, this poem is a collage, a whole poem made out of cutouts from other texts. What are the functions of these allusions? Compare them with T. S. Eliot's same strategy in *The Waste Land*.

(4) We can find a sense of bitter irony and ambivalence from the lines like "Let me be/ Not by art have we lived,/Not by graven images forbidden to us/ Not by letters I fancy,/ Do we dare say/ With Spinoza grinding lenses, Rabbaisi,/ After living on Cathedral Parkway?" What are the conflicts between Zukofsky's Jewishness and Modernism?

(5) At the beginning of "The," Christianity and modernism are imagined to be a triangulated relationship, with the Mother serving as the third term. Could you interpret this relationship in terms of Freud's Oedipus Complex and the conflicts between Christian tradition and Jewish tradition?

(6) Charles Bernstein gives us an example of Zukofky's homophonic translation (see the "Assigned Reading"). What are the features and effects of homophonic translation?

(7) Charles Bernstein thinks "Poem beginning 'The' anticipates many of the major formal and thematic concerns in much of Zukofsky's subsequent work." What are the formal and thematic concerns in Poem beginning "The"?

5.3 Assigned Reading

Louis Zukofsky: An Introduction

Charles Bernstein

The melody! The rest is accessory:
My one voice. My other: is
An objective—rays of the object brought to a focus,
An objective—nature as creator—desire

for what is objectively perfect
Inextricably the direction of historic and
contemporary particulars
—*from A*—6

Louis Zukofsky is the most formally radical poet to emerge among the second wave modernists who composed in the wake of such first-generation innovators as Ezra Pound, T. S. Eliot, Wallace Stevens, James Joyce, William Carlos Williams, and Gertrude Stein. Each one of these older poets was an important source for Zukofsky, whose response to his modernist predecessors was precise and comprehensive. In place of a sometimes overwhelming monumentalism of "*the*" great poem, Zukofsky emphasized the need for "*a*" series of poems. He rejected the major keys for minor chords, universals for particulars, the grandiose for discreteness. In the process, he created a ravishing, yet sometimes forbidding, body of work notable for its intricacy of detail as well as for its resistance to sweeping pronouncements and vague generalizations. Zukofsky's poetry is both emotional and accessible, but it demands much of its readers because of its refusal to separate intellect from feeling, or complexity from clarity.

Louis Zukofsky was born in 1904 on the Lower East Side of New York, the child of Yiddish-speaking parents who had emigrated from Russia (or, more precisely, Lithuania), just before Louis was born. His father Pinchos (1860—1950) and mother Chana (1862—1927) figure significantly in his work.

Zukofsky attended Columbia University, part of the unprecedented spike in Jewish students admitted to Ivy League colleges immediately after World War Ⅰ, following the introduction of test-based admissions. At Columbia, Zukofsky studied with Mark Van Doren, then a prominent poet, and John Dewey, the philosopher so influential for artists of Zukofsky's and the immediately subsequent generation. A precocious student, he was only 20 when he got his M. A., writing a dissertation on Henry Adams. (Zukofsky never got his B. A., having failed to take a necessary Phys Ed class.) While at Columbia, Zukofsky's closest literary comrade was Whittaker Chambers, who, at the time, was involved with the Communist Party, but who later turned on his fellow travelers on the left, becoming famous as one of Alger Hiss' principal accusers.

Among the first-wave modernists, Pound cast the biggest shadow for

Zukofsky. In 1927, the 23-year-old poet sent Pound "Poem beginning 'The.'" Pound published it in*The Exile* and also recommended that Harriet Monroe let Zukofsky put together a special number of her magazine, *Poetry.* Editing the "'Objectivists' 1931" issue was a turning point for Zukofsky, firmly establishing his "objectivist" aesthetic in both his lead essay and his selection of poets, including several who, along with Lorine Niedecker, who he met slightly later, would become his most significant companions-in-poetry-George Oppen, Charles Reznikoff, and the British poet Basil Bunting.

Zukofsky supported himself in a decidedly ad-hoc manner until 1934, when he got a research job with a federal works program and soon after with the Works Projects Administration (WPA), where he stayed until 1942, most significantly working on a history of American handicrafts. He met Celia Thaew in 1933 and they were married six years later. The Zukofskys had one child, Paul, born in 1943, the same year Louis left the WPA to work as a substitute public school teacher and a technical writer. Paul and Celia, both musicians, figure prominently in Zukofsky's poems, most movingly in the lyric rondo *A*—11. (Paul went on to become a prominent violinist and conductor.) Moreover, domestic themes become more pronounced in Zukofksy's poems written after World War II. In 1947, he took a job as an instructor in the English Department of the Polytechnic Institute of Brooklyn, where he would teach until retiring in 1966. For most of his life, Zukofsky lived in the heart of New York City and certainly his poems are as much in, of, and about New York—itself an urban collage of energy 24 hours each day—as anything else. In 1972, the Zukofskys moved to Port Jefferson, New York, on Long Island. Zukofsky died there in 1978.

After a prescient early poem from 1922, the selection of Zukofsky's poems included in this volume begins with three of the six movements of "Poem beginning 'The.'" The complete poem begins with an untranslated epigraph (in Persian) by Omar Khayyám, followed by a full page of sources given by name and line (this index is included in the notes section of the present edition). "Poem beginning 'The'" is a powerful response to Eliot's *The Waste Land*; it's list of sources is a wry comment on Eliot's appended notes to his poem. But that is just an opening gambit of the poem. "Poem beginning 'The'" anticipates many of the major formal and thematic concerns in much of Zukofsky's subsequent work. Composed of 333 separately numbered lines, including one left blank, the poem is a masterpiece of pointillist collage, in which the basic unit of composition, the numbered line, is allowed to stand by itself, as discrete, while simultaneously being stitched together with the other lines. This concern for the relation of part to the whole—specifically, that the part is neither consumed by the whole nor isolated from it—is a key aspect of Zukofsky's poetics and politics. Thematically, the poem addresses a central concern for the immigrant generation: the problem of assimilation, both cultural and poetical.

In contrast to Eliot, Zukofsky's list of sources is ethnically inflected, local, comic, as well as deeply responsive to the canon of British poetry. In particular, Zukofsky gives prominent mention to, and translates, the Yiddish-American poet Yehoash (Solomon Bloomgarden), most famous for his Yiddish translation of the Torah. "Poem beginning 'The'" raises the problem of the poet, through his newly acquired, lofty education, his socialist views, and his atheism, losing connection with his religious familial culture. This is evident, especially in its poignant address to Zukofsky's mother in the fifth movement of the poem, "Autobiography,"—"If horses but could sing Bach, mother—/ Remember how I wished it once—/ Now I kiss you who could never sing Bach, never read Shakespeare." In contrast to Pound and Eliot, Zukofsky—from this earliest poem—recognized the founding significance of difference for American poetry. The final lines of "Autobiography" are emblematic: "Keine Kadish wird man sagen." The passage is adapted from Heinrich Heine's "Gedächtnisfeier" (Memorial)—"Keine Messe wird man singen, / Keinen Kadosch wird man sagen, / Nichts gesagt und nichts gesungen / Wird an meinen Sterbetagen" ("No Mass will anyone sing / Neither Kaddish will anyone say / Not said and not sung / When I lay dead"). These same issues are addressed in the excerpts included from *A*—12, where Zukofsky's father figures prominently.

Louis Zukofsky's poems operate within an interval that he describes, in *A*—12, as "Lower limit speech / Upper limit music." The music of poetry, in Zukofsky's sense, refers to the intricate patterning of sound that everywhere pervades his work. This poetry leads with sound and you can never go wrong following the sound sense, for it is only after you hear the words that you are able to locate their meanings. In other words, these poems are not representations of ideas but enactments of thoughts in motion, articulated as sound. Zukofsky loved to create patterns, some of which are apparent and some of which operate subliminally. Often in reading one of his poems, you can sense multiple patterns at play; indeed, reading Zukofsky induces this sensation. But these poems are not multi-dimensional crossword puzzles: no solution is required, or, for that matter, even desired. The experience made possible through the crafting of the poems is "when the meanings are" (as Emily Dickinson puts it): the meaning is not behind the words but in the words as they unfold, and refold, in the ear.

Often Zukofsky's poems have no speaker; they are what are, things in the world, handmade. *I's* (pronounced *eyes*) (the title of one of Zukofsky's collections of short poems) is his now-classic formulation for the I that becomes an other. The I in the eye, and the eye in I (aye aye; the ayes have it). In Zukofsky's lyric, the personally expressive poem is not replaced by the poem as thing seen (recall Pound's injunction to use no word that does not contribute to the sense of a thing seen). For Zukofsky, it's all about toggling: between I and I, it and we, eye and you, seen and unseen, present and absent, here and there; a re-doubling-as-re-doubting of the senses. "See sun, and think shadow" (#21, *Anew*).

Zukofsky's poems-as-objects are not impersonal so much as autonomous; "small (or large) machine(s) made of words" (Williams); "nature as creator" (*A*—6). There is no better example of self-reflectivity in poetry than #20 of *Anew*, a poem that does what it says it's doing: "The tunes image holding the line." Thinking in psychoanalytic terms, the "objectivist" poem is a transitional object, a thing that takes its meaning by means of our relation to it. Or to put it more baldly: the materiality in Zukofsky's poetry is always a social materiality. It's not a matter of what it says, but of what it is; or, better, it is not a matter of what it is, but of what it does. Words are things too, and in Zukofsky's poetry they have a heft, a stuffness, a thickness that we can count on and which counts on us. These poems are not well-wrought urns but crystalline vessels of light; when we hold them in our hands we see our hands.

Immediately following "Poem Beginning 'The,'" we present a spectrum of Zukofsky's short poems, from the late 1920s to the early 1960s. These poems build their meaning one word at a time, the words tug at you as soon as you let the poem take you in tow. These short lyrics are not about overhearing but hearing again; each word, like a stone dropped in a pond, creates a ripple around it. The intersecting ripples on the surface of the pond are the pattern of the poem. Listen for the figures rather than try to figure anything out.

In September, 2004, before a standing-room only crowd at the Zukofsky centennial at Columbia and Barnard, Peter Quartermain spoke of "Thinking with the Poem," citing "The," from *After I's* (1961—1964):

The
The
desire
of
towing

"A one-word title," Quartermain noted. "Followed by four one-word lines ... Zukofsky explained to (Ian Hamilton) Finlay that he'd been thinking of tugboats, which tow very seriously." Zukofsky also pointed out the modulating vowel sounds in the poem. The kind of microtonal attention required of a Zukofsky poem is not a matter of deciphering but of close listening, of evenly hovering attention to the sonic, linguistic, and lexical dimensions of the poem, as much for their discrepant engagements as for their fit. I love the simple fact of the title, *The*, by the author of *A*. In his talk Quartermain asked: Is *A* pronounced ay or uh? Eh? And now we have another poem beginning "The." Is the title pronounced *thuh* or *thee*? Beats me. Both. Syllable count: 1/2/1/2. Tow the line? But, they say it's supposed to be toe the line. So much depends upon ... whether you want to be towed, since this is "the" desire not "a" desire. Now, go back to the image: Tiny tug drags large barge. Perhaps this poem's a counter-poetics: Do you want a poem to tow you or to do some towing yourself? A Zukofsky poem does not tow you along for a ride; that's what Quartermain means by emphasizing "thinking with the poem." In contrast to "the" desire of towing, we might speak of "a" desire not to be towed. Or anyway, told.

Perhaps Zukofsky's most exquisite realization of the microtonal shifting of vowels in one of his permutational poems, or rounds, is the Valentine "Songs of Degrees," which creates constellations among nine seed words: *hear*, *her*, *clear*, *mirror*, *care*, *error*, *in*, *his*, *is*. There is a moebius effect as the same words shift from noun to verb. Another striking example of word-by-word permutation, approaching fugue, is "Julia's Wild," from *Bottom: on Shakespeare*, whose multiple variants of the word order and phrasing of this eight-word, decasyllabic string: come-shadow-come-and-take-this-shadow-up, is a tour-de-force of polymetrical imagination in its aversion *of* (not *to*) pentameter.

At the other side of the spectrum from "The" and "Songs of Degree" is "Mantis," a much-cited poem from 1934, regrettably not included in this selection. The elaborate conceit of the piece is a praying mantis "lost in the subway"—"fact," Zukofsky notes, not "symbol," of the "oppression" and "helplessness" of the poor. In his most explicitly proletarian mode, the author produced the single work of his that is most conducive to New Critical close reading. Indeed, "Mantis" displays how Zukofsky is able to use the closed-form sestina as a means for social reflection:

> Mantis! praying mantis! since your wings' leaves
> And your terrified eyes, pins, bright, black and poor
> Beg—"Look, take it up " (thought's torsion)! "save it!"
> I who can't bear to look, cannot touch, —You—
> You can—but no one sees your steadying lost
> In the cars' drafts on the lit subway stone.
> ...
> Fly, mantis, on the poor, arise like leaves
> The armies of the poor, strength: stone on stone
> And build the new world in your eyes, Save it!

More remarkable, however, is "*Mantis*, An Interpretation," Zukofsy's extensive commentary-in-verse, which suggests the insufficiency of the poem and the necessity for interpretation—not as closure but as dialectical method for opening the word's work into a social world: "The mantis might have heaped up upon itself a / Grave of verse,/ But the facts are not a symbol. "The final lines of the poem do not represent an idea but enfold "the simultaneous, / The diaphanous, historical / in one head. " As if directly confronting Kafka, Zukofsky wryly concludes: "No human being wishes to become / An insect for the sake of a symbol. "

A is Zukofsky's lifelong long poem in 24 parts, one for each hour of the day, written from 1928 to 1974 (though not in chronological order). The complete poem runs about 800 pages in the Johns Hopkins University Press edition. Most of the movements begin with an "A" or an "an. " A is a serial collage, an explicit turning away from Pound's desire, in the *Cantos*, for montage, for the parts to cohere. As such, *A* opens a "z-sited path" (*A*—23) for the long serial poems of Zukofsky's most immediate heirs in the following generation—Robert Creeley, Robert Duncan, Jack Spicer, Robin Blaser, Hannah Weiner, Charles Olson, Larry Eigner, and Jerome Rothenberg. Ideas in *"A"* are not proclaimed but threaded into successions of voicings. The sources, themes, and forms in *A* are plural and overlaid; there is much taken from daily life, much from family life, many literary and philosophical threads, alongside explicitly addressed political and aesthetic commitments. These are Zukofsky's "historic and contemporary particulars," which together make up a tissue of allusion and articulation that is everywhere localized and embodied in and as the poem.

A—1—first word A—opens on the night of April 5, 1928—both the first night of Passover and Good Friday—at a performance that Zukofsky attended of St. Matthew's Passion at Carnegie Hall. Bach weaves through *A*, whose intricate pattern of recurrences, recapitulations, and extensions can be compared, at least metaphorically, to the form of a fugue—from the chordal arrangement of syllables to the recurrences both between and within the movements of the work.

"There's naw-thing / lak po—ee try," Zukofsky writes in "It's a gay li - ife," "it's a delicacy / for a horse." Is this the horse Zukofsky evokes in "Poem Beginning 'The,'" the one he told his mother he wished could sing Bach? *A*—7 returns to horses—there are many plays on horse in Zukofsky—here it's police sawhorses closing a street, sawhorses that look like a capital letter "A" in this poem of seven sonnets.

A —9 is the crux of *A*—a supreme realization of what Zukofsky called "rested totality"; that is, "desire for what is objectively perfect." The poem takes its form, and rhyme scheme, directly from Calvalcanti's "Donna Mi Prega," which had also been the subject of an influential translation by Pound. *A*—9 has two halves, written, respectively, before and after Word War Ⅱ. The second half of the poem is a mirror image of the first. Its sources include Marx and Spinoza (the two liminal figures for secular American Jewish thought), as well as a scientific treatise on quantum physics (related scientific material is also found in "It's hard to see but think of a sea," #12 of *Anew*, included in this volume). *A*—9's intricate system of patterning goes from its eleven-syllable lines, mostly in sonnet-length stanzas, to what Zukfosky called the "conical" distribution of n's and r's, to the syntactic rotation of the same words shifting to different parts of speech (as in the "Songs of

Degrees" and "Julia's Wild"). *A*—9 presents the shimmering figure of a crystal turning on its axis to an imagined beat, leaning leftward, arriving at song. The poem's recurrent motif is for a rescaling of values toward that which is created by "hands" and "hearts"—that is, by the production of good and goods made by human hands; rather than by commodity value, that is, by how much a thing is sold for. "Labor as creator," as Zukofsky puts it in *A*—8, from the 1930s.

One outtake from *A*—9 is the hilarious and charming "A Foin Lass Bodders," a translation of "Donna Mi Prega" into Brooklynese. *A*—15 begins its second stanza with a homophonic translation of *The Book of Job*: if you listen closely you can almost hear the Hebrew percolating through the English: "He neigh ha lie low"; but this is also a horse's song (its neigh), or "An hinny," which is not only a backside but a cross between a "she-ass" and a stallion.

Zukofsky's iconoclastic approach to translation would flower with *Catullus*, which he wrote with Celia Zukofsky, working on it from 1958—1966. For *Catullus*, the Zukofsky developed a technique that has come to be called homophonic translation—translation with special emphasis to the sound rather than the lexical meaning. Since Latin and English share many cognates, the results are sometimes uncannily resonant even passionate, versions, of the original poems. It is worth comparing the Zukofskys' versions of the poems with the Catullus originals, which is easy enough to do since editions of Catullus are available online and in print. The numbers for each poem is the same (note that #22 of *Anew*, included here, is an early version *Catullus* 8). Let's take #112 as an example. The Latin is—

> Multus home es, Naso, neque tecum multus homost qui
> descendit: Naso, multus es et pathicus.

Literal translation by Celia Zukofsky:

> Much a man you are, Naso, and that you much a man it is who
> comes down: Naso, much you are and pathetic/lascivious.

Cornish edition in the Loeb Classical Library (used by the Zukofskys):

You are many men's man, Naso, but not many men go down town with you: Naso, you are many men's man and minion.

Finally, the homophonic version:

> Mool 'tis homos, 'Naso, 'n 'queer take 'im mool 'tis ho most he
> descended: Naso, mool'tis—is it pathic, cuss.

The Zukofsky version is able to take on a certain texture that brings us closer to the Latin while at the same allowing the queerness of the original to come out. Leading with the sound, homophonic translation reframes what is significant in translation, challenging the idea that the translation should focus on content or create poems that sound fluent in their new language. Zukofsky insists that the mark of the translator be pronounced, and that in making the translation strange, we may provide a way to come closer to its core.

Following *Catullus*, Zukofsky completed the remaining movements of *A*, writing *A*—22 and *A*—23 from 1970 to 1974. He then went on to 80 *Flowers*, a work in which the density and overlays of *A*—23, let's call it the mulching of sources and reflections, is extended and formalized. The work consists of 81 poems, each with eight five-word lines. After 80 *Flowers*, Zukofsky planned one more work, *Gamut*, but was only able to complete the first poem of the projected series.

Zukofsky's work is too varied to create a representative selection. For this gathering, we have necessarily left out his prose writings, both essay and fiction (I should have liked to begin with "An Objective"). Since *A* is best read as a single long poem of 24 parts, the scale of that work cannot be reflected here. In the limited space available, I have tried to give a visceral sense of a range of formal, thematic, and aesthetic possibilities that exists within the highly articulated constellation of Zukofsky's work as a whole.

The selection is built around three long poems that are included: First, "Poem Beginning 'The,'" inaugural for second-wave (Jewish) modernism. Second, "4 Other Countries," based on a European trip Zukofsky took in 1957, with its capacious range of references and locations, and also its intimation of the five-word line. (Williams expressed his enthusiastic response to this poem in a letter that was very encouraging to Zukofsky.) Last, the late, majestically refractive (not to say sublimely refractory) *A*—23, with its 1000 five-word lines, Zukofsky's most linguistically radical achievement and a foundational work for the thickly textual American poetry of the last part of the 20th century. Those three works make a perfect interrelated set and key into the other selections. The unit of composition is not the part but the whole 160-page book: each section must contribute toward that whole but also hold its own. That is, I have tried to use Zukofsky's principle of collage and arrangement in *A* to create an historically grounded constellation of particulars. To achieve this goal, it has been necessary to make excerpts from poems, a precarious practice that is only justified because it is part of an overall design; excerpts from single moments of *A*, published by themselves or in an anthology selection, would not be justified (nor approved by the copyright holder).

Naturally, many significant poems have had to be omitted. Zukofsky's ode to his wash-stand (from 29 *Poems*) remains a useful example of the poetics of the common and the reversal of values from the worship of/at "the" altar to "a" secular everyday, with relevance to Reznikoff, for example:

To my wash-stand
in which I wash
my left hand
and my right hand

To my wash-stand
whose base is Greek
whose shaft
is marble and fluted

The first part of the three-line "partita" of *A*—13, with its twirling aphorisms is one of the highlights of *A*. Those seeking out the complete *A* will be sure to take in the turn from one-to two-to three-word lines in *A*—14 and the full flowering, in *A*—22, of the five-word line (often in stanzas of five lines) that is a basic unit of late Zukofsky. *A*—22 starts with what has become something of a signature piece for Zukofsky, a Valentine tercet, made with 9 vowels and 9 consonants that concatenate multiple plays on era/anno/aer/are, and on a/an/any, and also on year/ear; perhaps you can hear, mirrored, an *error* in that other poem for Valentine time, "Songs of Degrees." A round of these six words shows the care in all to come anon.

AN ERA
ANY TIME
OF YEAR

[Selected from Charles Bernstein. Louis Zukofsky: An Introduction. *Foreign Literature Studies*, 2006(2).]

6. Elizabeth Bishop

6.1 Presentation Topics

(1) Bishop's complex negotiation of formal and historical imperatives.

(2) Bishop's poetic objects, tonal and grammatical shifts and poetic structures.

6.2 Selected Reading

Ⅰ. Central issue of concern

The tension between Elizabeth Bishop's seemingly traditional form and the rich and subversive meaning.

Ⅱ. Text

The Map

Land lies in water; it is shadowed green.
Shadows, or are they shallows, at its edges
showing the line of long sea-weeded ledges
where weeds hang to the simple blue from green.
Or does the land lean down to life the sea from under,
drawing it unperturbed around itself?
Along the fine tan sandy shelf
is the land tugging at the sea from under?

The shadow of Newfoundland lies flat and still.
Labrador's yellow, where the moony Eskimo
has oiled it. We can stroke these lovely bays,
under a glass as if they were expected to blossom,
or as if to provide a clean cage for invisible fish.
The names of seashore towns run out to sea,
the names of cities cross the neighboring mountains
—the printer here experiencing the same excitement

as when emotion too far exceeds its cause.
These peninsulas take the water between thumb and finger
like women feeling for the smoothness of yard-goods.

Mapped waters are more quiet than the land is,
lending the land their waves' own conformation:
and Norway's hare runs south in agitation,
profiles investigate the sea, where land is.
Are they assigned, or can the countries pick their colors?
—What suits the character or the native waters best.
Topography displays no favorites; North's as near as West.
More delicate than the historians' are the map-makers' colors.

[Selected from Elizabeth Bishop. *The Complete Poems, 1927—1979*. New York: Farrar, Straus and Girous, 1983.]

The Moose

For Grace Bulmer Bowers

From narrow provinces
of fish and bread and tea,
home of the long tides
where the bay leaves the sea
twice a day and takes
the herrings long rides,

where if the river
enters or retreats
in a wall of brown foam
depends on if it meets
the bay coming in,
the bay not at home;

where, silted red,
sometimes the sun sets
facing a red sea,
and others, veins the flats'

lavender, rich mud
in burning rivulets;

on red, gravelly roads,
down rows of sugar maples,
past clapboard farmhouses
and neat, clapboard churches,
bleached, ridged as clamshells,
past twin silver birches,

through late afternoon
a bus journeys west,
the windshield flashing pink,
pink glancing off of metal,
brushing the dented flank
of blue, beat-up enamel;

down hollows, up rises,
and waits, patient, while
a lone traveler gives
kisses and embraces
to seven relatives
and a collie supervises.

Goodbye to the elms,
to the farm, to the dog.
The bus starts. The light
grows richer; the fog,
shifting, salty, thin,
comes closing in.

Its cold, round crystals
form and slide and settle
in the white hens' feathers,
in gray glazed cabbages,
on the cabbage roses

and lupins like apostles;

the sweet peas cling
to their wet white string
on the whitewashed fences;
bumblebees creep
inside the foxgloves,
and evening commences.

One stop at Bass River.
Then the Economies
Lower, Middle, Upper;
Five Islands, Five Houses,
where a woman shakes a tablecloth
out after supper.

A pale flickering. Gone.
The Tantramar marshes
and the smell of salt hay.
An iron bridge trembles
And a loose plank rattles
but doesn't give way.

On the left, a red light
swims through the dark:
a ship's port lantern.
Two rubber boots show,
illuminated, solemn.
A dog gives one bark.

A woman climbs in
with two market bags,
brisk, freckled, elderly.
"A grand night. Yes, sir,
all the way to Boston."

She regards us amicably.

Moonlight as we enter
the New Brunswick woods,
hairy, scratchy, splintery;
moonlight and mist
caught in them like lamb's wool
on bushes in a pasture.

The passengers lie back.
Snores. Some long sighs.
A dreamy divagation
begins in the night,
a gentle, auditory,
slow hallucination...

In the creakings and noises,
an old conversation
—not concerning us,
but recognizable, somewhere,
back in the bus:
Grandparents' voices

uninterruptedly
talking, in Eternity:
names being mentioned,
things cleared up finally;
what he said, what she said,
who got pensioned;

deaths, deaths and sicknesses;
the year he remarried;
the year (something) happened.
She died in childbirth.
That was the son lost
when the schooner foundered.

He took to drink. Yes.
She went to the bad.
When Amos began to pray
even in the store and
finally the family had
to put him away.

"Yes..." that peculiar
affirmative. "Yes..."
A sharp, indrawn breath,
half groan, half acceptance,
that means "life's like that.
We know it (also death)."

Talking the way they talked
in the old featherbed,
peacefully, on and on,
dim lamplight in the hall,
down in the kitchen, the dog
tucked in her shawl.

Now, it's all right now
even to fall asleep
just as on all those nights.
—Suddenly the bus driver
stops with a jolt,
turns off his lights.

A moose has come out of
the impenetrable wood
and stands there, looms, rather,
in the middle of the road.
It approaches; it sniffs at
the bus' hot hood.

Towering, antlerless,

high as a church,
homely as a house
(or, safe as houses).
A man's voice assures us
"Perfectly harmless..."

Some of the passengers
exclaim in whispers,
childishly, softly,
"Sure are big creatures."
"It's awful plain."
"Look! It's a she!"

Taking her time,
she looks the bus over,
grand, otherworldly.
Why, why do we feel
(we all feel) this sweet
sensation of joy?

"Curious creatures,"
says our quiet driver,
rolling his r's.
"Look at that, would you."
Then he shifts gears.
For a moment longer,

by craning backward,
the moose can be seen
on the moonlit macadam;
then there's a dim
smell of moose, an acrid
smell of gasoline.

[Selected from Elizabeth Bishop. *The Complete Poems, 1927—1979*. New York: Farrar, Straus and Girous, 1983.]

Ⅲ. Questions for discussion

(1) As to the question "What is a map," Bishop will cite "First Lessons in Geography" for answer: "A picture of the whole, or a part, of the Earth's surface." But in "The Map," the map is surely metaphorical. History and geography, political and economic unity, aesthetic value all are bound together throughout the history of mapmaking. Then what does map symbolize in this poem?

(2) In an introductory note to her Phi Beta Kappa reading at Harvard, Bishop calls "The Moose" a "sort of ballad, a rather simple record of a bus trip from N. S." But obviously it is an over simplified statement. Beneath the simple narrative about the bus trip, there is a grand thematic concern. What is it? And what it the function of this combination?

(3) "The Moose" is an autobiographical narrative poem which is dedicated to Bishop's deceased aunt. And because of this, it is classified as a post-confessional lyric. Could you sum up certain basic features of post-confessional lyric? Take "The Moose" as an example.

(4) What does the moose symbolize? What is Bishop's attitude towards death?

(5) In "The Moose," Bishop's repetition of words is quite marked. What are the functions of these repetitions?

(6) Bishop once said, "the choice is never wide and never free." What is Mutlu Konuk Blasing's comment? What do you think of Bishop's remark and Blasing's interpretation?

6.3 Assigned Reading

Elizabeth Bishop: "Repeat, Repeat, Repeat; Revise, Revise, Revise"

Mutlu Konuk Blasing

Costume and custom are complex.
The headgear of the other sex
inspires us to experiment.

—Bishop

Elizabeth Bishop's refusal to be classified and anthologized as a woman poet is well known; less well known, perhaps, is her statement "I've always considered myself a strong feminist." Taken together, these positions suggest that her being a "feminist"—whatever she may mean by it, she is not evading the political issue—does not entail her perceiving her work as a woman poet's, and she demands to be read from this double perspective. For in order to read Bishop as a feminist, we need to place her all the more firmly within a patriarchal tradition so as to see how her revisions of it signify politically as well as poetically. Formally, her work is traditional: her lines are usually metrical, her stanzas often have intricate rhyme schemes, and her forms range from blank verse and sonnets to sestinas and villanelles. Her conventional stanzas and meters, together with her grammatical syntax, place her within the symbolic order, and while she challenges its assumptions and hierarchies, her dissension—including "feminist" revisions—register within this framework. However, given her historical position after modernism, her conventional forms and language themselves serve a critical function: by aligning herself with a patriarchal tradition and observing conventional verse forms, she can critique a different—and, from her position, more dangerous because more naturalized—set of assumptions that underwrite the investment of authority in the person and experience of the poet, who is historically male.

Bishop's work, with its complex negotiation of formal and historical imperatives, forces us to question the idea of a separate women's poetic "language" or "tradition"—even a foreshortened version that would align her with Marianne Moore, her primary woman predecessor. Granted, her descriptive strategies owe something to Moore, and both poets play with scale and point of view in order to preclude consistent, totalizing perspectives and to signal the constructedness of the world they describe. A poem like "The Steeple-Jack," for example, clearly shows what Moore may have taught Bishop. Similarly, both poets question the alignment of women with nature, a dominant metaphor written into the very language they use. "Turn to the letter M," Moore writes, "and you will find / that 'a wife is a coffin.'" The "letter M" links matter, mother, and mortality—a literal given exploited by others, including H. D. But the initial "M" also doubles as doubles as "Marianne's monogram" and suggests that a woman poet finds herself already written up in a cultural sourcebook or dictionary. The dualisms of letters, woman, nature, and death versus spirit, man, mind, and life are engendered and gendered by idealism, which Moore and Bishop equally resist. Being a "literalist of the imagination," who skews discourse by "arguments" based on literal accidents, is one strategy of subverting the symbolic economy of idealism that Moore—among other poets, male and female alike—sometimes follows. Moore tends to rely on a special linguistic, formal, and moral dispensation to attack the assumptions that make for a center, author, or poem.

But this is not Bishop's stylistic strategy. She avoids Moore's formal and syntactic eccentricities and denies herself the privileged perspective of such marginality. Although Bishop admired Moore's "true originality," she also acknowledged "the sort of alienation it might involve." She is careful to distinguish her work from Moore's idiosyncratic poetry: "She looked like no one else; she talked like no one else; her poems showed a mind not much like anyone else's; and her notions of meter and rhyme were unlike all the conventional notions—so why not believe that the old English meters that still seem natural to most of us (or seemed to, at any rate) were not natural to her at all?" Bishop's backtracking to stress "seemed" is telling and suggests that she is perfectly aware of what is at stake in employing traditional forms.

From the beginning Bishop never strays too far from "the old English meters," and her work increasingly addresses all that is involved in this "seeming"—this alignment with a tradition that is common property, with always a more or less loose fit on several counts. As Helen Carr puts it, "The complex of history and flesh that we each are can never be represented accurately in a shared discourse." Yet to wander too far from this shared discourse is not to get nearer one's particular "complex of history and flesh," whatever that may be; at the risk of simplifying Moore and the historical pressures that shape her work, I would propose her as a case in point. In poetic language, not only one's particular history but "flesh" itself must register, if it is to register at all, in historically coded and publicly recognizable conventions of patterning the physical properties of a given language, such as rhythm, rhyme, and meters. In Bishop's words, "the choice is never wide and never free," for poetry is not a matter of creating one's own subjectivity but of choosing how to reappropriate an already overdetermined subjectivity.

While Bishop stays with meters, her remark that they only "seem" natural seems also to resist the alignment of the physical, bodily, "natural" face of language with such poetic devices as rhythm, meter, and lineation. A version of this alignment informs, for example, Julia Kristeva's argument that rhythm in poetry resists the deadly repression of the physical word by the signifying function. Poetry (by men or women) cultivates the "semiotic" function—gendered female—and enables it to hold its own against the paternal, symbolic order. All poetry is thus subversive: it weakens gender divisions and challenges the symbolic order itself. For this reason, all who would stabilize a social order—from Plato to Stalin and the Fascists—must root out poetry: "The poet is put to death because he wants to turn rhythm into a dominant element; because he wants to make a language perceive what it doesn't want to say, provide it with its matter independently of the sign, and free it from denotation. For it is this eminently parodic gesture that changes the system."

Yet this "gesture" signifies as such only within "the system"; furthermore, the semiotic dimension has its own systemically determined margins and centers. The criteria that define certain kinds of semiotic language as "poetic" are historically and culturally regulated—if not by tradition, then by contemporary consensus. In other words, poetry's formalism is determined, and even if a poet rejects conventional meters, stanzas, or rhyme schemes, she still must set up some artificial, formal order, combining in different ways available patterns for organizing the material aspects of the signifier, in order to have a pattern—with "repeats"—to mark the special or poetic nature of her language. Moore is only one example. What seems to subvert the symbolic order, then, also duplicates it in another register by instituting its own hierarchies. For example, meter or what registers as rhythm is not a natural quality of the semiotic dimension; it is an abstract pattern that metonymically substitutes for the physical qualities of a given language. Whether conventional or experimental, forms only represent the semiotic, as it is figured and positioned within the symbolic order, to signify the "natural" face of language. Thus poetic language destabilizes and constantly reverses all simple oppositions like semiotic—symbolic and signifier—signified, as well as the metaphorical alignment of these formal and linguistic dualisms with hierarchical distinctions. This systemic and unstable subversiveness, I would argue, is the larger, discursive function of poetry's formalism, one that Bishop fully exploits.

Any discussion of women's poetry in general from a feminist perspective is complicated by at least two other considerations, more historical than generic. The first is the cultural gendering of poetry itself. Especially since the eighteenth century, the increasing separation of subjective and material realms, together with the gendering of these opposites, has aligned poetry with the "feminine" realm of the imagination, the emotions, and personal experience as opposed to the "masculine" values of reason, utility, empirical truth, and public experience. Since the Romantics, the male poet's cultural position of authority has itself come into question. Thus the modernists' poetic anxieties—how to "make it new"—tend to get cast in gender terms—how to write "like a man." This anxiety affects someone like Moore as much as Pound or Wallace Stevens, whose complex of gender and poetic anxieties Frank Lentricchia examines in *Ariel and the Police*.

Poetry is a special, sacramental language, a privileged hieratic discourse—historically, a jealously guarded male domain. Especially since the Romantics, however, it may focus on personal experience—historically, a female province. In other words, poetry is an elitist discourse that may deal with culturally disadvantaged material. Moreover, while thoroughly intertextual, it may articulate private experience. Again, poetry would appear to maintain and question cultural binarism like elitist versus communal or public versus private. Yet, as Carr points out, while popular forms of prose are now subject to critical study by feminists, the hierarchical distinction between poetry and "mere verse" remains virtually unchallenged. Poetry maintains its privileged position—ironically, at the cost of becoming culturally marginal—partly because it already radically destabilizes oppositional thinking, including cultural typing not only of gender but of what constitutes individual versus public experience. These terms are neither oppositional nor identical: each is articulated through the other and can play the other's part. And poetry will not reduce to discourse any more than it will reduce to individual expression or formalist sacrament. Feminist criticism of poetry, then, is not well served by arguments for a separate women's poetic tradition or language, for reasons apart from the universalism of such a position that a number of feminist critics have objected to.

The second historical consideration involves the history of 20th century poetry. When the idea of an authoritative norm (the consensus of a literary generation about the way to write) disappears with modernism and all historical styles become equally usable, the political efficacy and charge of "deviant" styles become limited. Conversely, after modernism, styles that observe historical conventions are able increasingly to question the rhetoric of their forms and may indeed have greater rhetorical flexibility than organicist experimental styles, which cannot afford to question their own rhetoric. For the only authority organicist experimentalism can claim is that it is ostensibly non-rhetorical—that it can access truths and processes beyond those available to conventional forms, which alone are seen as rhetorical. Organicist experimental writers end up with less room to question the values (ethical, political, or natural) that they invoke to authorize their forms, for without the identification of forms with certain moral, political, or metaphysical truths, the poet has no authority save that of individual talent, which in poetry is no authority at all. Thus ostensibly free forms, which must invest in authorities "above" or "below" the historical, conventional, or rhetorical, may enjoy less rhetorical freedom than conservative forms. Bishop takes full advantage of the "narrow" freedom her conventional forms offer, including release from the authority of "natural" truths, and her work increasingly registers the complexity of a woman poet's historical position, not only post eighteen century but post modernism.

[Selected from Mutlu Konuk Blasing. *Politics and Form in Postmodern Poetry*. Cambridge: Cambridge University Press, 1995.]

Chapter 8 Poetry After 1945

1. Introduction

Postmodernism is a reaction to modernism, representing a new mode of perception and a new way of writing. In poetry it strives to go against the vogue of the New Critical poem and its parent style, the High Modernism of the precious decades. However, it is closely linked with the previous period as it acknowledges part of it as the sources of its inspiration. As well, its reaction against Eliot and the New Criticism is also an indication of its debt to High Modernism.

Like any other literary group, postmodernism owes a lot to its historical background, the postwar period. Together with economic growth and the increasing affluence, this era witnesses abundant new experiences: memories of war savageries, the cold war, nuclear bomb, McCarthyism, Civil Rights and race relations, awareness of ethnic and cultural diversity and difference, the Vietnam war, the Beat Generation, communal living and drugs, the impact of TV, feminism and the fight against patriarchy, the fight for sexual freedom, the self-assertion of gays, the computer and the information explosion that has followed in its wake, the increase in self-awareness and identity, the consciousness of environmental protection including the ozone layer, greenhouse effect, and species preservation, the exploration of space and the new vistas of vision it has opened up for humankind, etc. With all these changes, human perceptions, sensibility and values all have altered. Experience becomes more individualized and expression tends to be more personal, even idiosyncratic. Therefore, new ways of expression are urgently needed.

Additionally, in the 1950s the poetic atmosphere encouraged the younger generation to rebel against the tradition. Codifying values and methods, the New

Criticism, which dominated over literary creation and criticism as an academic orthodoxy for over thirty years, eventually became a dogmatic straightjacket to the imagination. Thus many people, especially the young generation, were encouraged to struggle out of its bondage. What's more, people were tired of a style (i.e. the High Modernist style) unchanged for over 40 years (1910—1950). Bounded by the restrictions and inhibitions of the New Criticism, and the hardship to follow the traditionalism, internationalism, intellectualism and impersonality of the High Modernist style, they found no leeway for anything reflective, meditative and conversational. Therefore, they cased their interest on new and fashionable ways which always easily attracted notice and made a stir.

What's more, some masters of modernism like T. S. Eliot, Ezra Pound and Williams Carols Williams also experienced change in their poetry writing. Eliot's move from High Modernist to the meditative mode was obvious in the *Four Quartets*. But what was more attractive was Pound's *Pisan Cantos* and Williams' *Paterson* which appealed to the imagination of the young generation. Departing from the High Modernist concrete and fragmentary mode of presentation and its doctrine of impersonality, *Pisan Cantos* offered a new, spontaneous, free, autobiographical, and reflective way of writing. Meanwhile, appearing to be open, changing, forever in process, William's *Paterson* acted on the impulse of the moment rather than planned. Under all these conditions, nothing could stop the wind of changing from blowing.

With regards to the changes in taste and values that occurred in the 1950s and 1960s, the very idea of art has changed. Different from the 1890s and early 20th century when art and poetry were regarded as the end of thought, the finished products of the creative process, closed in form, with rhymes and stanzas, coherent images and figures and completed in plot enacted, now art and poetry are considered as open, ongoing, the process of the mind thinking, stressing motion, not previously well-planned but created on the impulse of the moment. Instead of aiming at an elite leadership as the finely metered Modernist poem did, postmodern poetry endeavors to reach the common people as much as possible.

As regards thematic concerns, postmodern poetry portrays daily experiences, events and emotions. Accepting life for what it is, it tries to represent life as with strengths and weakness, as something inconsistent, ever changing and never wholly knowable. Man envisioned by postmodern poetry, vulnerable and helpless, is at the mercy of overwhelming odds. Thus what the poets need to do, according to some people, is to seize the moment and make the best of it for themselves as well as the world at large. In formal aspects, postmodern poetry welcomes open form. The poem is often autobiographic as the poet is always speaking himself with personal and emotional tone, and intense but qualified feelings like humor amid remorse, disgust or anguish. The diction is mostly from daily speech, while the style is conversational, colloquial, discursive and meditative with a generally casual and relaxed mood. However, much of postmodern poetry is very hard to understand due to the private nature of the poet's thinking and expression, and their self-indulgence encouraged by the postmodern tendency of extreme individualization.

Though postmodern poetry sounds like monolithic, it is actually a blanket term covering a wide range of diverse experimentation and a bunch of schools. The 1950s and 1960s witnessed the rising of several different poetic groups, such as the Beat Generation with Allen Ginsberg as the leading figure, the Black Mountain poets very much influenced by the rector Charles Olson, the Confessional School including Sylvia Plath, the New York School held together by the friendship and enthusiasm of Frank O'Hara and so on. Beginning with the 1970s, American poetry has become too heterogeneous to group and define. However, there are still some prominent ones like the "Language" poet Charles Bernstein, and Anne Waldman as an active member of the "Outrider" experimental poetry community. Due to its diversity and abundance postmodern poetry contributes a lot to the prosperity of contemporary poetry.

Key Words

Beat Generation

A group of poets and writers who rose to prominence during the 1950s represented by Allen Ginsberg and Jack Kerouac as well as many others. In its purest from, Beat writing is characterized by a distinctive blending of comic exuberance and prophetic aspirations. With their disdain for bourgeois values and their readiness to shock middle-class sensibilities, the Beat writers opened the way for the much broader counter-culture of the 1960s.

Confessional Poetry

In which the author describes parts of his life which would not be in the public domain. Confessional poetry derives from the Romantics and Ezra Pound, but rose as a school of American poetry in the 1950s. The term "Confessional verse" was first made current in a review of Robert Lowell's *Life Studies*.

Language Poetry

Language poetry is not so much a movement as a theory-generated method of poetic composition that emerged in the early 1970s in North America. Despite its seeming rejection of the past, has a strong connection with the North American poetic traditions such as the 1930s Objectivist movement and the Black Mountain poetry.

2. Allen Ginsberg

2.1 Presentation Topics

(1) Allen Ginsberg and the Beat Generation.

(2) Counter Culture.

(3) Linguistic features of his poems.

2.2 Selected Reading

Ⅰ. Central issue of concern

Allen Ginsberg's sense of social breakdown and his tone of social protest.

Ⅱ. Text

Howl

① ***for Carl Solomon***

(1)

① A wardmate of Ginsberg while both were patients in the Columbia Psychiatric Institute in 1949. Many details in "Howl" come from their conversation.

I saw the best minds of my generation destroyed by madness, starving hysterical naked,
dragging themselves through the negro streets at dawn looking for an angry fix,
angelheaded hipsters burning for the ancient heavenly connection① to the starry dynamo in the machinery of night,
who poverty and tatters and hollow-eyed and high sat up smoking in the supernatural darkness of cold-water flats floating across the tops of cities contemplating jazz,
who bared their brains to Heaven under the El② and saw Mohammedan angels staggering on tenement roofs illuminated,
who passed through universities with radiant cool eyes hallucinating Arkansas and Blake-light③ tragedy among the scholars of war,
who were expelled from the academies for crazy & publishing obscene odes on the windows of the skull,
who cowered in unshaven rooms in underwear, burning their money in wastebaskets and listening to the Terror through the wall,
who got busted in their pubic beards returning through Laredo④ with a belt of marijuana for New York,
who ate fire in paint hotels or drank turpentine in Paradise Alley⑤, death, or purgatoried their torsos night after night
with dreams, with drugs, with waking nightmares, alcohol and cock and endless balls,
incomparable blind streets of shuddering cloud and lightning in the mind leaping towards poles of Canada & Paterson⑥, illuminating all the motionless world of Time between,
Peyote solidities of halls, backyard green tree cemetery dawns, wine drunkenness over the rooftops, storefront boroughs of teahead joyride neon blinking traffic

---

① One who supplies drugs.

② The elevated railway in New York City; also, a Hebrew word meaning God.

③ One summer Ginsberg had an auditory vision of William Blake reciting his poems "Ah! Sunflower" and "The Sick Rose."

④ A city in southern Texas.

⑤ A tenement courtyard in New York's East Village, the setting of one of Kerouac's novels.

⑥ Ginsberg's hometown in New Jersey, also the town celebrated by William Carlos Williams in *Paterson*.

light, sun and moon and tree vibrations in the roaring winter dusks of Brooklyn①, ashcan rantings and kind king light of mind,
who chained themselves to subways for the endless ride from Battery to holy Bronx② on benzedrine until the noise of wheels and children brought them down shuddering mouth-wracked and battered bleak of brain all drained of brilliance in the drear light of Zoo,
who sank all night in submarine light of Bickford's③ floated out and sat through the stale beer afternoon in desolate Fugazzi's④, listening to the crack of doom on the hydrogen jukebox,
who talked continuously seventy hours from park to pad to bar to Bellevue⑤ to museum to the Brooklyn Bridge,
a lost batallion of platonic conversationalists jumping down the stoops off fire escapes off windowsills off Empire State⑥ out of the moon,
yacketayakking screaming vomiting whispering facts and memories and anecdotes and eyeball kicks and shocks of hospitals and jails and wars,
whole intellects disgorged in total recall for seven days and nights with brilliant eyes, meat for the Synagogue cast on the pavement,
who vanished into nowhere Zen New Jersey leaving a trail of ambiguous picture postcards of Atlantic City Hall,
suffering Eastern sweats and Tangerian bone-grindings and migraines of China under junk-withdrawal in Newark's⑦ bleak furnished room,
who wandered around and around at midnight in the railway yard wondering where to go, and went, leaving no broken hearts,
who lit cigarettes in boxcars boxcars boxcars racketing through snow toward lonesome farms in grandfather night,

---

① A borough of New York City in southeast New York on western Long Island.
② Opposite ends of a New York subway line. Bronx Zoo was the northern terminus.
③ An all-night cafeteria where Ginsberg once worked.
④ Name of a bar.
⑤ A hospital for psychiatric patients.
⑥ New York State.
⑦ A city in western California.

who studied Plotinus Poe St John of the Cross① telepathy and bop kaballah② because the cosmos instinctively vibrated at their feet in Kansas,
who loned it through the streets of Idaho seeking visionary Indian angels who were visionary Indian angels,
who thought they were only mad when Baltimore③ gleamed in supernatural ecstasy,
who jumped in limousines with the Chinaman of Oklahoma on the impulse of winter midnight streetlight smalltown rain,
who lounged hungry and lonesome through Houston④ seeking jazz or sex or soup, and followed the brilliant Spaniard to converse about America and Eternity, a hopeless task, and so took ship to Africa,
who disappeared into the volcanoes of Mexico leaving behind nothing but the shadow of dungarees and the larva and ash of poetry scattered in fireplace Chicago,
who reappeared on the West Coast investigating the FBI in beards and shorts with big pacifist eyes sexy in their dark skin passing out incomprehensible leaflets,
who burned cigarette holes in their arms protesting the narcotic tobacco haze of Capitalism,
who distributed Supercommunist pamphlets in Union Square⑤ weeping and undressing while the sirens of Los Alamos⑥ wailed them down, and wailed down Wall⑦, and the Staten Island ferry also wailed,
who broke down crying in white gymnasiums naked and trembling before the machinery of other skeletons,
who bit detectives in the neck and shrieked with delight in policecars for committing no crime but their own wild cooking pederasty and intoxication,
who howled on their knees in the subway and were dragged off the roof waving

---

① Plotinus (205—270), a visionary philosopher; Poe, Edgar Allan Poe; St. John of the Cross, Spanish visionary and poet (1542—1591).

② Bop, jazz style of the 1940s; kaballah, a mystical tradition of interpretation of Hebrew scripture.

③ A city in northern Maryland.

④ A port city in Texas.

⑤ A gathering place for radical speakers in New York in the 1930s.

⑥ In New Mexico, a center for the development of the atomic bomb.

⑦ Wall Street, or the Wailing Wall in Jerusalem.

genitals and manuscripts,
who let themselves be fucked in the ass by saintly motorcyclists, and screamed with joy,
who blew and were blown by those human seraphim, the sailors, caresses of Atlantic and Caribbean love,
who balled in the morning in the evenings in rosegardens and the grass of public parks and cemeteries scattering their semen freely to whomever come who may,
who hiccuped endlessly trying to giggle but wound up with a sob behind a partition in a Turkish Bath when the blonde & naked angel came to pierce them with a sword①,
who lost their loveboys to the three old shrews of fate② the one eyed shrew of the heterosexual dollar the one eyed shrew that winks out of the womb and the one eyed shrew that does nothing but sit on her ass and snip the intellectual golden threads of the craftsman's loom,
who copulated ecstatic and insatiate with a bottle of beer a sweetheart a package of cigarettes a candle and fell off the bed, and continued along the floor and down the hall and ended fainting on the wall with a vision of ultimate cunt and come eluding the last gyzym of consciousness,
who sweetened the snatches of a million girls trembling in the sunset, and were red eyed in the morning but were prepared to sweeten the snatch of the sunrise, flashing buttocks under barns and naked in the lake,
who went out whoring through Colorado in myriad stolen night-cars, N. C. ③, secret hero of these poems, cocksman and Adonis of Denver④—joy to the memory of his innumerable lays of girls in empty lots & diner backyards, moviehouses' rickety rows, on mountaintops in caves or with gaunt waitresses in familiar roadside lonely petticoat upliftings & especially secret gas-station solipsism of johns, & hometown alleys too,

---

① This refers to the sculpture *The Ecstasy of St. Teresa* by Lorenzo Bernini (1598—1680).

② In Greek mythology, the three goddesses who determine a mortal's life by spinning out a length of thread and cutting it at the time of death.

③ Neal Cassady, hip companion of Kerouac and the original Dean Moriarty, one of the leading characters in *On the Road*.

④ Adonis, a strikingly handsome youth loved by Aphrodite; Denver, one of the shrines of the Beat Generation.

who faded out in vast sordid movies, were shifted in dreams, woke on a sudden
  Manhattan, and picked themselves up out of basements hungover with heartless
  Tokay① and horrors of Third Avenue iron dreams & stumbled to unemployment
  offices,
who walked all night with their shoes full of blood on the snowbank docks waiting
  for a door in the East River to open to a room full of steamheat and opium,
who created great suicidal dramas on the apartment cliff-banks of the Hudson under
  the wartime blue floodlight of the moon & their heads shall be crowned with
  laurel in oblivion,
who ate the lamb stew of the imagination or digested the crab at the muddy bottom
  of the rivers of the Bowery②,
who wept at the romance of the streets with their pushcarts full of onions and bad
  music,
who sat in boxes breathing in the darkness under the bridge, and rose up to build
  harpsichords in their lofts,
who coughed on the sixth floor of Harlem crowned with flame under the tubercular
  sky surrounded by orange crates of theology,
who scribbled all night rocking and rolling over lofty incantations which in the
  yellow morning were stanzas of gibberish,
who cooked rotten animals lung heart feet tail borsht & tortillas dreaming of the
  pure vegetable kingdom,
who plunged themselves under meat trucks looking for an egg,
who threw their watches off the roof to cast their ballot for Eternity outside of
  Time & alarm clocks fell on their heads every day for the next decade,
who cut their wrists three times successively unsuccessfully, gave up and were
  forced to open antique stores where they thought they were growing old and
  cried,
who were burned alive in their innocent flannel suits on Madison Avenue③ amid
  blasts of leaden verse & the tanked-up clatter of the iron regiments of fashion &

① A naturally sweet wine made in Hungary.
② Southern extension of Third Avenue in New York City.
③ Center of New York advertising industry.

the nitroglycerine shrieks of the fairies of advertising & the mustard gas of sinister intelligent editors, or were run down by the drunken taxicabs of Absolute Reality,

who jumped off the Brooklyn Bridge this actually happened and walked away unknown and forgotten into the ghostly daze of Chinatown soup alleyways & firetrucks, not even one free beer,

who sang out of their windows in despair, fell out of the subway window, jumped in the filthy Passaic①, leaped on negroes, cried all over the street, danced on broken wineglasses barefoot smashed phonograph records of nostalgic European 1930s German jazz finished the whiskey and threw up groaning into the bloody toilet, moans in their ears and the blast of colossal steamwhistles,

who barreled down the highways of the past journeying to each other's hotrod-Golgotha② jail-solitude watch Birmingham jazz incarnation,

who drove crosscountry seventy-two hours to find out if I had a vision or you had a vision or he had a vision to find out Eternity,

who journeyed to Denver, who died in Denver, who came back to Denver & waited in vain, who watched over Denver & brooded & loned in Denver and finally went away to find out the Time, & now Denver is lonesome for her heroes,

who fell on their knees in hopeless cathedrals praying for each other's salvation and light and breasts, until the soul illuminated its hair for a second,

who crashed through their minds in jail waiting for impossible criminals with golden heads and the charm of reality in their hearts who sang sweet blues to Alcatraz③,

who retired to Mexico to cultivate a habit, or Rocky Mount to tender Buddha or Tangiers to boys or Southern Pacific④ to the black locomotive or Harvard to Narcissus to Woodlawn⑤ to the daisychain or grave,

who demanded sanity trials accusing the radio of hypnotism & were left with their insanity & their hands & a hung jury,

---

① River flowing past Paterson.

② The place in ancient Judea where Jesus was believed to have been crucified.

③ A rocky island of western California in San Francisco Bay, the site of a prison before 1963.

④ Rocky Mount, city in North Carolina, where Kerouac once lived; Tangiers, a place in Morocco, where William Burroughs (1914—1997) lived; Southern Pacific, a railroad company for which Neal Cassady once worked.

⑤ A cemetery in the Bronx.

who threw potato salad at CCNY lecturers on Dadaism① and subsequently presented themselves on the granite steps of the madhouse with the shaven heads and harlequin speech of suicide, demanding instantaneous lobotomy,
and who were given instead the concrete void of insulin metrasol electricity hydrotherapy psychotherapy occupational therapy pingpong & amnesia,
who in humorless protest overturned only one symbolic pingpong table, resting briefly in catatonia,
returning years later truly bald except for a wig of blood, and tears and fingers, to the visible madman doom of the wards of the madtowns of the East,
Pilgrim State's Rockland's and Greystone's② foetid halls, bickering with the echoes of the soul, rocking and rolling in the midnight solitude-bench dolmen-realms of love, dream of life a nightmare, bodies turned to stone as heavy as the moon,
with mother finally * * * * *, and the last fantastic book flung out of the tenement window, and the last door closed at 4AM and the last telephone slammed at the wall in reply and the last furnished room emptied down to the last piece of mental furniture, a yellow paper rose twisted on a wire hanger in the closet, and even that imaginary, nothing but a hopeful little bit of hallucination—
ah, Carl, while you are not safe I am not safe, and now you're really in the total animal soup of time—
and who therefore ran through the icy streets obsessed with a sudden flash of the alchemy of the use of the ellipse the catalog the meter & the vibrating plane,
who dreamt and made incarnate gaps in Time & Space through images juxtaposed, and trapped the archangel of the soul between 2 visual images and joined the elemental verbs and set the noun and dash of consciousness together jumping with sensation of Pater Omnipotens Aeterna Deus③
to recreate the syntax and measure of poor human prose and stand before you speechless and intelligent and shaking with shame, rejected yet confessing out

① CCNY, City College of New York; Dadaism, artistic cult of absurdity (1916—1920).

② Names of three psychiatric hospitals near New York. Carl Solomon was institutionalized at Pilgrim State and Rockland; Ginsberg's mother, Naomi, was institutionalized at Greystone.

③ All Powerful Father, Eternal God (Latin). This is an allusion to a phrase used by the French painter Paul Cezanne (1839—1906), in a letter describing the effects of nature (1904).

the soul to conform to the rhythm of thought in his naked and endless head,
the madman bum and angel beat in Time, unknown, yet putting down here what might be left to say in time come after death,
and rose incarnate in the ghostly clothes of jazz in the goldhorn shadow of the band and blew the suffering of America's naked mind for love into an eli eli lamma lamma sabacthani① saxophone cry that shivered the cities down to the last radio
with the absolute heart of the poem of life butchered out of their own bodies good to eat a thousand years.

(2)

What sphinx② of cement and aluminium bashed open their skulls and ate up their brains and imagination?
Moloch③! Solitude! Filth! Ugliness! Ashcans and unobtainable dollars! Children screaming under the stairways! Boys sobbing in armies! Old men weeping in the parks!
Moloch! Moloch! Nightmare of Moloch! Moloch the loveless! Mental Moloch! Moloch the heavy judger of men!
Moloch the incomprehensible prison! Moloch the crossbone soulless jailhouse and Congress of sorrows! Moloch whose buildings are judgement! Moloch the vast stone of war! Moloch the stunned governments!
Moloch whose mind is pure machinery! Moloch whose blood is running money! Moloch whose fingers are ten armies! Moloch whose breast is a cannibal dynamo! Moloch whose ear is a smoking tomb!
Moloch whose eyes are a thousand blind windows! Moloch whose skyscrapers stand in the long streets like endless Jehovas! Moloch whose factories dream and croak in the fog! Moloch whose smokestacks and antennae crown the cities!
Moloch whose love is endless oil and stone! Moloch whose soul is electricity and banks! Moloch whose poverty is the specter of genius! Moloch whose fate is a cloud of sexless hydrogen! Moloch whose name is the Mind!

---

① My God, my God, why have you forsaken me? (Aramaic, Christ's last words on the Cross.)

② A figure in Egyptian myth having the body of a lion and the head of a man, ram or hawk.

③ Ginsbertg's own annotation in the facsimile edition of the poem reads: "'Moloch': or Molech, the Canaanite fire god, whose worship was marked by parents' burning their children as proprietary sacrifice. 'And thou shalt not let any of thy seed pass through the fire to Molech' (Leviticus 18:21)."

Moloch in whom I sit lonely! Moloch in whom I dream angels! Crazy in Moloch! Cocksucker in Moloch! Lacklove and manless in Moloch!
Moloch who entered my soul early! Moloch in whom I am a consciousness without a body! Moloch who frightened me out of my natural ecstasy! Moloch whom I abandon! Wake up in Moloch! Light streaming out of the sky!
Moloch! Moloch! Robot apartments! invisible suburbs! skeleton treasuries! blind capitals! demonic industries! spectral nations! invincible madhouses! granite cocks! monstrous bombs!
They broke their backs lifting Moloch to Heaven! Pavements, trees, radios, tons! lifting the city to Heaven which exists and is everywhere about us!
Visions! omens! hallucinations! miracles! ecstacies! gone down the American river!
Dreams! adorations! illuminations! religions! the whole boatload of sensitive bullshit!
Breakthroughs! over the river! flips and crucifixions! gone down the flood! Highs! Epiphanies! Despairs! Ten years' animal screams and suicides! Minds! New loves! Mad generation! down on the rocks of Time!
Real holy laughter in the river! They saw it all! the wild eyes! the holy yells! They bade farewell! They jumped off the roof! to solitude! waving! carrying flowers! Down to the river! into the street!

(3)

Carl Solomon! I'm with you in Rockland①
    where you're madder than I am
I'm with you in Rockland
    where you must feel strange
I'm with you in Rockland
    where you imitate the shade of my mother
I'm with you in Rockland
    where you've murdered your twelve secretaries
I'm with you in Rockland
    where you laugh at this invisible humour

---

① A town in eastern Massachusetts, southeast of Boston.

I'm with you in Rockland
    where we are great writerson the same dreadful typewriter
I'm with you in Rockland
    where your condition has become serious and is reported on the radio
I'm with you in Rockland
    where the faculties of the skull no longer admit the worms of the senses
I'm with you in Rockland
    where you drink the tea of the breasts of the spinsters of Utica①
I'm with you in Rockland
    where you pun on the bodies of your nurses the harpies of the Bronx
I'm with you in Rockland
    where you scream in a straightjacket that you're losing the game of the actual pingpong of the abyss
I'm with you in Rockland
    where you bang on the catatonic piano the soul is innocent and immortal it should never die ungodly in an armed madhouse
I'm with you in Rockland
    where fifty more shocks will never return your soul to its body again from its pilgrimage to a cross in the void
I'm with you in Rockland
    where you accuse your doctors of insanity and plot the Hebrew socialist revolution against the fascist national Golgotha
I'm with you in Rockland
    where you will split the heavens of Long Island and resurrect your living human Jesus from the superhuman tomb
I'm with you in Rockland
    where there are twenty-five thousand mad comrades all together singing the final stanzas of the Internationale②
I'm with you in Rockland
    where we hug and kiss the United States under our bedsheets the United States

---

① A city in middle New York State.
② Name of a song and the official Soviet anthem until 1944.

that coughs all night and won't let us sleep
I'm with you in Rockland
where we wake up electrified out of the coma by our own souls' airplanes roaring over the roof they've come to drop angelic bombs the hospital illuminates itself imaginary walls collapse O skinny legions run outside O starry-spangled shock of mercy the eternal war is here O victory forget your underwear we're free
I'm with you in Rockland
in my dreams you walk dripping from a sea-journey on the highway across America in tears to the door of my cottage in the Western night

[Selected from *The Norton Anthology of American Literature* (Sixth Edition, Vol. E). New York: W. W. Norton & Company, 2003.]

Ⅲ. Questions for discussion

(1) What do you think connects three parts of the poem?

(2) What can we learn about the lifestyle of the beatniks from this poem? How does the language in the poem help to develop it?

(3) Do you think lines 11, 35, 36, 38, 41, and 71 pornographic? Why or why not?

(4) Why did the author mention so many place names like Bowery, Harlem, Rocky Mount, Madison Avenue, Union Square, Denver, and Tangiers in the poem? Why did he mention the mental institutions/psychiatric hospitals repeatedly? Why did he mention Los Alamos?

(5) Are writers like John of the Cross, Poe, and philosophers like Plotinus popular among the beats? Why?

(6) What is the attitude of beats toward capitalism and communism?

(7) The poem has been read aloud to audiences many times. What has made it suitable for stage performance and attractive to listeners?

(8) Comment on the influence American literary inheritance has on the the poem and its author.

2.3 Assigned Reading

Foreword to *The Beats Book*

Allen Ginsberg

The phrase "Beat generation" arose out of a specific conversation between Jack Kerouac and John Clellon Holmes in 1948. They were discussing the nature of generations, recollecting the glamour of the Lost Generation, and Kerouac said, "Ah, this is nothing but a beat generation" (as Kerouac sometimes called it), an "angelic generation," or some other epithet. But Kerouac waved away the question and said beat generation—not meaning to name the generation, but to unname it.

John Clellon Holmes' celebrated article in late 1952 in the *New York Times Magazine* carried the headline title "This Is the Beat Generation." That caught the public eye. Then Kerouac anonymously published a fragment of *On the Road* called "Jazz of the Beat Generation," and that reinforced the curiously poetic phrase. So that's the early history of the term.

Herbert Huncke, author of *The Evening Sun Turned Crimson*, and friend of Kerouac, Burroughs, and others of that literary circle from the forties, introduced them to what was then known as "hip language." In that context, the word "beat" is carnival, "subterranean" (subcultural) term—a term much used then in Times Square: "Man, I'm beat," meaning without money and without a place to stay. It could also refer to those "who walked all night with shoes full of blood on the snowbank docks waiting for a door in the East River to open to a room full of steam and opium" (*Howl*). Or the word would be used as in conversation: "Would you like to go to the Bronx Zoo?" "Nah, man, I'm too 'beat,' I was up all night." So, the original street usage meant exhausted, at the bottom of the world, looking up or out, sleepless, wide-eyed, perspective, rejected by society, on your own, streetwise. Or, as it once implied, "beat" meant finished, completed, in the dark night of the soul or in the cloud of unknowing. It could mean open, as in the Whitmanesque sense of "openness," equivalent to humility. So "beat" was interpreted in various circles to mean emptied out, exhausted, and at the same time wide-open and receptive to vision.

A third meaning of "beat," as in beatific, was publicly articulated in 1959 by

Kerouac, to counteract the abuse of the term in the media (where it was being interpreted as meaning "beaten completely," a "loser," without the aspect of humble intelligence, or of "beat" as "the beat of drums" and "the beat goes on"—all varying mistakes of interpretation or etymology). Kerouac (in various interviews and lectures) was trying to indicate the correct sense of the word by pointing out its connection to words like "beatitude" and "beatific"—the necessary beatness or darkness that precedes opening up to light, egolessness, giving room for religious illumination.

A fourth meaning that accumulated around the word is found in the phrase "Beat generation literary movement." This phrase referred to a group of friends who had worked together on poetry, prose, and cultural conscience from the mid-forties until the term became popular nationally in the late fifties. The group consisted of Kerouac, Neal Cassady (Kerouac's prototype hero of *On the Road*), William Burroughs, Herbert Huncke, John Clellon Holmes (author of *Go*, *The Horn*, and other books), and myself. We met Carl Solomon and Philip Lamantia in 1948, encountered Gregory Corso in 1950, and first saw Lawrence Ferlinghetti and Peter Orlovsky in 1954.

By the mid-fifties, this smaller circle—through natural affinity of modes of thought, literary style, or planetary perspective—was augmented in friendship and literary endeavor by a number of writers in San Francisco, including Michael McClure, Gary Snyder, Philip Whalen, and by 1958 some other powerful but lesser-known poets, such as Bob Kaufman, Jack Micheline, and Ray Bremser, and the better-known black poet LeRoi Jones. All of us accepted the term "beat" at one time or anther, humorously or seriously, but sympathetically, and were included in a survey of Beat manners, morals, and literature by *Life* magazine in a lead article in 1959 by Paul O'Neil, and by the journalist Alfred Aronowitz in a twelve-part series entitled "The Beat Generation" in the *New York Post*.

By the mid-fifties a sense of some mutual trust and interest was developed with Frank O'Hara and Kenneth Koch as well as with Robert Creeley and other alumni of Black Mountain College in North Carolina. Of that literary circle, Kerouac, Whalen, Synder, poets Lew Welch, Diane di Prima, Joanne Kyger, and Orlovsky, as well as myself and others were interested in meditation and Buddhism. (A discussion of the relationship between Buddhism and the Beat generation can be found in a scholarly survey of the evolution of Buddhism in America, *How the Swans Came to the Lake*, by Rick Fields.)

The fifth meaning of the phrase "Beat generation" refers to the broader influence of literary and artistic activities of poets, filmmakers, painters, writers, and novelists who were working in concert in anthologies, publishing houses, independent filmmaking, and other media. These groups refreshed the longlived bohemian cultural tradition in America. Among major interactive figures were: in film and still photography, Robert Frank and Alfred Leslie; in music, David Amram; in painting, Larry Rivers; in poetry and publishing, Cid Corman, Jonathan Williams, Don Allen, Barney Rosset, Lawrence Ferlinghetti. This energy fell out into the youth movement of the day, which was growing, and was absorbed by the mass and middle-class culture of the late fifties and early sixties.

Some essential ideals of the original artistic movement can be traced clearly in these poets' writings, and continued intergenerational interest decade after decade has been magnetized by a number of consistent themes which might be summarized as follows: An inquisitiveness into the nature of consciousness, leading to acquaintance with Eastern thought, meditation practice, art as extension or manifestation of exploration of the texture of consciousness, spiritual liberation as a result. This led toward sexual liberation, particularly gay liberation, which historically had a part in catalyzing women's lib and black lib. A tolerant nontheistic view developed out of exploring the texture of consciousness, thus cosmic anti-fascism, a peaceable nonviolent approach to politics, multiculturalism, the absorption of black culture into mainstream literature and music, as, for example, Kerouac's spontaneous "bop prosody" or the odd identity of the group of poets later called the "Beat generation": Burroughs, white Protestant; Kerouac, American Indian and Breton; Corso, Italian Catholic; myself, Jewish radical; Orlovsky, White Russian; Gary Snyder, Scotch-German; Lawrence Lamentia, Italian authentic Surrealists; Michael McClure, Midwest U. S. Scotch; Bob Kaufman, Surrealistic African-American; LeRoi Jones, Black Powerful, among others. So art's viewed as sacred practice, with sacramental approach to each other as characters. The color of candor emerges with good humor and an inadvertent spontaneous frankness, unpremeditated directness in life and in art, the end of secrecy and paranoia that runs beneath macho sexual politics and demagoguery all the way up through CIA-KGB and nuclear machinations. There's further realization we can destroy the human residence on the planet if we don't trust and exercise out better natures, thus an end to 19th century Marxist-Capitalist myth of progress with expansionist imperial rivalry.

Our interest in psychedelic substances as educational tools, particularly marijuana, mushrooms, and LSD, let to a more realistic approach to drug laws, recognizing that tobacco and alcohol are physically more destructive than all other drugs except cocaine. Thus the junk problem should be transformed into an asset for the failing family farm to help reinhabit the countryside and provide some sustainable product (cloth, rope, et al.) as alternative to plastic consciousness.

And finally, appreciation of eros, sacramental approach to sexual joy. Those are the main themes that have run through the art and poetry and prose of the writers I mentioned from the very beginning in the forties through the public poetry readings that surfaced in mid-fifties into common consciousness. Many of these values have entered mainstream thought—e. g. , ecology, grass, gay lib, multiculturalism—but haven't seen fruition in government behavior, so that now we have more folk in our prisons or under government surveillance than any country West or East.

This "Beat generation" or "sixties" tolerant worldview provoked an intoxicated right wing to go into "Denial" (as in AA terminology) of reality, and reinforced its codependency with repressive laws, incipient police state, death-penalty demagoguery, sex demagoguery, art censorship, fundamentalist monotheist televangelist quasi-fascist wrath, racism, and homophobia. This counterreaction seems a by-product of the further gulf between the rich and poor classes, growth of a massive abused underclass, increased power and luxury for the rich who control politics and their minions in the media. Prescription: more art, meditation, lifestyle of relative penury, avoidance of conspicuous consumption that's burning down the planet.

I think younger generations have been attracted by the exuberance, libertarian optimism, erotic humor, frankness, continuous energy, invention, and collaborative amity of these poets and singers. We had a great job to do, and we're doing it, trying to save and heal the spirit of America.

[Selected from Anne Waldman, (ed.). *The Beat Book: Writings from the Beat Generation*. Bostom: Shambhala, 2007.]

3. Charles Olson

3.1 Presentation Topics

(1) Projective or Open verse.

(2) Charles Olson and Black Mountain College.

(3) Artistic features of his poems.

3.2 Selected Reading

Ⅰ. Central issue of concern

Charles Olson's quest for meaning of life and death in his "composition by field."

Ⅱ. Text

Maximus, to Gloucester, Sunday, July 19①

(1)

and they stopped before that bad sculpture of a fisherman

—"as if one were to talk to a man's house,
knowing not what gods or heroes are" —
not knowing what a fisherman is
instead of going straight to the Bridge
and doing no more than—saying no more than—
in the Charybdises② of the
Cut waters the flowers tear off

① Maximus, the author's poetic persona; Gloucester, the name of an island and fishing town in Massachussetts, where the author was brought up; July 19, the date of an annual ceremony during which the people of Gloucester commemorate the fishermen drowned on the sea.

② Charybdis and Scylla are two sea monsters in Greek mythology. The former is a whirlpool and the latter lives on a reef close enough to the whirlpool that they pose a threat to passing sailors and boats.

the wreaths

the flowers
turn
the character of the sea   The sea jumps
the fate of the flower   The drowned men are undrowned
in the eddies
        of the eyes
        of the flowers
        opening
        the sea's eyes

The disaster
is undone
What was received as alien
—the flower
on the water, that a man drowns
that he dies in water as he dies on earth, the impossible
    that this gross fact can return to us
        in this upset
on a summer day
of a particular tide

that the sensation is true,
that the transformations of fire are, first of all, sea—
    "as gold for wares wares for gold"

    Let them be told who stopped first
    by a bronze idol

    A fisherman is not a successful man
    he is not a famous man he is not a man
    of power, these are the damned by God

(2)

whose surface bubbles
with these gimlets

which screw-in like

potholes, caustic
caked earth of painted
pools, Yellowstone
Park[①] of holes
is death the diseased
presence on us, the spilling lesion

of the brilliance
it is to be alive: to walk onto it
as Jim Bridger[②] the first into it,

it is more true a scabious
field than it is a pretty
meadow

When a man's coffin is the sea
the whole of creation shall come to his funeral,

it turns out; the globe
is below, all lapis

and its blue surface golded
by what happened

this afternoon: there are eyes
in this water

the flowers
from the shore,

awakened
the sea

---

① A national reserve in the Rocky Mountains, U. S., mainly in Wyoming. It has many geysers and hot springs.

② Bridger (1804—1881), a fur trader and one of the first white men to see the geysers and other natural wonders of the Yellowstone Park. He is considered the first white American to see the Great Salt Lake in 1824.

Men are so sure they know very many things,
they don't even know night and day are one

A fisherman works without reference to
that difference. It is possible he also

by lying there when he does lie, jowl
to the sea, has another advantage: it is said,

"You rectify what can be rectified," and when a man's heart cannot see
this, the door of his divine intelligence is shut

let you who paraded to the Cut today
to hold memorial services to all fishermen
who have been lost at sea in a year
when for the first time not one life was lost

    radar sonar radio telephone good engines
    bed-check seaplanes goodness over and under us

no difference
when men come back

[Selected from *The Norton Anthology of American Literature* (Second Edition, Vol. 2). New York: W. W. Norton & Company, 1985.]

Ⅲ. Questions for discussion

(1) In what way is the poem different from those by previous poets, for example T. S. Eliot?

(2) What kind of man, according to your common sense, is a fisherman? What's the author's idea? Sculptures are usually done for "gods or heroes." How about the one mentioned in this poem?

(3) Why does the author mention "Charybdise"?

(4) What does the word "bad" in line one suggest?

(5) What does the author mean by "these are the damned by God"? How about "not one life was lost"?

(6) What can we learn from the last four lines of the poem?

(7) Do you think this poem a good example of "composition by field?" Why or why not?

(8) It is said that in theme Olson is critical of the American way of life. What

do you think he wants to tell the reader in this poem?

3.3 Assigned Reading

Projective Verse VS. *The Non-Projective Verse*

Charles Olson

(Or what a French critic① calls "closed" verse, that verse which print bred and which is pretty much what we have had, in English & American, and have still got, despite the work of Pound & Williams: it led Keats, already a hundred years ago, to see it (Wordsworth's, Milton's) in the light of "the Egotistical Sublime"②; and it persists, at this latter day, as what you might call the private-soul-at-any-public-wall)

Verse now, 1950, if it is to go ahead, if it is to be of essential use, must, I take it, catch up and put into itself certain laws and possibilities of the breath, of the breathing of the man who writes as well as of his listenings. (The revolution of the year, 1910③, the trochee's heave, asks it of the younger poets.)

I want to do two things: Ⅰ, try to show what projective or OPEN verse is, what it involves, in its act of composition, how, in distinction from the non-projective, it is accomplished; and Ⅱ, suggest a few ideas about what stance toward reality brings such verse into being, what the stance does, both to the poet and to his reader. (The stance involves, for example, a change beyond, and larger than, the technical, and may, the way things look, lead to a new poetics and to new concepts from which some sort of drama, say, or of epic, perhaps, may emerge.)

(1)

First, some simplicities that a man learns, if he works in OPEN, or what can also be called COMPOSITION BY FIELD, as opposed to inherited line, stanza, over-all form, what is the "old" base of the non-projective.

(1) the kinetics of the thing. A poem is energy transferred from where the poet got it (he will have some several causations), by way of the poem itself to, all the way over to, the reader. Okay. Then the poem itself must, at all points, be a high-energy construct and, at all points, an energy-discharge. So: how is the poet to accomplish same energy, how is he, what is the process by which a poet gets in,

---

① Identified by Ralph Maud as René Nelli.
② Keats' description of Wordsworth.
③ Olson's birth year.

at all points energy at least the equivalent of the energy which propelled him in the first place, yet an energy which is peculiar to verse alone and which will be, obviously, also different from the energy which the reader, because he is the third term, will take away?

This is the problem which any poet who departs from closed form is specially confronted by. And it involves a whole series of new recognitions. From the moment he ventures into FIELD COMPOSITION—puts himself in the open—he can go by no track other than the one the poem under hand declares, for itself. Thus he has to behave, and be, instant by instant, aware of some several forces just now beginning to be examined. (It is much more, for example, this push, than simply such a one as Pound put, so wisely, to get us started: "the musical phrase," go by it, boys, rather than by, the metronome.)

(2) is the *principle*, the law which presides conspicuously over the composition, and, when obeyed, is the reason why a projective poem can come into being. It is this: FORM IS NEVER MORE THAN AN EXTENSION OF CONTENT. (Or so it got phrased by one, R. Creeley, and it makes absolute sense to me, with this possible corollary, that right form, in any given poem, is the only and exclusively possible extension of content under hand.) There it is, brothers, sitting there, for USE.

Now (3) the *process* of the thing, how the principle can be made so to shape the energies that the form is accomplished. And I think it can be boiled down to one statement (first pounded into my head by Edward Dahlberg): ONE PERCEPTION MUST IMMEDIATELY AND DIRECTLY LEAD TO A FURTHER PERCEPTION. It means exactly what it says, is a matter of, at all points (even, I should say, of our management of daily reality as of the daily work) get on with it, keep moving, keep in, speed, the nerves, their speed, the perceptions, theirs, the acts, the split second acts, the whole business, keep it moving as fast as you can, citizen. And if you also set up as a poet, USE USE USE the process at all points, in any given poem always, always one perception must must must MOVE, INSTANTER, ON ANOTHER!

So there we are, fast, there's the dogma. And its excuse, its usableness, in practice. Which gets us, it ought to get us, inside the machinery, now, 1950, of how projective verse is made.

If I hammer, if I recall in, and keep calling in, the breath, the breathing as distinguished from the hearing, it is for cause, it is to insist upon a part that breath plays in verse which has not (due, I think, to the smothering of the power of the line by too set a concept of foot), has not been sufficiently observed or practiced, but which has to be if verse is to advance to its proper force and place in the day, now, and ahead. I take it that PROJECTIVE VERSE teaches, is, this lesson, that that verse will only do in which a poet manages to register both the acquisitions of his ear and the pressure of his breath.

Let's start from the smallest particle of all, the syllable. It is the king and pin of versification, what rules and holds together the lines, the larger forms, of a poem. I would suggest that verse here and in England dropped this secret from the late Elizabethans to Ezra Pound, lost it, in the sweetness of meter and rime, in a honey-head. (The syllable is one way to distinguish the original success of blank verse, and its falling off, with Milton.)

It is by their syllables that words juxtapose in beauty, by these particles of sound as clearly as by the sense of the words which they compose. In any given instance, because there is a choice of words, the choice, if a man is in there, will be, spontaneously, the obedience of his ear to the syllables. The fineness, and the practice, lie here, at the minimum and source of speech.

O western wynd, when wilt thou blow①
And the small rain down shall rain
O Christ that my love were in my arms
And I in my bed again

It would do no harm, as an act of correction to both prose and verse as now written, if both rime and meter, and, in the quantity words, both sense and sound, were less in the forefront of the mind than the syllable, if the syllable, that fine creature, were more allowed to lead the harmony on. With this warning, to those who would try: to step back here to this place of the elements and minims of language, is to engage speech where it is least careless—and least logical. Listening for the syllables must be so constant and so scrupulous, the exaction must be so complete, that the assurance of the ear is purchased at the highest—40 hours a day—price. For from the root out, from all over the place, the syllable comes, the figures of, the dance:

"Is" comes from the Aryan root, as, to breathe. The English "not" equals the Sanscrit "na,"

① An anonymous poem from the sixteenth century.

which may come from the root "na," to be lost, to perish. "Be" is from bhu, to grow.

I say the syllable, king, and that it is spontaneous, this way: the ear, the ear which has collected, which has listened, the ear, which is so close to the mind that it is the mind's, that it has the mind's speed... it is close, another way: the mind is brother to this sister and is, because it is so close, is the drying force, the incest, the sharpener... it is from the union of the mind and the ear that the syllable is born.

But the syllable is only the first child of the incest of verse (always, that Egyptian thing, it produces twins!). The other child is the LINE. And together, these two, the syllable and the line, they make a poem, they make that thing, the—what shall we call it, the Boss of all, the "Single Intelligence." And the line comes (I swear it) from the breath, from the breathing of the man who writes, at the moment that he writes, and thus is, it is here that, the daily work, the WORK, gets in, for only he, the man who writes, can declare, at every moment, the line its metric and its ending—where its breathing, shall come to, termination.

The trouble with most work, to my taking, since the breaking away from traditional lines and stanzas, and from such wholes as, say, Chaucer's *Troilus* or S's *Lear*, is: contemporary workers go lazy RIGHT HERE WHERE THE LINE IS BORN.

Let me put it baldly. The two halves are:

the HEAD, by way of the EAR, to the SYLLABLE
the HEART, by way of the BREATH, to the LINE

And the joker? that it is in the 1st half of the proposition that, in composing, one lets-it-rip; and that it is in the 2nd half, surprise, it is the LINE that's the baby that gets, as the poem is getting made, the attention, the control, that it is right here, in the line, that the shaping takes place, each moment of the going.

I am dogmatic, that the head shows in the syllable. The dance of the intellect is there, among them, prose or verse. Consider the best minds you know in this here business: where does the head show, is it not, precise here, in the swift currents of the syllable? Can't you tell a brain when you see what it does, just there? It is true, what the master says he picked up from Confusion: all the thots men are capable of can be entered on the back of a postage stamp. So, is it not the PLAY of a mind we are after, is not that that shows whether a mind is there at all?

The elements of language are finite, but the poet through his attentiveness (Play of mind) is the person who makes use of words in a particular sophisticated way.

And the threshing floor for the dance? Is it anything but the LINE? And when the line has, is, a deadness, is it not a heart which has gone lazy, is it not, suddenly, slow things, similes, say, adjectives, or such, that we are bored by?

For there is a whole flock of rhetorical devices which have now to be brought under a new bead, now that we sight within the line. Simile is only one bird who comes down, too easily. The descriptive functions generally have to be watched, every second, in projective verse, because of their easiness, and thus their drain on the energy which composition by field allows into a poem. Any slackness takes off attention, that crucial thing, from the job in hand, from the push of the line under hand at the moment, under the reader's eye, in his moment. Observation of any kind is, like argument in prose, properly previous to the act of the poem, and, if allowed in, must be so juxtaposed, apposed, set in, that it does not, for an instant, sap the going energy of the content toward its form.

It comes to this, this whole aspect of the newer problems. (We now enter, actually, the large area of the whole poem, into the FIELD, if you like, where all the syllables and all the lines must be managed in their relations to each other.) It is a matter, finally of OBJECTS, what they are, what they are inside a poem, how they got there, and, once there, how they are to be used. This is something I want to get to in another way in Part Ⅱ, but, for the moment, let me indicate this, that every element in an open poem (the syllable, the line, as well as the image, the sound, the sense) must be taken up as participants in the kinetic of the poem just as solidly as we are accustomed to take what we call the objects of reality; and that these elements are to be seen as creating the tensions of a poem just as totally as do those other objects create what we know as the world.

The objects which occur at every given moment of composition (of recognition, we can call it) are, can be, must be treated exactly as they do occur therein and not by any ideas or preconceptions from outside the poem, must be handled as a series of objects in field in such a way that a series of tensions (which they also are) are made to hold, and to hold exactly inside the content and the context of the poem which has forced itself, through the poet and them, into being.

Because breath allows all the speech-force of language back in (speech is the "solid" of verse, is the secret of a poem's energy), because, now, a poem has, by speech, solidity, everything in it can now be treated as solids, objects, things;

and, though insisting upon the absolute difference of the reality of the verse from that other dispersed and distributed thing, yet each of these elements of a poem can be allowed to have the play of their separate energies and can be allowed, once the poem is well composed, to keep, as those other objects do, their proper confusions.

Which brings us up, immediately, bang, against tenses, in fact against syntax, in fact against grammar generally, that is, as we have inherited it. Do not tenses, must they not also be kicked around anew, in order that time, that other governing absolute may be kept, as must the space-tensions of a poem, immediate, contemporary to the acting-on-you of the poem? I would argue that here, too, the LAW OF THE LINE, which projective verse creates, must be hewn to, obeyed, and that the conventions which logic has forced on syntax must be broken open as quietly as must the too set feet of the old line. But an analysis of how far a new poet can stretch the very conventions on which communication by language rests, is too big for these notes, which are meant, I hope it is obvious, merely to get things started.

Let me just throw in this. It is my impression that all parts of speech suddenly, in composition by field, are fresh for both sound and percussive use, spring up like unknown, unnamed vegetables in the patch, when you work it, come spring. Now take Hart Crane. What strikes me in him is the singleness of the push to the nominative, his push along that one arc of freshness, the attempt to get back to word as handle. (If logos is word as thought, what is word as noun, as, pass me that, as Newman Shea① used to ask, at the galley table, put a jib on the blood, will ya.) But there is a loss in Crane of what Fenollosa is so right about, in syntax, the sentence as first act of nature, as lightning, as passage of force from subject to object, quick, in this case, from Hart to me, in every case, from me to you, the VERB, between two nouns. Does not Hart miss the advantages, by such an isolated push, miss the point of the whole front of syllable, line, field, and what happened to all language, and to the poem, as a result?

I return you now to London, to beginnings, to the syllable, for the pleasures of it, to intermit:

> If music be the food of love, play on,

---

① A Gloucester fisherman.

Give me excess of it, that, surfeiting,
The appetite may sicken, and so die.
That strain again! It had a dying fall:
O, it came o'er my ear like the sweet sound,
That breathes upon a bank of violets,
Stealing and giving odour! ①

What we have suffered from, is manuscript, press, the removal of verse from its producer and its reproducer, the voice, a removal by one, by two removes from its place of origin and its destination. For the breath has a double meaning which Latin had not yet lost.

The irony is, from the machine has come one gain not yet sufficiently observed or used, but which leads directly on toward projective verse and its consequences. It is the advantage of the typewriter that, due to its rigidity and its space precisions, it can, for a poet, indicate exactly the breath, the pauses, the suspensions even of syllables, the juxtapositions even of parts of phrases, which he intends. For the first time the poet has the stave and the bar a musician has had. For the first time he can, without the convention of rime and meter, record the listening he has done to his own speech and by that one act indicate how he would want any reader, silently or otherwise, to voice his work.

It is time we picked the fruits of the experiments of Cummings, Pound, Williams, each of whom has, after his way, already used the machine as a scoring to his composing, as a script to its vocalization. It is now only a matter of the recognition of the conventions of composition by field for us to bring into being an open verse as formal as the closed, with all its traditional advantages.

If a contemporary poet leaves a space as long as the phrase before it, he means that space to be held, by the breath, an equal length of time. If he suspends a word or syllable at the end of a line (this was most Cummings' addition) he means that time to pass that it takes the eye—that hair of time suspended—to pick up the next line. If he wishes a pause so light it hardly separates the words, yet does not want a comma—which is an interruption of the meaning rather than the sounding of the line—follow him when he uses a symbol the typewriter has ready to hand:

"What does not change / is the will to change." ②

---

① From Shakespeare's *Twelfth Night*.

② Opening line of Olson's poem "The Kingfishers."

Observe him, when he takes advantage of the machine's multiple margins, to juxtapose:

Sd he:
    to dream takes no effort
        to think is easy
        to act is more difficult
    but for a man to act after he has taken thought, this!
is the most difficult of all①

Each of these lines is a progressing of both the meaning and the breathing forward, and then a backing up, without a progress or any kind of movement outside the unit of time local to the idea.

There is more to be said in order that this convention be recognized, especially in order that the revolution out of which it came may be so forwarded that work will get published to offset the reaction now afoot to return verse to inherited forms of cadence and rime. But what I want to emphasize here, by this emphasis on the typewriter as the personal and instantaneous recorder of the poet's work, is the already projective nature of verse as the sons of Pound and Williams are practicing it. Already they are composing as though verse was to have the reading its writing involved, as though not the eye but the ear was to be its measurer, as though the intervals of its composition could be so carefully put down as to be precisely the intervals of its registration. For the ear, which once had the burden of memory to quicken it (rime & regular cadence were its aids and have merely lived on in print after the oral necessities were ended) can now again, that the poet has his means, be the threshold of projective verse.

(2)

Which gets us to what I promised, the degree to which the projective involves a stance toward reality outside a poem as well as a new stance towards the reality of a poem itself. It is a matter of content, the content of Homer or of Euripides or of Seami② as distinct from that which I might call the more "literary" masters. From the moment the projective purpose of the act of verse is recognized, the content does—it will—change. If the beginning and the end is breath, voice in its largest sense, then the material of verse shifts. It has to. It starts with the composer. The

① From Olson's "The Praises."

② A Japanese writer of the late fourteenth and early fifteenth centuries, also known as Motekiyo.

dimension of his line itself changes, not to speak of the change in his conceiving, of the matter he will turn to, of the scale in which he imagines that matter's use. I myself would pose the difference by a physical image. It is no accident that Pound and Williams were both involved variously in a movement which got called "objectivism." But that word was then used in some sort of a necessary quarrel, I take it, with "subjectivism." It is now too late to be bothered with the latter. It has excellently done itself to death, even though we are all caught in its dying. What seems to me a more valid formulation for present use is "objectism," a word to be taken to stand for the kind of relation of man to experience which a poet might state as the necessity of a line or a work to be as wood is, to be as clean as wood is as it issues from the hand of nature, to be as shaped as wood can be when a man has had his hand to it. Objectism is the getting ride of the lyrical interference of the individual as ego, of the "subject" and his soul, that peculiar presumption by which western man has interposed himself between what he is as a creature of nature (with certain instructions to carry out) and those other creations of nature which we may, with no derogation, call objects. For a man is himself an object, whatever he may take to be his advantages, the more likely to recognize himself as such the greater his advantages, particularly at that moment that he achieves an humilitas sufficient to make him of use.

It comes to this: the use of a man, by himself and thus by others, lies in how he conceives his relation to nature, that force to which he owes his somewhat small existence. If he sprawl, he shall find little to sing but himself, and shall sing, nature has such paradoxical ways, by way of artificial forms outside of himself. But if he stays inside himself, if he is contained within his nature as he is participant in the larger force, he will be able to listen, and his hearing through himself will give him secrets objects share. And by an inverse law his shapes will make their own way. It is in this sense that the projective act, which is the artist's act in the larger field of objects, leads to dimensions larger than the man. For a man's problem, the moment he takes speed up in all its fullness, is to give his work his seriousness, a seriousness sufficient to cause the thing he makes to try to take its place alongside the things of nature. This is not easy. Nature works from reverence, even in her destructions (species go down with a crash). But breath is man's special qualification as animal. Sound is a dimension he has extended. Language is one of his proudest acts. And when a poet rests in these as they are in himself (in his physiology, if you like, but the life in him, for all that) then he, if he chooses to speak from these roots, works in that area where nature has given him size, projective size.

It is projective size that the play, *The Trojan Women*①, possesses, for it is able to stand, is it not, as its people do, beside the Aegean—and neither Andromache or the sea suffer diminution. In a less "heroic" but equally "natural" dimension Seami causes the Fisherman and the Angel to stand clear in *Hagoromo*②. And Homer, who is such an unexamined cliché that I do not think I need to press home in what scale Nausicaa's girls wash their clothes.

Such works, I should argue—and I use them simply because their equivalents are yet to be done—could not issue from men who conceived verse without the full relevance of human voice, without reference to where lines come from, in the individual who writes. Nor do I think it accident at that, at this end point of the argument, I should use, for examples, two dramatists and an epic poet. For I would hazard the guess that, if projective verse is practiced long enough, is driven ahead hard enough along the course I think it dictates, verse again can carry much larger material than it has carried in our language since the Elizabethans. But it can't be jumped. We are only at the beginnings, and if I think that the *Cantos* make more "dramatic" sense than do the plays of Mr. Eliot, it is not because I think they have solved the problem but because the methodology of the verse in them points a way by which, one day, the problem of a larger content and of larger forms may be solved. Eliot is, in fact, a proof of a present danger, of "too easy" a going on in the practice of verse as it has been, rather than as it must be, practiced. There is no question, for example, that Eliot's line, from "Prufrock"③ on down, has speech-force, is "dramatic," is, in fact, one of the most notable lines since Dryden. I suppose it stemmed immediately to him from Browning, as did so many of Pound's early things. In any case Eliot's line has obvious relations backward to the Elizabethans, especially to the soliloquy. Yet O. M. Eliot is not projective. It could even be argued (and I say this carefully, as I have said all things about the non-projective, having considered how each of us must save himself after his own fashion and how much, for that matter, each of us owes to the non-projective, and

① A play by Euripides.

② One of the Noh plays translated by Pound.

③ T. S. Eliot's poem "The Love Song of J. Alfred Prufrock."

will continue to owe, as both go alongside each other) but it could be argued that it is because Eliot has stayed inside the non-projective that he fails as a dramatist—that his root is the mind alone, and a scholastic mind at that (no high intelletto despite his apparent clarities)—and that, in his listenings he has stayed there where the ear and the mind are, has only gone from his fine ear outward rather than, as I say a projective poet will, down through the workings of his own throat to that place where breath comes from, where breath has its beginnings, where drama, has come from, where, the coincidence is, all acts spring.

[Selected from Donald Allen, Benjamin Friedlander, (ed.). *Collected Prose*. Berkeley: University of California Press, 1997.]

4. Sylvia Plath

4.1 Presentation Topics

(1) Confessional poetry.

(2) Sylvia Plath's poetry characterized by the intense coupling of its violent or disturbed imagery and its playful use of alliteration and rhyme.

4.2 Selected Reading

Ⅰ. Central issues of concern

Sylvia Plath as a confessional poet.

Ⅱ. Text

The Colossus

I shall never get you put together entirely,
Pieced, glued, and properly jointed.
Mule-bray, pig-grunt and bawdy cackles
Proceed from your great lips.
It's worse than a barnyard.

Perhaps you consider yourself an oracle,
Mouthpiece of the dead, or of some god or other.
Thirty years now I have labored

To dredge the silt from your throat.
I am none the wiser.

Scaling little ladders with glue pots and pails of Lysol
I crawl like an ant in mourning
Over the weedy acres of your brow
To mend the immense skull-plates and clear
The bald, white tumuli of your eyes.

A blue sky out of the Oresteia
Arches above us. O father, all by yourself
You are pithy and historical as the Roman Forum.
I open my lunch on a hill of black cypress.
Your fluted bones and acanthine hair are littered

In their old anarchy to the horizon-line.
It would take more than a lightning-stroke
To create such a ruin.
Nights, I squat in the cornucopia
Of your left ear, out of the wind,

Counting the red stars and those of plum-color.
The sun rises under the pillar of your tongue.
My hours are married to shadow.
No longer do I listen for the scrape of a keel
On the blank stones of the landing.

Ariel

Stasis in darkness.
Then the substanceless blue
Pour of tor and distances.

God's lioness,
How one we grow,
Pivot of heels and knees! —The furrow

Splits and passes, sister to
The brown arc
Of the neck I cannot catch,

Nigger-eye
Berries cast dark
Hooks—

Black sweet blood mouthfuls,
Shadows.
Something else

Hauls me through air—
Thighs, hair;
Flakes from my heels.

White
Godiva, I unpeel—
Dead hands, dead stringencies.

And now I
Foam to wheat, a glitter of seas.
The child's cry

Melts in the wall.
And I
Am the arrow,

The dew that flies,
Suicidal, at one with the drive
Into the red
Eye, the cauldron of morning.

[Selected from Ted Hughes, (ed.). *The Collected Poems*. New York: Harper & Row, 1981.]

Ⅲ. Questions for discussion

(1) In the poem "Colossus," how is the image of "Colossus" presented in this poem?

(2) How is the speaker, as a female, view the Colossus and herself?

(3) In the poem, what do the lines of "I am none the wiser" and "My hours are married to shadow" mean?

(4) Ariel is the imprisoned spirit that is condemned to serve an unbending and demanding master in Shakespeare's play, *The Tempest*, and in Plath poem "Ariel," it is generally believed to be the horse of the speaker. How do you think this poem reveals the speaker's feelings of imprisonment, suffocation and the inability to release herself from the everyday demands of life?

(5) The poem "Ariel" seems to presents a ride from darkness to sunrise. What does this riding experience bring to the speaker? What do the images of "the arrow" and "the dew that flies. / suicidal" suggest in the ending stanza?

(6) Plath's poetry is deceptively simple in language and form, but usually fragments them into unusual and sometimes painful combinations by using surprising and occasionally brutal imagery. Read these two poems again to see how this is reflected.

4.3 Assigned Reading

A 1962 Interview with Sylvia Plath

Peter Orr

ORR: Sylvia, what started you writing poetry?

PLATH: I don't know what started me, I just wrote it from the time was quite small. I guess I liked nursery rhymes and I guess I thought I could do the same thing. I wrote my first poem, my first published poem, when I was eight-and-a-half years old. It came out in *The Boston Traveller* and from then on, I suppose, I've been a bit of a professional.

ORR: What sort of thing did you write about when you began?

PLATH: Nature, I think: birds, bees, spring, fall, all those subjects which are absolute gifts to the person who doesn't have any interior experience to write about. I think the coming of spring, the stars overhead, the first snowfall and so on are gifts for a child, a young poet.

ORR: Now, jumping the years, can you say, are there any themes which particularly attract you as a poet, things that you feel you would like to write about?

PLATH: Perhaps this is an American thing: I've been very excited by what I feel is the new breakthrough that came with, say, Robert Lowell's *Life Studies*, this intense breakthrough into very serious, very personal, emotional experience which I feel has been partly taboo. Robert Lowell's poems about his experience in a mental hospital, for example, interested me very much. These peculiar, private and taboo subjects, I feel, have been explored in recent American poetry. I think particularly the poetess Ann Sexton, who writes about her experiences as a mother, as a mother who has had a nervous breakdown, is an extremely emotional and feeling young woman and her poems are wonderfully craftsmanlike poems and yet they have a kind of emotional and psychological depth which I think is something perhaps quite new, quite exciting.

ORR: Now you, as a poet, and as a person who straddles the Atlantic, if I can put it that way, being an American yourself....

PLATH: That's a rather awkward position, but I'll accept it!

ORR:[...]On which side does your weight fall, if I can pursue the metaphor?

PLATH: Well, I think that as far as language goes I'm an American, I'm afraid, my accent is American, my way of talk is an American way of talk, I'm an old-fashioned American. That's probably one of the reasons why I'm in England now and why I'll always stay in England. I'm about fifty years behind as far as my preferences go and I must say that the poets who excite me most are the Americans. There are very few contemporary English poets that I admire.

ORR: Does this mean that you think contemporary English poetry is behind the times compared with American?

PLATH: No, I think it is in a bit of a strait-jacket, if I may say so. There was an essay by Alvarez, the British critic: his arguments about the dangers of gentility in England are very pertinent, very true. I must say that I am not very genteel and I feel that gentility has a stranglehold: the neatness, the wonderful tidiness, which is so evident everywhere in England is perhaps more dangerous than it would appear on the surface.

ORR: But don't you think, too, that there is this business of English poets who are labouring under the whole weight of something which in block capitals is called "English Literature"?

PLATH: Yes, I couldn't agree more. I know when I was at Cambridge this appeared to me. Young women would come up to me and say "How do you dare to write, how do you dare to publish a poem, because of the criticism, the terrible criticism, that falls upon one if one does publish?" And the criticism is not of the poem as poem. I remember being appalled when someone criticized me for beginning just like John Donne, but not quite managing to finish like John Donne, and I first felt the full weight of English Literature on me at that point. I think the whole emphasis in England, in universities, on practical criticism (but not that so much as on historical criticism, knowing what period a line comes from) this is almost paralyzing. In America, in University, we read—what? —T. S. Eliot, Dylan Thomas, Yeats, that is where we began. Shakespeare flaunted in the background. I'm not sure I agree with this, but I think that's for the young poet, the writing poet, it is not quite so frightening to go to university in America as it is in England, for these reasons.

ORR: You say, Sylvia, that you consider yourself an American, but when we listen to a poem like "Daddy," which talks about Dachau and Auschwitz and Mein Kampf, I have the impression that this is the sort of poem that a real American could not have written, because it doesn't mean so much, these names do not mean so much, on the other side of the Atlantic, do they?

PLATH: Well now, you are talking to me as a general American. In particular, my background is, may I say, German and Austrian. On one side I am a first generation American, on one side I'm second generation American, and so my concern with concentration camps and so on is uniquely intense. And then, again, I'm rather a political person as well, so I suppose that's what part of it comes from.

ORR: And as a poet, do you have a great and keen sense of the historic?

PLATH: I am not a historian, but I find myself being more and more fascinated by history and now I find myself reading more and more about history. I am very interested in Napoleon, at the present: I'm very interested in battles, in wars, in Gallipoli, the First World War and so on, and I think that as I age I am becoming more and more historical. I certainly wasn't at all in my early twenties.

ORR: Do your poems tend now to come out of books rather than out of your own life?

PLATH: No, no. I would not say that at all. I think my poems immediately come out of the sensuous and emotional experiences I have, but I must say I cannot sympathise with these cries from the heart that are informed by nothing except a needle or a knife, or whatever it is. I believe that one should be able to control and manipulate experiences, even the most terrific, like madness, being tortured, this sort of experience, and one should be able to manipulate these experiences with an informed and an intelligent mini I think that personal experience is very important, but certainly it shouldn't be a kind of shut-box and mirror looking, narcissistic experience. I believe it should be relevant, and relevant to the larger things, the bigger things such as Hiroshima and Dachau and so on.

ORR: And so, behind the primitive, emotional reaction there must be an intellectual discipline.

PLATH: I feel that very strongly: having been an academic, having been tempted by the invitation to stay on to become a Ph. D., a professor, and all that, one side of me certainly does respect all disciplines, as long as they don't ossify.

ORR: What about writers who have influenced you, who have meant a lot to you?

PLATH: There were very few. I find it hard to trace them really. When I was at College I was stunned and astounded by the moderns, by Dylan Thomas, by Yeats, by Auden even: at one point I was absolutely wild for Auden and everything I wrote was desperately Audenesque. Now I again begin to go backwards, I begin to look to Blake, for example. And then, of course, it is presumptuous to say that one is influenced by someone like Shakespeare: one reads Shakespeare, and that is that.

ORR: Sylvia, one notices in reading your poems and listening to your poems that there are two qualities which emerge very quickly and clearly; one is their lucidity (and I think these two qualities have something to do one with the other), their lucidity and the impact they make on reading. Now, do you consciously design your poems to be both lucid and to be effective when they are read aloud?

PLATH: This is something I didn't do in my earlier poems. For example, my first book, *The Colossus*, I can't read any of the poems aloud now. I didn't write them to be read aloud. They, in fact, quite privately, bore me. These ones that I have just read, the ones that are very recent, I've got to say them, I speak them to myself, and I think that this in my own writing development is quite a new thing with me, and whatever lucidity they may have comes from the fact that I say them to myself, I say them aloud.

ORR: Do you think this is an essential ingredient of a good poem, that it should be able to be read aloud effectively?

PLATH: Well, I do feel that now and I feel that this development of recording poems, of speaking poems at readings, of having records of poets, I think this is a wonderful thing. I'm very excited by it. In a sense, there's a return, isn't there, to the old role of the poet, which was to speak to a group of people, to come across.

ORR: Or to sing to a group?

PLATH: To sing to a group of people, exactly.

ORR: Setting aside poetry for a moment, are there other things you would like to write, or that you have written?

PLATH: Well, I always was interested in prose. As a teenager, I published short stories. And I always wanted to write the long short story, I wanted to write a novel. Now that I have attained, shall I say, a respectable age, and have had experiences, I feel much more interested in prose, in the novel. I feel that in a novel, for example, you can get in toothbrushes and all the paraphernalia that one finds in dally life, and I find this more difficult in poetry. Poetry, I feel, is a tyrannical discipline, you've got to go so far, so fast, in such a small space that you've just got to turn away all the peripherals. And I miss them! I'm a woman, I like my little *Lares* and *Penates*, I like trivia, and I find that in a novel I can get more of life, perhaps not such intense life, but certainly more of life, and so I've become very interested in novel writing as a result.

ORR: This is almost a Dr. Johnson sort of view, isn't it? What was it he said, 'There are some things that are fit for inclusion in poetry and others which are not'?

PLATH: Well, of course, as a poet I would say pouf! I would say everything should be able to come into a poem, but I can't put toothbrushes into a poem, I really can't!

ORR: Do you find yourself much in the company of other writers, of poets?

PLATH: I much prefer doctors, midwives, lawyers, anything but writers. I think writers and artists are the most narcissistic people. I mustn't say this, I like many of them, in fact a great many of my friends happen to be writers and artists. But I must say what I admire most is the person who masters an area of practical experience, and can teach me something. I mean, my local midwife has taught me how to keep bees. Well, she can't understand anything I write. And I find myself liking her, may I say, more than most poets. And among my friends I find people who know all about boats or know all about certain sports, or how to cut somebody open and remove an organ. I'm fascinated by this mastery of the practical. As a poet, one lives a bit on air. I always like someone who can teach me something practical.

ORR: Is there anything else you would rather have done than writing poetry? Because this is something, obviously, which takes up a great deal of one's private life, if one's going to succeed at it. Do you ever have any lingering regrets that you didn't do something else?

PLATH: I think if I had done anything else I would like to have been a doctor. This is the sort of polar opposition to being a writer, I suppose. My best friends when I was young were always doctors. I used to dress up in a white gauze helmet and go round and see babies born and cadavers cut open. This fascinated me, but I could never bring myself to disciplining myself to the point where I could learn all the details that one has to learn to be a good doctor. This is the sort of opposition: somebody who deals directly with human experiences, is able to cure, to mend, to help, this sort of thing. I suppose if I have any nostalgias it's this, but I console myself because I know so many doctors. And I may say, perhaps, I'm happier writing about doctors than I would have been being one.

ORR: But basically this thing, the writing of poetry, is something which has been a great satisfaction to you in your life, is it?

PLATH: Oh, satisfaction! I don't think I could live without it. It's like water or bread, or something absolutely essential to me. I find myself absolutely fulfilled when I have written a poem, when I'm writing one. Having written one, then you fall away very rapidly from having been a poet to becoming a sort of poet in rest, which isn't the same thing at all. But I think the actual experience of writing a poem is a magnificent one.

[Selected from Peter Orr, (ed.). *The Poet Speaks: Interviews with Contemporary Poets Conducted by Hilary Morrish, Peter Orr, John Press, and Ian Scott-Kilvery*. London: Routledge 1966.]

5. Charles Bernstein

5.1 Presentation Topics

(1) Charles Bernstein as a leading poet and theorist.

(2) Bernstein as a representative of Language poetry.

(3) The influence of Gertude Stein on Bernstein and other Language poets.

5.2 Selected Reading

Ⅰ. Central issue of concern

Language to create, instead of conveying, meanings in Charles Berntein's poems.

Ⅱ. Text

My God Has an Attitude Problem

Being splints
it being hard
being Being
going on being
Being
being face-to-
face with Itself
rendering Its
rent replicants
rootless
writhing in
incontinence

[Selected from Charles Bernstein. *With Strings*. Chicago: University of Chicago Press, 2001.]

The Kiwi Bird in the Kiwi Tree

I want no paradise only to be
drenched in the downpour of words, fecund

with tropically. Fundament be
yond relation, less "real" than made, as arms
surround a baby's gurgling: encir-
ling mesh pronounces its promise (not bars
that pinion, notes that ply). The tailor tells
of other tolls, the seam that binds, the trim,
the waste, & having spelled these names, move on
to toys or talcums, skates & scores. Only
the imaginary is real—not trumps
beclouding the mind's acrobatic vers-
ions. The first fact is the social body,
one from another, nor needs no other.

[Selected from Charles Bernstein. *Rough Trades*. Los Angeles: Sun & Moon Press, 1991.]

Ⅲ. Questions for discussion

(1) How does the poet break the practices and rules of language in the poems?

(2) What do you think of the relationship between the signifier and the signified as shown in the poems?

(3) Language poets believes that language is not used to convey but create ideas. Do you think so?

(4) How do you think Charles Bernstein is different from other poets?

(5) For what purpose do you think the poet breaks the existing linguistic rules? Can it be understood as politically—as well as artistically—oriented?

5.3 Assigned Reading

Interview with Charles Bernstein

Nie Zhenzhao

Nie Zhenzhao (Nie for short hereafter): With the magazine L=A=N=G=U=A=G=E, your essays and your poems, you are generally considered the leading representative poet and theoretician of what is called Language Poetry, so I would like to begin my questions here. Language Poetry was first introduced to Chinese readers in 1993 when an anthology entitled *The Selected Poems from Language Poets* was published by Sichuan Arts & Literature Publishing House, China, with a circulation of around 2000 copies. Since then there have been few publications on Language Poetry in China. As a result, this work is still unfamiliar to most Chinese scholars and students. Would you please make a brief introduction to the occurrence, the development and the status quo of this school of poetry?

Charles Bernstein(CB for short hereafter): Language Poetry is a term that has come to stand for a rather raucous period in American poetry, from the mid-70s onward, in which a group of writers, mostly in New York, San Francisco, and Washington, D. C. , engaged in a large-scale collective effort to champion poetic invention both in our own work and the work of other English language poets of the 20th century. Because most of the established magazines, presses, and poetry organizations favored a different approach to poetry, we relied on our own resources, as far as publishing and presenting our work in performance. This was collective action without dogma, perhaps brought together as much by we didn't like as what we shared stylistically. And while from time to time someone would try to impose order or a neat history on our unruly and diffident practice, many of us took those interventions as an opportunity to define ourselves against just such labeling and schooling. There is no one history here and no one poetics.

In 1978, Bruce Andrews and I started *L=A=N=G=U=A=G=E*, a forum for poetics and discussion, something we felt was crucial and also lacking, both in the mainstream and in the alternative poetry scenes, in which there was an antipathy to critical thinking bordering on anti-intellectualism. The poets of *L=A=N=G=U=A=G=E*, and there were dozens of us, were interested in both a historical and an ideological approach to poetics and aesthetics and also a stand of dissent, both to prevailing poetry norms but also to U. S. government policies. We questioned all the "given" features of poetry, from voice and expression to clarity and exposition; and in the process, came up with many different, indeed contradictory, approaches to poetry and poetics. Our desire to link our poetry and poetics with the contemporary critical, philosophical, speculative, and political thinking—with a visceral connection to the civil rights movement, feminism, and the antiwar movement—has become a significant mark of our work, and one that has perhaps given rise to our various collective names, which have been both praised and condemned.

Nie: In China some people think that the poetry associated with *L=A=N=G*

$=U=A=G=E$ is the outcome of the influence of structuralism, post-structuralism, and postmodernism. How do you think of that?

CB: That's a common view based on the fact that many people are more familiar with these cultural developments than they are with what was going on in poetry. In truth, you can say that our work was contemporary with those other developments but not derived from them. Although, in the long view, mutual interactions and cross-connections will be more apparent. The poets of $L=A=N=G=U=A=G=E$ often offered a very sharp critique of structuralism, post-structuralism and postmodernism; certainly, that was a significant part of my critical writing of the period. But all of us shared much, if contrasted with technorationality, religious fundamentalism, and market suprematism.

Nie: Some people say, "Language Poetry is not so much a movement as a theory-generated method of poetic composition that emerged from the post-modernist tendency in contemporary North American poetry." As a theorist of Language Poetry, would you please make a comment on its theory and its background?

CB: Well I am not so much a theorist as a practitioner who reflects on his practice. Much of my poetics is pragmatic; none of it is systematic. This distinction between poetics and theory, though, would fall on deaf ears to those who are against "thinking" or against critical reflection, favoring instead what they claim to be unmediated personal expression. I won't get into a chicken-or-egg debate here about which comes first; poetics and poetry are mutually informing. But those who wish to deny the conceptual basis of their writing in favor of unmediated expression risk falling into a dogmatic rigidity about writing. I am especially interested in extreme forms of poetry, odd and eccentric forms, constructed procedures and procedural constructions. I never assume that the words I use represent a given world; I make the work anew with each word. Poetry is as much a product of delusion as illumination, illusion as reality.

Nie: How about the aesthetic principles and writing rules of this school?

CB: You are asking the wrong person or should I say the wronged person. Each poem can set forth its own rules and my primary aesthetic principle is to intensify the experience of the aesthetic. I left school as soon as I was able. I am working on my own now.

Nie: OK, but are there any rules or defining qualities of Language Poetry?

CB: Dominique Fourcade proposes: be ready but not prepared. I guess I could say also be prepared but not ready. Discrepancy is the key. I want a poetry that makes up its own rules and then doesn't follow those either.

Nie: Well then, in terms of practice, what are the most distinctive artistic features/techniques of the poets associated with *L=A=N=G=U=A=G=E*?

CB: You'd certainly notice some strong stylistic tendencies in work from around 1980: lots of disjunction (one phrase or line or sentence having no obvious logical connection to the next), an absence of simple lyric expression purporting to be the poet's feeling or expressing her or his subjective experience, structural and formal novelty (invented forms), a feeling of the constructedness of the poem's form, an exploration of discrepancies between word and object, metaphor and representation, truth and logic. But none of those things would be defining except maybe to say, paradoxically, that the lack of assumption about what defines a poem as a poem is perhaps defining.

Nie: Some people believe that Language Poetry is deeply involved politically from the very beginning, with a clear agreement with Neo-Marxism and New Leftism in America. But others thought that Language Poetry is detached from the real life. These two opinions seem sharply opposite to each other. As far as you are concerned, which do you think is true? And what do you think is the cause of such a difference?

CB: That's a useful problem to contemplate. Within a kind of hyper-empirical American approach to reality, ideas, ideologies, theories, philosophies, psychic structures, psychoanalytic or economic or linguistic structures, indeed the imaginary, are all debunked as removed from "real life." I try to stay out of the way of people who have this view of the real, because, in the end, for them what's real is a fist in the face of a gun against the temple. I prefer my imaginary life.

Nie: How do you think of the relationship between politics and poetry in general?

CB: The problem for politics, as much as for poetry, is how you define the real, how you describe the state of things. We see reality through metaphors and respond to those metaphors. No writing is innocent. Poetry marks the end of innocence for writing and the beginning of the imaginary.

Nie: *L=A=N=G=U=A=G=E* is generally regarded as a renegade brand, but in what way it is rebellious while to what extent it has connections with English poetic traditions?

CB: The English poetic tradition—just as the European and North and South American traditions—has a long line of renegade poets. Let's just say: renegades for the particularity of individual human experience and against both the uniformity of "correct language" that imposes preformed orders on live thinking and also against moral and religious laws that unnecessarily regulate individual behavior and expression. Dissident thought is valuable just because it is dissident. The wildness of the imagination is the greatest guarantor not only of freedom, but also of reality.

Nie: What is the relationship between *L=A=N=G=U=A=G=E* and other post-modern poetic schools such as New Formalism?

CB: There is an incredible variety of poetry being written in the U. S. at this time, from highly conventional to astonishingly inventive, from professional to amateur, from rural to urban to post-urban, from spiritual to erotic, from materialist to post-materialist. It would probably make more sense to assume that these different approaches to poetry have little or nothing in common than to think of them as part of the same activity, which tends to level some of the most interesting differences. New Formalism is one among these many contemporary manifestations of American poetry, as is "Language Poetry," and perhaps they are most easily understood as opposites: one emphasizing the invention of new forms, the other emphasizing the use of traditional forms, but that would make it seem almost like the old line between "free verse" and metrical verse. Most American poetry is now written in free verse formats, including much that is fairly straight forward at the level of form. I've always been interested in fractured, demented, asymmetrical, incongruous textures, and indeed what I call "dysprosody"—the prosody of distressed sounds.

Nie: Generally speaking, the poetry you focused on in *L=A=N=G=U=A=G=E* puts more emphasis on the written (visual) dimension of poetry than on the spoken (oral) dimension. Maybe this partly accounts for why you have collaborated with visual artists. However, in *Close Listening*: *Poetry and the Performed Word*, which you edited, you emphasize the sound of poetry. Does this reflect a shift in your own approach?

CB: I think as I began to perform my work more and more, and also as I organized more and more readings and poetry events, I began to feel that I had not sufficiently addressed the performative and sound dimensions of the poetry with which I was most engaged. Also I became interested in sound not as a natural extension of the written word but as a discrepant element, another layer of the complex that is the poetics work. And my major project of the last two years, working with Al Filreis, has been to develop a large archive of digital recordings of poetry readings, available for free at PennSound.

Nie: In "Sentences," the first section of Parsing, your 1975 book that is collected in Republics of Reality 1975—1995, you start each line of each poem with "they," "I," "you," "it," or "was." Why do you deliberately choose the same word to start a line and to adopt such grammatical structure? In the conventional structure of the poetic line, poets try to avoid recurrence of a word in the beginning of all lines in a stanza for the aesthetic variance of reading. So why do you intentionally use the same word to start a line, or to compose a stanza, for example, the stanza consisting of "contextual disruption," which could be, to me, a feature of your poems?

CB: *Parsing* is one of my earliest works. The title refers to breaking sentences or phrases into their syntactic parts, itself a form of contextual disruption. In *Parsing* all the words being with a pronoun, some of which can operate as "shifters," that is they take on different references depending on the context. There are two sources for "Sentences," both oral histories: *Working* by Studs Terkel and *Yessir, I've Been Here a Long Time: Faces and Words of Americans* by George Mitchell. I lifted and arranged lots of those "I" and "You" sentences from these vernacular speech transcriptions, and placed them amidst mostly sentences I generated myself. The final poem, numbered 1 & 2 is all first lines of Emily Dickinson's poems.

In this work I was interested in repetition as a form of reiteration, insistence in Gertrude Stein's sense. There is also a relation to the minimalist music of Steve Reich and also his own interest in repetitive and highly rhythmical chanting. One of Ron Silliman's most influential early essays, "The New Sentence" discusses the non-syllogistic logic of this kind of sentence organization. In "Sentences" I was interested in getting to a basic unit of speech and then using that to make rhythmic compositions. Much of the content of the sentences is plaintive, so that is part of the pull for me. A kind of collective *plaint* of despair or melancholy or disappointment or separation, which is something that threads through my work and connects it, perhaps unexpectedly, to fado, blues, mourning prayers, or other forms of lament that also use repetition.

Nie: In "Space and Poetry" in *Parsing*, and in many other poems, we can conclude that you fracture discursive language by rearranging phrases into lines that together produce non-grammatical sentences. It seems that you divide a sentence in parts and then reconfigure these parts. Here is a sentence in "Space and Poetry" as example, "space, and poetry / dying and transforming words, before / arbitrary, period locked / with meaning and which / preposterousness," which you divide it into 5 lines. I wonder how to understand their special poetic quality of this fractured sentence. Could you give me some hints?

CB: This is phase two of *Parsing*, after "Sentences." You could see it as a kind of analytic cubism. Apparently prior sentences (no original set of sentences is provided) are divided (cut-up) into component parts and these are opened up into a field layout (not flush left, spread over the whole page). The lines form a kind of music of changing or shifting parts that cannot be parsed on a linear level. This opens the page out to something that is not a two-dimensional Euclidean space but a curved space, a space with n-dimensionality. Let me now reinsert the space you deliberately subtracted for your question, so you can feel the torque:

space, and poetry
dying and transforming words, before
arbitrary, period locked
with meaning and which
preposterousness. Still

Nie: In some poems such as "Roseland" (*Parsing*), "Of course ..." and "St. McC." (*Shade*), "Some nights" and "Type" (*Stigma*), you intentionally omit punctuation marks just like James Joyce did in Ulysses to express for expression of stream of consciousness. Of course, there are many poems composed by other poets without punctuation marks, but their grammatical structure is clear for us to read and interpret. Compared with them, it seems that you fracture the regular grammatical structure to compose lines to create new meaning, which could be difficult for readers to get. What is your aesthetic purpose to use this technique to compose poems? How can we get your exact meaning of a poem without punctuation marks?

CB: There is no exact meaning, no prior meaning which I transform into verse, no single or paraphrasable meaning for the reading to grasp. A structure, or perhaps better to say an environment is created for the reader to respond, to interenact. This is frustrating if you are reading to try to extract a meaning, pleasurable if you are comfortable trolling within meanings. By the way, "Roseland" has as its source some phrases from David Antin's "the sociology of art" from talking at the boundaries, so it's cut-up from Antin's transcription of his original "spoken" talk. That's a very specific example of the kind of speech/writing tension or disjunction I was interested in for *Parsing*.

Nie: From some of your poems I realize that you admire irregular arrangement of lines or like to fracture sentences to form stanzas and poems. For example, you break the sentences in the poems such as "The Hand Gets Scald but the Heart Grows Colder" in Controlling Interests and "The Puritan Ethic and the Spirit of Capitalization" in *Rough Trades* into many parts and then organize them into a new poetic form. Do you have rules when you fracture a sentence and rearrange the fractured sentence? What kind of poetic art do you strive for?

CB: Mostly I work intuitively, arranging the words on the page so as to maximize the ping and pong of word against word, phrase against phrase, to intensify the visceral verbal sensation, to find sense, indeed make sense with what is at hand. Many of the poems that may seem to be rearrangements of prior texts—cut-ups—are actually freely composed, though sometimes they have gone through a series of erasures and rewritings and rearrangements of my own original seed text. The formal prototype for the poems you mention is "Asylums" (Islets/Irritations), which is one of my first poems, from 1974. In that poem I cut out snippets from a source text, Erving Goffman's *Asylum*, mostly focusing on the words just before and after the period, in other words the interstitial dynamics of the text, the literal place of transition from one sentence to the next. Another way to look at it would be to say I took a prior text and erased most it, or that the only parts "left" are the nodal points around the sentences. So then the process resembles sculpting from a slab of stone, creating the work by means of chiseling away at the surface of the rock. These poems, then, appear to have gone through a process of textual erosion. "The Puritan Ethic and the Spirit of Capitalization" is the most eroded of these works. The title comes from Max Weber's turn-of-the-20th century sociological study *The Protestant Ethic and the Spirit of Capitalism*, which emphasized the connection between accumulation, capitalism, and the Protestant ethic. The poem enacts an erosion of accumulated meanings or perhaps simply a turn away from a semiotics of accumulated meaning. "The Hand Gets Scald but the Heart Grows Colder" is somewhat more typical of my work from *Controlling Interests* and the period immediately following, which has a mix of eroded (or erased) textual fragments, aphorism, lists, metacommentaries, lyric strains, instructions, found language, commands; in other words a collage of various elements, which are fused together through thematic, rhythmic, associational, and structural dynamics, most of which are come upon—that is, just made up—in the process of writing the poem.

Nie: Generally speaking, to understand a poem is to understand its meaning, therefore the title is significant as the guide for understanding, or the topic of the poem. However, some titles of your poems are different from those we read from conventional way. I can take your poem "Mao Tse Tung Wore Khakis" as example. From the conventional reading, we should understand this poem first from understanding of its title but the title seems to have nothing to do with the content of the poem. How do you think of this question? What is the function of "Mao Tse Tung Wore Khakis" as the title of the poem? There are several other names mentioned in the poem. Are Paul McCartney and Bob Dylan the well-known American singers and songwriters? And is Perry Como one of the most American popular vocalists? What significance of their names is mentioned in the poem? What is your intent of Thunderbirds and THE LIONS in the poem? In this poem, some lines are printed in black, some in capital letters, and some in italic. What do you mean by acting like this? In general, could you help to show us the meaning of this poem?

CB: The difficulty of this poem for you is probably more related to its local (American) cultural references than to the kind of aesthetic and formal issues we have been talking about. Although I do often like titles whose relation to the poem is oblique, oblique more than dissociated. In this case, the poem refers to a set of ads by the Gap clothing story chain, a brand of closing that emphasizes "informal" styles, denim jeans being the quintessential example. The ads featured blow-up photos of all kinds of hip artists and intellectuals, including Allen Ginsberg, Miles Davis, and Jack Kerouac, with the tag line "... Wore Khakis." Needless to say, Chairman Mao was not included in the ads, though didn't he wear khakis, too? The references to Bob Dylan are a bit obscure even for the entertainment news junky of 2007; at the time the poem was written, Dylan chose to go to more commercial Woodstock 25th anniversary concert in Saugerties, New York, rather than the "alternative" celebration at the site of the original festival. Perry Como, a decidedly square singer of an earlier generation, is compared to the presumably hip McCartney.

The poem is a sonnet and there are some procedural interruptions including a warning message from the then current, now hopeless outmoded, e-mail system of the time. The Thunderbird was a cool car (and now also an e-mail program, but not then). The lions are still on the loose.

Nie: I am confused about the style of some of the works in *Poetic Justice* (collected in *Republics of Reality*): "Palukaville," "Lo Disfruto," "electric," "Azoot D'Puund," "Out of This Inside," "Hotel Empire," "Lift off," "Appropriation," "Faculty Politics," and "The Taste is What Counts." Could you tell me whether they are essays or poems or what kind of other style we should call them?

CB: They are poems but in a prose format, though as you can see many different approaches to the "prose" format, to such an extent that prose becomes, rather than something neutral, something visually specific, what Marjorie Perloff recently calls "Concrete Prose" (thinking of Haroldo de Campos' *Galaxias*). *Poetic Justice* is the companion collection to *Shade*, which had mostly very thin poems; the poems in *Poetic Justice* are so thick as to exceed the margins. A few of these are serial sentences prose, what Ron Silliman dubbed "the new sentence": a quick succession of complete sentences, juxtaposed one to the next, without logical connectives (paratactic). Ron's *Sunset Debris* is a prose poem made up of all questions. "Palukaville" (names after Joe Palooka the cartoon boxer, in the sense of "punch drunk") is made up of all answers, responding to the questions of *Sunset Debris*. "The Taste Is What Counts" and "Lo Disfruto" are imploded syntax prose, made up of periods not sentences, where phrase is grafted on to phrase to make intricately recombinant rhythmic patterns. "electric," and "Out of this Inside" are more closely related to free-associative, diaristic/journal writing, though with some visual overlays (the expressive use of capital letters in the middle of words) and other structural elements added to create more traction/tension. "Azoot D'Puund" is written with entirely invented words, so it's a sound poem, but again in a prose format. "Lift Off," in contrast, appears to be something of a visual poem, though it looks like prose, it is actually lineated. It is based on the series of letters on the "lift off" or correction tape of an IBM Selectric Ⅱ typewriter. I originally published this book as an offset edition, typing the pages myself on my Selectric. So the right margin is ragged, but mostly the lines go to the end of the page. Still, those versions of the work were ambiguous as to whether they were prose or verse lines. But for *Republics of Reality*, we set most of the pieces as prose, meaning we did not respect line endings. Still, as you noticed, there are many different paragraph and line arrangement: the visual space of the "prose" is plural. The prose is arose.

Nie: I notice that you use a number of different formats for your poems. As you have discussed, some are written in prose but you also have some with a mixture of prose poems and free verse. Although you don't work with traditional metrical forms, I believe that you have your own prosodic rules because I can feel strong rhythms in the poem, which I can't describe conclusively. I don't know if my intuition is right or not. Can you say anything about meter and rhythm of your poetry?

CB: Metricality is an ideal system that is independent of performance and, to some degree, independent of pronunciation (the articulation and duration of syllables). In contrast, rhythm is something heard. Metrical verse emphasizes symmetry and uniformity. My own impulses are toward asymmetry and syncopation: the off-balance, the slant, the microtonal, but still with a pulse. It's possible to create a strong acoustic rhythm with dissonance (clashing sounds and clashing sound patterns). Patterns don't have to be linear they can be fractal. I use all kinds of forms and also count in a variety of ways. If you look under the hood, from time to time, you will see patterns in the words per line or lines per stanza, syllable counting that is a metrical, and many passages with traditional metric but right up against ones that are not. Poems whose rhythm is driven primarily by alliteration. And when I perform the poems the sonic shapes are all important, but I want that shape to stretch, bend, snap, break down into a virtually acoustic vocable noise, lapse into song by day, lullaby by night, interrupted by the whirring and wailing of the fire engines I hear outside my window.

Nie: I have some small questions. Why do you number the 1st stanza as the 3rd and the ending stanza as the 788th while there are factually only 13 stanzas in "The Manufacture of Negative Experience" in *With Strings*? "The Order of a Room" is the most particular poem in its form, I suppose. It seems that you borrowed techniques from concrete poems somewhat, but I am not sure. How to read this poem composed in irregular alignment of words with figures? And how to understand this kind of poems? Could you give some advice?

CB: The many stanzas that are left blank in "The Manufacture of Negative Experience" leave room for thought; they are the blank spots of a negative dialectics, writ large. "The Order of Room" uses many different sources to contemplate what we have been discussing throughout this interview: what makes for order? Can you have nonlinear order? Is order something fixed and controlling, as in "law and order" or do our imposed orders make us dead and blind to other, harder to perceive orders, orders of the universe, but also of our souls?

[Selected from Nie Zhenzhao. Interview with Charles Bernstein. *Foreign Literature Studies*, 2007 (3).]

6. Anne Waldman

6.1 Presentation Topics

(1) Anne Waldman as a performance poet.

(2) Anne Waldman's inheriting the traditions of Beat poetry and New York School.

(3) Anne Waldman as a feminist and cultural activist.

6.2 Selected Reading

Ⅰ. Central issue of concern

Anne Waldman's serious concern with the role of language and the being of the self as a (wo)man in the contemporary power structure.

Ⅱ. Text

Suppose a Game

Suppose language is a game
  whose rules are dreamed
    by an agreement of players

Once broken, the speakers are tossed
  & know no rude tongue but their own
    no (fixed) meaning in solipsism

But always in a process of being stranded
  are spectators of solipsism
  stuck with themselves, empirical data

Theirs is private demon language
  obstruction, ownership, demand
    Is the door open?

Rain here yet?
  Have their ideas entered all heads?
    Is this the end of the game?

They quickly become the ex-modern
  and you, poet, enter the arena
    an animating principle to a touch of words

Seduce them to your page
  caress plosiveness
    beat them to a fine shapelessness

Or sentences are for the first time stark & clear

not untrue to what flaunts style:
webs of cloth, a mirror you hold

The players conjure nihilism, their only way
to be curious, vain, a waste of strength
as confusion weakens the vocal art

Cybernetics is the exchange of their news for yours
Yours is: However abundant the nectar,
the bees stop dancing as the sugar drops

They tell you nothing, their lips are sealed, you keep dancing
Was the agreement that words shine like sun,
or glint as weapons in moonlight?

Why I Meditate

—A reply for Allen Ginsberg

I sit because I'm wing'd with awe
I sit because the poetry scene got sour in America in 1980
I sit because Milarepa did
I sit because Padmasamb have buried the Bardo Thotrol in the Gampo Hills & gave endless transmission to discover how death is liberating
I sit because Yeshe Tsogyal appeared in a dream & showed me her cervix like an ocean
I sit because the Dakinis dance over my forehead
I sit because thoughts chase thoughts
I sit in Puri they won't let me in the Hindu temple
I sit in Bodnath under the 8 eyes of the great stupa
I sit in Calcutta like being in Preta realm
I prostrate 1,000 times under the descendant of Buddha's bodhi tree
I sit like a frog on Cherry Valley's poetry farm
I sit by her hospital door, breathe in my mother's eyeball pain
I sit like an agent provocateur on the Orient Express
I sit like a cow in farmer Lang's meadow

I sit inside the body of a nursing mother
I sit to scandalize
I sit because I won't take it lying down
I sit to test old friends & loves
I sit because passion burns me up
I sit because I'm a paranoid speed freak
I sit because I deserted the poetry wars
I sit to be exile from Ego's land.

[Selected from Anne Waldman. *In the Room of Never Grieve*. Minneapolis, MN: Coffee House Press, 2003.]

Ⅲ. Questions for discussion

(1) Anne Waldman is usually seen as a representative of so-called post-Beats. Can you find some evidence to support this idea?

(2) Anne Waldman is known for her efforts in poetry performance. How do you think these two poems carry some qualities for performance?

(3) What view of language does the first poem present?

(4) Do you think the second poem reveals the poet's acceptance of the Buddhist culture? How can you compare this with Allen Ginsberg's influence of Buddhism?

(5) Do you think the poet demonstrates her special concern with women in the second poem? How?

6.3 Assigned Reading

Preface to *In the Room of Never Greive*

Anne Waldman

Will writing ever be enough to explicate the poet's days and hours and some of the rest of the world too? We live in "interesting times," a dire historical moment dominated by the American government's insatiable hegemonic empire-building. "Rome Fell"—a heady prophetic reminder—proclaims an antiwar slogan. It's not as if we need to quibble about the motives of the ruling powers and how they have scant use for poetry. What, poetry? No poetry for the masses? They might get wise to us, the masters of war mutter. We struggle against a new world order and will not fall victim to the language of euphemism propagated by illegal rulers and their corporate/media lackeys. *Poetry is* news that stays news—that was a bias from the start. Yet what is the place of writing—of *poetry*—everybody asks—in such a state of affairs? And why do I offer this particular book, this retrospective, this "package," these choices, at this time?

To reclaim the imagination, to free our language from the stench of manipulation, my voices tell me. Examine how the mind moves in language that seeks to create alternative ways to live, to survive, and to sing. These are the tasks, the disciplines. Thus for this book I wanted the most dynamic, most feminist, most oral/public interventions that include efficacious possibility. I wanted them both on and off the page. I wanted to change the dominant "master narratives" and question the role of language as it plays with its own markers. I wanted to posit: if the very future of this planet is at stake, is it enough to deconstruct, to mystify, to obviate? Would beauty still be the call? Or love? Of course, along with the Buddhist sense of boddhicitta—awakened heart. One conjures from that tradition as well, the sense of upaya, skillful means, and prajna, wisdom. I wanted a book that would speak to my community of family and friends as co-conspirators who struggle to keep the world safe for poetry. Testimony? You could say that. I wanted the sense of the book as a "reader," with accompanying compact disc, in collaboration with my son Ambrose Bye, as "sounder."

I wanted a document that would offer a range of the various projects over these pre-and post-millennial years. Some of the disparate forms: vocal, visual, visible, political, performative.

I fuss a lot over a "book." How it moves, how it is distinguished from a random sheaf of poems. *In the Room of Never Grieve*, the book, is meant to honor and carry the flavor of the other books. My friend Anselm Hollo proffers "survival dancing" as a modus operandi. I want a sense of urgency that's the psycho-physical shape of thought and body and sensibility, dancing around and about the book. Dance as a spiral. Also: research, scholarship, inspiration, renunciation. Thus a "selected" from some eighteen intense published years and two unpublished recent compilations. Eleven sections in all. What were the favorites? What seemed most relevant now, personally? What would pick up where my previous new and selected, *Helping the Dreamer*, left off, with the sense of an ongoing trajectory and a hint of overlap? So the process included showing a larger picture—almost three-dimensional—of the work. And out of this selection, another selection or compendium of performance, in part, with musical collaboration. I wanted *In the Room of Never Grieve*, the disc, to work conceptually as a performance as if one were in fact in a room as a state of mind. The disc does not follow the order of the book. I invited Ambrose to create a soundscape for the poems he selected. He has grown up, lived with many of these pieces in his ear. This is his response. Selections within selections.

The cover reproduces a favorite painting by long-time friend and artist-collaborator George Schneeman. The egg tempura painting has graced my wall these past months. The photographs, not necessarily contemporaneous with each section, trace a public life perhaps and at times a life-in-performance.

The Book: I start with "Fast Speaking Woman, Part ii," from the early eighties, coming on the heels of the original "Fast Speaking Woman." Lines kept spilling out, it's that simple, with more variable riffs, greater breath phrasing on the page ["mincy mincy mincy mincy she cried/ mincy mincy mincy/ she was burning all right/ her house (the one she carried on her head) was afire"]. More played out, as it were, less predictable than the original chant. The voice hears itself as crone, assuming various personalities or guises that carry a meta—"I." Other pieces from the anniversary edition include a spel, a reggae, sung verses, and a sutra. Oral by intent and specificity.

Next cluster from *Skin Meat Bones* embeds modal structures as well—the title poem with its three primordial notes echoes the Buddhist chant ("om" "ah" "hum"), and the menses-dementia chant "Crack in the World" is to be read as performance-monologue. Yet "Science Times" is a mental discourse on the page. Locked in whose head?

The pieces in *Tell Me About It* are meditations around various artists and their work: Jasper Johns, Jane Freilicher, Larry Rivers, Elizabeth Murray, trying to say something of surface, of style, of kinesis.

Not a Male Pseudonym is a Sapphic paean, a reverie both lyrical and bittersweet. The first-person lover-of-women wants to be intimate, strong, irresistible, and chooses to use words as emotional jabs, albeit sparingly.

Troubairitz, a word referring to a female troubadour, is a long poem written with the Tibetan bardo or gap (between states of mind as it moves through states of love) as a trope or conceit. Composed over a forty-nine-day period, it makes extensive use of Buddhist psychological terms.

Iovis: *All Is Full of Jove*, *Iovis* Ⅱ, and the unpublished selection from *Iovis*, *Book* Ⅲ: *The Eternal War* on which this book concludes, are part of the same ongoing epic *Iovis* (literally "of Jove") trilogy begun in the mid-eighties and continuing with rhizomic adventure and roar into the present. The *Iovis* project has an exalted tone and purpose: total assault on and transmutation of patriarchy—through imagination, compassion, and magic. It undermines and subsumes dominant patriarchal mindsets and fabrications. As reclaimed tantric female epic it challenges assumptions of form, intervenes and torques narrative, disgorges themes, and shunts war again and again. It names and calls out enemy, weaponry, swagger. The presenter is a hermaphroditic hierophant with vatic power. Her/His mind surveys topics of male dominance, beauty, war, crime, parentage, and explores ceremonial rites for respected elders. Voices dance here through the female cycle: child, virgin, lover, mother, hag. The poem is a collaboration with history—personal, dreamed, mythic—virtual as well as actual. It attempts to claim, magnetize, harness magical power, transmute war through language. It attempts to tell all the stories of place in all manner of genre. It shows off its erudition, it retreats into the prehistoric cave at night to paint fantastic shapes on the walls in ocher. Its weave is narrative yet circular. It emulates Sappho, William Blake, Dante, Charles Olson, Ezra Pound, William Carlos Williams of *Paterson*, H. D. of *Trilogy* and *Helen in Egypt*, and others, yet it fights for its right to be a feminist form. The final section from *Iovis*, *Book* Ⅲ: *The Eternal War* cries out against the bifurcation of experience and imagination. What's seen, what's hidden, what's beautiful, what's ugly. It's as if the poet were both child and seer, trying to make sense of a world gone mad under the thumb of restraint and dangerously calculated power. Many of the themes in *Iovis* (the trilogy) are resonant in most of the other works in this book. Much of my writing "hovers" around these engaged poetic centers.

Kill or Cure displays prose poems that call the writer out to perform and challenge preconceived notions of the poem. Monologues perhaps. Talky, didactic. Some of the pieces here were written for specific occasions such as "Paean: May I

Speak Thus?" which was "composed on the tongue" at a fundraiser for AIDS research with Allen Ginsberg in Aspen, Colorado.

Marriage: A Sentence, written very much for the page, is a serial poem exploring themes and mores of marriage, but also of gender assumption. It arose out of a series of haibun (the Japanese prose poem that has a clinching haiku at its end) I had written for one of my classes at Naropa University. The prose parts were interspersed with poem bits—extended haiku as it were—as a kind of bonding material. So back and forth between prose and poetry, between genders, between voices and veneers. But it is the challenge of the sentence that rules. How far may the serial poem stretch to materialize the complexities and ironies of marriage as a measure of a dynamic that pushes and pulls through time and space and still puzzles the grammarian-minded poet?

In the Room of Never Grieve is very elegiac in tone. It's the little girl biting the bullet: I will stay in this room, forever, I will be strong, I will never grieve. The subtext: I love, therefore I meditate on death and suffer loss.

Today I joined several poets on the steps of the New York Public Library. The "Shock & Awe" campaign had just begun over Baghdad. It was the first day of spring. We stood beneath our Poets For Peace Banner and read poems by poets from all over the world. I sang "Rogue State." The war goes on and this particularly horrific and senseless invasion will reap years of negative snarling karma, and be the paradigm for the next wars, the next imperious interventions. Poets oppose this monstrous aggression and further aggressions with our voices, breath, our wits, our bodies, our words, our cultural/activist interventions. We continue our activity in the nation's streets and in concert with other outraged citizens of the world. We as poets witness and continue to proclaim ourselves, in Shelley's phrase: the true legislators of the race.

[Selected from Anne Waldman. *In the Room of Never Grieve*. MN: Coffee House Press, 2003.]

Chapter 9 Drama

1. Introduction

Drama inAmerica was slow to develop as a self-conscious literary form. It was not until 1920 (the year of Eugene O'Neill's *Beyond the Horizon*) that America produced a playwright.

Healthy changes in American theater are often in reaction against Broadway, a pattern observable as early as 1915 with the formation of the Washington Square Players and the Provincetown Players. European influence was strong. By 1915, Henrik Ibsen in Europe and George Bernard Shaw inEngland had shown that the theater could be an arena for serious ideas. The American tours of European companies, in particular the Moscow Art Theatre in 1923, further exposed Americans to the theatrical avant-garde. American playwrights in the 1920s and 1930s were united not so much by a common cause of ideas, European or American, as by the new assumption that drama could be a branch of contemporary literature.

The era's leading playwright is Eugene O'Neill. O'Neill is generally acclaimed as one of the greatest American playwright, who has exerted extensive and profound influences on American drama. O'Neill has won Nobel Prize for Literature, and has won Pulitzer Prize for Drama for four times for the power, honesty and deep-felt emotions of his dramatic works. The power of his drama lies not only in its external action, but also in the depth of his characterization and the deep concerns for human fate. He experimented less in language than in dramatic structure and in new production methods available through technology (e. g., lighting) or borrowed from the stylized realism of German expressionism.

Almost as famous at the time was Maxwell Anderson, whose best plays—the tragic *Winterset* (1935) and the romantic comedy *High Tor* (1937) embody a stylized blank verse. Playwrights such as Sidney Howard, Lillian Hellmam, and Robert Sherwood explored problems of the modern characters in serious realistic plays. George Kaufman and his many collaborators, especially Moss Hart, invented a distinctively American form, the wisecracking domestic and social comedy, while S. N. Behrman and Philip Barry wrote higher comedies of ideas. The musical comedy is another distinctively American invention. Social commentary and satire had been a thread in the bright weave of American drama since the early 1920s, beginning with Elmer Rice's fiercely expressionistic play about a rebellious nonentity, *The Adding Machine* (1923). After the Depression, social criticism became a much more important dramatic theme. Perhaps the most significant is Clifford Odets' *Waiting for Lefty* (1935). It was in this period that drama moved decisively into the Amcrican literary mainstream.

American theatre since World War Ⅱ enjoyed a steady growth, specifically in tragedy and tragi-comedy. The new generation of dramatists, on the one hand, clings to traditional realism in themes constantly searching for the meaning of life in a world in which man seems to have been lost. On the other hand, modern drama is extremely experimental as far as the theatrical techniques are concerned. Many of them are worthy of study, but Arthur Miller, Tennessee Williams and Edward Albee are the three giants in drama.

Tennessee Williams (1911—1983) was an American playwright who received many top theatrical awards for his dramas, including the Pulitzer Prize for Drama (*A Streetcar Named Desire*, 1948, and *Cat on a Hot Tin Roof*, 1955), and in 1980 was presented with the Presidential Medal of Freedom by President Jimmy Carter. Williams is the great romantic of the American drama. He is fascinated with the poignant side of the human condition: the suffering and death of the young, the pains of the defeated, the fading of youth and beauty, the self-destruction, the violence in love, the vicissitudes of the gay world, the and deep despair. Sexuality and cruelty are frequent themes in Williams' plays.

Arthur Miller (1915—2005) is an American playwright and essayist. He is a prominent figure in American theatre, writing dramas that include awards-winning plays such as *All My Sons* (1947), *Death of a Salesman* (1949), *The Crucible* (1953) and *After the Fall* (1964). As a playwright, Miller is a follower of Ibsen both in dramaturgy and in themes, and his is generally believed to embody the conscience of America in the 20th century. Fascinated by the potential capacities of humans, he wrote thesis plays, challenging an audience to make moral judgments, indicting bourgeois society for its selfishness while insisting on the collective responsibility of all human beings for each other.

Edward Albee (1928—) is an American playwright best known for *Who's Afraid of Virginia Woolf?*, *The Zoo Story*, *A Delicate Balance* and *Three Tall Women*. His works are considered well-crafted, often unsympathetic examinations of the modern condition. His early works reflect a mastery and Americanization of the Theatre of the Absurd that found its peak in works by European playwrights such as Jean Genet, Samuel Beckett, and Eugène Ionesco.

It is obvious that American drama was dominated mainly by white males in the first half of the 20th century. In the second half of the 20th century, however, American theatre has shown signs that it has become more accessible to female dramatists and those from ethnic minorities. Yet even within this relatively "closed shop" of the American theatre, the range of voices has been extensive. At its best, American theatre has reflected the diversity of American society. All kinds of American idioms and regional speech crop up in American drama, reminding us that this is a vast country with many currents contributing to the mainstream of American life. It is in this diversity that the American theatre and its dramatists find their unique voice. Some new developments deserve mentioning, especially the African American drama, feminist drama, gay and lesbian drama.

The first African American dramatist to receive national attention was Langston Hughes, whose plays, such as *Mulatto* in 1935, were popular with black and white audiences—but in Harlem, not on Broadway. The Broadway breakthrough for African American dramatists came in 1941 with Richard Wright's stage adaptation of his famous novel *Native Son*. In the 1950s Broadway welcomed Louis Peterson's *Take a Giant Step* in 1953, and Lorraine Hansberry's *Raisin in the Sun* (1959) became the most successful and most often performed African American play up through the present. In the 1960s the African American civil rights revolution brought African American dramatists to the forefront of American drama both on and off Broadway right through to the present. The greatest living African American dramatist is August Wilson, whose series of plays referred to as the Pittsburg Cycle are already an important part of the history of American drama. After Arthur Miller, Wilson is the most significant living American playwright.

Although Zona Gale, Rachel Crothers, Susan Glaspell, Zoe Akins, Lulu Vollmer, Edna Ferber, Lillian Hellman, Carson McCullers, and Lorraine Hansberry made significant contributions to American drama in their time, it was not until the women's movement in the late 1960s and 1970s that a feminist agenda reached the American stage. This agenda included defining issues of gender, studying sex and power, supporting equality for women, differentiating the language and experience of woman, empowering women writers in a patriarchal and sexist society, and contradicting the often distorted depiction of women in plays written by men. Additionally, women dramatists strove to create a contemporary canon of women's plays. Feminist drama foregrounds a woman's struggle for autonomy. Arguably, however, it does not have to be written by a woman. Outstanding among the women dramatists inspired by and participating in the women's movement are the African American Ntozake Shange, whose 1976 play*For Colored Girls Who Have Considered Suicide/When the Rainbow Is Enuf* symbolized the connection with, and the debt to, the Civil Rights movement of the 1960s; Beth Henley (*Crimes of the Heart*, 1977); Marsha Norman (*'Night Mother*, 1983); Tina Howe (*Painting Churches*, 1983); and Wendy Wasserstein (*The Heidi Chronicles*, 1988, and *The Sisters Rosensweig*, 1992).

As early as 1934 the possibility of a lesbian relationship was broached on the American stage in Lillian Hellman's*The Children Hour*. But it was not until Mart Crowley's *The Boys in the Band* in 1968 that the pleasures and the pains, the humor and the pathos of gay life in the United States entered the mainstream of American drama (and film).

Key words

The Theatre of the Absurd

A designation for particular plays written by a number of primarily European playwrights in the late 1940s, 1950s, and 1960s, as well as to the style of theatre which has evolved from their work. Edward Albee, to some extent, is a representative of this movement in America. The Absurd plays takes the form of man's reaction to a world apparently without meaning or man as a puppet controlled or menaced by an invisible outside force. Some characteristics that coincide in the plays are: broad comedy mixed with horrific or tragic images; characters caught in hopeless situations forced to do repetitive or meaningless actions; dialogue full of clichés, wordplay, and nonsense; plots that are cyclical or absurdly expansive; either a parody or dismissal of realism and the concept of the "well-made play."

Broadway theatre

Commonly called simply Broadway, refers to theatrical performances presented in one of the 40 large professional theaters with 500 seats or more located in the Theatre District, New York (plus one theatre in Lincoln Center) in Manhattan. Along with London's West End theatre, Broadway theatre is usually considered to represent the highest level of commercial theatre in the English-speaking world.

2. Eugene O'Neill

2.1 Presentation Topics

(1) Eugene O'Neill is acclaimed as the "Father of American drama," how do you comment on it?

(2) Cite evidences to illustrate the autobiographical features of O'Neill's plays.

2.2 Selected Reading

Ⅰ. Central issue of concern

Naturalism, realism and Ecological awareness.

Ⅱ. Text

The Moon of the Caribbees

A Play in One Act

CHARACTERS
YANK
DRISCOLL
OLSON
DAVIS, seaman of the British tramp steamer, Glencairn
COCKY
SMITTY
PAUL
LAMPS, the lamptrimmer
CHIPS, the carpenter
OLD TOM, the donkeyman
BIG FRANK
DICK, firemen on the Glencairn
MAX
PADDY
BELLA
SUSIE, West Indian Negresses
VIOLET
PEARL
THE FIRST MATE

Two other seamen—SCOTTY and IVAN—and several other members of the stokehole-engine-room crew.

The Moon of the Caribbees

SCENE—A forward section of the main deck of the British tramp Steamer Glencairn, at anchor off an island in the West Indies. The full moon, half-way up the sky, throws a clear light on the deck. The sea is calm and the ship motionless.

On the left two of the derrick booms of the foremast jut out at an angle of forty-five degrees, black against the sky. In the rear the dark outline of the port bulwark is sharply defined against a distant strip of coral beach, white in the moonlight, fringed with coco palms whose tops rise clear of the horizon. On the right is a forecastle with an open doorway in the center leading to the seamen's and firemen's compartments. On either side of the doorway are two closed doors opening on the quarters of the Bo'sun, the ship's carpenter, the messroom steward, and the donkeyman—what might be called the petty officers of the ship. Near each bulwark there is also a short stairway, like a section of fire escape, leading up to the forecastle head (the top of the forecastle) —the edge of which can be seen on the right.

In the center of the deck, and occupying most of the space, is the large, raised square of the number one batch, covered with canvas, battened down for the night.

A melancholy negro chant, faint and far-off, drifts, crooning, over the water.

Most of the seamen and firemen are reclining or sitting on the batch. Paul is leaning against the port bulwark, the upper part of his stocky figure outlined against the sky. Smitty and Cocky are sitting on the edge of the forecastle head with their legs dangling over. Nearly all are smoking pipes or cigarettes. The majority are dressed in patched suits of dungaree. Quite few are in their bare feet and some of them, especially the firemen, have nothing on but a pair of pants and an undershirt. A good many wear caps.

There is the low murmur of different conversations going on in the separate groups as the curtain rises. There is followed by a sudden silence in which the singing from the land can be plainly heard.

DRISCOLL—(*a powerful built Irishman who is sitting on the edge of the batch, front—irritably*) Will ye listen to them naygurs? I wonder now, do they call that keenin' a song?

SMITTY—(*a young Englishman with a blond musache. He is sitting on the forecastle head looking out over the water with his chin supported on his hands.*) It doesn't make a chap feel very cheerful, does it? (*He sighs.*)

COCKY—(*a wizened runt of a man with a straggling gray mustache—slapping Smitty on the back*) Cheero, ole dear! Down't be ser dawhn in the marf, Duke. She loves yer.

SMITTY—(*gloomily*) Shut up, Cocky! (*He turns away from Cocky and falls to dreaming again, staring toward the spot on the shore where the singing seems to come from.*)

BIG FRANK—(*a huge fireman sprawled out on the right of the batch—waving a hand toward the land*) They bury somebody—py chiminy Christmas, I tink so from way it sounds.

YANK—(*a rather good-looking rough who is sitting beside Driscoll*) What d'yuh mean, bury? They don't plant 'em down here, Dutchy. They eat 'em to save fun'ral expenses. I guess this guy went down the wrong way an' they got indigestion.

COCKY—Indigestion! Ho yus, not 'arf! Down't yer know as them blocks' as two stomacks like a bleedin' camel?

DAVIS—(*a short, dark man seated on the right of batch*) An' you seen the two, I s'pect, ain't you?

COCKY—(*scornfully*) Down't be showin' yer igerance be tryin' to make a mock o' me what has seen more o' the world than yeself ever will.

MAX—(*a Swedish fireman—from the rear of the batch*) Spin dat yarn, Cocky.

COCKY—It's Gawd's troof, what I tole yer. I 'eard it from a bloke what was captured pris'ner by 'em in the Solomon Islands. Shipped wiv 'im one voyage. 'Twas a rare treat to 'ear 'im tell what 'appened to 'im among 'em. (*musingly*) 'E was a funny bird, ' e was—' ailed from Mile End, 'e did.

DRISCOLL—(*with a snort*) Another lyin' Cockney, the loike av yourself!

LAMPS—(*a fat Swede who is sitting on a camp stool in front of his door talking with Chips*) Where you meet up with him, Cocky?

CHIPS—(*a lanky Scotchman—derisively*) In New Guinea, I'll lay my oath!

COCKY—(*defiantly*) Yus! It was in New Guinea, time I was shipwrecked there. (*There is a perfect storm of groans and laughter at this speech.*)

YANK—(*getting up*) Yuh know what we said yuh'd get if yuh sprung any of that lyin' New Guinea dope on us again, don't yuh? Close that trap if yuh don't want a duckin' over the side.

COCKY—Ow, I was on'y tryin' to edicate yer a bit. (*He sinks into dignified silence.*)

YANK—(*nodding toward the shore*) Don't yuh know this is the West Indies, yuh crazy mut? There ain't no cannibals here. They're only common niggers.

DRISCOLL—(*irritably*) Whativer they are, the divil take their cryin'. It's enough to give a man the jigs listenin' to 'em.

YANK—(*with a grin*) What's the matter, Drisc? Yuh're as sore as a boil about somethin'.

DRISCOLL—I'm dyin' sid impatience to have a dhrink; an' that blarsted bumboat naygur woman took her oath she'd bring back rum enough for the lot av us whin she came back on board to-night.

BIG FRANK—(*overhearing this—in a loud eager voice*) You say the bumboat voman vill bring booze?

DRISCOLL—(*sarcastically*) That's right—tell the Old Man about ut, an' the Mate, too. (*All of the crew have edged nearer to Driscoll and are listening to the conversation with an air of suppressed excitement. Driscoll lowers his voice impressively and addresses them all.*) She said she cud snake ut on board in the bottoms av thim baskets av fruit they're goin' to bring wid 'em to sell to us for'ard.

THE DONKEYMAN—(*an old gray-headed man with a kindly, wrinkled face. He is sitting on a camp stool in front of his door, right front.*) She'll be bringin' some black women with her this time—or times has changed since I put in here last.

DRISCOLL—She said she wud—two or three—more, maybe, I dunno. (*This announcement is received with great enthusiasm by all hands.*)

COCKY—Wot a bloody lark!

OLSON—Py yingo, we have one hell of a time!

DRISCOLL—(*warningly*) Remimber ye must be quiet about ut, ye scuts—wid the dhrink, I mane—ivin if the bo'sun is ashore. The Old Man ordered her to bring no booze on board or he wudn't by a thing off av her for the ship.

PADDY—(*a squat, ugly Liverpool Irishman*) To the divil wid him!

BIG FRANK—(*turning on him*) Shud up, you tamn fool, Paddy! You want make trouble? (*to Driscoll*) You und me, ve keep dem quiet, Drisc.

DRISCOLL—Right ye are, Dutchy. I'll split the skull av the first wan av ye starts to foight. (*Three bells are heard striking.*)

DAVIS—Three bells. When's she comin', Drisc?

DRISCOLL—She'll be here any minute now, surely. (*to Paul, who has returned to his position by the bulwark after hearing Driscoll's news*) D'you see'm comin', Paul?

PAUL—I don't see anyting like bumboat. (*They all set themselves to wait, lighting pipes, cigarettes, and making themselves comfortable. There is a silence broken only by the mournful singing of the negroes on shore.*)

SMITTY—(*slowly—with a trace of melancholy*) I wish they'd stop that song. It makes you think of —well —things you ought to forget. Rummy go, what?

COCKY—(*slapping him on the back*) Cheero, ole love! We'll be 'avin our rum in arf a mo', Duke. (He comes down to the deck, leaving Smitty alone on the forecastle head.)

BIG FRANK—Sing something, Drisc. Den ve don't hear dot yelling.

DAVIS—Give us a chanty, Drisc.

PADDY—Wan all av us knows.

MAX—We all sing in on chorus.

OLSON—"Rio Grande," Drisc.

BIG FRANK—No, ve don't know dot. Sing "Viskey Johnny."

CHIPA—"Flyin' cloud."

COCKY—Now! Guv us "Maid o' Amsterdam."

LAMPS—"Santa Anna" iss good one.

DRISCOLL—Shut your mouths, all av you. (*scornfully*) A chanty is ut ye want? I'll bet me whole pay day there's not wan in the crowd 'ceptin' Yank here, an' Ollie, an' meself, an' Lamps an' Cocky, maybe, wud be sailors enough to know the main from the mizzen on a windjammer. Ye've heard the names av chanties but divil note av the tune or a loine av the words do ye know. There's hardly a rale deep-water sailor lift on the seas, more's the pity.

YANK—Give us "Blow The Man Down." We all know some of that. (*A chorus of assenting voices: Yes! —Righto! —Let 'er drive! Start 'er, Drisc! etc.*)

DRISCOLL—Come in then, all av ye. (*He sings*) As I was a-roamin' down Paradise Street—

ALL—Wa-a-ay, blow the man down!

DRISCOLL—As I was a-roamin' down Paradise Street—

ALL—Give us some time to blow the man down!

CHORUS

Blow the man down, boys, oh, blow the man down!
Wa-a-ay, blow the man down!
As I was a-roamin' down Paradise Street—
Give us some time to blow the man down!

DRISCOLL—A pretty young maiden I chanced for to meet.

ALL—Wa-a-ay, blow the man down!

DRISCOLL—A pretty young maiden I chanced for to meet.

ALL—Give us some time to blow the man down!

CHORUS

Blow the man down, boys, oh, blow the man down!

Wa-a-ay, blow the man down!

A pretty youngmaiden I chanced for to meet.

Give us some time to blow the man down!

PAUL—(*just as Driscoll is clearing his throat preparatory to starting the next* verse) Hay, Drisc! Here she come, I tink. Some bumboat comin' dis way. (*They all rush to the side and look toward the land.*)

YANK—There's five or six of them in it—and they paddle like skirts.

DRISCOLL—(*wildly elated*) Hurroo, ye scuts!' Tis thim right enough. (*He does a few jig steps on the deck.*)

OLSON—(*after a pause during which all are watching the approaching boat*) Py yingo, I see six in boat, yes, sir.

DAVIS—I kin make out the baskets. See 'em there amidships?

BIG FRANK—Vot kind booze dey bring—viskey?

DRISCOLL—Rum, foine West Indy rum wid a kick in ut loike a mule's hoind leg.

LAMPS—Maybe she don't bring any; maybe skipper scare her.

DRISCOLL—Don't be throwin' cold water, Lamps. I'll skin her black hoide off av her if she goes back on her worrd.

YANK—Here they come. Listen to 'em gigglin'. (*calling*) Oh, you kiddo! (*The sound of women's voices can be heard talking and laughing.*)

DRISCOLL—(*calling*) Is ut you, Mrs. Old Black Joe?

A WOMAN'S VOICE—Ullo, Mike! (*There is loud femine laughter at this retort.*)

DRISCOLL—Shake a leg an' come abord thin.

THE WOMAN'S VOICE—We're a-comin'.

DRISCOLL—Come on, Yank. You an' me'd best be goin' to give 'em a hand wid their truck. 'Twill put 'em in good spirits.

COCKY—(*as they start off left*) Ho, you ain't 'arf a fox, Drisc. Down't drink it all afore we sees it.

DRISCOLL—(*over his shoulder*) You'll be havin' yours, me sonny bye, don't fret. (*He and Yank go off left.*)

COCKY—(*lifting his lips*) Gawd blimey, I can do wiv a wet.

DAVIS—Me, too!

CHIPS—I'll bet there ain't none of us'll let any go to waste.

BIG FRANK—I could trink a whole barrel mineself, py chimminy Christmas!

COCKY—I 'opes all the gels ain't as bloomin' ugly as 'er. Looked like a bloody organ-grinder's monkey, she did. Gawd, I couldn't put up wiv the likes of 'er!

PADDY—Ye'll be lucky if any of thim looks at ye, ye squinteyed runt.

COCKY—(*angrily*) Ho, yus? You ain't no bleedin' beauty prize yeself, me man. A 'airy ape, I calls yer.

PADDY—(*walking toward him—truculently*) Whot's thot? Say ut again if ye dare.

COCKY—(*his hand on his sheath knife—snarling*) 'Airy ape! That's wot I says! (*Paddy tries to reach him but the others keep them apart.*)

BIG FRANK—(*pushing Paddy back*) Vot's the matter mit you, Paddy. Don't you hear vat Driscoll say—no fighting?

PADDY—(*grumblingly*) I don't take no back talk from that deck-scrubbin' shrimp.

COCKY—Blarsted coal-puncher! (*Driscoll appears wearing a broad grin of satisfaction. The fight is immediately forgotten by the crowd who gather around him with exclamations of eager curiosity. How is it, Drisc? Any luck? Vot she bring, Drisc? Where's the gels? Etc.*)

DRISCOLL—(*with an apprehensive glance back at the bridge*) Not so loud, for the love av hivin! (*the clamor dies down.*) Yis, she has ut wid her. She'll be here in a minute wid a pint bottle or two for each wan av ye—three shillin's a bottle. So don't be impashunt.

COCKY—(*indignantly*) Three bob! The bloody cow!

SMITTY—(*with an ironic smile*) Grand larceny, by God! (*They all turn and look up at him, surprised to hear him speak.*)

OLSON—Py yingo, we don't pay so much.

BIG FRANK—Tamn black tief!

PADDY—We'll take ut away from her and give her nothin'.

THE CROWD—(*growling*) Dirty thief! Dot's right! Give her nothin'! Not bloomin' 'apenny! Etc.

DRISCOLL—(*grinning*) Ye can take ut or lave ot, me sonny byes. (*He casts a glance in the direction of the bridge and then reaches inside his shirt and pulls out a pint bottle.*) 'Tis foine rum, the rale stuff. (*He drinks.*) I slipped this wan out av wan av the baskets whin they wasn't lookin'. (*He bands the bottle to Olson who is nearest him.*) Here ye are, Ollie. Take a small sup an' pass ut to the inxt. 'Tisn't much but 'twill serve to take the black taste out av your mouths if ye go aisy wid ut. An' there's buckets more av ut comin'. (*The bottle passes from hand to hand, each man taking his and smacking his lips with a deep "Aaah" of satisfaction.*)

DAVIS—Where's she now, Drisc?

DRISCOLL—Up havin' a worrd wid the skipper, makin' arrangements about the money, I s'pose.

DAVIS—An' where's the other gels?

DRISCOLL—Wid her. There's foive av thim she took aboard—two swate little slips av things, near as white as you an' me are, for that gray-whiskered auld fool, an' the mates—an' the engineers too, maybe. The rist av thim'll be comin' for'ard whin she comes.

COCKY—'E ain't 'arf a funny ole bird, the skipper. Gawd blimey! 'Member when we sailed from 'ome 'ow 'e stands on the bridge lookin' like a bloody ole sky pilot? An' 'is missus dawn on the bloomin' dock 'owlin' fit to kill 'erself? An' 'is kids 'owlin' an' wavin' their 'andkerchiefs? (*with great moral indignation*) An' 'ere 'e is making up to a bleedin' nigger! There's a captain for yer! Gawd blimey! Bloody crab, I calls 'im!

DRISCOLL—Shut up, ye insect! Sure, it's not you should be talkin', an' you wid a woman an' childer weepin' for ye in iviry divil's port in the wild worrld, if we can believe your own tale av ut.

COCKY—(*still indignant*) I ain't no bloomin' captain, I ain't. I ain't got no missus—reg'lar married, I means. I ain't —

BIG FRANK—(*putting a huge paw over Cocky's mouth*) You ain't going talk so much, you hear? (*Cocky wiggles away from him.*) Say, Drisc, how ve pay dis voman for booze? Ve ain't got no cash.

DRISCOLL—It's aisy enough. Each girl'll have a slip av paper wid her an' whin you buy anythin' you write ut down and the price beside ut and sign your name. If ye can't write have some one who can do it for ye. An' rimimber this: Whin ye buy a bottle av dhrink or (*with a wink*) somethin' else forbid, ye must write down tobaccy or fruit or somethin' the loike av that. Whin she laves the skipper'll pay what's owin' on the paper an' take ut out av your pay. Is ut clear to ye now?

ALL—Yes—Clear as day—Aw right, Drisc—Righto—Sure. Etc.

DRISCOLL—An' don't forgit what I said about bein' quiet wid the dhrink, or the Mate'll be down on our necks an' spile the fun. (*a chorus of assent*)

DAVIS—(*looking aft*) Ain't this them comin'? (*They all look in that direction. The silly laughter of a woman is heard.*)

DRISCOLL—Look at Yank, wud ye, wid his arrm around the middle av wan av thim. That lad's not watin' any toime. (*The four women enter from the left, giggling and whispering to each other. The first three carry baskets on their heads. The youngest and best-looking comes last. Yank has his arm about her waist and is carrying her basket in his other hands. All four are distinct negro types. They wear light-colored, loose-fitting clothes down their baskets on the batch and sit down beside them. The men crowd around, grinning.*)

BELLA—(*she is the oldest, stoutest, and homeliest of the four—grnning back at them*) Ullo, boys.

THE OTHER GIRLS—'Ullo, boys.

THE MEN—Hello, yourself—Evenin'—Hello—How are you? Etc.

BELLA—(*genially*) Hope you had a nice voyage. My name's Bella, this heres' Susie, yander's Violet, and her there (*pointing to the girl with Yank*) is Pearl. Now we all knows each other.

PADDY—(*roughly*) Never mind the girls. Where's the dhrink?

BELLA—(*tartly*) You are a hawg, ain't you? Don't talk so loud or you don't git any—you nor no man. Think I want the ole captain to put me off the ship, do you?

YANK—Yes, nix on hollerin', you! D'yuh wanta queer all of us?

BELLA—(*casting a quick glance over her shoulder*) Here! Some of you big strapping boys sit back of us on the hatch there so's them officers can't see what we're doin'. (*Driscoll and several of the others sit and stand in back of the girls on the hatch. Bella turns to Driscoll.*) Did you tell'em they gotter sign for what they gits—and how to sign?

DRISCOLL—I did—what's your name again—oh, yis—Bella, darlin'.

BELLA—Then it's all right; but you boys has gotter go inside the fo'castle when you gits your bottle. No drinkin' out here on deck. I ain't talkin' no chances. (*An impatient murmur of assent goes up from the crowd.*) Ain't that right, Mike?

DRISCOLL—Right as rain, darlin'. (*Big Frank leans over and says something to him in a low voice. Driscoll laughs and slaps his thigh.*) Listen, Bella, I've somethin' to ask ye for my little friend here who's bashful. Ut has to do wid the ladies so I'd best be whisperin' ut to ye meself to kape them from blushin'. (*He leans over and asks her a question.*)

BELLA—(*firmly*)Four shillin's.

DRISCOLL—(*laughing*) D'you hear that, all av ye? Four shillin's ut is.

PADDY—(*angrily*)To hell wid this talkin'. I want a dhrink.

BELLA—Is everything all right, Mike?

DRISCOLL—(*after a look back at the bridge*) Sure. Let her droive!

BELLA—All right, girls. (*The girls reach down in their baskets in under the fruit which is on top and each pulls out a pint bottle. Four of the men crowd up and take the bottles.*) Fetch a light, Lamps, that's a good boy. (*Lamps goes to his room and returns with a candle. This is passed from one girl to another as the men sign the sheets of paper for their bottles.*) Don't you boys forget to mark down cigarettes or tobacco or fruit, remember! There shillin's is the price. Take it into the fo'castle. For Gawd's sake, don't stand out here drinkin' in the moonlight. (*The four go into the forecastle. Four mor take their places. Paddy plants himself in front of Pearl who is sitting by Yank with his arm still around her.*)

PADDY—(*gruffly*)Gimme thot! (*She holds out a bottle which he snatches from her hand. He turns to go away.*)

YANK—(*sharply*) Here, you! Where d'yuh get that stuff? You ain't signed for that yet.

PADDY—(*sullenly*) I can't write me name.

YANK—Then I'll write it for yuh. (*He takes paper from Pearl and writes.*) There ain't goin' to be no welchin' on little Bright Eyes here—not when I'm around, see? Ain't I right, kiddo?

PEARL—(*with a grin*) Yes, suh.

BELLA—(*seeing all four are served*) Take it into the fo'castle, boys. (*Paddy defiantly raises his bottle and gulps down a drink in the full moonlight. Bella sees him.*) Look at 'im! Look at the dirty swine! (*Paddy slouches into the forecastle.*) Wants to git me in trouble. That settles it! We all got to git inside, boys, where we won't git caught. Come on, girls. (*The girls pick up their baskets and follow Bella. Yank and Pearl are the last to reach the doorway. She singers behind him, her eyes fixed on Smitty, who is still sitting on the forecastle head, his chin on his hands, staring off into vacancy.*)

PEARL—(*waving a hand to attract his attention*) Come ahn in, pretty boy. Ah likes you.

SMITTY—(*coldly*) Yes; I want to buy a bottle, please. (*He goes down the steps and follows her into the forecastle. No one remains on deck but the Donkeyman, who sits smoking his pipe in front of his door. There is the subdued babble of voices from the crowed inside but the mournful cadence of the song from the shore can again be faintly heard. Smitty reappears and closes the door to the forecastle after him. He shudders and shakes his shoulders as if flinging off something which disgusted him. Then he lifts the bottle which is in his hand to his lips and gulps down a long drink. The Donkeyman watches him impassively. Smitty sits down on the batch facing him. Now that the closed door has shut off nearly all the noise the singing from shore comes clearly over the moonlit water.*)

SMITTY—(*listening to it for a moment*) Damn that song of theirs. (*He takes another big drink.*) What do you say, Donk?

THE DONKEYMAN—(*quietly*) Seems nice an' sleepy-like.

SMITTY—(*with a hard laugh*) Sleepy! If I listened to it long—sober—I'd never go to sleep.

THE DONKEYMAN—'Tain't sich bad music, is it? Sounds kinder pretty to me—low an' mournful—same as listenin' to the organ outside o' church of a

Sunday.

SMITTY—(*with a touch of impatience*) I didn't mean it was bad music. It isn't. It's the beastly memories the damn thing brings up—for some reason. (*He takes another pull at the bottle.*)

THE DONKEYMAN—Ever hear it before?

SMITTY—No; never in my life. It's just a something about the rotten thing which makes me think of—well—oh, the devil! (*He forces a laugh.*)

THE DONKEYMAN—(*spitting placidly*) Queer things, mem'ries. I ain't ever been bothered much by 'em.

SMITTY—(*looking at him fixedly for a moment—with quiet scorn*) No, you wouldn't be.

THE DONKEYMAN—Not that I ain't had my share o' things goin' wrong; but I puts 'em out o' me mind, like, an' fergets 'em.

SMITTY—But suppose you couldn't put them out of your mind? Suppose they haunted you when you were awake and when you were asleep—what then?

THE DONKEYMAN—(*quietly*) I'd git drunk, same's you're doin'.

SMITTY—(*with a harsh laugh*) Good advice. (*He takes another drink. He is beginning to show the effect of the liquor. His face is flushed and he talks rather wildly.*) We are poor little lambs who have lost our way, eh, Donk? Damned from here to eternity, what? God have mercy on such as we! True, isn't it, Donk?

THE DONKEYMAN—Maybe; I dunno. (*after a slight pause*) Whatever set you goin' to sea? You ain't made for it.

SMITTY—(*laughing wildly*) My old friend in the bottle here, Donk.

THE DONKEYMAN—I done my share o' drinkin' in my time. (*regretfully*) Them was good times, those days. Can't hold up under drink no more. Doctor told me I'd got to stop or die. (*He spits contently.*) So I stops.

SMITTY—(*with a foolish smile*) Then I'll drink one for you. Here's your health, old top! (He drinks.)

THE DONKEYMAN—(*after a pause*) S'pose there's a gel mixed up in it someplace, ain't there?

SMITTY—(*stiffly*) What makes you think so?

THE DONKEYMAN—Always is when a man lets music bother 'im. (*after a few puffs at his pipe*) An' she said she threw you over 'cause you was drunk; an' you said you drunk 'cause she threw you over. (*He spits leisurely.*) Queer thing, love, ain't it?

SMITTY—(*rising to his feet with drunken dignity*) I'll trouble you not to pry into my affairs, Donkeyman.

THE DONKEYMAN—(*unmoved*) That's everybody's affair, what I said. I been through it many's the time. (*genially*) I always hit'em a whack on the ear an' went out and got drunker'n ever. When I come home again they always had somethin' special nice cooked fur me to eat. (*puffing at his pipe*) That's the on'y way to fix 'em when they gits on their high horse. I don't s'pose you ever tried that?

SMITTY—(*pompously*) Gentlemen don't hit women.

THE DONKEYMAN—(*placidly*) No; that's why they has mem'ries when they hears music. (*Smitty does not deign to reply to this but sinks into a scornful silence. Davis and the girl Violet come out of the forecastle and close the door behind them. He is staggering a bit and she is laughing shrilly.*)

DAVIS—(*turning to the left*) This way, Rose, or Pany, or Jessamine, or black Tulip, or Violet, or whatever the hell flower your name is. No one'll see us back here. (*They go off left.*)

THE DONKEYMAN—There 's love at first sight for you—an' plenty more o' the same in the fo'c's'tle. No mem'ries jined with that.

SMITTY—(*rearlly repelled*) Shut up, Donk. You're disgusting. (*He takes a long drink.*)

THE DONKEYMAN—(*philosophically*) All depends on how you was brung up, I s'pose. (*Pearl comes out of the forecastle. There is a roar of voices from inside. She shuts the door behind her, sees Smitty on the batch, and comes over and sits beside him and put her arm over his shoulder.*)

THE DONKEYMAN—(*chuckling*) There's love for you, Duke.

PEARL—(*patting Smith's hand with her hand*) 'Ullo, pretty boy. (*Smitty pushes her hand away coldly.*) What you doin' out here all alone by yourself?

SMITTY—(*with a twisted grin*) Thinking and—(*he indicates the bottle in his hand*)drinking to stop thinking. (*He drinks and laughs maudlinly. The bottle is three-quarters empty.*)

PEARL—You oughtn't drink so much, pretty boy. Don' you know dat? You have big, big headache come mawnin'.

SMITTY—(*dryly*) Indeed?

PEARL—Tha's true. Ah knows what Ah say. (*cooingly*) Why you run 'way from me, pretty boy? Ah likes you. Ah don' like them other fellahs. They act too rough. You ain't rough. You're a gentleman. Ah knows. Ah can tell a genelman fahs Ah can see 'im.

SMITTY—Thank you for the compliment; but you're wrong, you see. I'm merely—a ranker. (*He adds bitterly*) And a rotter.

PEARL—(*patting his arm*) No, you ain't. Ah knows better. You're a genelman. (*insinuatingly*) Ah wouldn't have nothin' to do with them other men, but (she smiles at him enticingly) you is diff'rent. (*He pushes her away from him disgustedly. She pouts*) Don' you like me, pretty boy?

SMITTY—(*a bit ashamed*) I beg your pardon. I didn't mean to be rude, you know, really. (*His politeness is drunkenly exaggerated.*) I'm a bit off color.

PEARL—(*brightening up*) Den you do like me—little ways?

SMITTY—(*carelessly*) Yes, yes, why shouldn't I? (*He suddenly laughs wildly and puts his arm around her waist and presses her to him.*) Why not? (*He pulls his arm back quickly with a shudder of disgust, and takes a drink. Pearl looks at him curiously, puzzled by his strange actions. The door from the forecastle is kicked open and Yank comes out. The uproar of shouting, laughing and singing voices has increased in violence. Yank staggers over toward Smitty and Pearl.*)

YANK—(*blinking at them*) What the hell—oh, it's you, Smitty and the Duke. I was goin' to turn one loose on the jaw of any guy' d cop my dame, but seein' it's you—(*sentimentally*) Pals is pals and any pal of mine c'n have anythin' I got, see? (*holding out his hand*) Shake, Duke. (*Smitty takes his hand and he pumps it up and down.*) You'n me's frens. Ain't I right?

SMITTY—Right it is, Yank. But you're wrong about this girl. She isn't with me. She was just going back to the fo'c's'tle to you. (*Pearl looks at him with hatred gathering in her eyes.*)

YANK—Tha' right?

SMITTY—On my word!

YANK—(*grabbing her arm*) Come on then, you, Pearl! Le's have a drink with the bunch. (*He pulls her to the entrance where she shakes off his hand long enough to turn on Smitty furiously.*)

PEARL—You swine! You can go to hell! (*She goes in the forecastle, slamming the door.*)

THE DONKEYMAN—(*spitting calmly*) There's love for you. They are all the same—white, brown, yeller 'n' black, a whack on the ear's the only thing'll learn 'em. (*Smitty makes no reply but laughs harshly and takes another drink then sits staring before him, the almost empty bottle tightly clutched in one hand. There is an increase in volume of the muffled clamor from the forecastle and a moment later the door is thrown open and the Whole mob, led by Driscoll, pours out on deck. All of them are very drunk and several of them carry bottles in their hands. Bella is the only one of the women who is absolutely sober. She tries in vain to keep the men quiet. Pearl drinks from Yank's bottle every moment or so, laughing shrilly, and leaning against Yank, whose arm is about her waist. Paul comes out last carrying an accordion. He staggers over and stands on top of the hatch, his instrument under his arm.*)

DRISCOLL—Play us a dance, ye square-head swab! —a rale, Godforsaken son av a turkey trot wid guts to ut.

YANK—Straight from the old Barbary Coast in Frisco!

PAUL—I don't know. I try. (*He commences tuning up.*)

YANK—Ataboy! Let'er rip! (*Davis and Biolte come back and join the crowd. The Donkeyman looks on them all with a detached, indulgent air. Smitty startes before him and does not seem to know there is any one on deck but himself.*)

BIG FRANK—Dance? I don't dance. I trink! (*He suits the action to the word and roars with meaningless laughter.*)

DRISCOLL—Git out av the way thin, ye big huld, an'give us some room. (*Big Frank sits down on the hatch, right. All of the others who are not going to dance either follow his example or lean against the port bulwark.*)

BELLA—(*on the verge of tears at her inability to keep them in the forecastle or make them be quiet now they are out*) For Gawd's sake, boys, don't shout so loud! Want to git me in trouble?

DRISCOLL—(*grabbing her*) Dance wid me, me cannibal quane. (*Some one drops a bottle on deck and it smashes.*)

BELLA—(*hysterically*) There they goes! There they goes! Captain'll hear that! Oh, my Lawd!

DRISCOLL—Be damned to him! Here's the music! Off ye go! (*Paul starts playing "You Great Big Beautiful Doll" with a note left out every now and then. The four couples commence dancing—a jerk-shouldered version of the old Turkey Trot as it was done in the sailor-town dives, made more grotesque by the fact that all the couples are drunk and keep lurching into each other every moment. Two of the men start dancing together, intentionally bumping into the others. Yank and Pearl slaps him across the side of the face with all her might, and laughs viciously. He jumps to his feet with his fists clenched but sees who hit him and sits down again smiling bitterly. Yank laughs boisterously.*)

YANK—Wow! Some wallop! One on you, Duke.

DRISCLLL—(*hurling his cap at Paul*) *Faster, ye toad*! (*Paul makes frantic efforts to speed up and the music suffers in the process.*)

BELLA—(*puffing*) Let me go. I'm wore out with you steppin' on my toes, you clumsy Mick. (*She struggles but Driscoll holds her tight.*)

DRISCOLL—God blarst you for havin' such big feet, thin. Aisy, aisy, Mrs. Old Black Joe! Tis dancin'll take the blubber off ye. (*He whirls her around the deck by main force. Cocky, with Susie, is dancing near the batch, right, when Paddy, who is sitting on the edge with Big Frank, sticks his foot out and the wavering couple stumble over it and fall flat on the deck. A roar of laughter goes up. Cocky rises to his feet, his face livid with rage, and springs at Paddy, who promptly knocks him down. Driscoll his Paddy and Big Frank hits Driscoll. In a flash a wholesale fight has broken out and the deck is a surging crowd of drink-maddened men hitting out at each other indiscriminately, although the general ideas seems to be battle between seamen and firemen. The women shriek and take refuge on top of the hatch, where they huddle in a frightened group. Finally there is the flash of a knife held high in the moonlight and a loud yell of pain.*)

DAVIS—(*somewhere in the crowd*) Here's the Mate comin'! Let's git out o'this! (*There is a general rush for the forecastle. In a moment there is no one left on deck but the little group of women pn the hatch; Smitty, still dazedly rubbing his check; the Donkeyman quietly smoking on his stool; and Yank and Driscoll, their faces battered up considerably, their undershirts in shreds, bending over the still form of Paddy, which lies stretched out on the deck between them. In the silence the mournful chant from the shore creeps slowly out to the ship.*)

DRISCOLL—(*quickly—in a low voice*) Who knoifed him?

YANK—(*stupidly*) I didn't see it. How do I know? Cocky, I'll bet. (*The First Mate enters from the the left. He is a tall, strongly-built man dressed in a plain blue uniform.*)

THE MATE—(*angrily*) What's all this noise about? (*He sees the man lying on the deck.*) *Hello! What's this?* (*He bends down on one knee beside Paddy.*)

DRISCOLL—(*stammering*) All av us—was in a bit av a harmless foight, sir—an'—I dunno—(*The Mate rolls Paddy over and sees a knife wound on his shoulder.*)

THE MATE—Knifed, by God. (*He takes an electric flash from his pocket and examines the cut.*) Lucky it's only a flesh wound. He must have hit his head on deck when he fell. That's what knocked him out. This is only a scratch. Take him aft and I'll bandage him up.

DRISCOLL—Yis, sor. (*They take Paddy by the shoulders and feet and carry him off left. The Mate looks up and sees the women on the hatch for the first time.*)

THE MATE—(*surprised*) Hello! (*He walks over to them.*) Go to the cabin and get your money and clear off. If I had my way, you'd never—(*His foot hits a bottle. He stoops down and picks it up and smells of it.*) Rum, by God! So that's the trouble! I thought their breaths smelled damn queer. (*to the women, harshly*) You needn't go to the skipper for any money. You won't get any. That'll teach you to smuggle rum on a ship and start a riot.

BELLA—But, Mister—

THE MATE—(*sternly*) You know the agreement—rum—no money.

BELLA—(*indignantly*) Honest to Gawd, Mister, I never brung no—

THE MATE—(*fiercely*) You're a liar! And none of your lip or I'll make a complaint ashore to-morrow and have you locked up.

BELLA—(*subdued*) Please, Mister—

THE MATE—Clear out of this, now! Not another word out of you! Tumble over the side damn quick! The two others are waiting for you. Hop, now! (*They walk quickly—almost run—off to the left. The Mate follows them, nodding to *the Donkeyman, and ignoring the oblivious Smitty.*)

(*There is absolute silence on the ship for a few moments. The melancholy song of the negroes drifts crooning over the water. Smitty listens to it intently for a time; then sighs heavily, a sigh that is half a sob.*)

SMITTY—God! (*He drinks the last drop in the bottle and throws it behind him on the hatch.*)

THE DONKEYMAN—(*spitting tranquilly*) More mem'ries? (*Smitty does not answer him. The ship's bell tolls four bells. The Donkeyman knocks out his pipe.*) I think I'll turn in. (*He opens the door to his cabin, but turns to look at Smitty—kindly*) You can't hear it in the fo'c's'tle—the music, I mean—an' there'll likely be more drink in there, too. Good night. (*He goes in and shuts the door.*)

SMITTY—Good night, Donk. (*He gets wearily to his feet and walks with bowed shoulders, staggering a bit, to the forecastle entrance and goes in. there is silence for a second or so, broken only by the haunted, saddened voice of that brooding music, faint and far-off, like the mood of the moonlight made audible.*)

(The Curtain Falls)

[Selected from Eugene O'Neill. *Complete Plays*. (Vol. I). New York: The Library of America, 1988.]

Ⅲ. Questions for discussion

(1) Cite evidences to illustrate the ecological awareness of O'Neill permeated in this play.

(2) How do you evaluate the naturalistic features of this play?

(3) What is O'Neill's ideal man-and-nature relation reflected in this play?

(4) What are the realistic features of this play?

(5) What is the position of *The Moon of the Caribbees* in O'Neill's writing career?

(6) What are the elements that contribute to the accomplishment of his achievements?

2.3 Assigned Reading

Eugene O'Nell's Last Plays: Separating Art from Autobiography

Doris Alexander

In his foreword to the letters of Oskar Kokoschka (*Letters.* New York: Thames and Hudson, 1992), the Austrian painter, playwright, and poet born two years before O'Neill, E. H. Gombrich writes:

> Those of our contemporaries who like to identify artistic creation with self-expression have rarely been able to avoid the trap of circularity. They fashion the image of the artist out of what they know of his work and interpret the work in terms of their image of the artist's personality. No wonder they are often disappointed when the documents contradict this imaginary equation. It so happens that Oskar Kokoschka belonged to the generation that launched this idea.

O'Neill was part of that generation as well, and how strange that a playwright frequently deemed an expressionist for much of his career and an avowed foe of realism should find almost all of his work judged in terms of the alleged facts of his own life. The facts, however, have been inspired by the playwright's own work.

Ever since the publication and first performance of *Long Day's Journey into Night*, O'Neill's reputation as one of the most autobiographical playwrights ever has been set in stone. Soon thereafter, the quest began to create the dramaturgical backstory for all of his plays. Critics and commentators have identified every stray character that appears or is even mentioned in his plays. An interesting pursuit, but recently questions have begun to surface about its validity as the best way to understand the plays. It is clear that O'Neill's life is compelling in its own right. Let us allow the biographies to stand alone and move them to a separate shelf from the plays. While we are at it, let us bar O'Neill biography from the rehearsal room and the stage itself.

When you read Doris Alexander's latest book on O'Neill you will understand why such steps are necessary. The book is a bombshell. The lifetime of research that Professor Alexander has put into it explodes not only myths, but much of what is now taken to be the foundation of O'Neill studies as well. The book's subtitle lets us know immediately what she has set out to do. Alexander concludes her preface:

Because this book compares the facts of the plays with the documentary evidence of the historical record, it offers what is really a first study in biography based on knowledge of what in a work are the facts of the author's life and what are not. From the publication day of *Long Day's Journey into Night*, books on Eugene O'Neill (up to Stephen Black's *Mourning and Tragedy*, which perhaps leans on it most heavily) have taken the play as reliable guide for interpreting the meaning of his life. So perhaps this study will alert O'Neill biographers and all biographers of the dangers in confusing the artistry of a work with its raw materials and of taking a revelation of an aspect of human life as literally the life story of its author.

This is the third of Alexander's books on O'Neill (*The Tempering of Eugene O'Neill* and *Eugene O'Neill's Creative Struggle* are the others). It is far more than a third installment; it is a radical revision of O'Neill studies that shines a searchlight on fundamental problems that have interfered with our understanding of O'Neill. Alexander fearlessly argues that we have been held bound by our fascination with his life and failed to grasp fully his artistry. Alexander's tone is so reserved, her demolition works so quietly and swiftly, that it leaves the reader breathless, a rare occurrence for a scholarly work.

To take but one example, at the opening of chapter eight she reveals that a central article of faith in our understanding of Ella O'Neill/Mary Tyrone probably never existed. There was no wedding gown. There was in fact no father around at all to plan a wedding, let alone to indulge a darling daughter's every whim. Thomas Joseph Quinlan died three years before Ella Quinlan married. (In *O'Neill Son and Playwright*, when Louis Sheaffer describes Ella Quinlan's wedding dress he uses almost verbatim O'Neill's language describing Mary Tyrone's wedding dress. The Gelbs' *Life With Monte Cristo* makes no such error.) Alexander demonstrates that it was a debutante ball gown of O'Neill's wife Carlotta that inspired the dress in the play. Indeed, she argues that there is much more of Mr. and Mrs. Eugene O'Neill than Mr. and Mrs. James O'Neill in this family portrait. Alexander reminds us that O'Neill could not possibly have known the things about his parents that he seems to be revealing in *Long Day's Journey*.

Theater historians familiar with the diary of the *Monte Cristo* company actress Elizabeth Robins are aware that Mr. and Mrs. O'Neill were quite different than Mr. and Mrs. Tyrone. What is more, Alexander reminds us that James O'Neill always had defenders among his surviving contemporaries. Old troupers spoke out *against Long Day's Journey* in 1956, but their voices have been overwhelmed. The crushing burden of biography has not only limited academic discussion of the play, it has virtually proscribed the play's performance unless its set conforms to the dimensions of a certain parlor in New London, Connecticut.

Beside *Long Day's Journey*, Alexander also discusses *The Iceman Cometh* and *A Moon for the Misbegotten*. She devotes six chapters to *Iceman*, seven to *Long Day's Journey*, and one to *Moon*. While there is much to be learned from her findings about Iceman, it is Alexander's commentary on *Long Day's Journey* that will raise the most controversy and consternation. Her argument offers a sober assessment of the contrast between what is so and what we think is so, making one aware of an almost Pirandellian cast to the way *Long Day's Journey* has been perceived by scholars even when the evidence of performance contradicts O'Neill's own text.

The original Broadway production is one of the most revered in American theater history, yet Alexander picks up a telling detail to illustrate a revealing anomaly. She draws our attention to the ascot worn by actor Fredric March, so different from the knotted handkerchief that O'Neill describes Tyrone as wearing. March transformed the unassuming gardener in a threadbare suit who doesn't give a damn how he looks to a bespoke-kitted-out gentleman of leisure. Alexander allows us to see that the original Broadway production is allowed such an idiosyncrasy. (Alexander does not comment on March's most famous stage business, the brogue he assumed during James' descent into alcohol-sodden despair.) Conversely, productions since then have been judged according to a standard of being true to the life of the O'Neills rather than the Tyrones, and the principle that the Tyrones of the original New York company were the embodiment of the O'Neills so it is best to follow their example, a perfect demonstration of Gombrich's trap of circularity.

In her final comments on the play Alexander points out another false lead, the famous inscription to Carlotta. Alexander argues that self-serving machinations by O'Neill's widow set the play on the autobiographical course followed so relentlessly by so many. The critic who was the bellwether for this was none other than Brooks Atkinson, who declared that the play was "as personal and as literal as drama can be." To counter this, as mentioned above, Alexander reports the little-remembered phenomenon of friends and fans of James O'Neill who were upset by his portrayal in the play. She offers the reasonable assertion that it was just this sort of reaction that O'Neill sought to avoid with his 25-year interdiction. She also refers to comments by George Jean Nathan, who knew the play before it was published and was a friend of O'Neill's, that O'Neill wished to withhold it.

Alexander takes O'Neill's wishes quite as seriously as did Bennett Cerf, who lost Random House a bestseller when he insisted on abiding by the contract he had signed with the playwright. While I for one am glad the play was made available, Alexander's argument is a strong one. To be sure, this controversy is not new; nevertheless, the context she provides for it is. Whether O'Neill knew what he was doing by giving complete control to his wife has been argued before, but Carlotta's manipulative wiles have never seemed so stark as in Alexander's account.

In sum, this concise, yet devastating study is neither a sweeping indictment nor any sort of bill of incrimination, but rather a straightforward suggestion that we fully recognize that O'Neill was an artist and forget that he was ever a son. The record speaks for itself; he cut off almost everyone in his life so that he could write his plays. Who among us would deny that it is the plays that matter now, not the man?

[Selected from Eugene O'Nell. *Last Plays*. Athens, GA: University of Georgia Press, 2005.]

3. Edward Albee

3.1 Presentation Topics

(1)The contributions of Albee.

(2)Comment on the relationship within the American families.

3.2 Selected Reading

Ⅰ. Central issue of concern

The Theatre of Absurd and the American Dream.

Ⅱ. Text

The American Dream

The Players:

MOMMY

DADDY

GRANDMA

MRS. BARKER

YOUNG MAN

THE SCENE: A living room. Two armchairs, one toward either side of the stage, facing each other diagonally out toward the audience. Against the rear wall, a sofa. A door, leading out from the apartment, in the rear wall, far stage-right. An archway, leading to other rooms, in the side wall, stage-left.

At the beginning, MOMMY and DADDY are seated in the armchairs, DADDY in the armchair stage—left. MOMMY in the other.

Curtain U P. A silence. Then:

MOMMY: I don't know what can be keeping them.

DADDY: They're late, naturally.

MOMMY: Of course, they're late; it never fails.

DADDY: That's the way things are today, and there's nothing you can do about it.

MOMMY: You're quite right.

DADDY: When we took this apartment, they were quick enough to have me sign the lease; they were quick enough to take my check for two months' rent in advance...

MOMMY: And one month's security...

DADDY: ... and one month's security. They were quick enough to check my references; they were quick enough about all that. But now! But now, try to get the icebox fixed, try to get the doorbell fixed, try to get the leak in the johnny fixed! Just try it... they aren't so quick about that.

MOMMY: Of course not; it never fails. People think they can get away with anything these days... and, of course they can. I went to buy a new hat yesterday. (*Pause.*) I said, I went to buy a new hat yesterday.

DADDY: Oh! Yes... yes.

MOMMY: Pay attention.

DADDY: I am paying attention, Mommy.

MOMMY: Well, be sure you do.

DADDY: Oh, I am.

MOMMY: All right, Daddy; now listen.

DADDY: I'm listening, Mommy.

MOMMY: You're sure!

DADDY: Yes... yes, I'm sure, I'm all ears.

MOMMY: (*giggles at the thought*; *then*) All right, now. I went to buy a new hat yesterday and I said, "I'd like a new hat, please." And so, they showed me a few hats, green ones and blue ones, and I didn't like any of them, not one bit. What did I say? What did I just say?

DADDY: You didn't like any of them, not one bit.

MOMMY: That's right; you just keep paying attention. And then they showed me one that I did like. It was a lovely little hat, and I said, "Oh, this is a lovely little hat; I'll take this hat; oh my, it's lovely. What color is it?" And they said, "Why, this is beige; isn't it a lovely little beige hat?" And I said, "Oh, it's just lovely." And so, I bought it. (*Stops*, *looks at* DADDY.)

DADDY: (to show he is paying attention) And so you bought it.

MOMMY: And so I bought it, and I walked out of the store with the hat right on my head, and I ran spang into the chairman of our woman's club, and she said, "Oh, my dear, isn't that a lovely little hat? Where did you get that lovely little hat? It's the loveliest little hat; I've always wanted a wheat-colored hat myself." And, I said, "Why, no, my dear; this hat is beige; beige." And she laughed and said, "Why no, my dear, that's a wheat—colored hat... wheat. I know beige from wheat." And I said, "Well, my dear, I know beige from wheat, too." What did I say? What did I just say?

DADDY: (*tonelessly*) Well, my dear, I know beige from wheat, too.

MOMMY: That's right. And she laughed, and she said, "Well, my dear, they certainly put one over on you. That's wheat if I ever saw wheat. But it's so lovely, just the same." And then she walked off. She's a dreadful woman, you don't know her: she has dreadful taste, two dreadful children, a dreadful house and an absolutely adorable husband who sits in a wheel chair all the time. You don't know him. You don't know anybody, do you? She's just a dreadful woman, but she is chairman of our woman's club, so naturally I'm terribly fond of her. So, I went right back into the hat shop, and I said, "Look here; what do you mean selling me a hat that you say is beige, when it's wheat all the time ... wheat! I can tell beige from wheat any day in the week, but not in this artificial light of yours. "They have artificial light, Daddy.

DADDY: Have they!

MOMMY: And I said, "The minute I got outside I could tell that it wasn't a beige hat at all: it was a wheat hat. "And they said to me, "How could you tell that when you had the hat on the top of your head? "Well, that made me angry, and so I made a scene right there; I screamed as hard as I could: I took my hat off and I threw it down on the counter, and oh, I made a terrible scene. I said, I made a terrible scene.

DADDY: (*snapping to*) Yes ... yes ... good for you!

MOMMY: And I made an absolutely terrible scene; and they became frightened, and they said, "Oh, madam; oh, madam. "But I kept right on, and finally they admitted that they might have made a mistake; so they took my hat into the back, and then they came out again with a hat that looked exactly like it. I took one look at it, and I said, "This hat is wheat-colored; wheat." Well, of course, they said, "Oh, no, madam, this hat is beige; you go outside and see. "So, I went outside, and lo and behold, it was beige. So I bought it.

DADDY: (*clearing his throat*) I would imagine that it was the same hat they tried to sell you before.

MOMMY: (*with a little laugh*) Well, of course it was!

DADDY: That's the way things are today; you just can't get satisfaction; you just try.

MOMMY: Well, I got satisfaction.

DADDY: That's right, Mommy. You did get satisfaction, didn't you?

MOMMY: Why are they so late? I don't know what can be keeping them.

DADDY: I've been trying for two weeks to have the leak in the johnny fixed.

MOMMY: You can't get satisfaction; just try. I can get satisfaction, but you can't.

DADDY: I've been trying for two weeks and it isn't so much for my sake; I can always go to the club.

MOMMY: It isn't so much for my sake, either; I can always go shopping.

DADDY: It's really for Grandma's sake.

MOMMY: Of course it's for Grandma's sake. Grandma cries every time she goes to the johnny as it is; but now that it doesn't work it's even worse, it makes Grandma think she's getting feeble-headed.

DADDY: Grandma is getting feeble-headed.

MOMMY: Of course Grandma is getting feeble headed, but not about her johnny-do's.

DADDY: No; that's true. I must have it fixed.

MOMMY: Why are they so late? I don't know what can be keeping them.

DADDY: When they came here the first time, they were ten minutes early; they were quick enough about it then.

(*Enter* GRANDMA *from the archway, stage-left. She is loaded down with boxes, large and small, neatly wrapped and tied.*)

MOMMY: Why Grandma, look at you! What is all that you're carrying?

GRANDMA: They're boxes. What do they look like?

MOMMY: Daddy! Look at Grandma; look at all the boxes she's carrying!

DADDY: My goodness, Grandma; look at all those boxes.

GRANDMA: Where'll I put them?

MOMMY: Heavens! I don't know. Whatever are they for?

GRANDMA: That's nobody's damn business.

MOMMY: Well, in that case, put them down next to Daddy; there.

GRANDMA: (*dumping the boxes down, On and around* DADDY'S *feet.*) I sure wish you'd get the john fixed.

DADDY: Oh, I do wish they'd come and fix it. We hear you ... for hours ... whimpering away ...

MOMMY: Daddy! What a terrible thing to say to Grandma!

GRANDMA: Yeah. For shame, talking to me that way.

DADDY: I'm sorry, Grandma.

MOMMY: Daddy's sorry, Grandma.

GRANDMA: Well, all right. In that case I'll go get the rest of the boxes. I suppose I deserve being talked to that way. I've gotten so old. Most people think that when you get so old, you either freeze to death, or you burn up.

But you don't. When you get so old, all that happens is that people talk to you that way.

DADDY:(*contrite*) I said I'm sorry, Grandma.

MOMMY:Daddy said he was sorry.

GRANDMA:Well, that's all that counts. People being sorry. Makes you feel better; gives you a sense of dignity, and that's all that's important ... a sense of dignity. And it doesn't matter if you don't care, or not, either. You got to have a sense of dignity, even if you don't care, 'cause, if you don't have that, civilization's doomed.

MOMMY:You've been reading my book club selections again!

DADDY:How dare you read Mommy's book club selections, Grandma!

GRANDMA:Because I'm old! When you're old you gotta do something. When you get old, you can't talk to people because people snap at you. When you get so old, people talk to you that way. That's why you become deaf, so you won't be able to hear people talking to you that way. And that's why you go and hide under the covers in the big soft bed, so you won't feel the house shaking from people talking to you that way. That's why old people die, eventually. People talk to them that way. I've got to go and get the rest of the boxes. (GRANDMA *exits.*)

DADDY:Poor Grandma, I didn't mean to hurt her.

MOMMY:Don't you worry about it; Grandma doesn't know what she means.

DADDY:She knows what she says, though.

MOMMY:Don't you worry about it; she won't know that soon. I love Grandma.

DADDY:I love her, too. Look how nicely she wrapped these boxes.

MOMMY:Grandma has always wrapped boxes nicely. When I was a little girl, I was very poor, and Grandma was very poor, too, because Grandpa was in heaven. And every day, when I went to school, Grandma used to wrap a box for me, and I used to take it with me to school; and when it was lunch-time, all the little boys and girls used to take out their boxes of lunch, and they weren't wrapped nicely at all, and they used to open them and eat their chicken legs and chocolate cakes; and I used to say, "Oh, look at my lovely lunch box; it's so nicely wrapped it would break my heart to open it. "And so, I wouldn't open it.

DADDY:Because it was empty.

MOMMY:Oh no. Grandma always filled it up, because she never ate the dinner she cooked the evening before; she gave me all her food for my lunch box the next day. After school, I'd take the box back to Grandma, and she'd open it and eat the chicken legs and chocolate cake that was inside. Grandma used to say, "I love day-old cake." That's where the expression day-old cake came from. Grandma always ate everything a day late. I used to eat all the other little boys' and girls' food at school, because they thought my lunch box was empty. They thought my lunch box was empty, and that's why I wouldn't open it. They thought I suffered from the sin of pride, and since that made them better than me, they were very generous.

DADDY: You were a very deceitful little girl.

MOMMY: We were very poor! But then I married you, Daddy, and now we're very rich.

DADDY: Grandma isn't rich.

MOMMY: No, but you've been so good to Grandma she feels rich. She doesn't know you'd like to put her in a nursing home.

DADDY: I wouldn't!

MOMMY: Well, heaven knows, I would! I can't stand it, watching her do the cooking and the housework, polishing the silver, moving the furniture...

DADDY: She likes to do that. She says it's the least she can do to earn her keep.

MOMMY: Well, she's right. You can't live off people. I can live off you, because I married you. And aren't you lucky all I brought with me was Grandma. A lot of women I know would have brought their whole families to live off you. All I brought was Grandma. Grandma is all the family I have.

DADDY: I feel very fortunate.

MOMMY: You should. I have a right to live off of you because I married you, and because I used to let you get on top of me and bump your uglies; and I have a right to all your money when you die. And when you do, Grandma and I can live by ourselves...if she's still here. Unless you have her put away in a nursing home.

DADDY: I have no intention of putting her in a nursing home.

MOMMY: Well, I wish somebody would do something with her!

DADDY: At any rate, you're very well provided for.

MOMMY: You're my sweet Daddy; that's very nice.

DADDY: I love my Mommy.

(*Enter* GRANDMA *again, laden with more boxes.*)

GRANDMA: (*dumping the boxes on and around* DADDY'S *feet*) There; that's the lot of them.

DADDY: They're wrapped so nicely.

GRANDMA: (*to* DADDY) You won't get on my sweet side that way...

MOMMY: Grandma.

GRANDMA: ... telling me how nicely I wrap boxes. Not after what you said: how I whimpered for hours...

MOMMY: Grandma!

GRANDMA: (*to* MOMMY) Shut up! (*To* DADDY) You don't have any feelings. That's what's wrong with you. Old people make all sorts of noises, half of them they can't help. Old people whimper, and cry, and belch, and make great hollow rumbling sounds at the table; old people wake up in the middle of the night screaming, and find out they haven't even been asleep; and when old people are asleep, they try to wake up, and they can't... not for the longest time.

MOMMY: Homilies, homilies!

GRANDMA: And there's more, too.

DADDY: I'm really very sorry, Grandma.

GRANDMA: I know you are, Daddy; it's Mommy over there makes all the trouble. If you'd listened to me, you wouldn't have married her in the first place. She was a tramp and a trollop and a trull to boot, and she's no better now.

MOMMY: Grandma!

GRANDMA: (*to* MOMMY) Shut up! (*To* DADDY) When she was no more than eight years old she used to climb up on my lap and say, in a sickening little voice, "When I grow up, I'm going to marry a rich old man; I'm going to set my wittle were end right down in a tub o' butter, that's what I'm going to do." And I warned you, Daddy; I told you to stay away from her type. I told you to. I did.

MOMMY: You stop that! You're my mother, not his!

GRANDMA: I am?

DADDY: That's right, Grandma. Mommy's right.

GRANDMA: Well, how would you expect somebody as old as I am to remember a thing like that? You don't make allowances for people. I want an allowance. I want an allowance!

DADDY: All right, Grandma; I'll see to it.

MOMMY: Grandma! I'm ashamed of you.

GRANDMA: Humf! It's a fine time to say that. You should have gotten rid of me a long time ago if that's the way you feel. You should have had Daddy set me up in business somewhere ... I could have gone into the fur business, or I could have been a singer. But no; not you. You wanted me around so you could sleep in my room when Daddy got fresh. But now it isn't important, because Daddy doesn't want to get fresh with you any more, and I don't blame him. You'd rather sleep with me, wouldn't you, Daddy?

MOMMY: Daddy doesn't want to sleep with anyone. Daddy's been sick.

DADDY: I've been sick. I don't even want to sleep in the apartment.

MOMMY: Yon see? I told you.

DADDY: I just want to get everything over with.

MOMMY: That's right. Why are they so late? Why can't they get here on time?

GRANDMA: (*an owl*) Who? Who? ... Who? Who?

MOMMY: You know, Grandma.

GRANDMA: No, I don't.

MOMMY: Well, it doesn't really matter whether you do or not.

DADDY: Is that true?

MOMMY: Oh, more or less. Look how pretty Grandma wrapped these boxes.

GRANDMA: I didn't really like wrapping them; it hurt my fingers, and it frightened me. But it had to be done.

MOMMY: Why, Grandma?

GRANDMA: None of your damn business.

MOMMY: Go to bed.

GRANDMA: I don't want to go to bed. I just got up. I want to stay here and watch. Besides ...

MOMMY: Go to bed.

DADDY: Let her stay up, Mommy; it isn't noon yet.

GRANDMA: I want to watch; besides ...

DADDY: Let her watch, Mommy.

MOMMY: Well, all right, you can watch; but don't you dare say a word.

GRANDMA: Old people are very good at listening; old people don't like to talk; old people have colitis and lavender perfume. Now I'm going to be quiet.

DADDY: She never mentioned she wanted to be a singer.

MOMMY: Oh, I forgot to tell you, but it was ages ago. (*The doorbell rings.*) Oh, goodness! Here they are!

GRANDMA: Who? Who?

MOMMY: Oh, just some people.

GRANDMA: The van people? Is it the van people? Have you finally done it? Have you called the van people to come and take me away?

DADDY: Of course not, Grandma!

GRANDMA: Oh, don't be too sure. She'd have you carted off too, if she thought she could get away with it.

MOMMY: Pay no attention to her, Daddy. (*An aside to* GRANDMA) My God, you're ungrateful! (*The doorbell rings again.*)

DADDY: (*wringing his hands*) Oh dear; oh dear.

MOMMY: (*still to* GRANDMA) Just you wait; I'll fix your wagon. (*Now to* DADDY.) Well, go let them in, Daddy. What are you waiting for?

DADDY: I think we should talk about it some more. Maybe we've been hasty... a little hasty, perhaps. (*Doorbell rings again.*) I'd like to talk about it some more.

MOMMY: There's no need. You made up your mind; you were firm; you were masculine and decisive.

DADDY: We might consider the pros and the...

MOMMY: I won't argue with you; it has to be done; you were right. Open the door.

DADDY: But I'm not sure that...

MOMMY: Open the door.

DADDY: Was I firm about it?

MOMMY: Oh, so firm; so firm.

DADDY: And was I decisive?

MOMMY: So decisive! oh, I shivered.

DADDY: And masculine? Was I really masculine?

MOMMY: Oh, Daddy, you were so masculine; I shivered and fainted.

GRANDMA: Shivered and fainted, did she? Humf!

MOMMY: You be quiet.

GRANDMA: Old people have a right to talk to themselves; it doesn't hurt the gums, and it's comforting. (*Doorbell rings again.*)

DADDY: I shall now open the door.

MOMMY: What a masculine Daddy! Isn't he a masculine Daddy?

GRANDMA: Don't expect me to say anything. Old people are obscene.

MOMMY: Some of your opinions aren't so bad. You know that?

DADDY: (*backing off from the door*) Maybe we can send them away.

MOMMY: Oh, look at you! You're turning into jelly; you're indecisive; you're a woman.

DADDY: All right. Watch me now; I'm going to open the door. Watch. Watch!

MOMMY: We're watching; we're watching.

GRANDMA: I'm not.

DADDY: Watch now; it's opening. (*He opens the door.*) It's open!

MRS. BARKER: (*steps into the room.*) Here they are!

MOMMY: Here they are!

GRANDMA: Where?

DADDY: Come in. You're late. But, of course, we expected you to be late; we were saying that we expected you to be late.

MOMMY: Daddy, don't be rude! We were saying that you just can't get satisfaction these days, and we were talking about you, of course, won't you come in?

MRS. BARKER: Thank you. I don't mind if I do.

MOMMY: We're very glad that you're here, late as you are. You do remember us, don't you? You were here once before. I'm Mommy, and this is Daddy, and that's Grandma doddering there in the corner.

MRS. BARKER: Hello, Mommy; hello, Daddy; and hello there, Grandma.

DADDY: Now that you're here, I don't suppose you could go away and maybe come back some other time.

MRS. BARKER: Oh no; we're much too efficient for that. I said, hello there,

Grandma.

MOMMY: Speak to them, Grandma.

GRANDMA: I don't see them.

DADDY: For shame, Grandma; they're here.

MRS. BARKER: Yes, we're here, Grandma. I'm Mrs. Barker. I remember you; don't you remember me?

GRANDMA: I don't recall. Maybe you were younger, or something.

MOMMY: Grandma! What a terrible thing to say!

MRS. BARKER: Oh now, don't scold her, Mommy; for all she knows she may be right.

DADDY: Uh ... Mrs. Barker, is it? Won't you sit down?

MRS. BARKER: I don't mind if I do.

MOMMY: Would you like a cigarette, and a drink, and would you like to cross your legs?

MRS. BARKER: You forget yourself, Mommy; I'm a professional woman. But I will cross my legs.

DADDY: Yes, make yourself comfortable.

MRS. BARKER: I don't mind if I do.

GRANDMA: Are they still here?

MOMMY: Be quiet, Grandma.

MRS. BARKER: Oh, we're still here. What an unattractive apartment you have!

MOMMY: Yes, but you don't know what a trouble it is. Let me tell you ...

DADDY: I was saying to Mommy ...

MRS. BARKER: Yes, I know. I was listening outside.

DADDY: About the icebox, and ... the doorbell ... and the ...

MRS. BARKER: ... and the Johnny. Yes, we're very efficient; we have to know everything in our work.

DADDY: Exactly what do you do?

MOMMY: Yes, what is your work?

MRS. BARKER: Well, my dear, for one thing, I'm chairman of your woman's club.

MOMMY: Don't be ridiculous. I was talking to the chairman of my woman's club just yester—Why, so you are, You remember, Daddy, the lady I was telling you about? The lady with the husband who sits in the swing? Don't you remember?

DADDY: No ... no ...

MOMMY: Of course you do. I'm so sorry, Mrs. Barker. I would have known you anywhere, except in this artificial light. And look! You have a hat just like the one I bought yesterday.

MRS. BARKER: (*with a little laugh*) No, not really; this hat is cream.

MOMMY: Well, my dear, that may look like a cream hat to you, but I can ...

MRS. BARKER: Now, now; you seem to forget who I am.

MOMMY: Yes, I do; don't I? Are you sure you're comfortable? Won't you take off your dress?

MRS. BARKER: I don't mind if I do. (*She removes her dress.*)

MOMMY: There. You must feel a great deal more comfortable.

MRS. BARKER: Well, I certainly look a great deal more comfortable.

DADDY: I'm going to blush and giggle.

MOMMY: Daddy's going to blush and giggle.

MRS. BARKER: (*pulling the hem of her slip above her knees*) You're lucky to have such a man for a husband.

MOMMY: Oh, don't I know it!

DADDY: I just blushed and giggled and went sticky wet.

MOMMY: Isn't Daddy a caution, Mrs. Barker?

MRS. BARKER: Maybe if I smoked ...?

MOMMY: Oh, that isn't necessary.

MRS. BARKER: I don't mind if I do.

MOMMY: No; no, don't. Really.

MRS. BARKER: I don't mind ...

MOMMY: I won't have you smoking in my house, and that's that! You're a professional woman.

DADDY: Grandma drinks AND smokes; don't you, Grandma?

GRANDMA: No.

MOMMY: Well, now, Mrs. Barker; suppose you tell us why you're here.

GRANDMA: (*as* MOMMY *walks through the boxes*) The boxes ... the boxes ...

MOMMY: Be quiet, Grandma.

DADDY: What did you say, Grandma?

GRANDMA: (*as* MOMMY *steps on several of the boxes*) The boxes, damn it!

MRS. BARKER: Boxes; she said boxes. She mentioned the boxes.

DADDY: What about the boxes, Grandma? Maybe Mrs. Barker is here because of the boxes. Is that what you meant, Grandma?

GRANDMA: I don't know if that's what I meant or not. It's certainly not what I thought I meant.

DADDY: Grandma is of the opinion that...

MRS. BARKER: Can we assume that the boxes are for us? I mean, can we assume that you had us come here for the boxes?

MOMMY: Are you in the habit of receiving boxes?

DADDY: A very good question.

MRS. BARKER: Well, that would depend on the reason we're here. I've got my fingers in so many little pies, you know. Now, I can think of one of my little activities in which we are in the habit of receiving baskets; but more in a literary sense than really. We might receive boxes, though, under very special circumstances. I'm afraid that's the best answer I can give you.

DADDY: It's a very interesting answer.

MRS. BARKER: I thought so. But, does it help?

MOMMY: No; I'm afraid not.

DADDY: I wonder if it might help us any if I said I feel misgivings, that I have definite qualms.

MOMMY: Where, Daddy?

DADDY: Well, mostly right here, right around where the stitches were.

MOMMY: Daddy had an operation, you know.

MRS. BARKER: Oh, you poor Daddy! I didn't know; but then, how could I?

GRANDMA: You might have asked; it wouldn't have hurt you.

MOMMY: Dry up, Grandma.

GRANDMA: There you go. Letting your true feelings come out. Old people aren't dry enough, I suppose. My sacks are empty, the fluid in my eyeballs is all caked on the inside edges, my spine is made of sugar candy, I breathe ice; but you don't hear me complain. Nobody hears old people complain because people think that's all old people do. And that's because old people are gnarled and sagged and twisted into the shape of a complaint. (*Signs off.*) That's all.

MRS. BARKER: What was wrong, Daddy?

DADDY: Well, you know how it is: the doctors took out something that was there and put in something that wasn't there. An operation.

MRS. BARKER: You're very fortunate, I should say.

MOMMY: Oh, he is; he is. All his life, Daddy has wanted to be a United States Senator; but now ... why now he's changed his mind, and for the rest of his life he's going to want to be Governor ... it would be nearer the apartment, you know.

MRS. BARKER: You are fortunate, Daddy.

DADDY: Yes, indeed; except that I get these qualms now and then, definite ones.

MRS. BARKER: Well, it's just a matter of things settling; you're like an old house.

MOMMY: Why Daddy, thank Mrs. Barker.

DADDY: Thank you.

MRS. BARKER: Ambition! That's the ticket. I have a brother who's very much like you, Daddy ... ambitious. Of course, he's a great deal younger than you; he's even younger than I am ... if such a thing is possible. He runs a little newspaper. Just a little newspaper ... but he runs it. He's chief cook and bottle washer of that little newspaper, which he calls *The Village Idiot*. He has such a sense of humor; he's so self-deprecating, so modest. And he'd never admit it himself, but he is the Village Idiot.

MOMMY: Oh, I think that's just grand. Don't you think so, Daddy?

DADDY: Yes, just grand.

MRS. BARKER: My brother's a dear man, and he has a dear little wife, whom he loves, dearly. He loves her so much he just can't get a sentence out without mentioning her. He wants everybody to know he's married, He's really a stickler on that point; he can't be introduced to anybody and say hello without adding, "Of course, I'm married. "As far as I'm concerned, he's the chief exponent of Woman Love in this whole country; he's even been written up in psychiatric journals because of it.

DADDY: Indeed!

MOMMY: Isn't that lovely.

MRS. BARKER: Oh, I think so. There's too much woman hatred in this country, and that's a fact.

GRANDMA: Oh, I don't know.

MOMMY: Oh, I think that's just grand. Don't you think so, Daddy?

DADDY: Yes, just grand.

GRANDMA: In case anybody's interested ...

MOMMY: Be quiet, Grandma.

GRANDMA: Nuts!

MOMMY: Oh, Mrs. Barker, you must forgive Grandma. She's rural.

MRS. BARKER: I don't mind if I do.

DADDY: Maybe Grandma has something to say.

MOMMY: Nonsense. Old people have nothing to say; and if old people did have something to say, nobody would listen to them. (*To* GRANDMA) You see? I can pull that stuff just as easy as you can.

GRANDMA: Well, you got the rhythm, but you don't really have the quality. Besides, you're middle-aged.

MOMMY: I'm proud of it!

GRANDMA: Look. I'll show you how it's really done. Middle-aged people think they can do anything, but the truth is that middle-aged people can't do most things as well as they used to. Middle-aged people think they're special because they're like everybody else. We live in the age of deformity. You see? Rhythm and content. You'll learn.

DADDY: I do wish I weren't surrounded by women; I'd like some men around here.

MRS. BARKER: You can say that again!

GRANDMA: I don't hardly count as a woman, so can I say my piece?

MOMMY: Go on. Jabber away.

GRANDMA: It's very simple; the fact is, these boxes don't have anything to do with why this good lady is come to call. Now, if you're interested in knowing why these boxes are here ...

DADDY: I'm sure that must be all very true, Grandma, but what does it have to do with why...pardon me, what is that name again?

MRS. BARKER: Mrs. Barker.

DADDY: Exactly. What does it have to do with why...that name again?

MRS. BARKER: Mrs. Barker.

DADDY: Precisely. What does it have to do with why what's-her-name is here?

MOMMY: They're here because we asked them.

MRS. BARKER: Yes. That's why.

GRANDMA: Now if you're interested in knowing why these boxes are here...

MOMMY: Well, nobody is interested!

GRANDMA: You can be as snippety as you like for all the good it'll do you.

DADDY: You two will have to stop arguing.

MOMMY: I don't argue with her.

DADDY: It will just have to stop.

MOMMY: Well, why don't you call a van and have her taken away?

GRANDMA: Don't bother; there's no need.

DADDY: No, now, perhaps I can go away myself...

MOMMY: Well, one or the other; the way things are now it's impossible. In the first place, it's too crowded in this apartment. (*To* GRANDMA) And it's you that takes up all the space, with your enema bottles, and your Pekinese①, and God-only-knows-what-else...and now all these boxes...

GRANDMA: These boxes are...

MRS. BARKER: I've never heard of enema bottles...

GRANDMA: She means enema bags, but she doesn't know the difference. Mommy comes from extremely bad stock. And besides, when Mommy was born... well, it was a difficult delivery, and she had a head shaped like a banana.

MOMMY: You ungrateful—Daddy? Daddy, you see how ungrateful she is after all these years, after all the things we've done for her? (*To* GRANDMA) One of these days you're going away in a van; that's what's going to happen to you!

GRANDMA: Do tell!

MRS. BARKER: Like a banana?

---

① A breed of a small dog which is originally bred in China.

GRANDMA: Yup, just like a banana.

MRS. BARKER: My word!

MOMMY: You stop listening to her; she'll say anything. Just the other night she called Daddy a hedgehog.

MRS. BARKER: She didn't!

GRANDMA: That's right, baby; you stick up for me.

MOMMY: I don't know where she gets the words; on the television, maybe.

MRS. BARKER: Did you really call him a hedgehog?

GRANDMA: Oh look; what difference does it make whether I did or not?

DADDY: Grandma's right. Leave Grandma alone.

MOMMY: (*to* DADDY) How dare you!

GRANDMA: Oh, leave her alone, Daddy; the kid's all mixed up.

MOMMY: You see? I told you. It's all those television shows. Daddy, you go right into Grandma's room and take her television and shake all the tubes loose.

DADDY: Don't mention tubes to me.

MOMMY: Oh! Mommy forgot! (*To* MRS. BARKER) Daddy has tubes now, where he used to have tracts.

MRS. BARKER: Is that a fact!

GRANDMA: I know why this dear lady is here.

MOMMY: You be still.

MRS. BARKER: Oh, I do wish you'd tell me.

MOMMY: No! No! That wouldn't be fair at all.

DADDY: Besides, she knows why she's here; she's here because we called them.

MRS. BARKER: La! But that still leaves me puzzled. I know I'm here because you called us, but I'm such a busy girl, with this committee and that committee, and the Responsible Citizens Activities I indulge in.

MOMMY: Oh my; busy, busy.

MRS. BARKER: Yes, indeed. So I'm afraid you'll have to give me some help.

MOMMY: Oh, no. No, you must be mistaken. I can't believe we asked you here to give you any help. With the way taxes are these days, and the way you can't get satisfaction in ANYTHING... no, I don't believe so.

DADDY: And if you need help ... why, I should think you'd apply for a

Fulbright Scholarship[1]...

MOMMY: And if not that...why, then a Guggenheim Fellowship[2]...

GRANDMA: Oh, come on; why not shoot the works and try for the Prix de Rome. (*Under her breath to* MOMMY *and* DADDY) Beasts!

MRS. BARKER: Oh, what a jolly family. But let me think. I'm kneedeep in work these days; there's the Ladies' Auxiliary Air Raid Committee, for one thing; how do you feel about air raids?

MOMMY: Oh, I'd say we're hostile.

DADDY: Yes, definitely; we're hostile.

MRS. BARKER: Then, you'll be no help there. There's too much hostility in the world these days as it is; but I'll not badger you! There's a surfeit of badgers as well.

GRANDMA: While we're at it, there's been a run on old people, too. The Department of Agriculture, or maybe it wasn't the Department of Agriculture—anyway, it was some department that's run by a girl—put out figures showing that ninety per cent of the adult population of the country is over eighty years old...or eighty per cent is over ninety years old...

MOMMY: You're such a liar! You just finished saying that everyone is middle-aged.

GRANDMA: I'm just telling you what the government says ... that doesn't have anything to do with what...

MOMMY: It's that television! Daddy, go break her television.

GRANDMA: You won't find it.

DADDY: (*wearily getting up*) If I must...I must.

MOMMY: And don't step on the Pekinese; it's blind.

DADDY: It may be blind, but Daddy isn't. (*He exits, through the archway, stage—left.*)

GRANDMA: You won't find it, either.

MOMMY: Oh, I'm so fortunate to have such a husband. Just think; I could

---

① J. William Fulbright (1905—1995) is a U. S. politician who proposed the Fulbright Act (1946), establishing an exchange program for educators and students.

② A family of U. S. industrialists and philanthropists who set up a foundation granting fellowships to scholars, writers and artists.

have a husband who was poor, or argumentative, or a husband who sat in a wheel chair all day... OOOOHHHH! *What* have I said? *What* have I said?

GRANDMA: You said you could have a husband who sat in a wheel...

MOMMY: I'm mortified! I could die! I could cut my tongue out! I could...

MRS. BARKER: (*forcing a smile*) Oh, now... now... don't think about it...

MOMMY: I could... why, I could...

MRS. BARKER: ... don't think about it... really...

MOMMY: You're quite right. I won't think about it, and that way I'll forget that I ever said it, and that way it will be all right. (*Pause.*) There ... I've forgotten. Well, now, now that Daddy is out of the room we can have some girl talk.

MRS. BARKER: I'm not sure that I...

MOMMY: You do want to have some girl talk, don't you?

MRS. BARKER: I was going to say I'm not sure that I wouldn't care for a glass of water. I feel a little faint.

MOMMY: Grandma, go get Mrs. Barker a glass of water.

GRANDMA: Go get it yourself. I quit.

MOMMY: Grandma loves to do little things around the house; it gives her a false sense of security.

GRANDMA: I quit! I'm through!

MOMMY: Now, you be a good Grandma, or you know what will happen to you. You'll be taken away in a van.

GRANDMA: You don't frighten me. I'm too old to be frightened. Besides...

MOMMY: WELL! I'll tend to you later. I'll hide your teeth... I'll...

GRANDMA: Everything's hidden.

MRS. BARKER: I am going to faint. I am.

MOMMY: Good heavens! I'll go myself. (*As she exits, through the archway, stage-left.*) I'll fix you, Grandma. I'll take care of you later. (*She exits*)

GRANDMA: Oh, go soak your head. (*To* MRS. BARKER) Well, dearie, how do you feel?

MRS. BARKER: A little better, I think. Yes, much better, thank you, Grandma.

GRANDMA: That's good.

MRS. BARKER: But ... I feel so lost ... not knowing why I'm here ... and, on top of it, they say I was here before.

GRANDMA: Well, you were. Yon weren't here, exactly, because we've moved around a lot, from one apartment to another, up and down the social ladder like mice, if you like similes.

MRS. BARKER: I don't ... particularly.

GRANDMA: Well, then, I'm sorry.

MRS. BARKER: (*suddenly*) Grandma, I feel I can trust you.

GRANDMA: Don't be too sure, it's every man for himself around this place ...

MRS. BARKER: Oh ... is it? Nonetheless, I really do feel that I can trust you. Please tell me why they called and asked US to come. I implore you!

GRANDMA: Oh my; that feels good. It's been so long since anybody implored me. Do it again. Implore me some more.

MRS. BARKER: You're your daughter's mother, all right!

GRANDMA: Oh, I don't mean to be hard. If you won't implore me, then beg me, or ask me, or entreat me ... just anything like that.

MRS. BARKER: You're a dreadful old woman!

GRANDMA: You'll understand some day, Please!

MRS. BARKER: Oh, for heaven's sake! ... I implore you ... I beg you ... I beseech you!

GRANDMA: Beseech! Oh, that's the nicest word I've heard in ages. You're a dear, sweet woman ... You ... beseech ... me. I can't resist that.

MRS. BARKER: Well, then ... please tell me why they asked us to come.

GRANDMA: Well, I'll give you a hint. That's the best I can do, because I'm a muddle headed old woman. Now listen, because it's important. Once upon a time, not too very long ago, but a long enough time ago ... oh, about twenty years ago ... there was a man very much like Daddy, and a woman very much like Mommy, who were married to each other, very much like Mommy and Daddy are married to each other; and they lived in an apartment very much like one that's very much like this one, and they lived there with an old woman who was very much like yours truly, only younger, because it was some time ago; in fact, they were all somewhat younger.

MRS. BARKER: How fascinating!

GRANDMA: Now, at the same time, there was a dear lady very much like you, only younger then, who did all sorts of Good Works... And one of the Good Works this dear lady did was in something very much like a volunteer capacity for an organization very much like the Bye-Bye Adoption Service, which is nearby and which was run by a terribly deaf old lady very much like the Miss Bye-Bye who runs the Bye-Bye Adoption Service nearby.

MRS. BARKER: How enthralling!

GRANDMA: Well, be that as it may. Nonetheless, one afternoon this man, who was very much like Daddy, and this woman who was very much like Mommy came to see this dear lady who did all the Good Works, who was very much like you, dear, and they were very sad and very hopeful, and they cried and smiled and bit their fingers, and they said all the most intimate things.

MRS. BARKER: How spellbinding! What did they say?

GRANDMA: Well, it was very sweet. The woman, who was very much like Mommy, said that she and the man who was very much like Daddy had never been blessed with anything very much like a bumble of joy.

MRS. BARKER: A what?

GRANDMA: A bumble; a bumble of joy.

MRS. BARKER: Oh, like bundle.

GRANDMA: Well, yes; very much like it. Bundle, bumble; who cares? At any rate, the woman, who was very much like Mommy, said that they wanted a bumble of their own, but that the man, who was very much like Daddy, couldn't have a bumble; and the man, who was very much like Daddy, said that yes, they had wanted a bumble of their own, but that the woman, who was very much like Mommy, couldn't have one, and that now they wanted to buy something very much like a bumble.

MRS. BARKER: How engrossing!

GRANDMA: Yes. And the dear lady, who was very much like you, said something that was very much like, "Oh, what a shame; but take heart...I think we have just the bumble for you." And, well, the lady, who was very much like Mommy, and the man, who was very much like Daddy, cried and smiled and bit their ringers, and said some more intimate things, which were totally irrelevant but which were pretty hot stuff, and so the dear lady, who was very much like you, and who had something very much like a penchant for pornography, listened with something very much like enthusiasm. "Whee," she said. "Whoooopeeeeee!" But that's beside the point.

MRS. BARKER: I suppose so. But how gripping!

GRANDMA: Anyway... they bought something very much like a bumble, and they took it away with them. But... things didn't work out very well.

MRS. BARKER: You mean there was trouble?

GRANDMA: You got it. (*With a glance through the archway.*) But, I'm going to have to speed up now because I think I'm leaving soon.

MRS. BARKER: Oh. Are you really?

GRANDMA: Yup.

MRS. BARKER: But old people don't go anywhere; they're either taken places, or put places.

GRANDMA: Well, this old person is different. Anyway ... things started going badly.

MRS. BARKER: Oh yes. Yes.

GRANDMA: Weeeeellll ... in the first place, it turned out the bumble didn't look like either one of its parents. That was enough of a blow, but things got worse. One night, it cried its heart out, if you can imagine such a thing.

MRS. BARKER: Cried its heart out! Well!

GRANDMA: But that was only the beginning. Then it turned out it only had eyes for its Daddy.

MRS. BARKER: For its Daddy! Why, any self-respecting woman would have gouged those eyes right out of its head.

GRANDMA: Well, she did. That's exactly what she did. But then, it kept its Bose up in the air.

MRS. BARKER: Ufggh! How disgusting!

GRANDMA: That's what they thought. But then, it began to develop an interest in its you-know-what.

MRS. BARKER: In its you-know-what! Well! I hope they cut its hands off at the wrists!

GRANDMA: Well, yes, they did that eventually. But first, they cut off its you-know-what.

MRS. BARKER: A much better idea!

GRANDMA: That's what they thought. But after they cut off its you-know-what, it still put its hands under the covers, looking for its you-know-what. So, finally, they had to cut off its hands at the wrists.

MRS. BARKER: Naturally!

GRANDMA: And it was such a resentful bumble. Why, one day it called its Mommy a dirty name.

MRS. BARKER: Well, I hope they cut its tongue out!

GRANDMA: Of course. And then, as it got bigger, they found out all sorts of terrible things about it, like: it didn't have a head on its shoulders, it had no guts, it was spineless, its feet were made of clay... just dreadful things.

MRS. BARKER: Dreadful!

GRANDMA: So you can understand how they became discouraged.

MRS. BARKER: I certainly can! And what did they do?

GRANDMA: What did they do? Well, for the last straw, it finally up and died; and you can imagine how that made them feel, their having paid for it, and all. So, they called up the lady who sold them the bumble in the first place and told her to come right over to their apartment. They wanted satisfaction; they wanted their money back. That's what they wanted.

MRS. BARKER: My, my, my.

GRANDMA: How do you like them apples?

MRS. BARKER: My, my, my.

DADDY: (*off stage*) Mommy! I can't find Grandma's television, and I can't find the Pekinese, either.

MOMMY: (*off stage*) Isn't that funny! And I can't find the water.

GRANDMA: Heh, heh, heh. I told them everything was hidden.

MRS. BARKER: Did you hide the water, too?

GRANDMA: (*puzzled*) No. No, I didn't do that.

DADDY: (*off stage*) The truth of the matter is, I can't even find Grandma's room.

GRANDMA: Heh, heh, heh.

MRS. BARKER: My! You certainly did hide things, didn't you?

GRANDMA: Sure, kid, sure.

MOMMY: (*sticking her head in the room*) Did you ever hear of such a thing, Grandma? Daddy can't find your television, and he can't find the Pekinese, and the truth of the matter is he can't even find your room.

GRANDMA: I told you. I hid everything.

MOMMY: Nonsense, Grandma! Just wait until I get my hands on you. You're a troublemaker ... that's what you are.

GRANDMA: Well, I'll be out of here pretty soon, baby.

MOMMY: Oh, you don't know how right you are! Daddy's been wanting to send you away for a long time now, but I've been restraining him. I'll tell you one thing, though ... I'm getting sick and tired of this fighting, and I might just let him have his way. Then you'll see what'll happen. Away you'll go; in a van, too. I'll let Daddy call the van man.

GRANDMA: I'm way ahead of you.

MOMMY: How can you be so old and so smug at the same time? You have no sense of proportion.

GRANDMA: You just answered your own question.

MOMMY: Mrs. Barker, I'd much rather you came into the kitchen for that glass of water, what with Grandma out here, and all.

MRS. BARKER: I don't see what Grandma has to do with it; and besides. I don't think you're very polite.

MOMMY: You seem to forget that you're a guest in this house ...

GRANDMA: Apartment!

MOMMY: Apartment! And that you're a professional woman. So, if you'll be so good as to come into the kitchen, I'll be more than happy to show you where the water is, and where the glass is, and then you can put two and two together if you're clever enough. (*She vanishes.*)

MRS. BARKER: (*after a moment's consideration*) I suppose she's right.

GRANDMA: Well, that's how it is when people call you up and ask you over to do something for them.

MRS. BARKER: I suppose you're right, too. Well, Grandma, it's been very nice talking to you.

GRANDMA: And I've enjoyed listening. Say, don't tell Mommy or Daddy that I gave you that hint, will you?

MRS. BARKER: Oh, dear me, the hint! I'd forgotten about it, if you can imagine such a thing. No, I won't breathe a word of it to them.

GRANDMA: I don't know if it helped you any...

MRS. BARKER: I can't tell, yet. I'll have to... what is the word I want? ... I'll have to relate it... that's it... I'll have to relate it to certain things that I know, and... draw... conclusions... What I'll really have to do is to see if it applies to anything. I mean, after all, I do do volunteer work for an adoption service, but it isn't very much like the Bye-Bye Adoption Service... it is the Bye-Bye Adoption Service... and while I can remember Mommy and Daddy coming to see me, oh, about twenty years ago, about buying a bumble, I can't quite remember anyone very much like Mommy and Daddy coming to see me about buying a bumble. Don't you see? It really presents quite a problem... I'll have to think about it... mull it... but at any rate, it was truly first-class of you to try to help me. Oh, will you still be here after I've had my drink of water?

GRANDMA: Probably... I'm not as spry as I used to be.

MRS. BARKER: Oh. Well, I won't say good-bye then.

GRANDMA: No. Don't. (MRS. BARKER *exits through the archway.*) People don't say good-by to old people because they think they'll frighten them. Lordy! If they only knew how awful "hello" and "my, you're looking chipper" sounded, they wouldn't say those things either. The truth is, there isn't much you can say to old people that doesn't sound just terrible. (*The doorbell rings.*) Come on in! (*The* YOUNG MAN *enters.* GRANDMA *looks* him *over.*) Well, now, aren't you a breath of fresh air!

YOUNG MAN: Hello there.

GRANDMA: My, my, my. Are you the van man?

YOUNG MAN: The what?

GRANDMA: The van man. The van man. Are you come to take me away?

YOUNG MAN: I don't know what you're talking about.

GRANDMA: Oh. (*Pause.*) Well. (*Pause.*) My, my, aren't you some thing!

YOUNG MAN: Hm?

GRANDMA: I said, my, my, aren't you something.

YOUNG MAN: Oh. Thank you.

GRANDMA: You don't sound very enthusiastic.

YOUNG MAN: Oh, I'm... I'm used to it.

GRANDMA: Yup... yup. You know, if I were about a hundred and fifty years younger I could go for you.

YOUNG MAN: Yes, I imagine so.

GRANDMA: Unh-hunh... will you look at those muscles!

YOUNG MAN: (*flexing his muscles*) Yes, they're quite good, aren't they?

GRANDMA: Boy, they sure are. They natural?

YOUNG MAN: Well, the basic structure was there, but I've done some work, too... you know, in a gym.

GRANDMA: I'll bet you have. You ought to be in the movies, boy.

YOUNG MAN: I know.

GRANDMA: Yup! Right up there on the old silver screen. But I suppose you've heard that before.

YOUNG MAN: Yes, I have.

GRANDMA: You ought to try out for them... the movies.

YOUNG MAN: Well, actually, I may have a career there yet. I've lived out on the West Coast almost all my life... and I've met a few people who... might be able to help me. I'm not in too much of a hurry, though. I'm almost as young as I look.

GRANDMA: Oh, that's nice. And will you look at that face!

YOUNG MAN: Yes, it's quite good, isn't it? Clean-cut, midwest farm boy type, almost insultingly good-looking in a typically American way. Good profile, straight nose, honest eyes, wonderful smile...

GRANDMA: Yup. Boy, you know what you are, don't you? You're the American Dream, that's what you are. All those other people, they don't know what they're talking about. You... you are the American Dream.

YOUNG MAN: Thanks.

MOMMY: (*off stage*) Who rang the doorbell?

GRANDMA: (*shouting off stage*) The American Dream!

MOMMY: (*off stage*) What? What was that, Grandma?

GRANDMA: (*shouting*) The American Dream! The American Dream! Damn it!

DADDY: (*off stage*) How's that, Mommy?

MOMMY: (*off stage*) Oh, some gibberish; pay no attention. Did you find

Grandma's room?

DADDY:(*off stage*) No. I can't even find Mrs. Barker.

YOUNG MAN:What was all that?

GRANDMA:Oh, that was just the folks, but let's not talk about them, honey:let's talk about you.

YOUNG MAN:All right.

GRANDMA:Well, let's see. If you're not the van man, what are you doing here?

YOUNG MAN:I'm looking for work.

GRANDNMA:Are you! Well, what kind of work?

YOUNG MAN: Oh, almost anything ... almost anything that pays. I'll do almost anything for money.

GRANDMA:Will you... Will you? Hmmmm. I wonder if there's anything you could do around here?

YOUNG MAN:There might be. It looked to be a likely building.

GRANDMA:It's always looked to be a rather unlikely building to me, but I suppose you'd know better than I.

YOUNG MAN:I can sense these things.

GRANDMA:There might be something you could do around here. Stay there! Don't come any closer.

YOUNG MAN:Sorry.

GRANDMA:I don't mean I'd mind. I don't know whether I'd mind, or not... But it wouldn't look well; it would look just awful.

YOUNG MAN:Yes; I suppose so.

GRANDMA:Now, stay there, let me concentrate. What could you do? The folks have been in something of a quandary around here today, sort of a dilemma, and I wonder if you mightn't be some help.

YOUNG MAN:I hope so... if there's money in it. Do you have any money?

GRANDMA:Money! Oh, there's more money around here than you'd know what to do with.

YOUNG MAN:I'm not so sure.

GRANDMA:Well, maybe not. Besides, I've got money of my own.

YOUNG MAN:You have?

GRANDMA: Sure. Old people quite often have lots of money; more often than most people expect. Come here, so I can whisper to you ... not too close. I might faint.

YOUNG MAN: Oh, I'm sorry.

GRANDMA: It's all right, dear. Anyway ... have you ever heard of that big baking contest they run? The one where all the ladies get together in a big barn and bake away?

YOUNG MAN: I'm ... not ... sure ...

GRANDMA: Not so close. Well, it doesn't matter whether you've heard of it or not. The important thing is—and I don't want anybody to hear this ... the folks think I haven't been Out of the house in eight years—the important thing is that I won first prize in that baking contest this year. Oh, it was in all the papers; not under my own name, though. I used a nom de boulangkre; I called myself Uncle Henry.

YOUNG MAN: Did you?

GRANDMA: Why not? I didn't see any reason not to. I look just as much like an old man as I do like an old woman. And you know what I called it ... what I won for?

YOUNG MAN: No. What did you call it?

GRANDMA: I called it Uncle Henry's Day-Old Cake.

YOUNG MAN: That's a very nice name.

GRANDMA: And it wasn't any trouble, either. All I did was go out and get a store-bought cake, and keep it around for a while, and then slip it in, unbeknownst to anybody. Simple.

YOUNG MAN: You're a very resourceful person.

GRANDMA: Pioneer stock.

YOUNG MAN: Is all this true? Do you want me to believe all this?

GRANDMA: Well, you can believe it or not ... it doesn't make any difference to me. All I know is, Uncle Henry's Day-Old Cake won me twenty-five thousand smackerolas.

YOUNG MAN: Twenty-five thou—

GRANDMA: Right on the old loggerhead. Now ... how do you like them apples?

YOUNG MAN: Love'em.

GRANDMA: I thought you'd be impressed.

YOUNG MAN: Money talks.

GRANDMA: Hey! You look familiar.

YOUNG MAN: Hm? Pardon?

GRANDMA: I said, you look familiar.

YOUNG MAN: Well, I've done some modeling.

GRANDMA: No ... no. I don't mean that. You look familiar.

YOUNG MAN: Well, I'm a type.

GRANDMA: Yup; you sure are. Why do you say you'd do anything for money ... if you don't mind my being nosy?

YOUNG MAN: No, no. It's part of the interviews. I'll be happy to tell you. It's that I have no talents at all, except what you see ... my person: my body, my face. In every other way I am incomplete, and I must therefore ... compensate.

GRANDMA: What do you mean, incomplete? You look pretty complete to me.

YOUNG MAN: I think I can explain it to you, partially because you're very old, and very old people have perceptions they keep to themselves, because if they expose them to other people ... well, you know what ridicule and neglect are.

GRANDMA: I do, child, I do.

YOUNG MAN: Then listen. My mother died the night that I was born, and I never knew my father; I doubt my mother did. But, I wasn't alone, because lying with me ... in the placenta ... there was someone else ... my brother ... my twin.

GRANDMA: Oh, my child.

YOUNG MAN: We were identical twins ... he and I ... not fraternal ... identical; we were derived from the same ovum; and in this, in that we were twins not from separate ova but from the same one, we had a kinship such as you cannot imagine. We ... we felt each other breathe ... his heartbeats thundered in my temples ... mine in his ... our stomachs ached and we cried for feeding at the same time ... are you old enough to understand?

GRANDMA: I think so, child; I think I'm nearly old enough.

YOUNG MAN: I hope so. But we were separated when we were still very young, my brother, my twin and I ... inasmuch as you can separate one being. We were torn apart ... thrown to opposite ends of the continent. I don't know what became of my brother ... to the rest of myself ... except that, from time to time, in the years that have passed, I have suffered losses ... that I can't explain. A fall from grace ... a departure of innocence ... loss ... loss. How can I put it to you? All right; like this: Once ... it was as if all at once my heart ... became numb ... almost as though I ... almost as though ... just like that ... it had been wrenched from my body ... and from that time I have been unable to love. Once ... I was asleep at the time ... I awoke, and my eyes were burning. And since that time I have been unable to see anything, anything, with pity, with affection ... with anything but ... cool disinterest. And my groin ... even there ... since one time ... one specific agony ... since then I have not been able to love anyone with my body. And even my hands ... I cannot touch another person and feel love. And there is more ... there are more losses, but it all comes down to this: I no longer have the capacity to feel anything. I have no emotions. I have been drained, torn asunder ... disemboweled. I have, now, only my person ... my body, my face. I use what I have ... I let people love me ... I accept the syntax around me, for while I know I cannot relate ... I know I must be related to. I let people love me ... I let people touch me ... I let them draw pleasure from my groin ... from my presence ... from the fact of me ... but, that is all it comes to. As I told you, I am incomplete ... I can feel nothing. I can feel nothing. And so ... here I am ... as you see me. I am ... but this ... what you see. And it will always be thus.

GRANDMA: Oh, my child; my child. (*Long pause; then:*) I was mistaken ... before. I don't know you from somewhere, but I knew ... once ... someone very much like you ... or, very much as perhaps you were.

YOUNG MAN: Be careful; be very careful. What I have told you may not be true. In my profession ...

GRANDMA: Shhhhhh. (*The* YOUNG MAN *bows his head, in acquiescence.*) Someone ... to be more precise ... who might have turned out to be very much like you might have turned out to he. And ... unless I'm terribly mistaken ... you've found yourself a job.

YOUNG MAN: What are my duties?

MRS. BARKER: (*off stage*) Yoo—hoo! Yoo—hoo!

GRANDMA: Oh—oh. You'll ... you'll have to play it by ear, my dear ... unless

I get a chance to talk to you again. I've got to go into my act, now.

YOUNG MAN: But, I...

GRANDMA: Yoo—hoo!

MRS. BARKER: (*coming through archway*) Yoo—hoo...oh, there you are, Grandma. I'm glad to see somebody. I can't find Mommy or Daddy. (*Double takes.*) Well...who's this?

GRANDMA: This? Well...un...oh, this is the...uh...the van man. That's who it is...the van man.

MRS. BARKER: So! It's true! They did call the van man. They are having you carted away.

GRANDMA: (*shrugging*) Well, you know. It figures.

MRS. BARKER: (*to* YOUNG MAN) How dare you cart this poor old woman away!

YOUNG MAN: (*after a quick look at* GRANDMA, *who nods*) I do what I'm paid to do. I don't ask any questions.

MRS. BARKER: (*after a brief pause*) Oh. (*Pause.*) Well, you're quite right, of course, and I shouldn't meddle.

GRANDMA: (*to* YOUNG MAN) Dear, will you take my things out to the van? (*She points to the boxes.*)

YOUNG MAN: (*after only the briefesthesitation*) Why certainly.

GRANDMA: (*as the* YOUNG MAN *takes up half the boxes, exits by the front door*) Isn't that a nice young van man?

MRS. BARKER: (*shaking her head in disbelief, watching the* YOUNG MAN *exit*) Unh—hunh...some things have changed for the better. I remember when I had my mother carted off...the van man who came for her wasn't anything near as nice as this one.

GRANDMA: Oh, did you have your mother carted off, too?

MRS. BARKER: (*cheerfully*) Why certainly! Didn't you?

GRANDMA: (*puzzling*) No ... no, I didn't. At least, I can't remember. Listen dear; I got to talk to you for a second.

MRS. BARKER: Why certainly, Grandma.

GRANDMA: Now, listen.

MRS. BARKER: Yes, Grandma. Yes.

GRANDMA: Now listen carefully. You got this dilemma here with Mommy and Daddy ...

MRS. BARKER: Yes! I wonder where they've gone to?

GRANDMA: They'll be back in. Now, LISTEN!

MRS. BARKER: Oh, I'm sorry.

GRANDMA: Now, you got this dilemma here with Mommy and Daddy, and I think I got the way out for you. (*The* YOUNG MAN *re-enters through the front door.*) Will you take the rest of my things out now, dear? (*To* MRS. BARKER, *while the* YOUNG MAN *takes the rest of the boxes, exits again by the front door.*) Fine. Now listen, dear. (*She begins to whisper in* MRS. BARKER'S *ear.*)

MRS. BARKER: Oh! Oh! Oh! I don't think I could ... do you really think I could? Well, why not? What a wonderful idea ... what an absolutely wonderful idea!

GRANDMA: Well, yes, I thought it was.

MRS. BARKER: And you so old!

GRANDMA: Heh, hell, heh.

MRS. BARKER: Well, I think it's absolutely marvelous, anyway. I'm going to find Mommy and Daddy right now.

GRANDMA: Good. You do that.

MRS. BARKER: Well, now. I think I will say good-by. I can't thank you enough. (*She starts to exit through the archway.*)

GRANDMA: You're welcome. Say it!

MRS. BARKER: Huh? What?

GRANDMA: Say good-by.

MRS. BARKER: Oh. Good-by. (*She exits.*) Mommy! I say, Mommy! Daddy!

GRANDMA: Good-by. (*By herself now, she looks about.*) Ah me. (*Shakes her head.*) Ah me. (*Takes in the room.*) Good-by. (*The* YOUNG MAN *re-enters.*)

GRANDMA: Oh, hello, there.

YOUNG MAN: All the boxes are outside.

GRANDMA: (*a little sadly*) I don't know why I bother to take them with me. They don't have much in them ... some old letters, a couple of regrets ...

Pekinese ... blind at that ... the television ... my Sunday teeth ... eighty-six years of living ... some sounds ... a few images, a little garbled by now ... and, well ... (*She shrugs.*)... you know ... the things one accumulates.

YOUNG MAN: Can I get you ... a cab, or something?

GRANDMA: Oh no, dear ... thank you just the same. I'll take it from here.

YOUNG MAN: And what shall I do now?

GRANDMA: Oh, you stay here, dear. It will all become clear to you. It will be explained. You'll understand.

YOUNG MAN: Very well.

GRANDMA: (*after one more look about*) Well ...

YOUNG MAN: Let me see you to the elevator.

GRANDMA: Oh, that would be nice, dear.

(*They both exit by the front door, slowly.*)

(*Enter* MRS. BARKER, *followed by* MOMMY *and* DADDY.)

MRS. BARKER: And I'm happy to tell you that the whole thing's settled. Just like that.

MOMMY: Oh, we're so glad. We were afraid there might be a problem, what with delays, and all.

DADDY: Yes, we're very relieved.

MRS. BARKER: Well, now; that's what professional women are for.

MOMMY: Why ... where's Grandma? Grandma's not here! Where's Grandma? And look! The boxes are gone, too. Grandma's gone, and so are the boxes. She's taken off, and she's stolen something! Daddy!

MRS. BARKER: Why, Mommy, the van man was here.

MOMMY: (*startled*) The what?

MRS. BARKER: The van man. The van man was here.

(*The lights might dim a little, suddenly.*)

MOMMY: (*shakes her head*) No, that's impossible.

MRS. BARKER: Why, I saw him with my own two eyes.

MOMMY: (*near tears*) No, no, that's impossible. No. There's no such thing as the van man. There is no van man. We ... we made him up. Grandma? Grandma?

DADDY: (*moving to* MOMMY) There, there, now.

MOMMY: Oh Daddy ... where's Grandma?

DADDY: There, there, now.

(*While* DADDY *is comforting* MOMMY, GRANDMA *comes out, stage-right, near the footlights.*)

GRANDMA: (*to the audience*) Shhhhhh! I want to watch this.

(*She motions to* MRS. BARKER *who, with a secret smile, tiptoes to the front door and opens it. The* YOUNG MAN *is framed therein. Lights up full again as he steps into the room.*)

MRS. BARKER: Surprise! Surprise! Here we are!

MOMMY: What? What?

DADDY: Hm? What?

MOMMY: (her tears merely sniffles now) What surprise?

MRS. BARKER: Why, I told you. The surprise I told you about.

DADDY: You ... you know, Mommy.

MOMMY: Sur ... prise?

DADDY: (*urging her to cheerfulness*) You remember, Mommy; why we asked ... uh ... what's-her-name to come here?

MRS. BARKER: Mrs. Barker, if you don't mind.

DADDY: Yes. Mommy? You remember now? About the bubble ... about wanting satisfaction?

MOMMY: (*her sorrow turning into delight*) Yes. Why yes! Of course! Yes! Oh, how wonderful!

MRS. BARKER: (*to the* YOUNG MAN) This is Mommy.

YOUNG MAN: How ... how do you do?

MRS. BARKER: (*stage whisper*) Her name's Mommy.

YOUNG MAN: How ... how do you do, Mommy?

MOMMY: Well! Hello there!

MRS. BARKER: (*to the* YOUNG MAN) And that is Daddy.

YOUNG MAN: How do you do, sir?

DADDY: How do you do?

MOMMY: (*herself again, circling the* YOUNG MAN, *feeling his arm, poking him*) Yes, sir! Yes, sirree! Now this is more like it. Now this is a great deal more like it! Daddy! Come see. Come see if this isn't a great deal more like it.

DADDY: I… I can see from here, Mommy. It does look a great deal more like it.

MOMMY: Yes, sir. Yes sirree! Mrs. Barker, I don't know how to thank you.

MRS. BARKER: Oh, don't worry about that. I'll send you a bill in the mail.

MOMMY: What this really calls for is a celebration. It calls for a drink.

MRS. BARKER: Oh, what a nice idea.

MOMMY: There's some sauterne in the kitchen.

YOUNG MAN: I'll go.

MOMMY: Will you? Oh, how nice. The kitchen's through the archway there. (*As the* YOUNG MAN *exits: to* MRS. BARKER.) He's very nice. Really top notch: much better than the other one.

MRS. BARKER: I'm glad you're pleased. And I'm glad everything's all straightened out.

MOMMY: Well. at least we know why we sent for you. We're glad that's cleaned up. By the way, what's his name?

MRS. BARKER: Ha! Call him whatever you like. He's yours. Call him what you called the other one.

MOMMY: Daddy? What did we call the other one?

DADDY: (*puzzled*) Why…

YOUNG MAN: (*re-entered with a tray on which are a bottle of sauterne and five glasses*) Here we are!

MOMMY: Hooray! Hooray!

MRS. BARKER: Oh, good!

MOMMY: (*moving to the tray*) So, Let's—Five glasses? Why five? There are only four of us. Why five?

YOUNG MAN: (*catches* GRANDMA'S *eye;* GRANDMA *indicates she is not there*) Oh, I'm sorry.

MOMMY: You must learn to count. We're a wealthy family, and you must learn to count.

YOUNG MAN: I will.

MOMMY: Well, everybody take a glass. (*They do.*) And we'll drink to celebrate. To satisfaction! Who says you can't get satisfaction these days!

MRS. BARKER: What dreadful sauterne!

MOMMY: Yes, isn't it? (*To* YOUNG MAN, *her voice already a little fuzzy from the wine.*) You don't know how happy I am to see you! Yes sirree. Listen, that time we had with ... with the other one. I'll tell you about it some time. (*Indicates* MRS. BARKER) After she's gone. She was responsible for all the trouble in the first place. I'll tell you all about it. (*Sidles up to him a little.*) Maybe ... maybe later tonight.

YOUNG MAN: (*not moving away*) Why yes. That would be very nice.

MOMMY: (puzzles) something familiar about you ... you know that? I can't quite place it ...

GRANDMA: (*interrupting ... to audience*) Well, I guess that just about wraps it up. I mean, for better or worse, this is a comedy, and I don't think we'd better go any further. No, definitely not. So, let's leave things as they are right now ... while everybody's happy ... while everybody's got what he wants ... or everybody's got what he thinks he wants. Good night, dears.

CURTAIN

[Selected from Edward Albee. *Two Plays by Edward Albee*. New York: New American Library, 1959.]

Ⅲ. Questions for discussion

(1) What are the messages that Albee wants to convey in *The American Dream*?

(2)Comment on the characterization of this play.

(3)Some critics say that the relationship within the American family is based on money, how do you evaluate it?

(4)In what sense is this play a realistic one?

(5)Albee has been called an absurdist playwright, how accurately can the term "absurdist" be applied to his play?

(6)What are the common features of Albeeand O'Neill?

3.3 Assigned Reading

Allegory in Edward Albee's *The American Dream*

Ervin Beck

Our understanding of Edward Albee's achievement in *The American Dream*

(1960) has come a long way since 1961 when Martin Esslin hailed it as a "brilliant first example of an American contribution to the Theatre of the Absurd" and 1966 when Nicholas Canaday, Jr. labeled it America's "best example of what has come to be known as 'the theatre of the absurd'"①.

The shrewdest assessment of absurdism in Albee is byBrian Way, who shows convincingly that, although Albee has successfully mastered the techniques of theatrical absurdism, he has nevertheless shied away from embracing the metaphysics that the style implies. That is, Albee knows that Theatre of the Absurd is "an absorption-in-art of certain existentialist and post-existentialist philosophical concepts having to do, in the main, with man's attempts to make sense for himself out of his senseless position in a world which makes no sense"②. But Albee nevertheless believes in the validity of reason—that things can be proved, or that events can be shown to have definite meanings. Structurally, the chief evidence for this claim is that Albee's plays, including *The American Dream*, move toward resolution, denouement and completion rather than the circularity or open-endedness typical of Theatre of the Absurd.

In regard to content, Way's point may be extended by contrasting the implications of the titles of *The American Dream* and Eugene Ionesco's *The Bald Soprano* , an absurdist drawing room comedy to which Albee's play seems indebted in many ways. Ionesco's title derives from the Fireman's passing reference to the woman who always wears her hair in the same style. She is not a character in the play, nor is she ever referred to again. She is a non-sequitur, as is everything else in that circular play, since nothing follows logically from what precedes it.

Albee's title, on the other hand, is rich in intellectual and moral substance, since it refers to a host of ideas and feelings associated with the fondest hopes of participants in the American experience, both historic and contemporary. The title is also a fitting thematic label for the play since the dialogue explicitly refers to the American Dream after the Young Man appears on stage. Ionesco's title—like all titles, an authorial comment on the text—rightly says that the play lacks meaning;

---

① Nicholas Canaday, Jr.. Albee's *The American Dream* and the Existential Vacuum, *South Central Bulletin*, 1966 (26). p. 28.

② Edward Albee. Which Theatre is the Absurd One?. Horst Frenz, (ed.). *American Playwrights on Drama*. New York, 1965. p. 170.

Albee says that it refers to a lot of meaning.

That meaning is most obviously associated with the Young Man, since he is specifically identified as the American Dream by the dialogue of the play. The less obvious—but more important—meaning is embodied in Grandma. The goal of this essay will be to clarify how Grandma's character and experience bear most of the meaning of the American Dream that Albee wants to communicate in this play. As we shall see, that meaning fits squarely within the mainstream American humanist tradition stretching back to the early, idealistic years of the American republic.

Even though she is a physical disaster, many critics have noticed various kinds of attractive qualities in Grandma. Don D. Moore finds her the most appealing, the most refreshing and the wisest figure in the play. Canaday, who has written the most about Grandma, praises her for her realism, clear vision, enjoyment of living, and creative response to life, especially the way she resolves the knot of the plot. Daniel R. Brown rightly, in my opinion, finds in Grandma a licensed speaker, someone who tells us what to think and therefore becomes a kind of mouthpiece for the author. A few critics have also associated Grandma with the American Dream, among them being A. Robert Lee, George E. Wellworth and Ronald Hayman. For instance, Hayman says, "There are hints that Albee intends her to be ... an incarnation of the American nineteenth-century liberal values which were still alive earlier in the twentieth (century)."① However, all such comments have been incidental, made in passing. They do not do justice to the major role that Grandma plays in the drama. After all, she is the main character in the play, appearing on stage more of the time and having more speeches than any other character. It is, in effect, her play, and she deserves detailed examination as the main bearer of traditional values in the play.

Indeed, she fits squarely within the archetype of "The American Adam" sketched persuasively by R. W. B. Lewis in his seminal book by the same name on American intellectual history. The American Adam is, of course, the archetype of a new kind of human being, freed from the corrupt institutions of the Old World and facing an unspoiled garden utopia, armed with power derived from youthful vigor and spiritual innocence. On a rather superficial level, Grandma is Lewis'

---

① *Ronald Hayman. Edward Albee.* New York, 1973. pp. 35-36.

agrarian hero subduing the American Eden of a wilderness with industry and ingenuity. Mommy verifies Grandma's association with the American countryside by saying "Oh, Mrs. Barker, you must forgive Grandma. She's rural"①. Mommy also acknowledges Grandma's continued industry, despite her old age: "I can't stand it, watching her do the cooking and the housework, polishing the silver, moving the furniture." And Grandma herself claims the role by saying, "Pioneer stock," when the Young Man admires her resourcefulness in the bakeoff contest, where she has indeed shown a kind of Yankee ingenuity.

Of course, Grandma represents this ideal in its declining, hence less attractive and potent, years. "My sacks are empty, the fluid in my eyeballs is all caked on the inside edges, my spine is made of sugar candy; I breathe ice," she says. But for an otherwise absurdist play, she embodies and speaks the truths associated with America's earliest and best impulses.

Her explicit identification with the American Adam is depicted by Albee in two rather subtle, cryptic ways. First, when Grandma examines the Young Man for the first time, she exclaims: "Yup ... yup. You know, if I were about a hundred and fifty years younger I could go for you." Here literary criticism must become mathematical: The play was written in 1960, which means that Grandma literally has in mind the year 1810, when the United States (with its new constitution) was 21 years old—newly come of age, full of idealism and on the verge of its incredible expansion. At that time in history, the Young Man would have made a perfect mate for Grandma.

Second, although Grandma is literally a woman—the American Eve? —Albee has worked into his characterization and text elements that help bridge the gender gap, making his American Dream androgynous if not wholly masculine. "I look just as much like an old man as I do like an old woman," "Grandma declares." And in the bake-off contest, of course, her nom de boulangere is "Uncle Henry." The "Henry" gives Grandma a masculine dimension. The "Uncle" even associates her with "Uncle Sam," that ubiquitous image in popular culture that approximates the American Adam in Lewis' literary culture.

---

① Edward Albee. *The American Dream and The Zoo Story*. New York: American Library Books, 1963. p. 85.

In fact, Albee may have designed his play fully conscious of the early American theatrical convention of depicting a true blue American hero on the stage in the form of an Uncle Sam stage type. Walter Meserve points out that, in early American theater, the Yankee character, the Negro character and the Indian character were the three stage types that American playwrights added to the caricatures that they had inherited fromEurope. This Yankee character, first called "Jonathan," appears in over 100 American plays from 1800 to 1850—early (1787) as Master Jonathan in Tyler's *The Contrast* and late (1845) as *Adam Trueman* in Mowatt's *Fashion.* The type even developed a stylized red, white and blue costume, ""much after the present caricature of Uncle Sam, minus the stars but glorifying in the stripes."

Theater historians and directors of the play will be struck by the many similarities indeed between Grandma and Adam Trueman, namely their blunt, outspoken natures; their support of the traditional American values that they see being undermined by newfangledness; and, most important, their prescience and practical ability that enable them to resolve by their own contrivings the very complicated knots in their respective plays. To communicate this role to twentieth-century audiences who may not be familiar with the convention, a director might want to make Grandma look something like the Jonathans, Uncle Sams and Adam Truemans in her stage ancestry.

Of course, Grandma also has the inner qualities that link her with the best that has been thought aboutAmerica. First of all, in the dehumanized, alienated society of Mommy and Daddy's apartment in which she lives, she alone bears the standard of benevolent humanism for which America has always stood. True, she has learned to insult, to give as well as take from Mommy. But she alone has a sense of human dignity, of the worth of the individual upon which American democracy is based.

In one of her first speeches Grandma states her philosophy of life: "Well, that's all that counts. People being sorry. Makes you feel better; gives you a sense of dignity, and that's all that's important ... a sense of dignity. And it doesn't matter if you don't care, or not, either. You got to have a sense of dignity, even if you don't care, 'cause, if you don't have that, civilization's doomed."

To Grandma's keynote statement, Mommy responds accusatorially: "You've been reading my book club selections again!" Of course! While Mommy has been glued to the television, Grandma has probably been reading Heritage Book Club selections by Plato, Moses, Shakespeare, Jefferson and other sources of America's enduring values. Grandma's eloquent view of history helps make her the only genuinely human, empathetic character in the play, as is seen particularly in her intimate scenes with Mrs. Barker and the Young Man, both of whom are moved by her ability to understand and sympathize with them.

This understanding of Grandma helps make sense out of the main stage property associated with her—her boxes. On a literal level, the boxes are simply the belongings that Grandma takes with her as she moves from the apartment. As Mommy finds out when she looks for the bathroom, however, Grandma is really emptying the apartment of all of its contents—even the water. These "contents" are, in effect, the "content" of the American dream. Grandma possesses the substance of it all, and leaves only the shell behind, in the form of empty-headed, vicious Mommy and passive, disemboweled Daddy.

The dispute between Mommy and Grandma over rhythm and content also alludes to the symbolic associations of Grandma's boxes. "You got the rhythm, but you don't really have the quality," Grandma claims. Then, following a tirade against middle-aged people, she repeats: "You see? Rhythm and content. You'll learn." The integration of form and content that Grandma claims (as opposed to the perversion of mere form in Mommy) is also embodied in Grandma's boxes, which are not only full of items but are also impressively wrapped. The taking out of the apartment of these neatly wrapped boxes is one of the most important image sequences in the logical structure of Albee's seemingly illogical play.

The function and meaning of Grandma as the American Dream emerges most precisely in the juxtaposition of her with her main foil, the Young Man. Although critics always identify the Young Man with Albee's stated theme, they almost never point out that the Young Man assumes that identify for us only because Grandma gives him that symbolic interpretation. Soon after she sees him she exclaims: "Yup. Boy, you know what you are, don't you? You're the American Dream, that's what you are. All those other people, they don't know what they're talking about. You ... you are the American Dream."

My point is that it takes one (American Dream, old style) to know one

(American Dream, new style).

The Young Man has often been explicated as the Hollywood-style American Dream of Success—sexy, materialistic, lacking values, superficially dazzling. There is no need to go further into that here. But it is important to consider how the young Man as American Dream relates to Grandma as American Dream.

In one respect, again it is the difference between form and content—the Young Man with the marvelous physique but "in every other way ... incomplete" and Grandma with all of the substance of the play but a decrepit body. This complementary set of needs draws the two together like a magnet. Grandma is especially affected by the Young Man, almost swooning, in fact, whenever he moves close to her. "Not too close," she says. "I might faint."

Yet, although Grandma empathizes deeply with the Young Man in his painful "fall from grace" and "departure of innocence"—"Oh, my child; my child," she exclaims—she is savvy enough to know that his fortuitous arrival requires her own immediate departure. After all, the apartment is too small to hold all four people, and crass, shallow Mommy has definitely rejected Grandma (and her humanistic American Dream) and chosen the Young Man (and his materialistic American Dream). This realization fills Grandma with anger and inspires her greatest emotional outburst in the play. In reply to Mommy's query, "Who rang the doorbell?" Grandma responds, "The American Dream!... (Shouting) The American Dream! The American Dream! Damn it!" On the surface level Grandma's "Damn it!" merely reflects annoyance at Mommy's deafness. On the other hand, her three—fold repetition of "The American Dream!" constitutes a rhetorical excess that suggests Grandma's deeper emotional and intellectual response. Her "Damn it!" may constitute Grandma's great recognition that she has been displaced. In effect, she also means, "Damn it! This is the American Dream that has come to displace me."

Mommy's choice of the Young Man and her rejection of Grandma are at the heart of the plot of the play. Albee's own comments on the play make this clear. In describing *The American Dream* Albee renders Mommy's exchange of characters abstract, even allegorical: "The play is an ... attack on the substitution of artificial for real values in our society." Read "Young Man" for "artificial values" and "Grandma" for "real values" and the heart of the play becomes clear.

Is *The American Dream* "nihilist, immoral, defeatist"? Albee asks rhetorically. If it had been written fully in the absurdist mode, it might suggest nihilism. If it lacked value-laden Grandma, it might be amoral. And if it showed Grandma killed, it might be defeatist. But it is none of these. For Grandma's manipulation of the plot, moving it as she does to resolution and "satisfaction," shows that life does have meaning and order and that human experience is to some degree within our rational control. And the fact that Grandma does not die suggests that the old American Dream lives on somehow, somewhere.

Indeed, Albee's final disposition of Grandma is optimistic in a rather extreme way, for this play. For although Grandma leaves the stage with her boxes, she does not leave the theater. In fact, she moves front stage, close to the audience, from which position she is able to communicate directly with both the Young Man, who remains inside the staged action, and the audience watching the play. At one point she signals to the Young Man that "she is not there," and at the very end she speaks directly to the audience: "Well, I guess that just about wraps it up. I mean, for better or worse, this is a comedy, and I don't think we'd better go any further. No, definitely not. So, let's leave things as they are right now ... while everybody's happy ... while everybody's got what he wants ... or everybody's got what he thinks he wants. Good night, dears."

Although her final lines are rather innocuous, the stance from which she speaks them is laden with significance. Grandma—the old American Dream, as this essay has claimed—is not dead. Albee has not been able to bring himself to have her carted off by the "van man." She may have been expelled from Mommy and Daddy's apartment, but she has found a new home—and a new set of friends—in the audience of the play. Albee has passed the dream on to us. Properly perceiving the norm upon which his satire is based, we are now responsible for nurturing it in our lives in real life.

The play has moved through three theatrical modes. In the opening dispute over the beige-cream-wheat colored hat, Albee establishes an absurd-seeming style and metaphysic, in which everything is relative and nothing can be known for certain. As soon as Grandma enters the scene, Albee tempers his absurdism with expressionism, the dominant mode of the play, as Grandma and the Young Man interact and their meanings are clarified. And when Grandma finally leaves the stage Albee even moves into theatricalism, creating the alienation effect of Brechtian drama to help us see and accept what his didactic drama has been aiming at.

Seen in these terms, *The American Dream* fits squarely within the American tradition of thought and theater. And Albee shows that his inspiration is less the Theatre of the Absurd of the Old World cynic Eugene Ionesco and more the theatrical expressionism of the New World optimist Thornton Wilder—who, we might recall, told Albee in 1953, "Why don't you try writing plays?"①

Of course, the allegorical interpretation offered here errs in straight jacketing and rendering abstract a play that is delightfully baffling in its wacky rendering of daily life inAmerica. But the allegorical perception is important not only because it gets at the heart of Albee's intentions in the play but also because it enables us to relate *The American Dream* to his other works and to understand his larger corpus better.

With its allegorical dimension, *The American Dream* (1960) anticipates the heavily allegorical *Tiny Alice* (1964) a few years later. More important, *The American Dream* constitutes an early miniature of Albee's masterpiece, *Who's Afraid of Virginia Woolf* (1962). By Albee's own admission, of course, the main characters in *Virginia Woolf* were named after George and Martha Washington and Nikita Khruschev, which allows the allegorical affirmation that the American Dream of democratic humanism (George = George Washington) will prevail over its recent threat, scientific materialism (Nick = Nikita Khruschev).

The plays, of course, are more than allegories of the American Dream. But they are at least that, and we might look at Albee's corpus again, expecting to find these essentials—allegorical core and obsession with the American Dream—throughout his works.

[Selected from Ervin Beck. Allegory in Edward Albee's *The American Dream*. *Explicator* 55, 1997 (1).]

① Gilbert A. Harrison, *The Enthusiast: A Life of Thornton Wilder*. New Haven: Yale University Press, 1983. p. 316.